CRIMINAL LAW

D1377380

Criminal Law

[Author removed at request of original publisher]

University of Minnesota Libraries Publishing edition, 2015. This edition adapted from a work originally produced in 2010 by a publisher who has requested that it not receive attribution.

Minneapolis, MN

Copyright: by Lumen Learning.

Contents

Publisher Information

Criminal Law is adapted from a work produced and distributed under a Creative Commons license (CC BY-NC-SA) in 2012 by a publisher who has requested that they and the original author not receive attribution. This adapted edition is produced by the University of Minnesota Libraries Publishing through the eLearning Support Initiative.

This adaptation has reformatted the original text, and replaced some images and figures to make the resulting whole more shareable. This adaptation has not significantly altered or updated the original 2012 text. This work is made available under the terms of a Creative Commons Attribution-NonCommercial-ShareAlike license. CC licensed content, Shared previously

- Criminal Law. **Provided by**: University of Minnesota Libraries Publishing . **Located at**: http://open.lib.umn.edu/criminallaw/. **License**: *CC BY-NC-SA: Attribution-NonCommercial-ShareAlike*

Preface

Welcome to *Criminal Law*, your guide to a fascinating yet challenging topic. This engaging and interactive textbook will enhance your ability to be successful in academics or a career in criminal justice.

Content

Criminal Law begins with the foundations of law and the legal system and then extensively explores criminal laws and defenses using general state principles, federal law, the Constitution, and the Model Penal Code as guidelines. Although it is neither possible nor desirable to discuss *every* criminal law, this textbook provides a basic yet thorough overview of the American criminal justice system. After completing *Criminal Law*, you will be familiar with the nature and sources of law, the court system, the adversarial process, the most prominent crimes, and accompanying criminal defenses.

Approach

Criminal Law uses a two-step process to augment learning, called the *applied* approach. First, after building a strong foundation from scratch, *Criminal Law* introduces you to crimes and defenses that have been broken down into separate components. It is so much easier to memorize and comprehend the subject matter when it is simplified this way. However, becoming proficient in the law takes more than just memorization. You must be trained to take the laws you have studied and apply them to various fact patterns. Most students are expected to do this automatically, but application must be seen, experienced, and practiced before it comes naturally. Thus the second step of the applied approach is reviewing examples of the application of law to facts after dissecting and analyzing each legal concept. Some of the examples come from cases, and some are purely fictional. All the examples are memorable, even quirky, so they will stick in your mind and be available when you need them the most (like during an exam). After a few chapters, you will notice that you no longer obsess over an explanation that doesn't completely make sense the first time you read it—you will just skip to the example. The examples clarify the principles for you, lightening the workload significantly.

Features

Let's face it, legal textbooks can be dry. This is unfortunate because law, especially criminal law, is an intrinsically compelling topic. To hold your attention and keep you alert, *Criminal Law* employs a variety of instructional techniques that should engage you from start to finish.

First, chapters contain embedded videos, ethical scenarios, charts, diagrams, and tables to demonstrate the legal concepts and examples provided. These enhancements break up the text and also appeal to various learning styles.

In addition, instead of wasting valuable textbook space by reprinting edited cases, *Criminal Law* links to cases online. You can read more cases that way, and cases are like examples—they demonstrate the application of law to facts. Also, you can read the entire case exactly the way the judge wrote it, instead of an edited version that has been shrunk to fit into a limited amount of pages.

Have you ever tried to check your answers to review questions in a textbook, only to find that the correct answers are nowhere in sight? *Criminal Law* gives you the answer to every question at the end of each chapter. Go ahead and check the answers first. Contrary to popular belief, this actually improves—and does not detract

---

from—learning.

In addition, *Criminal Law* includes hundreds of footnotes that link to online cases and statutes; supplementary links to articles, websites, and statistics online; and plenty of reference material for a term paper or other research project. In short, *Criminal Law* should contain everything you need to successfully complete your course. It is also a valuable guide to which you can refer throughout your criminal justice career.

Goals

Although academic success is important, *Criminal Law* hopes to increase your awareness as you read the newspaper (or read the news online), watch television, or discuss legal situations with friends and colleagues. Law is an integral part of life, yet most people lack the most fundamental understanding of legal concepts.It is hoped that once you have finished reading *Criminal Law*, you will become your own most trusted legal authority.

CC licensed content, Shared previously

- Criminal Law. **Provided by**: University of Minnesota Libraries Publishing . **Located at**: http://open.lib.umn.edu/criminallaw/. **License**: *CC BY-NC-SA: Attribution-NonCommercial-ShareAlike*

Chapter 1: Introduction to Criminal Law

1.1 Introduction

Roadsidepictures – 1st. Dodge Charger With A Police Package – CC BY-NC 2.0.

Elementary notions of fairness enshrined in our constitutional jurisprudence dictate that a person receive fair notice not only of the conduct that will subject him to punishment but also of the severity of the penalty that a State may impose.

—*BMW of North America, Inc. v. Gore*, cited in Section 1 "Damages"

Learning Objective

Define a crime.

This textbook introduces you to our legal system in the United States, the basic elements of a crime, the specific elements of commonly encountered crimes, and most criminal defenses. Criminal law always involves the government and government action, so you will also review the pertinent sections of the United States Constitution and its principles as they apply to criminal law. By the end of the book, you will be comfortable with the legal framework that governs the careers of criminal justice professionals.

Definition of a Crime

Let's begin at the beginning by defining a crime. The most basic definition of a crime is "an act committed in violation of a law prohibiting it, or omitted in violation of a law ordering it" (Yourdictionary.com, 2010). You learn about criminal act and omission to act in Chapter 4 "The Elements of a Crime". For now, it is important to understand that criminal act, omission to act, and criminal intent are **elements** or parts of every crime. **Illegality** is also an element of every crime. Generally, the *government* must enact a *criminal law* specifying a crime and its elements before it can punish an individual for criminal behavior. Criminal laws are the primary focus of this book. As you slowly start to build your knowledge and understanding of criminal law, you will notice some unique characteristics of the United States' legal system.

Laws differ significantly from state to state. Throughout the United States, each state and the federal government criminalize different behaviors. Although this plethora of laws makes American legal studies more complicated for teachers and students, the size, cultural makeup, and geographic variety of our country demand this type of legal system.

Laws in a democratic society, unlike laws of nature, are created by *people* and are founded in religious, cultural, and historical value systems. People from varying backgrounds live in different regions of this country. Thus you will see that different people enact distinct laws that best suit their needs. This book is intended for use in all states. However, the bulk of any criminal law overview is an examination of different crimes and their elements. To be accurate and representative, this book focuses on *general* principles that *many* states follow and provides frequent references to specific state laws for illustrative purposes. Always check the most current version of your state's law because it may vary from the law presented in this book.

Laws are not *static*. As society changes, so do the laws that govern behavior. Evolving value systems naturally lead to new laws and regulations supporting modern beliefs. Although a certain stability is essential to the enforcement of rules, occasionally the rules must change.

Try to maintain an open mind when reviewing the different and often contradictory laws set forth in this book. Law is not exact, like science or math. Also try to become comfortable with the gray area, rather than viewing situations as black or white.

Key Takeaway

- A crime is an act committed in violation of a law prohibiting it or omitted in violation of a law ordering it. In general, the criminal law must be enacted before the crime is committed.

Exercise

Answer the following question. Check your answer using the answer key at the end of the chapter.

Read *Gonzales v. Oregon*, 546 U.S. 243 (2006). Did the US Supreme Court preserve Oregon's right to legalize physician-assisted suicide? The case is available at this link: http://www.law.cornell.edu/supct/html/04-623.ZS.html.

References

Yourdictionary.com, "Definition of Crime," accessed August 15, 2010, http://www.yourdictionary.com/crime. CC licensed content, Shared previously

- Criminal Law. **Provided by**: University of Minnesota Libraries Publishing . **Located at**: http://open.lib.umn.edu/criminallaw/. **License**: *CC BY-NC-SA: Attribution-NonCommercial-ShareAlike*

1.2 Criminal Law and Criminal Procedure

Learning Objective

Compare criminal law and criminal procedure.

This book focuses on criminal law, but it occasionally touches on issues of criminal procedure, so it is important to differentiate between the two.

Criminal law generally defines the *rights* and *obligations* of individuals in society. Some common issues in criminal law are the elements of specific crimes and the elements of various criminal defenses. Criminal procedure generally concerns the *enforcement* of individuals' rights during the criminal process. Examples of procedural issues are individuals' rights during law enforcement investigation, arrest, filing of charges, trial, and appeal.

Example of Criminal Law Issues

Clara and Linda go on a shopping spree. Linda insists that they browse an expensive department store. Moments after they enter the lingerie department, Linda surreptitiously places a bra in her purse. Clara watches, horrified, but does not say anything, even though a security guard is standing nearby. This example illustrates two issues of criminal law: (1) Which crime did Linda commit when she shoplifted the bra? (2) Did Clara commit a crime when she failed to alert the security guard to Linda's shoplifting? You learn the answer to issue (1) in Chapter 11 "Crimes against Property" and issue (2) in Chapter 4 "The Elements of a Crime" and Chapter 7 "Parties to Crime".

Example of Criminal Procedure Issues

Review the example in Section 1.2.1 "Example of Criminal Law Issues". Assume that Linda and Clara attempt to leave the store and an alarm is activated. Linda begins sprinting down the street. Colin, a police officer, just happens to be driving by with the window of his patrol car open. He hears the store alarm, sees Linda running, and begins shooting at Linda from the car. Linda is shot in the leg and collapses. Linda is treated at the hospital for her injury, and when she is released, Colin arrests her and transports her to the police station. He brings her to an isolated room and leaves her there alone. Twelve hours later, he reenters the room and begins questioning Linda. Linda immediately requests an attorney. Colin ignores this request and continues to question Linda about the reason the department store alarm went off. Whether Colin properly arrested and interrogated Linda are **criminal procedure** issues beyond the scope of this book. However, this example does illustrate one criminal law issue: did Colin *commit a crime* when he shot Linda in the leg? You learn the answer to this question in Chapter 5 "Criminal Defenses, Part 1".

Figure 1.1 Criminal Law and Criminal Procedure

Key Takeaway

- Criminal law generally defines the rights and obligations of individuals in society. Criminal procedure generally concerns the enforcement of individuals' rights during the criminal process.

Exercises

Answer the following questions. Check your answers using the answer key at the end of the chapter.

Paul, a law enforcement officer, arrests Barney for creating a disturbance at a subway station. While Barney is handcuffed facedown on the ground, Paul shoots and kills him. Paul claims that he accidentally grabbed his gun instead of his Taser. Is this an issue of criminal law or criminal procedure?

Read *Payton v. New York*, 445 U.S. 573 (1980). In *Payton*, the US Supreme Court held a New York statute unconstitutional under the Fourth Amendment. Did the *Payton* ruling focus on criminal law or criminal procedure? The case is available at this link: http://supreme.justia.com/us/445/573.

CC licensed content, Shared previously

- Criminal Law. **Provided by**: University of Minnesota Libraries Publishing . **Located at**: http://open.lib.umn.edu/criminallaw/. **License**: *CC BY-NC-SA: Attribution-NonCommercial-ShareAlike*

1.3 The Difference between Civil and Criminal Law

Learning Objectives

Compare civil and criminal law.
Ascertain the primary differences between civil litigation and a criminal prosecution.

Law can be classified in a variety of ways. One of the most general classifications divides law into civil and criminal. A basic definition of civil law is "the body of law having to do with the private rights of individuals" (Yourdictionary.com, 2010). As this definition indicates, civil law is between individuals, not *the government*. Criminal law involves regulations enacted and enforced by government action, while civil law provides a remedy for individuals who need to enforce private rights against other individuals. Some examples of civil law are family law, wills and trusts, and contract law. If individuals need to resolve a *civil dispute*, this is called civil litigation, or a civil lawsuit. When the type of civil litigation involves an injury, the injury action is called a tort.

Characteristics of Civil Litigation

It is important to distinguish between civil litigation and criminal prosecution. Civil and criminal cases share the same courts, but they have very different goals, purposes, and results. Sometimes, one set of facts gives way to a civil lawsuit *and* a criminal prosecution. This does not violate double jeopardy and is actually quite common.

Parties in Civil Litigation

In civil litigation, an injured party sues to receive a court-ordered remedy, such as money, property, or some sort of performance. Anyone who is injured—an individual, corporation, or other business entity—can sue civilly. In a civil litigation matter, the injured party that is suing is called the plaintiff. A plaintiff must hire and pay for an attorney or represent himself or herself. Hiring an attorney is one of the many costs of litigation and should be carefully contemplated before jumping into a lawsuit.

The alleged wrongdoer and the person or entity being sued are called the defendant. While the term *plaintiff* is always associated with civil litigation, the wrongdoer is called a defendant in *both* civil litigation and a criminal prosecution, so this can be confusing. The defendant can be any person or thing that has caused harm, including an individual, corporation, or other business entity. A defendant in a civil litigation matter must hire and pay for an attorney *even if that defendant did nothing wrong*. The right to a free attorney does not apply in civil litigation, so a defendant who cannot afford an attorney must represent himself or herself.

Goal of Civil Litigation

The *goal* of civil litigation is to *compensate the plaintiff* for any injuries and to put the plaintiff back in the position that person held before the injury occurred. This goal produces interesting results. It occasionally creates liability or an obligation to pay when there is no fault on behalf of the defendant. The goal is to make the plaintiff whole, not to punish, so *fault* is not really an issue. If the defendant has the resources to pay, sometimes the law requires the defendant to pay so that society does not bear the cost of the plaintiff's injury.

A defendant may be liable without fault in two situations. First, the law that the defendant violated may not require fault. Usually, this is referred to as strict liability. Strict liability torts do not require fault because they do not include an intent component. Strict liability and other intent issues are discussed in detail in Chapter 4 "The Elements of a Crime". Another situation where the defendant may be liable without fault is if the defendant did not actually commit any act but is associated with the acting defendant through a *special relationship*. The policy of holding a separate entity or individual liable for the defendant's action is called vicarious liability. An example of vicarious liability is employer-employee liability, also referred to as respondeat superior. If an employee injures a plaintiff while on the job, the *employer* may be liable for the plaintiff's injuries, whether or not the employer is at fault. Clearly, between the employer and the employee, the employer generally has the better ability to pay.

Example of Respondeat Superior

Chris begins the first day at his new job as a cashier at a local McDonald's restaurant. Chris attempts to multitask and pour hot coffee while simultaneously handing out change. He loses his grip on the coffee pot and spills steaming-hot coffee on his customer Geoff's hand. In this case, Geoff can sue *McDonald's and Chris* if he sustains injuries. McDonald's is not technically at fault, but it may be liable for Geoff's injuries under a theory of respondeat superior.

Harm Requirement

The goal of civil litigation is to compensate the plaintiff for injuries, so the plaintiff must be a bona fide **victim** that can prove **harm**. If there is no evidence of harm, the plaintiff has no basis for the civil litigation matter. An example would be when a defendant rear-ends a plaintiff in an automobile accident without causing damage to the vehicle (property damage) or physical injury. Even if the defendant is at fault for the automobile accident, the plaintiff cannot sue because the plaintiff does not need compensation for any injuries or losses.

Damages

Often the plaintiff sues the defendant for money rather than a different, performance-oriented remedy. In a civil litigation matter, any money the court awards to the plaintiff is called damages. Several kinds of damages may be appropriate. The plaintiff can sue for compensatory damages, which compensate for injuries, costs, which repay the lawsuit expenses, and in some cases, punitive damages. Punitive damages, also referred to as **exemplary damages**, are *not* designed to compensate the plaintiff but instead focus on *punishing* the defendant for causing the injury (BMW of North America, Inc., 1996).

Characteristics of a Criminal Prosecution

A criminal prosecution takes place after a defendant violates a federal or state criminal statute, or in some jurisdictions, after a defendant commits a common-law crime. Statutes and common-law crimes are discussed in Section 1.6 "Sources of Law".

Parties in a Criminal Prosecution

The government institutes the criminal prosecution, rather than an individual plaintiff. If the defendant commits a federal crime, **the United States of America** pursues the criminal prosecution. If the defendant commits a state crime, the state government, often called the **People of the State** pursues the criminal prosecution. As in a civil lawsuit, the alleged wrongdoer is called the **defendant** and can be an individual, corporation, or other business entity.

The *attorney* who represents the government controls the criminal prosecution. In a federal criminal prosecution, this is the United States Attorney (United States Department of Justice, 2010). In a state criminal prosecution, this is generally a state prosecutor or a **district attorney** (Galaxy.com, 2010). A state prosecutor works for the state but is typically an elected official who represents the county where the defendant allegedly committed the crime.

Applicability of the Constitution in a Criminal Prosecution

The defendant in a criminal prosecution can be represented by a private attorney or a *free* attorney paid for by the state or federal government if he or she is *unable to afford attorney's fees* and *facing incarceration* (Alabama v. Shelton, 2001). Attorneys provided by the government are called public defenders (18 U.S.C., 2010). This is a significant difference from a civil litigation matter, where both the plaintiff and the defendant must hire and pay for their own private attorneys. The court appoints a free attorney to represent the defendant in a criminal prosecution because *the Constitution is in effect* in any criminal proceeding. The Constitution provides for the assistance of counsel in the Sixth Amendment, so *every* criminal defendant facing incarceration has the right to legal representation, regardless of wealth.

The presence of the Constitution at every phase of a criminal prosecution changes the proceedings significantly from the civil lawsuit. The criminal defendant receives many constitutional *protections*, including the right to remain silent, the right to due process of law, the freedom from double jeopardy, and the right to a jury trial, among others.

Goal of a Criminal Prosecution

Another substantial difference between civil litigation and criminal prosecution is the *goal*. Recall that the goal of civil litigation is to compensate the plaintiff for injuries. In contrast, the goal of a criminal prosecution is to *punish* the defendant.

One consequence of the goal of punishment in a criminal prosecution is that *fault* is almost always an element in any criminal proceeding. This is unlike civil litigation, where the ability to pay is a priority consideration. Clearly, it is unfair to punish a defendant who did nothing wrong. This makes criminal law justice oriented and very satisfying for most students.

Injury and a victim are *not* necessary components of a criminal prosecution because punishment is the objective, and there is no plaintiff. Thus behavior can be criminal even if it is essentially harmless. Society does not condone or pardon conduct simply because it fails to produce a tangible loss.

Examples of Victimless and Harmless Crimes

Steven is angry because his friend Bob broke his skateboard. Steven gets his gun, which has a silencer on it, and puts it in the glove compartment of his car. He then begins driving to Bob's house. While Steven is driving, he exceeds the speed limit on three different occasions. Steven arrives at Bob's house and then he hides in the bushes by the mailbox and waits. After an hour, Bob opens the front door and walks to the mailbox. Bob gets his mail, turns around, and begins walking back to the house. Steven shoots at Bob three different times but misses, and the bullets end up landing in the dirt. Bob does not notice the shots because of the silencer.

In this example, Steven has committed several crimes: (1) If Steven does not have a special permit to carry a concealed weapon, putting the gun in his glove compartment is probably a crime in most states. (2) If Steven does not have a special permit to own a silencer for his gun, this is probably a crime in most states. (3) If Steven does not put the gun in a locked container when he transports it, this is probably a crime in most states. (4) Steven committed a crime each time he exceeded the speed limit. (5) Each time Steven shot at Bob and missed, he probably committed the crime of attempted murder or assault with a deadly weapon in most states. Notice that none of the crimes Steven committed caused any discernible harm. However, common sense dictates that Steven should be punished so he does not commit a criminal act in the future that *may* result in harm.

Table 1.1 Comparison of Criminal Prosecution and Civil Litigation

Feature	Criminal Prosecution	Civil Litigation
Victim	No	Yes. This is the plaintiff.
Harm	No	Yes. This is the basis for damages.
Initiator of lawsuit	Federal or state government	Plaintiff
Attorney for the initiator	US Attorney or state prosecutor	Private attorney
Attorney for the defendant	Private attorney or public defender	Private attorney
Constitutional protections	Yes	No

Figure 1.2 Crack the Code

Crack the Code

Compare the following state laws:

Fla.Stat.Ann. §768.19:

768.19 Right of action.--When the death of a person is caused by the wrongful act, negligence, default, or breach of contract or warranty of any person, including those occurring on navigable waters, and the event would have entitled the person injured to maintain an action and recover damages if death had not ensued, the person or watercraft that would have been liable in damages if death had not ensued shall be liable for damages as specified in this act notwithstanding the death of the person injured, although death was caused under circumstances constituting a felony.

Fla.Stat.Ann. §782.04:

Murder. (1)(a) The unlawful killing of a human being:

1. When perpetrated from a premeditated design to effect the death of the person killed or any human being; ...

2. is murder in the first degree and constitutes a capital felony, punishable as provided in §775.082.

Comparison of civil wrongful death with criminal murder

Law and Ethics: The O. J. Simpson Case

Two Different Trials—Two Different Results

O. J. Simpson was prosecuted criminally and sued civilly for the murder and wrongful death of victims Ron Goldman and his ex-wife, Nicole Brown Simpson. In the criminal prosecution, which came first, the US Constitution provided O. J. Simpson with the right to a fair trial (due process) and the right to remain silent (privilege against self-incrimination). Thus the burden of proof was beyond a reasonable doubt, and

O. J. Simpson did *not* have to testify. O. J. Simpson was acquitted, or found *not guilty*, in the criminal trial (Linder, D., 2010).

In the subsequent civil lawsuit, the burden of proof was preponderance of evidence, which is 51–49 percent, and O. J. Simpson was forced to testify. O. J. Simpson was found *liable* in the civil lawsuit. The jury awarded $8.5 million in compensatory damages to Fred Goldman (Ron Goldman's father) and his ex-wife Sharon Rufo. A few days later, the jury awarded punitive damages of $25 million to be shared between Nicole Brown Simpson's children and Fred Goldman (Jones, T. L., 2010).

> Do you think it is ethical to give criminal defendants more legal protection than civil defendants? Why or why not?
> Why do you think the criminal trial of O. J. Simpson took place before the civil trial? Check your answers to both questions using the answer key at the end of the chapter.

Johnny Cochran Video

Johnny Cochran: If the Gloves Don't Fit…

This video presents defense attorney Johnny Cochran's closing argument in the O. J. Simpson criminal prosecution:
(click to see video)

Key Takeaways

- Civil law regulates the private rights of individuals. Criminal law regulates individuals' conduct to protect the public.
- Civil litigation is a legal action between individuals to resolve a civil dispute. Criminal prosecution is when the government prosecutes a defendant to punish illegal conduct.

Exercises

Answer the following questions. Check your answers using the answer key at the end of the chapter.

> Jerry, a law enforcement officer, pulls Juanita over for speeding. When Jerry begins writing Juanita's traffic ticket, she starts to berate him and accuse him of racial profiling. Jerry surreptitiously reaches into his pocket and activates a tape recorder. Juanita later calls the highway patrol where Jerry works and files a false complaint against Jerry. Jerry sues Juanita for $500 in small claims court for filing the false report. He uses the tape recording as evidence. Is this a **civil litigation matter** or a **criminal prosecution**?
> Read *Johnson v. Pearce*, 148 N.C.App. 199 (2001). In this case, the plaintiff sued the defendant for **criminal conversation**. Is this a civil litigation matter or a criminal prosecution? The case is available at this link: http://scholar.google.com/scholar_case?case=10159013992593966605&q=Johnson+v.+Pearce&hl=en&as_sdt=2,5.

References

Alabama v. Shelton, 535 U.S. 654 (2002), accessed August 16, 2010, http://www.law.cornell.edu/supct/html/00-1214.ZO.html.

BMW of North America, Inc. v. Gore, 517 U.S. 559 (1996), accessed February 13, 2010, http://www.law.cornell.edu/supct/html/94-896.ZO.html.

Galaxy.com website, "United States' Prosecuting Attorneys," accessed February 15, 2010, http://www.galaxy.com/dir968533/United_States.htm.

Jones, T. L., "Justice for the Dead," TruTV website, accessed August 18, 2010, http://www.trutv.com/library/crime/notorious_murders/famous/simpson/dead_16.html.

Linder, D., "The Trial of Orenthal James Simpson," UMKC website, accessed August 18, 2010, http://www.law.umkc.edu/faculty/projects/ftrials/Simpson/Simpsonaccount.htm.

United States Department of Justice, "United States Attorneys," accessed February 15, 2010, http://www.justice.gov/usao.

Yourdictionary.com, "Definition of Civil Law," accessed August 16, 2010, http://www.yourdictionary.com/civil-law.

18 U.S.C. § 3006A, accessed February 15, 2010, http://www.law.cornell.edu/uscode/18/3006A.html.
CC licensed content, Shared previously

- Criminal Law. **Provided by**: University of Minnesota Libraries Publishing . **Located at**: http://open.lib.umn.edu/criminallaw/. **License**: *CC BY-NC-SA: Attribution-NonCommercial-ShareAlike*

1.4 Classification of Crimes

Learning Objectives

Ascertain the basis for grading.
Compare malum in se and malum prohibitum crimes.
Compare the punishment options for felonies, misdemeanors, felony-misdemeanors, and infractions.
Compare jail and prison.

Crimes can be classified in many ways. Crimes also can be grouped by subject matter. For example, a crime like assault, battery, or rape tends to injure another person's body, so it can be classified as a "crime against the person." If a crime tends to injure a person by depriving him or her of property or by damaging property, it can be classified as a "crime against property." These classifications are basically for convenience and are not imperative to the study of criminal law.

More important and substantive is the classification of crimes according to the severity of punishment. This is called grading. Crimes are generally graded into four categories: felonies, misdemeanors, felony-misdemeanors, and infractions. Often the criminal intent element affects a crime's grading. Malum in se crimes, murder, for example, are evil in their nature and are generally graded higher than malum prohibitum crimes, which are regulatory, like a failure to pay income taxes.

Felonies

Felonies are the *most serious* crimes. They are either supported by a heinous intent, like the intent to kill, or accompanied by an extremely serious result, such as loss of life, grievous injury, or destruction of property. Felonies are serious, so they are graded the highest, and all sentencing options are available. Depending on the jurisdiction and the crime, the sentence could be execution, prison time, a fine, or alternative sentencing such as probation, rehabilitation, and home confinement. Potential consequences of a felony conviction also include the inability to vote, own a weapon, or even participate in certain careers.

Misdemeanors

Misdemeanors are *less serious* than felonies, either because the intent requirement is of a lower level or because the result is less extreme. Misdemeanors are usually punishable by jail time of one year or less per misdemeanor, a fine, or alternative sentencing like probation, rehabilitation, or community service. Note that incarceration for a misdemeanor is in jail rather than prison. The difference between jail and prison is that cities and counties operate jails, and the state or federal government operates prisons, depending on the crime. The restrictive nature of the confinement also differs between jail and prison. Jails are for defendants who have committed less serious offenses, so they are generally less restrictive than prisons.

Felony-Misdemeanors

Felony-misdemeanors are crimes that the government can prosecute and punish as *either* a felony or a misdemeanor, depending on the particular circumstances accompanying the offense. The discretion whether to prosecute the crime as a felony or misdemeanor usually belongs to the *judge*, but in some instances the *prosecutor* can make the decision.

Infractions

Infractions, which can also be called **violations**, are the least serious crimes and include minor offenses such as jaywalking and motor vehicle offenses that result in a simple traffic ticket. Infractions are generally punishable by a fine or alternative sentencing such as traffic school.

Figure 1.3 Diagram of Grading

Most Serious	
Less Serious	
Less Serious	
Least Serious	

Key Takeaways

- Grading is based on the severity of punishment.
- Malum in se crimes are evil in their nature, like murder. Malum prohibitum crimes are regulatory, like a failure to pay income taxes.

- Felonies are graded the highest. Punishment options for felonies include the following:
    - Execution
    - Prison time
    - Fines
    - Alternative sentencing such as probation, rehabilitation, and home confinement

- Misdemeanors are graded lower than felonies. Punishment options for misdemeanors include the following:
    - Jail time of one year or less per misdemeanor
    - Fines
    - Alternative sentencing such as probation, rehabilitation, and community service
- Felony-misdemeanors are punished as either a felony or a misdemeanor.

- Infractions, also called violations, are graded lower than misdemeanors and have less severe punishment options:
    - Fines
    - Alternative sentencing, such as traffic school
- One difference between jail and prison is that cities and counties operate jails, and the state or federal government operates prisons, depending on the crime. The restrictive nature of the confinement is another difference. Jails are for defendants who have committed less serious offenses, so they are generally less restrictive than prisons.

Exercises

Answer the following questions. Check your answers using the answer key at the end of the chapter.

Harrison kills Calista and is prosecuted and sentenced to one year in jail. Did Harrison commit a felony or a misdemeanor?

Read *State v. Gillison*, 766 N.W. 2d 649 (2009). In *Gillison*, why did the Iowa Court of Appeals rule that the defendant's prior convictions were felony convictions? What impact did this ruling have on the defendant's sentence? The case is available at this link:

http://scholar.google.com/scholar_case?case=8913791129507413362&q= State+v.+Gillison&hl=en&as_sdt=2,5&as_vis=1.

CC licensed content, Shared previously

- Criminal Law. **Provided by**: University of Minnesota Libraries Publishing . **Located at**: http://open.lib.umn.edu/criminallaw/. **License**: *CC BY-NC-SA: Attribution-NonCommercial-ShareAlike*

1.5 The Purposes of Punishment

Learning Objective

Ascertain the effects of specific and general deterrence, incapacitation, rehabilitation, retribution, and restitution.

Punishment has five recognized purposes: *deterrence*, *incapacitation*, *rehabilitation*, *retribution*, and *restitution*.

Specific and General Deterrence

Deterrence prevents future crime by frightening the *defendant* or the *public*. The two types of deterrence are specific and general deterrence. Specific deterrence applies to an *individual defendant*. When the government punishes an individual defendant, he or she is theoretically less likely to commit another crime because of fear of another similar or worse punishment. General deterrence applies to the *public* at large. When the public learns of an individual defendant's punishment, the public is theoretically less likely to commit a crime because of fear of the punishment the defendant experienced. When the public learns, for example, that an individual defendant was severely punished by a sentence of life in prison or the death penalty, this knowledge can inspire a deep fear of criminal prosecution.

Incapacitation

Incapacitation prevents future crime by removing the defendant from society. Examples of incapacitation are incarceration, house arrest, or execution pursuant to the death penalty.

Rehabilitation

Rehabilitation prevents future crime by altering a defendant's behavior. Examples of rehabilitation include educational and vocational programs, treatment center placement, and counseling. The court can combine rehabilitation with incarceration or with probation or parole. In some states, for example, nonviolent drug offenders must participate in rehabilitation in combination with probation, rather than submitting to incarceration (Ariz. Rev. Stat., 2010). This lightens the load of jails and prisons while lowering recidivism, which means reoffending.

Retribution

Retribution prevents future crime by removing the desire for *personal* avengement (in the form of assault, battery, and criminal homicide, for example) against the defendant. When victims or society discover that the defendant has been adequately punished for a crime, they achieve a certain satisfaction that our criminal procedure is working effectively, which enhances faith in law enforcement and our government.

Restitution

Restitution prevents future crime by punishing the defendant *financially*. Restitution is when the court orders the criminal defendant to pay the victim for any harm and resembles a civil litigation damages award. Restitution can be for physical injuries, loss of property or money, and rarely, emotional distress. It can also be a *fine* that covers some of the costs of the criminal prosecution and punishment.

Figure 1.4 Different Punishments and Their Purpose

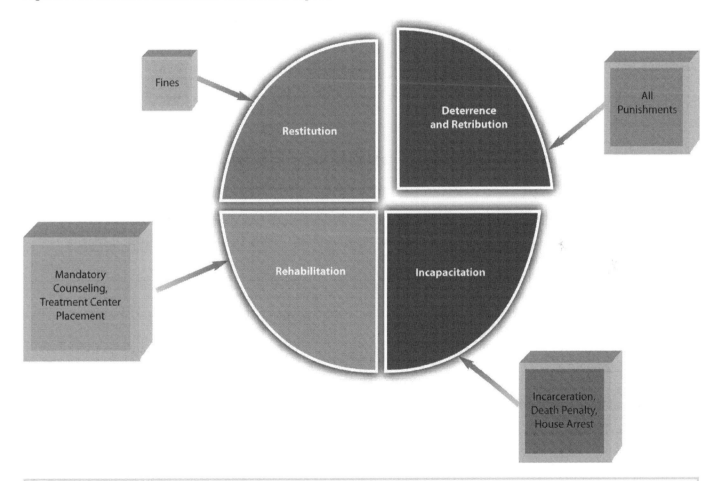

Key Takeaways

- Specific deterrence prevents crime by frightening an individual defendant with punishment. General deterrence prevents crime by frightening the public with the punishment of an individual defendant.
- Incapacitation prevents crime by removing a defendant from society.
- Rehabilitation prevents crime by altering a defendant's behavior.
- Retribution prevents crime by giving victims or society a feeling of avengement.
- Restitution prevents crime by punishing the defendant financially.

Exercises

Answer the following questions. Check your answers using the answer key at the end of the chapter.

What is one difference between criminal victims' restitution and civil damages?
Read *Campbell v. State*, 5 S.W.3d 693 (1999). Why did the defendant in this case claim that the restitution award was too high? Did the Texas Court of Criminal Appeals agree with the defendant's claim? The case is available at this link:
http://scholar.google.com/scholar_case?case=11316909200521760089&hl=en&as_sdt=2&as_vis=1&oi=scholarr.

References

Ariz. Rev. Stat. §13-901.01, accessed February 15, 2010, http://law.justia.com/arizona/codes/title13/00901-01.html.
CC licensed content, Shared previously

- Criminal Law. **Provided by**: University of Minnesota Libraries Publishing . **Located at**: http://open.lib.umn.edu/criminallaw/. **License**: *CC BY-NC-SA: Attribution-NonCommercial-ShareAlike*

1.6 Sources of Law

Learning Objectives

Identify the three sources of law.
Rank the three sources of law, from highest to lowest.
Ascertain the purpose of the US and state constitutions.
Ascertain one purpose of statutory law.
Ascertain the purpose of case law.
Define judicial review.
Diagram and explain the components of a case brief.

Law comes from three places, which are referred to as the **sources of law**.

Constitutional Law

The first source of law is **constitutional law**. Two constitutions are applicable in every state: the federal or US Constitution, which is in force throughout the United States of America, and the state's constitution. The US Constitution created our legal system, as is discussed in Chapter 2 "The Legal System in the United States". States' constitutions typically focus on issues of local concern.

The purpose of federal and state constitutions is to *regulate government action*. Private individuals are protected by the Constitution, but they do not have to follow it themselves.

Example of Government and Private Action

Cora stands on a public sidewalk and criticizes President Obama's health-care plan. Although other individuals may be annoyed by Cora's words, the government *cannot* arrest or criminally prosecute Cora for her speech because the First Amendment of the US Constitution guarantees each individual the right to speak freely. On the other hand, if Cora walks into a Macy's department store and criticizes the owner of Macy's, Macy's could eject Cora immediately. Macy's and its personnel are *private*, not government, and they *do not* have to abide by the Constitution.

Exceptions to the Constitution

The federal and state constitutions are both written with words that can be subject to more than one interpretation. Thus there are many *exceptions* to any constitution's protections. Constitutional protections and exceptions are discussed in detail in Chapter 3 "Constitutional Protections".

For safety and security reasons, we see more exceptions to constitutional protections in *public schools* and *prisons*. For example, public schools and prisons can mandate a certain style of dress for the purpose of ensuring safety. Technically, forcing an individual to dress a specific way could violate the right to self-expression, which the First Amendment guarantees. However, if wearing a uniform can lower gang-related conflicts in school and prevent prisoners from successfully escaping, the government can constitutionally suppress free speech in these locations.

Superiority of the Constitution

Of the three sources of law, constitutional law is considered the *highest* and should not be supplanted by either of the other two sources of law. Pursuant to principles of federal supremacy, the *federal* or US Constitution is the most preeminent source of law, and state constitutions cannot supersede it. Federal constitutional protections and federal supremacy are discussed in Chapter 2 "The Legal System in the United States" and Chapter 3 "Constitutional Protections".

Statutory Law

The second source of law is **statutory law**. While the Constitution applies to government action, statutes apply to and regulate *individual* or *private* action. A **statute** is a written (and published) law that can be enacted in one of two ways. Most statutes are written and voted into law by the *legislative* branch of government. This is simply a group of individuals elected for this purpose. The US legislative branch is called Congress, and Congress votes federal statutes into law. Every state has a legislative branch as well, called a state legislature, and a state legislature votes state statutes into law. Often, states codify their *criminal* statutes into a penal code.

State citizens can also vote state statutes into law. Although a state legislature adopts *most* state statutes, citizens voting on a ballot can enact some very important statutes. For example, a majority of California's citizens voted to enact California's medicinal marijuana law (California Compassionate Use Act of 1996, 2010). California's three-strikes law was voted into law by both the state legislature and California's citizens and actually appears in the California Penal Code in two separate places (Brown, B., and Jolivette, G., 2010).

Statutory Law's Inferiority

Statutory law is inferior to **constitutional law**, which means that a statute cannot conflict with or attempt to supersede constitutional rights. If a conflict exists between constitutional and statutory law, the courts must resolve the conflict. Courts can invalidate unconstitutional statutes pursuant to their power of **judicial review**, which is discussed in an upcoming section.

Administrative Laws and Ordinances

Other written and published laws that apply to individuals are administrative laws and ordinances. Administrative laws and ordinances should not supersede or conflict with statutory law.

Administrative laws are enacted by administrative agencies, which are governmental agencies designed to regulate in specific areas. Administrative agencies can be federal or state and contain not only a legislative branch but also an executive (enforcement) branch and judicial (court) branch. The Food and Drug Administration (FDA) is an example of a federal administrative agency. The FDA regulates any food products or drugs produced and marketed in the United States.

Ordinances are similar to statutes, except that *cities* and *counties* vote them into law, rather than a state's legislature or a state's citizens. Ordinances usually relate to health, safety, or welfare, and violations of them are typically classified as **infractions** or **misdemeanors**, rather than **felonies**. A written law prohibiting jaywalking within a city's or county's limits is an example of an ordinance.

Model Penal Code

State criminal laws differ significantly, so in the early 1960s a group of legal scholars, lawyers, and judges who were members of the American Law Institute drafted a set of suggested criminal statutes called the Model Penal Code. The intent of the Model Penal Code was to provide a standardized set of criminal statutes that all states could adopt, thus simplifying the diversity effect of the United States' legal system. While the Model Penal Code has not been universally adopted, a majority of the states have incorporated portions of it into their penal codes, and the Model Penal Code survives as a guideline and focal point for discussion when state legislatures modify their criminal statutes.

Case Law

The third source of law is **case law**. When judges rule on the facts of a particular case, they create case law. *Federal* case law comes from federal courts, and *state* case law comes from state courts. Case law has its origins in English common law.

English Common Law

In Old England, before the settlement of the United States, case law was the most prevalent source of law. This was in contrast to countries that followed the Roman Law system, which primarily relied on written codes of conduct enacted by legislature. Case law in England was mired in tradition and local customs. Societal principles of law and equity were the guidelines when courts issued their rulings. In an effort to be consistent, English judges made it a policy to follow previous judicial decisions, thereby creating a uniform system of laws throughout the country for the first time. Case law was named common law because it was common to the entire nation (Duhaime, L., 2010).

The English system of jurisprudence made its way to the United States with the original colonists. Initially, the thirteen colonies unanimously adopted common law as the law of the land. All crimes were common-law crimes, and cases determined criminal elements, defenses, and punishment schemes. Gradually, after the Revolutionary War, hostility toward England and modern reform led to the erosion of common-law crimes and a movement toward codification. States began replacing common-law crimes with statutes enacted by state legislatures. Oxford professor Sir William Blackstone's *Commentaries on the Law of England,* which interpreted and summarized English common law, became an essential reference as the nation began the process of converting common-law principles into written statutes, ordinances, and penal codes (Duhaime, L., 2010).

Limitations on Common-Law Crimes

In modern society, in many states and the federal government (United States v. Hudson & Goodwin, 2010), judges *cannot* create crimes. This violates notions of fairness. Making up a new crime and punishing the defendant for it does not provide consistency or predictability to our legal system. It also violates the principle of legality, a core concept of American criminal justice embodied in this phrase: "Nullum crimen sine lege, nulla poena sine crimen" (No crime without law, no punishment without crime).

In states that do not allow common-law crimes, **statutes** must define criminal conduct. If no statute exists to criminalize the defendant's behavior, the defendant *cannot be criminally prosecuted*, even if the behavior is abhorrent. As the Model Penal Code states, "[n]o conduct constitutes an offense unless it is a crime or violation under this Code or another statute of this State" (Model Penal Code § 1.05(1)).

The common law still plays an important role in criminal lawmaking, even though most crimes are now embodied in statutes. Classification of crimes as felonies and misdemeanors is a reflection of English common law. Legislatures often create statutes out of former common-law crimes. Judges look to the common law when defining statutory terms, establishing criminal procedure, and creating defenses to crimes. The United States is considered a common-law country. Every state except Louisiana, which is based on the French Civil Code, adopts the common law as the law of the state *except* where a statute provides otherwise (Legal Definition, 2010).

Example of a Court's Refusal to Create a Common-Law Crime

Read *Keeler v. Superior Court*, 470 P.2d 617 (1970). In *Keeler*, the defendant attacked his pregnant ex-wife, and her baby was thereafter stillborn. The California Supreme Court disallowed a murder charge against Keeler under California Penal Code § 187 because the statute criminalized only the malicious killing of a "human being." The court reached its decision after examining the common-law definition of human being and determining that the definition did not include a fetus. The court reasoned that it *could not create a new crime* without violating the due process clause, separation of powers, and California Penal Code § 6, which prohibits the creation of common-law crimes. After the *Keeler* decision, the California Legislature changed Penal Code § 187 to include a fetus, excepting abortion (Cal. Penal Code, 2010).

Powerful Nature of Case Law

Generally, if there is a statute on an issue, the statute is *superior* to case law, just as the Constitution is superior to statutory law. However, judges *interpret* constitutional and statutory law, making case law a *powerful* source of law. A judge can interpret a constitution in a way that adds or creates exceptions to its protections. A judge can also interpret a statute in a way that makes it unconstitutional and unenforceable. This is called the power of judicial review (Marbury v. Madison, 2010).

Example of Judicial Review

An example of judicial review is set forth in *Texas v. Johnson*, 491 U.S. 397 (1989). In *Johnson*, the US Supreme Court ruled that burning a flag is protected self-expression under the First Amendment to the US Constitution. Thus the Court reversed the defendant's conviction under a Texas statute that criminalized the desecration of a venerated object. Note how *Johnson* not only *invalidates* a state statute as being inferior to the US Constitution but also *changes* the US Constitution by adding flag burning to the First Amendment's protection of speech.

Figure 1.5 Diagram and Hierarchy of the Sources of Law

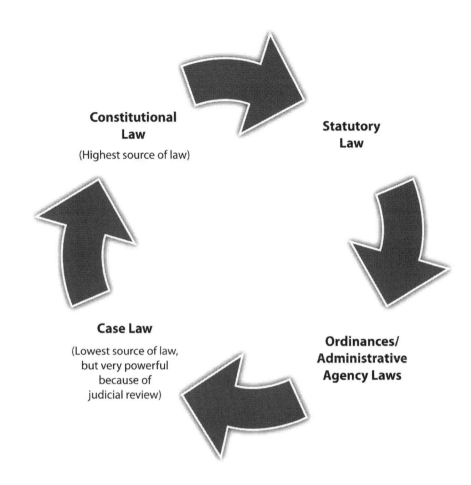

Constitutional
Law
(Highest source of law)

Statutory
Law

Ordinances/
Administrative
Agency Laws

Case Law
(Lowest source of law,
but very powerful
because of
judicial review)

Stare Decisis and Precedent

Cases are diverse, and case law is not really *law* until the judge rules on the case, so there must be a way to ensure case law's *predictability*. It would not be fair to punish someone for conduct that is not yet illegal. Thus judges adhere to a policy called stare decisis. Stare decisis is derived from English common law and compels judges to follow rulings in previous cases. A previous case is called precedent. Once judges have issued a ruling on a particular case, the public can be assured that the resulting precedent will continue to be followed by other judges. Stare decisis is not absolute; judges can deviate from it to update the law to conform to society's modern expectations.

Rules of Stare Decisis and Use of Precedent

Case precedent is generally an *appeal* rather than a *trial*. There is often more than one level of appeal, so some appeals come from higher courts than others. This book discusses the court system, including the appellate courts, in Chapter 2 "The Legal System in the United States".

Many complex rules govern the use of **precedent**. Lawyers primarily use precedent in their arguments, rather than **statutes** or the **Constitution**, because it is so specific. With proper research, lawyers can usually find precedent that matches or comes very close to matching the facts of any particular case. In the most general sense, judges tend to follow precedent that is *newer*, from a *high court*, and from the *same court system*, either federal or state.

Example of Stare Decisis and Use of Precedent

Geoffrey is a defense attorney for Conrad, who is on trial for first-degree murder. The murder prosecution is taking place in New Mexico. Geoffrey finds case precedent from a New York Court of Appeals, dated 1999, indicating that Conrad should have been prosecuted for *voluntary manslaughter*, not first-degree murder. Brandon, the prosecuting attorney, finds case precedent from the *New Mexico Supreme Court*, dated *2008*, indicating that a first-degree murder prosecution is appropriate. The trial court will probably follow the precedent submitted by Brandon because it is newer, from a higher court, and from the same court system as the trial.

Case Citation

Cases must be *published* to become case law. A published case is also called a judicial opinion. This book exposes you to many judicial opinions that you have the option of reading on the Internet. It is essential to understand the meaning of the case citation. The case citation is the series of numbers and letters after the title of the case and it denotes the case's published location. For example, let's analyze the case citation for *Keeler v. Superior Court*, 470 P.2d 617 (1970).

Figure 1.6 Keeler Case Citation

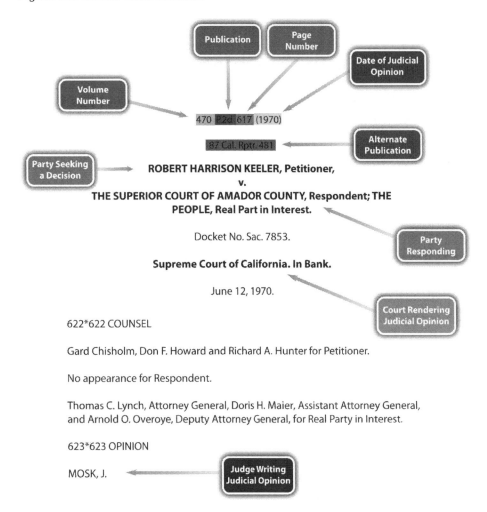

As you can see from the diagram, the number 470 is the volume number of the book that published the *Keeler* case. The name of that book is "P.2d" (this is an abbreviation for *Pacific Reports, 2d Series*). The number 617 is the page number of the *Keeler* case. The date (1970) is the date the California Supreme Court ruled on the case.

Case Briefing

It is useful to condense judicial opinions into case brief format. The *Keeler* case brief is shown in Figure 1.7 "Keeler Case Brief".

Figure 1.7 Keeler Case Brief

1. *Keeler v. Superior Court*, 470 P.2d 617 (1970).
2. A. (Procedural Facts) The defendant seeks a writ of prohibition, CA Supreme Court.
   B. (Substantive Facts) The defendant became upset when he saw that his ex-wife was pregnant. After stating "I'm going to stomp it out of you," he kneed his ex-wife in the abdomen. She survived, but the baby was stillborn, the cause of death a fractured skull. The defendant was charged with murder under Cal. Penal Code § 187, which defined murder as the malicious and unlawful killing of a human being. The defendant sought a writ of prohibition to disallow the murder charge, because he killed a fetus.
3. (Issue) Can a defendant be charged with murder for killing a fetus in a state that statutorily defines murder as the malicious and unlawful killing of a human being?
4. A. (Substantive Holding) A defendant cannot be charged with murder for killing a fetus in a state that statutorily defines murder as the malicious and unlawful killing of a human being.
5. B. (Procedural Holding) Writ of prohibition granted, murder charge disallowed.
6. (Rationale) The Court examined the common-law definition of human being, and held that it did not include a fetus. Charging the defendant with murder of a fetus, when the murder statute criminalizes only murder of a human being born alive, would violate: due process by not giving the defendant notice of what is criminal, separation of powers by allowing a court to create crimes, which is the legislature's responsibility, and California Penal Code §6, which specifically prohibits common-law crimes.

Read this case at the following link: http://scholar.google.com/scholar_case?case=2140632244672927312&hl=en&as_sdt=2&as_vis=1&oi=scholarr.

Published judicial opinions are written by judges and can be lengthy. They can also contain more than one case law, depending on the number of issues addressed. Case briefs reduce a judicial opinion to its essentials and can be instrumental in understanding the most important aspects of the case. Standard case brief formats can differ, but one format that attorneys and paralegals commonly use is explained in the following paragraph.

Review the *Keeler* case brief. The case brief should begin with the **title of the case**, including the **citation**. The next component of the case brief should be the **procedural facts**. The procedural facts should include two pieces of information: *who is appealing* and *which court* the case is in. As you can see from the *Keeler* case brief, Keeler brought an application for a writ of prohibition, and the court is the California Supreme Court. Following the procedural facts are the **substantive facts**, which should be a short description of the facts that instigated the court trial and appeal. The procedural and substantive facts are followed by the **issue**. The issue is the question the court is examining, which is usually the grounds for appeal. The case brief should phrase the issue as a question. Cases usually have more than one issue. The case brief can state all the issues or only the issue that is most important. The **substantive holding** comes after the issue, is *actually the case law*, and answers the issue question. If more than one issue is presented in the case brief, a substantive holding should address each issue.

Figure 1.8 Example of a Substantive Holding

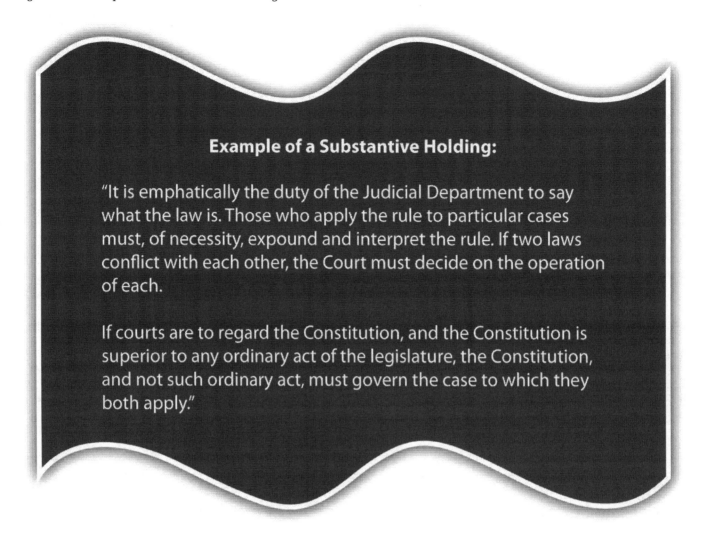

Example of a Substantive Holding:

"It is emphatically the duty of the Judicial Department to say what the law is. Those who apply the rule to particular cases must, of necessity, expound and interpret the rule. If two laws conflict with each other, the Court must decide on the operation of each.

If courts are to regard the Constitution, and the Constitution is superior to any ordinary act of the legislature, the Constitution, and not such ordinary act, must govern the case to which they both apply."

Marbury v. Madison, 5 U.S. (1 Cranch) 137 (1803), http://www.law.cornell.edu/supct/html/historics/USSC_CR_0005_0137_ZS.html.

A **procedural holding** should follow the substantive holding. The procedural holding discusses what the court did procedurally with the case. This could include reversing the lower court's ruling, affirming the lower court's ruling, or *adjusting a sentence* issued by the lower court. This book discusses court procedure in detail in Chapter 2 "The Legal System in the United States". Last, but still vital to the case brief, is the **rationale**. The rationale discusses the *reasoning* of the judges when ruling on the case. Rationales can *set policy*, which is not technically case law but can still be used as precedent in certain instances.

One judge writes the judicial opinion. Judges vote how to rule, and not all cases are supported by a unanimous ruling. Occasionally, other judges will want to add to the judicial opinion. If a judge agrees with the judicial opinion, the judge could write a **concurring opinion**, which explains why the judge agrees. If a judge disagrees with the judicial opinion, the judge could write a **dissenting opinion** explaining why the judge disagrees. The dissenting opinion will not change the judicial opinion, but it may also be used as precedent in a future case if there are grounds for changing the law.

Key Takeaways

- The three sources of law are constitutional, statutory, and case law.
- The sources of law are ranked as follows: first, constitutional; second, statutory; and third, case law. Although it is technically ranked the lowest, judicial review makes case law an extremely powerful

source of law.
- The purpose of the US and state constitutions is to regulate government action.
- One purpose of statutory law is to regulate individual or private action.
- The purpose of case law is to supplement the law when there is no statute on point and also to interpret statutes and the constitution(s).
- The court's power to invalidate statutes as unconstitutional is called judicial review.

- The components of a case brief are the following:
    - The title, plus citation. The citation indicates where to find the case.
    - The procedural facts of the case. The procedural facts discuss who is appealing and in which court the case is located.
    - The substantive facts. The substantive facts discuss what happened to instigate the case.
    - The issue. The issue is the question the court is examining.
    - The substantive holding. The substantive holding answers the issue question and is the case law.
    - The procedural holding. The procedural holding discusses what the court did procedurally with the case.
    - The rationale. The rationale is the reason the court held the way it did.

Exercises

Answer the following questions. Check your answers using the answer key at the end of the chapter.

Hal invents a new drug that creates a state of euphoria when ingested. Can Hal be criminally prosecuted for ingesting his new drug?

Read *Shaw v. Murphy*, 532 U.S. 223 (2001). Did the US Supreme Court allow prison inmates the First Amendment right to give other inmates legal advice? Why or why not? The case is available at this link:
http://scholar.google.com/scholar_case?case=9536800826824133166&hl=en&as_sdt=2&as_vis=1&oi=scholarr.

Read Justice Scalia's dissenting opinion in *Lawrence v. Texas*, 539 U.S. 558 (2003). What is the *primary* reason Justice Scalia dissented to the US Supreme Court's opinion in *Lawrence*? The dissenting opinion is available at this link: http://www.law.cornell.edu/supct/html/02-102.ZD.html. The judicial opinion in *Lawrence v. Texas* is available at this link: http://www.law.cornell.edu/supct/html/02-102.ZS.html.

References

Brown, B., and Jolivette, G., "A Primer: Three Strikes—The Impact after More Than a Decade," Legislative Analyst's Office website, accessed February 15, 2010, http://www.lao.ca.gov/2005/3_strikes/3_strikes_102005.htm.

Cal. Penal Code § 187, accessed August 23, 2010, http://codes.lp.findlaw.com/cacode/PEN/3/1/8/1/s187.

California Compassionate Use Act of 1996, Cal. Health and Safety Code § 11362.5, accessed February 15, 2010, http://www.cdph.ca.gov/programs/mmp/Pages/Medical%20Marijuana%20Program.aspx.

Duhaime, L., "Common Law Definition," Duhaime.org website, accessed September 26, 2010, http://www.duhaime.org/LegalDictionary/C/CommonLaw.aspx.

Legal Definition, "Common Law," Lectlaw.com website, accessed September 26, 2010, http://www.lectlaw.com/def/c070.htm.

Marbury v. Madison, 5 U.S. (1 Cranch) 137 (1803), accessed February 15, 2010, http://www.law.cornell.edu/supct/html/historics/USSC_CR_0005_0137_ZS.html.

United States v. Hudson & Goodwin, 11 U.S. 32 (1812), accessed September 24, 2010, http://openjurist.org/11/us/32/the-united-states-v-hudson-and-goodwin.

CC licensed content, Shared previously

- Criminal Law. **Provided by**: University of Minnesota Libraries Publishing . **Located at**: http://open.lib.umn.edu/criminallaw/. **License**: *CC BY-NC-SA: Attribution-NonCommercial-ShareAlike*

1.7 End-of-Chapter Material

Summary

A crime is action or inaction in violation of a criminal law. Criminal laws vary from state to state and from state to federal.

The study of criminal law defines crimes and defenses to crimes. The study of criminal procedure focuses on the enforcement of rights by individuals while submitting to government investigation, arrest, interrogation, trial, and appeal.

A civil lawsuit or civil litigation matter resolves a dispute between individuals, called a plaintiff (the injured party) and defendant (the alleged wrongdoer). Every civil litigation matter includes a victim (the plaintiff), which has suffered harm. The goal of the civil litigation matter is to compensate the plaintiff for injury. The court can compensate the plaintiff by awarding money, which is called damages. Both parties in a civil litigation matter must represent themselves or hire private attorneys.

A criminal prosecution takes place when the government, represented by a prosecutor, takes legal action against the defendant (the alleged wrongdoer) for committing a crime. Some criminal prosecutions do not include a victim, or harm, because the goal of the criminal prosecution is punishment, not compensation. Every criminal prosecution involves the government, so the US and state constitutions provide the criminal defendant with extra protections not present in a civil lawsuit, such as free counsel when the defendant is indigent and facing incarceration.

Crimes can be classified according to the severity of punishment. The most serious crimes with the entire range of sentencing options available are felonies. Misdemeanors are less serious than felonies and have less severe sentencing options. Felony-misdemeanors can be prosecuted and punished as a felony or a misdemeanor, depending on the circumstances. Infractions, also called violations, are the least serious crimes and generally do not involve incarceration. The purposes of punishing a criminal defendant are both specific and general deterrence, incapacitation, rehabilitation, retribution, and restitution.

Law comes from three sources: the Constitution, a statute, or a case. The Constitution is the highest source of law but is only applicable when there is government action. Statutory law applies to individuals but is inferior to constitutional law. Case law is law made by judges when they rule on the facts of a case. Although case law is technically inferior to statutory law, judges must interpret statutes and the Constitution, so case law can be the most powerful source of law. When a case invalidates a statute as unconstitutional, this action is called judicial review. Case law stays consistent because judges follow previous court decisions, called precedent. This policy, called stare decisis, lends predictability to case law but is not absolute, and courts can deviate from it to update the law.

You Be the Lawyer

Read the prompt, review the case, and then decide whether you would accept or reject the case if you were the lawyer. Check your answers using the answer key at the end of the chapter.

You are an expert in *criminal law*, not *civil litigation*. Would you **accept** or **reject** this case? Read

Cetacean Community v. Bush, 386 F.3d 1169 (9th Cir. 2004). The case is available at this link: http://scholar.google.com/scholar_case?case=14748284771413043760&hl=en&as_sdt=2&as_vis=1 &oi=scholarr.

You are an expert in *criminal law*, not *criminal procedure*. Would you **accept** or **reject** this case? Read *People v. Wrotten*, 2010 N.Y. Slip Op 04501 (2010). The case is available at this link: http://law.justia.com/cases/new-york/appellate-division-first-department/2010/2010-04501.html You are an expert in *constitutional law*. Would you **accept** or **reject** this case? Read *Wilson v. Layne*, 526 U.S. 603 (1999). The case is available at this link: http://www.law.cornell.edu/supct/html/98-83.ZS.html.

Reread question 3. Change your expertise to constitutional law as it applies to *criminal prosecutions*. Would you **accept** or **reject** the *Wilson* case?

Cases of Interest

- *Padilla v. Gonzales*, 397 F.3d 1016 (2005), discusses malum in se and malum prohibitum crimes: http://scholar.google.com/scholar_case?case=5187582705718052419&q= malum+in+se+ malum+in+prohibitum&hl=en&as_sdt=2,5&as_ylo=2004&as_vis=1.
- *Rogers v. Tennessee*, 532 U.S. 451 (2001), discusses a state's ability to create a common-law crime: http://www.law.cornell.edu/supct/html/99-6218.ZS.html.
- *Roe v. Wade*, 410 U.S. 113 (1973), is the case in which the US Supreme Court invalidates a state statute criminalizing abortion: http://www.law.cornell.edu/supct/html/historics/USSC_CR_0410_0113_ZO.html.

Articles of Interest

- Model Penal Code: http://legal-dictionary.thefreedictionary.com/Model+Penal+Code
- Stare decisis: http://civilliberty.about.com/od/historyprofiles/g/stare_decisis.htm

Websites of Interest

- Federal criminal statutes: http://www.law.cornell.edu/uscode/18
- State criminal statutes: http://www.legallawhelp.com/state_law/
- Government agencies in alphabetical order: https://www.usa.gov/federal-agencies/a
- Complete federal Constitution: http://topics.law.cornell.edu/constitution
- State constitutions: http://www.thegreenpapers.com/slg/links.phtml

Statistics of Interest

- State prosecutors in the United States: http://bjs.ojp.usdoj.gov/index.cfm?ty=pbse&sid=9
- Felony convictions in the US state courts: http://bjs.ojp.usdoj.gov/index.cfm?ty=pbdetail&iid=2152
- Estimated crime statistics in the United States: http://www.ucrdatatool.gov/Search/Crime/State/RunCrimeStatebyState.cfm

References

Shaw v. Murphy, 532 U.S. 223, 229 (2001), accessed October 4, 2010, http://scholar.google.com/scholar_case?case=9536800826824133166&hl=en&as_sdt=2&as_vis=1&oi=scholarr.

CC licensed content, Shared previously

- Criminal Law. **Provided by**: University of Minnesota Libraries Publishing . **Located at**: http://open.lib.umn.edu/criminallaw/. **License**: *CC BY-NC-SA: Attribution-NonCommercial-ShareAlike*

Chapter 2: The Legal System in the United States

2.1 Federalism

Brent Moore – Gordon County Courthouse – Calhoun, GA – CC BY-NC 2.0.

The requirement of proof beyond a reasonable doubt has this vital role in our criminal procedure for cogent reasons. The accused, during a criminal prosecution, has at stake interests of immense importance, both because of the possibility that he may lose his liberty upon conviction and because of the certainty that he would be stigmatized by the conviction.

—*In re: Winship*, cited in Section 2 "Burden of Proof in a Criminal Prosecution"

Learning Objectives

Define federalism.
Ascertain the sections of the Constitution that give Congress regulatory authority.
Ascertain the basis for Congress's authority to enact criminal laws.
Compare federal regulatory authority with state regulatory authority.
Compare federal criminal laws with state criminal laws.
Define federal supremacy.

The United States' system of government is called federalism. Federalism, as set forth in the US Constitution, divides governmental power between the *federal government* and each of the *states*. This prevents a concentrated source of governmental power in one individual or small group of individuals. Because of federalism, the United States has one federal legal system, and each state has its own state legal system. Thus in the United States, a plethora of legal systems all operate harmoniously at the same time.

The Scope of Federal Law

The government's power to regulate comes from the US Constitution. The *federal* government derives its authority to create law from Article I, § 8, which discusses federal Congress's *exclusive* or **delegated powers**. These include the power to regulate currency and coin, establish a post office, promote science and art by regulating the rights to discoveries and writings, declare war and raise armies, conduct foreign affairs, regulate interstate and foreign commerce, and make laws necessary and proper to execute other powers expressly granted in the Constitution. Courts have interpreted the last two powers mentioned in the commerce clause and the necessary and proper clause to be the *broadest* sources of federal regulatory authority.

To simplify and summarize precedent defining federal regulatory authority, federal laws are meant to regulate in two areas. First, federal laws regulate issues that concern the *country*, rather than just one city, county, or state. The federal government regulates in the area of foreign affairs, for example, because this affects the United States of America, not just one particular region. Second, federal laws regulate commerce, which is economic activity, that *crosses from state to state*. Some common examples are television broadcasts, the Internet, and any form of transportation such as the airlines.

Federal Criminal Laws

The original intent was for the federal government to be a *limited* government, with the bulk of regulatory authority residing in the *states*. The only *crimes* Congress is specifically authorized to punish are piracies and felonies on the high seas, counterfeiting, and treason; however, case precedent has expanded the federal government's power to enact criminal laws based on the commerce clause and the necessary and proper clause (McCulloch v. Maryland, 2010). Still, there must be *some* connection to an issue of national character and interstate commerce, or the federal government will overstep its authority. In general, federal criminal laws target conduct that occurs on federal property or conduct involving federal employees, currency, coin, treason, national security, rights secured by the Constitution, or commerce that crosses state lines. Currently, over five hundred crimes are listed in Part I, Title 18 of the United States Code, which codifies criminal laws for the federal government.

Figure 2.1 Diagram of Federal Laws

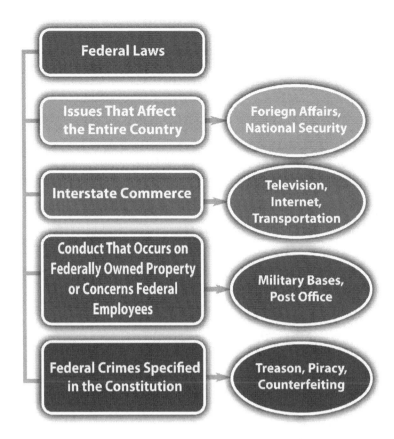

The Scope of State Law

The US Constitution designates the states as the *primary regulatory authority*. This is clarified in the Tenth Amendment, which reads, "The powers not delegated to the United States by the Constitution, nor prohibited to it by the States, are reserved to the States respectively, or the people." State laws are also supposed to regulate in two areas. First, state laws regulate issues of a *local* character or concern. A state may regulate, for example, its water ownership and use because water can be scarce and is not generally provided to other states. Second, state laws regulate issues or things that remain within a state's border. A state generally regulates, for example, the operation of a small business whose products are only sold locally and not shipped out of the state.

Federal laws are *the same* in every state, but state laws *differ* from state to state. Something that is legal in one state may be illegal in another state. This inconsistency makes our system of federalism complicated for students (and lawyers). However, with a country as large and varied as the United States, it is sensible to allow each state to choose for itself which laws will be most suitable.

State Criminal Laws

The power to enact criminal laws belongs almost *exclusively* to the states. This is because of the Tenth Amendment, which vests in states a police power to provide for the health, safety, and welfare of state citizens. Approximately 90 percent of all criminal laws are state, rather than federal. Often, federal crimes are also state crimes and can be prosecuted and punished by both the state and federal government without violating the principle of double jeopardy.

Example of the Diversity of State Laws

In Nevada, prostitution is legal under certain circumstances (N.R.S., 2010). An individual who engages in prostitution inside a licensed "house of prostitution" in Nevada is not exposed to criminal liability. However, if the *same individual* engages in prostitution in a *different state*, he or she may be subject to a criminal prosecution. Prostitution will be discussed in detail in Chapter 12 "Crimes against the Public".

Figure 2.2 Crack the Code

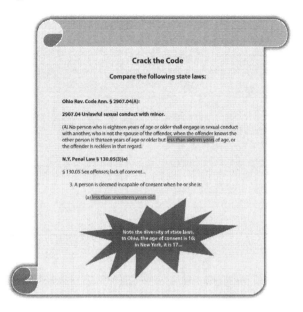

Federal Supremacy

Our legal system is divided up to conform to the principle of federalism, so a potential exists for conflict between federal law and state law. A federal law may make something *illegal*; a state law may insist that it is *legal*. Whenever a conflict occurs between federal and state law, courts must follow the federal law. This is called federal supremacy. As the Supremacy Clause of Article VI of the federal Constitution states, "This Constitution, and the Laws of the United States which shall be made in Pursuance thereof; and all Treaties made, or which shall be made, under the Authority of the United States, shall be the supreme Law of the Land; and the Judges in every State shall be bound thereby, any Thing in the Constitution or Laws of any State to the Contrary notwithstanding."

Example of Federal Supremacy

In Washington and several other states, an individual may possess and use marijuana for medicinal purposes with a prescription (Washington State Medicinal Marijuana Act, 2010; ProCon.org, 2010). Federal law prohibits possession and use of marijuana under *any circumstances* (21 U.S.C., 2010). Technically, this could be a conflict that violates **federal supremacy**. Until the courts address the federal supremacy issue, however, medical marijuana statutes can continue to stay in effect. Read about a recent ruling regarding the constitutionality of Michigan's medicinal marijuana law under the Supremacy Clause: http://www.pressandguide.com/articles/2011/04/09/news/doc4d9f557b8ab37805648033.txt.

Figure 2.3 Diagram of State Laws

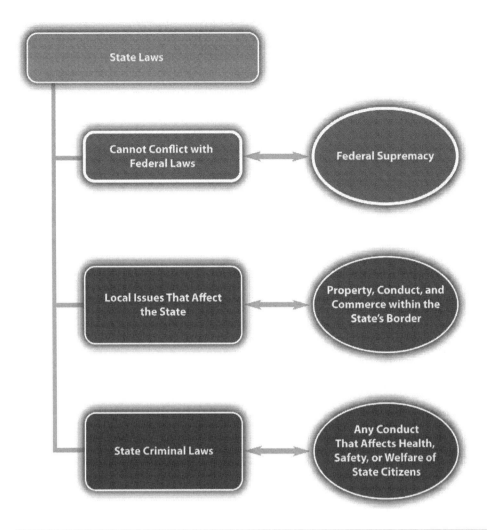

Law and Ethics: The Arizona Immigration Law

Can a State Regulate Immigration?

Arizona passed a comprehensive immigration law designed to seek out and deport illegal immigrants. This law created a national furor, and its detractors insisted it would lead to unethical racial profiling. The federal government attacked the law in Federal District Court (Archibold, R. C., 2010). Judge Susan Bolton issued a preliminary injunction that stopped enforcement of the sections of the law that required state law enforcement to check an immigrant's status while enforcing other laws and that required immigrants to prove they were in the country legally or risk state charges (Archibold, R. C., 2010). Read the District Court's preliminary injunction ruling, which is available at this link: http://graphics8.nytimes.com/packages/pdf/national/20100729_ARIZONA_DOC.pdf.

What is the basis for Judge Bolton's decision? Check your answer using the answer key at the end of the chapter.

Read about the most recent ruling on Arizona's immigration law by the US Court of Appeals for the Ninth Circuit: http://latindispatch.com/2011/05/10/arizonas-jan-brewer-to-appeal-immigration-law-to-u-s-supreme-court/.

Read about Utah's immigration law: http://www.cnn.com/2011/POLITICS/05/11/utah.immigration.bill/.

Read about Alabama's immigration law: http://www.reuters.com/article/2011/06/10/tagblogsfindlawcom2011-freeenterprise-idUS123058502120110610.

U.S. v. State of Arizona Video

10-16645 *U.S. v. State of Arizona*

This video is the Arizona governor's appeal of the district court preliminary injunction:
(click to see video)

Key Takeaways

- Federalism is a system of government in which power is divided between one national, federal government and several independent state governments.

- Congress gets its regulatory authority from Article I § 8 of the federal Constitution. This includes several delegated powers, the commerce clause, and the necessary and proper clause.
    - The commerce clause gives Congress the power to regulate commerce that crosses state lines.
    - The necessary and proper clause gives Congress the power to regulate if necessary to carry out all other powers listed in the Constitution.
- The Constitution specifically authorizes Congress to punish piracies and felonies on the high seas, counterfeiting, and treason. Case precedent has also expanded the federal government's power to enact criminal laws based on the commerce clause and the necessary and proper clause.
- The federal government is intended to be limited, with the bulk of regulatory authority residing in the states. The federal government is restricted to regulating in the areas designated in Article I § 8 of the federal Constitution. The states can regulate for the health, safety, and welfare of citizens pursuant to their police power, which is set forth in the Tenth Amendment of the federal Constitution.
- Federal criminal laws criminalize conduct that occurs on federal property or involves federal employees, currency, coin, treason, national security, rights secured by the Constitution, or commerce that crosses state lines. State criminal laws make up 90 percent of all criminal laws, are designed to protect state citizens' health, safety, and welfare, and often criminalize the same conduct as federal criminal laws.
- Federal supremacy, which is set forth in the Supremacy Clause of the federal Constitution, requires courts to follow federal laws if there is a conflict between a federal and state law.

Exercises

Answer the following questions. Check your answers using the answer key at the end of the chapter.

Congress passes a law criminalizing the posting of child pornography on the Internet. Where does Congress get the authority to pass this criminal law? If a state has a criminal law criminalizing the same conduct, can both the state *and* federal government prosecute a defendant for one act of downloading child pornography?
Read *U.S. v. Morrison*, 529 U.S. 518 (2000). Which part(s) of the Constitution did the US Supreme Court rely on when it held that 42 U.S.C. § 13981 is unconstitutional? The case is available at this link: http://www.law.cornell.edu/supct/html/99-5.ZS.html.
Read *Pennsylvania v. Nelson*, 350 U.S. 497 (1956). Why did the US Supreme Court invalidate the Pennsylvania Sedition Act? The case is available at this link: http://supreme.justia.com/us/350/497/case.html.

References

Archibold, R. C., "Judge Blocks Arizona's Immigration Law," The *New York Times* website, accessed October 1, 2010, http://www.nytimes.com/2010/07/29/us/29arizona.html.

McCulloch v. Maryland, 17 U.S. (4 Wheat.) 316 (1819), accessed August 28, 2010, http://www.law.cornell.edu/supct/html/historics/USSC_CR_0017_0316_ZS.html.

N.R.S. § 201.354, accessed September 24, 2010, http://www.leg.state.nv.us/nrs/NRS-201.html#NRS201Sec354.

Washington State Medicinal Marijuana Act, Chapter 69.51A RCW, accessed August 28, 2010, http://apps.leg.wa.gov/RCW/default.aspx?cite=69.51a&full=true.

ProCon.org website, see all states that legalize medicinal marijuana: "16 Legal Medical Marijuana States and DC," accessed August 28, 2010, http://medicalmarijuana.procon.org/view.resource.php?resourceID=000881.

21 U.S.C. Ch. 13 § 801 et. seq., accessed October 1, 2010, http://www.deadiversion.usdoj.gov/21cfr/21usc/index.html.

CC licensed content, Shared previously

- Criminal Law. **Provided by**: University of Minnesota Libraries Publishing . **Located at**: http://open.lib.umn.edu/criminallaw/. **License**: *CC BY-NC-SA: Attribution-NonCommercial-ShareAlike*

2.2 The Branches of Government

Learning Objectives

Identify the three branches of government.
Ascertain the head of the federal and state legislative branches of government.
Compare the Senate and the House of Representatives.
Ascertain the head of the federal and state executive branches of government.
Ascertain the head of the federal and state judicial branches of government.

The federal Constitution was written to ensure that government power is distributed and never concentrated in one or more areas. This philosophy is served by **federalism**, where the federal government shares power with the states. It is also further served by dividing the government into three branches, all responsible for different government duties and all *checking and balancing* each other. The three branches of government are detailed in Articles I–III of the federal Constitution and are the legislative branch, the executive branch, and the judicial branch. While the federal Constitution identifies only the federal branches of government, the principle of checks and balances applies to the states as well. Most states identify the three state branches of government in their state constitution.

Each branch of government has a distinct authority. When one branch encroaches on the duties of another, this is called a violation of separation of powers. The *courts* decide whether a government branch has overstepped its boundaries because courts interpret the Constitution, which describes each branch's sphere of influence. Thus the judicial branch, which consists of all the courts, retains the balance of power.

The Legislative Branch

The **legislative branch** is responsible for creating statutory laws. Citizens of a state can vote for some state statutes by ballot, but the **federal legislative branch** enacts all federal statutes. In the federal government, the legislative branch is headed by Congress. States' legislative branches are headed by a state legislature. Congress is bicameral, which means it is made up of two houses. This system provides equal representation among the several states and by citizens of the United States. States are represented by the Senate. Every state, no matter how large or small, gets two senators. Citizens are represented by the House of Representatives. Membership in the House of Representatives is based on population. A heavily populated state, like California, has more representatives than a sparsely populated state, like Alaska. States' legislatures are generally bicameral and have a similar structure to the federal system.

Figure 2.4 Diagram of the Legislative Branch

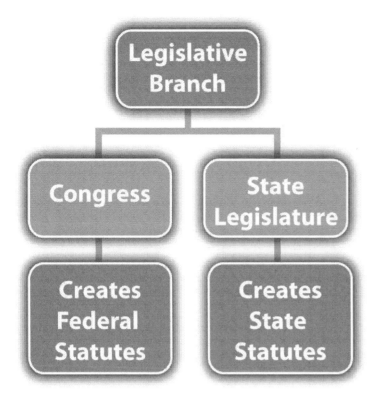

Examples of Legislative Branch Checks and Balances

The legislative branch can check and balance both the *executive* branch and the *judicial* branch. Congress can impeach the president of the United States, which is the first step toward removal from office. Congress can also enact statutes that supersede judicial opinions, as discussed in Chapter 1 "Introduction to Criminal Law". Similarly, state legislature can also impeach a governor or enact a state statute that supersedes a state case law.

The Executive Branch

The **executive branch** is responsible for enforcing the statutes enacted by the legislative branch. In the federal government, the executive branch is headed by the president of the United States. States' executive branches are headed by the governor of the state.

Figure 2.5 Diagram of the Executive Branch

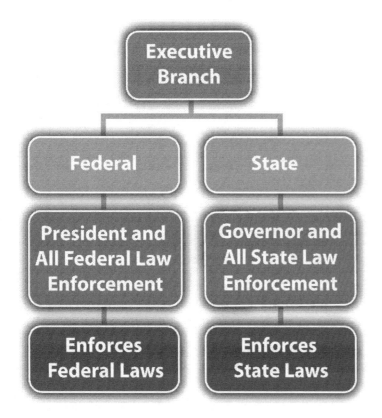

Examples of Executive Branch Checks and Balances

The executive branch can check and balance both the *legislative* branch and the *judicial* branch. The president of the United States can veto statutes proposed by Congress. The president also has the authority to nominate federal justices and judges, who thereafter serve for life. State executive branches have similar check and balancing authority; a governor can generally veto statutes proposed by state legislature and can appoint some state justices and judges.

The Judicial Branch

The **judicial branch** is responsible for interpreting all laws, including statutes, codes, ordinances, and the federal and state constitutions. This power is all encompassing and is the basis for **judicial review**, referenced in Chapter 1 "Introduction to Criminal Law". It allows the judicial branch to invalidate any unconstitutional law in the statutory source of law and also to change the federal and state constitutions by interpretation. For example, when a court creates an exception to an amendment to the constitution, it has made an informal change without the necessity of a national or state consensus. The federal judicial branch is headed by the US Supreme Court. Each state's judicial branch is headed by the highest-level state appellate court. Members of the judicial branch include all judges and justices of every federal and state court in the court system, which is discussed shortly.

Figure 2.6 Diagram of the Judicial Branch

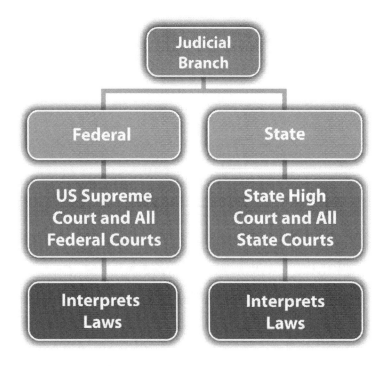

Examples of Judicial Branch Checks and Balances

The judicial branch can check and balance both the *legislative* branch and the *executive* branch. The US Supreme Court can invalidate statutes enacted by Congress if they conflict with the Constitution. The US Supreme Court can also prevent the president from taking action if that action violates separation of powers. The state courts can likewise nullify unconstitutional statutes passed by the state legislature and void other executive branch actions that are unconstitutional.

Table 2.1 The Most Prominent Checks and Balances between the Branches

Government Branch	Duty or Authority	Check and Balance	Government Branch Checking and Balancing
Legislative	Create statutes	President can veto	Executive
Executive	Enforce statutes	Congress can override presidential veto by 2/3 majority	Legislative
Judicial	Interpret statutes and Constitution	President nominates federal judges and justices	Executive
Executive	Enforce statutes	Senate can confirm or reject presidential nomination of federal judges and justices	Legislative
Executive	Enforce statutes	Congress can impeach the president	Legislative
Legislative	Create statutes	Courts can invalidate unconstitutional statutes	Judicial

Government Branch	Duty or Authority	Check and Balance	Government Branch Checking and Balancing
Executive	Enforce statutes	Courts can invalidate unconstitutional executive action	Judicial
Judicial	Interpret statutes and Constitution	Statutes can supersede case law	Legislative

Key Takeaways

- The three branches of government are the legislative branch, the executive branch, and the judicial branch.
- The head of the federal legislative branch of government is Congress. The head of the state legislative branch of government is the state legislature.
- The Senate represents every state equally because each state has two senators. The House of Representatives represents each citizen equally because states are assigned representatives based on their population.
- The head of the federal executive branch of government is the president. The head of each state executive branch of government is the governor.
- The head of the federal judicial branch of government is the US Supreme Court. The head of each state judicial branch of government is the highest-level state appellate court.

Exercises

Answer the following questions. Check your answers using the answer key at the end of the chapter.

A mayor enacts a policy that prohibits police officers in his city from enforcing a state law prohibiting the possession and use of marijuana. The mayor's policy specifically states that within the city limits, marijuana is legal to possess and use. Which constitutional principle is the mayor violating? Which branch of government should check and balance the mayor's behavior in this matter?

Read *Youngstown Sheet & Tube Co. v. Sawyer*, 343 U.S. 579 (1952). In *Youngstown*, President Truman seized control of steel mills to avert a strike, using his authority as commander in chief of the armed forces. President Truman wanted to ensure steel production during the Korean War. Did the US Supreme Court uphold President Truman's action? Why or why not? The case is available at this link: http://supreme.justia.com/us/343/579/.

Read *Hamdi v. Rumsfeld*, 542 U.S. 507 (2004). In *Hamdi*, the US Supreme Court reviewed the US Court of Appeals for the Fourth Circuit's decision prohibiting the release of a US citizen who was held as an enemy combatant in Virginia during the Afghanistan War. The citizen's detention was based on a federal statute that deprived him of the opportunity to consult with an attorney or have a trial. Did the US Supreme Court defer to the federal statute? Why or why not? The case is available at this link: http://scholar.google.com/scholar_case?case=6173897153146757813&hl=en&as_sdt=2&as_vis=1&oi=scholarr.

CC licensed content, Shared previously

- Criminal Law. **Provided by**: University of Minnesota Libraries Publishing . **Located at**: http://open.lib.umn.edu/criminallaw/. **License**: *CC BY-NC-SA: Attribution-NonCommercial-ShareAlike*

2.3 The Court System

Learning Objectives

Compare federal and state courts.
Define jurisdiction.
Compare original and appellate jurisdiction.
Identify the federal courts and determine each court's jurisdiction.
Identify the state courts and determine each court's jurisdiction.

Every state has *two* court systems: the *federal* court system, which is the same in all fifty states, and the *state* court system, which varies slightly in each state. Federal courts are fewer in number than state courts. Because of the Tenth Amendment, discussed earlier in Section 2.1.2 "The Scope of State Law", most laws are state laws and therefore most legal disputes go through the state court system.

Federal courts are exclusive; they adjudicate only *federal* matters. This means that a case can go through the federal court system only if it is based on a federal *statute* or the federal *Constitution*. One exception is called **diversity of citizenship** (28 U.S.C. § 1332, 2010).If citizens from different states are involved in a civil lawsuit and the amount in controversy exceeds $75,000, the lawsuit can take place in federal court. All federal *criminal prosecutions* take place in federal courts.

State courts are nonexclusive; they can adjudicate state or federal matters. Thus an individual who wants to sue civilly for a federal matter has the option of proceeding in state or federal court. In addition, someone involved in a lawsuit based on a federal statute or the federal Constitution can remove a lawsuit filed in state court to federal court (28 U.S.C. § 1441, 2010). All state *criminal prosecutions* take place in state courts.

Jurisdiction

Determining which court is appropriate for a particular lawsuit depends on the concept of jurisdiction. Jurisdiction has two meanings. A court's jurisdiction is the power or authority to hear the case in front of it. If a court does not have jurisdiction, it cannot hear the case. Jurisdiction can also be a geographic area over which the court's authority extends.

There are two prominent types of court jurisdiction. Original jurisdiction means that the court has the power to hear a trial. Usually, only *one* opportunity exists for a trial, although some actions result in both a criminal and a civil trial, discussed previously in Chapter 1 "Introduction to Criminal Law". During the trial, evidence is presented to a trier of fact, which can be either a judge or a jury. The trier of fact determines the facts of a dispute and decides which party prevails at trial by applying the law to those facts. Once the trial has concluded, the next step is an appeal. During an appeal, *no evidence is presented*; the appellate court simply reviews what took place at trial and determines whether or not any major errors occurred.

The power to hear an appeal is called appellate jurisdiction. Courts that have appellate jurisdiction review the **trial record** for error. The trial record includes a court reporter's **transcript**, which is typed notes of the words spoken during the trial and pretrial hearings. In general, with exceptions, appellate courts cannot review a trial record until the trial has ended with a *final judgment*. Once the appellate court has made its review, it has the ability to take three actions. If it finds no compelling or prejudicial errors, it can affirm the judgment of the trial court, which means that the judgment remains the same. If it finds a significant error, it can reverse the judgment of the trial court, which means that the judgment becomes the opposite (the winner loses, the loser wins). It can also remand, which means send the case back to the trial court, with instructions. After remand, the trial court can take action that the appellate court cannot, such as adjust a sentence or order a new trial.

Some courts have only original jurisdiction, but most courts have a little of original and appellate jurisdiction. The US Supreme Court, for example, is primarily an appellate court with appellate jurisdiction. However, it also has original jurisdiction in some cases, as stated in the Constitution, Article III, § 2, clause 2: "In all Cases affecting Ambassadors, other public Ministers and Consuls, and those in which a State shall be Party, the supreme Court shall have original Jurisdiction. In all the other Cases before mentioned, the supreme Court shall have appellate jurisdiction."

Example of Original and Appellate Jurisdiction

Paulina is prosecuted for the attempted murder of Ariana. Paulina is represented by public defender Pedro. At Paulina's trial, in spite of Pedro's objections, the judge rules that Paulina's polygraph examination results are admissible, but prohibits the admission of certain witness testimony. Paulina is found guilty and appeals, based on the judge's evidentiary rulings. While Pedro is writing the appellate brief, he discovers case precedent barring the admission of polygraph examination results. Pedro *can include* the case precedent in his appellate brief but *not the prohibited witness testimony*. The appellate court has the jurisdiction to hold that the objection was improperly overruled by the trial court, but is limited to reviewing the trial record for error. The appellate court *lacks* the jurisdiction to admit new evidence not included in the trial record.

The Federal Courts

For the purpose of this book, the focus is the federal trial court and the intermediate and highest level appellate courts because these courts are most frequently encountered in a criminal prosecution. Other federal specialty courts do exist but are not discussed, such as bankruptcy court, tax court, and the court of military appeals.

The federal trial court is called the **United States District Court**. Large states like California have more than one district court, while smaller states may have only one. District courts hear all the federal trials, including civil and criminal trials. As stated previously, a dispute that involves only state law, or a state criminal trial, cannot proceed in district court. The exception to this rule is the diversity of citizenship exception for civil lawsuits.

After a trial in district court, the loser gets one appeal of right. This means that the intermediate appellate federal court *must* hear an appeal of the district court trial if there are sufficient grounds. The intermediate appellate court in the federal system is the **United States Court of Appeals**. There is less federal law than state law, so only thirteen US Courts of Appeals exist for all fifty states. The US Courts of Appeals are spread out over thirteen judicial circuits and are also referred to as Circuit Courts.

Circuit Courts have appellate jurisdiction and can review the district court criminal and civil trials for error. The Circuit Court reviews only trials that are federal in nature, with the exception of civil lawsuits brought to the district court under diversity of citizenship. As noted in Chapter 1 "Introduction to Criminal Law", the federal Constitution governs criminal trials, so *only a guilty defendant* can appeal. In general, with exceptions, appeal of a not-guilty verdict (also called an acquittal) violates a defendant's double jeopardy protection.

After a Circuit Court appeal, the loser has one more opportunity to appeal to the highest-level federal appellate court, which is the **United States Supreme Court**. The US Supreme Court is the highest court in the country and is located in Washington, DC, the nation's capital. The US Supreme Court has eight associate justices and one chief justice: all serve a lifetime appointment.

The US Supreme Court is a discretionary court, meaning it does not have to hear appeals. Unlike the Circuit Courts, the US Supreme Court can pick and choose which appeals it wants to review. The method of applying for review with the US Supreme Court is called filing a petition for a writ of certiorari.

Any case from a Circuit Court, or a case *with a federal matter at issue* from a state's highest-level appellate court, can petition for a writ of certiorari. If the writ is granted, the US Supreme Court reviews the appeal. If the writ is denied, which it is the majority of the time, the ruling of the Circuit Court or state high court is the final ruling. For this reason, the US Supreme Court reverses many cases that are accepted for review. If the US Supreme Court wants to "affirm" the intermediate appellate court ruling, all it has to do is deny the petition and let the lower court ruling stand.

The State Courts

For the purpose of this book, a representative state court system is reviewed. Slight variations in this system may occur from state to state.

Most states offer their citizens a "people's court," typically called small claims court. **Small claims court** is a civil court designed to provide state citizens with a low-cost option to resolve disputes where the amount in controversy is minimal. A traditional small claims court only has the jurisdiction to award money damages. This means that it cannot adjudicate criminal matters or family court matters such as granting a petition for divorce. Small claims courts also limit the amount of money damages available, typically less than $10,000.

Small claims court has special rules that make it amenable to the average individual. Attorneys cannot represent clients in small claims court, although they certainly can represent themselves just like any other individual. Small claims court proceedings are generally informal, and usually no court reporter types what is said. Therefore, no court record exits for appeal. Small claims court *appeals* are the exception to the general rule and are usually new trials where evidence is accepted.

States generally have a **state trial court** that can also be the appellate court for small claims court appeals. This trial court is usually called superior court, circuit court, or county court. State trial courts are generally all-purpose and hear civil litigation matters, state criminal trials, and nonlitigation cases including family law, wills and probate, foreclosures, and juvenile adjudications. States can, however, create "specialty courts" to hear special matters and free up the trial courts for basic criminal prosecutions and civil litigation trials. Some states divide their trial courts into lower and higher levels. The lower-level trial court adjudicates infractions and misdemeanors, along with civil lawsuits with a smaller amount in controversy. The higher-level trial court adjudicates felonies and civil lawsuits with a higher amount in controversy.

The intermediate appellate court for the state court system is usually called the **state court of appeals**, although some smaller or low-population states may have only *one* appellate court called the **state supreme court**. The state courts of appeal provide appeals of right, meaning they *must* hear an appeal coming from the state's trial court if adequate grounds are present. Appeals can be of any case adjudicated in the state trial court. In state criminal prosecutions, as stated earlier in the discussion of federal appeals, only a guilty defendant can appeal without violating the protection against double jeopardy. At the appellate level, the state court of appeal simply reviews the trial court record for error and does not have the **jurisdiction** to hear new trials or accept evidence.

The highest appellate court for the state court system is usually called the state supreme court. In states that have both intermediate and high-level appellate courts, the state supreme court is a discretionary court that gets to select the appeals it hears, very similar to the US Supreme Court. The state supreme court generally grants a petition for writ of certiorari, or a **petition for review**, if it decides to hear a civil or criminal case coming out of the state court of appeal. If review is denied, the state court of appeal ruling is the final ruling on the case. If review is granted and the state supreme court rules on the case, the loser has one more chance to appeal, *if there is a federal matter*, to the US Supreme Court.

Figure 2.7 Diagram of the Court System

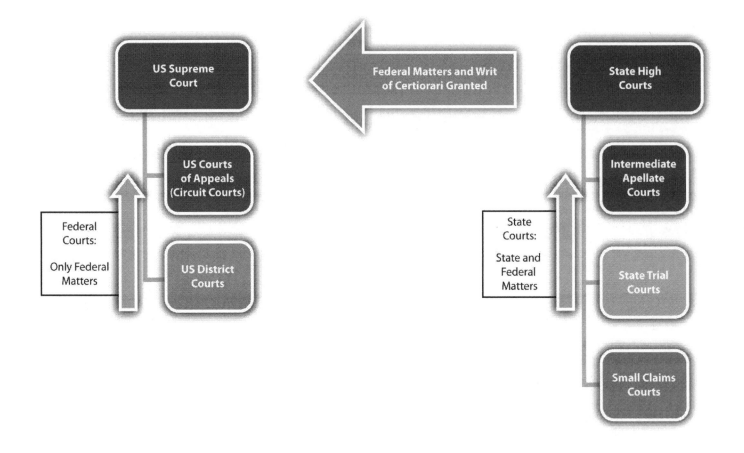

Key Takeaways

- Federal courts are exclusive and hear only federal matters or cases involving diversity of citizenship. State courts are nonexclusive and can hear state and federal matters. All federal criminal prosecutions take place in federal court, and all state criminal prosecutions take place in state court.
- Jurisdiction is either the court's power to hear a matter or a geographic area over which a court has authority.
- Original jurisdiction is a court's power to hear a trial and accept evidence. Appellate jurisdiction is a court's power to hear an appeal and review the trial for error.
- Three federal courts adjudicate criminal matters: the trial court, which is called the United States District Court; the intermediate court of appeal, which is called the United States Court of Appeals or Circuit Court; and the high court of appeal, which is called the United States Supreme Court. The district court has original jurisdiction; the Circuit Court and US Supreme Court have primarily appellate jurisdiction.
- State courts are usually limited to four, and only three adjudicate criminal matters. Small claims court is a "people's court" and hears only civil matters with a low threshold of damages. The state trial court, often called superior, circuit, or county court, is the trial court for the state system. Some states have an intermediate court of appeal, which is generally called the state court of appeals. Some states have a high court of appeal, which is generally called the state supreme court. The trial court has original jurisdiction; the state court of appeal and state supreme court primarily have appellate jurisdiction.

Exercises

Answer the following questions. Check your answers using the answer key at the end of the chapter.

Jenna sues Max for $25,000, based on a car accident that occurs in Indiana. Jenna loses at trial and appeals to the highest state appellate court in Indiana, where she loses again. Can Jenna appeal her case to the US Supreme Court? Why or why not?

Read *United States v. P.H.E., Inc.*, 965 F.2d 848 (1992). In *P.H.E., Inc.*, the defendant never went to trial but was *indicted*. The defendant challenged the indictment, which was upheld by the trial court. The government claimed that the Court of Appeals for the Tenth Circuit could not hear an appeal of the trial court's decision, because there was never a "final judgment." Did the Circuit Court agree? Why or why not? The case is available at this link:
http://scholar.google.com/scholar_case?case=16482877108359401771&hl=en&as_sdt=2&as_vis=1&oi=scholarr.

Read *Hertz Corp. v. Friend*, 130 S. Ct. 1181 (2010). How did the US Supreme Court determine citizenship of a *corporation* for the purpose of diversity jurisdiction? The case is available at this link:
http://scholar.google.com/scholar_case?case=11481058059843290042&hl=en&as_sdt=2&as_vis=1&oi=scholarr.

References

28 U.S.C. § 1332, accessed August 30, 2010, http://www.law.cornell.edu/uscode/28/1332.html.

28 U.S.C. § 1441 et. seq., accessed August 30, 2010, http://www.law.cornell.edu/uscode/28/1441.html.
CC licensed content, Shared previously

- Criminal Law. **Provided by**: University of Minnesota Libraries Publishing . **Located at**: http://open.lib.umn.edu/criminallaw/. **License**: *CC BY-NC-SA: Attribution-NonCommercial-ShareAlike*

2.4 The Burden of Proof

Learning Objectives

Define the burden of proof.
Distinguish between the burden of production and the burden of persuasion.
Compare the civil and criminal burden of proof.
Compare inference and presumption.
Compare circumstantial and direct evidence.

The key to the success of a civil or criminal trial is meeting the burden of proof. A *failure* to meet the burden of proof is also a common ground for appeal. In this section, you learn the burden of proof for the plaintiff, prosecution, and defendant. You also are introduced to different classifications of evidence and evidentiary rules that can change the outcome of the trial.

Definition of the Burden of Proof

The burden of proof is a party's responsibility to prove a disputed charge, allegation, or defense (Yourdictionary.com, 2010). The burden of proof has two components: the burden of production and the burden of persuasion. The burden of production is the obligation to *present* evidence to the judge or jury. The burden of persuasion is the duty to *convince* the judge or jury to a certain standard, such as beyond a reasonable doubt, which is defined shortly. This standard is simply a measuring point and is determined by examining the quantity and quality of the evidence presented. "Meeting the burden of proof" means that a party has introduced enough compelling evidence to reach the standard defined in the burden of persuasion.

The plaintiff or prosecutor generally has the burden of proving the case, including every element of it. The defendant often has the burden of proving any defense. The trier of fact determines whether a party met the burden of proof at trial. The trier of fact would be a judge in a nonjury or bench trial. In a *criminal* case, the trier of fact is almost always a jury because of the right to a jury trial in the Sixth Amendment. Jurors are not legal experts, so the judge explains the burden of proof in jury instructions, which are a common source of appeal.

Burden of Proof in a Civil Case

Burdens of proof vary, depending on the type of case being tried. The plaintiff's burden of proof in a civil case is called preponderance of evidence. Preponderance of evidence requires the plaintiff to introduce slightly more or slightly better evidence than the defense. This can be as low as 51 percent plaintiff to 49 percent defendant. When preponderance of evidence is the burden of proof, the judge or jury must be convinced that it is "more likely than not" that the defendant is liable for the plaintiff's injuries. Preponderance of evidence is a fairly low standard, but the plaintiff must still produce more and better evidence than the defense. If the plaintiff offers evidence of questionable quality, the judge or jury can find that the burden of proof is not met and the plaintiff loses the case.

The defendant's burden of proof when proving a defense in a civil case is also preponderance of evidence. For example, in the O. J. Simpson civil case discussed in Chapter 1 "Introduction to Criminal Law", O. J. Simpson failed to meet the burden of proving the defense of *alibi*. The defendant does not always have to prove a defense in a civil case. If the plaintiff does not meet the burden of proof, the defendant is victorious without having to present *any evidence at all*.

Burden of Proof in a Criminal Prosecution

The prosecution's burden of proof in a criminal case is the most challenging burden of proof in law; it is **beyond a reasonable doubt**. Judges have struggled with a definition for this burden of proof. As Chief Justice Shaw stated nearly a century ago,

[w]hat is reasonable doubt? It is a term often used, probably pretty well understood, but not easily defined. It is not mere possible doubt; because every thing relating to human affairs, and depending on moral evidence, is open to some possible or imaginary doubt. It is that state of the case, which, after the entire comparison and consideration of all the evidence, leaves the minds of jurors in that condition that they cannot say they feel an abiding conviction, to a moral certainty, of the truth of the charge (Commonwealth v. Webster, 2010).

In general, the prosecution's evidence must overcome the defendant's presumption of innocence, which the Constitution guarantees as due process of law (In re Winship, 2010). This fulfills the policy of criminal prosecutions, which is to punish the guilty, not the innocent. If even a slight chance exists that the defendant is innocent, the case most likely lacks convincing and credible evidence, and the trier of fact should acquit the defendant.

States vary as to their requirements for the defendant's burden of proof when asserting a defense in a criminal prosecution (Findlaw.com, 2010). Different defenses also have different burdens of proof, as is discussed in detail in Chapter 5 "Criminal Defenses, Part 1" and Chapter 6 "Criminal Defenses, Part 2". Some states require the defendant to meet the burden of production, but require the prosecution to thereafter meet the burden of persuasion, *disproving* the defense to a preponderance of evidence or, in some states, beyond a reasonable doubt. Other states require the defendant to meet the burden of production *and* the burden of persuasion. In these states, the defendant's standard is typically preponderance of evidence, *not* beyond a reasonable doubt. The defendant does not always have to prove a defense in a criminal prosecution. If the prosecution does not meet the burden of proof, the defendant is acquitted without having to present any evidence at all.

Example of a Failure to Meet the Burden of Proof

Ann is on trial for first-degree murder. The only key piece of evidence in Ann's trial is the murder weapon, which was discovered in Ann's dresser drawer during a law enforcement search. Before Ann's trial, the defense makes a motion to suppress the murder weapon evidence because the search warrant in Ann's case was signed by a judge who was inebriated and mentally incompetent. The defense is successful with this motion, and the judge rules that the murder weapon is *inadmissible* at trial. The prosecution decides to proceed anyway. If there is no other convincing and credible evidence of Ann's guilt, Ann does not need to put on a defense in this case. The prosecution will fail to meet the burden of proof and Ann will be acquitted.

Figure 2.8 Diagram of the Criminal Burden of Proof

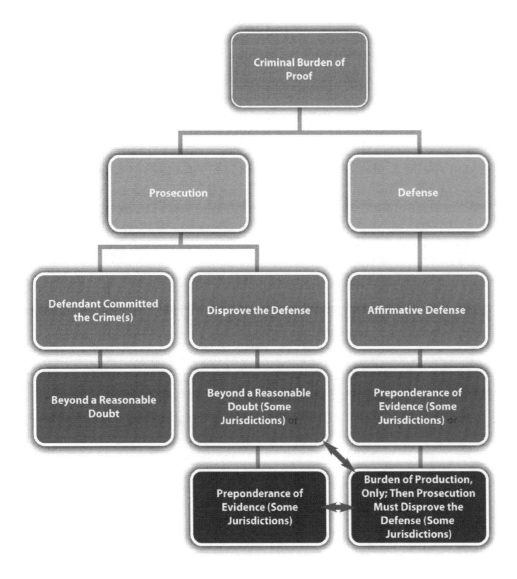

Inference and Presumption

Parties can use two tools to help meet the burden of proof: inference and presumption. Jury instructions can include inferences and presumptions and are often instrumental in the successful outcome of a case.

An inference is a conclusion that the judge or jury *may* make under the circumstances. An inference is never mandatory but is a choice. For example, if the prosecution proves that the defendant punched the victim in the face after screaming, "I hate you!" the judge or jury can infer that the punch was thrown intentionally.

A presumption is a conclusion that the judge or jury *must* make under the circumstances. As stated previously, all criminal defendants are presumed innocent. Thus the judge or jury *must* begin any criminal trial concluding that the defendant is not guilty.

Presumptions can be rebuttable or irrebuttable. A party can disprove a *rebuttable* presumption. The prosecution can rebut the presumption of innocence with evidence proving beyond a reasonable doubt that the defendant is guilty. An irrebuttable presumption is irrefutable and *cannot* be disproved. In some jurisdictions, it is an irrebuttable presumption that children under the age of seven are incapable of forming criminal intent. Thus in these jurisdictions children under the age of seven cannot be criminally prosecuted (although they may be subject to a juvenile adjudication proceeding).

Circumstantial and Direct Evidence

Two primary classifications are used for evidence: circumstantial evidence or direct evidence.

Circumstantial evidence indirectly proves a fact. Fingerprint evidence is usually circumstantial. A defendant's fingerprint at the scene of the crime *directly* proves that the defendant placed a finger at that location. It *indirectly* proves that because the defendant was present at the scene and placed a finger there, the defendant committed the crime. Common examples of circumstantial evidence are fingerprint evidence, DNA evidence, and blood evidence. Criminal cases relying on circumstantial evidence are more difficult for the prosecution because circumstantial evidence leaves room for doubt in a judge's or juror's mind. However, circumstantial evidence such as DNA evidence can be very reliable and compelling, so the prosecution can and often does meet the burden of proof using *only* circumstantial evidence.

Direct evidence directly proves a fact. For example, eyewitness testimony is often direct evidence. An eyewitness testifying that he or she saw the defendant commit the crime *directly* proves that the defendant committed the crime. Common examples of direct evidence are eyewitness testimony, a defendant's confession, or a video or photograph of the defendant committing the crime. Criminal cases relying on direct evidence are easier to prove because there is less potential for reasonable doubt. However, direct evidence can be unreliable and is not necessarily preferable to circumstantial evidence. If an eyewitness is impeached, which means he or she loses credibility, the witness's testimony lacks the evidentiary value of reliable circumstantial evidence such as DNA evidence.

Table 2.2 Comparison of Circumstantial and Direct Evidence in a Burglary Case

Evidence	Circumstantial	Direct
Fiber from the defendant's coat found in a residence that has been burglarized	Yes	No—directly proves **presence at the scene**, not that the defendant committed burglary
GPS evidence indicating the defendant drove to the burglarized residence	Yes	No—same explanation as fiber evidence
Testimony from an eyewitness that she saw the defendant go into the backyard of the burglarized residence	Yes	No—could prove trespassing because it directly proves **presence at the scene**, but it does not directly prove burglary
Surveillance camera footage of the defendant purchasing burglar tools	Yes	No—does not directly prove they were used on the residence
Cell phone photograph of the defendant burglarizing the residence	No	Yes—directly proves that the defendant committed the crime
Witness testimony that the defendant confessed to burglarizing the residence	No	Yes—directly proves that the defendant committed the crime
Pawn shop receipt found in the defendant's pocket for items stolen from the residence	Yes	No—directly proves that the items were pawned, not stolen

Casey Anthony Trial Video

Casey Anthony Verdict: Found Not Guilty of Murder

In this video, the jury foreperson in the Casey Anthony trial reads the trial verdict. Casey Anthony was acquitted of murder, manslaughter, and child abuse of her daughter, Caylee Anthony. The evidence in the case was all *circumstantial*, and the coroner did not determine the cause of the victim's death (Lohr, D., 2011).

(click to see video)

Key Takeaways

- The burden of proof is a party's obligation to prove a charge, allegation, or defense.
- The burden of production is the duty to present evidence to the trier of fact. The burden of persuasion is the duty to convince the trier of fact to a certain standard, such as preponderance of evidence or beyond a reasonable doubt.

- The civil burden of proof is preponderance of evidence, for both the plaintiff and the defendant. The criminal burden of proof for the prosecution is beyond a reasonable doubt.
    - The criminal burden of proof for the defense is generally preponderance of evidence. States vary on whether they require the criminal defendant to meet both the burden of production and persuasion or just the burden of production. Different defenses also require different burdens of proof.
    - In states that require the defendant to meet only the burden of production, the prosecution must disprove the defense to a preponderance of evidence or beyond a reasonable doubt, depending on the state and on the defense.
- An inference is a conclusion the trier of fact may make, if it chooses to. A presumption is a conclusion the trier of fact must make. A rebuttable presumption can be disproved; an irrebuttable presumption cannot.
- Circumstantial evidence indirectly proves a fact. A fingerprint at the scene of the crime, for example, indirectly proves that because the defendant was present at the scene, the defendant committed the crime. Direct evidence directly proves a fact. If the defendant confesses to a crime, for example, this is direct evidence that the defendant committed the crime.

Exercises

Answer the following questions. Check your answers using the answer key at the end of the chapter.

Bria is asserting the insanity defense in her criminal prosecution for murder. In Bria's state, defendants have the burden of production and persuasion to a preponderance of evidence when proving the insanity defense. Bria offers her own testimony that she is insane and incapable of forming criminal intent. Will Bria be successful with her defense? Why or why not?

Read *Patterson v. New York*, 432 U.S. 197 (1977). In *Patterson*, the defendant was on trial for murder. New York law reduced murder to manslaughter if the defendant proved extreme emotional disturbance to a **preponderance of evidence**. Did the US Supreme Court hold that it is *constitutional* to put this burden on the defense, rather than forcing the prosecution to disprove extreme emotional disturbance beyond a reasonable doubt? Which part of the Constitution did the Court analyze to justify its holding? The case is available at this link: http://supreme.justia.com/us/432/197/case.html.

Read *Sullivan v. Louisiana*, 508 U.S. 275 (1993). In *Sullivan*, the jury was given a constitutionally deficient jury instruction on beyond a reasonable doubt. Did the US Supreme Court hold that this was a prejudicial error requiring reversal of the defendant's conviction for murder? Which part of the Constitution did the Court rely on in its holding? The case is available at this link: http://scholar.google.com/scholar_case?case=1069192289025184531&hl=en&as_sdt=2002&as_vis=1.

References

Commonwealth v. Webster, 59 Mass. 295, 320 (1850), accessed September 26, 2010, http://masscases.com/cases/sjc/59/59mass295.html.

Findlaw.com, "The Insanity Defense among the States," findlaw.com website, accessed October 1, 2010, http://criminal.findlaw.com/crimes/more-criminal-topics/insanity-defense/the-insanity-defense-among-the-states.html.

In re Winship, 397 U.S. 358 (1970), accessed September 26, 2010, http://www.law.cornell.edu/supct/html/historics/USSC_CR_0397_0358_ZO.html.

Lohr, D., "Casey Anthony Verdict: NOT GUILTY of First-Degree Murder," Huffingtonpost.com website, accessed August 24, 2011, http://www.huffingtonpost.com/2011/07/05/casey-anthony-trial-verdict_n_890173.html#s303265&title=Casey_Anthony_Verdict.

Yourdictionary.com, "Definition of Burden of Proof," accessed September 26, 2010, http://www.yourdictionary.com/burden-of-proof.

CC licensed content, Shared previously

- Criminal Law. **Provided by**: University of Minnesota Libraries Publishing . **Located at**: http://open.lib.umn.edu/criminallaw/. **License**: *CC BY-NC-SA: Attribution-NonCommercial-ShareAlike*

2.5 End-of-Chapter Material

Summary

The United States' system of government is called federalism and consists of one federal government regulating issues of a national concern and separate state governments regulating local issues. The bulk of criminal lawmaking resides with the states because of the police power granted to the states in the Tenth Amendment. Ninety percent of all criminal laws are state laws. Many federal crimes are also state crimes, and a defendant can be prosecuted federally and by a state without triggering double jeopardy protection. If a federal statute exists on an issue, a state statute cannot conflict with it because of the Constitution's Supremacy Clause.

The Constitution sets forth three branches of government. The legislative branch consists of Congress and has the authority to create laws. The executive branch is headed by the president of the United States and has the authority to enforce the laws created by the legislative branch. The judicial branch is headed by the US Supreme Court and has the authority to interpret laws and the Constitution. Each branch checks and balances each other, and the judicial branch ensures that no branch oversteps its authority and violates separation of powers. State governments mimic the federal branches of government at the state level and set forth authorities in each state's constitution.

The federal court system exclusively adjudicates federal matters and consists primarily of the US District Court, the US Court of Appeals or Circuit Court, and the US Supreme Court. Each state has its own court system consisting primarily of a trial court, intermediate court of appeal, and possibly a high court of appeal. Trial courts have original jurisdiction and can accept evidence. Appellate courts have appellate jurisdiction and are limited to reviewing the trial courts' decisions for error.

Each party in a civil or criminal trial must meet a burden of proof, which consists of a burden of producing evidence and a burden of persuading the trier of fact. The burden of proof for a civil plaintiff or defendant is preponderance of evidence, which means that the trier of fact must be convinced it is more likely than not that a party should prevail. The burden of proof for the prosecution in a criminal case is beyond a reasonable doubt, which is a stricter standard than preponderance of evidence and consists of enough compelling evidence to rebut the defendant's presumption of innocence. The burden of proof for a criminal defense varies but is often preponderance of evidence. Inferences, which are conclusions the trier of fact may make, and presumptions, which are conclusions the trier of fact must make, can help meet the burden of proof. The evidence presented to meet the burden of proof can be circumstantial, which indirectly proves a fact, or direct, which directly proves a fact. Circumstantial evidence leaves room for reasonable doubt, but it can be reliable and the basis of a successful criminal prosecution.

You Be the Juror

Read the prompt, review the case, and then decide whether enough evidence exists to meet the burden of proof. Check your answers using the answer key at the end of the chapter.

The defendant was convicted of possession of a handgun with an altered serial number. The defendant contended that he *did not know* the serial number had been altered. The prosecution offered evidence that the gun was "shiny" in the location of the serial number. The prosecution also proved that the defendant was in possession of the handgun for a week. Is this sufficient evidence to prove beyond a reasonable doubt that the defendant knew the serial number had been altered? Read *Robles v. State*, 758 N.E.2d 581 (2001). The case is available at this link: http://scholar.google.com/scholar_case?case=7369971752262973607&q= Indiana+2001+%22Robles+v.+State%22&hl=en&as_sdt=2,5.

The defendant was convicted of attempted first-degree murder of a peace officer when he shot a sheriff. The defendant contended that he *did not know* the victim was a peace officer. The sheriff was in a vehicle with a whip antenna, was armed, and was well known as a sheriff in Angola Prison, where the defendant was incarcerated previous to the shooting incident. However, the sheriff was in an unmarked car with the red light covered, out of uniform, and his badge was obscured. Is this sufficient evidence to prove beyond a reasonable doubt that the defendant knew the victim was a peace officer? Read *Donahue v. Burl Cain*, 231 F.3d 1000 (2000). The case is available at this link: http://openjurist.org/231/f3d/1000/larry-donahue-v-burl-cain.

The defendant was convicted of third-degree robbery, which requires a threat of immediate use of physical force. The defendant entered a McDonald's restaurant twenty minutes before closing dressed in sunglasses, a leather jacket, and a bandana that covered his hair. The defendant beckoned the clerk and thereafter demanded that she put money from different cash register drawers into his bag. The defendant did not appear armed, nor did he raise his voice or verbally threaten the clerk. Is this sufficient evidence to prove beyond a reasonable doubt that the defendant threatened immediate use of physical force? Read *State v. Hall*, 966 P.2d 208 (1998). The case is available at this link: http://www.publications.ojd.state.or.us/docs/S44712.htm.

The defendant was convicted of possession of cocaine with intent to sell. The defendant possessed seven individual packages of white powdery substance, but only one package was tested (and it tested positive for cocaine). Is this sufficient evidence to prove beyond a reasonable doubt that the defendant possessed cocaine with intent to sell? Read *Richards v. Florida*, No. 4008-4216 (2010). The case is available at this link: http://www.4dca.org/opinions/June%202010/06-09-10/4D08-4216.op.w-dissent.pdf.

Cases of Interest

- *Clinton v. Jones*, 520 U.S. 681 (1997), discusses separation of powers: http://scholar.google.com/scholar_case?case=1768307810279741111&q= Clinton+v.+Jones&hl=en&as_sdt=2,5.
- *Gonzales v. Raich*, 545 U.S. 1 (2005), discusses the reach of the commerce clause: http://scholar.google.com/scholar_case?case=15669334228411787012&q= %22criminal+burden+of+proof%22&hl=en&as_sdt=2,5&as_ylo=2000.
- *Sabri v. United States*, 541 U.S. 600 (2004), discusses the federal government's ability to criminalize bribery of a local government official: http://www.law.cornell.edu/supct/html/03-44.ZS.html.
- *U.S. v. Comstock*, 627 F.3d 513 (2010), discusses criminal and civil burdens of proof: http://scholar.google.com/scholar_case?case=15669334228411787012&q= %22criminal+burden+of+proof%22&hl=en&as_sdt=2,5&as_ylo=2000.

Articles of Interest

- Connections between federalism and homeland security: https://www.hsaj.org/articles/163
- Video court: http://www.businessweek.com/ap/financialnews/D9N3D24G0.htm
- Burden of proof: http://law.jrank.org/pages/4927/Burden-Proof.html
- Federal and state court systems: http://www.uscourts.gov/about-federal-courts/court-role-and-structure/comparing-federal-state-courts

Websites of Interest

- US Supreme Court: http://www.supremecourt.gov
- Federal courts: http://www.uscourts.gov/
- Civic participation: http://www.congress.org

Statistics of Interest

- US Supreme Court: http://www.allcountries.org/uscensus/356_u_s_supreme_court_cases_filed.html

References

Order, *U.S. v. Arizona*, No. CV 10-1413-PHX-SRB, U.S. District Court, accessed October 1, 2010, http://graphics8.nytimes.com/packages/pdf/national/20100729_ARIZONA_DOC.pdf.
CC licensed content, Shared previously

- Criminal Law. **Provided by**: University of Minnesota Libraries Publishing . **Located at**: http://open.lib.umn.edu/criminallaw/. **License**: *CC BY-NC-SA: Attribution-NonCommercial-ShareAlike*

Chapter 3: Constitutional Protections

3.1 Applicability of the Constitution

arbyreed – Mountain Flag – CC BY-NC 2.0.

Those who wrote our constitutions knew from history and experience that it was necessary to protect against unfounded criminal charges brought to eliminate enemies and against judges too responsive to the voice of higher authority.

—*Duncan v. Louisiana*, cited in Section 3.2 "The Due Process and Equal Protection Clauses"

Learning Objectives

Distinguish between the two types of constitutional protections.
Compare unconstitutional on its face with unconstitutional as applied.
Distinguish among different standards of judicial review.
Compare bill of attainder with ex post facto laws.
Ascertain the three types of ex post facto laws.

In addition to statutory and common-law defenses, a criminal defendant has extensive protections that are set forth in the United States Constitution. As stated earlier in this book, the federal Constitution is applicable in all criminal cases because the government is prosecuting. State constitutions typically mirror the federal Constitution because it sets the *minimum* standard of protection that is guaranteed to all citizens. States can and often do provide *more* constitutional protections to criminal defendants than the federal Constitution, as long as those state protections do not violate notions of federal supremacy. In this chapter, the federal Constitution is analyzed with reference to state constitutional protections when relevant.

Constitutional Protections

Generally, two types of constitutional protections exist. First, a defendant can challenge the constitutionality of a criminal statute or ordinance (from this point forward, the term *statute* includes ordinances unless otherwise noted). Recall from Chapter 1 "Introduction to Criminal Law" that these codified laws cannot conflict with or attempt to supersede the Constitution. An attack on the constitutionality of a statute can be a claim that the statute is unconstitutional on its face, is unconstitutional as applied, or *both*. A statute is unconstitutional on its face when its wording is unconstitutional. A statute is unconstitutional as applied when its enforcement is unconstitutional. The difference between the two is significant. If a statute is unconstitutional on its face, it is invalid under *any circumstances*. If the statute is unconstitutional as applied, it is only unconstitutional under certain circumstances.

A second type of constitutional protection is *procedural*. The defendant can protest an unconstitutional procedure that occurs during prosecution. Procedure during prosecution includes, but is not limited to, arrest, interrogation, search, filing of charges, trial, and appeal. The defendant can make a motion to dismiss the charges, suppress evidence, or declare a mistrial. The defendant can also appeal and seek to reverse a conviction, among other remedies.

This book concentrates on criminal law rather than criminal procedure, so the bulk of this chapter is devoted to unconstitutional criminal statutes, rather than unconstitutional *procedures*. The exception is the right to a jury trial, which is discussed shortly.

Example of Constitutional Protections

Bill is on trial for obstructing a public sidewalk. Bill was arrested for standing in front of a restaurant's entrance with a sign stating "will eat any and all leftovers." The city ordinance Bill violated makes it a misdemeanor to "stand or sit on a public sidewalk with a sign." To save money, the judge presiding over Bill's trial declares that Bill will have a bench trial, rather than a jury trial. In this example, Bill can constitutionally attack the city *ordinance* for violating his freedom of speech because it prohibits holding a sign. The city ordinance appears unconstitutional *on its face* and *as applied* to Bill. Bill can also constitutionally attack *his bench trial* because he has the right to a jury trial. He could do this by making a motion to declare a mistrial, by petitioning an appellate court to halt the trial, or by appeal after a judgment of conviction.

Figure 3.1 Constitutional Protections

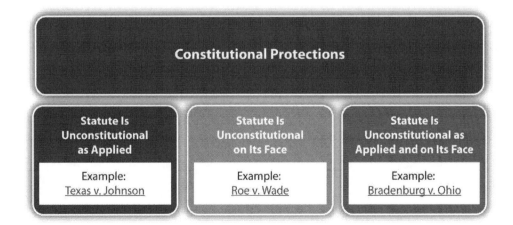

Judicial Review

As stated previously in this book, courts review statutes to ensure that they conform to the Constitution pursuant to their power of **judicial review**. Courts generally use different standards of review when constitutional protections are at stake. Typically, a court balances the *government's* interest in regulating certain conduct against an *individual's* interest in a constitutionally protected right. This balancing of interests varies depending on the right at stake. If a constitutional right is fundamental, the court uses strict scrutiny to analyze the statute at issue. A statute that violates or inhibits fundamental constitutional protections is presumptively invalid and can be upheld only if it uses the least restrictive means possible. The government also must prove the statute is supported by a compelling government interest. When the challenge is based on discrimination under the equal protection clause, the court may use a lower standard, called the rational basis test. The rational basis test allows a statute to discriminate if the statute is rationally related to a legitimate government interest. Most constitutional rights are considered fundamental and trigger the strict scrutiny of the courts.

Example of Strict Scrutiny

Review the example regarding Bill, who was arrested essentially for standing and holding a sign. The US Supreme Court has held that freedom of speech is a *fundamental right*. Thus a court reviewing the ordinance in Bill's case will hold the ordinance presumptively invalid, unless the government can demonstrate a compelling interest in enacting it, and that it used the least restrictive means possible. The ordinance is broadly written to include all signs, and preventing individuals from holding signs does not serve a compelling government interest, so this difficult standard will probably result in the court holding the ordinance *unconstitutional*.

The Legislative Branch's Prohibited Powers

The legislative branch cannot punish defendants without a trial or enact retroactive criminal statutes pursuant to the Constitution's prohibition against bill of attainder and ex post facto laws. Article 1, § 9, clause 3 states, in pertinent part, "No Bill of Attainder or ex post facto Law shall be passed." The prohibition on bill of attainder and ex post facto laws is extended to the states in Article 1, § 10, clause 1: "No State shall...pass any Bill of Attainder, ex post facto Law." Many state constitutions also prohibit ex post facto legislative action, mirroring the federal Constitution (Indiana Constitution, 2010).

Bill of Attainder

Bill of attainder is when the legislative branch of government punishes the defendant without a trial. The drafters of the Constitution wanted to ensure that criminal defendants have a full and fair adjudication of their rights before the government imposes punishment. Bill of attainder is usually accomplished by a statute that targets an individual or group of individuals for some type of government sanction. Bill of attainder protection enforces *separation of powers* by eliminating the ability of the legislature to impose criminal punishment without a trial conducted by the judicial branch (U.S. v. Brown, 2010).

Example of Bill of Attainder

Brianne is a member of the Communist party. Brianne applies for a job as a teacher at her local elementary school and is refused, based on this statute: "Members of any subversive group, including the Communist party, cannot hold public office nor teach for a public institution." Brianne could attack this statute as a bill of attainder. Its provisions, targeting members of the Communist party or any other subversive group, *punish* by eliminating career opportunities. The members targeted are punished without a trial or any adjudication of their rights. Thus this statute allows the legislature to impose a sanction without a trial in violation of the Constitution's prohibited powers.

Ex Post Facto

An ex post facto law punishes an individual *retroactively*, and severely encroaches on notions of fairness. There are three types of ex post facto laws. First, a law is ex post facto if it punishes behavior that occurred before the law was in effect. Second, ex post facto laws may increase the punishment for the offense after the crime occurred. Third, a law can be ex post facto if it increases the possibility of conviction after the crime occurred.

Example of an Ex Post Facto Law Punishing Behavior Retroactively

A state murder statute defines murder as the killing of a human being, *born alive*. The state legislature amends this statute to include the killing of a fetus, with the exception of abortion. The amendment extends the application of the statute to all criminal fetus killings that occurred *before* the statute was changed. This language punishes defendants for behavior that was legal when committed. If the state attempts to include this language, a court can strike the statute for violating the prohibition against ex post facto laws.

Example of an Ex Post Facto Law Increasing Punishment Retroactively

In the preceding example about amending the murder statute, the state also amends the statute to increase the penalty for murder to the *death penalty*. Before the amendment, the penalty for murder was *life in prison* without the possibility of parole. The state cannot give the death penalty to defendants who committed murder before the statute was amended. This is considered ex post facto because it increases the punishment for the offense after the crime is committed.

Example of an Ex Post Facto Law Increasing the Possibility of Conviction Retroactively

In the preceding example, the state amends the murder statute to remove the statute of limitations, which is the time limit on prosecution. Before the amendment, the statute of limitations was fifty years. The state cannot prosecute defendants who committed murder *more than fifty years ago*, pursuant to the amendment. This is considered ex post facto because it increases the chance of conviction after the crime is committed.

Changes That Benefit a Defendant Retroactively

Changes that *benefit* a criminal defendant are not considered ex post facto and may be applied retroactively. In the preceding example, if the state amended the murder statute to *shorten* the statute of limitations, this change actually benefits defendants by making it more difficult to convict them. Thus this amendment would be constitutional.

Ex Post Facto Applies Only to Criminal Laws

Ex post facto protection applies only to *criminal* laws. Laws that raise fees or taxes after payment are civil rather than criminal in nature. Thus these retroactive increases do not exceed governmental authority and are constitutional.

Figure 3.2 The Constitution's Prohibited Powers

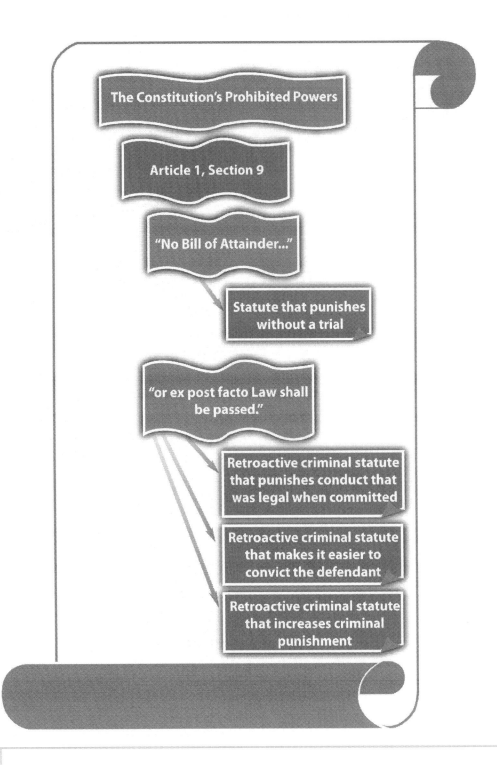

The Constitution's Prohibited Powers

Article 1, Section 9

"No Bill of Attainder..."

Statute that punishes without a trial

"or ex post facto Law shall be passed."

Retroactive criminal statute that punishes conduct that was legal when committed

Retroactive criminal statute that makes it easier to convict the defendant

Retroactive criminal statute that increases criminal punishment

Key Takeaways

- The Constitution protects individuals from certain statutes and certain governmental procedures.
- A statute is unconstitutional on its face when its wording is unconstitutional. A statute is unconstitutional as applied when its enforcement is unconstitutional.
- A court reviews a statute for constitutionality using strict scrutiny if the statute inhibits a fundamental constitutional right. Strict scrutiny means that the statute is presumptively invalid, and the government must prove it is supported by a compelling government interest and uses the least restrictive means. Occasionally, a court reviews a statute for constitutionality under the equal protection clause using the rational basis test, which means that the statute is constitutional if rationally related to a legitimate government interest.
- A bill of attainder is when the legislative branch punishes a defendant without a trial. Ex post facto laws punish criminal defendants retroactively.

- Ex post facto laws punish defendants for acts that were not criminal when committed, increase the punishment for a crime retroactively, or increase the chance of criminal conviction retroactively.

Exercises

Answer the following questions. Check your answers using the answer key at the end of the chapter.

A public university raises tuition in the middle of the semester after students have already paid and sends all registered students a bill for "fees past due." Does this violate the prohibition on ex post facto laws? Why or why not?

Read *Smith v. Doe*, 538 U.S. 84 (2003). Why did the US Supreme Court hold that Alaska's Megan's Law is constitutional? The case is available at this link: http://scholar.google.com/scholar_case?case=14879258853492825339&hl=en&as_sdt=2&as_vis=1&oi=scholarr.

Read *Stogner v. California*, 539 U.S. 607 (2003). Why did the US Supreme Court hold that California's Sex Offender statute of limitations was unconstitutional? The case is available at this link: http://supreme.justia.com/us/539/607.

References

Indiana Constitution, art. I, § 24, accessed October 4, 2010, http://www.law.indiana.edu/uslawdocs/inconst/art-1.html.

U.S. v. Brown, 381 U.S. 437 (1965), accessed October 2, 2010, http://supreme.justia.com/us/381/437/case.html. CC licensed content, Shared previously

- Criminal Law. **Provided by**: University of Minnesota Libraries Publishing . **Located at**: http://open.lib.umn.edu/criminallaw/. **License**: *CC BY-NC-SA: Attribution-NonCommercial-ShareAlike*

3.2 The Due Process and Equal Protection Clauses

Learning Objectives

Define the Bill of Rights.
Define the principle of selective incorporation.
Distinguish between substantive and procedural due process.
Compare void for vagueness and overbreadth.
Ascertain the purpose of the equal protection clause as it applies to criminal laws.

Although the legislative branch's prohibited powers are in Article I of the Constitution, the Bill of Rights contains most of the constitutional protections afforded to criminal defendants. The Bill of Rights is the first ten amendments to the Constitution. In addition, the Fourteenth Amendment, which was added to the Constitution after the Civil War, has a plethora of protections for criminal defendants in the due process and equal protection clauses.

The Bill of Rights was originally written to apply to the federal government. However, US Supreme Court precedent has held that *any* constitutional amendment that is implicit to due process's concept of ordered liberty must be incorporated into the Fourteenth Amendment's protections and applied to the states (Duncan v. Louisiana, 2010). This doctrine is called selective incorporation, and it includes virtually all the constitutional protections in the Bill of Rights. Thus although the original focus of the Bill of Rights may have been limiting the federal government, modern interpretations of the Constitution ensure that its protections also extend to all levels of state and local government.

The Meaning of Due Process of Law

The due process clause states, "No person shall...be deprived of life, liberty, or property, without due process of law." The due process clause in the Fifth Amendment applies to *federal* crimes and federal criminal prosecutions. The federal due process clause is mirrored in the Fourteenth Amendment, which guarantees due process of law in *state* criminal prosecutions. Most states have a similar provision in their constitutions (Missouri Constitution, 2010).

Substantive due process protects individuals from an unreasonable loss of substantive rights, such as the right to speak freely and the right to privacy. Procedural due process protects individuals from being criminally punished without notice and an opportunity to be heard. Both substantive and procedural due processes ensure that individuals are not denied their life (capital punishment), liberty (incarceration), or property (forfeiture) *arbitrarily*.

Void for Vagueness

Void for vagueness challenges the wording of a statute under the due process clause. A statute is void for vagueness if it uses words that are indefinite or ambiguous. Statutes that are not precisely drafted do not provide

---

notice to the public of exactly what kind of behavior is criminal. In addition, and *more important*, they give too much discretion to law enforcement and are unevenly enforced (U.S. v. White, 2010). With a void for vagueness challenge, the statute must be so unclear that "men of common intelligence must guess at its meaning," (Connally v. General Construction Co., 2010) which is an objective standard.

Example of a Statute That Is Void for Vagueness

A state legislature enacts a statute that criminalizes "inappropriate attire on public beaches." Larry, a law enforcement officer, arrests Kathy for wearing a two-piece bathing suit at the beach because in his belief, women should wear one-piece bathing suits. Two days later, Burt, another law enforcement officer, arrests Sarah for wearing a one-piece bathing suit at the beach because in his belief, women should not be seen in public in bathing suits. Kathy and Sarah can attack the statute on its face and as applied as void for vagueness. The term "inappropriate" is unclear and can mean different things to different people. Thus it gives too much discretion to law enforcement, is subject to uneven application, and does not give Kathy, Sarah, or the public adequate notice of what behavior is criminal.

Overbreadth

A statute is overbroad if it criminalizes both constitutionally protected and constitutionally unprotected conduct. This challenge is different from **void for vagueness**, although certain statutes can be attacked on both grounds. An overbroad statute criminalizes *too much* and needs to be revised to target only conduct that is outside the Constitution's parameters.

Example of an Overbroad Statute

A state legislature enacts a statute that makes it criminal to photograph "nude individuals who are under the age of eighteen." This statute is probably overbroad and violates due process. While it prohibits constitutionally *unprotected* conduct, such as taking obscene photographs of minors, it also criminalizes First Amendment *protected* conduct, such as photographing a nude baby.

Figure 3.3 The Due Process Clause

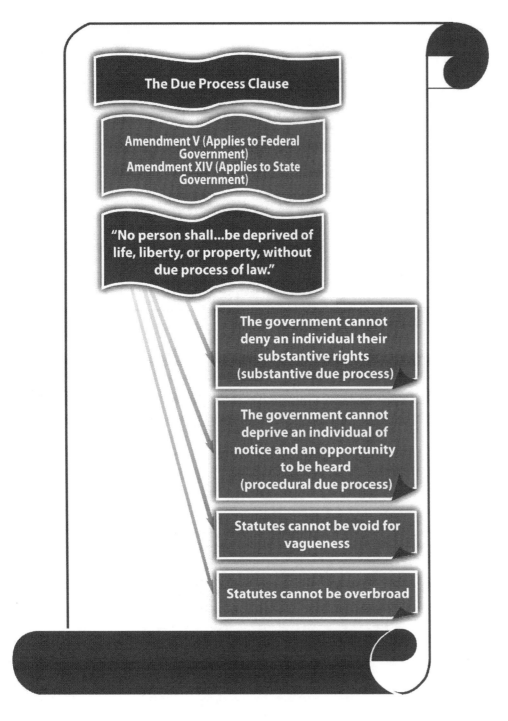

The Equal Protection Clause

The Fourteenth Amendment states in relevant part, "nor shall any State...deny to any person within its jurisdiction the equal protection of the laws." The equal protection clause applies to the *state* government. State constitutions generally have a similar provision (California Constitution, 2010). The equal protection clause prevents the state government from enacting criminal laws that *discriminate* in an unreasonable and unjustified manner. The Fifth Amendment due process clause prohibits the federal government from discrimination if the discrimination is so unjustifiable that it violates due process of law (Bolling v. Sharpe, 2010).

The prohibition on governmental discrimination is not absolute; it depends on the class of persons targeted for special treatment. In general, court scrutiny is heightened according to a sliding scale when the subject of discrimination is an arbitrary classification. Arbitrary means random and often includes characteristics an individual is born with, such as race or national origin. The most arbitrary classifications demand **strict scrutiny**, which means the criminal statute must be supported by a *compelling* government interest. Statutes containing classifications that are not arbitrary must have a **rational basis** and be supported by a *legitimate* government interest.

Criminal statutes that classify individuals based on their race must be given strict scrutiny because race is an arbitrary classification that cannot be justified. Modern courts do not uphold criminal statutes that classify based on race because there is no government interest in treating citizens of a different race more or less harshly (Loving v. Virginia, 2010).

Criminal statutes that have a rational basis for discrimination and are supported by a legitimate government interest *can* discriminate, and frequently do. Criminal statutes that punish felons more severely when they have a history of criminal behavior, for example, three-strikes statutes, are supported by the legitimate government interests of specific and general deterrence and incapacitation. Note that the basis of the discrimination, a criminal defendant's *status as a convicted felon*, is rational, not arbitrary like race. Thus although these statutes discriminate, they are constitutional pursuant to the equal protection clause.

Figure 3.4 The Equal Protection Clause

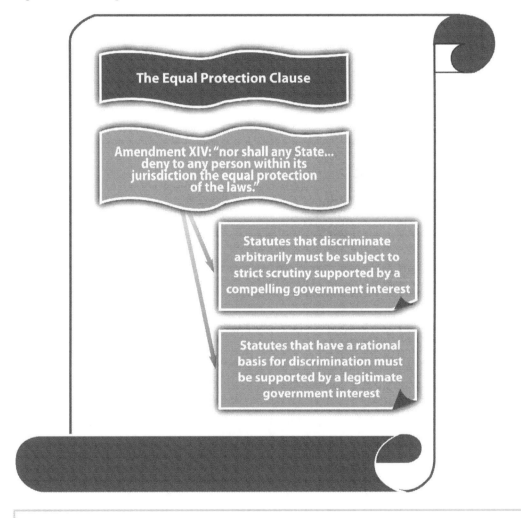

Key Takeaways

- The Bill of Rights is the first ten amendments to the Constitution and contains many protections for criminal defendants.
- Selective incorporation applies most of the constitutional protections in the Bill of Rights to the states.
- Substantive due process protects criminal defendants from unreasonable government intrusion on their substantive constitutional rights. Procedural due process provides criminal defendants with notice and an opportunity to be heard before imposition of a criminal punishment.
- A statute that is void for vagueness is so imprecisely worded that it gives too much discretion to law

enforcement, is unevenly applied, and does not provide notice of what is criminal. A statute that is overbroad includes constitutionally protected conduct and therefore unreasonably encroaches upon individual rights.

- The equal protection clause prevents the state government from enacting criminal laws that arbitrarily discriminate. The Fifth Amendment due process clause extends this prohibition to the federal government if the discrimination violates due process of law.

Exercises

Answer the following questions. Check your answers using the answer key at the end of the chapter.

A local ordinance makes it a misdemeanor to dress in "gang attire." Is this ordinance constitutional? Why or why not?

Read *Smith v. Goguen*, 415 U.S. 566 (1974). Why did the US Supreme Court strike down the Massachusetts flag misuse statute? The case is available at this link: http://scholar.google.com/scholar_case?case=14723025391522670978&hl=en&as_sdt=2&as_vis=1&oi=scholarr.

Read *Grayned v. City of Rockford*, 408 U.S. 104 (1972). In *Grayned*, the US Supreme Court analyzed an ordinance prohibiting individuals from willfully making a noise or disturbance on grounds adjacent to a school building that disturbs the peace or good order of the school session. Did the Court hold that this ordinance was constitutional? Why or why not? The case is available at this link: http://supreme.justia.com/us/408/104/case.html.

Read Justice Sandra Day O'Connor's concurring opinion in *Lawrence v. Texas*, 539 U.S. 558 (2003). Why did Justice O'Conner feel that Texas's sodomy law was unconstitutional? The case is available at this link: http://www.law.cornell.edu/supct/html/02-102.ZC.html.

References

Bolling v. Sharpe, 347 U.S. 497 (1954), accessed October 4, 2010, http://scholar.google.com/scholar_case?case=16234924501041992561&hl=en&as_sdt=2&as_vis=1&oi=scholarr.

California Constitution, art. I, § 7, accessed October 4, 2010, http://www.leginfo.ca.gov/.const/.article_1.

Connally v. General Construction Co., 269 U.S. 385 (1926), accessed October 3, 2010, http://supreme.justia.com/us/269/385/case.html.

Duncan v. Louisiana, 391 U.S. 145 (1968), accessed October 20, 2010, http://caselaw.lp.findlaw.com/scripts/getcase.pl?court=us&vol=391&invol=145.

Loving v. Virginia, 388 U.S. 1 (1967), accessed October 4, 2010, http://www.law.cornell.edu/supct/html/historics/USSC_CR_0388_0001_ZO.html.

Missouri Constitution, art. I, § 10, accessed October 10, 2010, http://www.sos.mo.gov/pubs/missouri_constitution.pdf.

U.S. v. White, 882 F.2d 250 (1989), accessed October 6, 2010, http://scholar.google.com/scholar_case?case=12667022335593752485&hl=en&as_sdt=2&as_vis=1&oi=scholarr.
CC licensed content, Shared previously

- Criminal Law. **Provided by**: University of Minnesota Libraries Publishing . **Located at**: http://open.lib.umn.edu/criminallaw/. **License**: *CC BY-NC-SA: Attribution-NonCommercial-ShareAlike*

3.3 Freedom of Speech

Learning Objectives

Define speech under the First Amendment.
Identify five types of speech that can be governmentally regulated in spite of the First Amendment.
Ascertain the constitutional parameters for statutes that criminalize speech.

The First Amendment states, in relevant part, "Congress shall make no law...abridging the freedom of speech." Although this language specifically targets *federal Congress*, the First Amendment has been held applicable to the states by virtue of selective incorporation (Gitlow v. New York, 2010). Most state constitutions have a similar provision protecting freedom of speech (Illinois Constitution, 2010).

Freedom of speech has been the focus of countless judicial opinions. To summarize US Supreme Court precedent, the word *speech* has been interpreted to cover virtually any *form* of expression, including verbal and written words, pictures, photographs, videos, and songs. First Amendment speech also includes expressive *conduct* such as dressing a certain way (Tinker v. Des Moines Independent Community School District, 2011), flag burning (Texas v. Johnson, 2010), and cross burning (R.A.V. v. St. Paul, 2010).

Exceptions to the First Amendment's Protection of Free Speech

In general, courts have examined the history of the Constitution and the policy supporting freedom of speech when creating exceptions to its coverage. Modern decisions afford freedom of speech the strictest level of scrutiny; only a compelling government interest can justify an exception, which must use the least restrictive means possible (Sable Communis. of California, Inc. v. FCC, 2010). For the purpose of brevity, this book reviews the constitutional exceptions to free speech in statutes criminalizing **fighting words**, **incitement to riot**, **hate crimes**, and **obscenity**.

Figure 3.5 The First Amendment

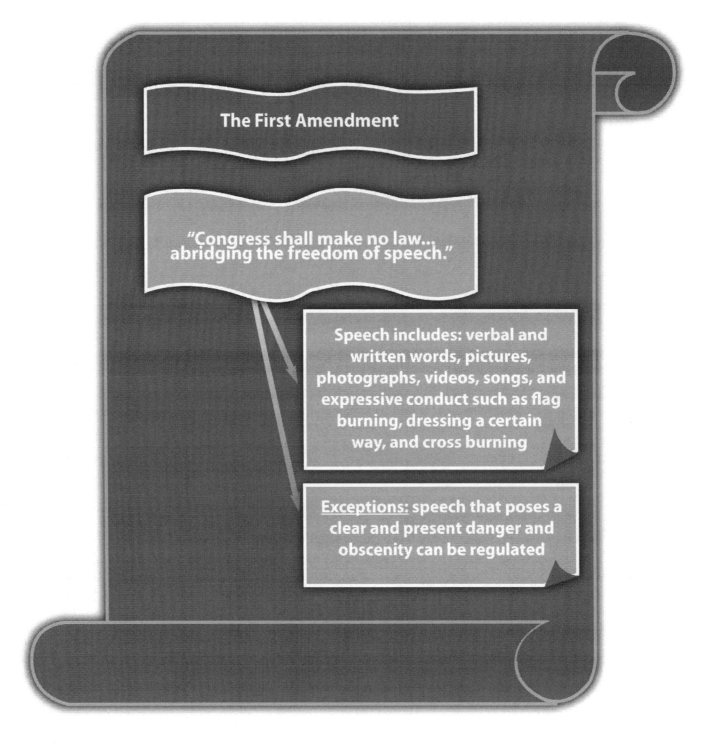

Fighting Words

Although the First Amendment protects *peaceful* speech and assembly, if speech creates a **clear and present danger** to the public, it can be regulated (Schenck v. U.S., 2010). This includes fighting words, "those which by their very utterance inflict injury or tend to incite an immediate breach of the peace" (Chaplinsky v. New Hampshire, 2010).

Any criminal statute prohibiting fighting words must be narrowly tailored and focus on *imminent* rather than *future* harm. Modern US Supreme Court decisions indicate a tendency to favor freedom of speech over the government's interest in regulating fighting words, and many fighting words statutes have been deemed unconstitutional under the First Amendment or void for vagueness and overbreadth under the Fifth Amendment and Fourteenth Amendment due process clause (Lewis v. City of New Orleans, 2010).

Example of an Unconstitutional Fighting Words Statute

Georgia enacted the following criminal statute: "Any person who shall, without provocation, use to or of another, and in his presence...opprobrious words or abusive language, tending to cause a breach of the peace...shall be guilty of a misdemeanor" (Ga. Code § 26-6303). The US Supreme Court determined that this statute was overbroad, void for vagueness, and unconstitutional under the First Amendment (Gooding v. Wilson, 2010).

The Court held that the dictionary definitions of "opprobrious" and "abusive" give them greater reach than fighting words. Thus the statute is overbroad and does not restrict its prohibition to *imminent* harm. Opprobrious and abusive have various meanings, so the statute is also subject to uneven enforcement and is void for vagueness. As the Court stated, this language "licenses the jury to create its own standard in each case" (Gooding v. Wilson, 1972; Herndon v. Lowry, 2010).

Incitement to Riot

Incitement to riot can also be regulated under the clear and present danger exception. Similar to fighting words, an incitement to riot statute must prohibit *imminent* lawless action (Brandenburg v. Ohio, 2010).Statutes that prohibit simple advocacy with no imminent threat or harm cannot withstand the First Amendment's heightened scrutiny.

Example of an Unconstitutional Incitement to Riot Statute

Ohio enacted a statute that criminalized "advocat[ing]...the duty, necessity, or propriety of crime, sabotage, violence, or unlawful methods of terrorism as a means of accomplishing industrial or political reform" and "voluntarily assembl[ing] with any society, group or assemblage of persons formed to teach or advocate the doctrines of criminal syndicalism" (Ohio Rev. Code Ann. § 2923.13). A Ku Klux Klan leader was convicted under the statute after the media broadcast films of him leading a KKK meeting. The US Supreme Court held, "Accordingly, we are here confronted with a statute which, by its own words and as applied, purports to punish mere advocacy and to forbid, on pain of criminal punishment, assembly with others merely to advocate the described type of action. Such a statute falls within the condemnation of the First and Fourteenth Amendments" (Brandenburg v. Ohio, 2010).

Hate Crimes

Many states and the federal government have enacted hate crimes statutes. When hate crimes statutes criminalize speech, including expressive conduct, a First Amendment analysis is appropriate. When hate crimes statutes enhance a penalty for criminal conduct that is *not expressive*, the First Amendment is not applicable (Wisconsin v. Mitchell, 2010).

Hate crimes statutes punish conduct that is targeted at specific classifications of people. These classifications are listed in the statute and can include race, ethnicity, gender, sexual orientation, or religion. Hate crimes statutes that criminalize speech can be constitutional under the clear and present danger exception if they are tailored to apply only to speech or expressive conduct that is supported by the *intent to intimidate* (Virginia v. Black, 2010). This can include speech and expressive conduct such as threats of imminent bodily injury, death, or cross burning. Hate crimes statutes must be narrowly drafted, and cannot be void for vagueness or overbroad.

Hate crimes statutes that criminalize the *content* of speech, like a prejudicial *opinion* about a certain race, ethnicity, gender, sexual orientation, or religion are unconstitutional under the First Amendment (R.A.V. v. St. Paul, 2010). Statutes of this nature have been held to have a "chilling effect" on free expression by deterring individuals from expressing unpopular views, which is the essence of free speech protection. Although this type of speech can stir up anger, resentment, and possibly trigger a violent situation, the First Amendment protects content-based speech from governmental regulation without strict scrutiny exposing a compelling government interest.

Example of an Unconstitutional Statute Prohibiting Cross Burning

St. Paul, Minnesota, enacted the Bias-Motivated Crime Ordinance, which prohibited the display of a symbol that a person knows or has reason to know "arouses anger, alarm or resentment in others on the basis of race, color, creed, religion or gender" (Ordinance, St. Paul, Minn., Legis. Code § 292.02 (1990)). In *R.A.V. v. St. Paul*, 505 U.S. 377 (1992), the US Supreme Court held that this ordinance was unconstitutional on its face because regulation was based on the *content* of speech, with no additional requirement for *imminent lawless action*. The Court held that the ordinance did not proscribe the use of fighting words (the display of a symbol) toward specific groups of individuals, which would be an equal protection clause challenge. Instead, the Court determined that the statute prohibited the use of specific *types of fighting words,* for example, words that promote racial hatred, and this is impermissible as viewpoint-based censorship. As the Court stated, "[c]ontent-based regulations are presumptively invalid" (R.A.V. v. St. Paul, 2010).

Example of a Constitutional Statute Prohibiting Cross Burning

Virginia enacted a statute that makes it criminal "for any person..., with the intent of intimidating any person or group..., to burn...a cross on the property of another, a highway or other public place" (Va. Code Ann. § 18.2-423). The US Supreme Court held this statute constitutional under the First Amendment because it did not single out cross burning *indicating racial hatred*, as the Minnesota cross-burning ordinance did. The Court stated, "Unlike the statute at issue in *R. A. V.*, the Virginia statute does not single out for opprobrium only that speech directed toward 'one of the specified disfavored topics.' *Id.*, at 391." It does not matter whether an individual burns a cross with intent to intimidate because of the victim's race, gender, or religion, or because of the victim's "political affiliation, union membership, or homosexuality" (Virginia v. Black, 2010).

Obscenity

Another exception to free speech is *obscenity.* Obscenity is usually conveyed by speech, such as words, pictures, photographs, songs, videos, and live performances. However, obscenity is not *protected* speech under the First Amendment (Roth v. United States, 2010).

In *Miller v. California*, 413 U.S. 15 (1973), the US Supreme Court devised a three-part test to ascertain if speech is obscene and subject to government regulation. Generally, speech is obscene if (1) the average person, applying contemporary community standards would find that the work, taken as a whole, appeals to the prurient interest in sex; (2) it depicts sexual conduct specifically defined by the applicable state law in a patently offensive way; and (3) it lacks serious literary, artistic, political, or scientific value (Miller v. California, 2010).

Example of Speech That Is Not Obscene

In *Jenkins v. Georgia*, 418 U.S. 153 (1974), the US Supreme Court viewed the film *Carnal Knowledge* to determine whether the defendant could be constitutionally convicted under an obscenity statute for showing it at a local theater. The Court concluded that most of the film's sexual content was suggestive rather than explicit, and the only direct portrayal of nudity was a woman's bare midriff. Thus although a jury convicted the defendant after viewing the film, the Court reversed the conviction, stating that the film does not constitute the hard-core pornography that the three-part test for obscenity isolates from the First Amendment's protection. The Court stated, "Appellant's showing of the film 'Carnal Knowledge' is simply not the 'public portrayal of hard core sexual conduct for its own sake, and for the ensuing commercial gain' which we said was punishable in *Miller*, Id., at 35" (Jenkins v. Georgia, 2010).

Nude Dancing

Statutes that regulate nude dancing have also been attacked under the First Amendment. Although the US Supreme Court has ruled that nude dancing is constitutionally protected expression, it has also upheld reasonable restrictions on nudity, such as requirements that nude dancers wear pasties and a g-string (City of Erie et al v. Pap's A.M., 2010).

Table 3.1 Statutes Prohibiting Speech under a First Amendment Exception

Conduct Prohibited	Potential Constitutional Challenge	Necessary Statutory Requirements
Fighting words	First Amendment, vague, overbreadth	Must proscribe imminent lawless action, be narrowly drafted, precise
Incitement to riot	First Amendment, vague, overbreadth	Must proscribe imminent lawless action, be narrowly drafted, precise; cannot prohibit simple advocacy
Hate speech	First Amendment, vague, overbreadth	Must be narrowly drafted, precise; must target speech supported by the intent to intimidate; cannot be content based without a compelling government interest
Obscenity	First Amendment, vague, overbreadth	Must be narrowly drafted, precise; must target speech that appeals to a prurient interest in sex, depicts sex in a patently offensive way, lacks serious social value
Nude dancing	First Amendment, vague, overbreadth	Can be reasonably restricted

Law and Ethics

Should Depictions of Animal Cruelty Be Protected by the First Amendment?

Congress enacted 18 U.S.C. § 48, which criminalizes commercial creation, sale, or possession of a visual or auditory depiction in which a living animal is intentionally maimed, mutilated, tortured, wounded, or killed, if that conduct violates federal or state law where the creation, sale, or possession takes place. In *United States v. Stevens*, 552 U.S. 442 (2010), the US Supreme Court held that this statute is *facially overbroad* and violative of the *First Amendment*. Specifically, the Court held that depictions of animal cruelty are entitled to First Amendment protection, and the statute is *presumptively invalid* because it is *content based*. In addition, the Court stated that the government's interest in censoring this type of material is not compelling enough to outweigh the prohibition on protected speech and that the statute on its face included material that may have redeeming social value. The Court's opinion is available at this link: http://www.law.cornell.edu/supct/html/08-769.ZO.html.

Do you think the First Amendment should protect material depicting animal cruelty? Why or why not?
What are some possible consequences of criminalizing this type of speech?

Check your answers to both questions using the answer key at the end of the chapter.

U.S. v. Stevens Video

American Civil Liberties Union (ACLU) Explains the *U.S. v. Stevens* Case

This video of ACLU legal director Steven R. Shapiro analyzes the *U.S. v. Stevens* case:
(click to see video)

Key Takeaways

- Speech under the First Amendment is any form of expression, such as verbal or written words, pictures, videos, and songs. Expressive conduct, such as dressing a certain way, flag burning, and cross burning, is also considered First Amendment speech.
- Five types of speech that can be governmentally regulated are fighting words, incitement to riot, hate speech, obscenity, and nude dancing.
- Statutes that prohibit fighting words and incitement to riot must be narrowly drafted to include only speech that incites imminent unlawful action, not future harm or general advocacy. Statutes that prohibit hate speech must be narrowly drafted to include only speech that is supported by the intent to intimidate. Statutes that prohibit obscenity must target speech that appeals to a prurient interest in sex, depicts sexual conduct in a patently offensive way, and has little or no literary, artistic, political, or scientific value. Nude dancing can be regulated as long as the regulation is reasonable, such as requiring dancers to wear pasties and a g-string.

Exercises

Answer the following questions. Check your answers using the answer key at the end of the chapter.

A state statute enhances the penalty for battery if the crime is committed "because of the victim's race." To prove race-biased intent, it is frequently necessary to admit evidence of the defendant's statements indicating racial hatred and intolerance. Does this statute violate the First Amendment's free speech protection? Why or why not? Read the case on which this question is based, *Wisconsin v. Mitchell*, 508 U.S. 47 (1993). The case is available at this link: http://www.law.cornell.edu/supct/html/92-515.ZO.html.

Read *Reno v. American Civ. Liberties Union*, 521 U.S. 844 (1997). This case reviews the constitutionality of a federal statute regulating Internet activity to protect minors. Why did the US Supreme Court hold that certain provisions of the federal Communications Decency Act of 1996 were unconstitutional? The case is available at this link: http://caselaw.lp.findlaw.com/scripts/getcase.pl?court=us&vol=000&invol=96-511.

Read *Holder v. Humanitarian Law Project*, 130 S. Ct. 2705 (2010). Did the US Supreme Court uphold a federal statute prohibiting aid to terrorist groups? Why or why not? The case is available at this link: http://scholar.google.com/scholar_case?case=3116082426854631219&hl=en&as_sdt=2&as_vis=1&oi=scholarr.

References

Brandenburg v. Ohio, 395 U.S. 444 (1969), accessed October 6, 2010, http://supreme.justia.com/us/395/444/case.html.

Chaplinsky v. New Hampshire, 315 U.S. 568, 572 (1942), accessed October 6, 2010, http://caselaw.lp.findlaw.com/cgi-bin/getcase.pl?friend=wisbar&navby=case&court=us&vol=315&invol=568&pa

geno=574.

City of Erie et al v. Pap's A.M., 529 U.S. 277 (2000), accessed October 11, 2010, http://caselaw.lp.findlaw.com/scripts/getcase.pl?court=us&vol=000&invol=98-1161.

Gitlow v. New York, 268 U.S. 652 (1925), accessed October 5, 2010, http://supreme.justia.com/us/268/652/case.html.

Gooding v. Wilson, 405 U.S. 518 (1972), accessed October 7, 2010, http://scholar.google.com/scholar_case?case=3138831397470557431&hl=en&as_sdt=2&as_vis=1&oi=scholarr.

Herndon v. Lowry, 301 U.S. 242, 263 (1937), accessed October 7, 2010, http://scholar.google.com/scholar_case?case=3138831397470557431&hl=en&as_sdt=2&as_vis=1&oi=scholarr.

Illinois Constitution, art. I, § 4, accessed October 9, 2010, http://www.ilga.gov/commission/lrb/con1.htm.

Jenkins v. Georgia, 418 U.S. 153, 161 (1974), accessed October 7, 2010, http://caselaw.lp.findlaw.com/scripts/getcase.pl?navby=case&court=us&vol=418&invol=153.

Lewis v. City of New Orleans, 415 U.S. 130 (1974), accessed October 7, 2010, http://caselaw.lp.findlaw.com/scripts/getcase.pl?navby=case&court=us&vol=415&invol=130.

Miller v. California, 413 U.S. 15 (1973), accessed October 7, 2010, http://scholar.google.com/scholar_case?case=287180442152313659&hl=en&as_sdt=2&as_vis=1&oi=scholarr.

R.A.V. v. St. Paul, 505 U.S. 377 (1992), accessed October 5, 2010, http://caselaw.lp.findlaw.com/scripts/getcase.pl?court=us&vol=505&invol=377.

Roth v. United States, 354 U.S. 476 (1957), accessed October 7, 2010, http://supreme.justia.com/us/354/476/case.html.

Sable Communis. of California, Inc. v. FCC, 492 U.S. 115 (1989), accessed October 5, 2010, http://supreme.justia.com/us/492/115/case.html.

Schenck v. U.S., 249 U.S. 47 (1919), accessed October 5, 2010, http://supreme.justia.com/us/249/47/case.html.

Texas v. Johnson, 491 U.S. 397 (1989), accessed October 5, 2010, http://caselaw.lp.findlaw.com/scripts/getcase.pl?court=us&vol=491&invol=397.

Tinker v. Des Moines Independent Community School District, 393 U.S. 503 (1969), accessed October 8, 2011, http://supreme.justia.com/us/393/503/case.html.

Virginia v. Black, 535 U.S. 343 (2003), accessed October 5, 2010, http://caselaw.lp.findlaw.com/scripts/getcase.pl?court=us&vol=000&invol=01-1107.

Wisconsin v. Mitchell, 508 U.S. 47 (1993), accessed October 7, 2010, http://www.law.cornell.edu/supct/html/92-515.ZO.html.
CC licensed content, Shared previously

- Criminal Law. **Provided by**: University of Minnesota Libraries Publishing . **Located at**: http://open.lib.umn.edu/criminallaw/. **License**: *CC BY-NC-SA: Attribution-NonCommercial-ShareAlike*

3.4 The Right to Privacy

Learning Objectives

Ascertain the constitutional amendments that support a right to privacy.
Ascertain three constitutionally protected individual interests that are included in the right to privacy.

The federal Constitution does not explicitly protect privacy. However, several of the amendments in the Bill of Rights ensure and protect individual decision making and autonomy from governmental intrusion. Thus modern interpretations of the Constitution by the US Supreme Court have created a right to privacy (Griswold v. Connecticut, 2010). This right is considered fundamental and subject to strict scrutiny; only a compelling government interest can justify a statute encroaching on its protections. Many states include an explicit right to privacy in their state constitutions (Hawaii Consitution, 2010).

The Constitutional Amendments Protecting Privacy

US Supreme Court precedent has held that the right to privacy comes from the First, Third, Fourth, Fifth, Ninth, and Fourteenth Amendments. The First Amendment protects the right to speak freely, assemble peacefully, and worship according to individual choice. The Third Amendment prohibits the government from forcing individuals to quarter, house, or feed soldiers. The Fourth Amendment prevents the government from unreasonably searching or seizing an individual or an individual's property. The Fifth and Fourteenth Amendments provide due process of law before the government can deprive an individual of life, liberty, or property. The Ninth Amendment states that rights not explicitly set forth in the Constitution may still exist. Taken together, these amendments indicate that the Constitution was written to erect a barrier between individuals and an *overly intrusive* and *regulatory* government. In modern society, this right to privacy guarantees the right to use *birth control*, the right to an *abortion*, and the right to *participate in consensual sexual relations*.

The Right to Use Birth Control

The right to privacy was first established in the US Supreme Court case of *Griswold v. Connecticut*, 381 U.S. 479 (1965). In *Griswold*, the defendants, Planned Parenthood employees, were convicted of prescribing birth control as accessories under two Connecticut statutes that criminalized the use of birth control. The Court found the statutes unconstitutional, holding that the First, Third, Fourth, Fifth, and Ninth Amendments created a "penumbra" of unenumerated constitutional rights, including zones of privacy (Griswold v. Connecticut, 2010). The Court stated that *marital privacy*, especially, deserved the utmost protection from governmental intrusion. The *Griswold* case set the stage for other fundamental privacy rights related to intimacy, including the right to an abortion and the right to consensual sexual relations.

The Right to an Abortion

The right to an abortion was set forth in the seminal US Supreme Court case of *Roe v. Wade*, 410 U.S. 113 (1973). In *Roe*, which examined a Texas statute criminalizing abortion, the Court held that every woman has the right to a legal abortion through the first trimester of pregnancy. In the aftermath of the *Roe* decision, more than half of the nation's state laws criminalizing abortion became unconstitutional and unenforceable. The Court held that state government has a *legitimate* interest in protecting a pregnant woman and her fetus from harm, which becomes a *compelling* interest when she has reached full term. However, during the first trimester, health concerns from abortion do not justify the erosion of a woman's right to make the abortion decision (Roe v. Wade, 2010). The Court thereafter struck down the Texas antiabortion statute as overbroad under the Fourteenth Amendment due process clause. Specifically, the Court held that during the first trimester of pregnancy, the abortion decision must be left to the pregnant woman and her attending physician (Roe v. Wade, 2010). In a recent decision post-*Roe*, the Court upheld a federal statute criminalizing partial-birth abortion, on the grounds that it was not void for vagueness or overbroad under the Fifth Amendment due process clause (Gonzales v. Carhat, 2010).

The Right to Consensual Sexual Relations

Even in the aftermath of *Roe v. Wade*, courts were reluctant to interfere with states' interests in enacting and enforcing statutes that criminalized sexual conduct. In *Bowers v. Hardwick*, 478 U.S. 186 (1986), the US Supreme Court upheld a Georgia statute that made it a crime to engage in consensual sodomy (Bowers v. Hardwick, 2010). The Court stated that there is no *fundamental* right to engage in sodomy and that the history of protecting marriage and family relationships should not be extended in this fashion (Bowers v. Hardwick, 2010). Many years later, the Court changed its stance and overruled *Bowers* in *Lawrence v. Texas*, 539 U.S. 558 (2003). In *Lawrence*, a Texas statute criminalizing homosexual sodomy was attacked on its face and as applied to two men who were discovered engaging in sex in their bedroom during a law enforcement search for weapons. The *Lawrence* decision rested on the due process clause of the Fourteenth Amendment. The Court held that *intimate choices* are a form of liberty protected by the due process clause, whether or not consenting individuals are married. The Court thereafter struck down the Texas sodomy statute because it was not justified by a sufficient government interest (Lawrence v. Texas, 2010).

Example of a Right to Privacy Analysis

Most states have statutes criminalizing consensual incest, which is sexual intercourse between family members who cannot legally marry. If an individual attacks a consensual incest statute as unconstitutional under the right to privacy, the court will balance the state's interest in preventing harm to an infant, such as birth defects, with an individual's interest in having consensual sexual intercourse with a family member, using *strict scrutiny*. If the court finds that the government interest is compelling, it can uphold the statute as long as it is not vague or overbroad.

Figure 3.6 The Right to Privacy

The Right to Privacy

Amendments I, III, IV, V, IX, and XIV

Includes the following:
• Right to use birth control
• Right to an abortion
• Right of adults to have consensual sexual relations

Statutes that invade privacy are subject to strict scrutiny

Key Takeaways

- The constitutional amendments supporting the right to privacy are the First, Third, Fourth, Fifth, Ninth, and Fourteenth Amendments.
- The right to privacy in the Constitution protects an individual's right to use contraceptives, to receive an abortion through the first trimester, and to engage in consensual sexual relations.

Exercises

Answer the following questions. Check your answers using the answer key at the end of the chapter.

A state statute prohibits inmates in state prison from engaging in consensual sodomy. An inmate is prosecuted under the statute. How will a court determine whether this statute is constitutional? Read the statute on which this exercise is based: California Penal Code § 286(e), http://law.onecle.com/california/penal/286.html.

Read *Planned Parenthood v. Casey*, 505 U.S. 833 (1992). In *Casey*, Pennsylvania modified its abortion statute to include a twenty-four-hour waiting period and informed consent for minors. Did the US Supreme Court uphold the Pennsylvania abortion statute? The case is available at this link: http://www.law.cornell.edu/supct/html/91-744.ZS.html.

References

Bowers v. Hardwick, 478 U.S. 186 (1986), accessed October 11, 2010, http://caselaw.lp.findlaw.com/scripts/getcase.pl?court=us&vol=478&invol=186.

Gonzales v. Carhart, 127 S. Ct. 1610 (2007), accessed October 11, 2010, http://scholar.google.com/scholar_case?case=7079370668659431881&hl=en&as_sdt=2&as_vis=1&oi=scholarr.

Griswold v. Connecticut, 381 U.S. 479 (1965), accessed October 9, 2010, http://caselaw.lp.findlaw.com/scripts/getcase.pl?court=us&vol=381&invol=479.

Hawaii Constitution, art. I, § 6, accessed October 9, 2010, http://hawaii.gov/lrb/con/conart1.html.

Lawrence v. Texas, 539 U.S. 558 (2003), accessed October 11, 2010, http://caselaw.lp.findlaw.com/scripts/getcase.pl?court=us&vol=000&invol=02-102.

Roe v. Wade, 410 U.S. 113, 162 (1973), accessed October 10, 2010, http://www.law.cornell.edu/supct/html/historics/USSC_CR_0410_0113_ZO.html.
CC licensed content, Shared previously

- Criminal Law. **Provided by**: University of Minnesota Libraries Publishing . **Located at**: http://open.lib.umn.edu/criminallaw/. **License**: *CC BY-NC-SA: Attribution-NonCommercial-ShareAlike*

3.5 The Right to Bear Arms

Learning Objective

Ascertain the constitutional parameters of an individual's right to possess a handgun under the Second Amendment.

Although the federal Constitution specifically references a right to bear arms in the Second Amendment, the US Supreme Court has not interpreted this amendment in a significant fashion until recently. The Second Amendment provides "[a] well regulated Militia, being necessary to the security of a free state, the right of the people to keep and bear Arms, shall not be infringed." Many state constitutions have a similar provision (Volokh, E., 2010). In 2008, the US Supreme Court explored the Second Amendment and its effect on weapons possession in a case attacking Washington, DC, firearms legislation (District of Columbia v. Heller, 2010).

In *District of Columbia v. Heller*, 128 S. Ct. 2783 (2008), the Court affirmed the Court of Appeals for the D.C. Circuit in striking provisions of the Firearms Control Regulations Act of 1975. The Court struck the portions of this act that banned the possession of handguns and mandated that all legal firearms must be kept unloaded and disassembled while in the home. Although the District Court held that the Second Amendment applies only to the militia, the US Supreme Court emphasized that the Second Amendment is exercised individually and belongs to all Americans. The Court also expanded previous interpretations of the Second Amendment to cover an individual's right to possess a usable handgun in the home for self-defense. The *Heller* case is unprecedented and is the first to address individual handgun possession under the Second Amendment. However, the *Heller* ruling is narrow and specifically excludes firearms restrictions on *felons*, the *mentally ill*, firearm possession in or near *schools* or government buildings, and the *commercial sale* of firearms. The *Heller* decision also fails to extend the Second Amendment's protections to the *states* because Washington, DC, is a federal enclave.

In *McDonald v. Chicago*, 130 S.Ct. 3020 (2010), the US Supreme Court revisited the gun possession issue by reviewing and rejecting as unconstitutional a handgun ban in the city of Chicago, Illinois. In *McDonald*, the Court took the extra step of extending the *Heller* ruling to the states, holding that the Second Amendment applies to the states via its **selective incorporation** into the due process clause. However, *McDonald* did not expand the ruling in *Heller* in other ways and reemphasized the Heller exceptions of firearms restrictions on felons, the mentally ill, firearm possession in or near schools or government buildings, and the commercial sale of firearms.

Example of an Appropriate Restriction on Firearms

Dirk is a public middle-school janitor. Occasionally, with the permission of the principal, Dirk stays overnight in an outbuilding on campus when he works a particularly late shift. Dirk wants to keep a handgun in the outbuilding, for protection. If Dirk's state has a statute prohibiting the possession of a handgun within one mile of any public school, Dirk *cannot* keep a handgun in the outbuilding for self-defense. Modern US Supreme Court precedent holds that the Second Amendment protects an individual's right to possess a handgun in the home for self-defense. However, this precedent specifically *exempts* firearm possession near schools. Unless newer precedent expands the ruling to include firearm possession near schools, the statute in Dirk's state is constitutional.

Figure 3.7 The Second Amendment

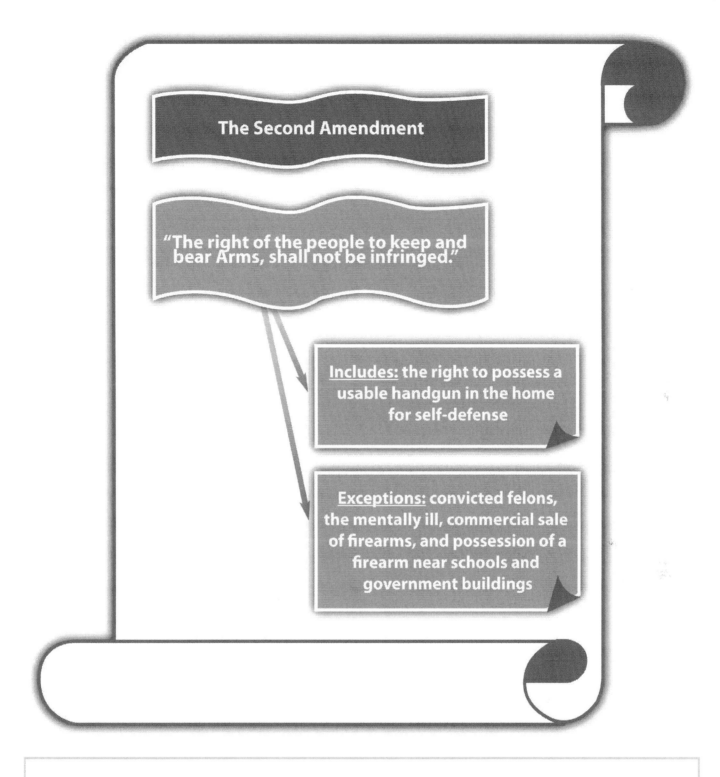

The Second Amendment

"The right of the people to keep and bear Arms, shall not be infringed."

Includes: the right to possess a usable handgun in the home for self-defense

Exceptions: convicted felons, the mentally ill, commercial sale of firearms, and possession of a firearm near schools and government buildings

Key Takeaway

- Pursuant to recent US Supreme Court precedent, the Second Amendment protects an individual's right to possess a usable handgun in the home for self-defense. This protection does not cover felons, the mentally ill, firearm possession near schools and government buildings, or the commercial sale of firearms.

Exercises

Answer the following questions. Check your answers using the answer key at the end of the chapter.

A state court order forbids the defendant from possessing a handgun while on probation. This makes it impossible for the defendant to resume his career as a police officer. How will this court order be analyzed under recent US Supreme Court precedent interpreting the Second Amendment?
Read *Lewis v. U.S.*, 445 U.S. 55 (1980). In *Lewis*, the defendant, a felon, was convicted under a federal statute for possession of a firearm by a convicted felon. The defendant claimed that this was unconstitutional because he was not represented by counsel during his trial on the original felony. The defendant never sought a pardon or reversal of his conviction for the original felony on appeal. Did the US Supreme Court uphold the defendant's conviction for possession of a firearm by a convicted felon? The case is available at this link:
http://scholar.google.com/scholar_case?case=1988023855177829800&hl=en&as_sdt=2&as_vis=1&oi=scholarr.
Read *U.S. v. Lopez*, 514 U.S. 549 (1995). In *Lopez*, the US Supreme Court held that a federal statute prohibiting firearms near schools was unconstitutional because it regulated conduct that had no effect on interstate commerce and thus exceeded Congress's authority under the commerce clause. If a state enacts a similar statute, would this be constitutional under the Second Amendment? The case is available at this link:
http://scholar.google.com/scholar_case?case=18310045251039502778&hl=en&as_sdt=2&as_vis=1&oi=scholarr.

References

District of Columbia v. Heller, 128 S. Ct. 2783 (2008), accessed October 13, 2010, http://www.law.cornell.edu/supct/html/07-290.ZO.html.

Volokh, E., "State Constitutional Right to Keep and Bear Arms Provisions," UCLA website, accessed October 22, 2010, http://www.law.ucla.edu/volokh/beararms/statecon.htm.
CC licensed content, Shared previously

- Criminal Law. **Provided by**: University of Minnesota Libraries Publishing . **Located at**: http://open.lib.umn.edu/criminallaw/. **License**: *CC BY-NC-SA: Attribution-NonCommercial-ShareAlike*

3.6 Excessive Punishment

Learning Objectives

Compare an inhumane procedure with disproportionate punishment under the Eighth Amendment.

Identify the most prevalent method of execution pursuant to the death penalty.

Ascertain crime(s) that merit capital punishment.

Identify three classifications of criminal defendants who cannot be constitutionally punished by execution.

Define three-strikes laws, and ascertain if they constitute cruel and unusual punishment pursuant to the Eighth Amendment.

Ascertain the constitutionality of sentencing enhancements under the Sixth Amendment right to a jury trial.

The prohibition against cruel and unusual punishment comes from the Eighth Amendment, which states, "Excessive bail shall not be required, nor excessive fines imposed, nor cruel and unusual punishments inflicted." State constitutions often have similar provisions (Texas Constitution, 2010). Although the ban on cruel and unusual punishment relates directly to *sentencing*, which is a criminal *procedure* issue, criminal statutes mandating various penalties can be held unconstitutional under the Eighth Amendment just like statutes offending the due process clause, so a brief discussion is relevant to this chapter. Another facet of excessive punishment is a criminal sentencing enhancement that is based on facts not found beyond a reasonable doubt by a jury. This has been held to violate the Sixth Amendment, which states, "In all criminal prosecutions, the accused shall enjoy the right to a...trial, by an impartial jury of the State and district wherein the crime shall have been committed."

In this section, three issues are analyzed and discussed: the infliction of *cruel punishment*, a criminal sentence that is *too severe*, and a criminal sentence that is invalid under the right to a *jury trial*.

Infliction of Cruel Punishment

In general, the government must refrain from inflicting cruel or barbaric punishments on criminal defendants in violation of the Eighth Amendment. In particular, cases asserting that a criminal punishment is inhumane often focus on capital punishment, which is the death penalty.

Synopsis of the History of Capital Punishment

The death penalty has been used as a criminal punishment since the eighteenth century BC. American death penalty law is influenced by the British because the colonists brought English common-law principles, including capital punishment, with them to the New World. The first execution in America took place in 1608, for spying (Death Penalty Information Center, 2010). Methods of execution and capital crimes varied from colony to colony. In the late 1700s, a movement to abolish the death penalty began, and in 1846 Michigan was the first state to eliminate the death penalty for all crimes except treason (Death Penalty Information Center, 2010). Throughout the nineteenth and twentieth centuries, the United States fluctuated in its attitude toward capital punishment. Executions were at an all-time high in the 1930s (Death Penalty Information Center, 2010). However, in 1972, in the landmark decision of *Furman v. Georgia*, 408 U.S. 238 (1972), the US Supreme Court held that Georgia's death penalty statute, which gave the jury complete discretion to sentence a criminal defendant to death, was *arbitrary* and therefore authorized *cruel and unusual* punishment in violation of the Eighth Amendment. This decision invalidated death penalty statutes in forty states. Later, in 1976, the US Supreme Court case of *Gregg v. Georgia*, 428 U.S. 153 (1976), affirmed the procedure of a bifurcated trial, separating the guilt phase from the penalty phase for death penalty cases. *Gregg* also affirmed the death penalty's constitutionality under the Eighth Amendment. Currently, thirty-four states and the federal government authorize the death penalty, while sixteen states and the District of Columbia do not (Death Penalty Information Center, 2010).

Inhumane Capital Punishment

A claim that capital punishment is *inhumane* and therefore unconstitutional under the Eighth Amendment focuses on the *method* of execution. Throughout the history of the death penalty, many methods of execution have been employed, including shooting, hanging, electrocution, the gas chamber, and lethal injection. At the time of this writing, the law is in a state of flux as to which methods of execution are constitutional because many state and federal decisions have stricken virtually every method available. The current focus of the courts is *lethal injection* because it is one of the few methods that has not been condemned as unconstitutional. Most states that authorize the death penalty use lethal injection as the primary method of execution. In a recent statement on this issue, the US Supreme Court in *Baze v. Rees*, 128 S. Ct. 1520 (2008), held that Kentucky's four-drug lethal injection procedure was *not* cruel and unusual punishment under the Eighth Amendment. In other states, including Missouri and Tennessee, federal courts using different facts have ruled the multidrug procedure *unconstitutional* (Death Penalty Information Center, 2010). It is impossible to predict the future of death penalty methodology under the Eighth Amendment because each case will be decided based on the circumstances presented. However, it is clear that the law in this area is ripe for a definitive statement of constitutionality under the Eighth Amendment's cruel and unusual punishment clause.

Disproportionate Punishment

Disproportionate punishment is a different issue than inhumane punishment, but it is still within the parameters of the Eighth Amendment. Disproportionate punishment asserts that a criminal punishment is *too severe* for the crime. Two criminal punishments garner many disproportionate punishment claims: **capital punishment** and punishment pursuant to three-strikes statutes.

Capital Punishment as Disproportionate

Capital punishment can be disproportionate because it is too severe for the *crime* or because it is too severe for the *criminal defendant*.

Examples of Capital Punishment That Is Disproportionate to the Crime

Death is the ultimate punishment, so it must be equivalent to the crime the defendant committed. Although the states and the federal government have designated many capital crimes that may not result in death, for example, treason that does not lead to death, the US Supreme Court has confirmed that the death penalty is too severe for most crimes. In *Coker v. Georgia*, 433 U.S. 584 (1977), the Court held that capital punishment is disproportionate for the crime of raping an adult woman. Many years later in *Kennedy v. Louisiana*, 128 S. Ct. 2641 (2008), the Court extended the disproportionality principle to invalidate the death penalty for child rape. *Kennedy* maintained the distinction between crimes committed against *individuals* and crimes committed against the *government*, like treason. The only crime against an individual that currently merits the death penalty is criminal homicide, which is the unlawful killing of one human being by another. Criminal homicide is discussed in detail in Chapter 9 "Criminal Homicide".

Figure 3.8 Crack the Code

Crack the Code

Compare the following state laws:

Ga. Code § 16- 6-1:

(a) A person commits the offense of rape when he has carnal knowledge of:

   (1) A female forcibly and against her will; or

   (2) A female who is less than ten years of age.

Carnal knowledge in rape occurs when there is any penetration of the female sex organ by the male sex organ. The fact that the person allegedly raped is the wife of the defendant shall not be a defense to a charge of rape.

(b) A person convicted of the offense of rape shall be punished by death...

Mont. Code Ann. § 45-5-503:

45-5-503. Sexual intercourse without consent.

(1) A person who knowingly has sexual intercourse without consent with another person commits the offense of sexual intercourse without consent...

   c) If the offender was previously convicted of an offense under this section or of an offense under the laws of another state or of the United States that if committed in this state would be an offense under this section and if the offender inflicted serious bodily injury upon a person in the course of committing each offense, the offender shall be:

   (i) punished by death...

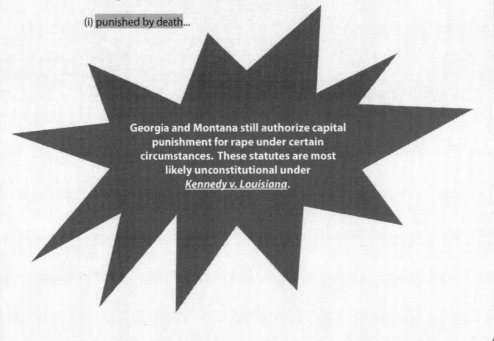

Georgia and Montana still authorize capital punishment for rape under certain circumstances. These statutes are most likely unconstitutional under *Kennedy v. Louisiana*.

Examples of Capital Punishment That Are Disproportionate to the Criminal Defendant

Recent US Supreme Court precedent has targeted specific classifications of criminal defendants for whom capital punishment is overly severe. Recent cases hold that the death penalty is cruel and unusual punishment for a criminal defendant who was a *juvenile* when the crime was committed (Roper v. Simmons, 2010), who is *mentally ill* (Ford v. Wainwright, 2010), or has an *intellectual disability* (Atkins v. Virginia, 2010) at the time of the scheduled execution. Although states vary in their classifications of juveniles (discussed in detail in Chapter 6 "Criminal Defenses, Part 2"), the Eighth Amendment prohibits capital punishment for an individual who was under eighteen years of age when he or she committed criminal homicide. Mental illness could cover a variety of disorders, but the US Supreme Court has held that a criminal defendant has a constitutional right to a determination of sanity before execution (Ford v. Wainwright, 2010). Intellectual disability is distinct from mental illness and is defined by the US Supreme Court as a substantial intellectual impairment that impacts everyday life, and was present at the defendant's birth or during childhood (Atkins v. Virginia, 2010). However, this standard is broad, so states vary in their legislative definitions of this classification (Death Penalty Information Center, 2010).

Example of Capital Punishment That Is Inhumane and Disproportionate to the Crime and the Criminal Defendant

Jerry is sentenced to death for rape. The state death penalty statute specifies death by decapitation. While on death row, Jerry begins to hear voices and is diagnosed as schizophrenic by the prison psychiatrist. The state schedules the execution anyway. In this example, the state death penalty statute is *inhumane* because death by decapitation is too severe a punishment for any crime. The death penalty statute is also *disproportionate* to the *crime* because execution is not a constitutional punishment for the crime of rape. Lastly, the death penalty statute is *disproportionate* to Jerry, *the criminal defendant*, because it is cruel and unusual to execute someone who is mentally ill.

Disproportionate Punishment Pursuant to Three-Strikes Laws

California was the first state to enact a "three strikes and you're out" law (Cal. Penal Code § 667, 2010). Generally, three-strikes statutes punish habitual offenders more harshly when they commit a second or third felony after an initial serious or violent felony (Cal. Penal Code § 667, 2010). To date, California's three-strikes law is the toughest in the nation; it mandates a minimum twenty-five-year- to life sentence for felons convicted of a third strike. California enacted its three-strikes legislation after the kidnapping, rape, and murder of Polly Klaas by a habitual offender. Twenty-four states followed, indicating public support for the incapacitation of career criminals (Three Strikes and You're Out, 2010).

Three-strikes statutes vary, but those most likely to be attacked as disproportionate count *any* felony as a strike after an initial *serious* or *violent* felony. Counting any felony might levy a sentence of *life in prison* against a criminal defendant who commits a *nonviolent* felony. However, the US Supreme Court has upheld lengthy prison sentences under three-strikes statutes for relatively minor second or third offenses, holding that they are not cruel and unusual punishment under the Eighth Amendment (Ewing v. California, 2010).

Figure 3.9 The Eighth Amendment

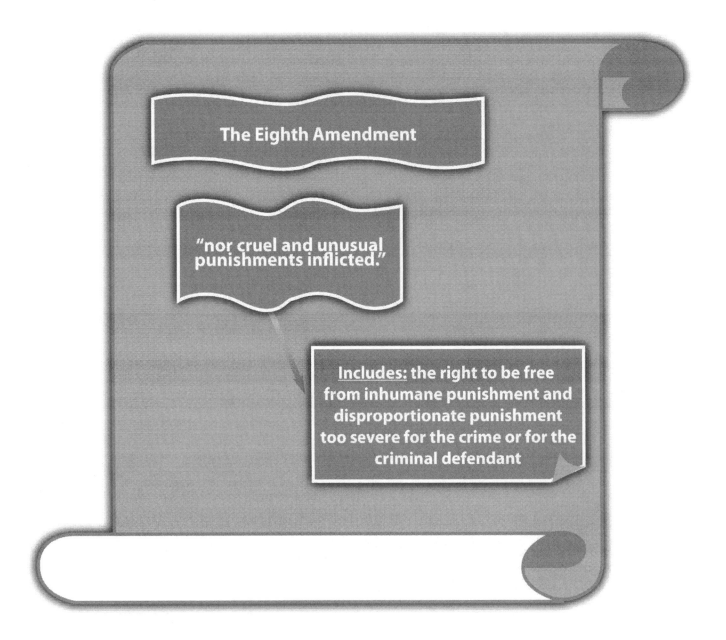

Sentencing that Violates the Right to a Jury Trial

Modern US Supreme Court precedent has expanded the jury's role in sentencing pursuant to the Sixth Amendment. Although a detailed discussion of sentencing procedure is beyond the scope of this book, a brief overview of sentencing and the roles of the judge and jury is necessary to a fundamental understanding of this important trial right, as is set forth in the following section.

The Role of the Judge and Jury in Sentencing Fact-Finding

As stated in Chapter 2 "The Legal System in the United States", the trier of fact decides the facts and renders a decision on innocence or guilt using **beyond a reasonable doubt** as the standard for the burden of proof. The trier of fact in a criminal prosecution is almost always a *jury* because of the right to a jury trial in the Sixth

Amendment. Occasionally, the defendant waives the right to a jury trial and has a bench trial with a judge playing the role of trier of fact. Although the jury determines innocence or guilt during a jury trial, the verdict defines the end of their role as the trier of fact, and the *judge* sets the sentence. The death penalty is an exception to the jury's limited role in sentencing; a jury must decide whether to sentence the defendant to death at a separate hearing after the trial has concluded.

Generally, criminal sentencing takes place after the trial. Although the sentencing procedure varies from state to state and from state to federal, a sentencing hearing is typically held after guilt has been determined at trial or after a guilty plea. For many years, judges have had almost *exclusive* control of sentencing. Although judges are restricted by the fact-finding done at trial, they can receive new evidence at sentencing if it is relevant. For example, a judge is bound by a jury determination that the defendant used a weapon when committing an armed robbery. However, the judge can accept new evidence at sentencing that reveals the defendant had two prior convictions for armed robbery and can enhance the sentence under a habitual offender or three-strikes statute.

Sentencing Enhancement by Judges

Until recently, judges could use evidence received at the sentencing hearing to enhance a sentence beyond the statutory maximum by making a determination of the *new* facts to a **preponderance of evidence**. However, in *Apprendi v. New Jersey*, 530 U.S. 466 (2000), the US Supreme Court held that the right to a jury trial prohibits judges from enhancing criminal sentences beyond the statutory maximum based on facts not determined by a jury **beyond a reasonable doubt**. In *Apprendi*, the trial court enhanced the defendant's sentence beyond the statutory maximum for possession of a firearm with an unlawful purpose under New Jersey's hate crimes statute. Although the jury did not determine that the defendant's crime was a hate crime, the judge accepted new evidence at sentencing that indicated the defendant's shooting into a residence was racially motivated. The US Supreme Court reversed the New Jersey Supreme Court, which upheld the sentencing procedure. The Court held that *other than evidence of a prior conviction*, a judge cannot enhance a defendant's sentence beyond the statutory maximum unless there has been a factual determination by a jury beyond a reasonable doubt of the facts supporting the sentencing enhancement. The Court based its holding on the Sixth Amendment right to a jury trial as incorporated and applied to the states through the Fourteenth Amendment due process clause.

Post-*Apprendi*, this holding was extended to federal sentencing guidelines in *U.S. v. Booker*, 543 U.S. 220 (2005). In *Booker*, a federal judge enhanced a sentence following mandatory US Sentencing Guidelines, which permitted judges to find the sentencing enhancement facts using the preponderance of evidence standard. The US Supreme Court ruled that the enhancement was invalid under the Sixth Amendment right to a jury trial and held that the US Sentencing Guidelines would be *advisory* only, never mandatory. *Booker* was based on *Blakely v. Washington*, 542 U.S. 296 (2004), which invalidated a similar Washington State sentencing procedure.

Pursuant to *Apprendi*, *Booker*, and *Blakely*, a criminal defendant's sentence is unconstitutional under the Sixth Amendment right to a jury trial if it is *enhanced* beyond the statutory maximum by facts that were *not* determined by a jury beyond a reasonable doubt. This premise applies in *federal* and *state* courts and also to *guilty pleas* rather than jury verdicts (Blakely v. Washington, 2010).

Example of an Unconstitutional Sentence Enhancement

Ross is tried and convicted by a jury of simple kidnapping. The maximum sentence for simple kidnapping is five years. At Ross's sentencing hearing, the judge hears testimony from Ross's kidnapping victim about the physical and mental torture Ross inflicted during the kidnapping. The victim did not testify at trial. The judge finds that the victim's testimony is credible and rules that Ross used cruelty during the kidnapping by a **preponderance of evidence**. The judge thereafter enhances Ross's sentence to eight years, based on a statutory sentencing enhancement of three years for "deliberate cruelty inflicted during the commission of a crime." The three-year sentencing enhancement is most likely unconstitutional. Under the Sixth Amendment right to a jury trial, the jury must find deliberate cruelty **beyond a reasonable doubt**. A court can strike the enhancement of three years on appeal, and on remand, the trial court cannot increase the sentence beyond the five-year maximum.

Figure 3.10 The Sixth Amendment

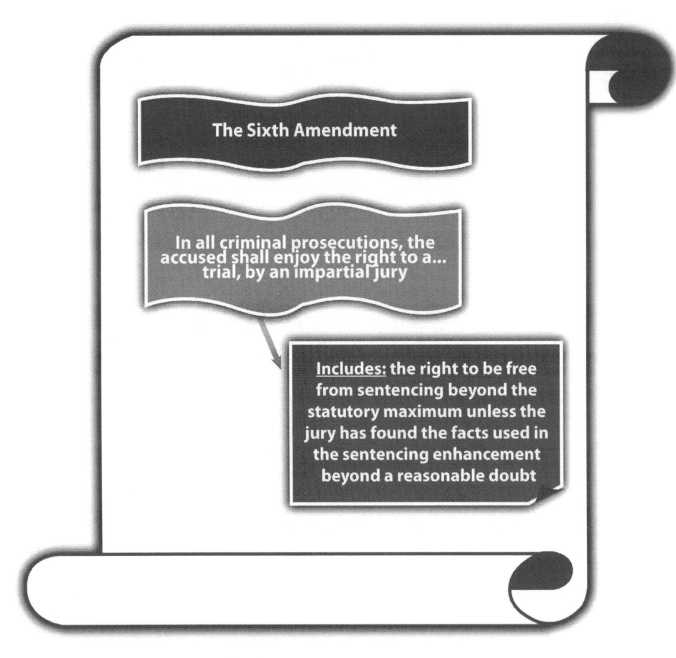

Figure 3.11 Diagram of Constitutional Defenses

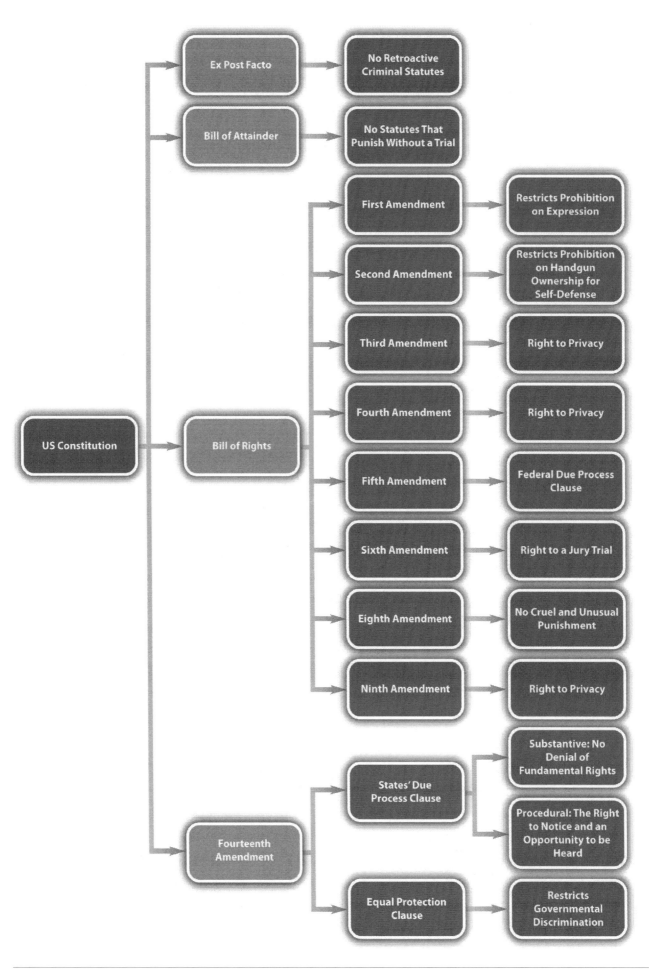

Key Takeaways

- An inhumane procedure punishes a defendant too severely for any crime. A disproportionate punishment punishes a defendant too severely for the crime he or she committed.
- Lethal injection is the most prevalent method of execution pursuant to the death penalty.
- Criminal homicide is the only crime against an individual that merits capital punishment.
- Criminal defendants who were juveniles when the crime was committed, are mentally incompetent, or have an intellectual disability cannot be subjected to capital punishment.
- Three-strikes laws punish criminal defendants more severely for committing a felony after they have committed one or two serious or violent felonies. Three-strikes laws have been held constitutional under the Eighth Amendment, even when they levy long prison sentences for relatively minor felonies.
- Sentencing enhancements beyond the statutory maximum are unconstitutional unless they are based on facts determined by a jury beyond a reasonable doubt under the Sixth Amendment right to a jury trial.

Exercises

Answer the following questions. Check your answers using the answer key at the end of the chapter.

Andrew is sentenced to death for torture. In Andrew's state, there is an "eye-for-an-eye" statute that mandates punishment that mimics the crime the defendant committed. Pursuant to this statute, Andrew will be tortured to death. Is the state's eye-for-an-eye statute constitutional under the Eighth Amendment? Why or why not?

Read *Lockyer v. Andrade*, 538 U.S. 63 (2003). What was the defendant's sentence in *Lockyer*? What was the defendant's crime? Did the US Supreme Court hold that the defendant's sentence was constitutional under the Eighth Amendment? The case is available at this link: http://scholar.google.com/scholar_case?case=18105647395364233477&hl=en&as_sdt=2&as_vis=1&oi=scholarr.

Read *Fierro v. Gomez*, 77 F.3d 301 (1996). Did the US Court of Appeals for the Ninth Circuit hold that the gas chamber procedure in California was constitutional under the Eighth Amendment? The case is available at this link: http://scholar.google.com/scholar_case?case=26906922262871934&hl=en&as_sdt=2&as_vis=1&oi=scholarr.

Read *Gall v. U.S.*, 128 S. Ct. 586 (2007). In *Gall*, the federal judge departed from the US Sentencing Guidelines and imposed a sentence of probation because the defendant had reformed and rejected his criminal lifestyle. Did the US Supreme Court uphold this sentence? Why or why not? The case is available at this link: http://scholar.google.com/scholar_case?case=5158806596650877502&q=Gall+v.+U.S.&hl=en&as_sdt=2,5&as_vis=1.

References

Atkins v. Virginia, 536 U.S. 304 (2002), accessed October 15, 2010, http://scholar.google.com/scholar_case?case=2043469055777796288&hl=en&as_sdt=2&as_vis=1&oi=scholarr.

Blakely v. Washington, 542 U.S. 296 (2004), accessed October 18, 2010, http://www.law.cornell.edu/supct/html/02-1632.ZO.html.

Cal. Penal Code § 667, accessed October 15, 2010, http://www.threestrikes.org/tslaw.html.

Death Penalty Information Center, "Introduction to the Death Penalty," deathpenaltyinfo.org website, accessed October 17, 2010, http://www.deathpenaltyinfo.org/part-i-history-death-penalty.

Death Penalty Information Center, "Lethal Injection: Constitutional Issue," deathpenaltyinfo.org website, accessed October 14, 2010, http://www.deathpenaltyinfo.org/lethal-injection-constitutional-issue.

Death Penalty Information Center, "State Statutes Prohibiting the Death Penalty for People with Mental Retardation," deathpenaltyinfo.org website, accessed October 14, 2010, http://www.deathpenaltyinfo.org/state-statutes-prohibiting-death-penalty-people-mental-retardation.

Death Penalty Information Center, "States with and without the Death Penalty," deathpenaltyinfo.org website, accessed October 14, 2010, http://www.deathpenaltyinfo.org/states-and-without-death-penalty.

Ewing v. California, 538 U.S. 11 (2003), accessed October 15, 2010, http://caselaw.lp.findlaw.com/scripts/getcase.pl?court=us&vol=000&invol=01-6978.

Ford v. Wainwright, 477 U.S. 399 (1986), accessed October 15, 2010, http://scholar.google.com/scholar_case?case=7904262174469084060&hl=en&as_sdt=2&as_vis=1&oi=scholarr.

Roper v. Simmons, 543 U.S. 551 (2005), accessed October 15, 2010, http://scholar.google.com/scholar_case?case=16987406842050815187&hl=en&as_sdt=2&as_vis=1&oi=scholarr.

Texas Constitution, art. I, § 13, accessed October 22, 2010, http://www.statutes.legis.state.tx.us/SOTWDocs/CN/htm/CN.1.htm.

Three Strikes and You're Out, "States That Have Three Strikes Laws," threestrikes.org website, accessed October 15, 2010, http://www.threestrikes.org/3strikestates.html.
CC licensed content, Shared previously

- Criminal Law. **Provided by**: University of Minnesota Libraries Publishing . **Located at**: http://open.lib.umn.edu/criminallaw/. **License**: *CC BY-NC-SA: Attribution-NonCommercial-ShareAlike*

3.7 End-of-Chapter Material

Summary

The US Constitution protects criminal defendants from certain statutes and procedures. State constitutions usually mirror the federal and occasionally provide more protection to criminal defendants than the federal Constitution, as long as the state constitutions do not violate federal supremacy. Statutes can be unconstitutional as written or as enforced and must be supported by a sufficient government interest. Statutes that punish without a trial (bills of attainder) or criminal statutes that are applied retroactively (ex post facto) are unconstitutional under Article 1 §§ 9 and 10. Other constitutional protections are in the Bill of Rights, which is the first ten amendments, and the Fourteenth Amendment, which contains the due process clause and the equal protection clause.

The due process clause prohibits the government from taking an individual's life, liberty, or property arbitrarily, without notice and an opportunity to be heard. Statutes that are vague or criminalize constitutionally protected conduct (overbroad) violate due process. The Fifth Amendment due process clause applies to the federal government, and the Fourteenth Amendment due process clause applies to the states. The Fourteenth Amendment due process clause also selectively incorporates fundamental rights from the Bill of Rights and applies them to the states. Rights incorporated and applied to the states are the right to free speech, the right to privacy, the right to bear arms, the right to be free from cruel and unusual punishment, and the right to a jury trial. The Fourteenth Amendment also contains the equal protection clause, which prevents the government from enacting statutes that discriminate without a sufficient government interest.

The First Amendment protects speech, expression, and expressive conduct from being criminalized without a compelling government interest and a statute that uses the least restrictive means possible. Some exceptions to the First Amendment are precise statutes targeting fighting words, incitement to riot, hate crimes, obscenity, and nude dancing. The First, Third, Fourth, Fifth, Ninth, and Fourteenth Amendments also create a right to privacy that prevents the government from criminalizing the use of birth control, abortion, or consensual sexual relations.

The Second Amendment protects an individual's right to possess a usable handgun in the home for self-defense. This right is not extended to convicted felons, the mentally ill, commercial sale of firearms, and firearm possession near schools and government buildings. The Eighth Amendment protects criminal defendants from inhumane and excessive punishments. The Sixth Amendment ensures that all facts used to extend a criminal defendant's sentencing beyond the statutory maximum must be determined by a jury beyond a reasonable doubt.

You Be the Legislative Analyst

You are an expert on *constitutional law*. Your state's legislature has hired you to analyze some proposed statutes to ensure that they are constitutional. Read each proposed statute and determine the following: (1) which **part** of the constitution is relevant, (2) whether the statute is **constitutional**, and (3) your **reasoning**. Check your answers using the answer key at the end of the chapter.

The proposed statute increases penalties for overdue state income tax **retroactively**. Is the proposed statute constitutional?

The proposed statute makes it a misdemeanor to display **nude art** in a public place. Is the proposed statute constitutional?

The proposed statute enhances the sentence for rape by three years of imprisonment if the defendant is infected with **AIDS**. Is the proposed statute constitutional?

The proposed statute prohibits a defendant with a conviction for any crime involving **alcohol** to possess a handgun in the home. Is the proposed statute constitutional?

The proposed statute mandates fifteen years of **solitary confinement** in prison if the defendant is convicted of forcible rape. Is the proposed statute constitutional?

Cases of Interest

- *South Dakota v. Asmussen*, 668 N.W.2d 725 (2003), discusses void for vagueness and overbreadth: http://caselaw.findlaw.com/sd-supreme-court/1080212.html.
- *Christian Legal Society v. Martinez*, 130 S. Ct. 2971 (2010), discusses the First Amendment: http://scholar.google.com/scholar_case?case=10772194664096336702&q=Christian+Legal+Society+v.+Martinez&hl=en&as_sdt=2,5.
- *U.S. v. Alvarez*, 617 F.3d 1198 (2010), discusses freedom of speech: http://scholar.google.com/scholar_case?case=3332503989513069132&q=U.S.+v.+Alvarez&hl=en&as_sdt=2,5&as_ylo=2010.
- *Snyder v. Phelps*, No. 09-751 (2011), discusses the First Amendment: http://www.law.cornell.edu/supct/html/09-751.ZO.html.
- *Robinson v. California*, 370 U.S. 660 (1962), discusses cruel and unusual punishment: http://caselaw.findlaw.com/us-supreme-court/370/660.html.

Articles of Interest

- Selective incorporation: http://www.law.umkc.edu/faculty/projects/ftrials/conlaw/incorp.htm
- Violent video games and the First Amendment: http://www.huffingtonpost.com/2011/06/27/supreme-court-violent-video-games_n_884991.html
- Ohio abortion bill: http://abcnews.go.com/Politics/ohio-heartbeat-bill-abortion-paves-roe-wade-challenge/story?id=12876224
- Second Amendment and gun control: http://usgovinfo.about.com/od/guncontrol/
- Recent US Supreme Court case on three strikes and its application to juveniles: http://www.correctionsone.com/juvenile-offenders/articles/2050079-High-Court-Calif-can-apply-3-strikes-law-to-juveniles

Websites of Interest

- First Amendment information: http://www.firstamendmentcenter.org/
- Hate crimes: http://www.fbi.gov/about-us/investigate/civilrights/hate_crimes/hate_crimes
- Death penalty information: http://www.deathpenaltyinfo.org

Statistics of Interest

- Hate crimes in the United States: http://www2.fbi.gov/ucr/hc2009/index.html
- US executions pursuant to the death penalty: http://www.deathpenaltyinfo.org/number-executions-state-and-region-1976

References

Smith v. Goguen, 415 U.S. 566, 582 (1974), accessed October 3, 2010, http://scholar.google.com/scholar_case?case=14723025391522670978&hl=en&as_sdt=2&as_vis=1&oi=scholarr.
CC licensed content, Shared previously

- Criminal Law. **Provided by**: University of Minnesota Libraries Publishing . **Located at**: http://open.lib.umn.edu/criminallaw/. **License**: *CC BY-NC-SA: Attribution-NonCommercial-ShareAlike*

Chapter 4: The Elements of a Crime

4.1 Criminal Elements

Wikimedia Commons – public domain.

Thus, an Olympic swimmer may be deemed by the community as a shameful coward, or worse, for not rescuing a drowning child in the neighbor's pool, but she is not a criminal.

—*State ex rel. Kuntz v. Thirteenth Jud. Dist.*, cited in Section 4 "Duty to Act Based on a Special Relationship"

Learning Objectives

List the elements of a crime.
Define the criminal act element.
Identify three requirements of criminal act.
Describe an exception to the criminal act element.
Ascertain three situations where an omission to act could be criminal.
Distinguish between actual and constructive possession.
Identify the criminal intent element required when possession is the criminal act.

Crimes can be broken down into elements, which the prosecution must prove beyond a reasonable doubt. Criminal elements are set forth in criminal statutes, or cases in jurisdictions that allow for common-law crimes. With exceptions, *every* crime has at least three elements: a criminal act, also called actus reus; a criminal **intent**, also called mens rea; and **concurrence** of the two. The term conduct is often used to reflect the criminal act and intent elements. As the Model Penal Code explains, "'conduct' means an action or omission and its accompanying state of mind" (Model Penal Code § 1.13(5)).

Figure 4.1 Criminal Code of Georgia

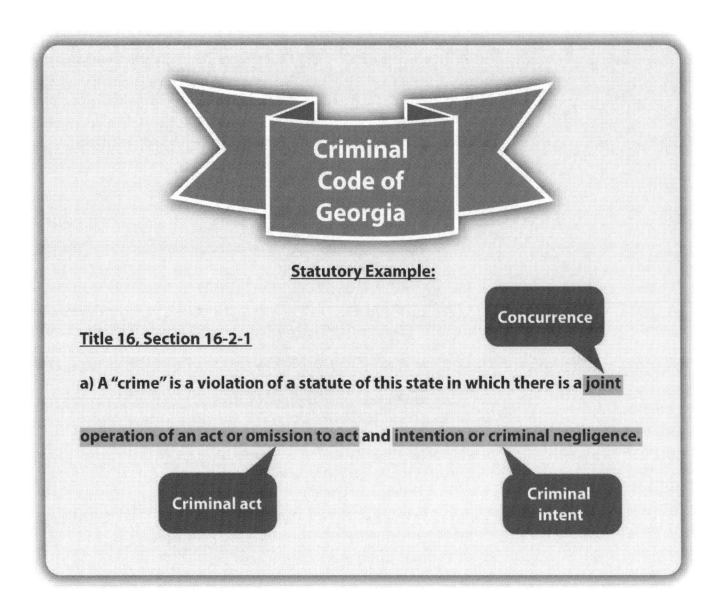

Recall from Chapter 1 "Introduction to Criminal Law" that not all crimes require a bad *result*. If a crime *does* require a bad result, the prosecution must also prove the additional elements of **causation** and **harm**.

Another requirement of some crimes is attendant circumstances. Attendant circumstances are specified factors that must be present when the crime is committed. These could include the crime's methodology, location or setting, and victim characteristics, among others.

This chapter analyzes the elements of every crime. Chapter 7 "Parties to Crime" through Chapter 13 "Crimes against the Government" analyze the elements of specific crimes, using a general overview of most states' laws, the Model Penal Code, and federal law when appropriate.

Example of a Crime That Has Only Three Elements

Janine gets into a fight with her boyfriend Conrad after the senior prom. She grabs Conrad's car keys out of his hand, jumps into his car, and locks all the doors. When Conrad strides over to the car, she starts the engine, puts the car into drive, and tries to run him down. It is dark and difficult for Janine to see, so Conrad easily gets out of her way and is unharmed. However, Janine is thereafter arrested and charged with attempted murder. In this case, the prosecution has to prove the elements of **criminal act**, **criminal intent**, and **concurrence** for attempted murder. The prosecution does *not* have to prove **causation** or that Conrad was **harmed** because attempt crimes, including attempted murder, do not have a bad result requirement. Attempt and other incomplete or inchoate crimes are discussed in Chapter 8 "Inchoate Offenses".

Criminal Act

Criminal act, or **actus reus**, is generally defined as an unlawful bodily movement (N.Y. Penal Law, 2010). The criminal statute, or case in jurisdictions that allow common-law crimes, describes the criminal act element.

Figure 4.2 Alabama Criminal Code

Statutory Example:

Section 13A-6-43 – Kidnapping in the first degree.

(a) A person commits a crime of kidnapping in the first degree if he abducts another person with intent to

(1) Hold him for ransom or reward; or

(2) Use him as a shield or hostage; or

Criminal act

(3) Accomplish or aid the commission of any felony or flight therefrom; or

(4) Inflict physical injury upon him, or to violate or abuse him sexually; or

(5) Terrorize him or a third person; or

(6) Interfere with the performance of any governmental or political function.

The Requirement of Voluntariness

One requirement of criminal act is that the defendant perform it *voluntarily*. In other words, the defendant must *control* the act. It would not serve the policy of specific deterrence to punish the defendant for irrepressible acts. The Model Penal Code gives the following examples of acts that are not voluntary and, therefore, not criminal: reflexes, convulsions, bodily movements during unconsciousness or sleep, conduct during hypnosis or resulting from hypnotic suggestion, or a bodily movement that otherwise is not a product of the effort or determination of the actor, either conscious or habitual (Model Penal Code § 2.01 (2)). *One voluntary act* is enough to fulfill the voluntary act requirement. Thus if a *voluntary* act is followed by an *involuntary* one, the court may still impose criminal liability depending on the circumstances (Govt. of Virgin Islands v. Smith, 2010).

Example of an Involuntary and Noncriminal Act

Perry is hypnotized at the local county fair. The hypnotist directs Perry to smash a banana cream pie into his girlfriend Shelley's face. Smashing a pie into a person's face is probably *battery* in most states, but Perry did not commit the act *voluntarily*, so he should not be convicted of a crime. Punishing Perry for battery would not specifically deter Perry from performing the act again while hypnotized because he is not in control of his behavior when experiencing this mental state.

Example of a Voluntary Act Followed by a Nonvoluntary Act

Timothy attends a party at a friend's house and consumes several glasses of red wine. Timothy then attempts to drive his vehicle home. While driving, Timothy passes out at the wheel and hits another vehicle, killing its occupant. Timothy can probably be convicted of one or more crimes in this situation. Timothy's acts of drinking several glasses of wine and then driving a vehicle are *voluntary*. Thus even though Timothy got into a car accident while unconscious, his involuntary act was preceded by conscious, controllable, and voluntary action. A punishment in this instance could *specifically deter* Timothy from drinking and driving on another occasion and is appropriate based on the circumstances.

Status as a Criminal Act

Generally, a defendant's **status** in society is not a criminal act. Status is *who* the defendant is, not what the defendant *does*. Similar to punishment for an involuntary act, when the government punishes an individual for status, it is essentially targeting that individual for circumstances that are outside his or her control. This punishment may be cruel and unusual pursuant to the Eighth Amendment if it is disproportionate to the defendant's behavior.

In *Robinson v. California*, 370 U.S. 660 (1962), the US Supreme Court held that it is unconstitutional as cruel and unusual punishment pursuant to the Eighth Amendment to punish an individual for the **status** of being a drug addict—even if the drugs to which the defendant is addicted are *illegal*. The Court compared drug addiction to an illness, such as leprosy or venereal disease. Punishing a defendant for being sick not only is inhumane but also does *not* specifically deter, similar to a punishment for an involuntary act.

If the defendant can control the actions at issue in spite of his or her status, the defendant's conduct can be constitutionally criminalized and punished pursuant to the Eighth Amendment. In *Powell v. Texas*, 392 U.S. 514 (1968), the US Supreme Court upheld the defendant's conviction for "drunk in public," in spite of the defendant's status as an alcoholic. The Court held that it is difficult *but not impossible* for an alcoholic to resist the urge to drink, so the behavior the statute criminalized was voluntary. Also, the Court ruled that the state has an interest in treating alcoholism and preventing alcohol-related crimes that could injure the defendant and others. Pursuant to *Powell*, statutes that criminalize *voluntary acts* that *arise* from status are constitutional under the Eighth Amendment.

Example of a Constitutional Statute Related to

Status

Refer to the example in Section 4 "Example of a Voluntary Act Followed by a Nonvoluntary Act", where Timothy drives under the influence of alcohol and kills another. A state statute that criminalizes killing another person while driving under the influence is constitutional as applied to Timothy, even if Timothy is an alcoholic. The state has an interest in treating alcoholism and preventing alcohol-related crimes that could injure or kill Timothy or another person. Timothy's act of driving while intoxicated is *voluntary*, even if his status as an alcoholic makes it more difficult for Timothy to control his drinking. Thus Timothy and other alcoholic defendants can be prosecuted and punished for killing another person while driving under the influence without violating the Eighth Amendment.

Thoughts as Criminal Acts

Thoughts are a part of **criminal intent**, *not* **criminal act**. Thoughts cannot be criminalized.

Example of Noncriminal Thoughts

Brianna, a housecleaner, fantasizes about killing her elderly client Phoebe and stealing all her jewelry. Brianna writes her thoughts in a diary, documenting how she intends to rig the gas line so that gas is pumped into the house all night while Phoebe is sleeping. Brianna includes the date that she wants to kill Phoebe in her most recent diary entry. As Brianna leaves Phoebe's house, her diary accidentally falls out of her purse. Later, Phoebe finds the diary on the floor and reads it. Phoebe calls the police, gives them Brianna's diary, and insists they arrest Brianna for attempted murder. Although Brianna's murder plot is sinister and is documented in her diary, an arrest is improper in this case. Brianna cannot be punished for her *thoughts alone*. If Brianna took substantial steps toward killing Phoebe, an attempted murder charge might be appropriate. However, at this stage, Brianna is only *planning* a crime, not *committing* a crime. Phoebe may be able to go to court and get a restraining order against Brianna to prevent her from carrying out her murder plot, but Brianna cannot be incapacitated by arrest and prosecution for attempted murder in this case.

Omission to Act

An exception to the requirement of a criminal act element is omission to act. Criminal prosecution for a *failure to act* is rare because the government is reluctant to compel individuals to put themselves in harm's way. However, under certain specific circumstances, omission to act can be criminalized.

An omission to act can only be criminal when the law imposes a *duty to act* (N.Y. Penal Law, 2010). This legal duty to act becomes an **element** of the crime, and the prosecution must prove it beyond a reasonable doubt, along with proving the defendant's inaction under the circumstances. Failure or omission to act is only criminal in three situations: (1) when there is a **statute** that creates a legal duty to act, (2) when there is a **contract** that creates a legal duty to act, or (3) when there is a **special relationship between the parties** that creates a legal duty to act. Legal duties to act vary from state to state and from state to federal.

Duty to Act Based on a Statute

When a duty to act is statutory, it usually concerns a government interest that is *paramount*. Some common examples of statutory duties to act are the duty to file state or federal tax returns (26 U.S.C., 2010), the duty of health-care personnel to report gunshot wounds (Fla. Stat. Ann., 2010), and the duty to report child abuse (Ky. Rev. Stat. Ann., 2010).

Figure 4.3 Kentucky Revised Statutes

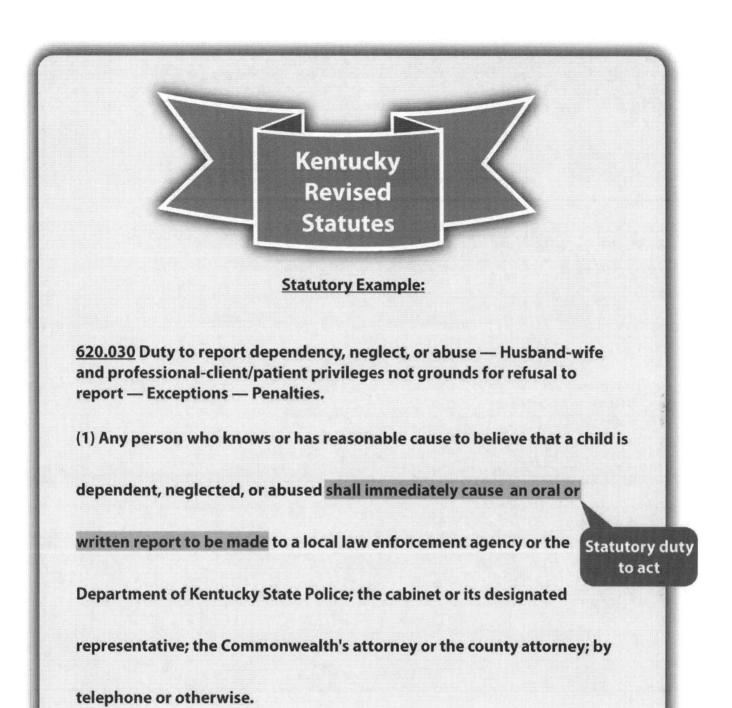

At common law, it was not criminal to stand by and refuse to help someone in danger. Some states *supersede* the common law by enacting Good Samaritan statutes that create a duty to assist those involved in an accident or emergency situation. Good Samaritan statutes typically contain provisions that insulate the actor from liability exposure when providing assistance (Minnesota Code, 2010).

Figure 4.4 Minnesota Good Samaritan Law

Read the Minnesota Good Samaritan Law:

604A.01 GOOD SAMARITAN LAW.

Subdivision 1. **Duty to assist.**

A person at the scene of an emergency who knows that another person is exposed to or has suffered grave physical harm shall, to the extent that the person can do so without danger or peril to self or others, give reasonable assistance to the exposed person. Reasonable assistance may include obtaining or attempting to obtain aid from law enforcement or medical personnel. A person who violates this subdivision is guilty of a petty misdemeanor.

Subd. 2. **General immunity from liability.**

(a) A person who, without compensation or the expectation of compensation, renders emergency care, advice, or assistance at the scene of an emergency or during transit to a location where professional medical care can be rendered, is not liable for any civil damages as a result of acts or omissions by that person in rendering the emergency care, advice, or assistance, unless the person acts in a willful and wanton or reckless manner in providing the care, advice, or assistance. This subdivision does not apply to a person rendering emergency care, advice, or assistance during the course of regular employment, and receiving compensation or expecting to receive compensation for rendering the care, advice, or assistance.

Note: Although the statute imposes a duty to rescue, it also protects individuals from civil liability. **Minn. Stat. Ann. § 604A.01;**

Good Samaritan Law Video

Good Samaritan Sued after Rescuing Woman in an Accident

This video is a news story on a California Supreme Court case regarding the civil liability of a Good Samaritan:
(click to see video)

Duty to Act Based on a Contract

A duty to act can be based on a contract between the defendant and another party. The most prevalent examples would be a physician's contractual duty to help a patient or a lifeguard's duty to save someone who is drowning. Keep in mind that *experts* who are *not* contractually bound can ignore an individual's pleas for help without committing a crime, no matter how morally abhorrent that may seem. For example, an expert swimmer can watch someone drown if there is no statute, contract, or special relationship that creates a legal duty to act.

Duty to Act Based on a Special Relationship

A special relationship may also be the basis of a legal duty to act. The most common special relationships are parent-child, spouse-spouse, and employer-employee. Often, the rationale for creating a legal duty to act when people are in a special relationship is the *dependence* of one individual on another. A parent has the obligation by law to provide food, clothing, shelter, and medical care for his or her children, because children are dependent on their parents and do not have the ability to procure these items themselves. In addition, if someone puts another person *in peril*, there may be a duty to *rescue* that person (State ex rel. Kuntz v. Thirteenth Jud. Dist., 2010). Although this is not exactly a special relationship, the victim may be dependent on the person who created the dangerous situation because he or she may be the only one present and able to render aid. On a related note, some jurisdictions also impose a duty to *continue to provide aid*, once aid or assistance has started (Jones v. U.S., 2010). Similar to the duty to rescue a victim the defendant has put in peril, the duty to continue to provide aid is rooted in the victim's dependence on the defendant and the unlikely chance that another person may come along to help once the defendant has begun providing assistance.

Example of a Failure to Act That Is Noncriminal

Recall the example from Chapter 1 "Introduction to Criminal Law", Section 1.2.1 "Example of Criminal Law Issues", where Clara and Linda are shopping together and Clara stands by and watches as Linda shoplifts a bra. In this example, Clara does *not* have a duty to report Linda for shoplifting. Clara does not have a *contractual* duty to report a crime in this situation because she is not a law enforcement officer or security guard obligated by an employment contract. Nor does she have a *special relationship* with the store mandating such a report. Unless a *statute* or ordinance exists to force individuals to report crimes committed in their presence, which is extremely unlikely, Clara can legally observe Linda's shoplifting without reporting it. Of course, if Clara assists Linda with the shoplifting, she has then performed a criminal act or actus reus, and a criminal prosecution is appropriate.

Example of a Failure to Act That Is Criminal

Penelope stands on the shore at a public beach and watches as a child drowns. If Penelope's state has a Good Samaritan law, she may have a duty to help the child based on a *statute*. If Penelope is the lifeguard, she may have a duty to save the child based on a *contract*. If Penelope is the child's mother, she may have a duty to provide assistance based on their *special relationship*. If Penelope threw the child in the ocean, she may have a duty to rescue the child she *put in peril*. If Penelope is just a bystander, and no Good Samaritan law is in force, she has no duty to act and cannot be criminally prosecuted if the child suffers harm or drowns.

Possession as a Criminal Act

Although it is passive rather than active, possession is still considered a criminal act. The most common objects that are criminal to possess are illegal contraband, drugs, and weapons. There are two types of possession: actual possession and constructive possession. Actual possession indicates that the defendant has the item on or very near his or her person. Constructive possession indicates that the item is not on the defendant's person, but is within the defendant's area of control, such as inside a house or automobile with the defendant (State v. Davis, 2011). More than one defendant can be in possession of an object, although this would clearly be a constructive possession for at least one of them.

Because it is passive, possession should be *knowing,* meaning the defendant is aware that he or she possesses the item (Connecticut Jury Instructions No. 2.11-1, 2011). As the Model Penal Code states in § 2.01(4), "[p]ossession is an act, within the meaning of this Section, if the possessor knowingly procured or received the thing possessed or was aware of his control thereof for a sufficient period to have been able to terminate his possession." In the vast majority of states, a statute permitting a conviction for possession *without* this knowledge or awareness lacks the criminal intent element and would be unenforceable.

Example of an Unenforceable Possession Statute

A state has a criminal statute that prohibits "being within 100 feet of any quantity of marijuana." Ricardo sits next to Jean on the subway. A law enforcement officer smells marijuana and does a pat-down search of Jean. He discovers that Jean has a large baggie of marijuana in his jacket pocket and arrests Jean and Ricardo for marijuana possession. Ricardo was within one hundred feet of marijuana as prohibited by the statute, but Ricardo *should not* be prosecuted for marijuana possession. No evidence exists to indicate that Ricardo knew Jean, or knew that Jean possessed marijuana. Thus Ricardo does not have the **criminal intent** or mens rea for possession, and the state's possession statute should not be enforced against him.

Key Takeaways

- The elements of a crime are criminal act, criminal intent, concurrence, causation, harm, and attendant circumstances. Only crimes that specify a bad result have the elements of causation and harm.
- Criminal act is usually an unlawful bodily movement that is defined in a statute, or a case in jurisdictions that allow common-law crimes.
- The criminal act must be voluntary and cannot be based solely on the status of the defendant or the defendant's thoughts.
- An exception to the criminal act element is omission to act.
- Omission to act could be criminal if there is a statute, contract, or special relationship that creates a legal duty to act in the defendant's situation.
- Actual possession means that the item is on or very near the defendant's person. Constructive possession means that the item is within the defendant's control, such as inside a house or vehicle with the defendant.
- In most states, the defendant must be aware that he or she possesses the item to be convicted of possession.

Exercises

Answer the following questions. Check your answers using the answer key at the end of the chapter.

Jacqueline is diagnosed with epilepsy two years after receiving her driver's license. While driving to a concert, Jacqueline suffers an epileptic seizure and crashes into another vehicle, injuring both of its occupants. Can Jacqueline be convicted of a crime in this situation? Why or why not?
Read *Oler v. State,* 998 S.W.2d 363 (1999). In *Oler,* the defendant was convicted of possession of a controlled substance by misrepresentation. The defendant solicited and received prescriptions for Dilaudid, a controlled substance, from four different physicians without informing them that he already had a prescription for Dilaudid. The defendant appealed, arguing that he had no *legal duty* to disclose his previous receipt of the drug to the physicians, and was therefore unlawfully punished for an **omission to act**. Did the Texas Court of Appeals uphold the defendant's conviction? Why or

why not? The case is available at this link:
http://scholar.google.com/scholar_case?case=460187562193844690&q=
998+S.W.2d+363&hl=en&as_sdt=10000000000002.
Read *Staples v. U.S.*, 511 U.S. 600 (1994). In *Staples*, the defendant was convicted of possession of an unregistered automatic weapon in violation of the National Firearms Act. The defendant claimed the conviction was improper because the prosecution did not prove that *he knew* the weapon was automatic, and the prosecution must prove this knowledge to convict under the statute. Did the US Supreme Court reverse the defendant's conviction? Why or why not? The case is available at this link: http://www.law.cornell.edu/supct/html/92-1441.ZO.html.

References

Connecticut Jury Instructions No. 2.11-1, accessed February 13, 2011, http://www.jud.ct.gov/ji/criminal/part2/2.11-1.htm.

Fla. Stat. Ann. § 790.24, accessed October 25, 2010, http://law.onecle.com/florida/crimes/790.24.html.

Govt. of Virgin Islands v. Smith, 278 F.2d 169 (1960), accessed October 26, 2010, http://openjurist.org/278/f2d/169/government-of-the-virgin-islands-v-smith.

Jones v. U.S., 308 F.2d 307 (1962), accessed October 25, 2010, http://scholar.google.com/scholar_case?case=14703438613582917232&hl=en&as_sdt=2002&as_vis=1.

Ky. Rev. Stat. Ann. § 620.030, accessed October 25, 2010, http://www.lrc.ky.gov/krs/620-00/030.pdf.

Minnesota Code § 604A.01, accessed October 25, 2010, http://law.justia.com/minnesota/codes/2005/595/604a-s01.html.

N.Y. Penal Law § 15.00, accessed October 25, 2010, http://law.onecle.com/new-york/penal/PEN015.00_15.00.html.

State ex rel. Kuntz v. Thirteenth Jud. Dist., 995 P.2d 951 (2000), accessed October 25, 2010, http://caselaw.findlaw.com/mt-supreme-court/1434948.html.

State v. Davis, 84 Conn. App. 505 (2004), accessed February 13, 2011, http://scholar.google.com/scholar_case?case=12496216636522596448&hl=en&as_sdt=2&as_vis=1&oi=scholarr.

26 U.S.C. § 7203, accessed October 25, 2010, http://www.law.cornell.edu/uscode/26/usc_sec_26_00007203—-000-.html.

CC licensed content, Shared previously

- Criminal Law. **Provided by**: University of Minnesota Libraries Publishing . **Located at**: http://open.lib.umn.edu/criminallaw/. **License**: *CC BY-NC-SA: Attribution-NonCommercial-ShareAlike*

4.2 Criminal Intent

Learning Objectives

Describe one important function of criminal intent.

List the three common-law criminal intents, ranking them in order of culpability.

Compare specific and general intent.

Describe an inference that makes it easier for the prosecution to prove a general intent crime.

Differentiate between motive and criminal intent.

List and define the Model Penal Code mental states, ranking them in order of culpability.

Identify an exception to the requirement that every crime contain a criminal intent element.

Explain how transferred intent promotes justice.

Describe the circumstances that give rise to vicarious criminal liability.

Define concurrence of criminal act and intent.

Although there are exceptions that are discussed shortly, criminal intent or mens rea is an essential element of most crimes. Under the common law, *all* crimes consisted of an act carried out with a guilty mind. In modern society, criminal intent can be the basis for *fault*, and punishment according to intent is a core premise of criminal justice. As stated in Chapter 1 "Introduction to Criminal Law", **grading** is often related to the criminal intent element. Crimes that have an "evil" intent are **malum in se** and subject the defendant to the most severe punishment. Crimes that *lack* the intent element are less common and are usually graded lower, as either misdemeanors or infractions.

Figure 4.5 New York Penal Law

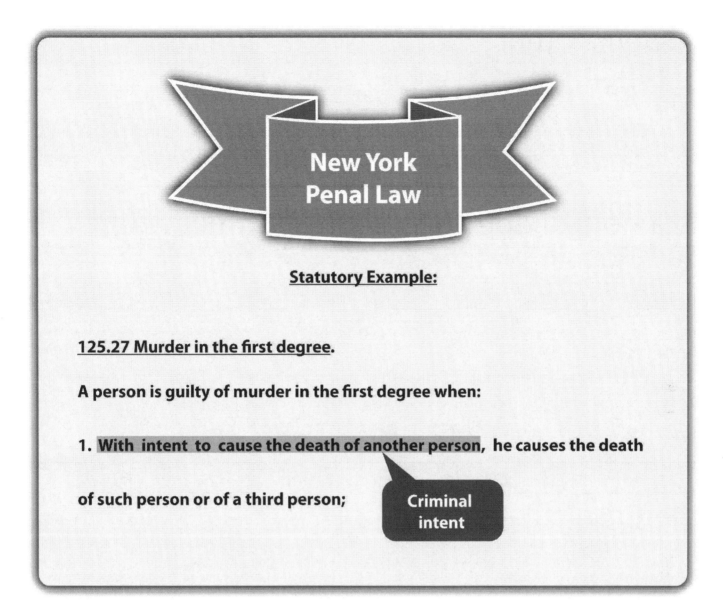

States and the federal government vary in their approach to defining criminal intent, and each jurisdiction describes the criminal intent element in a criminal statute, or case, in jurisdictions that allow common-law crimes. In this section, common-law definitions of criminal intent are explored, along with definitions of the criminal mental states in the Model Penal Code.

Common-Law Criminal Intent

The common-law criminal intents ranked in order of culpability are malice aforethought, specific intent, and general intent. Statutes and cases use different words to indicate the appropriate level of intent for the criminal offense, so what follows is a basic description of the intent definitions adopted by many jurisdictions.

Malice Aforethought

Malice aforethought is a special common-law intent designated for only one crime: *murder*. The definition of malice aforethought is "intent to kill." Society considers intent to kill the most evil of all intents, so malice aforethought crimes such as first- and second-degree murder generally mandate the most severe of punishments, including the death penalty in jurisdictions that allow for it. Malice aforethought and criminal homicide are discussed in detail in Chapter 9 "Criminal Homicide".

Specific Intent

Specific intent is the intent with the highest level of culpability for crimes other than murder. Unfortunately, criminal statutes rarely describe their intent element as "specific" or "general," and a judge may be required to define the level of intent using the common law or a dictionary to explain a word's ordinary meaning. Typically, specific intent means that the defendant acts with a more sophisticated level of awareness (Connecticut Jury Instructions No. 2.3-1, 2011). Crimes that require specific intent usually fall into one of three categories: either the defendant intends to cause a certain bad *result*, the defendant intends to do *something more* than commit the criminal act, or the defendant acts with knowledge that his or her conduct is illegal, which is called scienter.

Example of Specific Intent to Bring about a Bad Result

A state statute defines mayhem as "physical contact with another, inflicted with the intent to maim, disfigure, or scar." This statute describes a specific intent crime. To be guilty of mayhem under the statute, the defendant must inflict the physical contact with the intent of causing the bad *result* of maiming, disfigurement, or scarring. If the prosecution cannot prove this high-level intent, the defendant may be acquitted (or charged and convicted of a lower-level intent crime like battery).

So if Pauline says, "It's time to permanently mess up that pretty face," and thereafter takes out a razor and slices Peter's cheek with it, Pauline might be found guilty of mayhem. On the other hand, if Pauline slaps Peter while he is shaving without making the comment, and the razor bites into his cheek, it is more challenging to prove that she *intended a scarring*, and Pauline might be found guilty only of battery.

Example of Specific Intent to Do More than the Criminal Act

A state statute defines theft as "a permanent taking of property belonging to another." This statute describes a specific intent crime. To be guilty of theft under the statute, the defendant must intend to do more than "take the property of another," which is the criminal act. The defendant must also *intend to keep* the property permanently.

So if Pauline borrows Peter's razor to shave her legs, she has "taken the property of another," but she has not committed theft for the simple reason that she intends to return the property after use.

Example of Scienter

Although the terms mens rea and **scienter** are sometimes used interchangeably, many jurisdictions define scienter as knowledge that an act is *illegal*. Scienter can be the basis of **specific intent** in some statutes. So a statute that makes it a crime to "willfully file a false tax return" may require knowledge that the tax return includes false information *and* that it will be *unlawful* to file it (U.S. v. Pompanio, 2010). If the prosecution fails to prove beyond a reasonable doubt that the defendant knew his or her conduct was *illegal*, this could nullify scienter, and the prosecution cannot prove specific intent.

General Intent

General intent is less sophisticated than specific intent. Thus general intent crimes are easier to prove and can also result in a less severe punishment. A basic definition of general intent is the intent to perform the criminal act or actus reus. If the defendant acts intentionally but *without the additional desire* to bring about a certain result, or do anything other than the criminal act itself, the defendant has acted with general intent (People v. McDaniel,

2011).

Inference of General Intent

Intent is a notoriously difficult element to prove because it is locked inside the defendant's mind. Ordinarily, the only direct evidence of intent is a defendant's confession, which the government cannot forcibly obtain because of the Fifth Amendment privilege against self-incrimination. Witnesses who hear the defendant express intent are often unable to testify about it because of evidentiary rules prohibiting hearsay. However, many jurisdictions allow an **inference** of general intent based on the criminal *act* (Commonwealth v. Ely, 2011). In essence, if the jury accepts the inference, the prosecution does not have the burden of proving intent for a general intent crime.

Example of a General Intent Crime and an Inference of Intent

A state statute defines battery as "intentional harmful or offensive physical contact with another." This statute describes a general intent crime. To be guilty of battery under the statute, the defendant must *only* intend the harmful or offensive contact. The defendant does not have to desire that the contact produces a specific *result*, such as scarring, or death; nor does the defendant need **scienter**, or awareness that the physical contact is illegal.

If Addie balls up her fist and punches Eddie in the jaw after Eddie calls her a "stupid idiot," Addie has probably committed battery under the statute. A prosecutor could prove that Addie committed the *act* of harmful or offensive contact using Eddie's testimony and a physician's report. The jury could thereafter be instructed to "infer intent from proof of the act." If the jury accepts the inference and determines that Addie committed the criminal act, the jury could find Addie guilty of battery without additional evidence of intent.

Figure 4.6 Common Law Intents

Most Serious	
Less Serious	
Least Serious	

Motive

Intent should not be confused with motive, which is the *reason* the defendant commits the criminal act or actus reus. Motive can generate intent, support a defense, and be used to determine sentencing. However, motive *alone* does not constitute mens rea and does not act as a *substitute* for criminal intent.

Example of Motive

Isabella, a housewife with no criminal record, sits quietly in court waiting to hear the jury verdict in a trial for the rape of her teenage daughter by Ignatius. Ignatius has been convicted of child rape in three previous incidents. The jury foreman announces the decision finding Ignatius not guilty. Ignatius looks over his shoulder at Isabella and smirks. Isabella calmly pulls a loaded revolver out of her purse, and then shoots and kills Ignatius. In this case, Isabella's *motive* is *revenge* for the rape of her teenage daughter, or the desire to protect other women from Ignatius' conduct. This motive generated Isabella's criminal *intent*, which is malice aforethought or intent to kill. In spite of Isabella's motive, which is probably understandable under the circumstances, Isabella can be found guilty of murder because she acted with the murder mens rea. However, Isabella's motive may be introduced at sentencing and may result in a reduced sentence such as life in prison rather than the death penalty. In addition, Isabella's motive may affect a prosecutor's decision to seek the death penalty at all because this would probably be disfavored by the public.

Model Penal Code Criminal Intent

The Model Penal Code divides criminal intent into four states of mind listed in order of culpability: purposely, knowingly, recklessly, and negligently.

Purposely

A defendant who acts **purposely** intends to engage in conduct of that nature and intends to cause a certain result (N.H. Rev. Stat. Ann., 2011). Purposeful criminal intent resembles **specific intent** to cause harm, which was discussed previously. As the Model Penal Code states, "[a] person acts purposely with respect to a material element of an offense when: (i) if the element involves the nature of his conduct or a result thereof, it is his conscious object to engage in conduct of that nature or to cause such a result" (Model Penal Code § 2.02 (2) (a)).

Example of Purposely

Review the example given in Section 4 "Example of Specific Intent to Bring about a Bad Result", where Pauline takes out a razor and slices Peter's cheek. In this example, Pauline is aware of the nature of the act (slicing someone's cheek with a razor). Pauline also appears to be acting with the intent to cause a specific result, based on her statement to Peter. Thus Pauline is acting with **specific intent** or **purposely** and can probably be convicted of some form of aggravated battery or mayhem in most jurisdictions.

Knowingly

Knowingly indicates that the defendant is aware of the nature of the act and its probable consequences (Utah Code Ann., 2011). Knowingly differs from purposely in that the defendant is not acting *to cause* a certain result but is acting with the awareness that the result is *practically certain* to occur (State v. Huff, 2011). The Model Penal Code describes knowingly as follows: "A person acts knowingly with respect to a material element of an offense when...he is aware that his conduct is of that nature...if the element involves a result of his conduct, he is aware that it is practically certain that his conduct will cause such a result" (Model Penal Code in § 2.02(2) (b)).

Example of Knowingly

Victor brags to his girlfriend Tanya that he can shoot into a densely packed crowd of people on the subway train without hitting any of them. Tanya dares Victor to try it. Victor removes a concealed weapon from his waistband and shoots, aiming at a group of people standing with their back to him. The shot kills Monica, who is standing the closest to Victor. In this case, Victor did not *intend* to shoot Monica. In fact, Victor's goal was to shoot and miss all the standing subway passengers. However, Victor was *aware* that he was shooting a loaded gun (the nature of the act) and was also *practically certain* that shooting into a crowd would result in somebody getting hurt or killed. Thus Victor acted knowingly according to the Model Penal Code. If the state in which Victor shoots Monica defines murder intent as **knowingly** under the Model Penal Code, then Victor has most likely committed murder in this case.

Figure 4.7 Crack the Code

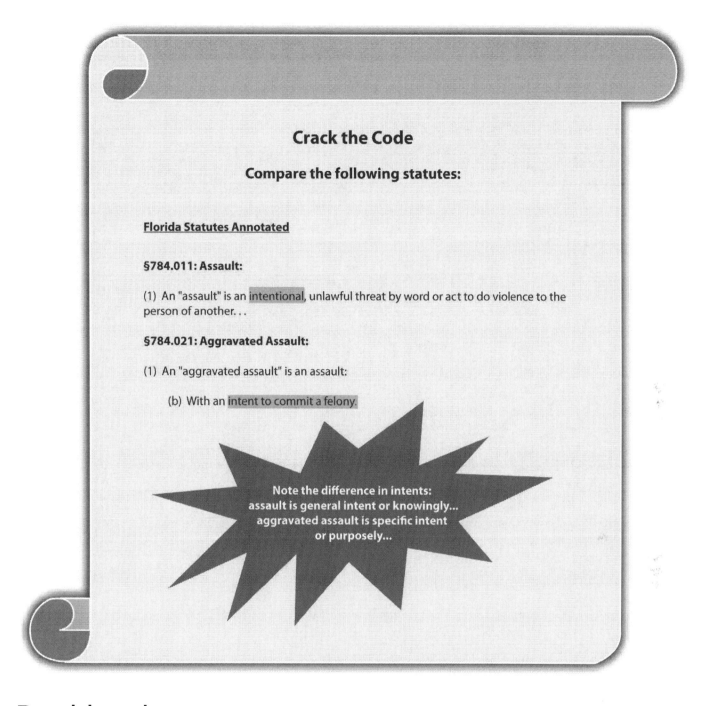

Crack the Code

Compare the following statutes:

Florida Statutes Annotated

§784.011: Assault:

(1) An "assault" is an intentional, unlawful threat by word or act to do violence to the person of another...

§784.021: Aggravated Assault:

(1) An "aggravated assault" is an assault:

(b) With an intent to commit a felony.

Note the difference in intents: assault is general intent or knowingly... aggravated assault is specific intent or purposely...

Recklessly

Recklessly is a lower level of culpability than knowingly, and reckless intent crimes are not as common as offenses criminalizing purposeful, knowing conduct. The *degree* of risk awareness is key to distinguishing a reckless intent crime from a knowing intent crime. A defendant acts recklessly if he or she consciously disregards a substantial and unjustifiable risk that the bad result or harm will occur (Colo. Rev. Stat. Ann., 2011). This is different from a knowing intent crime, where the defendant must be "practically certain" of the bad results. The reckless intent test is two pronged. First, the defendant must consciously disregard a substantial risk of harm. The standard is subjective; the *defendant* must know of the substantial risk. Second, the defendant must take an unjustifiable risk, meaning that no valid reason exists for the risk. The standard for this prong is objective; if a *reasonable person* would not take the risk, then the defendant's action in taking it is **reckless**. As the Model Penal Code states, "[t]he risk must be of such a nature and degree that...its disregard involves a gross deviation from the standard of conduct that a law-abiding person would observe in the actor's situation" (Model Penal Code § 2.02(2) (c)).

Example of Recklessly

Review the example in Section 4 "Example of Knowingly", where Victor shoots into a crowd of subway travelers and kills Monica. Change the example, and imagine that the subway train has only three passengers. Victor easily shoots in between them, yet the bullet ricochets off one of the seats and strikes Monica, killing her. Victor would be acting with **reckless** rather than **knowing** intent in this situation. Victor's knowledge and awareness of the *risk* of injury or death when shooting a gun inside a subway car containing three passengers is probably *substantial*. A reasonable, law-abiding person would probably *not* take this action under these circumstances. Thus Victor might be charged with a lower-level form of criminal homicide like **manslaughter** in this case. The difference between murder and manslaughter is discussed in detail in Chapter 9 "Criminal Homicide".

Negligently

Negligent intent crimes are less culpable than reckless intent crimes and are also less common. The difference between reckless and negligent intent is the defendant's *lack of awareness*. While defendants committing negligent intent crimes are also faced with a **substantial** and **unjustifiable** risk, they are *unaware* of it, even though a reasonable person would be (Idaho Code Ann., 2011). Thus the first prong of the reckless intent test is simply changed from a subjective to objective standard. As the Model Penal Code states, "[a] person acts negligently...when he should be aware of a substantial and unjustifiable risk that the material element exists or will result from his conduct"(Model Penal Code § 2.02(2) (d)).

Example of Negligently

Review the example in Section 4 "Example of Knowingly", where Victor shoots into a crowd of subway travelers and kills Monica. Change the example, and imagine that the subway train has no passengers. Victor brags to Tanya that he can shoot a crumpled napkin on the floor. Tanya challenges him to try it. Victor shoots at the napkin and misses, and the bullet ricochets three times off three different seats, travels backward, and strikes Tanya in the forehead, killing her instantly. In this case, Victor may be *unaware* of the bullet's potential to ricochet several times and actually travel backward. However, the trier of fact can determine that a "reasonable person" would be aware that shooting a gun inside a small subway train could result in injury or death. This would be a finding that Victor acted **negligently**, under the circumstances. If the state in which Victor shot Tanya criminalizes negligent killings, then Victor could be found guilty of criminal homicide in this case.

Figure 4.8 Model Penal Code Criminal Intents Ranked from Most Serious to Least Serious

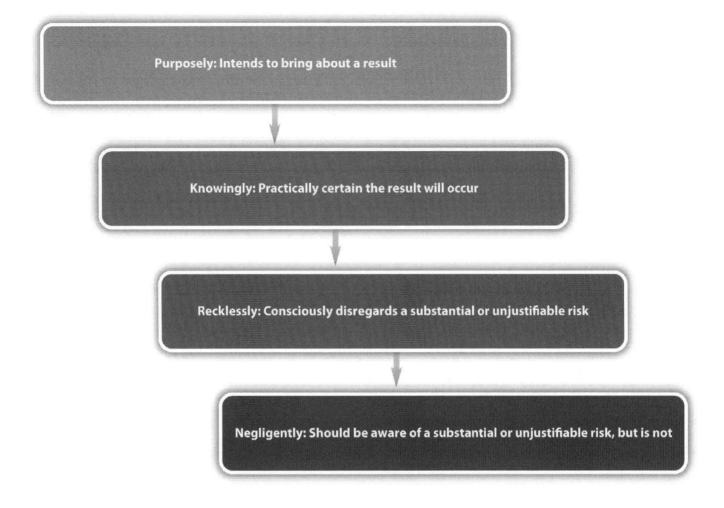

Elements and Criminal Intent

Occasionally, *different* criminal intents support the various elements of an offense. If a crime requires more than one criminal intent, each criminal intent must be proven beyond a reasonable doubt for each element.

Under the common law, every offense had just *one* criminal intent. In modern society, every offense has one criminal intent *unless* a statute specifies otherwise. As the Model Penal Code states, "[w]hen the law defining an offense prescribes the kind of culpability that is sufficient for the commission of an offense, without distinguishing among the material elements thereof, such provision shall apply to all of the material elements of the offense, unless a contrary purpose plainly appears" (Model Penal Code § 2.02(4)).

Example of a Crime That Requires More Than One Criminal Intent

A state statute defines burglary as "breaking and entering into a residence at nighttime with the intent to commit a felony once inside." In this statute, the elements are the following: (1) breaking, (2) and entering, (3) into a residence, (4) at nighttime. Breaking and entering are two **criminal act** elements. They must be committed with the *specific intent*, or *purposely*, to commit a felony once inside the residence. The elements of residence and nighttime are two **attendant circumstances**, which most likely have the lower level of *general intent* or *knowingly*. Thus this statute has *four* separate criminal intents that the prosecution must prove beyond a reasonable doubt for conviction.

Strict Liability

An *exception* to the requirement of a criminal intent element is strict liability. Strict liability offenses have *no* intent element (Ala. Code, 2011). This is a modern statutory trend, which abrogates the common-law approach that behavior is only criminal when the defendant commits acts with a guilty mind. Sometimes the rationale for strict liability crimes is the protection of the public's health, safety, and welfare. Thus strict liability offenses are often vehicle code or tax code violations, mandating a less severe punishment (Tex. Penal Code, 2011). With a strict liability crime, the prosecution has to prove only the criminal act and possibly causation and harm or attendant circumstances, depending on the elements of the offense.

Example of a Strict Liability Offense

A vehicle code provision makes it a crime to "travel in a vehicle over the posted speed limit." This is a **strict liability** offense. So if a law enforcement officer captures radar information that indicates Susie was traveling in a vehicle five miles per hour over the posted speed limit, Susie can probably be convicted of speeding under the statute. Susie's protests that she "didn't know she was traveling at that speed," are *not* a valid defense. Susie's *knowledge* of the nature of the act is irrelevant. The prosecution only needs to prove the **criminal act** to convict Susie because this statute is strict liability and does not require proof of criminal intent.

Transferred Intent

Occasionally, the defendant's criminal intent is *not directed toward the victim*. Depending on the jurisdiction, this may result in a *transfer* of the defendant's intent from the intended victim to the eventual victim, for the purpose of fairness (N.Y. Penal Law, 2011). Although this is a legal fiction, it can be necessary to reach a just result. Transferred intent is only relevant in crimes that require a bad result or victim. In a case where intent is transferred, the defendant could receive more than one criminal charge, such as a charge for "attempting" to commit a crime against the intended victim. Attempt and transferred intent are discussed in detail in Chapter 8 "Inchoate Offenses".

Example of Transferred Intent

Billy and his brother Ronnie get into an argument at a crowded bar. Billy balls up his fist and swings, aiming for Ronnie's face. Ronnie ducks and Billy punches *Amanda* in the face instead. Billy did not intend to batter Amanda. However, it is unjust to allow this protective action of Ronnie's to excuse Billy's conduct. Thus Billy's intent to hit Ronnie transfers in some jurisdictions over to Amanda. Billy can also be charged with attempted battery, which is assault, of Ronnie, resulting in *two* crimes rather than one under the **transferred intent** doctrine.

Vicarious Liability

Vicarious liability is similar to respondeat superior, a civil law concept discussed in Chapter 1 "Introduction to Criminal Law". Vicarious liability transfers a defendant's responsibility for the crime to a *different defendant*, on the basis of a *special relationship*. Under a theory of vicarious liability, the defendant does not need to commit the criminal act supported by criminal intent. The defendant just has to be involved with the criminal actor in a legally defined relationship. As in civil law, vicarious liability is common between employers and employees.

Corporate liability is a type of vicarious liability that allows a corporation to be prosecuted for a crime apart from its owners, agents, and employees (720 ILCS 5/5-4, 2011). This is a modern concept that did not exist at early common law. Although corporations cannot be incarcerated, they can be fined. Vicarious liability and corporate liability are discussed in more detail in Chapter 7 "Parties to Crime".

Example of Vicarious Liability

Don hires James to work in his liquor store. James is specially trained to ask for the identification of any individual who appears to be under the age of thirty and attempts to buy alcohol. One night, James sells alcohol to Ashley and does not request identification because Ashley is attractive and James wants to ask her out on a date. Unfortunately, Ashley is underage and is participating in a sting operation with local law enforcement. Certain statutes could *subject Don* to criminal prosecution for selling alcohol to an underage person like Ashley, even though Don did not *personally* participate in the sale. Because Don is James's employer, he may be vicariously liable for James's on-the-job conduct in this instance.

Concurrence of Act and Intent

Another element of most criminal offenses is the requirement that the criminal act and criminal intent exist at the same moment (California Criminal Jury Instructions No. 252, 2011). This element is called concurrence. Concurrence is rarely an issue in a criminal prosecution because the criminal intent usually generates the bodily response (criminal act). However, in some rare instances, the criminal act and intent are separated by time, in which case concurrence is lacking and the defendant cannot be convicted of a crime.

Example of a Situation Lacking Concurrence

Sherree decides she wants to kill her husband using a handgun. As Sherree is driving to the local gun shop to purchase the handgun, her husband is distracted and steps in front of her car. Sherree slams on the brakes as a reflex, but unfortunately she is unable to avoid striking and killing her husband. Sherree cannot be prosecuted for criminal homicide in this case. Although Sherree had formulated the intent to kill, the intent to kill did not exist at the moment she committed the criminal act of hitting her husband with her vehicle. In fact, Sherree was trying to *avoid* hitting her husband at the moment he was killed. Thus this case lacks **concurrence** of act and intent, and Sherree is not guilty of criminal homicide.

Key Takeaways

- One important function of intent is the determination of punishment. In general, the more evil the intent, the more severe the punishment.
- The three common-law intents ranked in order of culpability are malice aforethought, specific intent, and general intent.
- Specific intent is the intent to bring about a certain result, do something other than the criminal act, or scienter. General intent is simply the intent to perform the criminal act.
- With a general intent crime, the trier of fact may infer intent from the criminal act. This alleviates the prosecution's burden of proving criminal intent.
- Motive is the reason the defendant commits the criminal act. Motive standing alone is not enough to prove criminal intent.
- The Model Penal Code's criminal states of mind ranked in order of culpability are purposely, knowingly, recklessly, and negligently. Purposely is similar to specific intent to cause a particular result. Knowingly is awareness that results are practically certain to occur. Recklessly is a subjective awareness of a risk of harm, and an objective and unjustified disregard of that risk. Negligently is not being aware of a substantial risk of harm when a reasonable person would be.
- The exception to the requirement that every crime contain a criminal intent element is strict liability.
- Transferred intent promotes justice by holding a defendant responsible for his or her criminal conduct, even though the conduct was intended to harm a different victim.
- Vicarious liability is the transfer of criminal liability from one criminal defendant to another based on a special relationship.
- Concurrence requires that act and intent exist at the same moment.

Exercises

Answer the following questions. Check your answers using the answer key at the end of the chapter.

As Jordan is driving to school, she takes her eyes off the road for a moment and rummages through her purse for her phone. This causes her to run a stop sign. Jordan is thereafter pulled over by law enforcement and issued a traffic ticket. What is Jordan's criminal intent in this case? Is Jordan criminally responsible for running the stop sign? Why or why not?

Read *Morissette v. U.S.*, 342 U.S. 246 (1952). In *Morissette*, the defendant was convicted of unlawful conversion of federal property for gathering and selling spent bomb casings dropped during US Air Force practice maneuvers. The statute required "knowing" conversion of the property, and the defendant claimed he believed the property was *abandoned*. Did the US Supreme Court uphold the defendant's conviction? Why or why not? The case is available at this link: http://scholar.google.com/scholar_case?case=787130527265701764&hl=en&as_sdt=2&as_vis=1&oi=scholarr.

Read *State v. Crosby*, 154 P.3d 97 (2007). In *Crosby*, the defendant was convicted of manslaughter of a dependent person by neglect. The defendant's mother died of "sepsis" and was brought to the hospital covered with feces and bedsores. The defendant was her mother's caregiver. The jury was instructed that the defendant possessed the mental state of "recklessness" under the statute if she disregarded a substantial risk of **harm** or **circumstances**. The jury asked the judge if "circumstances" included the *bedsores* or *just death*. He responded that the risk could be more than just death and left it up to the jury to decide. Did the Supreme Court of Oregon uphold the defendant's conviction? Why or why not? The case is available at this link: http://scholar.google.com/scholar_case?case=10006178173306648171&q= State+v.+Crosby+S53295&hl=en&as_sdt=2,5.

Read *State v. Horner*, 126 Ohio St. 3d 466 (2010). In *Horner*, the defendant pleaded no contest to aggravated robbery. The defendant's pre-plea indictment did not contain a mens rea element for aggravated robbery, just the mens rea for theft. The defendant moved to dismiss the no contest plea, based on the fact that the indictment was defective for lacking the mens rea element. Did the Ohio Supreme Court find the indictment defective? Why or why not? The case is available at this link: http://www.supremecourt.ohio.gov/rod/docs/pdf/0/2010/2010-ohio-3830.pdf.

Law and Ethics: *Dean v. U.S.*

Ten Years Imprisonment for an Accident?

"Accidents happen. Sometimes they happen to individuals committing crimes with loaded guns." Read *Dean v. U.S.*, 129 S. Ct. 1849 (2009)), which is available at this link: http://scholar.google.com/scholar_case?case=10945987555184039397&q= Dean+v.+U.S.&hl=en&as_sdt=2,5.

In *Dean*, the defendant was sentenced to ten years imprisonment under a federal sentencing enhancement for an accidental discharge of his firearm during a bank robbery. The prosecution presented evidence at trial indicating that the defendant went into the bank wearing a mask and carrying a loaded firearm. The defendant told everyone in the bank to "get down," and then went behind the tellers' station and began grabbing money with his left hand. The gun in his right hand discharged. The defendant seemed surprised by the discharge, cursed, and ran out of the bank. No one was injured or hurt during the robbery.

The defendant thereafter admitted he committed the robbery. The US Supreme Court upheld the defendant's sentencing, in spite of the fact that there was *no* evidence of *intent* to discharge the firearm. The Court based its holding on the plain meaning of the statute requiring a minimum sentence of ten years imprisonment when a firearm is discharged during a robbery. The statute, 18 U.S.C. § 924(c) (1) (A), does not expressly state a criminal intent requirement. The Court further held that a presumption of criminal intent was not required. As the Court stated, "[i]t is unusual to impose criminal punishment for the consequences of purely accidental conduct. But it is not unusual to punish individuals for the unintended consequences of their *unlawful* acts" (*Dean v. U.S.*, 129 S. Ct. 1849, 1855 (2009)).

Do you think it is ethical to sentence Dean to ten years' imprisonment for his accidental conduct in this case? Why or why not?

Check your answer using the answer key at the end of the chapter.

References

Ala. Code § 13A-2-3, accessed February 14, 2011, http://law.onecle.com/alabama/criminal-code/13A-2-3.html.

California Criminal Jury Instructions No. 252, accessed February 14, 2011, http://www.justia.com/criminal/docs/calcrim/200/252.html.

Colo. Rev. Stat. Ann. § 18-1-501(8), accessed February 14, 2011, http://www.michie.com/colorado/lpext.dll?f=templates&fn=main-h.htm&cp=.

Commonwealth v. Ely, 444 N.E.2d 1276 (1983), accessed February 13, 2011, http://scholar.google.com/scholar_case?case=369554378994187453&hl=en&as_sdt=2&as_vis=1&oi=scholarr.

Connecticut Jury Instructions No. 2.3-1, accessed February 14, 2011, http://www.jud.ct.gov/ji/criminal/part2/2.3-1.htm.

Idaho Code Ann. § 18-101(2), accessed February 14, 2011, http://www.legislature.idaho.gov/idstat/Title18/T18CH1SECT18-101.htm.

N.H. Rev. Stat. Ann. § 626:2(II)(a), accessed February 14, 2011, http://www.gencourt.state.nh.us/rsa/html/LXII/626/626-2.htm.

People v. McDaniel, 597 P.2d 124 (1979), accessed February 14, 2011, http://scholar.google.com/scholar_case?case=8266915507346002022&hl=en&as_sdt=2&as_vis=1&oi=scholarr.

State v. Huff, 469 A.2d 1251 (1984), accessed February 14, 2011, http://scholar.google.com/scholar_case?case=4287195880403875631&hl=en&as_sdt=2&as_vis=1&oi=scholarr.

Tex. Penal Code § 49.04, accessed February 14, 2011, http://law.onecle.com/texas/penal/49.04.00.html.

Utah Code Ann. § 76-2-103(2), accessed February 14, 2011, http://le.utah.gov/~code/TITLE76/htm/76_02_010300.htm.

U.S. v. Pompanio, 429 U.S. 10 (1976), accessed October 28, 2010, http://supreme.justia.com/us/429/10/case.html.

720 ILCS 5/5-4, accessed February 14, 2011, http://law.onecle.com/illinois/720ilcs5/5-4.html.
CC licensed content, Shared previously

- Criminal Law. **Provided by**: University of Minnesota Libraries Publishing . **Located at**: http://open.lib.umn.edu/criminallaw/. **License**: *CC BY-NC-SA: Attribution-NonCommercial-ShareAlike*

4.3 Causation and Harm

Learning Objectives

Distinguish between factual and legal cause.
Define intervening superseding cause, and explain the role it plays in the defendant's criminal liability.
Define one and three years and a day rules.

As stated previously, causation and harm can also be elements of a criminal offense if the offense requires a bad result. In essence, if injury is required under the statute, or the case is in a jurisdiction that allows for common-law crimes, the defendant must *cause* the requisite *harm*. Many incidents occur when the defendant technically initiates circumstances that result in harm, but it would be unjust to hold the defendant criminally responsible. Thus causation should not be rigidly determined in every instance, and the trier of fact must perform an analysis that promotes fairness. In this section, causation in fact and legal causation are examined as well as situations where the defendant may be insulated from criminal responsibility.

Figure 4.9 Oregon Revised Statutes

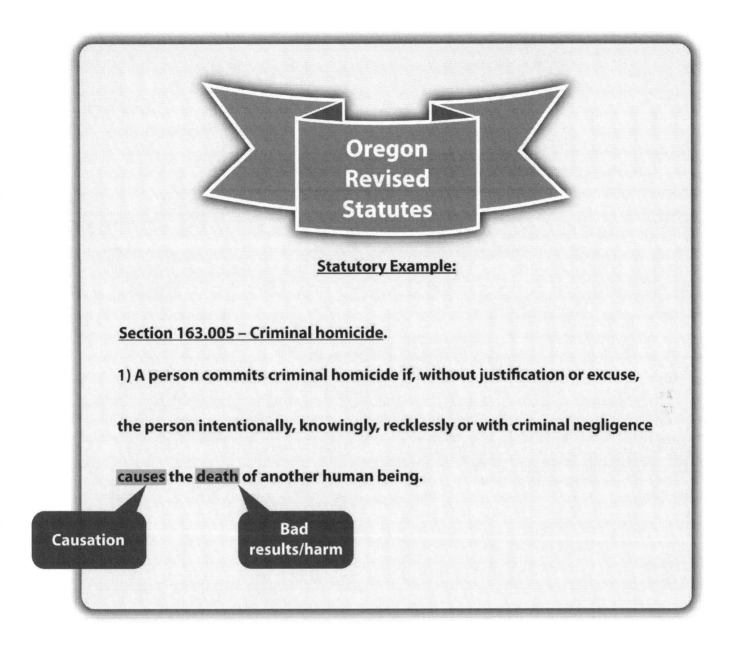

Causation in Fact

Every causation analysis is twofold. First, the defendant must be the factual or but for cause of the victim's harm. The *but for* term comes from this phrase: "but for the defendant's act, the harm would not have occurred" (Del. Code Ann. tit. II, 2011). As the Model Penal Code states, "[c]onduct is the cause of a result when...(a) it is an antecedent but for which the result in question would not have occurred" (Model Penal Code § 2.03(1)(a)). Basically, the defendant is the factual or but for cause of the victim's harm if the defendant's act starts the chain of events that leads to the eventual result.

Example of Factual Cause

Henry and Mary get into an argument over their child custody agreement. Henry gives Mary a hard shove. Mary staggers backward, is struck by lightning, and dies instantly. In this example, Henry's act forced Mary to move into the area where the lighting happened to strike. However, it would be *unjust* to punish Henry for Mary's death in this case because Henry could not have imagined the eventual result. Thus although Henry is the **factual or but for cause** of Mary's death, he is probably not the legal cause.

Legal Causation

It is the second part of the analysis that ensures fairness in the application of the causation element. The defendant must also be the **legal** or **proximate cause** of the harm. Proximate means "near," so the defendant's conduct must be closely related to the harm it engenders. As the Model Penal Code states, the actual result cannot be "too remote or accidental in its occurrence to have a [just] bearing on the actor's liability" (Model Penal Code § 2.03 (2) (b)).

The test for legal causation is objective foreseeability (California Criminal Jury Instructions No. 520, 2011). The trier of fact must be convinced that when the defendant acted, a *reasonable person* could have *foreseen* or predicted that the end result would occur. In the example given in Section 4 "Example of Factual Cause", Henry is not the legal cause of Mary's death because a reasonable person could have neither foreseen nor predicted that a shove would push Mary into a spot where lightning was about to strike.

The Model Penal Code adjusts the legal causation foreseeability requirement depending on whether the defendant acted purposely, knowingly, recklessly, or negligently. If the defendant's behavior is reckless or negligent, the legal causation foreseeability requirement is analyzed based on the *risk* of harm, rather than the *purpose* of the defendant.

Example of Legal Causation

Imagine that Henry and Mary get into the same argument over their child custody agreement, but this time they are in their garage, which is crowded with furniture. Henry gives Mary a hard shove, even though she is standing directly in front of a large entertainment center filled with books and a heavy thirty-two-inch television set. Mary staggers backward into the entertainment center and it crashes down on top of her, killing her. In this situation, Henry is the factual cause of Mary's death because he started the chain of events that led to her death with his push. In addition, it is *foreseeable* that Mary might suffer a serious injury or death when shoved directly into a large and heavy piece of furniture. Thus in this example, Henry could be the factual *and* legal cause of Mary's death. It is up to the trier of fact to make this determination based on an assessment of objective foreseeability and the attendant circumstances.

Intervening Superseding Cause

Another situation where the defendant is the factual but not the legal cause of the requisite harm is when something or someone interrupts the chain of events started by the defendant. This is called an intervening superseding cause. Typically, an intervening superseding cause cuts the defendant off from criminal liability because it is much closer, or *proximate*, to the resulting harm (Connecticut Jury Instructions No. 2.6-1, 2011). If an intervening superseding cause is a different individual acting with criminal intent, the *intervening* individual is criminally responsible for the harm caused.

Example of an Intervening Superseding Cause

Review the example with Henry and Mary in Section 4 "Example of Legal Causation". Change the example so that Henry pulls out a knife and chases Mary out of the garage. Mary escapes Henry and hides in an abandoned shed. Half an hour later, Wes, a homeless man living in the shed, returns from a day of panhandling. When he discovers Mary in the shed, he kills her and steals her money and jewelry. In this case, Henry is still the **factual cause** of Mary's death, because he chased her into the shed where she was eventually killed. However, Wes is probably the **intervening superseding cause** of Mary's death because he interrupted the chain of events started by Henry. Thus *Wes* is subject to prosecution for Mary's death, and Henry may be prosecuted only for assault with a deadly weapon.

One and Three Years and a Day Rules

In criminal homicide cases, the causation analysis could be complicated by a victim's *survival* for an extended time period. Because of modern technology, victims often stay alive on machines for many years after they have been harmed. However, it may be unreasonable to hold a defendant responsible for a death that occurs several years after the defendant's criminal act. A few states have rules that solve this dilemma.

Some states have either a one year and a day rule or a three years and a day rule (S.C. Code Ann., 2011). These rules create a timeline for the victim's death that changes the causation analysis in a criminal homicide case. Under one or three years and a day rules, the victim of a criminal homicide must die within the specified time limits for the defendant to be criminally responsible. If the victim does not die within the time limits, the defendant may be charged with *attempted murder*, rather than criminal homicide. California makes the timeline a *rebuttable presumption* that can be overcome with evidence proving that the conduct was criminal and the defendant should still be convicted (Cal. Penal Code, 2011).

Figure 4.10 California Penal Code

California Penal Code

Statutory Example:

Section 194

To make the killing either murder or manslaughter, it is not requisite that the party die within three years and a day after the stroke received or the cause of death administered. If death occurs beyond the time of three years and a day, there shall be a rebuttable presumption that the killing was not criminal. The prosecution shall bear the burden of overcoming this presumption. In the computation of time, the whole of the day on which the act was done shall be reckoned the first.

Death timeline rule

Death timeline rules are often embodied in a state's common law and have lost popularity in recent years (Key v. State, 2011). Thus many states have abolished arbitrary time limits for the victim's death in favor of ordinary principles of legal causation (Rogers v. Tennessee, 2011). Death timeline rules are not to be confused with the **statute of limitations**, which is the time limit the government has to *prosecute* a criminal defendant.

Figure 4.11 Diagram of the Elements of a Crime

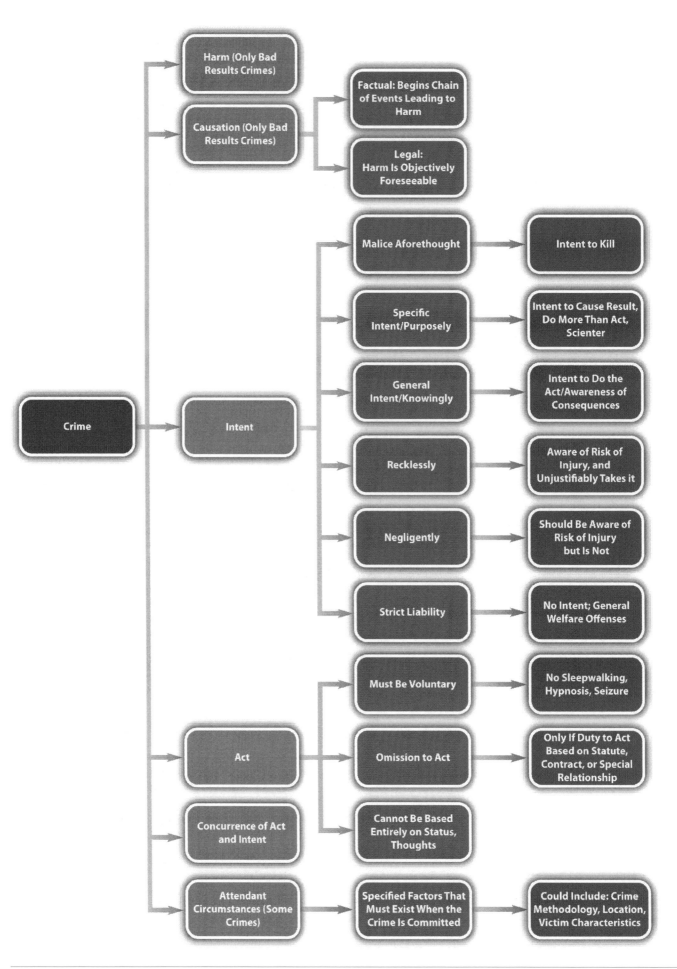

Key Takeaways

- Factual cause means that the defendant starts the chain of events leading to the harm. Legal cause means that the defendant is held criminally responsible for the harm because the harm is a foreseeable result of the defendant's criminal act.
- An intervening superseding cause breaks the chain of events started by the defendant's act and cuts the defendant off from criminal responsibility.
- One and three years and a day rules create a timeline for the victim's death in a criminal homicide.

Exercises

Answer the following questions. Check your answers using the answer key at the end of the chapter.

Phillipa sees Fred picking up trash along the highway and decides she wants to frighten him. She drives a quarter of a mile ahead of Fred and parks her car. She then hides in the bushes and waits for Fred to show up. When Fred gets close enough, she jumps out of the bushes screaming. Frightened, Fred drops his trash bag and runs into the middle of the highway where he is struck by a vehicle and killed. Is Phillipa's act the **legal cause** of Fred's death? Why or why not?

Read *Bullock v. State*, 775 A.2d. 1043 (2001). In *Bullock*, the defendant was convicted of manslaughter based on a vehicle collision that occurred when his vehicle hit the victim's vehicle in an intersection. The defendant was under the influence of alcohol and traveling thirty miles per hour over the speed limit. The victim was in the intersection *unlawfully* because the light was red. The defendant claimed that the victim was the **intervening superseding cause** of her own death. Did the Supreme Court of Delaware agree? The case is available at this link: http://caselaw.findlaw.com/de-supreme-court/1137701.html.

Read *Commonwealth v. Casanova*, 429 Mass. 293 (1999). In *Casanova*, the defendant shot the victim in 1991, paralyzing him. The defendant was convicted of assault with intent to murder and two firearms offenses. In 1996, the victim died. The defendant was thereafter indicted for his murder. Massachusetts had abolished the year and a day rule in 1980. Did the Massachusetts Supreme Judicial Court uphold the indictment, or did the court establish a new death timeline rule? The case is available at this link: http://scholar.google.com/scholar_case?case=16055857562232849296&hl=en&as_sdt=2&as_vis=1&oi=scholarr.

References

Cal. Penal Code § 194, accessed February 14, 2011, http://codes.lp.findlaw.com/cacode/PEN/3/1/8/1/s194.

California Criminal Jury Instructions No. 520, accessed February 14, 2011, http://www.justia.com/criminal/docs/calcrim/500/520.html.

Connecticut Jury Instructions No. 2.6-1, accessed February 14, 2011, http://www.jud.ct.gov/ji/criminal/part2/2.6-1.htm.

Del. Code Ann. tit. II, § 261, accessed February 14, 2011, http://delcode.delaware.gov/title11/c002/index.shtml#261.

Key v. State, 890 So.2d 1043 (2002), accessed February 15, 2011, http://www.lexisone.com/lx1/caselaw/freecaselaw?action=OCLGetCaseDetail&format=FULL&sourceID=beehed&searchTerm=efiQ.QLea.aadj.eaOS&searchFlag=y&l1loc=FCLOW.

Rogers v. Tennessee, 532 U.S. 541 (2001), accessed February 14, 2011, http://caselaw.lp.findlaw.com/scripts/getcase.pl?court=us&vol=000&invol=99-6218.

S.C. Code Ann. § 56-5-2910, accessed February 15, 2011, http://www.scstatehouse.gov/code/t56c005.htm.
CC licensed content, Shared previously

- Criminal Law. **Provided by**: University of Minnesota Libraries Publishing . **Located at**: http://open.lib.umn.edu/criminallaw/. **License**: *CC BY-NC-SA: Attribution-NonCommercial-ShareAlike*

4.4 End-of-Chapter Material

Summary

Crimes are made up of parts, referred to as elements. The criminal elements are criminal act or actus reus, criminal intent or mens rea, concurrence, causation, harm, and attendant circumstances. Only crimes that specify a bad result require the causation and harm elements.

Criminal acts must be voluntary or controllable and cannot consist solely of the defendant's status or thoughts. Just one voluntary act is needed for a crime, so if a voluntary act is followed by an involuntary act, the defendant can still be criminally responsible. Omission or failure to act can also be criminal if there is a duty to act based on a statute, contract, or special relationship. Possession is passive, but it can still be a criminal act. The most common items that are criminal to possess are illegal contraband, drugs, and weapons. Possession can be actual if the item is on or very near the defendant's person, or constructive if within an area of the defendant's control, like inside the defendant's house or vehicle. More than one defendant can be in possession of one item. Criminal possession should be supported by the intent of awareness because it is passive.

Criminal intent is an important element because it is often one factor considered in the grading of criminal offenses. The three common-law criminal intents are malice aforethought, which is intent to kill, specific intent, and general intent. Specific intent is the intent to bring about a particular result, a higher level of awareness than is required to perform the criminal act, or scienter, which is knowledge that a criminal act is unlawful. General intent is the intent to do the act and can often give rise to an inference of criminal intent from proof of the criminal act. Motive should not be confused with or replace intent. Motive is the reason the defendant develops criminal intent.

The Model Penal Code describes four criminal states of mind, which are purposely, knowingly, recklessly, and negligently. Purposely is similar to specific intent to cause a particular result. Knowingly is awareness that results are practically certain to occur. Recklessly is a subjective awareness of a risk of harm and an objective and unjustified disregard of that risk. Negligently is not being aware of a substantial risk of harm when a reasonable person would be. Offense elements, including specified attendant circumstances, may require different mental states. If so, the prosecution must prove each mental state for every element beyond a reasonable doubt.

Strict liability crimes do not require an intent element and are generally malum prohibitum, with a less severe punishment. Transferred intent is a legal fiction that transfers a defendant's criminal intent to an unintended victim for the purpose of fairness. Pursuant to transferred intent, the defendant may be responsible for two crimes: attempt and the completed crime, depending on the circumstances. Vicarious liability transfers a defendant's criminal liability to a different defendant based on a special relationship. Corporate liability is a type of vicarious liability that holds a corporation responsible for crimes apart from its owners, agents, and employees. Concurrence is also a criminal element that requires the criminal act and criminal intent exist at the same moment.

When the crime requires a bad result, the defendant must cause the harm. The defendant must be the factual and legal cause. Factual cause means that the defendant starts the chain of events that leads to the bad result. Legal or proximate cause means that it is objectively foreseeable that the end result will occur when the defendant commits the criminal act. An intervening superseding cause breaks the chain of events started by the defendant's criminal act and insulates the defendant from criminal liability. When the intervening superseding cause is an individual, the intervening individual is criminally responsible for the crime. Some states have rules that protect the defendant from criminal responsibility for homicide when the victim lives a long time after the criminal act. These death timeline rules require the victim to die within one or three years and a day from the defendant's criminal act and are becoming increasingly unpopular. Many states have abolished death timeline rules in favor of ordinary principles of legal causation.

You Be the Law Student

Read the prompt, review the case, and then decide whether the issue is the defendant's **criminal act** or **criminal intent**. Check your answers using the answer key at the end of the chapter.

Read *State v. Andrews*, 572 S.E.2d 798 (2002). In *Andrews*, the defendant took Prozac and Effexor for one day. The next day, the defendant ran his wife and her friend down with his car. After hitting both victims, the defendant jumped out of the car and stabbed his wife three times. He was convicted of attempted murder and assault with a deadly weapon against *both victims*. He appealed on the grounds that the jury was given an improper instruction as to his criminal responsibility for the crimes committed against his wife's *friend*. Did the Court of Appeals of North Carolina hold that this is an issue of **criminal act** or **criminal intent**? The case is available at this link: http://caselaw.findlaw.com/nc-court-of-appeals/1197459.html.

Read *State v. Sowry*, 155 Ohio App. 3d 742 (2004). In *Sowry*, Ohio police arrested the defendant and brought him to jail. Before booking the defendant, the police asked him whether he had any drugs on his person. He responded "no." The police thereafter searched him and discovered a plastic bag of marijuana in his pocket. The defendant was later convicted of knowingly conveying drugs onto the grounds of a detention facility. The defendant appealed and was successful. Did the Court of Appeals of Ohio hold that this is an issue of **criminal act** or **criminal intent**? The case is available at this link: http://www.supremecourt.ohio.gov/rod/docs/pdf/2/2004/2004-Ohio-399.pdf.

Read *Regalado v. U.S.*, 572 A.2d 416 (1990). In *Regalado*, the defendant was convicted of animal cruelty for punching a puppy repeatedly in the face. The defendant appealed, claiming that he was merely "disciplining" the puppy. Did the District of Columbia Court of Appeals hold that this is an issue of **criminal act** or **criminal intent**? The case is available at this link: http://scholar.google.com/scholar_case?case=10084482120424691457&hl=en&as_sdt=2&as_vis=1&oi=scholarr.

Read *State v. Slayton*, 154 P.3d 1057 (2007). In *Slayton*, the defendant received a hunting permit, hired a guide, and thereafter shot an elk and carried it out of the area. The defendant's hunting permit was valid in only a limited location, and the defendant shot the elk outside that location. The defendant was convicted of unauthorized hunting and transporting wildlife. The Arizona Superior Court vacated the defendant's convictions, the state appealed, and the Court of Appeals of Arizona reversed. Did the Court of Appeals of Arizona hold that this is an issue of **criminal act** or **criminal intent**? The case is available at this link: http://scholar.google.com/scholar_case?case=13377680343653410685&q=State+v.+Slayton&hl=en&as_sdt=2,5&as_ylo=2006.

Cases of Interest

- *State v. Kanavy*, 4 A.3d 991 (2010), discusses omission to act:
  http://scholar.google.com/scholar_case?case=13238547420575358722&q=State+v.+Kanavy&hl=en&as_sdt=2,5&as_vis=1.
- *U.S. v. Grajeda*, 581 F.3d 1186 (2009), discusses criminal intent:
  http://scholar.google.com/scholar_case?case=10326332733812062874&hl=en&as_sdt=2&as_vis=1&oi=scholarr.
- *People v. Roberts*, 826 P.2d 274 (1992), discusses proximate cause:
  http://scholar.google.com/scholar_case?case=128455976362726317&hl=en&as_sdt=2&as_vis=1&oi=scholarr.

Articles of Interest

- The duty to rescue: http://papers.ssrn.com/sol3/papers.cfm?abstract_id=796384
- Strict liability:
  http://www.bu.edu/law/central/jd/organizations/journals/bulr/volume86n2/documents/CARPENTERv2.pdf
- Vicarious liability: http://www.nj.com/news/index.ssf/2010/05/jury_finds_godinez_guilty_in_n.html

Websites of Interest

- State and federal laws and cases: http://law.onecle.com
- State and federal laws and cases: http://www.findlaw.com

CC licensed content, Shared previously

- Criminal Law. **Provided by**: University of Minnesota Libraries Publishing . **Located at**: http://open.lib.umn.edu/criminallaw/. **License**: *CC BY-NC-SA: Attribution-NonCommercial-ShareAlike*

Chapter 5: Criminal Defenses, Part 1

5.1 Criminal Defenses

Daniel Hoherd – Broken Latch – CC BY-NC 2.0.

A person who unlawfully and by force enters or attempts to enter a person's dwelling, residence, or occupied vehicle is presumed to be doing so with the intent to commit an unlawful act involving force or violence...

—Fla. Stat. Ann. §776.013(4), cited in Section 5.3.3 "Defense of Habitation"

Learning Objectives

Distinguish between a denial or failure of proof defense and an affirmative defense.
Distinguish between imperfect and perfect defenses.
Distinguish between factual and legal defenses.
Give examples of factual and legal defenses.
Distinguish between defenses based on justification and excuse.

A plethora of criminal defenses exist. Defenses may completely *exonerate* the criminal defendant, resulting in an acquittal, or *reduce the severity* of the offense. Chapter 3 "Constitutional Protections" discussed defenses based on the federal Constitution. This chapter reviews the categorization of nonconstitutional criminal defenses, along with the elements of various defenses sanctioning the use of force.

Categorization of Defenses

Defenses can be categorized as denial or failure of proof, affirmative, imperfect, or perfect. Defenses can also be categorized as factual, legal, based on justification, or excuse. Lastly, defenses can be created by a court (common law), or created by a state or federal legislature (statutory).

Definition of Denial or Failure of Proof and Affirmative Defenses

As stated in Chapter 2 "The Legal System in the United States", a criminal defendant will be acquitted if the prosecution cannot prove *every element* of the offense beyond a reasonable doubt. In certain cases, the defendant can either *deny* that a criminal element(s) exists or simply sit back and wait for the prosecution to fail in meeting its burden of proof. This legal strategy is sometimes referred to as either a denial or failure of proof defense.

An affirmative defense is not connected to the prosecution's burden of proof. When the defendant asserts an affirmative defense, the defendant raises a *new* issue that must be proven to a certain evidentiary standard. State statutes often specify whether a defense is affirmative. The Model Penal Code defines an affirmative defense as a defense that is deemed affirmative in the Code or a separate statute, or that "involves a matter of excuse or justification peculiarly within the knowledge of the defendant" (Model Penal Code § 1.12 (3) (c)). Procedurally, the defendant must assert any affirmative defense before or during the trial, or the defense cannot be used as grounds for an appeal.

Example of an Affirmative Defense

A fight breaks out at a party, and Juan is severely injured. Jasmine and Jerome are arrested and charged for battering Juan. Jerome claims that *he* did not touch Juan; *someone else* battered him. Jasmine claims that *she* did not batter Juan because she was legally defending herself against *Juan's* attack. Jerome's claim focuses on the elements of battery and asserts that these elements cannot be proven beyond a reasonable doubt. Technically, Jerome can do nothing and be acquitted if the prosecution fails to prove that he was the criminal actor. Jasmine's self-defense claim is an **affirmative** defense. Jasmine must do something to be acquitted: she must prove that Juan attacked *her* to a certain evidentiary standard.

Figure 5.1 Denial and Affirmative Defenses

Denial/Failure of Proof	
Affirmative	

Burden of Proof for Affirmative Defenses

As stated in Chapter 2 "The Legal System in the United States", states vary as to their requirements for the defendant's burden of proof when asserting an affirmative defense (Findlaw.com, 2010). Different defenses also have different burdens of proof. Some states require the defendant to meet the burden of production, but require the prosecution to thereafter meet the burden of persuasion, *disproving* the defense to a preponderance of evidence, or in some states, beyond a reasonable doubt. Other states require the defendant to meet the burden of production and the burden of persuasion. In such states, the defendant's evidentiary standard is preponderance of evidence, *not* beyond a reasonable doubt. In the example given in Section 5 "Example of an Affirmative Defense", for Jasmine's self-defense claim, Jasmine must prove she was defending herself by meeting either the burden of production or the burden of production and persuasion to a preponderance of evidence, depending on the jurisdiction.

Figure 5.2 Diagram of the Criminal Burden of Proof

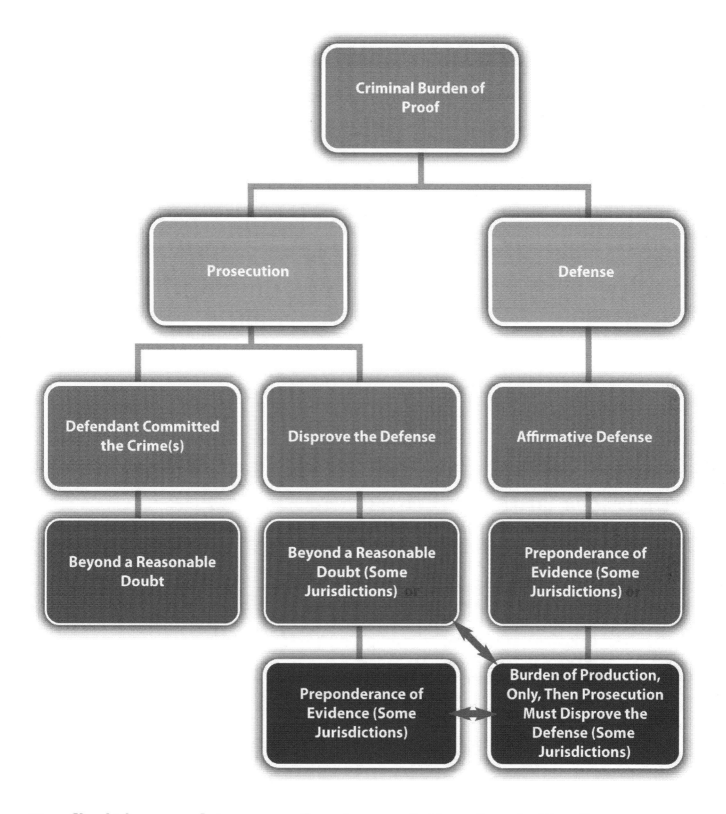

Definition of Imperfect and Perfect Defenses

As stated previously, a defense can reduce the severity of the offense, or completely exonerate the defendant from criminal responsibility. If a defense reduces the severity of the offense, it is called an imperfect defense. If a defense results in an acquittal, it is called a perfect defense. The difference between the two is significant. A defendant who is successful with an imperfect defense is still *guilty* of a crime; a defendant who is successful with a perfect defense is *innocent*.

Example of Imperfect and Perfect Defenses

LuLu flies into a rage and kills her sister Lola after she catches Lola sleeping with her fiancé. LuLu is thereafter charged with first-degree murder. LuLu decides to pursue two defenses. First, LuLu claims that the killing should be *manslaughter* rather than first-degree murder because she honestly but unreasonably believed Lola was going to attack *her*, so she thought she was acting in self-defense. Second, LuLu claims she was insane at the time the killing occurred. The claim of manslaughter is an **imperfect** defense that will reduce LuLu's sentence, but will not acquit her of criminal homicide. The claim of insanity is a **perfect** defense that will result in an acquittal.

Definition of Factual and Legal Defenses

A defense must be based on specific *grounds*. If a defense is based on an issue of **fact**, it is a factual defense. If a defense is based on an issue of **law**, it is a legal defense.

Example of Factual and Legal Defenses

Armando is charged with the burglary of Roman's residence. Armando decides to pursue two defenses. First, Armando claims that he was with Phil on the date and time of the burglary. This is called an alibi defense. Second, Armando claims that it is too late to prosecute him for burglary because of the expiration of the statute of limitations. Armando's alibi defense is a **factual** defense; it is based on the *fact* that Armando could not have committed the burglary because he was somewhere else at the time it occurred. Armando's statute of limitations defense is a **legal** defense because it is based on a *statute* that limits the amount of time the government has to prosecute Armando for burglary.

Definition of Justification and Excuse

With the exception of alibi, most affirmative defenses are based on either justification or excuse. Typically, justification and excuse defenses admit that the defendant committed the criminal act with the requisite intent, but insist that the conduct should not be criminal.

A defense based on justification focuses on the *offense*. A justification defense claims that the defendant's conduct should be legal rather than criminal because it supports a principle valued by society. A defense based on excuse focuses on the *defendant*. An excuse defense claims that even though the defendant committed the criminal act with criminal intent, the defendant should not be responsible for his or her behavior.

Example of Justification and Excuse

Review the examples of affirmative, imperfect, and perfect defenses given in Section 5.1.1 "Categorization of Defenses". Jasmine's self-defense claim is based on **justification**. Society believes that individuals should be able to protect themselves from harm, so actions taken in self-defense are justified and noncriminal. Note that a self-defense claim focuses on the *offense* (battery) in light of the circumstances (to prevent imminent harm). LuLu's insanity claim is based on **excuse**. Although LuLu killed Lola with criminal intent, if LuLu is truly insane it is not be fair or just to punish her for her behavior. Note that an insanity claim focuses on the *defendant* (a legally insane individual) and whether he or she should be criminally responsible for his or her conduct.

Table 5.1 Categorization of Defenses

Defense Type	Characteristics
Common-law	Created by a court

Defense Type	Characteristics
Statutory	Created by a state or federal legislature
Denial or failure of proof	Creates doubt in one or more elements of the offense and prevents the prosecution from meeting its burden of proof
Affirmative	Raises an issue separate from the elements of the offense
Imperfect	Reduces the severity of the offense
Perfect	Results in an acquittal
Factual	Based on an issue of fact
Legal	Based on an issue of law
Alibi	Asserts that the defendant was somewhere else when the crime was committed
Expiration of the statute of limitations	Asserts that it is too late for the government to prosecute the defendant for the crime
Justification	Claims that the criminal conduct is justified under the circumstances
Excuse	Claims that the defendant should be excused for his or her conduct

Key Takeaways

- A denial or failure of proof defense focuses on the elements of the crime and prevents the prosecution from meeting its burden of proof. An affirmative defense is a defense that raises an issue separate from the elements of the crime. Most affirmative defenses are based on justification or excuse and must be raised before or during the trial to preserve the issue for appeal.
- An imperfect defense reduces the severity of the offense; a perfect defense results in an acquittal.
- If the basis for a defense is an issue of fact, it is called a factual defense. If the basis for a defense is an issue of law, it is called a legal defense.
- An example of a factual defense is an alibi defense, which asserts that the defendant could not have committed the crime because he or she was somewhere else when the crime occurred. An example of a legal defense is a claim that the statute of limitations has expired, which asserts that it is too late for the government to prosecute the defendant for the crime.
- An affirmative defense is based on justification when it claims that criminal conduct is justified under the circumstances. An affirmative defense is based on excuse when it claims that the criminal defendant should be excused for his or her conduct.

Exercises

Answer the following questions. Check your answers using the answer key at the end of the chapter.

Carol is on trial for battery, a general intent crime. Carol puts on a defense that proves her conduct was accidental, *not* intentional. Is this an affirmative defense? Why or why not?
Read *State v. Burkhart*, 565 S.E.2d 298 (2002). In *Burkhart*, the defendant was convicted of three counts of murder. The defendant claimed he acted in self-defense. The jury instruction given during the defendant's trial stated that the prosecution had the burden of disproving self-defense.

However, the instruction did not state that the prosecution's burden of disproving self-defense was *beyond a reasonable doubt*. Did the Supreme Court of South Carolina uphold the defendant's conviction for the murders? The case is available at this link: http://scholar.google.com/scholar_case?case=1066148868024499763&hl=en&as_sdt=2&as_vis=1& oi=scholarr.

Read *Hoagland v. State*, 240 P.3d 1043 (2010). In *Hoagland*, the defendant wanted to assert a **necessity** defense to the crime of driving while under the influence. The Nevada Legislature had never addressed or mentioned a necessity defense. Did the Supreme Court of Nevada allow the defendant to present the necessity defense? The case is available at this link: http://scholar.google.com/scholar_case?case=8002120339805439441&q= Hoagland+v.+State&hl=en&as_sdt=2,5&as_ylo=2009.

References

Findlaw.com, "The Insanity Defense among the States," findlaw.com website, accessed October 11, 2010, http://criminal.findlaw.com/crimes/more-criminal-topics/insanity-defense/the-insanity-defense-among-the-states.html.
CC licensed content, Shared previously

- Criminal Law. **Provided by**: University of Minnesota Libraries Publishing . **Located at**: http://open.lib.umn.edu/criminallaw/. **License**: *CC BY-NC-SA: Attribution-NonCommercial-ShareAlike*

5.2 Self-Defense

Learning Objectives

Define self-defense.
Define deadly force.
Ascertain the four elements required for self-defense.
Ascertain two exceptions to the unprovoked attack requirement.
Define the battered wife defense, and explain its justification under the imminence requirement.
Analyze when it is appropriate to use deadly force in self-defense.
Distinguish between the duty to retreat and stand-your-ground doctrines.
Define imperfect self-defense.

As stated previously, self-defense is a defense based on **justification**. Self-defense can be a defense to assault, battery, and criminal homicide because it always involves the use of force. In the majority of states, self-defense is a **statutory** defense (Mich. Comp. Laws, 2010). However, it can be modified or expanded by courts on a case-by-case basis.

Most states have special requirements when the defendant uses deadly force in self-defense. **Deadly force** is defined as any force that could potentially kill. An individual does not have to actually die for the force to be considered deadly. Examples of deadly force are the use of a knife, gun, vehicle, or even bare hands when there is a disparity in size between two individuals.

Self-defense can operate as a **perfect** or **imperfect** defense, depending on the circumstances. Defendants who commit criminal homicide justified by self-defense can be acquitted, or have a murder charge reduced from first to second or third degree, or have a charge reduced from murder to manslaughter. Criminal homicide is discussed in detail in Chapter 9 "Criminal Homicide".

To successfully claim self-defense, the defendant must prove four elements. First, with exceptions, the defendant must prove that he or she was confronted with an **unprovoked** attack. Second, the defendant must prove that the threat of injury or death was **imminent**. Third, the defendant must prove that the **degree of force** used in self-defense was objectively reasonable under the circumstances. Fourth, the defendant must prove that he or she had an **objectively reasonable fear** that he or she was going to be injured or killed unless he or she used self-defense. The Model Penal Code defines self-defense in § 3.04(1) as "justifiable when the actor believes that such force is immediately necessary for the purpose of protecting himself against the use of unlawful force by such other person on the present occasion."

Provocation

In general, if the defendant initiates an attack against another, the defendant cannot claim self-defense (State v. Williams, 2010). This rule has two exceptions. The defendant can be the initial aggressor and still raise a self-defense claim if the attacked individual responds with *excessive* force under the circumstances, or if the defendant *withdraws* from the attack and the attacked individual persists.

Excessive Force Exception

In some jurisdictions, an individual cannot respond to the defendant's attack using excessive force under the circumstances (State v. Belgard, 2010). For example, an individual cannot use **deadly force** when the defendant initiates an attack using **nondeadly force**. If an individual does resort to deadly force with a nondeadly force attack, the defendant can use reasonable force in self-defense.

Example of the Excessive Force Exception

Patty and Paige get into an argument over a loan Patty made to Paige. Paige calls Patty a spoiled brat who always gets her way. Patty slaps Paige across the face. Paige grabs a carving knife from the kitchen counter and tries to stab Patty. Patty wrestles the knife away and stabs Paige in the chest, killing her. In this example, Patty provoked the attack by slapping Paige across the face. However, the slap is **nondeadly force**. In many jurisdictions, Paige cannot respond to nondeadly force with **deadly force**, like a knife. Paige used excessive force in her response to Patty's slap, so Patty can use deadly force to defend herself and may *not* be responsible for criminal homicide under these circumstances.

Withdrawal Exception

In some jurisdictions, the defendant can be the initial aggressor and still use force in self-defense if the defendant withdraws from the attack, and communicates this withdrawal to the attacked individual (N.Y. Penal Law, 2010). If the attacked individual persists in using force against the defendant after the defendant's withdrawal, rather than notifying law enforcement or retreating, the defendant is justified in using force under the circumstances.

Example of Withdrawal

Change the excessive force exception example in Section 5 "Example of the Excessive Force Exception". Imagine that after Patty slaps Paige across the face, Paige begins pounding Patty with her fists. Patty manages to escape and runs into the garage. She huddles against the garage wall. Paige chases Patty into the garage. Patty says, "Please, please don't hurt me. I'm sorry I slapped you." Paige kicks Patty in the back. Patty turns around and karate chops Paige in the neck, rendering her unconscious. In many jurisdictions, Patty's karate chop is lawful under a theory of self-defense because she completely *withdrew* from the attack. Thus Patty is probably not criminally responsible for battery, based on the karate chop to the neck. However, Patty *could* be criminally responsible for battery based on the slap to Paige's face because this physical contact was unprovoked and not defensive under the circumstances.

Figure 5.3 New York Penal Law

Statutory Example:

§35.15 Justification; use of physical force in defense of a person.

1. A person may, subject to the provisions of subdivision two, use physical force upon another person when and to the extent he or she reasonably believes such to be necessary to defend himself, herself or a third person from what he or she reasonably believes to be the use or imminent use of unlawful physical force by such other person, unless:

> **(b) The actor was the initial aggressor; except that in such case the use of physical force is nevertheless justifiable if the actor has withdrawn from the encounter and effectively communicated such withdrawal to such other person but the latter persists in continuing the incident by the use or threatened imminent use of unlawful physical force;**

Withdrawal exception

Imminence

The defendant cannot use any degree of force in self-defense unless the defendant is faced with an **imminent** attack (State v. Taylor, 2010). Imminent means the attack is *immediate* and not something that will occur in the future. If the defendant is threatened with a future attack, the appropriate response is to inform law enforcement, so that they can incapacitate the threatening individual by arrest or prosecution. Another situation where imminence is lacking is when the attack occurred in the *past*. When the defendant uses force to remedy a previous attack, this is retaliatory, and a self-defense claim is not appropriate. The legal response is to inform law enforcement so that they can incapacitate the attacker by arrest or prosecution.

Some state courts have expanded the imminence requirement to include situations where a husband in a domestic violence situation uses force or violence regularly against the defendant, a battered wife, therefore creating a threat of imminent harm every day (Bechtel v. State, 2010). If a jurisdiction recognizes the battered wife defense, the defendant—the battered wife—can legally use force against her abusive husband in self-defense in situations where harm is not necessarily immediate.

Example of an Attack That Is Not Imminent

Vinny tells Fiona that if she does not pay him the $1,000 she owes him, he will put out a contract on her life. Fiona pulls out a loaded gun and shoots Vinny. Fiona cannot successfully argue self-defense in this case. Vinny's threat was a threat of future harm, *not* imminent harm. Thus Fiona had plenty of time to contact law enforcement to help protect her safety.

Example of an Attack That Is Retaliatory

Dwight and Abel get into a fist fight. Dwight knocks Abel unconscious. Dwight observes Abel for a few minutes, and then he picks up a large rock and crushes Abel's skull with it, killing him. Dwight cannot claim self-defense in this situation. Once Dwight realized that Abel was unconscious, he did not need to continue to defend himself against an imminent attack. Dwight's conduct appears *retaliatory* and is not **justified** under these circumstances.

Example of an Imminent Attack under the Battered Wife Defense

Spike severely beats and injures his wife Veronica every couple of days. Spike's beatings have become more violent, and Veronica starts to fear for her life. One night, Veronica shoots and kills Spike while he is sleeping. In states that have expanded self-defense to include the battered wife defense, Veronica may be successful on a theory of self-defense.

Mary Winkler Defense Video

Dr. Alan J. Lipman Catherine Crier on Winkler Spousal Abuse Murder Trial

Mary Winkler claimed the battered wife defense as an imperfect defense to the murder of her husband, a pastor (Gay, M., 2011).
(click to see video)

Proportionality

The defendant cannot claim self-defense unless the degree of force used is **objectively reasonable** under the circumstances. This requirement primarily focuses on the use of **deadly force** and when it is legally justified. In general, deadly force can by employed in self-defense when a reasonable person feels threatened with imminent **death**, **serious bodily injury**, and, in some jurisdictions, a **serious felony** (Or. Rev. Stat. 2010). Serious bodily injury and serious felony are technical terms that are defined in a statute or case, depending on the jurisdiction. The Model Penal Code states that deadly force is not justifiable "unless the actor believes that such force is necessary to protect himself against death, serious bodily harm, kidnapping or sexual intercourse compelled by force or threat" (Model Penal Code § 3.04(2)(b)).

Example of Appropriate Deadly Force

Nicholas, an intruder, pins Wanda to the floor of her garage and begins to forcibly remove her clothing. Wanda feels around the floor with her hand and finds a screwdriver. She plunges the screwdriver into Nicholas's neck, killing him. Wanda has used appropriate force and can claim self-defense in most jurisdictions. A reasonable person in Wanda's situation would feel deadly force is necessary to repel Nicholas's sexual assault. Nicholas's attack is a **serious felony** that could result in **serious bodily injury** or **death**. Thus the use of deadly force is legally **justified** under these circumstances.

Duty to Retreat

Early common law stated that the defendant had a duty to retreat to the wall before using deadly force against an attacker. The majority of states have rejected this doctrine and instead allow the defendant to stand his or her ground if the defendant is not the initial aggressor in the confrontation (State v. Sandoval, 2010). In jurisdictions that still follow the **retreat doctrine**, the defendant must retreat if there is an objectively reasonable belief that the attacker will cause death or serious bodily injury, and a retreat won't unreasonably increase the likelihood of death or serious bodily injury (Connecticut Criminal Jury Instructions, 2010). The Model Penal Code defines the duty to retreat by stating that the use of deadly force is not justifiable if "the actor knows that he can avoid the necessity of using such force with complete safety by retreating" (Model Penal Code § 3.04 (2) (b) (ii)). An established exception to the retreat doctrine in jurisdictions that follow it is the defense of the home, which is called the **castle doctrine**. The castle doctrine is discussed shortly.

Example of the Duty to Retreat

Sandy and Sue have an argument in the park. Sue pulls a knife out of a sheath that is strapped to her leg and begins to advance toward Sandy. Sandy also has a knife in her pocket. In a state that follows the **retreat doctrine**, Sandy must attempt to escape, if she can do so safely. In a state that follows the **stand-your-ground doctrine**, Sandy can defend herself using her own knife and claim lawful self-defense. Note that Sandy was not the *initial aggressor* in this situation. If Sandy pulled a knife first, she could *not* use the knife and claim self-defense, whether the state follows the stand-your-ground doctrine or the duty to retreat doctrine.

Objectively Reasonable Fear of Injury or Death

The defendant cannot claim self-defense unless a reasonable person in the defendant's situation would believe that self-defense is necessary to avoid injury or death. If the defendant honestly but *unreasonably* believes self-defense is necessary under the circumstances, a claim of imperfect self-defense may reduce the severity of the offense (State v. Faulkner, 2010). However, the defendant is still guilty of a crime, albeit a less serious crime.

Example of Unjustified Conduct

Justin, who weighs over two hundred pounds and is six feet tall, accidentally bumps into Wanda, a slender ten-year-old child. Wanda spins around and shakes her fist at Justin. Justin responds by shoving Wanda so hard that she crashes into a telephone pole and is killed. Justin probably *cannot* claim self-defense under these circumstances. A reasonable person would not believe Wanda is about to seriously injure or kill Justin. Thus Justin's response is unnecessary and unjustified in this case.

Example of Imperfect Self-Defense

Change the unjustified conduct example given in Section 5 "Example of Unjustified Conduct". Imagine that a slender, female ten-year-old severely abused Justin when he was younger. Since the abusive incident, Justin has an unreasonable fear of female children and honestly believes that they can and will hurt him if provoked. If the trier of fact determines that Justin honestly but unreasonably believed that Wanda was about to inflict serious bodily injury or kill him, any charge of murder could be reduced to manslaughter on a theory of **imperfect self-defense**.

Key Takeaways

- Self-defense is a defense based on justification that allows a defendant to use physical force to protect himself or herself from injury or death.
- Deadly force is any force that can produce death. An individual does not have to die for the force to be deemed deadly.
- Four elements are required for self-defense: (1) an unprovoked attack, (2) which threatens imminent injury or death, and (3) an objectively reasonable degree of force, used in response to (4) an objectively reasonable fear of injury or death.
- Two exceptions to the unprovoked attack rule are an individual's use of excessive force in response to an initial attack and the defendant's withdrawal from the initial attack.
- The battered wife defense asserts that a woman who is a victim of spousal abuse may use force in self-defense under certain circumstances, even when the threat of harm is not immediate. The battered wife defense is justified with respect to the imminence requirement: because the abuse is so constant, the battered wife faces an imminent threat every day.
- Deadly force is appropriate in self-defense when the attacker threatens death, serious bodily injury, and, in some jurisdictions, a serious felony.
- The duty to retreat doctrine is a common-law rule requiring a defendant to retreat if it is safe to do so, instead of using deadly force in self-defense. The stand-your-ground doctrine is a rule allowing the defendant to use deadly force if appropriate in self-defense, rather than retreating.
- Imperfect self-defense is a defense available when the defendant has an honest but unreasonable belief that force is necessary to defend against injury or death. Imperfect self-defense reduces the severity of the offense, but does not result in acquittal.

Exercises

Answer the following questions. Check your answers using the answer key at the end of the chapter.

Scott's wife Diane constantly physically abuses him. One night while Diane is sleeping, Scott places a pillow over her face and smothers her. Can Scott defend against a charge of criminal homicide by claiming **self-defense**? Why or why not?

Read *Rodriguez v. State*, 212 S.W.3d 819 (2006). In *Rodriguez*, the defendant was convicted of murder and attempted murder. The defendant appealed his convictions on the ground that the jury did not *unanimously* reject each element of self-defense. Did the Court of Appeals of Texas uphold the defendant's convictions? The case is available at this link: https://casetext.com/case/rodriguez-v-state-464.

Read *Shuler v. Babbitt*, 49 F.Supp.2d 1165 (1998). In *Shuler*, the defendant shot and killed a grizzly bear that charged him while he checked a sheep pasture to make sure his sheep were safe. The sheep had already been subjected to several bear attacks. The Fish and Wildlife Service thereafter fined the defendant under the Endangered Species Act. The defendant claimed **self-defense** against the bear. The Fish and Wildlife Service ruled that the defendant *provoked* the attack and could not claim self-defense. Did the US District Court for the District of Montana uphold the fine? The case is available at this link: http://www.gilalivestockgrowers.org/documents/ShulerVsBabbitt.pdf.

Law and Ethics: The Menendez Brothers

Were They Entitled to a Jury Instruction on Imperfect Self-Defense?

Read *Menendez v. Terhune*, 422 F.3d 1012 (2005). The case is available at this link: http://cases.justia.com/us-court-of-appeals/F3/422/1012/569492.

Lyle and Eric Menendez were tried and convicted of murder and conspiracy to commit murder of their parents. There were two series of trials. The first trial, which had two separate juries, resulted in two hung juries. At the first trial, the brothers introduced evidence of sexual abuse by their father, and the court instructed the jury on **imperfect self-defense**. The imperfect self-defense jury instruction was based on the brothers' *honest but unreasonable fear* that their father would hurt or kill them (Menendez v. Terhune, 2010). The second trial took place in front of one jury and resulted in the convictions. During the second trial, some evidence of abuse was excluded, Lyle Menendez refused to testify, and there was *no* jury instruction on **imperfect self-defense**. After sentencing, the brothers petitioned for a writ of habeas corpus based on several claims, including the exclusion of the abuse evidence and failure to instruct the jury on imperfect self-defense (Menendez v. Terhune, 2010). The US Court of Appeals for the Ninth Circuit affirmed the district court's denial of the petition on grounds that there was insufficient evidence to support the jury instruction on imperfect self-defense and no foundation to support the admissibility of the evidence of abuse. The court held that the evidence confirmed there was no *imminent* threat of serious bodily injury or death when the brothers killed their parents.

The facts of the case are lurid. Evidence included the sexual abuse of both boys by their father, surreptitiously taped psychotherapy sessions, spending sprees, fabricated mafia hit stories, and alleged will tampering by the brothers after the parents were killed.

Do you think the Menendez case should have been treated as a "battered child syndrome" case, easing the requirement of *imminence* and allowing for a jury instruction on **imperfect self-defense**?

Check your answer using the answer key at the end of the chapter.

Menendez Brothers Video

Lyle and Erik Menendez News Report

A news story on the conviction of the Menendez brothers is presented in this video: (click to see video)

References

Bechtel v. State, 840 P.2d 1 (1992), accessed November 13, 2010, http://scholar.google.com/scholar_case?case=14171263417876785206&hl=en&as_sdt=2&as_vis=1&oi=scholarr.

Connecticut Criminal Jury Instructions, No. 2.8-3, accessed November 13, 2010, http://www.jud.ct.gov/ji/criminal/part2/2.8-3.htm.

Gay, M., "Abused Wife Who Killed Preacher Husband Speaks Out," Huffingtonpost.com website, accessed August 25, 2011, http://www.aolnews.com/2010/11/05/abused-wife-who-killed-preacher-husband-speaks-out.

Menendez v. Terhune, 422 F.3d 1012, 1024 (2005), accessed November 19, 2010, http://cases.justia.com/us-court-of-appeals/F3/422/1012/569492.

Mich. Comp. Laws § 780.972, accessed November 13, 2010, http://www.legislature.mi.gov/(S(3li5rs55kkzn2pfegtskdunn))/mileg.aspx?page=getObject&objectName=mcl-780-972&highlight=self-defense.

N.Y. Penal Law § 35.15(1)(b), accessed November 13, 2010, http://law.onecle.com/new-york/penal/PEN035.15_35.15.html.

Or. Rev. Stat. § 161.219, accessed November 13, 2010, http://www.leg.state.or.us/ors/161.html.

State v. Belgard, 410 So.2d 720 (1982), accessed November 13, 2010, http://www.leagle.com/xmlResult.aspx?xmldoc=19821130410So2d720_1997.xml&docbase=CSLWAR1-1950-1985.

State v. Faulkner, 483 A.2d 759 (1984), accessed November 13, 2010, http://scholar.google.com/scholar_case?case=17158253875987176431&hl=en&as_sdt=2&as_vis=1&oi=scholarr.

State v. Sandoval, 130 P.3d 808 (2006), accessed November 13, 2010, http://www.publications.ojd.state.or.us/S53457.htm.

State v. Taylor, 858 P.2d 1358 (1993), accessed November 13, 2010, http://scholar.google.com/scholar_case?case=1539441759711884447&hl=en&as_sdt=2&as_vis=1&oi=scholarr.

State v. Williams, 644 P.2d 889 (1982), accessed November 13, 2010, http://scholar.google.com/scholar_case?case=18157916201475630105&hl=en&as_sdt=2&as_vis=1&oi=scholarr.
CC licensed content, Shared previously

- Criminal Law. **Provided by**: University of Minnesota Libraries Publishing . **Located at**: http://open.lib.umn.edu/criminallaw/. **License**: *CC BY-NC-SA: Attribution-NonCommercial-ShareAlike*

5.3 Other Use-of-Force Defenses

Learning Objectives

Ascertain the elements required for the defense of others.
Define real and personal property.
Explain the appropriate circumstances and degree of force a defendant can use when defending property.
Ascertain the elements required for the defense of ejection of trespasser.
Distinguish defense of property from defense of habitation.
Ascertain the three elements required for the use of deadly force in defense of habitation under modern castle laws.
Identify three common features of modern castle laws.
Ascertain the constitutional parameters of the use of force by law enforcement to arrest or apprehend criminal suspects.

Aside from self-defense, a defendant can legally use force to defend another *person*, real or personal *property*, and *habitation*. In addition, *law enforcement* can use force to arrest or capture individuals who reasonably appear to be committing crimes. In this section, the elements of several use-of-force defenses will be reviewed. Keep in mind that these defenses can be statutory, common-law, perfect, or imperfect, depending on the facts and the jurisdiction.

Defense of Others

According to early common law, a defendant could use force to defend another only when the defendant and the person defended had a *special relationship*, such as a family connection. Most jurisdictions now reject this common-law restriction on defense of others and allow a defendant to defend *anyone* to the same degree that he or she could use self-defense (People v. Kurr, 2010). Thus in a majority of jurisdictions, defense of others requires the same elements as self-defense: the individual defended must be facing an unprovoked, imminent attack, and the defendant must use a reasonable degree of force with a reasonable belief that force is necessary to repel the attack.

Occasionally, a defendant uses force to defend another who has no legal right to use force in self-defense. Under the common law, the defendant could not use force legally if the individual defended could not use force legally in self-defense. However, the majority of states now allow a defendant to use force to defend another person if it *reasonably appears* that use of force is justified under the circumstances (Commonwealth v. Miranda, 2010). The Model Penal Code allows the defense of another when "under the circumstances as the actor believes them to be, the person whom he seeks to protect would be justified in using such protective force" (Model Penal Code § 3.05(1) (b)). Thus if the defendant has a *subjective belief* that the individual defended could use force legally in self-defense, defense of others is appropriate under the Model Penal Code.

Example of Defense of Others

Alex and Shane, aspiring law enforcement officers, are performing a training maneuver in a rural area. Their instructor Devin is watching nearby. Alex pretends to attack Shane. Just as Devin is about to demonstrate a takedown, Timmy, who is jogging in the area, dashes over and begins beating Alex. Under the older common-law rule, Timmy could be successfully prosecuted for battery of Alex. Shane did not have the right to use self-defense during a practice maneuver, so neither did *Timmy*. In jurisdictions that allow defense of others if it reasonably appears that self-defense is warranted, Timmy could probably use the defense to battery because it *reasonably appeared* that Alex was about to unlawfully attack Shane. In jurisdictions that follow the Model Penal Code, Timmy can most likely use defense of others as a defense to battery because it is clear *Timmy* honestly believed Shane had the right to use self-defense in this situation.

Defense of Property

All jurisdictions allow individuals to use force in defense of property under certain specified circumstances. Property can be real or personal. Real property is land and anything permanently attached to it. This includes a home. However, defense of the home is discussed in Section 5.3.3 "Defense of Habitation". Personal property is any movable object.

In the majority of states, the defendant can use force only to defend real or personal property if the defendant has an objectively reasonable belief that an *imminent* threat of damage, destruction, or theft will occur (California Criminal Jury Instructions, 2010). The Model Penal Code provides "the use of force upon or toward the person of another is justifiable when the actor believes that such force is immediately necessary: (a) to prevent or terminate an unlawful entry or other trespass upon land or a trespass against or the unlawful carrying away of tangible, movable property" (Model Penal Code §3.06(1) (a)). Thus if the defendant has a *subjective belief* that force is immediately necessary to protect real or personal property, force is appropriate under the Model Penal Code.

The amount of force that a defendant may legally use to protect real or personal property is *reasonable* force, under the circumstances (K.S.A., 2010). The defendant can also chase someone who steals personal property and take the item back (Conn. Gen. Stat., 2010). The Model Penal Code provides "the use of force upon or toward the person of another is justifiable when the actor believes that such force is immediately necessary...to retake tangible movable property" (Model Penal Code §3.06(1) (b)). In general, the Model Penal Code and most states do not authorize the use of **deadly force** to protect property (other than the home) under any circumstances (Fla. Stat. Ann., 2010).

Example of Defense of Property

Kelsey sees Keith, her stepbrother, approaching her brand new car with a key in his hand. It appears that Keith is about to scrape the paint on the door of the car with this key. Kelsey tackles Keith to prevent him from vandalizing the car. Kelsey has probably used *reasonable* force under the circumstances and can claim defense of property as a defense to battery. If Keith testifies that he was simply going to hand Kelsey the key, which she left in the house, the attack could still be justified if the trier of fact determines that it was *objectively reasonable* for Kelsey to believe Keith was about to damage her property. In jurisdictions that follow the Model Penal Code, Kelsey can probably use defense of property as a defense to battery because it is clear *Kelsey* believed that force was immediately necessary to protect her personal property in this situation. Of course, if Kelsey pulls out a gun and shoots Keith, she could not claim defense of property because deadly force is never justifiable to protect real or personal property from harm.

Ejection of Trespasser

A simple trespasser is an individual who is present on real property without consent of the owner. Property owners have the legal right to *eject* trespassers under certain specified circumstances.

Most states authorize the ejection of a trespasser if the trespasser is first asked to leave and fails to comply within a reasonable time (N.J. Stat., 2010). The degree of force that can be used to eject the trespasser is *reasonable force*, under the circumstances (Iowa Code, 2010). Deadly force is never reasonable to eject a trespasser unless the trespasser threatens imminent deadly force against the defendant or another individual (State v. Curley, 2010). Deadly force under these circumstances is justified by **self-defense** or **defense of others**, *not* ejection of trespasser.

Example of Ejection of Trespasser

Sam sees Burt sitting on his lawn. Sam goes up to Burt and asks him to "move along." Burt looks up, but does not stand. Sam goes into the house and calls law enforcement, but they inform Sam that there is a local emergency, and they cannot come and eject Burt for at least five hours. Sam goes back outside and sees that Burt is now sprawled out across the lawn. Sam grabs Burt, lifts him to his feet, and pushes him off the lawn and onto the sidewalk. Sam can probably use **ejection of trespasser** as a defense to battery of Burt. Sam asked Burt the trespasser to leave, and Burt ignored him. Sam's attempt to rely on law enforcement was likewise unsuccessful. Sam's use of nondeadly force appears objectively reasonable. Thus Sam's ejection of a trespasser is most likely appropriate under these circumstances.

Defense of Habitation

Defense of habitation is a defense that applies specifically to the defendant's *residence*. At early common law, a person's home was as sacred as his or her person, and deadly force could be employed to protect it. The majority of states have since enacted modern castle laws that embody this common-law doctrine. Other than the use of deadly force, defense of habitation generally follows the same rules as defense of property, self-defense, and defense of others. Thus this defense of habitation discussion focuses primarily on the use of deadly force.

The first state to expand the defense of habitation to include the use of deadly force was Colorado, with its "make my day" self-defense statute (Colo. Rev. Stat. Ann., 2010). In 2005, Florida began a wave of castle law modifications that resulted in most states revising their defense of habitation laws (Fla. Stat. Ann., 2010). Generally, three elements must be present before the use of deadly force is appropriate to defend habitation under modern castle laws. First, the intruder must actually *enter* or be in the process of entering the residence owned by the defendant (Fla. Stat. Ann., 2010). This excludes intruders who are outside or in the curtilage, which is the protected area around the home. Second, the residence must be *occupied* when the entry occurs. This excludes devices like spring-guns that protect unoccupied dwellings with deadly force (People v. Ceballos, 2010). Third, the defendant must have an *objectively reasonable* belief that the intruder intends to commit a crime of *violence* against the occupant(s) after entry (Or. Rev. Stat., 2010). The Model Penal Code provides "[t]he use of deadly force is not justifiable...unless the actor believes that...the person against whom the force is used is attempting to dispossess him of his dwelling...or...attempting to commit...arson, burglary, robbery or other felonious theft...and either...has employed or threatened deadly force...or...the use of force other than deadly force would expose the actor or another in his presence to substantial danger of serious bodily harm" (Model Penal Code § 3.06 (3)(d)).

The majority of states' castle laws abolish any **duty to retreat** when inside the home (Alaska Stat., 2010). Florida's castle law creates a presumption that the defendant has a reasonable fear of imminent peril of death or great bodily injury when the intruder makes an unlawful or forceful entry (Fla Stat. Ann., 2010). This compels the prosecution to *disprove* the defendant's reasonable belief of death or great bodily injury beyond a reasonable doubt, which is extremely difficult. Additional features of many castle laws are civil immunity and criminal immunity from prosecution (720 ILCS, 2010). **Immunity from prosecution** means that a defendant who complies with the castle law requirements cannot be sued for damages or prosecuted for a crime based on injury or death to the intruder.

Figure 5.4 Crack the Code

Crack the Code

Compare the following state laws:

Alaska Stat. §11.81.335: Justification: Use of deadly force in defense of self.

(b) A person may not use deadly force under this section if the person knows that, with complete personal safety and with complete safety as to others being defended, the person can avoid the necessity of using deadly force by leaving the area of the encounter, except there is no duty to leave the area if the person is

> (1) on premises

>> (A) that the person owns or leases;

>> (B) where the person resides, temporarily or permanently

Fla. Stat. Ann. § 776.013 Home protection; use of deadly force;

. . .(3) A person who is not engaged in an unlawful activity and who is attacked in any other place where he or she has a right to be has no duty to retreat and has the right to stand his or her ground and meet force with force, including deadly force if he or she reasonably believes it is necessary to do so to prevent death or great bodily harm to himself or herself or another or to prevent the commission of a forcible felony

In Alaska, the stand your ground rule applies to *premises*; in Florida, it applies *anywhere* it is legal to be...

Example of Defense of Habitation under a

Castle Law

Nate, a homeowner with three children, hears the front door open in the middle of the night. Nate removes a handgun from the nightstand and creeps silently down the stairs. He sees Bob tiptoeing toward his daughter's bedroom. Nate shoots and kills Bob. Unfortunately, Bob is Nate's daughter's boyfriend, who was trying to enter her bedroom for a late-night get-together. Nate could probably assert the defense of **protection of habitation** under modern castle laws in most jurisdictions. Bob made **entry** into an **occupied residence**. It is difficult to identify individuals in the dark and to ascertain their motives for entering a residence without the owner's consent. Thus it was *objectively reasonable* for Nate to feel threatened by Bob's presence and to use deadly force to protect his domicile and its residents. If Nate is successful with his defense, he will also be **immune** from a *civil suit* for damages if the castle law in his jurisdiction provides this immunity.

Change the example with Nate and Bob so that Bob enters the residence during the day, and Nate identifies him as his daughter's boyfriend. Under these circumstances, the prosecution could rebut any presumption that Nate's actions were objectively reasonable. A reasonable person would ask Bob why he was entering the residence before shooting and killing him. The trier of fact might determine that Nate's intent was not to protect himself and his family, but to *kill* Bob, which would be malice aforethought. If Nate's actions are not justifiable by the defense of habitation, he could be charged with and convicted of first-degree murder in this situation.

Use of Force in Arrest and Apprehension of Criminal Suspects

Occasionally, law enforcement must use *force* to effectuate an arrest or apprehend a criminal suspect. The *appropriate* use of force during an arrest or apprehension can operate as a defense to assault, battery, false imprisonment, kidnapping, and criminal homicide. At early common law, law enforcement could use reasonable, nondeadly force to arrest an individual for a misdemeanor and reasonable, even deadly force, to arrest an individual for *any* felony. Modern law enforcement's ability to use deadly force is governed by the US Constitution.

The US Supreme Court clarified the constitutional standard for law enforcement's use of deadly force in *Tennessee v. Garner*, 471 U.S. 1 (1985). In *Garner*, the Court invalidated a Tennessee statute that allowed law enforcement to exercise *any* degree of force to apprehend and arrest a fleeing felon. The law enforcement officer in *Garner* admitted that he shot and killed a suspect, reasonably believing he was *unarmed*. The Court held that the Fourth Amendment governed law enforcement's use of deadly force in this situation because the use of deadly force is a **seizure**. Thus law enforcement's use of deadly force must be scrutinized pursuant to the standard of constitutional *reasonableness*. According to the Court, the only constitutionally reasonable circumstances under which law enforcement can use deadly force to arrest or apprehend a fleeing felon is when law enforcement has probable cause to believe that the suspect poses a significant threat of death or serious physical injury to the officer or others.

Currently, most jurisdictions have statutes protecting law enforcement's reasonable use of force when effectuating an arrest or apprehending a fleeing suspect. Under *Garner*, these statutes must restrict the lawful use of deadly force to potentially deadly situations. If a law enforcement officer exceeds the use of force permitted under the circumstances, the law enforcement officer could be prosecuted for a *crime* or sued for *civil damages* (or both).

Example of Reasonable Force by Law Enforcement to Arrest

Review the example in Chapter 1 "Introduction to Criminal Law", Section 1.2.1 "Example of Criminal Law Issues". In that example, Linda puts a bra in her purse without paying for it at an expensive department store. When she attempts to leave the store, an alarm is activated. Linda begins sprinting down the street. Colin, a police officer, just happens to be driving by with the window of his patrol car open. He hears the store alarm, sees Linda running, and begins shooting at Linda from the car. Linda is shot in the leg and collapses. In this example, no facts exist to indicate that Linda poses a potentially **deadly** threat to Colin or others. The fact that Linda is running down the street and an alarm is going off does not demonstrate that Linda has committed a crime necessitating deadly force to arrest. Thus Colin can use only **nondeadly** force to arrest Linda, such as his hands, or possibly a stun gun or Taser to subdue her. If Linda is *unarmed* and Colin uses a firearm to subdue her, the utilization of deadly force is excessive under these circumstances and Colin has no defense to assault with a deadly weapon or to attempted murder.

Change this example and imagine that Colin pulls over and attempts to arrest Linda. Linda removes a gun from her purse. Under most modern statutes, Colin does not have a duty to retreat and can use deadly force to arrest or apprehend Linda. Under *Garner*, it is reasonable to believe that Linda poses a danger of death or serious bodily injury to Colin or others. Thus Colin can constitutionally use **deadly force** to protect himself and the public from harm in this situation. Note that Linda's theft is probably a *misdemeanor*, not a *felony*. However, it is Linda's exhibition of deadly force to resist arrest that triggers Colin's deadly force response. Under these circumstances, Colin's use of deadly force is justified and can operate as a legal defense in a criminal prosecution or civil suit for damages.

Figure 5.5 Diagram of Use-of-Force Defenses

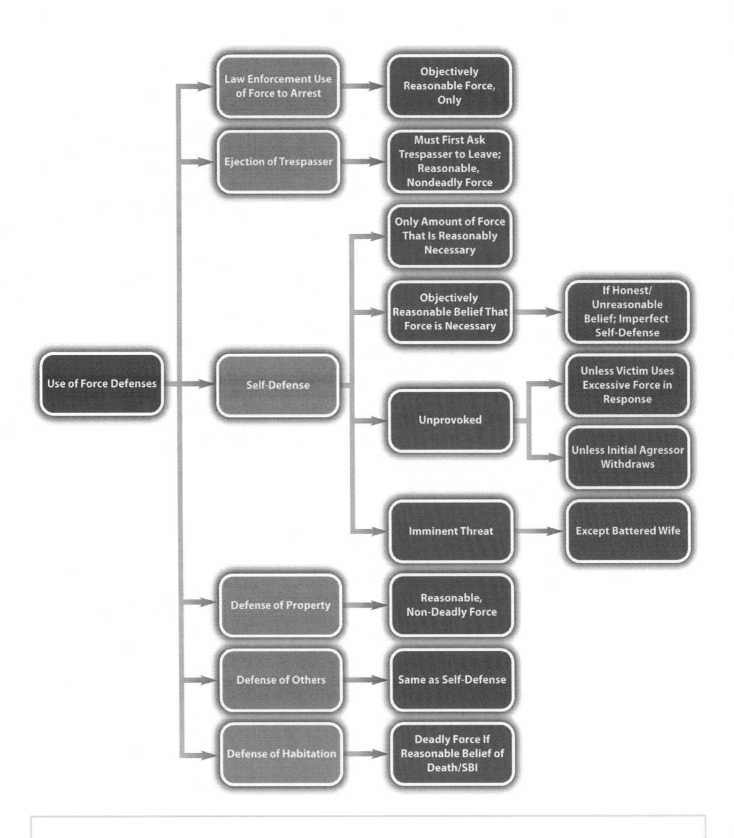

Key Takeaways

- Defense of others has the same elements as self-defense: the individual defended must be facing an unprovoked, imminent attack, and the defendant must use a reasonable degree of force with a reasonable belief that force is necessary to repel the attack.
- Real property is land and anything permanently attached to it. Personal property is any movable object.
- The defendant can use nondeadly force to defend real or personal property if the defendant has an

objectively reasonable belief that an imminent threat of damage, destruction, or theft will occur.
- Property owners can use reasonable nondeadly force to eject a trespasser after first asking the trespasser to leave.
- Only nondeadly force may be used to defend property; deadly force may be used to defend habitation.
- The defendant can use deadly force to defend habitation under modern castle laws if an intruder enters occupied premises, and the defendant has an objectively reasonable belief that the intruder will seriously injure or kill the occupants.
- Modern castle laws abolish the duty to retreat when inside the home, occasionally include a presumption that the defendant has an objectively reasonable belief the intruder is going to seriously injure or kill the occupants, and provide civil and criminal immunity from prosecution.
- Use of deadly force by law enforcement is considered a seizure under the Fourth Amendment, so law enforcement cannot use deadly force to apprehend or arrest a criminal suspect unless there is probable cause to believe the suspect will inflict serious physical injury or death upon the officer or others.

Exercises

Answer the following questions. Check your answers using the answer key at the end of the chapter.

Melanie watches as Betty verbally abuses Colleen. Betty is a known bully who verbally abused Melanie in the past. Betty calls Colleen an expletive and gives her a firm shove. Melanie walks up behind Betty, removes a knife from her pocket, and plunges the knife into Betty's back. Betty suffers internal injuries and later dies. Can Melanie use defense of others as a defense to criminal homicide? Why or why not?

Read *Commonwealth v. Alexander*, 531 S.E.2d 567 (2000). In *Alexander*, the defendant was convicted of brandishing a weapon when he pointed an *unloaded* rifle at an individual who was repossessing his vehicle in an aggressive and belligerent manner. Did the Supreme Court of Virginia uphold the defendant's conviction? The case is available at this link:
http://caselaw.findlaw.com/va-supreme-court/1454888.html.

Read *Dutton v. Hayes-Pupko*, No. 03-06-00438 (2008). In *Dutton*, a law enforcement officer asked the victim for her name and date of birth after she allegedly sprayed her neighbors with a hose. The victim refused to respond, and the law enforcement officer handcuffed her and forced her into his vehicle, injuring her wrist. The victim sued for use of *excessive* force in arrest. Did the Texas Court of Appeals hold that the victim had the right to sue the officer for use of excessive force in arrest? The case is available at this link:
http://scholar.google.com/scholar_case?case=17543977294597089197&q= Dutton+v.+Hayes-Pupko&hl=en&as_sdt=2,5&as_vis=1.

References

Alaska Stat. § 11.81.335(b), accessed November 16, 2010, http://touchngo.com/lglcntr/akstats/Statutes/Title11/Chapter81/Section335.htm.

California Criminal Jury Instructions No. 3476, accessed November 15, 2010, http://www.justia.com/criminal/docs/calcrim/3400/3476.html.

Colo. Rev. Stat. Ann. § 18-1-704.5, accessed November 16, 2010, http://www.co.jefferson.co.us/jeffco/sheriff_uploads/revised_statutes.htm.

Commonwealth v. Miranda, No. 08-P-2094 (2010), accessed November 14, 2010, http://www.socialaw.com/slip.htm?cid=19939&sid=119.

Conn. Gen. Stat. § 53a-21, accessed November 15, 2010, http://www.cga.ct.gov/2009/pub/chap951.htm#Sec53a-21.htm.

Fla. Stat. Ann. § 776.031, accessed November 16, 2010, http://law.justia.com/florida/codes/2007/TitleXLVI/chapter776/776_031.html.

Iowa Code § 704.4, accessed November 15, 2010, http://coolice.legis.state.ia.us/cool-ice/default.asp?category=billinfo&service=iowacode&ga=83&input=704#704.4.

K.S.A. § 21-3213, accessed November 15, 2010, http://kansasstatutes.lesterama.org/Chapter_21/Article_32/21-3213.html.

N.J. Stat. § 2C:3-6, accessed November 15, 2010, http://law.onecle.com/new-jersey/2c-the-new-jersey-code-of-criminal-justice/3-6.html.

Or. Rev. Stat. § 161.225, accessed November 16, 2010, http://www.leg.state.or.us/ors/161.html.

People v. Ceballos, 526 P.2d 241 (1974), accessed November 16, 2010, http://wings.buffalo.edu/law/bclc/web/calceballos.htm.

People v. Kurr, 654 N.W.2d 651 (2002), accessed November 14, 2010, http://scholar.google.com/scholar_case?case=14992698629411781257&hl=en&as_sdt=2&as_vis=1&oi=scholarr.

State v. Curley, Docket # 0000011.WA (Wash. App. 2010), accessed November 15, 2010, http://scholar.google.com/scholar_case?case=11648057948374905030&q=State+v.+Curley&hl=en&as_sdt=2,5&as_ylo=2009.

720 ILCS § 5/7-2 (b), accessed November 16, 2010, http://www.ilga.gov/legislation/ilcs/ilcs4.asp?DocName=072000050HArt.+7&ActID=1876&ChapAct=720.
CC licensed content, Shared previously

- Criminal Law. **Provided by**: University of Minnesota Libraries Publishing . **Located at**: http://open.lib.umn.edu/criminallaw/. **License**: *CC BY-NC-SA: Attribution-NonCommercial-ShareAlike*

5.4 Defenses Based on Choice

Learning Objectives

Ascertain the three elements required for the choice of evils defense.
Distinguish between the choice of evils defense and the duress defense.
Identify one crime that is not justifiable by the choice of evils defense or the duress defense.

Occasionally, the law protects a defendant from criminal responsibility when the defendant has *no choice* but to commit the crime. In this section, we review the choice of evils and duress defenses.

Choice of Evils Defense

The choice of evils defense (called the necessity defense in some jurisdictions) protects a defendant from criminal responsibility when the defendant commits a crime to avoid a greater, imminent harm. Under the Model Penal Code, "[c]onduct which the actor believes to be necessary to avoid harm or evil...is justifiable, provided that: (a) the harm or evil sought to be avoided by such conduct is greater than that sought to be prevented by the law defining the offense charged" (Model Penal Code § 3.02(1)(a)). The choice of evils defense can be statutory or common-law, perfect or imperfect, depending on the jurisdiction.

The choice of evils defense generally requires three elements. First, there must be more than one harm that will occur under the circumstances. Usually, the harms are the product of nature, or are circumstances beyond the defendant's control (State v. Holmes, 2010). Second, the harms must be ranked, with one of the harms ranked more severe than the other. The ranking is generally up to the legislature or common law. In many jurisdictions, the loss of life is never justifiable under this defense and cannot be ranked lower than any other harm (Ky. Rev. Stat. Ann., 2010). Third, the defendant must have an *objectively reasonable* belief that the greater harm is *imminent* and can only be avoided by committing the crime that results in the lesser harm (Tenn. Code Ann., 2010).

Figure 5.6 Kentucky Revised Statutes

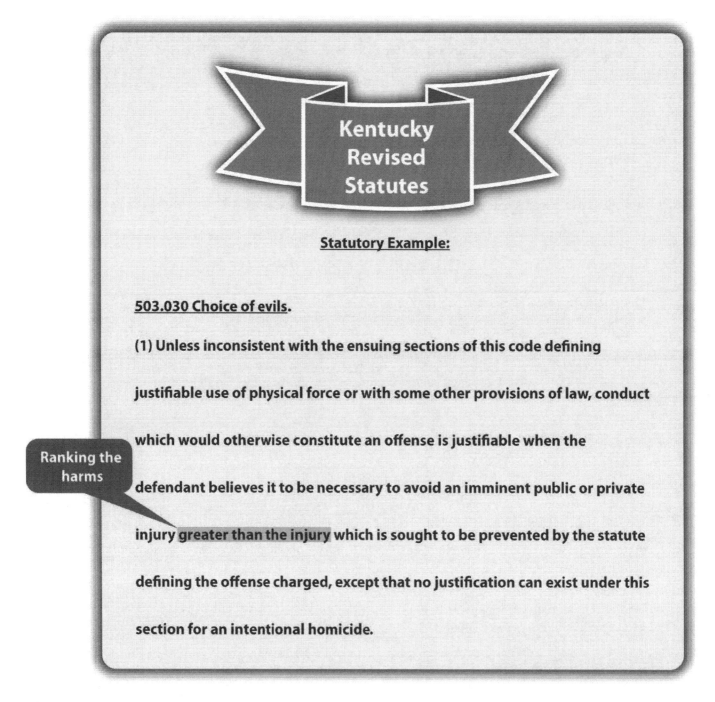

Statutory Example:

503.030 Choice of evils.

(1) Unless inconsistent with the ensuing sections of this code defining justifiable use of physical force or with some other provisions of law, conduct which would otherwise constitute an offense is justifiable when the defendant believes it to be necessary to avoid an imminent public or private injury greater than the injury which is sought to be prevented by the statute defining the offense charged, except that no justification can exist under this section for an intentional homicide.

Ranking the harms

The choice of evils defense is rarely used and is generally only a defense to the loss or destruction of property. When the defense is perfect, it results in an acquittal. When the defense is imperfect, it results in a reduction in sentence or the defendant's conviction of a lesser offense.

Example of the Choice of Evils Defense

Tamara gets lost while hiking in a remote, mountainous area. After wandering around for hours with the temperature dropping, Tamara finds a locked cabin. Tamara breaks a window and climbs inside. Once inside, Tamara prepares some canned chili, drinks tap water, and uses the telephone to call law enforcement. Tamara could probably plead and prove choice of evils as a defense to burglary and theft in many jurisdictions. Tamara was confronted with two harms: harm to her personal safety and well-being and harm to the real and personal property of another. The harm to Tamara's health and safety is ranked *more severe* than the minimal harm to property. It is *objectively reasonable* to break into and enter a cabin and use some of the supplies inside to prevent *imminent* injury or death. Thus although Tamara committed burglary and theft in many jurisdictions, she did so with the reasonable belief that she was saving her own life. A trier of fact could find that the harm avoided by Tamara's actions was greater than the harm caused by the burglary and theft, and Tamara could be acquitted, or have her sentence or crime reduced, depending on the jurisdiction.

Change the facts in the preceding example, and imagine that Tamara steals money and jewelry in addition to the chili and tap water. Tamara could not successfully prove the defense of choice of evils to this additional theft. No harm was avoided by Tamara's theft of the money and jewelry. Thus choice of evils cannot justify this crime.

Change the facts in the preceding example, and imagine that Tamara kills the cabin's owner because he refuses to allow her to enter. Tamara could not successfully prove the defense of choice of evils under these circumstances. Tamara's life is *no more important* than the cabin owner's. Thus Tamara cannot *rank* the harms, and choice of evils cannot justify criminal homicide in this case.

The Duress Defense

In some jurisdictions, the choice of evils defense is called the duress defense if the choice of evils is deliberately brought on by another *individual*, rather than by nature, an act of God, or circumstances outside the defendant's control. The Model Penal Code defines the duress defense as "an affirmative defense that the actor engaged in the conduct...because he was coerced to do so by the use of, or a threat to use, unlawful force against his person or the person of another" (Model Penal Code § 2.09(1)).

Three elements are required for the duress defense. First, the defendant or another person must face a threat of *imminent* serious bodily injury or death (Conn. Gen. Stat., 2010). Second, the defendant must have an *objectively reasonable* belief that the only way to avoid the serious bodily injury or death is to commit the crime at issue (Haw. Rev. Stat., 2010). Third, in most jurisdictions, the crime committed cannot be criminal homicide (RCW 9A.16.060, 2010). Like choice of evils, the duress defense is rarely used and can be statutory or common law, perfect or imperfect, depending on the jurisdiction.

Example of the Duress Defense

Keisha, a bank teller, hands Brian, a bank robber, money out of her drawer after he points a loaded gun at her head. Technically, Keisha embezzled the money from the bank, but she did so based on the *objectively reasonable* fear that Brian would kill her if she failed to comply with his demands. Keisha can successfully claim **duress** as a defense to any charge of theft. If Brian had pointed the gun at another client in line at the bank instead of Keisha, Keisha could still prevail using the duress defense because duress also applies when the threat of death or serious bodily injury is to *another* person.

Change the example with Keisha and Brian, and imagine that Brian's threat is made in a phone call, rather than in person. Brian threatens to kill Keisha if she doesn't place thousands of dollars in an envelope and mail it to him at a specified address. If Keisha complies, Keisha cannot prove duress as a defense to theft. Brian's threat by phone call is not a threat of *imminent* death. In addition, it is not objectively reasonable to be frightened by a voice on the telephone. Keisha could hang up the phone and contact law enforcement, instead of timidly complying with Brian's demands.

Change the preceding example with Keisha and Brian, and imagine that Brian orders Keisha to kill his ex-wife Pat, who works at the station next to Keisha. Brian thereafter hands Keisha a switchblade. Keisha cannot kill Pat and claim duress as a defense to murder in most states. Keisha's life is no more *valuable* than Pat's. Therefore, Keisha cannot legally choose to commit the crime of murder and justify the crime with the duress defense.

Key Takeaways

- Three elements are required for the choice of evils defense: the defendant must be faced with two or more evils, the evils must be ranked, and it must be objectively reasonable for the defendant to choose to commit the crime to avoid the imminent evil that is ranked higher.
- Choice of evils is often based on nature or an act of God; duress is generally brought on by another individual.

- Choice of evils and duress are generally not defenses to criminal homicide.

Exercises

Answer the following questions. Check your answers using the answer key at the end of the chapter.

A fire sweeps through a residential neighborhood. Clark and Manny light their neighbor's house on fire to create a firebreak. This prevents several houses from burning, including Clark's and Manny's. Do Clark and Manny have a defense to arson in this case? Why or why not?

Read *People v. Lovercamp*, 43 Cal. App. 3d 823 (1974). In *Lovercamp*, the defendants escaped from prison and were immediately captured. The defendants claimed they were forced to escape because a group of prisoners threatened them with sexual assault. The trial court did not allow the defendants to introduce evidence supporting the defense of **necessity**, and the defendants were convicted of escape. Did the Court of Appeals of California uphold their conviction for escape? The case is available at this link:
http://scholar.google.com/scholar_case?case=6496346791408865822&hl=en&as_sdt=2&as_vis=1&oi=scholarr.

Read *State v. Daoud*, 141 N.H. 142 (1996). In *Daoud*, the defendant was convicted of driving while under the influence. The defendant appealed because the trial court did not allow her to present evidence in support of the **duress** defense. Did the Supreme Court of New Hampshire uphold the defendant's conviction? The case is available at this link:
http://scholar.google.com/scholar_case?case=18389754229002463686&hl=en&as_sdt=2&as_vis=1&oi=scholarr.

References

Conn. Gen. Stat. § 53a-14, accessed November 22, 2010, http://search.cga.state.ct.us/dtsearch_pub_statutes.html.

Haw. Rev. Stat. § 702-231, accessed November 22, 2010, http://codes.lp.findlaw.com/histatutes/5/37/702/702-231.

Ky. Rev. Stat. Ann. § 503.030, accessed November 22, 2010, http://www.lrc.ky.gov/krs/503-00/030.PDF.

RCW 9A.16.060, accessed November 22, 2010, http://apps.leg.wa.gov/rcw/default.aspx?cite=9A.16&full=true#9A.16.060.

State v. Holmes, 129 Ohio Misc. 2d 38 (2004), accessed November 22, 2010, http://www.sconet.state.oh.us/rod/docs/pdf/98/2004/2004-ohio-7334.pdf.

Tenn. Code Ann. § 39-11-609, accessed November 22, 2010, http://www.michie.com/tennessee/lpext.dll?f=templates&fn=main-h.htm&cp=tncode.
CC licensed content, Shared previously

- Criminal Law. **Provided by**: University of Minnesota Libraries Publishing . **Located at**: http://open.lib.umn.edu/criminallaw/. **License**: *CC BY-NC-SA: Attribution-NonCommercial-ShareAlike*

5.5 Consent

Learning Objectives

Ascertain the two elements required for the consent defense.
Identify three situations where consent can operate as a legal defense.

Consent by the victim can also form the basis of a justification defense to criminal conduct. **Consent** is most commonly used as a defense to sex crimes such as rape, and lack of consent is a criminal **element** of most sexual offenses that must be proven beyond a reasonable doubt. Thus consent to sexual acts is discussed in Chapter 10 "Sex Offenses and Crimes Involving Force, Fear, and Physical Restraint". In this section, consent to *nonsexual* conduct is explored. Consent is a defense that can be statutory or common law, perfect or imperfect, depending on the jurisdiction.

Elements of the Consent Defense

Consent can be a valid defense to a crime only if the victim *chooses* to render it. Thus it must be proffered knowingly and voluntarily, or it is ineffective. Under the Model Penal Code, consent is ineffective if "it is given by a person who is legally incompetent to authorize the conduct...it is given by a person who by reason of youth, mental disease or defect or intoxication is manifestly unable to make a reasonable judgment...it is induced by force, duress or deception" (Model Penal Code § 2.11(3)). In general, consent is not **knowing** if it is given by an individual who is too young, mentally incompetent (Colo> Rev. Stat. Ann., 2010), or intoxicated. In general, consent is not **voluntary** if it is induced by force, threat of force, or trickery (Del. Code Ann. tit. 11, 2010).

Example of Unknowing Consent

Gina drinks six glasses of wine at a party and offers to be the "donkey" in a game of pin the tail on the donkey. Other party members watch as Gina staggers her way to the front of the room and poses in front of the pin the tail on the donkey poster. Geoff walks up to Gina and stabs her several times in the buttocks with a pin. Geoff probably cannot claim consent as a defense to battery in this case. Gina consented to battery while she was intoxicated, and clearly she was unable to make a reasonable judgment. Thus her consent was not given **knowingly** and was ineffective in this situation.

Example of Involuntary Consent

Change the example with Gina and Geoff. Imagine that Gina just arrived at the party and has not consumed any alcohol. Geoff tells Gina he will poke out her eye with a pin if she does not volunteer to be the donkey in the pin the tail on the donkey game. He exemplifies his threat by making stabbing gestures at Gina's eye with the pin. Frightened, Gina goes to the front of the room and poses in front of the donkey poster until Geoff stabs her in the buttocks with the pin. Geoff probably cannot claim **consent** as a defense to battery in this case. Gina consented in response to Geoff's threat of physical harm. Thus her consent was not given **voluntarily** and was ineffective in this situation.

Figure 5.7 Delaware Code Annotated

Statutory Example:

§453. Circumstances negativing consent as defense.

Unless otherwise provided by this Criminal Code or by the law defining the offense, consent of the victim does not constitute a defense if:

(1) It is given by a person who is legally incompetent to authorize the conduct charged to constitute the offense unless the defendant believes the victim is legally competent; or

Unknowing consent

(2) It is given by a person who, because of youth, mental illness, mental defect or intoxication is manifestly unable or known by the defendant to be unable to make a reasonable judgment as to the nature or harmfulness of the conduct charged to constitute the offense; or

(3) It is given by a person whose improvident consent is sought to be prevented by the law defining the offense; or

(4) It is induced by force, duress or deception.

Involuntary consent

Situations Where Consent Can Operate as a Defense

Consent is a defense to only a few crimes. In most jurisdictions, consent can operate only as a defense to *sexual* conduct, injury that occurs during a *sporting* event, and crimes that do not result in *serious bodily injury* or *death* (Me. Rev. Stat. Ann., 2010). As the Model Penal Code states, "[w]hen conduct is charged to constitute an offense because it causes or threatens bodily harm, consent to such conduct or to the infliction of such harm is a defense if: (a) the bodily harm consented to or threatened by the conduct consented to is not serious; or (b) the conduct and the harm are reasonably foreseeable hazards of joint participation in a lawful athletic contest or competitive sport" (Model Penal Code § 2.11(2)).

Example of Legal Consent

Review the examples with Gina and Geoff. Change the examples, and imagine that Gina did not consume any alcohol and was not threatened by Geoff. If Gina offers to be the donkey in the pin the tail on the donkey game and Geoff stabs her in the buttocks with the pin, Geoff may be able to use consent as a defense to battery. Gina's consent appears to be **knowing** and **voluntary**. Gina probably does not suffer **serious bodily injury** from the pin stab in the buttocks. Thus the elements of legal consent exist, and this situation is appropriate for the consent defense.

Figure 5.8 Diagram of Defenses, Part 1

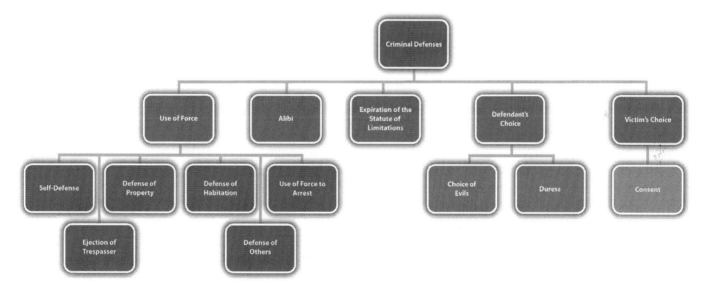

Key Takeaways

- Two elements are required for the consent defense: the defendant must consent knowingly (cannot be too young, mentally incompetent, or intoxicated) and voluntarily (cannot be forced, threatened, or tricked).
- Three situations where consent can operate as a defense are sexual offenses, situations that do not result in serious bodily injury or death, and sporting events.

Exercises

Answer the following questions. Check your answers using the answer key at the end of the chapter.

Allen tackles Brett during a high school football game, and Brett is severely injured. Can Allen be criminally prosecuted for battery? Why or why not?

Read *Donaldson v. Lungren*, 2 Cal. App. 4th 1614 (1992). In *Donaldson*, the defendant sought court permission to be cryogenically frozen because he had a brain tumor and wanted to be frozen until there was a cure. The defendant also sought to protect the individual who was going to help with the process and filed a lawsuit seeking an injunction and immunity from criminal prosecution for **assisted suicide**. The defendant claimed he had a constitutional right to **consent** to this procedure. Did the Court of Appeals of California uphold the defendant's right to be frozen—that is, to commit suicide? The case is available at this link: http://www.rickross.com/reference/alcor/alcor7.html.

Read *Ramey v. State*, 417 S.E.2d 699 (1992). In *Ramey*, the defendant, a police officer, was convicted of battery for beating the defendant with a flashlight and burning his nipples. The defendant claimed that the victim, who appeared to have mental problems, consented to this treatment. The trial court refused to instruct the jury on the consent defense. Did the Court of Appeals of Georgia uphold the defendant's conviction? The case is available at this link: http://scholar.google.com/scholar_case?case=10809733884390698075&hl=en&as_sdt=2002&as_vis=1.

References

Colo. Rev. Stat. Ann. § 18-1-505, accessed November 23, 2010, http://www.michie.com/colorado/lpext.dll?f=templates&fn=main-h.htm&cp=.

Del. Code Ann. tit. 11 § 453, accessed November 23, 2010, http://delcode.delaware.gov/title11/c004/index.shtml#451.

Me. Rev. Stat. Ann. 17-A § 109, accessed November 23, 2010, http://www.mainelegislature.org/legis/statutes/17-A/title17-Asec109.html.
CC licensed content, Shared previously

- Criminal Law. **Provided by**: University of Minnesota Libraries Publishing . **Located at**: http://open.lib.umn.edu/criminallaw/. **License**: *CC BY-NC-SA: Attribution-NonCommercial-ShareAlike*

5.6 End-of-Chapter Material

Summary

Defenses can be denial or failure of proof, affirmative, imperfect, perfect, factual, legal, common law (created by case law), or statutory (created by a state or federal legislature). A denial or failure of proof defense creates doubt in one or more of the elements of the offense and prevents the prosecution from meeting its burden of proof. An affirmative defense raises an issue separate from the elements of the offense and must be asserted before or during the trial or it cannot serve as the basis for an appeal. Defendants have either the burden of production or the burden of production and persuasion to a preponderance of evidence for an affirmative defense. An imperfect defense reduces the severity of the offense, or sentence. A perfect defense results in an acquittal. A factual defense is grounded in the facts of the case, while a legal defense depends on a statute or common-law principle. An example of a factual defense is an alibi defense, which asserts that the defendant could not have committed the crime because he or she was somewhere else at the time the crime occurred. An example of a legal defense is expiration of the statute of limitations, which means it is too late to prosecute the defendant for the offense.

Defenses can also be based on justification or excuse. A defense based on justification focuses on the offense and deems the conduct worthy of protection from criminal responsibility. A defense based on excuse focuses on the defendant and excuses his or her conduct under the circumstances.

Self-defense justifies the defendant's conduct in using physical force as protective. Self-defense is legal only when the defendant is faced with an unprovoked, imminent attack, and it is objectively reasonable that the degree of force used in response is necessary to avoid the attack. The defendant can be the initial aggressor and still use self-defense if the attacked individual uses too much force in response to the defendant's attack or if the defendant withdraws from the attack and is still pursued by the attacked individual. The attack does not necessarily have to be imminent if the defendant is a battered wife. Deadly force is any force that can kill under the circumstances. Deadly force can be used in self-defense only if the defendant is faced with imminent death, serious bodily injury, or the commission of a serious felony. Some jurisdictions require the defendant to retreat before resorting to deadly force, while others allow the defendant to stand his or her ground.

In most states, an individual can defend another to the same extent as self-defense. If a defendant is honestly but unreasonably mistaken about the fact that he or she needs to respond in self-defense or defense of others, imperfect self-defense or defense of others may be appropriate, depending on the jurisdiction. A defendant can also defend property using nondeadly force from an imminent threat of damage, loss, or theft. Real property is land and anything permanently attached to it, while personal property is any movable object. In many jurisdictions, a trespasser may be ejected from real property using nondeadly force after the trespasser has been requested to leave.

Defense of habitation is distinct from defense of real property in most states. Modern laws called castle laws expand the use of force to defend habitation. Castle laws eliminate the duty to retreat when in the home and provide civil and criminal immunity from prosecution for the use of deadly force. Deadly force can be used against a trespasser who enters occupied premises without consent of the owner when there is an objectively reasonable belief that the occupants will be seriously injured or killed.

Law enforcement can also use force to arrest or apprehend a criminal. If the force is deadly, it is considered a seizure under the Fourth Amendment and is scrutinized under an objectively reasonable standard.

The defense of choice of evils (called the necessity defense in some jurisdictions) permits the defendant to commit a crime if the harm caused is less severe than harm that will occur if the crime is not committed. In general, criminal homicide cannot be defended by choice of evils. Duress, a closely related defense, can sanction the use of force when the defendant is imminently threatened with serious bodily injury or death. Like choice of evils, the degree of force used pursuant to duress should be nondeadly.

The victim can also consent to the defendant's conduct, creating a consent defense, as long as the consent is given knowingly and voluntarily, the conduct is sexual or occurs during a sporting event, and the conduct does not involve serious bodily injury or death.

You Be the Defense Attorney

You are a well-known private defense attorney with a perfect record. Read the prompt, review the case, and then decide whether you would **accept** or **reject** it if you want to maintain your level of success. Check your answers using the answer key at the end of the chapter.

The defendant and his wife argued. She raised a knife above her head and stated, "Don't make me use this." The defendant took the knife away and thereafter stabbed the victim forty-three times in the head and chest with it. The defendant wants to make an *imperfect self-defense* argument. Will you accept or reject the case? Read *State v. Perez*, 840 P.2d 1118 (1992). The case is available at this link: http://scholar.google.com/scholar_case?case=7422940810428798296&hl=en&as_sdt=2&as_vis=1&oi=scholarr.

The defendants crossed a police tape and trespassed on a medical clinic's private property while protesting abortion. The defendants want to make arguments in support of *necessity*, *defense of others*, and *duress*. The basis of the defendants' claims is that they are protecting the lives of unborn children. Will you accept or reject the case? Read *Allison v. Birmingham*, 580 So.2d 1377 (1991). The case is available at this link: http://scholar.google.com/scholar_case?case=8254507993974001416&hl=en&as_sdt=2&as_vis=1&oi=scholarr.

The defendant, a police officer, shot the victim twice after being summoned to the victim's home by his wife. The victim was intoxicated and armed with two small steak knives. The defendant shot the victim subsequent to a somewhat lengthy encounter during which the victim lunged at him with the knives. The victim claimed he was putting the knives down or about to put the knives down. The victim is suing the defendant for damages based on use of *excessive force* in arrest or apprehension. Will you accept or reject the case? Read *Roy v. Inhabitants of Lewiston*, 42 F.3d 691 (1994). The case is available at this link: http://scholar.google.com/scholar_case?case=8822695050372354696&hl=en&as_sdt=2&as_vis=1&oi=scholarr.

The defendant, the Oakland Cannabis Buyers' Cooperative, distributes marijuana to qualified patients under California's Compassionate Use Act, which allows the possession and use of marijuana for medical purposes. The US government wants to stop this distribution under the federal Controlled Substances Act, which prohibits possession and use of marijuana under any circumstances. The defendant wants to continue distribution under a claim of *medical necessity*. Will you accept or reject the case? Read *U.S. v. Oakland Cannabis Buyers' Cooperative*, 532 U.S. 483 (2001). The case is available at this link: http://www.law.cornell.edu/supct/pdf/00-151P.ZO.

Cases of Interest

- *Acers v. United States*, 164 U.S. 388 (1896), discusses deadly force and self-defense: http://supreme.justia.com/us/164/388.
- *Graham v. Connor*, 490 U.S. 386 (1989), discusses force used in arrest: http://supreme.justia.com/us/490/386.
- *State v. Rogers*, 912 S.W.2d 670 (1995), discusses duress: http://scholar.google.com/scholar_case?case=4913796561906479282&hl=en&as_sdt=2&as_vis=1&

oi=scholarr.

Articles of Interest

- Affirmative defenses: https://www.law.cornell.edu/wex/affirmative_defense
- Self-defense and martial arts: http://www.ittendojo.org/articles/general-4.htm
- Castle laws: http://harvardjol.wpengine.com/wp-content/uploads/2013/10/Levin-Note1.pdf
- Necessity and duress defenses: http://papers.ssrn.com/sol3/papers.cfm?abstract_id=503462

Websites of Interest

- Castle laws by state:
  http://criminal.findlaw.com/criminal-law-basics/states-that-have-stand-your-ground-laws.html
- Criminal defense attorneys for all fifty states: http://www.hg.org/law-firms/USA-Criminal-Defense
  .html

Statistics of Interest

- Violence used during household burglaries in the United States:
  http://bjs.ojp.usdoj.gov/content/pub/press/vdhbpr.cfm
- US law enforcement officers killed and assaulted: https://www.fbi.gov/about-us/cjis/ucr/leoka

References

Menendez v. Terhune, 422 F.3d 1012, 1029 (2005), accessed November 19, 2010, http://cases.justia.com/us-court-of-appeals/F3/422/1012/569492.

Ramey v. State, 417 S.E.2d 699, 701 (1992), accessed November 23, 2010, http://scholar.google.com/scholar_case?case=10809733884390698075&hl=en&as_sdt=2002&as_vis=1.
CC licensed content, Shared previously

- Criminal Law. **Provided by**: University of Minnesota Libraries Publishing . **Located at**:
  http://open.lib.umn.edu/criminallaw/. **License**: *CC BY-NC-SA: Attribution-NonCommercial-ShareAlike*

Chapter 6: Criminal Defenses, Part 2

6.1 The Insanity Defense

Cabrera Photo – Ejercicio Fotográfico: Bodegón de Droga – CC BY-NC-ND 2.0.

The use of drugs or controlled substances, dependence on drugs or controlled substances or voluntary intoxication shall not, as such, constitute a defense to a criminal charge...

—Or. Rev. Stat. § 161.125(1), cited in Section 6.2.2 "Intoxication"

Learning Objectives

Identify four states that do not recognize an insanity defense.
Identify four versions of the insanity defense.
Ascertain the two elements required for the M'Naghten insanity defense.
Ascertain the two elements required for the irresistible impulse insanity defense.
Compare the M'Naghten, irresistible impulse, and substantial capacity tests.
Ascertain the basis of the Durham insanity defense.
Identify the various burdens of proof for the insanity defense.
Distinguish between diminished capacity and the insanity defense.
Compare the insanity defense with mental competence to stand trial.
Compare the insanity defense with the guilty but mentally ill verdict.
Compare different commitment procedures for an insane criminal defendant.
Distinguish temporary from permanent insanity.

With the exception of alibi and the expiration of the statute of limitations, Chapter 5 "Criminal Defenses, Part 1" explored criminal defenses based on **justification**. This chapter reviews criminal defenses based on **excuse**, including the insanity defense. Remember that defenses based on excuse focus on the *defendant* and claim that the defendant should be excused from criminal responsibility for his or her conduct under the circumstances.

Although controversial, most states and the federal government recognize an **insanity defense** (18 U.S.C., 2010). Montana, Utah, Kansas, and Idaho are the only states that do not (Findlaw.com, 2010). The insanity defense is the subject of much debate because it excuses even the most evil and abhorrent conduct, and in many jurisdictions, legal insanity functions as a perfect defense resulting in *acquittal*. However, the insanity defense is rarely used and hardly ever successful. This is generally because of the difficulty in proving *legal* insanity.

Many criminal defendants suffer from mental illness and can produce evidence of this illness such as psychiatric or layperson testimony. Often, mental disturbance is apparent from the defendant's conduct under the circumstances. However, legal insanity differs from *medical* insanity and is generally much more difficult to establish. The rationale behind creating a different standard for legal insanity is the goal of a criminal prosecution discussed in Chapter 1 "Introduction to Criminal Law". Criminal prosecution should deter as well as incapacitate. While the purpose of a medical diagnosis is to eventually *cure* the defendant's disorder, the purpose of criminal law is to *punish* the defendant. Thus the defendant's conduct is not excused if the defendant or society can benefit from punishment.

The policy supporting the insanity defense is twofold. First, an insane defendant does not have *control* over his or her conduct. This is similar to a defendant who is hypnotized, or sleepwalking. Second, an insane defendant does not have the ability to *form criminal intent*. Without the ability to control conduct, or the understanding that conduct is evil or wrong by society's standards, an insane defendant presumably will commit crimes again and again. Thus no deterrent effect is served by punishment, and treatment for the mental defect is the appropriate remedy.

Four variations of the insanity defense currently exist: M'Naghten, irresistible impulse, substantial capacity, and Durham.

M'Naghten Insanity Defense

The M'Naghten insanity defense, also called the **right-wrong test**, is the most common insanity defense in the United States. It is also the oldest and was created in England in 1843. The defense is named after Daniel M'Naghten. M'Naghten was under the paranoid delusion that the Prime Minister of England, Sir Robert Peel, was trying to kill him. When he tried to shoot Sir Peel from behind, he inadvertently shot Sir Peel's Secretary, Edward Drummond, who thereafter died. M'Naghten was put on trial for murder and, to the shock of the nation, the jury found him not guilty by reason of insanity (Queen v. M'Naghten, 2010). After a public outcry at this verdict, the British House of Lords developed a test for insanity that remains relatively intact today.

The M'Naghten insanity defense is *cognitive* and focuses on the defendant's awareness, rather than the ability to *control* conduct. The defense requires two elements. First, the defendant must be suffering from a *mental defect* at the time he or she commits the criminal act. The mental defect can be called a "defect of reason" or a "disease of the mind," depending on the jurisdiction (Iowa Code, 2010). Second, the trier of fact must find that because of the mental defect, the defendant did not know either the *nature and quality* of the criminal act or that the act was *wrong*.

The terms "defect of reason" and "disease of the mind" can be defined in different ways, but in general, the defendant must be cognitively impaired to the level of not knowing the nature and quality of the criminal act, or that the act is wrong. Some common examples of mental defects and diseases are psychosis, schizophrenia, and paranoia.

Jurisdictions vary as to the level of awareness the defendant must possess. Some jurisdictions use the term "know," or "understand," (Cal. Penal Code, 2010) while others use the term "appreciate" (Ala. Code, 2010). If know or understand is the standard, the trier of fact must ascertain a basic level of awareness under the attendant circumstances. If appreciate is the standard, the trier of fact must analyze the defendant's emotional state, and evidence of the defendant's character or personality may be relevant and admissible.

A defendant does not know the nature and quality of a criminal act if the defendant is completely oblivious to what he or she is doing. This is quite rare, so most defendants claiming insanity choose to assert that they did not know their act was *wrong*. However, jurisdictions differ as to the meaning of "wrong." Some jurisdictions define wrong as "legally wrong," meaning the defendant must be unaware that the act is against the law (State v. Crenshaw, 2010). Others define wrong as "legally *and morally*" wrong," meaning the defendant must also be unaware that the act is condemned by society (State v. Skaggs, 2010). Generally, the only instance where the defendant must be "morally wrong," standing alone, is when the defendant claims that the conduct was performed at the command of God, which is called the deific defense (State v. Worlock, 2010). Whether the standard is legally wrong or morally wrong, if there is any evidence of a cover-up or an attempt to hide or escape, it is apparent that the defendant knew the difference between right and wrong, defeating the claim of insanity under M'Naghten.

Example of a Case Inappropriate for the M'Naghten Insanity Defense

Susan wants to marry a single man, but he does not want the responsibility of caring for her children. Susan decides to kill her children. She drives her two sons, aged three and five, out to the lake. She puts the car in park, gets out, and then puts it in gear, watching as it drives into the water. Both of her sons drown. Later that day, Susan files a police report stating that a stranger kidnapped her children at gunpoint. While searching the area for the kidnapper, the police discover the children's bodies and evidence indicating that Susan killed them.

Susan recants her kidnapping story and admits she killed her children. However, she claims she is not guilty by reason of insanity. Susan's claim will probably not be successful if she killed her children in a jurisdiction that recognizes the M'Naghten insanity defense. Susan tried to mislead the police, demonstrating her awareness that she had done something wrong. Thus although Susan's behavior appears mentally imbalanced, she clearly *knew the difference* between right and wrong, and her conduct is not excusable under M'Naghten's rigid requirements.

Example of a Case Appropriate for the M'Naghten Insanity Defense

Andrea, a diagnosed schizophrenic, drowns five of her young children in the bathtub. Andrea promptly phones 911 and tells the operator that her children are dead. The operator dispatches an emergency call to law enforcement. When law enforcement officers arrive at Andrea's house, she informs them that she killed her children so that they could leave this earth and enter heaven.

Andrea thereafter claims she is not guilty for killing her children by reason of insanity. Andrea could be successful if the jurisdiction in which she killed her children recognizes the M'Naghten insanity defense. Andrea suffers from a **mental defect**, schizophrenia. In addition, there is *no* evidence indicating Andrea knew her conduct was **wrong**, such as an attempted escape, or cover-up. In fact, Andrea herself contacted law enforcement and immediately told them about her criminal acts. Thus both of the M'Naghten elements appear to be present, and Andrea's conduct may be excusable under the circumstances.

Figure 6.1 M'Naghten Insanity Defense

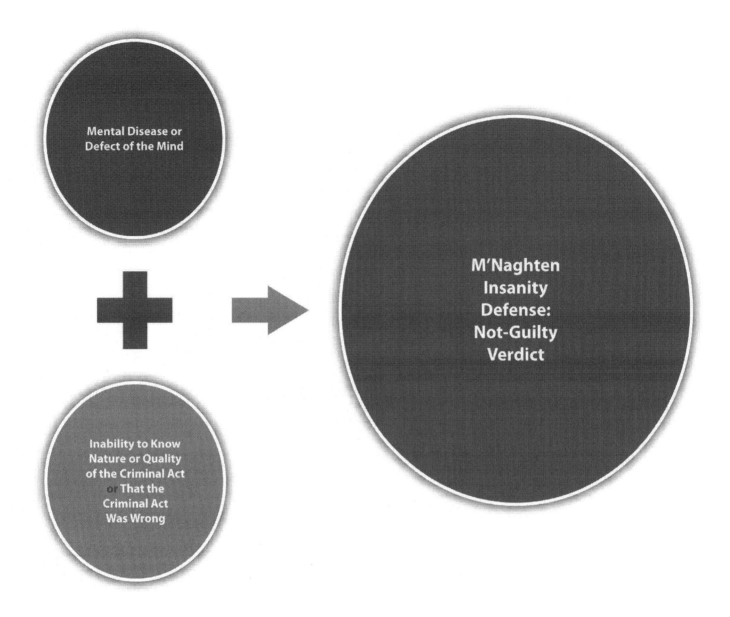

Irresistible Impulse Insanity Defense

Another variation of the insanity defense is the irresistible impulse defense. This defense has lost popularity over the years and is rejected by most of the states and the federal government (18 U.S.C., 2010). In some cases, the irresistible impulse insanity defense is *easier* to prove than the M'Naghten insanity defense, resulting in the acquittal of more mentally disturbed defendants.

The irresistible impulse insanity defense generally supplements M'Naghten, so the focus is on the defendant's awareness (cognitive) *and* the defendant's will (ability to control conduct). In jurisdictions that recognize the irresistible impulse insanity defense, the first element is the same as M'Naghten; the defendant must suffer from a mental defect or disease of the mind. However, the second element adds the concept of **volition**, or free choice. If the defendant cannot control his or her conduct because of the mental defect or disease, the defendant's conduct is excused even if the defendant understands that the conduct is wrong (State v. White, 2010). This is a softer stance than M'Naghten, which does *not* exonerate a defendant who is aware conduct is wrong. The challenge for the trier of fact in an irresistible impulse jurisdiction is distinguishing between conduct that can be *controlled* and conduct that cannot.

Example of a Case Inappropriate for the Irresistible Impulse Insanity Defense

Jolene, who has been diagnosed with paranoia, decides she must cut off all her sorority sisters' hair because they are "out to get her." She drives to the sorority house with a Taser and scissors in her backpack. Her plan is to subdue each sister with the stun gun and then hack off her hair. As she arrives at the house, she sees Agnes, one of her sorority sisters, trip and fall in the parking lot, ripping her cashmere sweater and scraping her chin. Feeling a stab of pity, Jolene ignores Agnes and walks hurriedly toward the building. As she enters, Ashley, another sorority sister, turns, scowls at Jolene, and barks, "What in the world are you wearing? You look like you just rolled out of bed!" Jolene pulls the stun gun out of her backpack and shoots Ashley. While Ashley is lying on the floor, Jolene takes out the scissors and cuts Ashley's hair off at the scalp.

Jolene claims she is not guilty for assault and battery of Ashley by reason of insanity. If Jolene attacked Ashley in a jurisdiction that recognizes the irresistible impulse insanity defense, she probably will not be successful with her claim. Jolene has been diagnosed with **paranoia**, which is a mental defect or disease. However, Jolene seems aware that shooting someone with a stun gun and cutting off her hair is *wrong* because she spared Agnes based on pity. In addition, Jolene's choice not to attack Agnes indicates she has *control* over her conduct. Thus Jolene is **cognitive** of the difference between right and wrong and has the **will** to suppress criminal behavior, defeating any claim of insanity under the irresistible impulse insanity defense.

Figure 6.2 Irresistible Impulse Insanity Defense

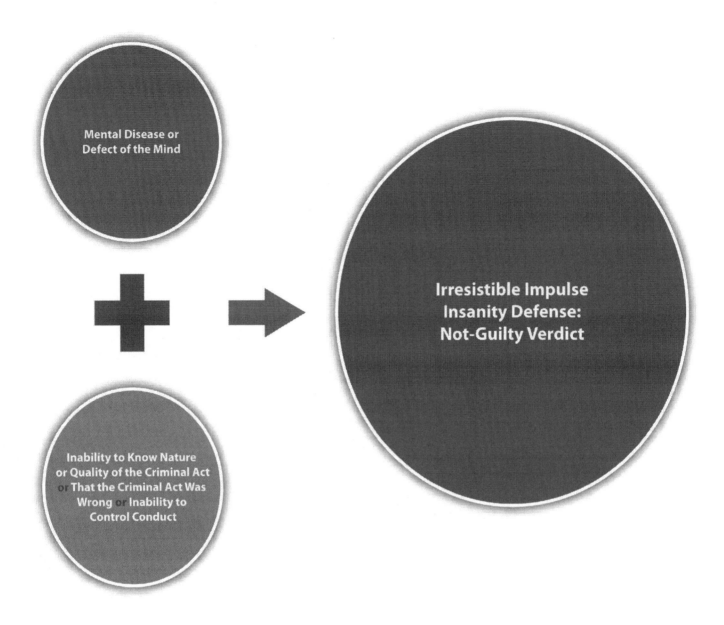

The Substantial Capacity Test

The substantial capacity test is the insanity defense created by the Model Penal Code. The Model Penal Code was completed in 1962. By 1980, approximately half of the states and the federal government adopted the substantial capacity test (also called the **Model Penal Code** or **ALI defense**) (Rolf, C. A., 2010). However, in 1982, John Hinckley successfully claimed insanity using the substantial capacity test in his federal trial for the attempted murder of then-President Ronald Reagan. Public indignation at this not-guilty verdict caused many states and the federal government to *switch* from the substantial capacity test to the more inflexible M'Naghten standard (18 U.S.C., 2010). In addition, jurisdictions that switched to M'Naghten also shifted the burden of proving insanity to the *defendant* (Rolf, C. A., 2010). The defendant's burden of proof for the insanity defense is discussed shortly.

The substantial capacity test is as follows: "A person is not responsible for criminal conduct if at the time of such conduct as a result of mental disease or defect he lacks substantial capacity either to appreciate the criminality [wrongfulness] of his conduct or to conform his conduct to the requirements of law" (Model Penal Code § 4.01(1)). The defense has two elements. The first element requires the defendant to have a mental disease or defect, like the M'Naghten and irresistible impulse insanity defenses. The second element combines the **cognitive** standard with **volitional**, like the irresistible impulse insanity defense supplementing the M'Naghten insanity defense.

In general, it is easier to establish insanity under the substantial capacity test because both the cognitive and volitional requirements are scaled down to more flexible standards. Unlike the M'Naghten insanity defense, the substantial capacity test relaxes the requirement for complete inability to understand or know the difference between right and wrong. Instead, the defendant must lack *substantial*, not total, capacity. The "wrong" in the substantial capacity test is "criminality," which is a *legal* rather than moral wrong. In addition, unlike the irresistible impulse insanity defense, the defendant must lack *substantial*, not total, ability to conform conduct to the requirements of the law. Another difference in the substantial capacity test is the use of the word "appreciate" rather than "know." As stated previously, appreciate incorporates an emotional quality, which means that evidence of the defendant's character or personality is relevant and most likely admissible to support the defense.

Example of the Substantial Capacity Test

Loreen has been diagnosed with psychosis and spent most of her life in a mental hospital. While at the mental hospital, Loreen made friends with many of the patients and health-care personnel. From time to time, Loreen would play jokes on these friends. Most of these "jokes" consisted of putting her antidepressants into their food. Loreen was always reprimanded and often sternly punished for these escapades. After her release from the mental hospital at age twenty-one, Loreen falls in love with Aidan, a man who works in a bookstore near her apartment. Loreen decides to make Aidan fall in love with her by feeding him a magic potion, which she concocts out of a mixture of her antidepressants. Loreen buys a book from Aidan and casually asks if he would like her to buy him a coffee. Aidan shrugs and says, "Sure, but I don't have a break for another two hours." Loreen offers to bring him the coffee. Before bringing the drink to Aidan, she puts her "magic potion" in it. While Aidan is sipping the coffee, Loreen declares her love for him. She then states, "I know I shouldn't have, but I put a love potion in your coffee. I hope it doesn't hurt you." Aidan becomes seriously ill after drinking the coffee and is hospitalized.

Loreen claims she is not guilty for battering Aidan by reason of insanity. If Loreen is in a jurisdiction that recognizes the substantial capacity test, she may be successful with her claim. Loreen has a mental disease or defect, **psychosis**. Loreen's statement to Aidan indicates that she lacks the *substantial* capacity to appreciate the criminality of her conduct. Note that if Loreen were in a M'Naghten jurisdiction, her statement "I know I shouldn't have" could prove her awareness that her conduct was *wrong*, defeating her claim. In addition, Loreen's behavior at the mental hospital indicates that she lacks the substantial capacity to conform or control her conduct. Even after a lifetime of being punished over and over for mixing her meds together and putting them in other people's food or drink, Loreen still does it. Lastly, in a substantial capacity jurisdiction, testimony from Loreen's friends at the mental hospital may be admissible to support her claim of insanity, and her lack of ability to "appreciate" the criminality of her conduct.

Figure 6.3 Substantial Capacity Insanity Defense

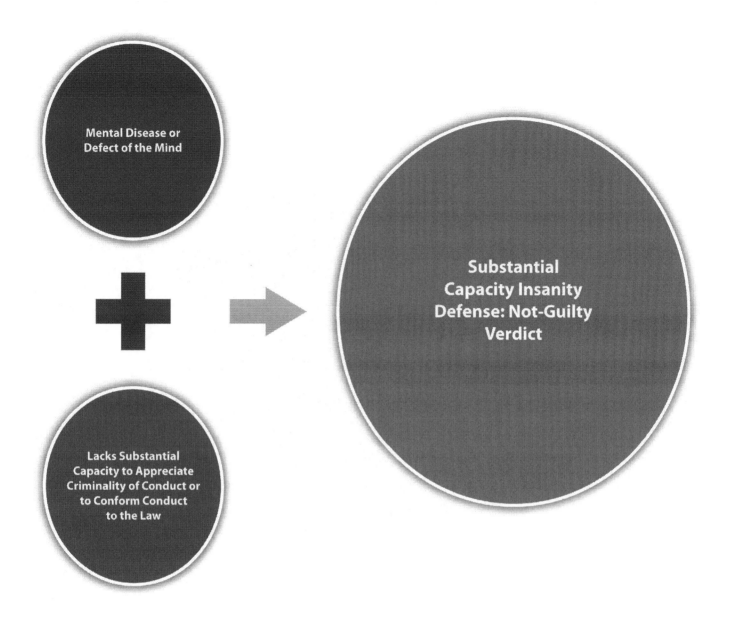

The Durham Insanity Defense

The Durham insanity defense is used only in New Hampshire and has been the established insanity defense in New Hampshire since the late 1800s. The Durham defense, also called the **Durham rule** or the **product test**, was adopted by the Circuit Court of Appeals for the District of Columbia in the case of *Durham v. U.S.*, 214 F.2d 862 (1954). The defense set forth in that case is as follows: "[A]n accused is not criminally responsible if his unlawful act was the product of mental disease or mental defect" (Durham v. U.S., 2010). However, the court failed to give definitions for product, mental disease, or mental defect. Thus the Durham insanity defense is extremely difficult to apply, and the D.C. Circuit rejected it in 1972 in the case of *U.S. v. Brawner*, 471 F.2d 969 (1972), which was later superseded by federal statute (18 U.S.C., 2010).

In general, the Durham insanity defense relies on ordinary principles of **proximate causation**. The defense has two elements. First, the defendant must have a mental disease or defect. Although these terms are not specifically defined in the *Durham* case, the language of the judicial opinion indicates an attempt to rely more on objective, psychological standards, rather than focusing on the defendant's subjective cognition. The second element has to do with **causation**. If the criminal conduct is "caused" by the mental disease or defect, then the conduct should be excused under the circumstances.

Example of the Durham Insanity Defense

Arianna has been diagnosed with **paranoia**. Most psychiatric experts agree that individuals afflicted with paranoia unreasonably believe that the human population is "out to get them." Arianna works under the direct supervision of Nora, who has a physical condition called "walleye." Nora's walleye makes it appear that she is looking to the side when she addresses people. Arianna gradually becomes convinced that Nora is communicating secret messages to their coworkers when she is speaking to Arianna. Arianna is genuinely frightened that Nora is telling their coworkers to kill her, and she decides she needs to defend herself. Arianna brings a gun to work one day, and when Nora begins talking to her about her tendency to take overlong lunches, Arianna pulls the gun out of her cubicle and shoots and kills Nora.

Arianna claims she is not guilty for killing Nora by reason of insanity. If Arianna killed Nora in New Hampshire, she might be successful with her claim. Arianna has a mental disease or defect, **paranoia**. Arianna can probably produce evidence, such as psychiatric expert testimony, that her paranoia "caused" or "produced" her criminal conduct, which was shooting Nora. Thus a trier of fact could acquit Arianna on the grounds that her conduct is excusable under these circumstances.

Figure 6.4 Durham Insanity Defense

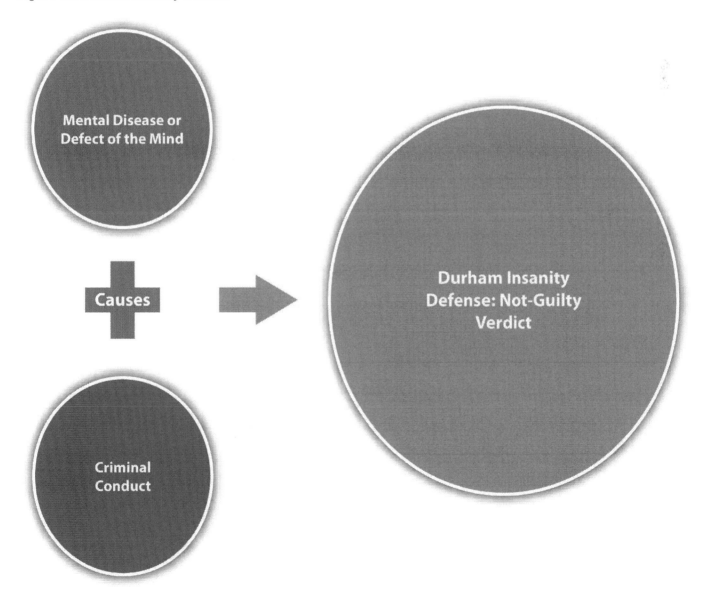

Proving Insanity

There is generally a **presumption** that criminal defendants are *sane*, just as there is a presumption that they are *innocent*. Therefore, at a minimum, a defendant claiming insanity must produce evidence that rebuts this presumption. Some states require the prosecution to thereafter prove sanity beyond a reasonable doubt or to a preponderance of evidence (Elkins, J.R., and students, 2010).

Post-*Hinckley*, many states have converted the insanity defense into an affirmative defense. Thus as discussed in Chapter 5 "Criminal Defenses, Part 1", the defendant may also have the burden of persuading the trier of fact that he or she is insane to a preponderance of evidence (New Jersey Jury Instruction on Insanity, 2010). The federal government and some other states require the defendant to prove insanity by **clear and convincing evidence**, which is a higher standard than preponderance of evidence (Tenn. Code Ann., 2010).

Diminished Capacity

A claim of diminished capacity differs from the insanity defense. Diminished capacity is an **imperfect failure of proof defense** recognized in a minority of jurisdictions. Diminished capacity could reduce a first-degree murder charge to second-degree murder or manslaughter if the defendant lacks the mental capacity to form the appropriate criminal intent **for first-degree murder**.

In California, diminished capacity was abolished as an affirmative defense after San Francisco Supervisor Dan White used it successfully in his trial for the murder of fellow Supervisor Harvey Milk. A jury convicted White of voluntary manslaughter rather than first-degree premeditated murder after reviewing evidence that proved his diet of junk food (Twinkies) created a chemical imbalance in his brain. In the aftermath of this highly publicized trial, California passed legislation eliminating the diminished capacity defense and limiting the admissibility of evidence of diminished capacity only to sentencing proceedings (Cal. Penal Code, 2010).

Similar to diminished capacity is the syndrome defense. A syndrome that negates the requisite intent for the crime could function as a **failure of proof defense** in a minority of jurisdictions. Some common examples of syndromes the American Psychiatric Association recognizes in the *Diagnostic and Statistical Manual of Mental Disorders*, fourth edition (*DSM-IV*), are antisocial personality disorder, posttraumatic stress disorder, and intermittent explosive disorder. Some common examples of syndromes identified but not recognized in *DSM-IV* are battered woman or battered wife syndrome (discussed in Chapter 5 "Criminal Defenses, Part 1") and caffeine withdrawal. Although successful use of the syndrome defense is rare, at least one case has excused a defendant's drunken driving and assault and battery against a police officer because of premenstrual syndrome (PMS) (Baltimore.com, 2011).

Mental Competence to Stand Trial

The insanity defense is different from mental competence to stand trial. The insanity defense pertains to the defendant's mental state when he or she commits the crime. If the insanity defense is successful, it *exonerates* the defendant from guilt. Mental competence to stand trial is analyzed at the time the trial is to take place. If the defendant is mentally incompetent to stand trial, the trial is delayed until the defendant regains competency. Although a detailed discussion of mental competence to stand trial is beyond the scope of this book, in general, a criminal defendant must be able to understand the charges against him or her, and be able to assist in his or her defense. As the Model Penal Code provides, "[n]o person who as a result of mental disease or defect lacks capacity to understand the proceedings against him or to assist in his own defense shall be tried, convicted or sentenced for the commission of an offense so long as such incapacity endures" (Model Penal Code § 4.04). A defendant who is mentally incompetent at the time of trial is subject to mental health treatment or even involuntary medication until competence is regained.

Guilty but Mentally Ill

Post-*Hinckley*, some states adopted the guilty but mentally ill verdict. A defendant who is found **guilty but mentally ill** is not *acquitted* but punished and treated for mental health simultaneously while in prison. Typically, the guilty but mentally ill verdict is available only when the defendant fails to prove legal insanity, and requires the defendant to prove mental illness at the time of the crime to a preponderance of evidence (725 ILCS, 2010).

Example of Guilty but Mentally Ill

Review the example with Jolene in Section 6 "Example of a Case Inappropriate for the Irresistible Impulse Insanity Defense". In this example, Jolene has been diagnosed with paranoia, but shows an ability to control and understand the wrongfulness of her conduct, so she probably will not be successful with an irresistible impulse insanity defense. If Jolene is in a state that offers a guilty but mentally ill verdict, Jolene may be an appropriate candidate because she was mentally ill at the time she assaulted and battered her sorority sister. If Jolene is found guilty but mentally ill, she will be treated for her mental health simultaneously while serving any prison sentence.

Figure 6.5 Effects (Circular Diagram) of Mental Competency Claims

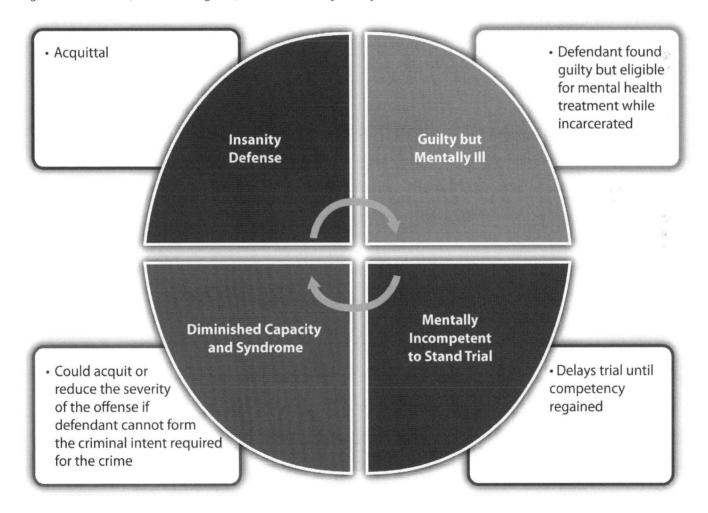

Figure 6.6 Diagram of the Insanity Defense

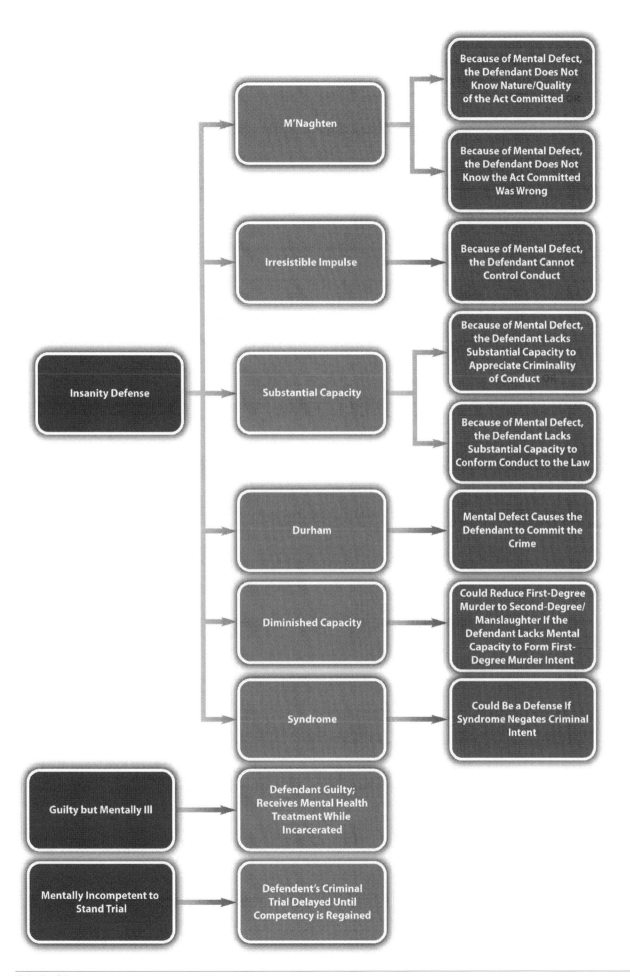

Hasan Fort Hood Shooting Video

Does Hasan Have an Insanity Defense? The Judge Rules!

In this news story on the legal implications of the Fort Hood shootings, Judge Napolitano discusses the upcoming prosecution of Nidal Hasan and the possibility of an insanity defense (Brown, A. K., 2011).
(click to see video)

Disposition of the Legally Insane

The not guilty by reason of insanity verdict means that the defendant is absolved from criminal responsibility and devoid of any criminal record for the offense. However, it does *not* mean that the defendant is free to return to society.

In several states and federally, a defendant who is found not guilty by reason of insanity is *automatically committed* to a treatment facility until there is a determination that mental health has been restored (18 U.S.C., 2010). This is also the Model Penal Code approach. As the Model Penal Code states in § 4.08(1), "[w]hen a defendant is acquitted on the ground of mental disease or defect excluding responsibility, the Court shall order him to be committed to the custody of the Commissioner of Mental Hygiene [Public Health] to be placed in an appropriate institution for custody, care and treatment."

Other states have a hearing on sanity after the judgment or verdict of not guilty by reason of insanity is returned. If the defendant is deemed mentally competent at the hearing, he or she is *released*. If the defendant is found mentally ill at the hearing, he or she is *committed* to the appropriate treatment facility (Ohio Rev. Code Ann., 2010).

Temporary Insanity

Many states also recognize temporary insanity, which does not differ in analysis from permanent insanity except for the duration of the mental illness (Malo, A., Barach, M. P., & Levin, J. A., 2010). In a state that recognizes temporary insanity, the elements of the state's insanity defense, either **M'Naghten**, **irresistible impulse**, **substantial capacity**, or **Durham**, must be present at the time the crime was committed. If the defendant is found not guilty by reason of insanity for the criminal offense, but regains mental competence at the time of prosecution, the defendant is *released* after the verdict is rendered. The trial court will order release based on the commitment procedure discussed in Section 6.1.9 "Disposition of the Legally Insane".

Example of Temporary Insanity

In Virginia in 1994, Lorena Bobbitt was tried for the crime of slicing off her husband's penis. Bobbitt pleaded not guilty to malicious wounding by reason of insanity. Bobbitt successfully established the **irresistible impulse insanity defense** by presenting evidence of years of spousal abuse, a forced abortion, and rape on the night of the incident (Bell, R., 2010; law.jrank.org, 2010). After the jury returned the verdict of not guilty by reason of insanity, Bobbitt was evaluated, deemed mentally competent, and released (Bell, R., 2010).

Lorena Bobbitt Trial Video

Lorena Bobbitt Trial, Day One

This news story discusses the first day of the Lorena Bobbitt trial (Simon, R., 2011).
(click to see video)

Key Takeaways

- The four states that do not recognize the insanity defense are Montana, Utah, Kansas, and Idaho.
- The four versions of the insanity defense are M'Naghten, irresistible impulse, substantial capacity, and Durham.

- The two elements of the M'Naghten insanity defense are the following:
  - The defendant must be suffering from a mental defect or disease at the time of the crime.
  - The defendant did not know the nature or quality of the criminal act he or she committed or that the act was wrong because of the mental defect or disease.

- The two elements of the irresistible impulse insanity defense are the following:
  - The defendant must be suffering from a mental defect or disease at the time of the crime.
  - The defendant could not control his or her criminal conduct because of the mental defect or disease.
- The substantial capacity test softens the second element of the M'Naghten and irresistible impulse insanity defenses. Under the substantial capacity test, the defendant must lack substantial, not total, capacity to appreciate the criminality of conduct or to control or conform conduct to the law.
- The Durham insanity defense excuses criminal conduct when it is caused by a mental disease or defect.
- The criminal defendant pleading not guilty by reason of insanity must produce evidence to rebut the presumption that criminal defendants are sane. Thereafter, either the prosecution has the burden of disproving insanity to a certain evidentiary standard or the defendant has the burden of proving insanity to a preponderance of evidence or clear and convincing evidence.
- The diminished capacity defense is a failure of proof imperfect defense that may reduce a first-degree murder to second-degree murder or manslaughter if the defendant did not have the mental capacity to form first-degree murder criminal intent. The insanity defense is generally a perfect affirmative defense in many jurisdictions.
- The insanity defense exonerates the defendant from criminal responsibility. Mental incompetence to stand trial delays the criminal trial until mental competency is regained.
- The guilty but mentally ill verdict finds the criminal defendant guilty but orders him or her to undergo mental health treatment while incarcerated. The insanity defense is generally a perfect affirmative defense in many jurisdictions.
- The federal government and some states automatically commit a criminal defendant to a mental health facility after an acquittal based on insanity. Other states have a postverdict hearing to rule on commitment.
- A claim of temporary insanity is the same as a claim of insanity except for the duration of the mental illness.

Exercises

Answer the following questions. Check your answers using the answer key at the end of the chapter.

Jeffrey is diagnosed with schizophrenia. For fifteen years, Jeffrey kidnaps, tortures, kills, and eats human victims. Jeffrey avoids detection by hiding his victims' corpses in various locations throughout the city. If the jurisdiction in which Jeffrey commits these crimes recognizes the M'Naghten insanity defense, can Jeffrey successfully plead and prove insanity? Why or why not? Read *State v. Guido*, 191 A.2d 45 (1993). In *Guido*, the defendant killed her husband and claimed insanity in a jurisdiction that recognizes the M'Naghten insanity defense. Psychiatric experts examined the defendant and deemed her legally sane at the time of the killing. The experts thereafter met with the defendant's attorney and changed their opinion to state that the defendant was legally *insane* at the time of the killing. The jury found the defendant sane after being made aware of this discrepancy. Did the New Jersey Supreme Court uphold the defendant's conviction? The case is available at this link: http://lawschool.courtroomview.com/acf_cases/8791-state-v-guido. Read *State v. Hornsby*, 484 S.E.2d 869 (1997). In *Hornsby*, the defendant sought to reverse his convictions for burglary and murder after jury verdicts of guilty but mentally ill. The defendant wanted to invalidate South Carolina's statute recognizing the verdict of guilty but mentally ill as unconstitutional. The defendant claimed that defendants incarcerated after guilty but mentally ill verdicts receive the same mental health treatment as defendants incarcerated under regular guilty verdicts, violating the Fourteenth Amendment due process clause. Did the Supreme Court of South Carolina uphold the statute? The case is available at this link: http://scholar.google.com/scholar_case?case=13615864613799310547&hl=en&as_sdt=2&as_vis=1&oi=scholarr.

Law and Ethics: The Elizabeth Smart Case

Two Prosecutions—Two Different Results

In 2002, Brian David Mitchell and his accomplice and wife, Wanda Barzee, kidnapped fourteen-year-old Elizabeth Smart from her home. Mitchell, a so-called street preacher, and Barzee held Smart captive for nine months, tethering her to a metal cable, subjecting her to daily rapes, and forcing her to ingest alcohol and drugs (Dobner, J., 2010). At one point, they transported Smart across state lines to California. Mitchell was put on trial for kidnapping and sexual assault in the state of Utah. The trial court found Mitchell incompetent to stand trial, and did not make a ruling forcing him to submit to medication to remedy the incompetency (Dobner, J., 2010). Unlike Mitchell, Barzee was involuntarily medicated pursuant to a state court order (by the same judge that heard Mitchell's incompetency claim), and pleaded guilty to federal and state kidnapping, sexual assault, and illegal transportation of a minor for sex, receiving two fifteen-year sentences, to be served concurrently (Dobner, J., 2010). The **federal** government also instituted a prosecution against Mitchell for kidnapping and taking Smart across state lines for sex. The US District Court judge held a competency hearing and found that Mitchell was *competent* to stand trial (Winslow, B., 2010). Mitchell pleaded not guilty by reason of **insanity**. Throughout the trial, Mitchell was often removed from the courtroom for loudly singing Christmas carols and hymns. A serious of experts testified regarding Mitchell's psychological ailments, including a rare delusional disorder, schizophrenia, pedophilia, and antisocial personality disorder. Nonetheless, the jury *rejected* the insanity defense and convicted Mitchell of kidnapping and transporting a minor across state lines for the purpose of illegal sex (Dobner, J., 2010).

If Mitchell had not committed federal crimes, he might *still* be awaiting trial in Utah.

What is the purpose of putting Mitchell on trial rather than delaying the trial for mental incompetency? Is this purpose *ethical*?

Check your answer using the answer key at the end of the chapter.

Read about Mitchell's sentencing at http://content.usatoday.com/communities/ondeadline/post/2011/05/elizabeth-smarts-kidnapper-sentenced-to-xx-years-in-prison/1.

Brian David Mitchell Video

Suspect Deemed Competent in Elizabeth Smart Case

This video is a news story on the federal court's ruling that Brian David Mitchell was mentally competent to stand trial in the Elizabeth Smart case:
(click to see video)

References

Ala. Code § 13A-3-1, accessed November 30, 2010, http://law.onecle.com/alabama/criminal-code/13A-3-1.html.

Baltimore.com website, "Successful PMS Defense in Virginia Case Revives Debate," accessed June 16, 2011, http://articles.baltimoresun.com/1991-06-16/news/1991167033_1_pms-richter-defense.

Bell, R., "Crimes Below the Belt: Penile Removal and Castration," TruTV website, accessed December 3, 2010, http://www.trutv.com/library/crime/criminal_mind/sexual_assault/severed_penis/index.html

Brown, A. K., "Fort Hood Shooting Suspect Major Nidal Hasan to Be Arraigned," Huffingtonpost.com website, accessed August 26, 2011, http://www.huffingtonpost.com/2011/07/20/fort-hood-shooting-suspect-in-court_n_904274.html.

Cal. Penal Code § 25, accessed November 30, 2010, http://law.onecle.com/california/penal/25.html.

Dobner, J., "Elizabeth Smart Kidnapper Convicted, Jury Rejects Insanity Defense," the *Christian Science Monitor* website, accessed December 11, 2010, http://www.csmonitor.com/USA/2010/1210/Elizabeth-Smart-kidnapper-convicted-jury-rejects-insanity-defense.

Dobner, J., "Wanda Barzee, Elizabeth Smart Kidnapper, Gets Fifteen Years, Including Seven Already Served," the *Huffington Post* website, accessed December 11, 2010, http://www.huffingtonpost.com/2010/05/21/wanda-barzee-elizabeth-smart_n_584787.html.

Durham v. U.S., 214 F.2d 862, 875 (1954), accessed December 2, 2010, http://scholar.google.com/scholar_case?case=12446862359488852364&hl=en&as_sdt=2&as_vis=1&oi=scholarr.

Elkins, J. R., and students at the West Virginia University College of Law, "Insanity Defense," West Virginia Homicide Jury Instructions Project, accessed December 2, 2010, http://myweb.wvnet.edu/~jelkins/adcrimlaw/insanity.html.

Findlaw.com, "The Insanity Defense among the States," findlaw.com website, accessed November 29, 2010, http://criminal.findlaw.com/crimes/more-criminal-topics/insanity-defense/the-insanity-defense-among-the-states.html.

Iowa Code § 701.4, accessed November 30, 2010, http://coolice.legis.state.ia.us/cool-ice/default.asp?category=billinfo&service=iowacode&ga=83&input=701.

law.jrank.org website, "John Wayne and Lorena Bobbitt Trials: 1993 and 1994—Lorena Bobbitt's Trial Begins," accessed December 3, 2010, http://law.jrank.org/pages/3594/John-Wayne-Lorena-Bobbitt-Trials-1993-1994-Lorena-Bobbitt-s-Trial-Begins.html.

Malo, A., Matthew P. Barach, and Joseph A. Levin, "The Temporary Insanity Defense in California," hastings.edu website, accessed December 3, 2010, http://www.uchastings.edu/public-law/docs/tempinsanity.pdf.

New Jersey Jury Instruction on Insanity, Based on N.J. Stat. Ann. § 2C: 4-1, accessed November 30, 2010, http://www.judiciary.state.nj.us/criminal/charges/respons1.pdf.

Ohio Rev. Code Ann. § 2945.40, accessed December 3, 2010, http://codes.ohio.gov/orc/2945.40.

Queen v. M'Naghten, 10 Clark & F.200, 2 Eng. Rep. 718 (H.L. 1843), accessed November 29, 2010, http://users.phhp.ufl.edu/rbauer/forensic_neuropsychology/mcnaghten.pdf.

Rolf, C. A., "From M'Naghten to Yates—Transformation of the Insanity Defense in the United States—Is It Still Viable?" *Rivier College Online Academic Journal* 2 (2006), accessed December 1, 2010, http://www.rivier.edu/journal/ROAJ-2006-Spring/J41-ROLF.pdf.

Simon, R., "Was Lorena Bobbitt's Act 'an Irresistible Impulse?'" Baltimoresun.com website, accessed August 26, 2011, http://articles.baltimoresun.com/1994-01-12/news/1994012071_1_lorena-bobbitt-insanity-defense-reason-of-insanity.

State v. Crenshaw, 659 P.2d 488 (1983), accessed November 30, 2010, http://lawschool.courtroomview.com/acf_cases/8790-state-v-crenshaw.

State v. Skaggs, 586 P.2d 1279 (1978), accessed November 30, 2010, http://www.leagle.com/xmlResult.aspx?xmldoc=1978587120Ariz467_1470.xml&docbase=CSLWAR1-1950-1985.

State v. White, 270 P.2d 727 (1954), accessed November 30, 2010,

http://scholar.google.com/scholar_case?case=15018626933471947897&hl=en&as_sdt=2&as_vis=1&oi=scholarr.

State v. Worlock, 569 A.2d 1314 (1990), accessed November 30, 2010, http://www.leagle.com/xmlResult.aspx?xmldoc=1990713117NJ596_1172.xml&docbase=CSLWAR2-1986-2006.

Tenn. Code Ann. § 39-11-501, accessed December 2, 2010, http://law.justia.com/tennessee/codes/2010/title-39/chapter-11/part-5/39-11-501.

Winslow, B., "Mitchell Ruled Competent to Stand Trial for Kidnapping Elizabeth Smart," Fox13now.com website, accessed December 11, 2010, http://www.fox13now.com/news/kstu-mitchell-competent-trial-kidnapping-smart,0,4261562.story.

18 U.S.C. § 17, accessed November 28, 2010, http://www.law.cornell.edu/uscode/18/usc_sec_18_00000017—-000-.html.

725 ILCS § 5/115-4(j), accessed December 3, 2010, http://law.onecle.com/illinois/725ilcs5/115-4.html.
CC licensed content, Shared previously

- Criminal Law. **Provided by**: University of Minnesota Libraries Publishing . **Located at**: http://open.lib.umn.edu/criminallaw/. **License**: *CC BY-NC-SA: Attribution-NonCommercial-ShareAlike*

6.2 Infancy, Intoxication, Ignorance, and Mistake

Learning Objectives

Define the infancy defense.
Distinguish a juvenile court adjudication from a criminal prosecution.
Ascertain four criteria that could support a juvenile court waiver of jurisdiction.
Identify a situation where voluntary intoxication may provide a defense.
Define involuntary intoxication.
Compare the defenses of voluntary and involuntary intoxication.
Identify a situation where mistake of law may provide a defense.
Identify a situation where mistake of law is not a valid defense.
Identify a situation where mistake of fact may provide a defense.
Identify a situation where mistake of fact is not a valid defense.

Infancy

Many states recognize the defense of infancy. **Infancy** asserts that the defendant is not subject to criminal prosecution because he or she is *too young* to commit a crime. The policy supporting the infancy defense is the belief that juvenile defendants are too immature to form criminal intent. The infancy defense is typically statutory and can be perfect or imperfect, depending on the jurisdiction.

States divide up the jurisdiction of criminal defendants between juvenile courts and adult courts. Juvenile court systems generally retain jurisdiction over criminal defendants under the age of sixteen, seventeen, or eighteen, with exceptions. The Model Penal Code position is that "[a] person shall not be tried for or convicted of an offense if: (a) at the time of the conduct charged to constitute the offense he was less than sixteen years of age, [in which case the Juvenile Court shall have exclusive jurisdiction]" (Model Penal Code § 4.10(1)(a)).

The primary purpose of a juvenile court adjudication is **rehabilitation**. The goal is to reform the minor before he or she becomes an adult. In most states, the infancy defense protects a youthful defendant from criminal prosecution as an *adult*; it does not prohibit a juvenile adjudication. Most minor defendants are adjudicated in juvenile court, so the infancy defense is rarely used.

Juveniles *can* be prosecuted as adults under certain specified circumstances. At early common law, criminal defendants were divided into three age groups. Those under the age of seven were deemed incapable of forming criminal intent, and could not be criminally prosecuted. Defendants between the ages of seven and fourteen were provided a **rebuttable presumption** that they lacked the mental capacity to form criminal intent. Once a defendant turned fourteen, he or she was subject to an adult criminal prosecution. Modern *statutes* codify the adult criminal prosecution standard for different age groups. Some states follow the early common law and set up rebuttable and irrebuttable presumptions based on the defendant's age (RCW 9A.04.050, 2010). Other states set forth a minimum age, such as fourteen or sixteen, and defendants who have reached that age are prosecuted as adults (N.Y. Penal Law § 30.00, 2010).

When a juvenile court has jurisdiction, the jurisdiction must be forfeited if the juvenile is to be prosecuted as an adult. This process is called waiver. Juvenile courts can have exclusive jurisdiction over minors under eighteen, or concurrent or simultaneous jurisdiction with adult courts, depending on the state.

States vary as to the waiver procedure. Some states allow judges to use discretion in granting the waiver, while others vest this power in the legislature or the prosecutor (Sickmund, M., 2010). A few factors serve as criteria supporting the waiver to adult criminal court: the nature of the offense, the sophistication it requires, the defendant's criminal history, and the threat the defendant poses to public safety (Kent v. United States, 2010).

Example of the Infancy Defense

Mario is ten years old. Mario shoplifts some candy from the local market and is arrested. The newly elected district attorney decides to make an example of Mario, and begins an adult criminal prosecution against him for theft. In Mario's state, the juvenile court has exclusive jurisdiction over individuals under the age of eighteen. Mario can probably claim **infancy** as a perfect defense to the theft charge. Mario should be adjudicated in juvenile court, not prosecuted as an adult. Therefore, the juvenile court has jurisdiction in this case and Mario's criminal prosecution should be dismissed.

Intoxication

Intoxication is another defense that focuses on the defendant's inability to form the requisite criminal intent. In general, intoxication can be based on the defendant's use of alcohol, legal drugs, or illegal drugs. The Model Penal Code defines intoxication as "a disturbance of mental or physical capacities resulting from the introduction of substances into the body" (Model Penal Code § 2.08(5) (a)). The intoxication defense could be perfect or imperfect, statutory or common law, depending on the jurisdiction.

Intoxication is a state that is achieved either *voluntarily* or *involuntarily*. Most states frown on the use of voluntary intoxication as a defense, and allow it only to reduce the severity of the crime charged (N.Y. Penal Law § 15.25, 2010). Recall from Chapter 4 "The Elements of a Crime" that if a defendant voluntarily undertakes action, such as drinking or ingesting drugs, the **voluntary act** requirement is met. Conduct that occurs *after* the voluntary intoxication probably is not excused unless the intoxication prevents the defendant from forming the criminal intent required for the offense (Or. Rev. Stat., 2010). If the crime charged is a reckless intent crime, voluntary intoxication rarely provides even an imperfect defense (Tenn. Code Ann., 2010).

Involuntary intoxication is more likely to provide a defense than voluntary intoxication. Generally, a defendant can claim involuntary intoxication if he or she ingested the drug or alcohol unknowingly or under force, duress, or fraud (California Jury Instructions No. 3427, 2010). Involuntary intoxication could affect the defendant's ability to form criminal intent, thus negating specific intent, dropping murder a degree, or converting murder to manslaughter. The Model Penal Code equates involuntary intoxication with the substantial capacity test, providing "[i]ntoxication which (a) is not self-induced...is an affirmative defense if by reason of such intoxication the actor at the time of his conduct lacks substantial capacity either to appreciate its criminality [wrongfulness] or to conform his conduct to the requirements of law" (Model Penal Code § 2.08 (4)).

Example of the Intoxication Defense

Clint slips a date rape drug into Delilah's drink at a fraternity party. Delilah is twenty-one and legally able to consume alcohol. The date rape drug produces a state of unconsciousness during which Delilah severely beats a sorority sister. Delilah can probably claim involuntary intoxication as a defense in this situation. Although Delilah voluntarily drank the alcohol, she became intoxicated from the date rape drug that she ingested *unknowingly*. Delilah could be acquitted or could have a charge of aggravated battery reduced, depending on the jurisdiction.

Figure 6.7 Crack the Code

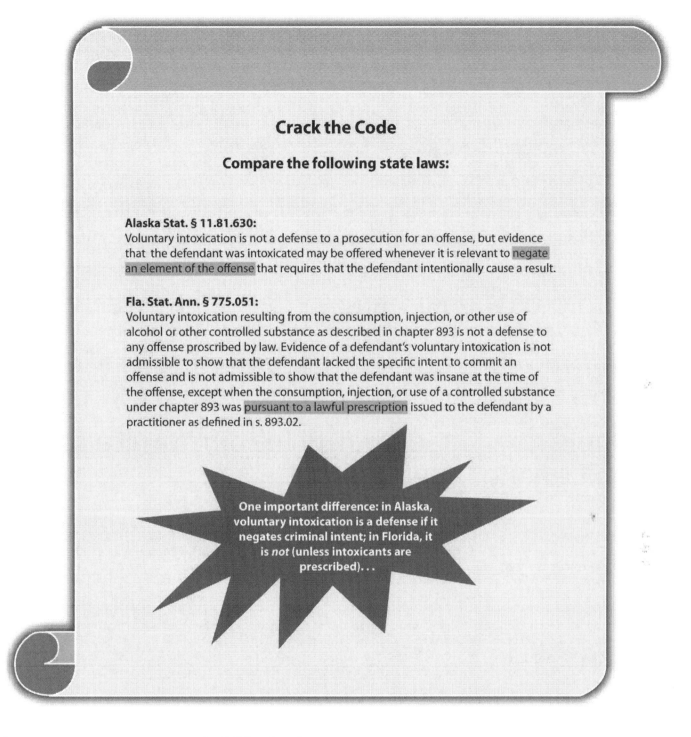

Crack the Code

Compare the following state laws:

Alaska Stat. § 11.81.630:
Voluntary intoxication is not a defense to a prosecution for an offense, but evidence that the defendant was intoxicated may be offered whenever it is relevant to negate an element of the offense that requires that the defendant intentionally cause a result.

Fla. Stat. Ann. § 775.051:
Voluntary intoxication resulting from the consumption, injection, or other use of alcohol or other controlled substance as described in chapter 893 is not a defense to any offense proscribed by law. Evidence of a defendant's voluntary intoxication is not admissible to show that the defendant lacked the specific intent to commit an offense and is not admissible to show that the defendant was insane at the time of the offense, except when the consumption, injection, or use of a controlled substance under chapter 893 was pursuant to a lawful prescription issued to the defendant by a practitioner as defined in s. 893.02.

One important difference: in Alaska, voluntary intoxication is a defense if it negates criminal intent; in Florida, it is *not* (unless intoxicants are prescribed). . .

Ignorance and Mistake

Occasionally, a defendant's **mistake** negates the criminal intent required for an offense. Mistakes can be a mistake of law or a mistake of fact. Mistake of law and fact defenses can be statutory or common law, perfect or imperfect, depending on the jurisdiction.

Mistake of Law

The basis of the mistake of law defense is that the defendant believes his or her *criminal* conduct is *legal*. The defense could be a failure of proof defense or an affirmative defense of excuse, depending on the jurisdiction (Tex.

Penal Code, 2010). The Model Penal Code provides, "Ignorance or mistake as to a matter of fact or law is a defense if: (a) the ignorance or mistake negatives the purpose, knowledge, belief, recklessness or negligence required to establish a material element of the offense; or (b) the law provides that the state of mind established by such ignorance or mistake constitutes a defense" (Model Penal Code § 2.04(1)).

Most states require that the mistake of law be founded on a *statute* or *judicial decision* that is later overturned (La. Rev. Stat. Ann, 2010). The Model Penal Code states, "A belief that conduct does not legally constitute an offense is a defense to a prosecution for that offense based upon such conduct when…the actor…acts in reasonable reliance upon an official statement of the law, afterward determined to be invalid…contained in…a statute or…judicial decision" (Model Penal Code § 2.04(3) (b)).

Incorrect advice from a licensed attorney *cannot* form the basis of a mistake of law defense (Hopkins v. State, 2010). Nor can mistake of law be rooted in *ignorance of the law* because all individuals are required to know the criminal laws effective in their jurisdiction. The Model Penal Code provides, "A belief that conduct does not legally constitute an offense is a defense to a prosecution for that offense based upon such conduct when: the statute or other enactment defining the offense is not known to the actor and has not been published or otherwise made available prior to the conduct" (Model Penal Code § 2.04(3) (a)).

Example of the Mistake of Law Defense

Shelby, an attorney, researches current case law and determines that it is legal to sell products over the Internet and not charge sales tax. Shelby starts selling designer clothing on eBay and does not charge her customers any sales tax. The case decision that Shelby relied on is *overturned* by a court of appeals. Shelby can probably assert **mistake of law** as a defense to the crime of evading payment of sales tax.

Example of a Case That Is Inappropriate for the Mistake of Law Defense

Review the mistake of law defense example given in Section 6 "Example of the Mistake of Law Defense". Assume that in Shelby's state, it is currently illegal to sell products over the Internet without charging sales tax. Jonathan meets with Shelby, and asks her to research whether he needs to charge sales tax when he sells products over the Internet. Shelby agrees to research the matter and get back to Jonathan the next day with an answer. After Jonathan leaves, Shelby is contacted by her friend Margaret, who wants to take an impromptu trip to New York City. Margaret asks Shelby if she would like to come along. Shelby agrees, rushes home, packs for the trip, and leaves with Margaret. The next day while Shelby is watching a Broadway play with Margaret, Jonathan calls Shelby on her cell phone and asks Shelby what her research revealed about the sales tax question. Even though she has *not* done any research on the matter, Shelby responds, "I just finished the research. You do not need to charges sales tax when you sell products over the Internet." If Jonathan thereafter relies on Shelby's incorrect advice, and sells products over the Internet without charging sales tax, he probably will *not* be able to assert **mistake of law** as a defense. Incorrect advice from an attorney cannot excuse criminal conduct, even if the crime is committed *because* of the faulty legal opinion. Therefore, Jonathan could be charged with tax evasion in this situation.

Mistake of Fact

Mistake of fact is more likely to provide a defense than mistake of law. If the facts *as the defendant believes them to be* negate the requisite intent for the crime at issue, the defendant can assert mistake of fact as a defense (N.H. Rev. Stat. Ann., 2010). Mistake of fact is generally not a defense to **strict liability** crimes because intent is not an element of a strict liability offense (People v. Olsen, 2010).

Example of the Mistake of Fact Defense

Mickie sees Rachel, his neighbor, riding his bicycle in her driveway. Mickie walks quickly up to Rachel and demands that she get off the bike and return it to his garage. Frightened, Rachel hops off and runs to her house, leaving the bike behind. Mickie walks the bike over to his garage. Once Mickie reaches the garage, he sees that his bike, which is an exact replica of Rachel's, is already inside. Mickie may be able to use **mistake of fact** as a defense to theft. As is discussed in Chapter 11 "Crimes against Property", the intent for theft is the intent to take the property of *another* person. Mickie believed Rachel's bike was *his*. Thus Mickie's mistake of fact negates the intent required for this offense.

Example of a Case That Is Inappropriate for the Mistake of Fact Defense

Tina is pulled over for speeding. Tina claims her speedometer is broken, so she was mistaken as to her speed. Tina probably *cannot* assert **mistake of fact** as a defense in this case. Speeding is generally a **strict liability** offense. Thus Tina's mistaken belief as to the facts is not *relevant* because there is no intent required for this crime.

Figure 6.8 Comparison of Infancy, Intoxication, and Mistake

Infancy	
Intoxication	
Mistake	

Key Takeaways

- Infancy is a defense to an adult criminal prosecution if the defendant is too young to form the requisite criminal intent for the offense.
- The purpose of an adult criminal prosecution is punishment; the purpose of a juvenile adjudication is rehabilitation of the minor before he or she becomes an adult.
- Four criteria that could support a juvenile court waiver of jurisdiction are the nature of the offense, the sophistication it requires, the defendant's criminal history, and the threat the defendant poses to public safety.
- Voluntary intoxication may provide a defense if the intoxication prevents the defendant from forming the requisite criminal intent for the offense.
- Involuntary intoxication is intoxication achieved unknowingly or pursuant to force, duress, or fraud.
- Voluntary intoxication is frowned on as a defense and in many states does not provide a defense to certain crimes, such as reckless intent crimes. Involuntary intoxication is more likely to serve as a defense any time the defendant is incapable of forming the requisite criminal intent for the offense.
- Mistake of law may provide a defense if the defendant believes his or her conduct is legal because of reliance on a statute or judicial opinion that is later overturned.
- Mistake of law is not a defense when the defendant believes his or her conduct is legal because of reliance on the incorrect advice of an attorney.
- If the facts as the defendant believes them to be prevent the defendant from forming the requisite intent for the crime, mistake of fact could be a valid defense.
- Mistake of fact is not a defense to strict liability crimes because intent is not an element.

Exercises

Answer the following questions. Check your answers using the answer key at the end of the chapter.

Burt, a sixteen-year-old, consumes alcohol for the first time at a party. Unaware of alcohol's effect, Burt drinks too much, attempts to walk home, and is cited for being drunk in public. In Burt's state, the juvenile court has concurrent jurisdiction over minors ages seventeen and under, with a waiver to adult court available at the judge's discretion. Burt has not broken any laws before. Is it likely that the judge will **waive** juvenile court jurisdiction in this case and allow the adult criminal prosecution of Burt? Why or why not?

Read *People v. Register*, 60 N.Y.2d 270 (1983). In *Register*, the defendant shot and killed an individual in a bar after drinking heavily for many hours. The defendant thereafter sought a jury instruction on the **intoxication** defense to a charge of depraved mind murder. The trial court refused, and the defendant was convicted. Did the Court of Appeals of the State of New York uphold the conviction? The case is available at this link:
http://scholar.google.com/scholar_case?case=9019321014077082981&hl=en&as_sdt=2&as_vis=1&oi=.

Read *Garnett v. State*, 632 A.2d 797 (1993). In *Garnett*, the defendant, an intellectually disabled twenty-year-old, had sexual intercourse with a thirteen-year-old girl whom he believed to be sixteen, and was prosecuted for statutory rape. Did the Court of Appeals of Maryland reverse the trial court and allow the defendant to assert **mistake of fact** (the victim's age) as a defense? Why or why not? The case is available at this link:
http://scholar.google.com/scholar_case?case=9331824442522694687&hl=en&as_sdt=2&as_vis=1&oi=scholarr.

References

California Jury Instructions No. 3427, accessed December 7, 2010, http://www.justia.com/criminal/docs/calcrim/3400/3427.html.

Hopkins v. State, 69 A.2d 456 (1949), accessed December 9, 2010, http://www.leagle.com/xmlResult.aspx?xmldoc=1949682193Md489_1637.xml&docbase=CSLWAR1-1950-1985.

Kent v. United States, 383 U.S. 541 (1966), accessed December 7, 2010, http://scholar.google.com/scholar_case?case=5405024647930835755&hl=en&as_sdt=2&as_vis=1&oi=scholarr.

La. Rev. Stat. Ann. § 14:17, accessed December 7, 2010, http://law.justia.com/louisiana/codes/2009/rs/title14/rs14-17.html.

N.H. Rev. Stat. Ann. § 626:3I (a), accessed December 9, 2010, http://www.gencourt.state.nh.us/rsa/html/lxii/626/626-mrg.htm.

N.Y. Penal Law § 30.00, accessed December 6, 2010, http://law.onecle.com/new-york/penal/PEN030.00_30.00.html.

N.Y. Penal Law § 15.25, accessed December 7, 2010, http://law.onecle.com/new-york/penal/PEN015.25_15.25.html.

Or. Rev. Stat. § 161.125, accessed December 7, 2010, https://www.oregonlaws.org/ors/161.125.

People v. Olsen, 685 P.2d 52 (1984), accessed December 9, 2010, http://lawschool.courtroomview.com/acf_cases/8639-people-v-olsen.

RCW 9A.04.050, accessed December 6, 2010, http://apps.leg.wa.gov/rcw/default.aspx?cite=9A.04.050.

Sickmund, M., OJJDP National Report Series Bulletin, "Juveniles in Court," National Center for Juvenile Justice website, accessed December 7, 2010, http://www.ncjrs.gov/html/ojjdp/195420/page4.html.

Tenn. Code Ann. § 39-11-503(b), accessed December 7, 2010, http://www.lawserver.com/law/state/tennessee/tn-code/tennessee_code_39-11-503.

Tex. Penal Code § 8.03, accessed December 7, 2010, http://www.statutes.legis.state.tx.us/docs/PE/htm/Pe.8.htm.

CC licensed content, Shared previously

- Criminal Law. **Provided by**: University of Minnesota Libraries Publishing . **Located at**: http://open.lib.umn.edu/criminallaw/. **License**: *CC BY-NC-SA: Attribution-NonCommercial-ShareAlike*

6.3 Entrapment

Learning Objective

Compare the subjective and objective entrapment defenses.

Historically, no legal limit was placed on the government's ability to induce individuals to commit crimes. The Constitution does not expressly prohibit this governmental action. Currently, however, all states and the federal government provide the defense of entrapment. The entrapment defense is based on the government's use of inappropriately persuasive tactics when apprehending criminals. Entrapment is generally a perfect affirmative statutory or common-law defense.

Entrapment focuses on the *origin* of criminal intent. If the criminal intent originates with the *government or law enforcement*, the defendant is entrapped and can assert the defense. If the criminal intent originates with the *defendant*, then the defendant is acting independently and can be convicted of the offense. The two tests of entrapment are subjective entrapment and objective entrapment. The federal government and the majority of the states recognize the subjective entrapment defense (Connecticut Jury Instruction on Entrapment, 2010). Other states and the Model Penal Code have adopted the objective entrapment defense (People v. Barraza, 2010).

Subjective Entrapment

It is entrapment pursuant to the subjective entrapment defense when law enforcement pressures the defendant to commit the crime against his or her will. The subjective entrapment test focuses on the *defendant's* individual characteristics more than on law enforcement's behavior. If the facts indicate that the defendant is *predisposed* to commit the crime without law enforcement pressure, the defendant will not prevail on the defense.

The defendant's criminal record is admissible if relevant to prove the defendant's criminal nature and predisposition. Generally, law enforcement can furnish criminal opportunities and use decoys and feigned accomplices without crossing the line into subjective entrapment. However, if it is clear that the requisite intent for the offense originated *with law enforcement*, not the *defendant*, the defendant can assert subjective entrapment as a defense.

Example of Subjective Entrapment

Winifred regularly attends Narcotics Anonymous (NA) for her heroin addiction. All the NA attendees know that Winifred is a dedicated member who has been clean for ten years, Marcus, a law enforcement decoy, meets Winifred at one of the meetings and begs her to "hook him up" with some heroin. Winifred refuses. Marcus attends the next meeting, and follows Winifred out to her car pleading with her to get him some heroin. After listening to Marcus explain his physical symptoms of withdrawal in detail, Winifred feels pity and promises to help Marcus out. She agrees to meet Marcus in two hours with the heroin. When Winifred and Marcus meet at the designated location, Marcus arrests Winifred for sale of narcotics. Winifred may be able to assert entrapment as a defense if her state recognizes the **subjective entrapment defense**. Winifred has not used drugs for ten years and did not initiate contact with law enforcement. It is unlikely that the intent to sell heroin *originated* with Winifred because she has been a dedicated member of NA, and she actually met Marcus at an NA meeting while trying to maintain her sobriety. Thus it appears that Marcus *pressured* Winifred to sell heroin against a natural *predisposition*, and the entrapment defense may excuse her conduct.

Objective Entrapment

The objective entrapment defense focuses on the *behavior of law enforcement*, rather than the individual defendant. If law enforcement uses tactics that would induce a *reasonable, law-abiding* person to commit the crime, the defendant can successfully assert the entrapment defense in an objective entrapment jurisdiction. The objective entrapment defense focuses on a reasonable person, not the actual defendant, so the defendant's predisposition to commit the crime is not relevant. Thus in states that recognize the objective entrapment defense, the defendant's criminal record is not admissible to disprove the defense.

Example of Objective Entrapment

Winifred has a criminal record for prostitution. A law enforcement decoy offers Winifred $10,000 to engage in sexual intercourse. Winifred promptly accepts. If Winifred's jurisdiction recognizes the **objective entrapment defense**, Winifred may be able to successfully claim entrapment as a defense to prostitution. A *reasonable, law-abiding person* could be tempted into committing prostitution for a substantial sum of money like $10,000. The objective entrapment defense focuses on *law enforcement* tactics, rather than the predisposition of the defendant, so Winifred's criminal record is irrelevant and is not admissible as evidence. Thus it appears that law enforcement used an excessive inducement, and entrapment may excuse Winifred's conduct in this case.

Figure 6.9 Comparison of Subjective and Objective Entrapment

Subjective Entrapment	
Objective Entrapment	

Figure 6.10 Diagram of Defenses, Part 2

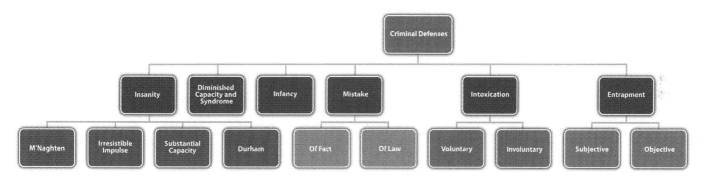

Key Takeaway

- The subjective entrapment defense focuses on the individual defendant, and provides a defense if law enforcement pressures the defendant to commit the crime against his or her will. If the defendant is predisposed to commit the crime without this pressure, the defendant will not be successful with the defense. Pursuant to the subjective entrapment defense, the defendant's criminal record is admissible to prove the defendant's predisposition. The objective entrapment defense focuses on law enforcement behavior, and provides a defense if the tactics law enforcement uses would convince a reasonable, law-abiding person to commit the crime. Under the objective entrapment defense, the defendant's criminal record is irrelevant and inadmissible.

Exercises

Answer the following questions. Check your answers using the answer key at the end of the chapter.

Allen has a criminal record for burglary. Roger, a law enforcement decoy, approaches Allen and asks if he would like to purchase methamphetamine. Allen responds that he would and is arrested. This interaction takes place in a jurisdiction that recognizes the **subjective entrapment defense**. If Allen claims entrapment, will Allen's criminal record be admissible to prove his predisposition to commit the crime at issue? Why or why not?

Read *Sosa v. Jones*, 389 F.3d 644 (2004). In *Jones*, the US District Court for the Eastern District of Michigan denied the defendant's petition for a writ of habeas corpus after he was sentenced to life in prison for conspiracy to sell and sale of cocaine. The defendant claimed he had been deprived of due process and was subjected to **sentencing entrapment** when federal agents delayed a sting operation to increase the amount of cocaine sold with the intent of increasing the defendant's sentencing to life in prison without the possibility of parole. Did the US Court of Appeals for the Sixth Circuit reverse the district court and grant the defendant's petition? The case is available at this link: http://openjurist.org/389/f3d/644/sosa-v-jones.

Read *Farley v. State*, 848 So.2d 393 (2003). In *Farley*, the government contacted the defendant, who had no criminal record, in a reverse sting operation with a mass e-mail soliciting individuals to purchase hard-core pornography. The defendant responded to the e-mail and was thereafter sent a questionnaire asking for his preferences. The defendant responded to the questionnaire, and an e-mail exchange ensued. In every communication by the government, protection from governmental interference was promised. Eventually, the defendant purchased child pornography and was arrested and prosecuted for this offense. The defendant moved to dismiss based on subjective and objective entrapment and the motion to dismiss was denied. The defendant was thereafter convicted. Did the Court of Appeal of Florida uphold the defendant's conviction? The case is available at this link:
http://www.lexisone.com/lx1/caselaw/freecaselaw?action=OCLGetCaseDetail&format=FULL&sourceID=bdjgjg&searchTerm= eiYL.TYda.aadj.ecCQ&searchFlag=y&l1loc=FCLOW.

References

Connecticut Jury Instruction on Entrapment, Based on Conn. Gen. Stats. Ann. § 53a-15, accessed December 10, 2010, http://www.jud.ct.gov/ji/criminal/part2/2.7-4.htm.

People v. Barraza, 591 P.2d 947 (1979), accessed December 10, 2010, http://scholar.google.com/scholar_case?case=4472828314482166952&hl=en&as_sdt=2&as_vis=1&oi=scholarr. CC licensed content, Shared previously

- Criminal Law. **Provided by**: University of Minnesota Libraries Publishing . **Located at**: http://open.lib.umn.edu/criminallaw/. **License**: *CC BY-NC-SA: Attribution-NonCommercial-ShareAlike*

6.4 End-of-Chapter Material

Summary

The federal government and every state except Montana, Utah, Kansas, and Idaho recognize the insanity defense. A not guilty by reason of insanity verdict is an acquittal for the offense. The policy supporting the insanity defense is the lack of deterrent effect when punishing the legally insane. Four insanity defenses are recognized in the United States: M'Naghten, irresistible impulse, substantial capacity, and Durham. The M'Naghten insanity defense is cognitive and excuses criminal conduct when the defendant is suffering from a mental defect or disease that prevents the defendant from knowing the nature or quality of conduct or from knowing that conduct is wrong. The irresistible impulse insanity defense adds a volitional component and excuses conduct the defendant cannot control because of a mental defect or disease. The substantial capacity test was created by the Model Penal Code and softens the requirements to substantial, rather than total, capacity to appreciate the criminality of conduct or to conform conduct to the law. The Durham insanity defense is recognized only in New Hampshire, and excuses conduct that is the product of or caused by a mental disease or defect. Jurisdictions vary as to the burden of proving insanity. All jurisdictions require the defendant to rebut a presumption that he or she is sane; some also require the defendant to persuade the trier of fact that he or she is legally insane to a preponderance of evidence or clear and convincing evidence (which is a higher standard than preponderance of evidence).

A minority of jurisdictions recognizes diminished capacity and the syndrome defense when the defendant cannot form the requisite criminal intent for the offense because of a mental impairment. The criminal defendant must also be mentally competent to stand trial, which means the defendant can understand the charges brought against him or her and can assist in any defense. Some jurisdictions recognize a guilty but mentally ill verdict, which does not exonerate the defendant, but provides for mental health treatment while incarcerated. Temporary insanity is also a defense in some jurisdictions and does not differ from the insanity defense except for the duration of the mental defect or disease.

The infancy defense excuses conduct when the defendant is too young to form criminal intent for the offense. The infancy defense is generally not available in juvenile adjudications, so it is rarely asserted because most youthful defendants are under the jurisdiction of juvenile courts. Juvenile courts can waive this jurisdiction and allow for an adult criminal prosecution under certain circumstances, considering the criteria of the nature of the offense, the sophistication it requires, the defendant's prior criminal history, and the threat the defendant poses to public safety.

Other excuse defenses are intoxication, ignorance, and mistake. Voluntary intoxication is frowned on as a defense, but will occasionally excuse conduct if it negates certain high-level criminal intent requirements. Involuntary intoxication, which is intoxication achieved unknowingly, or under duress or fraud, is more likely to provide a defense if it affects the defendant's capacity to form criminal intent. Ignorance of the law is not a defense because individuals are expected to know the laws of their jurisdiction. Mistake of law, which means the defendant does not know conduct is illegal, functions as a defense if the mistake is based on a judicial opinion or statute that is later overturned. Mistake of law is not a defense if the mistake is rooted in incorrect legal advice from an attorney. Mistake of fact is a defense if the facts as the defendant believes them to be negate the intent required for the offense.

Entrapment is also a defense in every jurisdiction. Most states and the federal government recognize the subjective entrapment defense, which focuses on the defendant's predisposition, and does not excuse conduct if the defendant would have committed the crime without law enforcement pressure. In a subjective entrapment jurisdiction, the defendant's criminal record is admissible to prove predisposition to commit the crime at issue. Objective entrapment is the Model Penal Code approach and excuses conduct if the pressure by law enforcement would induce a reasonable, law-abiding person to commit the crime. The defendant's criminal record is not admissible to show predisposition in an objective entrapment jurisdiction because the focus is on law enforcement tactics, not the defendant's nature.

You Be the Defense Attorney

You are a well-known private defense attorney with a perfect record. Read the prompt, review the case, and then decide whether you would **accept** or **reject** it if you want to maintain your level of success. Check your answers using the answer key at the end of the chapter.

The defendant shot and killed a police officer and then escaped on foot. He was thereafter charged with first-degree murder. The defendant wants to claim that his diagnosed paranoid schizophrenia affected his ability to form the intent required for murder. In your state (Arizona), the defendant cannot introduce this argument to negate intent; he can only plead insanity under an abbreviated version of M'Naghten, which requires proof that the defendant did not know his conduct was wrong because of a mental defect or disease. Will you accept or reject the case? Read *Clark v. Arizona*, 548 U.S. 735 (2006), which is available at this link:
http://scholar.google.com/scholar_case?case=5050526068124331217&q=
Clark+v.+Arizona&hl=en&as_sdt=2,5&as_vis=1.

The defendant, an eleven-year-old boy, had sexual intercourse with a seven-year-old boy and was charged with two counts of first-degree rape of a child. Three experts questioned the defendant, and two concluded he lacked the capacity to form the intent for rape. This conclusion was based on the defendant's response that the sexual contact was consensual and felt good. The defendant wants to present the *infancy* defense. Will you accept or reject the case? Read *State v. Ramer*, 86 P.3d 132 (2004), which is available at this link:
http://scholar.google.com/scholar_case?case=14834415223416879505&hl=en&as_sdt=2&as_vis=1&oi=scholarr.

The defendant, a diabetic, injected an abnormally large dose of insulin before his daughter's birthday party. He and his estranged wife went to the store to buy party supplies. When they returned to the defendant's vehicle, he hit her in the head with a hammer. She escaped the vehicle, and he caught up with her and ran her over. The defendant wants to claim *involuntary intoxication* as a defense to first-degree assault, domestic violence, and attempted first-degree murder. Will you accept or reject the case? Read *People v. Garcia*, 87 P.3d 159 (2003), which is available at this link:
http://www.leagle.com/decision/200324687P3d159_1238/PEOPLE%20v.%20GARCIA.

The defendant and a narcotics decoy have been acquainted for several years. The narcotics decoy set up a sale transaction between the defendant and a police officer, the defendant made the sale, and was thereafter charged with delivery of a controlled substance. The defendant claims that the decoy's status as his friend, and numerous phone calls to set up the narcotics sale pressured him to commit the crime and he wants to claim entrapment. Your state (Texas) allows the defense of *objective entrapment*, focusing on law enforcement tactics. Will you accept or reject the case? Read *Sebesta v. State*, 783 S.W.2d 811 (1990), which is available at this link:
http://scholar.google.com/scholar_case?case=7939192026130608711&hl=en&as_sdt=2002&as_vis=1.

Cases of Interest

- *U.S. v. Hinckley*, 493 F.Supp. 2d 65 (2007), discusses St. Elizabeth Hospital's proposal for the conditional release of John W. Hinckley:
  http://fl1.findlaw.com/news.findlaw.com/wp/docs/hinckley/ushinckley121703opn.pdf.
- *Graham v. Florida*, 130 S. Ct. 2011(2010), discusses sentencing a juvenile offender to life in prison:
  http://scholar.google.com/scholar_case?case=6982366090819046045&q=
  Graham+v.+Florida&hl=en&as_sdt=2,5.
- *Legue v. State*, 688 N.E.2d 408 (1997), discusses voluntary intoxication:
  http://scholar.google.com/scholar_case?case=15549524331562340362&hl=en&as_sdt=2&as_vis=1&oi=scholarr.

- *U.S. v. Albertini*, 830 F.2d 985 (1987), discusses mistake of law: http://lawschool.courtroomview.com/acf_cases/8647-united-states-v-albertini.

Articles of Interest

- The insanity defense and recent US Supreme Court decisions: http://www.repository.law.indiana.edu/cgi/viewcontent.cgi?article=1494&context=ilj
- The insanity defense for Jared Lee Loughner, the shooter of US Representative Gabrielle Giffords (D-AZ): http://www.nwherald.com/2011/01/10/insanity-defense-difficult-for-loughner/a8b43du
- The ruling that Jared Lee Loughner is incompetent to stand trial for the shooting of Representative Giffords: http://www.msnbc.msn.com/id/43165830/ns/us_news-crime_and_courts/t/ariz-shooting - spree-suspect-incompetent-trial
- The defense of caffeine overdose: http://www.cbsnews.com/news/murder-suspect-to-plead-insanity-by-caffeine/

Websites of Interest

- Insanity laws by state: http://criminal.findlaw.com/criminal-procedure/the-insanity-defense-among-the-states.html
- Information about entrapment: http://www.wopular.com/newsracks/entrapment

Statistics of Interest

- Juvenile crime in the United States: http://bjs.ojp.usdoj.gov/index.cfm?ty=pbdetail&iid=2028

CC licensed content, Shared previously

- Criminal Law. **Provided by**: University of Minnesota Libraries Publishing . **Located at**: http://open.lib.umn.edu/criminallaw/. **License**: *CC BY-NC-SA: Attribution-NonCommercial-ShareAlike*

Chapter 7: Parties to Crime

7.1 Parties to Crime

Tony Webster – National Law Enforcement Officers Memorial Visitors Center and Store – CC BY-NC 2.0.

Congress can impute to a corporation the commission of certain criminal offenses and subject it to criminal prosecution therefor.

—*New York Central R. Co. v. U.S.*, cited in Section 7.2.1 "Corporate Liability"

Learning Objectives

Identify the four parties to crime at early common law.
Identify the parties to crime in modern times.
Define the criminal act element required for accomplice liability.
Define the criminal intent element required for accomplice liability.
Define the natural and probable consequences doctrine.
Discuss the consequences of accomplice liability.
Determine whether an accomplice can be prosecuted when the principal is not prosecuted or acquitted.

Often more than one criminal defendant plays a role in the commission of a crime. Defendants working together with a common criminal purpose or design are acting with complicity. When the participation and criminal conduct varies among the defendants, an issue arises as to *who* is responsible for *which* crime and to *what degree*. This chapter analyzes different parties to crime, along with their accompanying criminal liability. Chapter 8 "Inchoate Offenses" examines crimes that necessarily involve more than one person such as **conspiracy** and **solicitation**, as well as another **inchoate** or incomplete crime, **attempt**.

Accomplice Liability

At early common law, parties to crime were divided into four categories. A principal in the first degree actually committed the crime. A principal in the second degree was present at the scene of the crime and assisted in its commission. An accessory before the fact was not present at the scene of the crime, but helped prepare for its commission. An accessory after the fact helped a party to the crime after its commission by providing comfort, aid, and assistance in escaping or avoiding arrest and prosecution or conviction.

In modern times, most states and the federal government divide parties to crime into two categories: principal, and **accessories** (Idaho Code Ann., 2010). The criminal actor is referred to as the **principal**, although all **accomplices** have equal criminal responsibility as is discussed in Section 7.1 "Parties to Crime".

Accomplice Elements

An accomplice under most state and federal statutes is responsible for the same crime as the criminal actor or **principal** (18 U.S.C., 2010). However, accomplice liability is **derivative**; the accomplice does not actually have to commit the crime to be responsible for it. The policy supporting accomplice liability is the idea that an individual who willingly participates in furthering criminal conduct should be accountable for it to the same extent as the criminal actor. The degree of participation is often difficult to quantify, so statutes and cases attempt to segregate blameworthy accomplices based on the **criminal act** and **intent** elements, as is discussed in Section 7.1 "Parties to Crime".

Accomplice Act

In the majority of states and federally, an accomplice must voluntarily act in some manner to *assist* in the commission of the offense. Some common descriptors of the **criminal act** element required for accomplice liability are aid, abet, assist, counsel, command, induce, or procure (K.S.A., 2010). Examples of actions that qualify as the accomplice criminal act are helping plan the crime, driving a getaway vehicle after the crime's commission, and luring a victim to the scene of the crime. The Model Penal Code defines the accomplice criminal act element as "aids...or attempts to aid such other person in planning or committing [the offense]" (Model Penal Code § 2.06(3) (a) (ii)).

In many states, **words** are enough to constitute the criminal act element required for accomplice liability (N.Y. Penal Law, 2010). On the other hand, mere presence at the scene of the crime, even presence at the scene combined with *flight*, is not sufficient to convert a bystander into an accomplice (Commonwealth v. Hargrave, 2010). However, if there is a **legal duty to act**, a defendant who is present at the scene of a crime without preventing its occurrence could be liable as an accomplice in many jurisdictions (People v. Rolon, 2010). As the Model Penal Code provides, "[a] person is an accomplice of another person in the commission of an offense if...having a legal duty to prevent the commission of the offense, fails to make proper effect so to do" (Model Penal Code § 2.06(3)(a)(iii)).

Example of a Case Lacking Accomplice Act

Review the criminal law issues example in Chapter 1 "Introduction to Criminal Law", Section 1.2.1 "Example of Criminal Law Issues". In that example, Clara and Linda go on a shopping spree. Linda insists that they browse an expensive department store. After they enter the lingerie department, Linda surreptitiously places a bra into her purse. Clara watches, horrified, but does not say anything, even though a security guard is standing nearby. As Linda and Clara leave the store, an alarm is activated. Linda and Clara run away with the security guard in pursuit. In this case, Clara has probably *not* committed the criminal act element required for accomplice liability. Although Clara was *present at the scene* of the crime and did not alert the security guard, mere presence at the scene is not sufficient to constitute the accomplice criminal act. Clara fled the scene when the alarm went off, but presence at the scene of a crime combined with flight is *still not enough* to comprise the accomplice criminal act. Thus Clara has probably not committed theft as an accomplice, and only Linda is subject to a criminal prosecution for this offense.

Example of Accomplice Act

Phoebe, the parent of a two-year-old named Eliza, watches silently as her live-in boyfriend Ricky beats Eliza. In Phoebe's state, parents have a duty to come to the aid of their children if their safety is threatened. Ricky severely injures Eliza, and both Phoebe and Ricky are arrested and charged with battery and child endangerment. Phoebe probably *has* committed the criminal act element required for accomplice liability in many jurisdictions. Phoebe does not personally act to physically harm her child. However, her *presence at the scene* combined with a *legal duty to act* could be enough to make her an accomplice. Thus Phoebe has most likely committed battery and child endangerment as an accomplice, and both *she* and *Ricky* are subject to a criminal prosecution for these offenses.

Accomplice Intent

The criminal intent element required for accomplice liability varies, depending on the jurisdiction. In many jurisdictions, the accomplice must act with **specific intent** or **purposely** when aiding or assisting the principal (Or. Rev. Stat., 2010). Specific intent or purposely means the accomplice desires the principal to commit the crime. The Model Penal Code follows this approach and requires the accomplice to act "with the purpose of promoting or facilitating the commission of the offense" (Model Penal Code § 2.06(3) (a)). In other jurisdictions, if the crime is *serious* and the accomplice acts with **general intent** or **knowingly** or has *awareness* that the principal will commit the crime with his or her assistance, intent to further the crime's commission could be inferred (People v. Lauria, 2010). In a minority of jurisdictions, only **general intent** or acting **knowingly** that the crime will be promoted or facilitated is required, regardless of the crime's seriousness (Washington Rev. Code Ann., 2010).

Example of Accomplice Intent

Joullian, a hotel owner, rents a hotel room to Winnifred, a prostitute. In a state that requires an accomplice to act with **specific intent** or **purposely**, Joullian must *desire* Winnifred to commit prostitution in the rented room to be Winnifred's accomplice. Evidence that Joullian stands to benefit from Winnifred's prostitution, such as evidence that he will receive a portion of the prostitution proceeds, could help prove this intent. If Joullian's state allows for an inference of **specific intent** or **purposely** with *serious* crimes when an accomplice acts with **general intent** or **knowingly**, it is unlikely that prostitution is a felony that would give rise to the inference. If Joullian's state requires only **general intent** or **knowingly** for accomplice liability regardless of the crime's seriousness, to be deemed an accomplice Joullian must simply be *aware* that renting Winnifred the room will promote or facilitate the act of prostitution.

The Natural and Probable Consequences Doctrine

Accomplice liability should be imputed only to blameworthy, deserving defendants. However, in some jurisdictions, if the crime the defendant intentionally furthers is *related* to the crime the principal actually commits, the defendant is deemed an accomplice. As with legal causation, discussed in Chapter 4 "The Elements of a Crime", foreseeability is the standard. Under the natural and probable consequences doctrine, if the defendant assists the principal with the intent to further a specific crime's commission, and the principal commits a *different* crime that is *foreseeable* at the time of the defendant's assistance, the defendant could be liable as an accomplice (ME Rev. Stat. Ann., 2010). Several jurisdictions have rejected this doctrine as an overly harsh extension of accomplice liability (Bogdanov v. People, 2010).

Example of the Natural and Probable Consequences Doctrine

José shows up drunk and unruly at his friend Abel's house and tells Abel he wants to "beat the hell" out of his girlfriend Maria. José asks Abel to drive him to Maria's house, and Abel promptly agrees. Abel drives José to Maria's house and waits in the car with the engine running. José forces his way into Maria's house and then beats and thereafter rapes her. If José and Abel are in a jurisdiction that recognizes the natural and probable consequences doctrine, the trier of fact could find that Abel is an accomplice to the battery, burglary, and rape of Maria. Abel appears to have the criminal intent required to be an accomplice to **battery** because he assisted José in his quest to *beat* Maria. If burglary and rape were *foreseeable* when Abel drove a drunk and angry José to Maria's house, the natural and probable consequences doctrine would extend Abel's accomplice liability to these crimes. If Abel is not in a natural and probable consequences jurisdiction, the trier of fact must separately determine that Abel had the criminal intent required to be an accomplice to *battery*, *burglary*, and *rape*; Abel's intent will be ascertained according to the jurisdiction's accomplice intent requirement—either **specific intent** or **purposely** or **general intent** or **knowingly**.

Figure 7.1 Diagram of Accomplice Liability

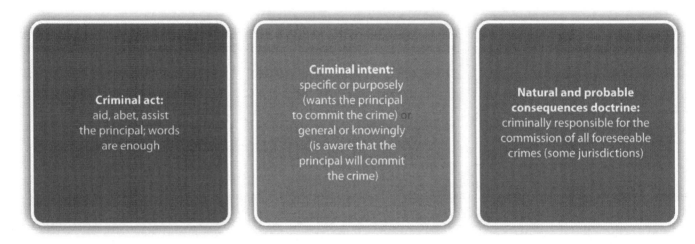

Consequences of Accomplice Liability

An accomplice is criminally responsible for the crime(s) the **principal** commits. Although the *sentencing* may vary based on a defendant-accomplice's criminal record or other extenuating circumstances related to sentencing, such as prior strikes, in theory, the accomplice is liable to the *same* degree as the principal. So if accomplice liability is established in the examples given in Section 7.1.2 "Accomplice Elements"; Phoebe is criminally responsible for battery and child endangerment, Joullian is criminally responsible for prostitution, and Abel is criminally responsible for battery and possibly burglary and rape. The **principal** should *also* be criminally responsible for his or her own actions. However, occasionally a situation arises where the principal is *not prosecuted* or *acquitted* because of a procedural technicality, evidentiary problems, or a plea bargain, as is discussed in Section 7 "Prosecution of an Accomplice When the Principal Is Not Prosecuted or Is Acquitted".

Prosecution of an Accomplice When the Principal Is Not Prosecuted or Is Acquitted

Although accomplice liability is derivative, in many jurisdictions the trier of fact can determine that a defendant is an accomplice even if the criminal actor or principal is not prosecuted or has been tried and acquitted for the offense (Standefer v. U.S., 2010). Thus a defendant can be liable for a crime even though he or she *did not* commit it and the defendant who *did* was spared prosecution or found *not guilty*. While this situation appears anomalous, if a defendant helps another commit a crime with the intent to further the crime's commission, punishment for the completed crime is appropriate. As the Model Penal Code states, "[a]n accomplice may be convicted on proof of the commission of the offense and of his complicity therein, though the person claimed to have committed the offense has not been prosecuted or convicted or has been convicted of a different offense or degree of offense...or has been acquitted" (Model Penal Code § 2.06(7)).

Example of Prosecution of an Accomplice When the Principal Is Not Prosecuted

Review the example in Section 7 "Example of the Natural and Probable Consequences Doctrine" with José and Abel. Assume that after José burglarizes, beats, and rapes Maria, local police arrest José and Abel. The police transport José and Abel to the police station and take them to separate rooms for interrogation. The police officer who interrogates José is a rookie and forgets to read José his Miranda rights. Thereafter, the police contact Maria, but she refuses to cooperate with the investigation because she fears reprisal from José. The district attorney decides not to prosecute José because of the tainted interrogation. In this case, Abel could *still be prosecuted* for battery and possibly rape and burglary as an accomplice in some jurisdictions. Although José is the **principal** and actually committed the crimes, it is not necessary for José to suffer the same criminal prosecution and punishment as Abel. If the elements required for accomplice liability are present, Abel can be fully responsible for the crimes *committed by José*, whether or not José is prosecuted for or convicted of these offenses.

Garrido Sentencing Video

Attorney: Nancy Garrido in Tears during Sentencing

Phillip Garrido, with his wife Nancy's help, kidnapped Jaycee Dugard, an eleven-year-old girl, and held her captive for eighteen years. During that time, Dugard was repeatedly raped, became pregnant twice, and gave birth to two children. Phillip Garrido pleaded guilty to multiple charges of rape and kidnapping and received a sentence of four hundred years to life in prison. Nancy was prosecuted as an accomplice, pleaded guilty and received a sentence of thirty-six years to life in prison (Martinez, M., 2011). Nancy Garrido's attorney discusses her sentencing as an **accomplice** in this video:
(click to see video)

Ghailani Verdict Video

Ghailani Guilty of One Count

Ahmed Ghailani, an alleged terrorist, was transferred from a military prison in Guantanamo Bay and tried as a civilian in a federal district court in New York. Ghailani was indicted for **accomplice liability** and conspiracy for the deaths of hundreds of citizens killed during Al Qaeda bombings of US embassies in Nairobi, Kenya, and Tanzania. At trial, the prosecution failed to convince the jury that Ghailani had the *criminal intent* required for accomplice liability. He was acquitted of the murders and attempted murders as an accomplice and convicted of one conspiracy charge. However, he received a sentence of life in prison without the possibility of parole for the conspiracy charge, the same sentence he would have received if convicted of all the murder and attempted murder charges (Weiser, B., 2011). A news story on the conviction of Ghailani is shown in this video:
(click to see video)

Key Takeaways

- The four parties to crime at early common law were principals in the first degree, principals in the second degree, accessories before the fact, and accessories after the fact. These designations signified the following:

- - Principals in the first degree committed the crime.
  - Principals in the second degree were present at the crime scene and assisted in the crime's commission.
  - Accessories before the fact were not present at the crime scene, but assisted in preparing for the crime's commission.
  - Accessories after the fact helped a party to the crime avoid detection and escape prosecution or conviction.
- In modern times, the parties to crime are principals and their accomplices, and accessories.
- The criminal act element required for accomplice liability is aiding, abetting, or assisting in the commission of a crime. In many jurisdictions, words are enough to constitute the accomplice criminal act element, while mere presence at the scene without a legal duty to act is not enough.
- The criminal intent element required for accomplice liability is either specific intent or purposely or general intent or knowingly.
- The natural and probable consequences doctrine holds an accomplice criminally responsible if the crime the principal commits is foreseeable when the accomplice assists the principal.
- The consequences of accomplice liability are that the accomplice is criminally responsible for the crimes the principal commits.
- In many jurisdictions, an accomplice can be prosecuted for an offense even if the principal is not prosecuted or is tried and acquitted.

Exercises

Answer the following questions. Check your answers using the answer key at the end of the chapter.

Justin asks his girlfriend Penelope, a bank teller, to let him know what time the security guard takes his lunch break so that he can successfully rob the bank. Penelope tells Justin the security guard takes his break at 1:00. The next day, which is Penelope's day off, Justin successfully robs the bank at 1:15. Has Penelope committed robbery? Why or why not?

Read *State v. Ulvinen*, 313 N.W.2d 425 (1981). In *Ulvinen*, the defendant sat guard and then helped her son clean up and dispose of evidence after he strangled and dismembered his wife. Thereafter, the defendant was convicted of murder as an accomplice. The defendant was asleep when the killing occurred, but before the killing her son told her that he planned to kill the victim. The defendant reacted with passive acquiescence by demurring and expressing disbelief that he would go through with his plans. Did the Supreme Court of Minnesota uphold the defendant's murder conviction? The case is available at this link:
http://scholar.google.com/scholar_case?case=5558442148317816782&hl=en&as_sdt=2&as_vis=1&oi=scholarr.

Read *Joubert v. State*, 235 SW 3d 729 (2007). In *Joubert*, the defendant was convicted and sentenced to death based on his participation in an armed robbery that resulted in the death of a police officer and employee. The jury convicted the defendant after hearing testimony from his accomplice and reviewing a video of the defendant confessing to the offense. The defendant appealed the conviction because in Texas, accomplice testimony must be corroborated by other evidence, and the defendant claimed that the other corroborating evidence was lacking in this case. Did the Court of Criminal Appeals of Texas uphold the defendant's conviction? Why or why not? The case is available at this link:
http://scholar.google.com/scholar_case?case=10119211983865864217&hl=en&as_sdt=2&as_vis=1&oi=scholarr.

References

Bogdanov v. People, 941 P.2d 247, 251 n. 8 (1997), accessed December 21, 2010, http://scholar.google.com/scholar_case?case=13910767150180460511&hl=en&as_sdt=2&as_vis=1&oi=scholarr #[8].

Cal. Penal Code § 31, accessed December 20, 2010,http://law.onecle.com/california/penal/31.html. and their accomplices.

Commonwealth v. Hargrave, 745 A.2d 20 (2000), accessed December 20, 2010, http://scholar.google.com/scholar_case?case=14481330811091769472&hl=en&as_sdt=2&as_vis=1&oi=scholarr.

Idaho Code Ann. § 18-205, accessed December 20, 2010, http://www.legislature.idaho.gov/idstat/Title18/T18CH2SECT18-205.htm.

K.S.A. § 21-3205, accessed December 20, 2010, http://kansasstatutes.lesterama.org/Chapter_21/Article_32/#21-3205.

Martinez, M., "Phillip, Nancy Garrido sentenced in Jaycee Dugard Kidnapping," CNN website, accessed August 15, 2011, http://articles.cnn.com/2011-06-02/justice/california.garridos.sentencing_1_jaycee-dugard-terry-probyn-phillip-garrido?_s=PM:CRIME.

ME Rev. Stat. Ann. tit. 17-A § 57 (3) (A), accessed December 21, 2010, http://www.mainelegislature.org/legis/statutes/17-a/title17-Asec57.html.

N.Y. Penal Law § 20.00, accessed December 26, 2010, http://law.onecle.com/new-york/penal/PEN020.00_20.00.html.

Or. Rev. Stat. § 161.155, accessed December 20, 2010, https://www.oregonlaws.org/ors/161.155.

People v. Lauria, 251 Cal. App. 2d 471 (1967), accessed December 21, 2010, http://scholar.google.com/scholar_case?case=686539897745974621&hl=en&as_sdt=2&as_vis=1&oi=scholarr.

People v. Rolon, 160 Cal. App. 4th 1206 (2008), accessed December 20, 2010, http://caselaw.findlaw.com/ca-court-of-appeal/1308666.html.

Standefer v. U.S., 447 U.S. 10 (1980), accessed December 22, 2010, http://scholar.google.com/scholar_case?case=11715693283858901517&hl=en&as_sdt=2&as_vis=1&oi=scholarr.

Washington Rev. Code Ann. § 9A.08.020 (3) (a), accessed December 21, 2010, http://apps.leg.wa.gov/rcw/default.aspx?cite=9A.08.020.

Weiser, B., "Ex-Detainee Gets Life Sentence in Embassy Blasts," *New York Times* website, accessed January 26, 2011, http://www.nytimes.com/2011/01/26/nyregion/26ghailani.html.

18 U.S.C. § 2, accessed December 20, 2010, http://codes.lp.findlaw.com/uscode/18/I/1/2.
CC licensed content, Shared previously

- Criminal Law. **Provided by**: University of Minnesota Libraries Publishing . **Located at**: http://open.lib.umn.edu/criminallaw/. **License**: *CC BY-NC-SA: Attribution-NonCommercial-ShareAlike*

7.2 Vicarious Liability

Learning Objectives

Distinguish between accomplice liability and vicarious liability.
Distinguish between corporate criminal vicarious liability and individual criminal vicarious liability.

Vicarious liability, a concept discussed in Chapter 4 "The Elements of a Crime", also transfers liability from one defendant to another. However, vicarious liability should not be confused with accomplice liability. Accomplice liability is based on the defendant's participation in a criminal enterprise and **complicity** with the criminal actor or principal, but vicarious liability transfers a defendant's criminal responsibility for the crime to a different defendant because of a *special relationship*. With vicarious liability, the acting defendant also is criminally responsible for his or her conduct. Similar to the civil law concept of respondeat superior discussed in Chapter 1 "Introduction to Criminal Law", vicarious liability in criminal law is common between employers and employees. It is also the basis of corporate liability, which is discussed in Section 7.2.1 "Corporate Liability".

Corporate Liability

At early common law, corporations were not criminally prosecutable as separate entities, which was most likely because in England, corporations were owned and operated by the government. In modern times, American corporations are private enterprises whose actions can seriously injure other individuals and the economy. Thus a corporation can be criminally responsible for conduct apart from its owners, agents, or employees (New York Central R. Co. v. U.S., 2010). In general, this is a **vicarious liability**, transferring criminal responsibility for an offense *from* an **agent** or **employee** of the corporation *to* the corporation itself, based on the employment relationship. Of course, the agent or employee also is responsible for the crime he or she commits.

A corporation is vicariously liable only if an agent or employee commits a crime *during* the agent or employee's scope of employment (720 ILCS, 2010). As the Model Penal Code states, "[a] corporation may be convicted of the commission of an offense if...the conduct is performed by an agent of the corporation acting in behalf of the corporation within the scope of his office or employment" (Model Penal Code § 2.07(1)(a)). The criminal punishment for a corporation is generally payment of a fine.

Example of Corporate Liability

Harry, an employee of Burger King Corporation, shreds corporate documents in his office when Burger King is sued civilly for sexual harassment in a multimillion-dollar class action suit. Under modern theories of corporate liability, both Harry and Burger King could be criminally prosecuted for obstruction of justice. Note that Burger King's liability is **vicarious** and depends on its relationship with Harry as an employer and the fact that Harry is acting within the scope of employment. Vicarious liability is distinguishable from **accomplice liability**, where the accomplice must be complicit with the criminal actor. The owners of Burger King, who are the corporate shareholders, did not actively participate in Harry's conduct, although they will share in the punishment if the corporation is fined.

Figure 7.2 Vicarious and Corporate Liability

Vicarious Liability		
Liability is imposed because of a special relationship	Corporate liability: the corporation is criminally liable for the actions of an agent or employee during the scope of employment	Employer-employee liability: the employer is criminally liable for the actions of an employee during the scope of employment

Individual Criminal Vicarious Liability

Generally speaking, criminal law disfavors **criminal vicarious liability**, the exception being corporate liability discussed in Section 7.2.1 "Corporate Liability". Criminal vicarious liability violates the basic precept that individuals should be criminally accountable for their own conduct, not the conduct of others (State v. Akers, 2010). Although accomplice liability appears to hold an accomplice responsible for principals' conduct, in reality the accomplice is committing a criminal act supported by criminal intent and is punished accordingly. In addition, other statutes that appear to impose criminal liability vicariously are actually holding individuals responsible for their *own* criminal conduct. Some examples are statutes holding **parents** criminally responsible when their **children** commit crimes that involve weapons belonging to the parents, and offenses criminalizing contributing to the delinquency of a minor. In both of these examples, the parents are held accountable for *their* conduct, such as allowing children to access their guns or be truant from school. The law is evolving in this area because the incidence of juveniles committing crimes is becoming increasingly prevalent.

Key Takeaways

- Accomplice liability holds an accomplice accountable when he or she is complicit with the principal; vicarious liability imposes criminal responsibility on a defendant because of a special relationship with the criminal actor.
- In many jurisdictions, corporations are vicariously liable for crimes committed by employees or agents acting within the scope of employment. Individual criminal vicarious liability is frowned on, but the law in this area is evolving as the incidence of juveniles committing crimes increases.

Exercises

Answer the following questions. Check your answers using the answer key at the end of the chapter.

Brad, the president and CEO of ABC Corporation, recklessly hits and kills a pedestrian as he is driving home from work. Could ABC Corporation be held vicariously liable for criminal homicide? Why or why not?

Read *People v. Premier House, Inc.*, 662 N.Y.S 2d 1006 (1997). In *Premier House*, the defendant, a housing cooperative that was incorporated, and members of the housing cooperative board of directors were ordered to stand trial for violating a New York law requiring that window guards be installed on apartment buildings. A child died after falling out of one of the windows. The members of the board of directors appealed on the basis that their positions were merely honorary, and they had no personal involvement in the crime. Did the Criminal Court of the City of New York uphold the order as to the members of the board of directors? Why or why not? The case is available at this link: http://scholar.google.com/scholar_case?case=6854365622778516089&hl=en&as_sdt=2&as_vis=1& oi=scholarr.

Read Connecticut General Statute § 53a-8(b), which criminalizes the sale or provision of a firearm to another for the purpose of committing a crime. The statute is available at this link: http://law.justia.com/connecticut/codes/2005/title53a/sec53a-8.html. Does this statute create **accomplice liability** or **vicarious liability**? Read the Connecticut Criminal Jury Instruction 3.1-4 for an explanation of the statute. The jury instruction is available at this link: http://www.jud.ct.gov/ji/criminal/part3/3.1-4.htm.

Law and Ethics: Life Care Centers of America, Inc.

Is a Corporation Criminally Accountable When Its Employees Are Not?

Read *Commonwealth v. Life Care Centers of America, Inc.*, 456 Mass. 826 (2010). The case is available at this link: http://scholar.google.com/scholar_case?case=12168070317136071651&hl=en&as_sdt=2&as_vis=1&oi=sc holarr. In *Life Care Centers*, a resident of the Life Care Center nursing home died in 2004 from injuries sustained when she fell down the front stairs while attempting to leave the facility in her wheelchair. The resident could try to leave the facility because she was not wearing a prescribed security bracelet that both set off an alarm and temporarily locked the front doors if a resident approached within a certain distance of those doors. The defendant, Life Care Centers of America, Inc., a corporation that operates the nursing home, was indicted for involuntary manslaughter and criminal neglect (Gillespie, G. G. & Scammon, K. S., 2011). The criminal intent element required for involuntary manslaughter and criminal neglect in Massachusetts is **reckless** intent. The evidence indicated that the order requiring the victim to wear a security bracelet was *negligently* edited out of the victim's treatment sheet, based on the actions of more than one employee. The individual employee who left the victim near the stairs without the security bracelet relied on the orders that did not indicate a need for the bracelet. There was no evidence that any *individual* employee of Life Care Centers of America, Inc. was **reckless**. The prosecution introduced a theory of "collective knowledge" of the actions or failure to act of the corporation's employees. The prosecution's premise was that the several individual instances of negligent conduct combined to create reckless conduct that could be imputed to the corporation vicariously. The Massachusetts Supreme Court unanimously held that the corporation *could not* be held criminally responsible unless *one individual employee* could be held criminally responsible (Commonwealth v. Life Care Centers of America, Inc., 2011).

Do you think it is *ethical* to allow a corporation to escape criminal responsibility for reckless involuntary manslaughter and criminal neglect when several employees' negligent conduct caused the death, rather than one employee's reckless conduct? Why or why not?

Check your answer using the answer key at the end of the chapter.

References

Commonwealth v. Life Care Centers of America, Inc., 456 Mass. 826 (2010), accessed January 24, 2011, http://scholar.google.com/scholar_case?case=12168070317136071651&hl=en&as_sdt=2&as_vis=1&oi=scholarr.

Gillespie, G. G. & Kristen S. Scammon, "SJC Limits Corporate Criminal Liability," Martindale.com website, accessed January 24, 2011, http://www.martindale.com/corporate-law/article_Mintz-Levin-Cohn-Ferris-Glovsky-Popeo-PC_1047124.htm.

New York Central R. Co. v. U.S., 212 U.S. 481 (1909), accessed December 21, 2010, http://supreme.justia.com/us/212/481.

State v. Akers, 400 A.2d 38 (1979), accessed December 26, 2010, http://scholar.google.com/scholar_case?case=12639244883487184852&hl=en&as_sdt=2&as_vis=1&oi=scholarr.

720 ILCS § 5/5-4, accessed December 26, 2010, http://law.onecle.com/illinois/720ilcs5/5-4.html.
CC licensed content, Shared previously

- Criminal Law. **Provided by**: University of Minnesota Libraries Publishing . **Located at**: http://open.lib.umn.edu/criminallaw/. **License**: *CC BY-NC-SA: Attribution-NonCommercial-ShareAlike*

7.3 Accessory

Learning Objectives

Distinguish between accomplice liability and the crime of accessory.
Define the criminal act element required for an accessory.
Define the criminal intent element required for an accessory.
Compare various approaches to grading the crime of accessory.

As stated in Section 7.1.1 "Accomplice Liability", at early common law, a defendant who helped plan the offense but was not present at the scene when the principal committed the crime was an **accessory before the fact**. A defendant who helped the principal avoid detection after the principal committed the crime was an **accessory after the fact**. In modern times, an accessory before the fact is an **accomplice**, and an accessory after the fact is an accessory, which is a separate and distinct offense. Some states still call the crime of accessory "accessory after the fact" (Mass. Gen. Laws ch. 274, 2011) or "hindering prosecution" (Haw. Rev. Stat., 2011).

The difference between an accomplice and an accessory is crucial. An accomplice is responsible for the offense the *principal* commits. An accessory, on the other hand, is guilty of a *separate crime* that is almost always a misdemeanor.

Accessory Act

The **criminal act** element required for an accessory in the majority of jurisdictions is aiding or assisting a principal in escape, concealment, or evasion of arrest and prosecution or conviction after the principal commits a **felony** (Va. Code Ann., 2010). In most states, a defendant cannot be an accessory to a misdemeanor, although in some states a defendant can be an accessory to a high-level or gross misdemeanor (N.R.S., 2010). In a minority of states, the defendant can be an accessory to any crime (Haw. Rev. Stat., 2011).

In many states, **words** are enough to constitute the accessory criminal act element (Minn. Stat. Ann., 2010). Often special categories of individuals are exempted from liability as an accessory, typically family members by blood or marriage (Vt. Stat. Ann. tit. 13, 2010).

Example of Accessory Act

Jim wakes up late at night to the sound of someone pounding on his door. He gets out of bed, walks down the stairs, and opens the door. His father James is on the doorstep. James's eyes are bloodshot and he is swaying slightly on his feet. He tells Jim that he just got into a car accident and needs to come inside before the police find out about it and begin an investigation. Jim steps aside and lets his father enter the house. The smell of alcohol on his father's breath is apparent. He thereafter allows his father to spend the night without contacting the police about the accident.

Jim has probably committed the **criminal act** element required for an accessory in many jurisdictions. Jim allowed his father to *escape arrest* and *evade* an alcohol screening after leaving the scene of a car accident, which is most likely **felony** drunk driving and hit and run. He also sheltered his father for the night, *concealing* him from law enforcement. If Jim is in a state that exempts family members from accessory liability, he may not be subject to prosecution because the principal to the crime(s) is his father. If Jim is not in a state that relieves family members

---

from accessory liability, he could be fully prosecuted for and convicted of this offense.

Figure 7.3 Crack the Code

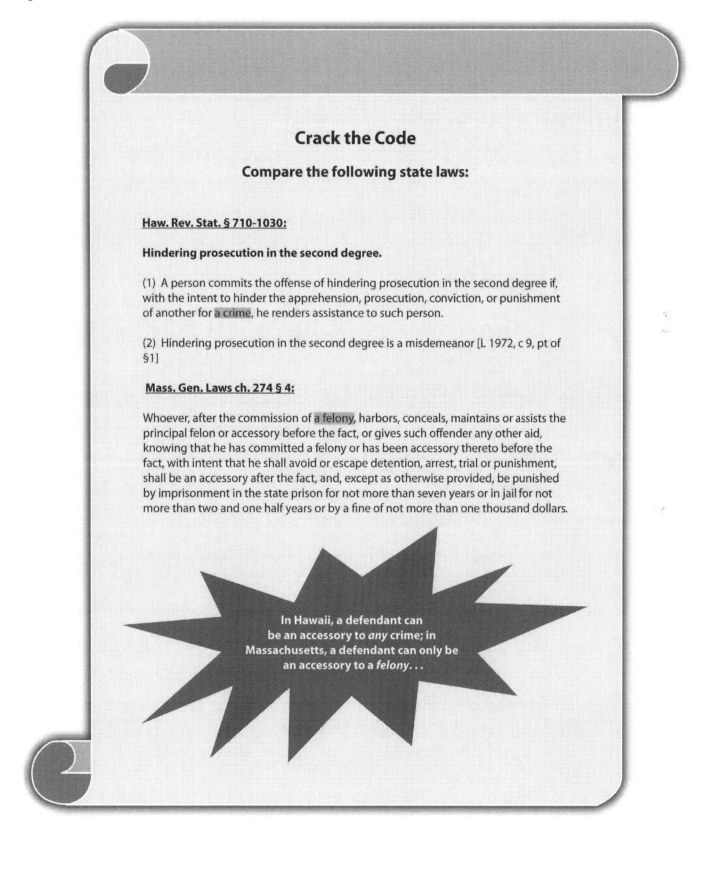

Crack the Code

Compare the following state laws:

Haw. Rev. Stat. § 710-1030:

Hindering prosecution in the second degree.

(1) A person commits the offense of hindering prosecution in the second degree if, with the intent to hinder the apprehension, prosecution, conviction, or punishment of another for a crime, he renders assistance to such person.

(2) Hindering prosecution in the second degree is a misdemeanor [L 1972, c 9, pt of §1]

Mass. Gen. Laws ch. 274 § 4:

Whoever, after the commission of a felony, harbors, conceals, maintains or assists the principal felon or accessory before the fact, or gives such offender any other aid, knowing that he has committed a felony or has been accessory thereto before the fact, with intent that he shall avoid or escape detention, arrest, trial or punishment, shall be an accessory after the fact, and, except as otherwise provided, be punished by imprisonment in the state prison for not more than seven years or in jail for not more than two and one half years or by a fine of not more than one thousand dollars.

In Hawaii, a defendant can be an accessory to *any* crime; in Massachusetts, a defendant can only be an accessory to a *felony*...

Accessory Intent

The criminal intent element required for an accessory has two parts. First, the defendant must act with **general intent** or **knowingly** or *awareness* that the principal committed a crime. Second, the defendant must help or assist the principal escape or evade arrest or prosecution for and conviction of the offense with **specific intent** or **purposely** (Mass. Gen. Laws ch. 274, 2010).

Example of Accessory Intent

Review the example with Jim and James given in Section 7 "Example of Accessory Act". In this case, Jim is **aware** that James committed a crime because James told Jim he got into an accident and James's intoxicated condition was apparent. Nonetheless, Jim **purposely** helped James evade arrest and an alcohol screening by sheltering him in his home while the effects of the alcohol dissipated. Thus Jim probably has the **criminal intent** required for liability as an accessory in most jurisdictions. If Jim is not in a state that exempts family members from accessory liability, he could be fully subject to prosecution for and conviction of this offense.

Accessory Grading

As stated in Section 7.3 "Accessory", in many jurisdictions accessory is an offense that is **graded** less severely than the crime committed by the principal. Accessory is typically graded as a misdemeanor (Haw. Rev. Stat., 2011), although in some jurisdictions it is graded as a felony (Idaho Code Ann., 2011).

Table 7.1 Comparison of Accomplice, Accessory, and Vicarious Liability

Type of Liability	Criminal Act	Criminal Intent
Accomplice	Aid, assist commission of a crime	Specific or purposely, or general or knowingly, depending on the jurisdiction
Accessory	Aid, assist evasion of prosecution or conviction for a felony, high-level misdemeanor, or any crime	General or knowingly (crime committed) plus specific or purposely (principal evades prosecution or conviction)
Vicarious	Committed by an individual in a special relationship with the defendant	Belongs to an individual in a special relationship with the defendant

Figure 7.4 Diagram of Parties to Crime

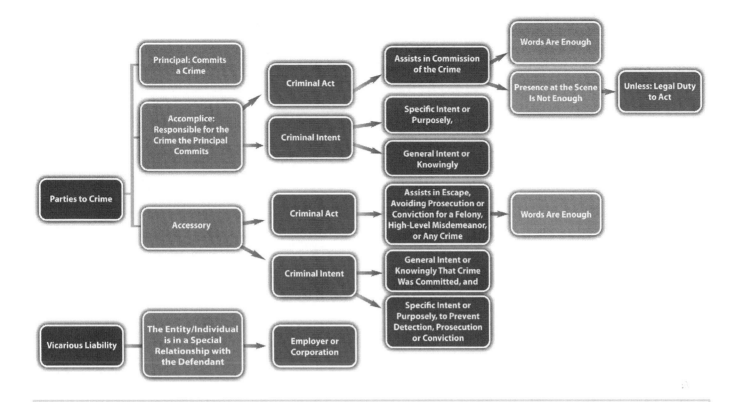

Key Takeaways

- Accomplice liability holds a complicit defendant accountable for the crime the principal commits; accessory is a separate crime that is typically a misdemeanor.
- The criminal act element required for an accessory is aiding or assisting the principal escape or evade arrest, prosecution for, or conviction of a felony, high-level misdemeanor, or any crime, depending on the jurisdiction. In many jurisdictions words are enough to constitute the accessory criminal act element.

- The criminal intent element required for an accessory has two parts. The defendant must act
    - with general intent or knowingly that the principal committed the crime,
    - with specific intent or purposely to help the principal escape or evade arrest, prosecution for, or conviction of the offense.
- In many jurisdictions, the crime of accessory is graded lower than the crime the principal committed; typically, it is graded as a misdemeanor, although in some jurisdictions, it is graded as a felony.

Exercises

Answer the following questions. Check your answers using the answer key at the end of the chapter.

Cory watches as her sister Amanda breaks into a parking meter across the street and starts scooping change into her purse. Amanda thereafter runs into a nearby alley and hides behind a dumpster. A police officer arrives on the scene and asks Cory if she witnessed the crime. Cory responds, "No, I didn't notice anything." The police officer does a search, does not find Amanda, and leaves. Has Cory committed a crime? If your answer is yes, which crime has Cory committed, and does Cory have a possible defense?

Read *U.S. v. Hill*, 268 F.3d 1140 (2001). In *Hill*, the defendant was convicted of harboring a fugitive and being an accessory when she helped her husband escape the country to avoid prosecution for a failure to pay child support. The defendant claimed that her convictions were unconstitutional because they contravened her right to privacy, association, marriage, and due process. Did the US

Court of Appeals for the Ninth Circuit uphold the defendant's convictions? The case is available at this link: http://caselaw.findlaw.com/us-9th-circuit/1215479.html.

Read *State v. Truesdell*, 620 P.2d 427 (1980). In *Truesdell*, the prosecution appealed the dismissal of the defendant's case that was a prosecution for accessory to her twelve-year-old son's felony shooting of her ex-husband. The lower court held that the defendant could not be an accessory to a felony because her son was not an adult who could be charged with a felony. Did the Oklahoma Court of Criminal Appeals reverse the lower court and permit the defendant to be tried as an accessory? Why or why not? The case is available at this link: http://scholar.google.com/scholar_case?case=14038267185437754114&q= State+v.+Truesdell+620+P.2d+427+%281980%29&hl=en&as_sdt=2,5.

References

Haw. Rev. Stat. § 710-1030, accessed January 26, 2011, http://law.justia.com/codes/hawaii/2009/volume-14/title-37/chapter-710/hrs-0710-1030-htm/.

Idaho Code Ann. § 18-206, accessed January 9, 2011, http://www.legislature.idaho.gov/idstat/Title18/T18CH2SECT18-206.htm.

Mass. Gen. Laws ch. 274 § 4, accessed January 16, 2011, http://law.onecle.com/massachusetts/274/4.html.

Minn. Stat. Ann. § 609.495, accessed December 23, 2010, https://www.revisor.mn.gov/statutes/?id=609.495&year=2010.

N.R.S. § 195.030, accessed December 26, 2010, http://law.onecle.com/nevada/crimes/195.030.html.

Va. Code Ann. § 18.2-19, accessed December 26, 2010, http://law.onecle.com/virginia/crimes-and-offenses-generally/18.2-19.html.

Vt. Stat. Ann. tit. 13 § 5, accessed December 23, 2010, http://www.leg.state.vt.us/statutes/fullchapter.cfm?Title=13&Chapter=001.
CC licensed content, Shared previously

- Criminal Law. **Provided by**: University of Minnesota Libraries Publishing . **Located at**: http://open.lib.umn.edu/criminallaw/. **License**: *CC BY-NC-SA: Attribution-NonCommercial-ShareAlike*

7.4 End-of-Chapter Material

Summary

Often more than one criminal defendant participates in the commission of a crime. Defendants working together with a common criminal purpose are acting with complicity and are responsible for the same crimes, to the same degree.

At early common law, there were four parties to a crime. A principal in the first degree actually committed the crime. A principal in the second degree was present at the crime scene and assisted in the crime's commission. An accessory before the fact was not present at the crime scene but helped prepare for the crime's commission. An accessory after the fact helped a party after he or she committed a crime by providing aid in escaping or avoiding arrest and prosecution or conviction. In modern times, there are only two parties to a crime: a principal, who is in the same category with his or her accomplice(s), and accessory(ies). Principals actually commit the crime, and they and their accomplices are criminally responsible for it. Accessories play the same role as accessories after the fact at common law.

The criminal act element required to be an accomplice in most jurisdictions is assistance in the commission of a crime. Words are enough to constitute the accomplice criminal act. Mere presence at the scene, even presence at the scene combined with flight after the crime's commission, is not enough to constitute the accomplice criminal act unless there is a legal duty to act.

The criminal intent element required for accomplice liability in many jurisdictions is specific intent or purposely to commit the crime at issue. In some states, general intent or knowingly that the principal will commit the crime creates an inference of intent if the offense is serious. In a minority of jurisdictions, general intent or knowingly that the principal will commit the crime is sufficient.

The natural and probable consequences doctrine holds accomplices criminally responsible for all crimes the principal commits that are reasonably foreseeable. In many jurisdictions an accomplice can be prosecuted for a crime the principal commits even if the principal is not prosecuted or acquitted.

Vicarious liability transfers criminal responsibility from one party to another because of a special relationship. Vicarious liability is common between employers and employees and is the basis for corporate criminal liability. Pursuant to modern corporate criminal liability, a corporation can be fined for a crime(s) a corporate agent or employee commits during the scope of employment. The corporate agent or employee also is criminally responsible for his or her conduct. In general, the law disfavors individual criminal vicarious liability. The law in this area is evolving as the incidence of juveniles committing crimes increases.

In modern times, an accessory is the equivalent of an accessory after the fact at common law. The criminal act element required for an accessory is providing assistance to a principal in escape, avoiding detection, or arrest and prosecution, or conviction for the commission of a felony, high-level misdemeanor, or any crime, depending on the jurisdiction. Words are enough to constitute the accessory criminal act. Several jurisdictions exempt family members from criminal responsibility for acting as an accessory.

The criminal intent element required for an accessory in most jurisdictions is general intent or knowingly that the principal committed a crime, and specific intent or purposely that the principal escape, avoid detection, or arrest and prosecution, or conviction for the offense. Accessory is a separate crime that is usually graded as a misdemeanor, although some jurisdictions grade accessory as a felony.

You Be the Law Professor

You are a law professor searching for cases to illustrate certain legal concepts for your students. Read the prompt, review the case, and then decide which **legal concept** it represents. Check your answers using the answer key at the end of the chapter.

The defendant's vehicle matched the description of a vehicle seen in the vicinity of a burglary before the burglary, during the burglary, and after the burglary. The defendant claimed that the evidence was insufficient to prove he was an accomplice to the burglary. Does this case illustrate the legal concept of **accomplice act**, **accomplice intent**, or **both**? Read *Collins v. State*, 438 So. 2d 1036 (1983). The case is available at this link:
http://scholar.google.com/scholar_case?case=8573128029213310764&hl=en&as_sdt=2,5&as_vis=1
.

The defendants, foster parents, were found guilty as accomplices to the felony murder of their two-year-old foster daughter. Although both defendants testified that the victim died from injuries experienced after a fall from a swing, medical experts reported that the victim's injuries were inconsistent with that testimony and appeared to be the result of child abuse. The jury convicted the defendants as accomplices to felony murder after a jury instruction stating that an omission to act could constitute the criminal act element for accomplice liability when there is a duty to act, and parents have a legal duty to come to the aid of their children. Does this case illustrate the legal concept of **omission to act**, **statutory interpretation**, or **both**? Read *State v. Jackson*, 137 Wn. 2d 712 (1999). The case is available at this link:
http://caselaw.findlaw.com/wa-supreme-court/1412039.html.

The defendant, an electrical contracting company, was found guilty of violating OSHA regulations that led to an employee's death. The victim, an apprentice in training, touched a live electrical wire and died from electrocution. The OSHA statute in question required "willful" conduct on behalf of the company. The jury instruction on willful stated that a company acted willfully or knowingly if individual employees of that company acted knowingly. The evidence indicated that some employees knew or were aware of live wiring in the vicinity of the accident. The defendant appealed and claimed that the jury instruction should have stated that a company acted willfully or knowingly if individual employees acted knowingly *and* had a *duty to report* that knowledge to the company. Does this case illustrate the legal concept of **criminal intent**, **vicarious liability**, or **both**? Read *U.S. v. L.E. Meyers Co.*, 562 F.3d 845 (2009). The case is available at this link:
http://scholar.google.com/scholar_case?case=2854285863509787279&hl=en&as_sdt=2&as_vis=1&oi=scholarr.

The defendant was convicted of both first-degree murder and accessory after the fact to that murder. The trial court did not instruct the jury that the offenses were mutually exclusive and that they could only convict the defendant of one or the other. The defendant appealed on the basis that he was entitled to a jury instruction that prevented a conviction on both murder and accessory after the fact to murder. Does this case illustrate the legal concept of the **criminal elements required for accessory after the fact**, the **criminal elements required for murder**, or **both**? Read *State v. Melvin*, No. 382PA09 (North Carolina 2010). The case is available at this link:
http://caselaw.findlaw.com/nc-supreme-court/1549865.html.

Cases of Interest

- *State v. Merida-Medina*, 191 P.3d 708 (2008), discusses accomplice liability:
  http://scholar.google.com/scholar_case?case=9533921177591527482&hl=en&as_sdt=2&as_vis=1&oi=scholarr.
- *State v. Guminga*, 395 N.W.2d 344 (1986), discusses vicarious liability and due process:
  http://scholar.google.com/scholar_case?case=9718401866480992202&hl=en&as_sdt=2&as_vis=1&oi=scholarr.
- *Staten v. State*, 519 So. 2d 622 (1988), discusses principal and accessory criminal responsibility:
  http://scholar.google.com/scholar_case?case=5691885691013540689&hl=en&as_sdt=2&as_vis=1&oi=scholarr.

Articles of Interest

- Spectator liability in gang rape: http://papers.ssrn.com/sol3/papers.cfm?abstract_id=1664162
- Corporate criminal liability: http://www.pointoflaw.com/feature/archives/2009/07/corporate-criminal-liability-s.php
- Criminal vicarious liability in general: http://www.lectlaw.com/mjl/cl048.htm

Website of Interest

- White collar crime blog site: http://lawprofessors.typepad.com/whitecollarcrime_blog/2009/12/recent-articles.html

Statistics of Interest

- FBI statistics on pending corporate and securities fraud cases: http://www.fbi.gov/stats-services/publications/financial-crimes-report-2009/financial-crimes-report-2009#corporate

References

Joubert v. State, 235 SW3d 729, 731 (2007), accessed January 22, 2011, http://scholar.google.com/scholar_case?case=10119211983865864217&hl=en&as_sdt=2&as_vis=1&oi=scholarr. CC licensed content, Shared previously

- Criminal Law. **Provided by**: University of Minnesota Libraries Publishing . **Located at**: http://open.lib.umn.edu/criminallaw/. **License**: *CC BY-NC-SA: Attribution-NonCommercial-ShareAlike*

Chapter 8: Inchoate Offenses

8.1 Attempt

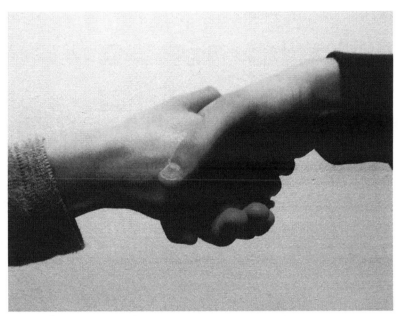

Chris-Håvard Berge – Shaking hands – CC BY-NC 2.0.

And so long as the partnership in crime continues, the partners act for each other in carrying it forward.

—*Pinkerton v. U.S.*, cited in Section 8.2.4 "Consequences of Conspiracy"

Learning Objectives

Define an inchoate crime.
Distinguish between general and specific attempt statutes.
Identify and describe the four tests jurisdictions use to ascertain the criminal act element required for attempt.
Define preparatory crimes.
Define the criminal intent element required for attempt.
Identify two potential defenses to attempt.
Distinguish between factual and legal impossibility.
Define voluntary abandonment.
Describe merger and explain the way it affects attempt crimes.
Analyze the relationship between transferred intent and attempt.
Distinguish between the grading of attempt and the completed crime.

Attempt, conspiracy, and solicitation are considered inchoate crimes. **Inchoate** means "just begun, incipient, in the early stages" (Yourdictionary.com, 2010). Inchoate crimes can be left unfinished, or incomplete. Although attempt never results in the finished criminal offense, both conspiracy and solicitation could give rise to separate completed crimes.

The rationale supporting punishment for an inchoate crime is **prevention** and **deterrence**. If a defendant could not be apprehended until a crime is finished, law enforcement would not be able to intervene and avert injury to victim(s) or property. In addition, a defendant who is unable to complete a crime would try again and again, free from any criminal consequences.

The difficulty in holding a defendant accountable for an inchoate or incomplete crime is ascertaining the *level of progress* necessary to impute criminal responsibility, which is especially daunting with **attempt**, because in every instance the crime is left unfinished, as is discussed in Section 8.1 "Attempt".

Synopsis of the History of Attempt

At early English common law, attempt was not a crime (Schulhofer, S. J. and Kahan, D. M., 2010). Gradually, the law evolved, and a defendant who committed attempt resulting in severe harm was punished for a minor crime, typically a misdemeanor. One of the first documented cases of attempt was *Rex v. Scofield*, Cald. 397 (1784) (Schulhofer, S. J. and Kahan, D. M., 2010). In *Scofield*, a servant was convicted of a misdemeanor for attempting to burn down his master's house with a lighted candle. A subsequent case, *Rex v. Higgins*, 102 Eng. Rep. 269 (K.B. 1801), upheld an indictment for attempted theft and firmly established the crime of attempt in English jurisprudence. In modern times, most states criminalize attempt, the majority in statutes, except in some states that permit common-law crimes. However, even in statutes, the word "attempt" is often left undefined, forcing courts to derive the meaning from common-law principles.

Attempt Statutes

In general, there are two types of attempt statutes. Some states have **general** attempt statutes that set forth attempt elements and apply them to *any* criminal offense (Tex. Penal Code, 2010). Other states and the federal government have **specific** attempt statutes that define attempt according to *specified* crimes, such as murder, robbery, or rape (18 U.S.C., 2011). Keep in mind that several states do not criminalize attempt in a statute and consider it a common-law crime (Grill v. State, 2010).

Attempt Act

The **criminal act** element required for attempt varies, depending on the jurisdiction. As Chapter 4 "The Elements of a Crime" stated, **thoughts** are *not* criminal acts. Thus a defendant does not commit attempt by plotting or planning an offense. An extension of this rule dictates that mere preparation is not enough to constitute the attempt criminal act element (People v. Luna, 2010). However, the crux of any attempt case is *how close* to completing the offense the defendant must get to fulfill the attempt criminal act requirement. In many statutes and cases, the attempt act is loosely defined to allow the trier of fact the flexibility needed to separate true criminal attempt from noncriminal preparation.

Jurisdictions use four tests to ascertain whether the defendant has committed the attempt criminal act: proximity test, res ipsa loquitur test, probable desistance test, and the Model Penal Code's substantial steps test.

Proximity Test

The **proximity test** measures the defendant's progress by examining how close the defendant is to completing the offense. The distance measured is the distance between preparation for the offense and successful termination. It is the amount *left to be done*, not what has *already been done*, that is analyzed (Commonwealth v. Hamel, 2010). In some jurisdictions, if the defendant's criminal intent is clear, the defendant does not need to come as close to completion of the offense (People v. Dillon, 2010). Generally, the defendant does not have to reach the last step before completion (People v. Dillon, 2010), although many defendants do.

Example of the Proximity Test

Melissa and Matthew decide they want to poison their neighbor's dog because it barks loudly and consistently every night. Melissa buys some rat poison at the local hardware store. Matthew coats a raw filet mignon with the poison and throws it over the fence into the neighbor's yard. Fortuitously, the neighbors are on an overnight camping trip, and the dog is with them. The next day, after a night of silence, Melissa feels regret and climbs over the fence to see what happened to the dog. When she sees the filet untouched on the ground, she picks it up and takes it back over the fence, later disposing of it in the trash. If Melissa and Matthew are in a jurisdiction that follows the **proximity test**, Melissa and Matthew have probably committed the criminal act element required for attempt. Melissa and Matthew finished *every act* necessary to commit the crime of destruction of property or animal cruelty (poisoning the dog). The only reason the crime was not successfully consummated was the absence of the dog, which is a circumstance outside their control. Thus Melissa and Matthew could most likely be charged with and convicted of this offense. If Melissa bought the rat poison but thereafter changed her mind and talked Matthew out of poisoning the dog, her actions would be a *preparation*, not a positive step toward commission of the crime. If Matthew coated the filet with poison but then changed his mind and threw the filet away, he would still be "too far" away from completing the offense. However, once the filet is thrown over the fence, the crime is *proximate* to completion; the only step left is the victim's (dog's) participation.

Res Ipsa Loquitur Test

Res ipsa loquitur means "the thing speaks for itself" (USLegal.com, 2010). The res ipsa loquitur test, also called the **unequivocality test**, analyzes the facts of each case independently. Under res ipsa loquitur or unequivocality, the trier of fact must determine that at the moment the defendant *stopped* progressing toward completion of the offense, it was clear that the defendant had *no other purpose* than commission of the specific crime at issue. This determination is based on the defendant's act—which manifests the intent to commit the crime (Hamiel v. Wisconsin, 2010).

Example of the Res Ipsa Loquitur Test

Harry wants to kill his wife Ethel for the proceeds of her life insurance policy. Harry contacts his friend Joe, who is reputed to be a "hit man," and sets up a meeting for the next day. Harry meets with Joe and asks him if he will murder Ethel for one thousand dollars. Joe agrees, and Harry pulls out a wad of cash and pays him. Unfortunately for Harry, Joe is a law enforcement decoy. If the state in which Harry paid Joe recognizes the **res ipsa loquitur** or **unequivocality test**, Harry has most likely committed attempted murder (along with **solicitation** to commit murder, which is discussed shortly). Harry's *actions* in contacting and thereafter hiring and paying Joe to kill Ethel indicate that he has no other purpose than the commission of Ethel's murder. Hiring and paying a hit man is more than just *preparation*. Note that evidence of Ethel's life insurance policy is not needed to prove the attempt act. Harry's conduct "speaks for itself," which is the essence of res ipsa loquitur or unequivocality.

Probable Desistance Test

The **probable desistance test** examines *how far* the defendant has progressed toward commission of the crime, rather than analyzing *how much* the defendant has left to accomplish. Pursuant to this test, a defendant commits attempt when he or she has crossed a line beyond which it is **probable** he or she will not **desist** unless there is an interruption from some outside source, law enforcement, or circumstances beyond his or her control (U.S. v. Mandujano, 2010).

Example of the Probable Desistance Test

Judy, who works at Zales jewelry store, tells her Facebook friends that she is going to steal a diamond necklace out of the safe that evening. Judy drives to Zales at eleven o'clock after the store has closed. She enters the building using her key and quickly disables the store alarm. She then turns off the store security camera. As she crouches down by the safe and begins to enter the combination, all the lights go on and she blinks, startled by the sight of several police officers pointing their guns at her. If the state in which Judy lives follows the **probable desistance** test, Judy has most likely committed attempted larceny, along with burglary. Judy informed others of her plan, drove to the crime scene, entered the building unlawfully, disabled the store alarm, and turned off the store security camera. This series of actions indicate that Judy crossed a point of no return. It is unlikely that Judy would have *desisted* without the law enforcement interruption, which fulfills the attempt act requirement pursuant to the probable desistance test.

Model Penal Code Substantial Steps Test

The Model Penal Code developed the **substantial steps** test in response to the large variance between different jurisdictions in evaluating the criminal act element required for attempt. The substantial steps test is intended to clarify and simplify the attempt act analysis, to prevent *arbitrary* application. It is also a test that is more likely to result in a conviction because it classifies as "substantial" those acts the other tests might consider only "preparatory" (People v. Dillon, 2011).

The substantial steps test has two parts. First, the defendant must take substantial steps toward completion of the crime. As the Model Penal Code states, "[a] person is guilty of an attempt to commit a crime if...he...does...anything which...is an act or omission constituting a substantial step in a course of conduct planned to culminate in his commission of the crime" (Model Penal Code § 5.01(1)(c)). Second, the defendant's actions must be "strongly corroborative of the actor's criminal purpose" (Model Penal Code § 5.01(2)). To further elucidate the test, the Model Penal Code provides seven examples of actions that constitute **substantial steps**, as long as they are *corroborative of* the defendant's *intent*. The seven examples are lying in wait; enticing the victim to go to the scene of the crime; investigating the potential scene of the crime; unlawfully entering a structure or vehicle where the crime is to be committed; possessing materials that are specially designed for unlawful use; possessing, collecting, or fabricating materials to be used in the crime's commission; and soliciting an innocent agent to commit the crime (Model Penal Code § 5.01(2)).

Example of the Substantial Steps Test

Kevin wants to rob an armored car that delivers cash to the local bank. After casing the bank for two months and determining the date and time that the car makes its delivery, Kevin devises a plan that he types on his computer. On the date of the next delivery, Kevin hides a weapon in his jacket pocket and makes his way on foot to the bank. Thereafter, he hides in an alley and waits for the truck to arrive. When the truck drives up and parks in front of the bank, Kevin walks over to the driver's door and reaches for his weapon. He is immediately apprehended by a security guard who saw him emerge from the alley. If Kevin is in a **substantial steps** jurisdiction, he has probably committed the criminal act element required for attempt. Kevin cased the bank, planned the robbery, showed up on the appointed date and time with a concealed weapon, and hid in an alley to wait for the truck to appear. These actions are (1) investigating the potential scene of the crime, (2) possessing materials to be used in the crime's commission, and (3) lying in wait. Thus Kevin has completed *three* substantial steps that corroborate his intent as expressed in the plan he typed, which is most likely sufficient to constitute the attempt criminal act element under the Model Penal Code.

Figure 8.1 Various Tests for Attempt Act

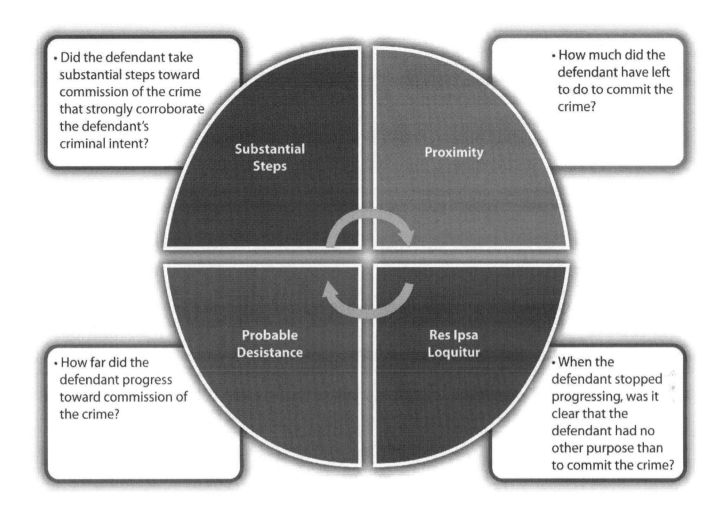

Figure 8.2 Crack the Code

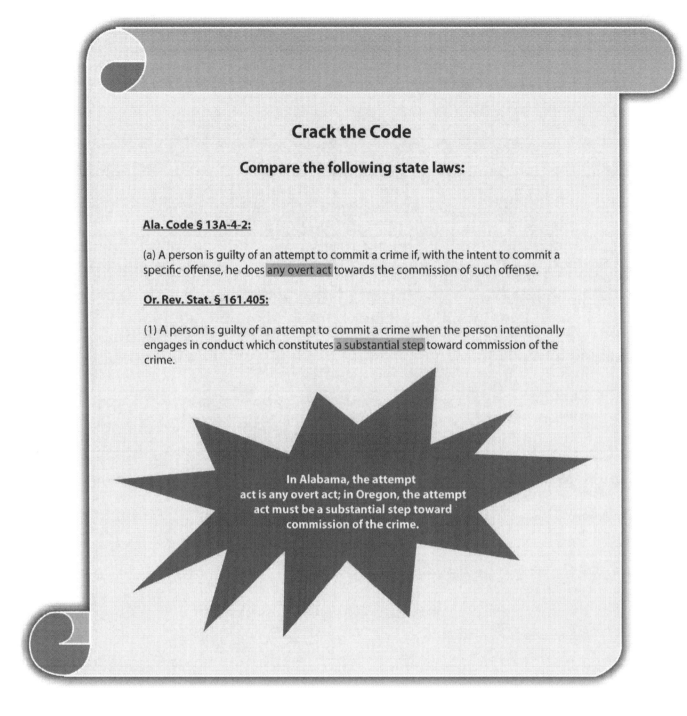

Crack the Code

Compare the following state laws:

Ala. Code § 13A-4-2:

(a) A person is guilty of an attempt to commit a crime if, with the intent to commit a specific offense, he does any overt act towards the commission of such offense.

Or. Rev. Stat. § 161.405:

(1) A person is guilty of an attempt to commit a crime when the person intentionally engages in conduct which constitutes a substantial step toward commission of the crime.

In Alabama, the attempt act is any overt act; in Oregon, the attempt act must be a substantial step toward commission of the crime.

Preparatory Crimes

Some states have statutes criminalizing behavior that would be considered *preparatory* under any of the four attempt act tests. For example, some statutes prohibit the mere *possession* of burglar's tools (N.Y. Penal Law, 2010) or even the *manufacture* of burglar's tools (Conn. Gen. Stat., 2010). A defendant could be convicted of a preparatory crime *and attempt* if the criminal act element for both is present under the circumstances.

Example of a Preparatory Crime and Attempt

Hal manufactures a lock pick and takes it to the local coin shop, which is closed. Hal takes the lock pick out and begins to insert it into the coin shop doorknob. A security guard apprehends Hal before he is able to pick the lock.

If Hal is in a jurisdiction that prohibits the manufacture of burglar's tools, he probably could be charged with and convicted of manufacture of burglar's tools *and* attempted burglary because he has committed the criminal act element required for both of these offenses.

Attempt Intent

The criminal intent element required for attempt in the majority of jurisdictions is the **specific intent** or **purposely** to commit the crime at issue (N.Y. Penal Law, 2010). Generally, no such thing exists as *reckless* or *negligent* attempt. Thus if the prosecution fails to prove beyond a reasonable doubt that the defendant acted purposefully with intent to commit the crime attempted, this could operate as a **failure of proof defense**.

Example of a Case Lacking Attempt Intent

Eric is hiking in a jurisdiction that criminalizes **reckless** burning. Eric pauses in front of a sign that states "Fire Danger Today: High." Eric reads the sign, pulls out a cigarette, lights it, and throws the lit match into some dry brush near the sign. He starts hiking and when he finishes his cigarette, he tosses the lit cigarette butt into some arid grass. Neither the brush nor the grass burns. Eric probably does *not* have the requisite criminal intent for attempted reckless burning. Attempt requires **purposeful** conduct. Eric's conduct is **reckless** because he is aware of a risk and disregards it. If Eric takes the match or lit cigarette and tries to ignite a fire with them, it is likely that he has the appropriate criminal intent for attempted arson. However, in this case Eric's actions demonstrate careless behavior that probably is not sufficient for the crime of attempt.

Defenses to Attempt

Along with failure of proof defenses to the criminal act and criminal intent elements, legal impossibility and voluntary abandonment can also function as affirmative defenses to attempt in many jurisdictions.

Impossibility as a Defense to Attempt

Two types of impossibility defenses exist: **legal impossibility**, which can function as a defense to attempt, and factual impossibility, which generally cannot. Legal impossibility means that the defendant believes what he or she is attempting to do is *illegal*, when it is not. Factual impossibility means that the defendant could not complete the crime attempted because the *facts* are not as he or she believes them to be. The Model Penal Code disallows factual impossibility as a defense by stating that conduct is an attempt when the defendant "purposely engages in conduct which would constitute the crime if the attendant circumstances were as he believes them to be" (Model Penal Code § 5.01(1) (a)).

Example of Legal Impossibility

Review the example given in Section 8 "Res Ipsa Loquitur Test" with Melissa and Matthew and the attempted poisoning of the neighbor's dog. Assume that Melissa is eighteen. Melissa believes that an individual must be twenty-one to purchase rat poison because that is the law in the state where she lived five years ago. Actually, the state in which Melissa currently resides allows the purchase of rat poison by those who are eighteen or older. The first store Melissa enters asks for identification when she tries to pay for the rat poison, so Melissa makes an excuse and leaves. The second store Melissa enters does not ask for identification, and she successfully makes the rat poison purchase. Melissa has probably *not* attempted to purchase rat poison illegally in the first store she entered. Melissa's act in attempting to purchase the rat poison is legal under the circumstances. Thus her mistaken belief that she is attempting to commit a crime does not transform this legal act into an *illegal* one.

Example of Factual Impossibility

Recall from the example given in Section 8 "Res Ipsa Loquitur Test" that Matthew threw a filet coated with rat poison over the fence into the neighbor's yard with the intent to poison the neighbor's dog. Both Melissa and Matthew are under the *mistaken* belief that the dog is present and will eat the filet. However, the dog is on an overnight camping trip with its owners. This **mistake of fact** probably will *not* excuse Melissa and Matthew's attempt. Melissa and Matthew purposely engaged in conduct that would result in the poisoning of the dog if the facts were as Melissa and Matthew believed them to be. Thus Melissa and Matthew have most likely committed attempted destruction of property or animal cruelty regardless of the fact that their plan could not succeed under the circumstances.

Voluntary Abandonment as a Defense to Attempt

Many jurisdictions allow a defendant who **voluntarily abandons** the planned offense to use this abandonment as an affirmative defense to attempt (Fla. Stat. Ann., 2010). The defense has two parts. First, the defendant must have a change of heart that is *not motivated* by an increased possibility of detection, or a change in circumstances that make the crime's commission more difficult. As the Model Penal Code states, "it is an affirmative defense that he abandoned his effort to commit the crime...under circumstances manifesting a complete and voluntary renunciation of his criminal purpose...[R]enunciation of criminal purpose is not voluntary if it is motivated...by circumstances...which increase the probability of detection...or which make more difficult the accomplishment of the criminal purpose" (Model Penal Code § 5.01(4)). Second, the abandonment must be complete and cannot simply be a postponement. Under the Model Penal Code, "[r]enunciation is not complete if it is motivated by a decision to postpone the criminal conduct until a more advantageous time or to transfer the criminal effort to another but similar...victim" (Model Penal Code § 5.01(4)). The voluntary abandonment defense gives defendants incentive to stop progressing toward consummation of the offense and prevents the crime from occurring without the need for law enforcement intervention.

Example of Voluntary Abandonment as a Defense to Attempt

Review the example with Melissa and Matthew in Section 8 "Res Ipsa Loquitur Test". If Melissa changes her mind after purchasing the rat poison and talks Matthew out of poisoning the neighbor's dog, Melissa has **voluntarily abandoned** the crime and cannot be charged with attempt. If Matthew changes his mind after coating the filet with rat poison and throws the filet away, Matthew has **voluntarily abandoned** the crime and cannot be charged with attempt. Note that both Melissa's and Matthew's actions are in the very early stages of the crime of destruction of property or animal cruelty and probably will be considered preparatory, rather than constituting the criminal act element required for attempt. When Melissa climbs over the fence, picks up the filet, and takes it back to her house for disposal, it is most likely too late to voluntarily abandon the crime. At this point, the crime of attempt has already been committed, and neither **voluntary abandonment** nor **factual impossibility** can function as defenses.

Merger

Attempt merges into the crime if the crime is completed in many jurisdictions, which means that the defendant cannot be charged with attempt *and* the completed crime (Ga. Code tit. 16, 2011).

Example of Merger

Review the example with Melissa and Matthew in Section 8 "Res Ipsa Loquitur Test". Change the facts, and assume that the neighbor's dog eats the poisoned filet and dies. Melissa and Matthew probably cannot be charged with attempted destruction of property or animal cruelty *and* destruction of property or animal cruelty in many jurisdictions. Once the crime is complete, the attempt crime **merges** into the consummated offense, and Melissa and Matthew may be charged only with destruction of property or animal cruelty.

Figure 8.3 Defenses to Attempt

Impossibility	
Voluntary Abandonment	
Merger	

Attempt and Transferred Intent

Recall from Chapter 4 "The Elements of a Crime" that a defendant's criminal intent can **transfer** from the *intended* victim to the *actual* victim in some jurisdictions. If the intent is transferred, the defendant may be criminally responsible for the consummated offense against the eventual victim and for **attempt** against the intended victim.

Example of Attempt and Transferred Intent

Review the example with Melissa and Matthew in Section 8 "Res Ipsa Loquitur Test". Change the facts, and assume that the neighbor's cat licks the poison off the filet and thereafter dies. If Melissa and Matthew are in a jurisdiction that recognizes **transferred intent**, they may be charged with **attempted** destruction of property or animal cruelty for *trying* to poison the neighbor's dog and destruction of property or animal cruelty for *actually* poisoning and killing the neighbor's cat.

Attempt Grading

Jurisdictions vary as to how they **grade** attempt. Some jurisdictions follow the common law and grade attempt *lower* than the completed offense (Mo. Ann. Stat., 2010). Other jurisdictions punish attempt *the same* as the attempted offense, with exceptions for certain specified crimes (Conn. Gen. Stat., 2010).

Figure 8.4 Diagram of Attempt

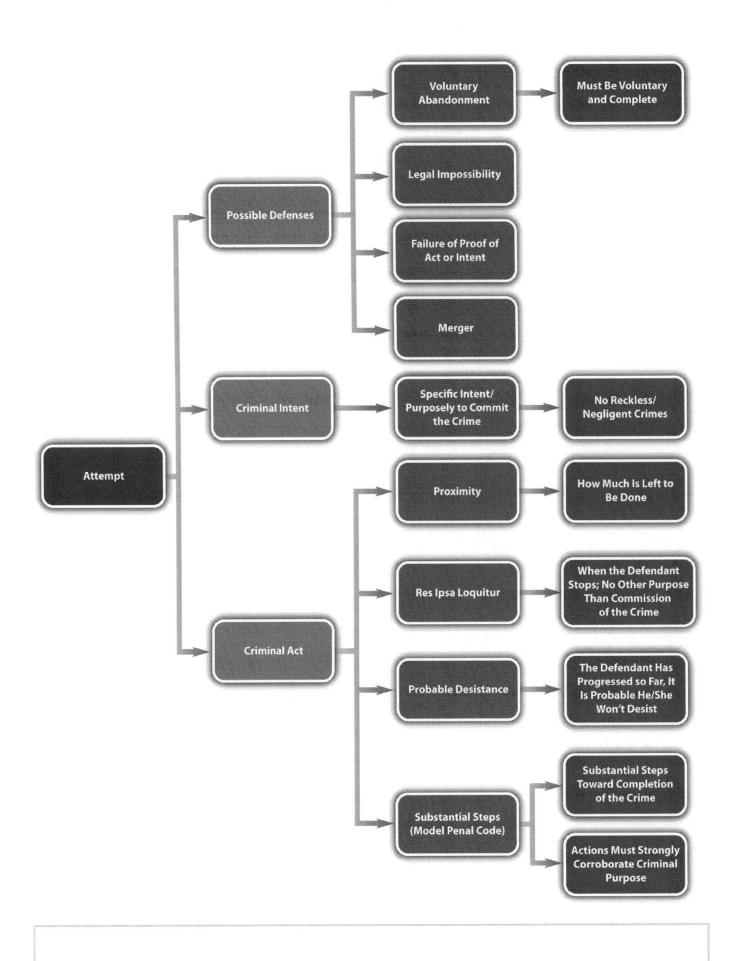

Key Takeaways

- An inchoate crime is a crime that might not be completed.
- General attempt statutes set forth the elements of attempt and apply them to any crime. Specific attempt statutes define attempt according to specified crimes, such as attempted murder, robbery, or rape.
- The four tests jurisdictions use to ascertain the criminal act element required for attempt are proximity, res ipsa loquitur, probable desistance, and substantial steps.
- The proximity test determines how close the defendant is to committing the crime by analyzing how much is left to accomplish after preparation for the offense.
- The res ipsa loquitur test, also called the unequivocality test, examines the defendant's actions at a moment in time to determine whether the defendant has no other purpose than committing the crime at issue.
- The probable desistance test analyzes whether the defendant has progressed so far that it is probable he or she will not desist without interruption from law enforcement or other intervening circumstances.
- The substantial steps test is the Model Penal Code test and ascertains whether the defendant has completed substantial steps toward commission of the crime that are corroborative of the defendant's criminal intent.
- Preparatory crimes criminalize preparing to commit a crime, which would be a stage that is too premature to constitute the criminal act element required for attempt.
- The criminal intent element required for attempt is specific intent or purposely to commit the crime at issue.
- Aside from failure of proof defenses to attempt act and intent, two potential defenses to attempt are legal impossibility and voluntary abandonment.
- Factual impossibility means the defendant cannot complete the crime because the facts are not as the defendant believes them to be. Factual impossibility is generally not a defense to attempt. Legal impossibility means the defendant believes he or she is attempting to commit a crime, but the defendant's actions are actually legal. Legal impossibility is generally a defense to attempt.
- Voluntary abandonment is when the defendant voluntarily and completely withdraws from commission of the offense before it is consummated.
- In many jurisdictions, attempt merges into the offense if it is completed, which means that a defendant cannot be charged with attempt and the completed crime.
- In a jurisdiction that allows for transferred intent, a defendant's intent can transfer from the intended victim to the actual victim. The defendant can thereafter be criminally responsible for the completed crime against the actual victim and attempt against the intended victim.
- Some jurisdictions grade attempt lower than the completed offense; others grade attempt the same as the completed offense, with exceptions.

Exercises

Answer the following questions. Check your answers using the answer key at the end of the chapter.

Carol shoots her father Carl with malice aforethought. He thereafter lingers in a coma for two months and then dies. Carol is in a jurisdiction that recognizes merger for attempt and that also requires a victim to die within one year and a day if the defendant is to be charged with murder. Can Carol be charged with attempted murder and murder? Why or why not?

Read *State v. Withrow*, 8 S.W.3d 75 (1999). In *Withrow*, the defendant made frequent visits to a house that was under law enforcement surveillance. While searching the house pursuant to a search warrant, law enforcement officers saw the defendant emerging from a bedroom that had a locked closet containing a jar with pills dissolving in it, which is the first step of methamphetamine production. The defendant was convicted of attempted methamphetamine production and received a sentence of eighteen years in prison. Did the Supreme Court of Missouri uphold the defendant's conviction? The case is available at this link: http://scholar.google.com/scholar_case?case=17239945130468444353&hl=en&as_sdt=2&as_vis=1&oi=scholarr.

Read *People v. Strand*, 539 N.W.2d 739 (1995). In *Strand*, the defendant was convicted of assault with intent to commit *attempted* kidnapping. Did the Michigan Court of Appeals uphold this conviction? The case is available at this link:

http://scholar.google.com/scholar_case?case=1507705469884283003&hl=en&as_sdt=2&as_vis=1&oi=scholarr.

References

Commonwealth v. Hamel, 52 Mass. App. Ct. 250 (2001), accessed December 29, 2010, http://scholar.google.com/scholar_case?case=3222223363179578849&hl=en&as_sdt=2&as_vis=1&oi=scholarr.

Conn. Gen. Stat. § 53a-106, accessed December 31, 2010, http://www.cga.ct.gov/2009/pub/chap952.htm#Sec53a-106.htm.

Fla. Stat. Ann. § 777.04(5) (a), accessed December 31, 2010, http://law.justia.com/florida/codes/2003/TitleXLVI/chapter777/777_04.html.

Ga. Code tit. 16 § 16-4-2, accessed January 28, 2011, http://law.onecle.com/georgia/16/16-4-2.html.

Grill v. State, 337 Md. 91 (1995), accessed December 27, 2010, http://www.leagle.com/xmlResult.aspx?xmldoc=1995428337Md91_1422.xml&docbase=CSLWAR2-1986-2006.

Hamiel v. Wisconsin, 285 N.W.2d 639 (1979), accessed December 30, 2010, http://scholar.google.com/scholar_case?case=3730801887783687670&hl=en&as_sdt=2002&as_vis=1.

Mo. Ann. Stat. § 564.011, accessed December 31, 2010, http://law.justia.com/missouri/codes/2005/t38/5640000011.html.

N.Y. Penal Law § 140.35, accessed December 31, 2010, http://law.onecle.com/new-york/penal/PEN0140.35_140.35.html.

People v. Dillon, 668 P.2d 697 (1983), accessed December 29, 2010, http://scholar.google.com/scholar_case?case=16336126005486548570&hl=en&as_sdt=2,5.

People v. Luna, 170 Cal. App. 4th 535 (2009), accessed December 27, 2010, http://scholar.google.com/scholar_case?case=11148942163253518924&hl=en&as_sdt=2&as_vis=1&oi=scholarr.

Schulhofer, S. J. and Dan M. Kahan, "Attempt," encyclopedia.com website, accessed December 26, 2010, http://www.encyclopedia.com/topic/Attempt.aspx.

Tex. Penal Code § 15.01, accessed December 27, 2010, http://law.onecle.com/texas/penal/15.01.00.html.

U.S. v. Mandujano, 499 F.2d 370, 373 fn. 5 (1974), accessed December 30, 2010, http://ftp.resource.org/courts.gov/c/F2/499/499.F2d.370.74-1445.html.

USLegal.com, "Definition of Res Ipsa Loquitur," accessed December 29, 2010, http://definitions.uslegal.com/r/res-ipsa-loquitur.

Yourdictionary.com, accessed December 28, 2010, "Definition of Inchoate," http://www.yourdictionary.com/inchoate.

18 U.S.C. § 1113, accessed June 28, 2011, http://www.law.cornell.edu/uscode/718/usc_sec_18_00001113—-000-.html.

CC licensed content, Shared previously

- Criminal Law. **Provided by**: University of Minnesota Libraries Publishing . **Located at**: http://open.lib.umn.edu/criminallaw/. **License**: *CC BY-NC-SA: Attribution-NonCommercial-ShareAlike*

8.2 Conspiracy

Learning Objectives

Explain why conspiracy is an inchoate crime.

Define the criminal act element required for conspiracy.

Compare the conspiracy overt act requirement with the criminal act element required for attempt.

Define the criminal intent element required for conspiracy.

Ascertain whether a coconspirator can be criminally responsible when another coconspirator is not prosecuted or acquitted.

Ascertain whether a coconspirator must know every other coconspirator to be guilty of conspiracy.

Distinguish between a wheel and chain conspiracy.

Define the Pinkerton rule.

Define Wharton's rule.

Identify an affirmative defense to conspiracy.

Ascertain whether merger applies to conspiracy.

Compare various approaches to conspiracy grading.

Define federal RICO.

Conspiracy punishes defendants for agreeing to commit a criminal offense. Conspiracy is an inchoate crime because it is possible that the defendants never will commit the planned offense. However, a conspiracy is complete as soon as the defendants become **complicit** and commit the **conspiracy act** with the **conspiracy intent**. The rationale for punishing defendants for planning activity, which generally is not sufficient to constitute the crime of attempt, is the increased likelihood of success when defendants work together to plot and carry out a criminal offense (Dennis v. U.S., 2011). If the defendants commit the crime that is the object of the conspiracy, the defendants are responsible for the conspiracy *and* the completed crime, as is discussed in Section 8.2.4 "Consequences of Conspiracy".

Conspiracy Act

In many jurisdictions, the **criminal act** element required for conspiracy is an agreement to commit any criminal offense (Fla. Stat. Ann., 2011). The agreement does not need to be formal or in writing (State v. Bond, 2011). Some states also criminalize as conspiracy the agreement to falsely indict another for a crime and the agreement to falsely maintain any lawsuit, even a civil lawsuit (Cal. Penal Code, 2011). Other states only criminalize as conspiracy the agreement to commit a felony (Tex. Penal Code, 2011).

In some states and federally, an **overt act** in furtherance of the conspiracy is also required (18 U.S.C., 2011). The Model Penal Code requires an overt act only when the planned crime is "other than a felony of the first or second degree" (Model Penal Code § 5.03(5)). The overt act does not have to be *criminal* and may be planning or preparatory activity that would be insufficient to constitute the criminal act element required for **attempt** (State v. Verive, 2011).

Example of Conspiracy Act

Review the example with Melissa and Matthew in Section 8 "Res Ipsa Loquitur Test". In this example, Melissa and Matthew agree to poison the neighbor's dog because it barks every night. After deciding they will poison the dog,

Melissa buys rat poison, and Matthew thereafter coats a filet mignon with it and throws it over the fence into the neighbor's yard. In a jurisdiction that defines the criminal act element for conspiracy as an agreement between two or more to commit a criminal offense, Melissa and Matthew probably committed the conspiracy criminal act *as soon as they agreed* to poison the dog. Their agreement could be verbal and does not need to be formal or in writing. If Melissa and Matthew are in a jurisdiction that requires an **overt act** in furtherance of the conspiracy, Melissa and Matthew probably have not committed the conspiracy criminal act until Melissa *buys the rat poison*. Note that the purchase of the rat poison is not sufficient to constitute the criminal act element required for **attempted** destruction of property or animal cruelty, as discussed in Section 8 "Res Ipsa Loquitur Test". However, it would likely be enough to support the **conspiracy** to commit destruction of property or animal cruelty.

Conspiracy Intent

The essence of conspiracy is agreement, which requires two or more parties. However, the modern approach is that a conspiracy may be formed as long as *one* of the parties has the appropriate intent (Ind. Code, 2011). Pursuant to this unilateral view of conspiracy, a conspiracy may exist between a defendant and a law enforcement decoy who is pretending to agree.

In the majority of jurisdictions, the criminal intent element required for conspiracy is **specific intent** or **purposely** to agree with another to commit the crime at issue (Connecticut Criminal Jury Instructions 3.3-1, 2011). As the Model Penal Code states, "[a] person is guilty of conspiracy...if with the purpose of promoting or facilitating its commission he: (a) agrees with such other person...that they...will engage in conduct which constitutes such crime" (Model Penal Code § 5.03(1) (a)). This intent has two components. The prosecution must prove that the conspirator intended to *agree* and also intended to *commit* the underlying offense (State v. Lewis, 2011).

Example of Conspiracy Intent

Shelley and Sam meet at a bar and discuss their lack of finances. Shelley mentions that she and her friend Steffy work at a convenience store. Sam asks Shelley if she would like to help him rob the convenience store when Steffy is working. Shelley agrees. The two plan the robbery. Shelley and Sam agree that Shelley will drive the getaway car on the appointed date and time. Shelley informs Sam that Steffy is extremely meek and fearful and will readily hand over cash out of the cash register if Sam uses a fake handgun. Shelley and Sam probably have the criminal intent element required for conspiracy. Shelley and Sam have the intent to *agree to work together* because they both need each other to successfully complete the convenience store robbery. In addition, Shelley and Sam have the intent to *successfully commit the robbery* because they both want the money the robbery will produce. Thus if no overt act is required in their jurisdiction, Shelley and Sam most likely have completed the crime of conspiracy and may be prosecuted for this offense whether or not the robbery actually takes place.

Conspiracy Parties

Similar to **accomplice liability**, the acquittal of or failure to prosecute one party to the conspiracy does not relieve a coconspirator from criminal responsibility in many states (Tex. Penal Code, 2011). In addition, a coconspirator does not need to *know* every other coconspirator to be accountable as a member of the conspiracy (Neb. Rev. Stat. Ann., 2011). As long as the conspiracy defendant is aware that other coconspirators exist, the mens rea for conspiracy is present. As the Model Penal Code states, "[i]f a person guilty of conspiracy...knows that a person with whom he conspires to commit a crime has conspired with another person or persons to commit the same crime, he is guilty of conspiring with such other person or persons, whether or not he knows their identity" (Model Penal Code § 5.03(2)). Large-scale conspiracies, such as conspiracies to distribute contraband or illegal firearms, may result in each member sharing criminal responsibility for the conspiracy and every separate conspiracy transaction.

A conspiracy that has more than one criminal objective still can be just *one* conspiracy. Under the Model Penal Code, "[i]f a person conspires to commit a number of crimes, he is guilty of only one conspiracy so long as such multiple crimes are the object of the same agreement or continuous conspiratorial relationship" (Model Penal

Code § 5.03(3)).

It is useful to understand two basic large-scale conspiracy organizational formats: wheel and chain conspiracies. A wheel conspiracy consists of a single conspirator, generally the ringleader who is interconnected to every other coconspirator. The ringleader is the hub; the other coconspirators are the spokes of the wheel. An example of a wheel conspiracy would be a mob boss linked to individual members of the mob following his or her commands. A chain conspiracy consists of coconspirators connected to each other like links in a chain but without a central interconnected ringleader. An example of a chain conspiracy is a conspiracy to manufacture and distribute a controlled substance, with the manufacturer linked to the transporter, who sells to a large-quantity dealer, who thereafter sells to a smaller-quantity dealer, who sells to a customer. Whether the conspiracy is wheel, chain, or otherwise, if the jurisdiction has a statute or common-law rule that each member does not need to personally know every other member as discussed previously, the coconspirators may be criminally responsible for the **conspiracy** *and* the crime(s) it furthers.

Figure 8.5 Comparison of Wheel and Chain Conspiracies

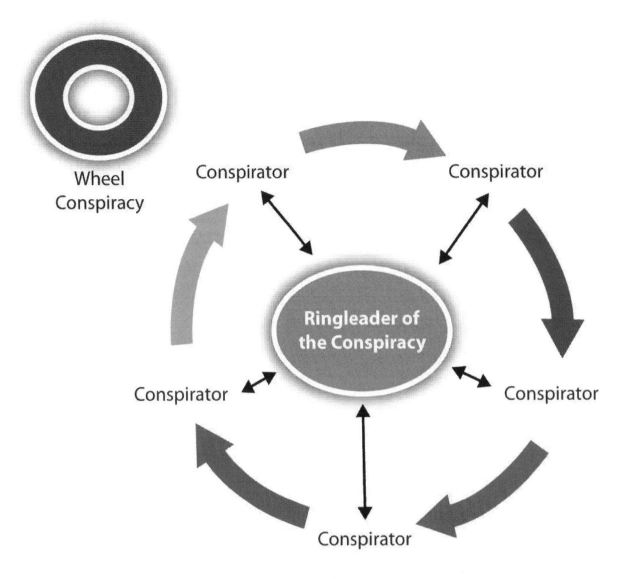

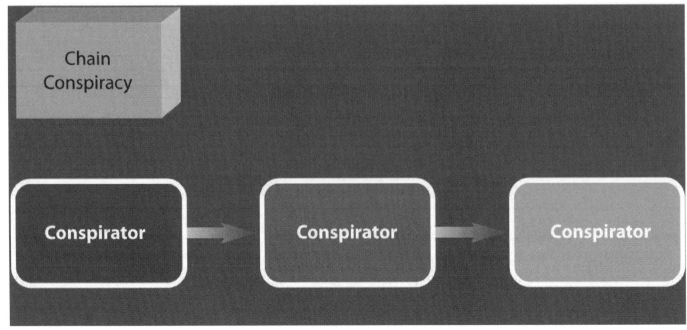

Consequences of Conspiracy

In some states and federally, individuals who enter into a conspiracy are criminally responsible for *every reasonably foreseeable* crime committed in furtherance of the conspiracy (U.S. v. Castaneda, 2011). This rule is called the Pinkerton rule, based on the US Supreme Court case that created it (*Pinkerton v. U.S.*, 328 U.S. 640 (1946).). One factor used to determine foreseeability is the degree of the defendant's involvement in the conspiracy. A defendant who plays a minor role is less likely to be criminally responsible than a defendant who has a more substantive involvement (U.S. v Castaneda, 2011).

Example of the Pinkerton Rule

Review the example in Section 8 "Example of Conspiracy Intent" with Shelley and Sam. Assume that on the night of the convenience store robbery, Lucy, an armed, off-duty police officer, wanders into the store to purchase cigarettes at the moment Sam pulls out his fake handgun. Lucy yanks her concealed handgun out of her waistband and tells Sam to drop the weapon. Jolene, another customer in the store, observes the two pointing guns at each other and suffers a fatal heart attack. In many jurisdictions, both Shelley and Sam probably could be criminally responsible for **conspiracy** to commit robbery, **attempted** robbery, and the **murder** of Jolene. Shelley and Sam attempted to commit the robbery *in furtherance* of the conspiracy. Both played a *major* role in the conspiracy and the attempted robbery. Thus both are accountable for the foreseeable consequences. Robbery is a crime of violence, so a death that occurs during a robbery is foreseeable, even though Sam is armed with only a pretend handgun. Thus Shelley and Sam may be charged with and convicted of Jolene's murder, which is most likely felony murder. Felony murder is discussed in detail in Chapter 9 "Criminal Homicide".

Wharton's Rule

A criminal offense that requires two parties cannot be the object of a conspiracy that consists of two parties. This rule is called Wharton's rule, or the **concert of action rule** (USLegal, 2011). However, a statute can expressly criminalize a conspiracy to commit any crime, *abrogating* the rule. Currently, Wharton's rule can operate as a judicial **presumption**, to be applied in the absence of legislative intent to the contrary (Ianelli v. U.S., 2011).

Example of a Case Where Wharton's Rule Is Inapplicable

Joanne and Robert conspire with Don, Joanne's pimp, to engage in prostitution. Joanne and Robert get caught in the act of engaging in prostitution by Edward, a police officer. Wharton's rule probably does not apply in this case. Although engaging in prostitution requires *two* parties, the conspiracy to engage in prostitution has *three* members—Don, Joanne, and Robert. Thus Wharton's rule is likely inapplicable, and Don, Joanne, and Robert might have committed conspiracy to engage in prostitution. Note that if only Joanne and Robert conspire to engage in prostitution, Wharton's rule may act as a judicial presumption that they cannot commit conspiracy *and* the crime it furthers.

Renunciation as a Defense to Conspiracy

One potential affirmative defense to conspiracy is renunciation. Similar to voluntary abandonment in attempt, **renunciation** can operate as a defense to conspiracy in some jurisdictions if the defendant completely and voluntarily renounces the conspiracy (N.J. Stat., 2011). The renunciation must also thwart the crime that is the object of the conspiracy. The Model Penal Code allows the defense and provides, "It is an affirmative defense that the actor, after conspiring to commit a crime, thwarted the success of the conspiracy, under circumstances manifesting a complete and voluntary renunciation of his criminal purpose" (Model Penal Code § 5.03(6)).

Example of Renunciation

Review the example with Shelley and Sam in Section 8 "Example of Conspiracy Intent". In this example, Shelley and Sam agree to commit a robbery at the convenience store where Steffy is a cashier. Adjust the example so that Shelley has a change of heart and contacts law enforcement about the robbery before she drives Sam to the convenience store in the getaway car. Law enforcement officers ask Shelley to help them apprehend Sam, and she agrees. Shelley drives Sam to the convenience store as planned. Two law enforcement officers dress in plainclothes and pretend to be shopping in the convenience store when Sam arrives. As soon as Sam pulls out his fake handgun, they arrest him. If Shelley is in a jurisdiction that recognizes the **renunciation** defense, she probably will have a valid defense to a charge of conspiracy. Although Shelley committed the criminal act for conspiracy with the requisite criminal intent, she *voluntarily* and *completely* renounced the conspiracy and *thwarted* the crime that was its object. Thus Shelly has likely met the requirements of renunciation, and only Sam may be charged with a crime or crimes in this scenario.

Merger

At early common law, conspiracy, which was a misdemeanor, **merged** into the completed felony that was its object. The merger was based on the significant procedural differences between misdemeanor and felony trials. As the differences diminished, so did the merger concept. In modern times, conspiracy does not merge into the completed offense (Callanan v. U.S., 2011). Thus a defendant can be charged with and convicted of conspiracy *and* any crime the conspiracy furthers, as is discussed more fully in Section 8.2.4 "Consequences of Conspiracy".

Figure 8.6 Defenses to Conspiracy

Renunciation	
Wharton's Rule	
Not: Merger	

Conspiracy Grading

Some states **grade** conspiracy the same as the most serious offense that is the conspiracy's object (18 Pa. Cons. Stat., 2011). Others grade conspiracy lower than the most serious conspired offense and do not criminalize the conspiracy to commit a simple, low-level misdemeanor (Tenn. Code Ann., 2011). Another view is to set a separate penalty for the conspiracy to commit specific crimes (Cal. Penal Code, 2011). It is not unconstitutional to punish conspiracy more severely than the crime conspired (Clune v. U.S., 2011).

Federal RICO

In response to an increase in organized crime, the federal government enacted the Racketeer Influenced and Corrupt Organization Act (RICO) (18 U.S.C. §§ 1961-1968)). RICO provides extensive criminal penalties and also a civil cause of action for **organized crime** and includes all offenses that are criminal under state or federal law. Although RICO was originally intended to focus on sophisticated criminal businesses such as loan sharking, mafia, and high-stakes gambling operations (Blakey, G. R., 2011), its modern application is much broader and encompasses many white-collar crimes and small-time conspiracies. A criminal organization always involves more than one member, and at the very least rudimentary planning, so conspiracy is a common RICO charge and is often easier to prove than a completed criminal offense. Recently, RICO has been criticized as being overused and applied in a manner inconsistent with its original purpose, especially when it targets smaller, low-member criminal "organizations." Some examples of highly publicized RICO defendants are Hell's Angels (Zimmerman, Keith and Zimmerman, Kent, 2011), Catholic priests in sex abuse cases (Smith, G., 2011), and Major League Baseball (Sportsbusinessdaily.com, 2011).

Table 8.1 Comparison of Conspiracy and Accomplice Liability

Type of Liability	Criminal Act	Criminal Intent
Conspiracy	Agreement to commit a crime, false criminal indictment, false lawsuit, or felony; some jurisdictions require an overt act in furtherance of the conspiracy	Specific intent or purposely to agree to commit the specified offense(s)
Accomplice	Aid, assist commission of a crime	Specific intent or purposely or general intent or knowingly, depending on the jurisdiction

Figure 8.7 Diagram of Conspiracy

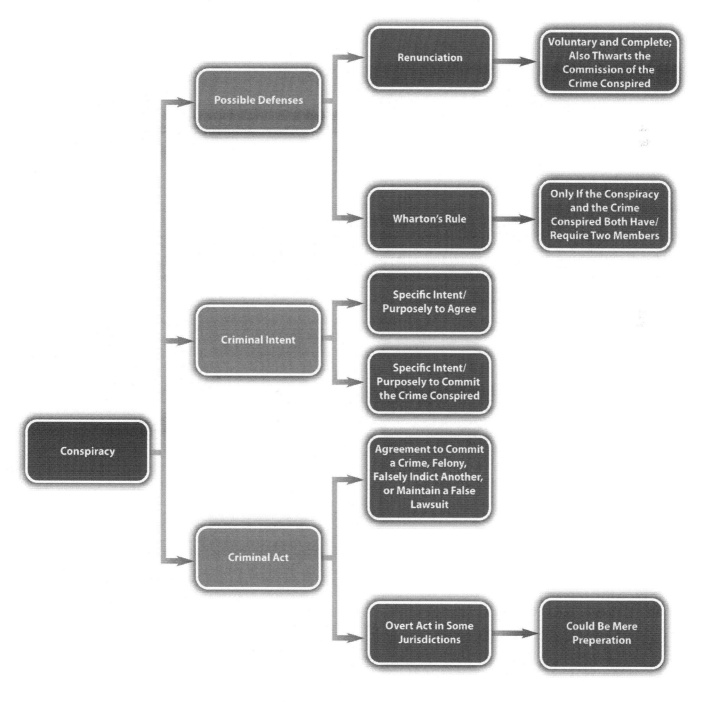

Tom DeLay Convicted of Conspiracy and Money Laundering Video

Judge Sentences Tom DeLay to Three Years in Prison

Tom DeLay, former US House Majority Leader, was convicted of conspiracy and money laundering (Meyer, P., 2011). His verdict is shown in this video:
(click to see video)

Key Takeaways

- Conspiracy is an inchoate crime because the defendants might never complete the offense that is the conspiracy's object.
- The criminal act element required for conspiracy is an agreement to commit any crime, commit a felony, falsely indict another for a crime, or falsely maintain any lawsuit, depending on the jurisdiction.
- The overt act required for conspiracy can be preparatory activity; the criminal act element required for attempt must be more than mere preparation.
- The criminal intent element required for conspiracy is specific intent or purposely to agree to commit the offense that is the conspiracy's object.
- The acquittal of or failure to prosecute one coconspirator does not prohibit the prosecution of other coconspirators in some jurisdictions.
- A coconspirator does not need to know every other coconspirator; as long as a coconspirator is aware that there are other members, he or she can be criminally responsible for conspiracy.
- A wheel conspiracy connects all members to one central member. A chain conspiracy interconnects the members in a linear fashion.
- The Pinkerton rule holds conspiracy members criminally responsible for every foreseeable crime committed in furtherance of the conspiracy.
- Wharton's rule could create a judicial presumption that a defendant cannot be criminally responsible for conspiracy and the crime that is its object if the conspiracy has only two members, and the crime that is its object requires two defendants.
- Renunciation is an affirmative defense to conspiracy in some jurisdictions if the defendant voluntarily and completely renounces the conspiracy and thwarts the crime that is its object.
- Generally, conspiracy does not merge like attempt; a defendant can be convicted of conspiracy and the crime conspired.
- Some jurisdictions grade conspiracy the same as the conspired offense; other jurisdictions grade conspiracy lower than the conspired offense. It is not unconstitutional to grade conspiracy higher than the offense that is its object.
- Federal RICO is a statute that is designed to punish organized crime.

Exercises

Answer the following questions. Check your answers using the answer key at the end of the chapter.

Gail and Roger conspire to commit a **misdemeanor**. In Gail and Roger's state, conspiracy is punishable as a **felony**. Can Gail and Roger be convicted of a felony for conspiring to commit a misdemeanor? Why or why not?
Read *State v. Blackmer*, 816 A.2d 1014 (2003). In *Blackmer*, the defendant appealed his conviction for conspiracy to possess marijuana with intent to sell because the individual with whom he was conspiring was a police decoy who did not have conspiracy intent. Did the Supreme Court of New Hampshire uphold the defendant's conviction? The case is available at this link:
http://scholar.google.com/scholar_case?case=10340846332108789820&q=
State+v.+Blackmer&hl=en&as_sdt=2,5.
Read *Commonwealth v. Roux*, 350 A.2d 867 (1976). In *Roux*, the defendant was convicted of murder and conspiracy to commit murder after a barroom brawl resulted in a victim's death. The defendant and others beat the victim with their fists. Thereafter the criminal actor took a knife from a

defendant who then walked away. The criminal actor stabbed the victim, who died as a result. The defendant who walked away claimed that he "abandoned" the conspiracy by leaving before the stabbing, and this should be an affirmative defense to the conspiracy and murder charges. Did the Supreme Court of Pennsylvania uphold the defendant's convictions? The case is available at this link: http://scholar.google.com/scholar_case?case=1692554406000599210&hl=en&as_sdt=2&as_vis=1&oi=scholarr.

Law and Ethics: The Han Murder Conspiracy

Did the Coconspirators Intend to Commit Murder?

Read *People v. Han*, 78 Cal. App. 4th 797 (2000). The case is available at this link: http://caselaw.lp.findlaw.com/data2/californiastatecases/g023433.pdf.

In *Han*, a lurid California case involving twins, three defendants were convicted of burglary, false imprisonment, and conspiracy to commit murder (Beloit Daily News, 2011). Two of the codefendants appealed on the grounds that the evidence was insufficient to support the verdict of conspiracy to commit murder. The codefendants claimed that the only **direct** evidence of intent to commit murder were statements made by the defendant Jeen Han *before* the conspiracy was formed, and defendant Han could not conspire with herself.

The defendant Jeen Han and her twin sister Sunny had a long history of violence against each other (People v. Han, 2011). Defendant Han became enraged when Sunny pressed charges against her for theft. Testimonial evidence presented at trial showed that she expressed the intent to kill her twin *before* any conspiracy was formed (People v. Han, 2011). She actively sought out individuals to help her with her sister's murder (People v. Han, 2011). Thereafter, she met up with her teenaged cousin and a friend, the other two codefendants. The three broke into Sunny Han's apartment, tied up Sunny and her roommate at gunpoint and placed them in the bathtub, and then ransacked Sunny's purse. Receipts produced at trial indicated a purchase of garbage bags, twine, utility tape, and Pine Sol previous to the incident. The Court of Appeal of California held that although circumstantial, the evidence supported the verdict. The court reasoned that the purchase of the twine, garbage bags, utility tape, and Pine Sol, combined with the actions of the defendants in breaking into the apartment, tying up the two roommates at gunpoint, and putting them in the bathtub, could be interpreted as circumstantial evidence of intent to kill, and the trier of fact did not err in making that conclusion (People v. Han, 2011).

Do you think it is *ethical* to impute Jeen Han's intent to murder her twin to the two other coconspirators, based on the circumstantial evidence presented at trial?

Check your answer using the answer key at the end of the chapter.

References

Beloit Daily News, "'Evil Twin' Found Guilty of Plotting to Kill Sister," *Beloit Daily News* website, accessed January 28, 2011, http://www.beloitdailynews.com/articles/1997/11/21/export7262.txt.

Blakey, G. R., "RICO: The Genesis of an Idea," Abstract, Social Science Research Network website, accessed January 4, 2011, http://papers.ssrn.com/sol3/papers.cfm?abstract_id=1142930.

Cal. Penal Code § 182(a) (2), (3), accessed January 2, 2011, http://law.justia.com/california/codes/2009/pen/182-185.html.

Callanan v. U.S., 364 U.S. 587 (1961), accessed January 4, 2011, http://scholar.google.com/scholar_case?case=10261023883092961366&hl=en&as_sdt=2&as_vis=1&oi=scholarr.

Clune v. U.S., 159 U.S. 590 (1895), accessed January 4, 2011, http://scholar.google.com/scholar_case?case=14126191414675975192&q=Clune+v.+US&hl=en&as_sdt=2002&as_vis=1.

Connecticut Criminal Jury Instructions 3.3-1, accessed January 1, 2011, http://www.jud.ct.gov/ji/criminal/part3/3.3-1.htm.

Dennis v. U.S., 341 U.S. 494 (1951), accessed January 3, 2011, http://scholar.google.com/scholar_case?case=13576454585730441281&hl=en&as_sdt=2&as_vis=1&oi=scholarr.

Fla. Stat. Ann. § 777.04(3), accessed January 1, 2011, http://www.leg.state.fl.us/statutes/index.cfm?App_mode=Display_Statute&Search_String=&URL=0700-0799/0777/Sections/0777.04.html.

Ianelli v. U.S., 420 U.S. 770, 785 (1975), accessed January 3, 2011, http://scholar.google.com/scholar_case?case=16942118715212641737&hl=en&as_sdt=2&as_vis=1&oi=scholarr.

Ind. Code § 35-41-5-2(5), accessed January 1, 2011, http://www.in.gov/legislative/ic/2010/title35/ar41/ch5.html.

Meyer, P., "Tom DeLay is sentenced to three years," *Los Angeles Times* website, accessed August 15, 2011, http://articles.latimes.com/2011/jan/11/nation/la-na-tom-delay-20110111.

Neb. Rev. Stat. Ann. § 28-202(2), accessed January 3, 2011, http://law.justia.com/nebraska/codes/2006/s28index/s2802002000.html.

N.J. Stat. § 2c: 5-2e, accessed January 4, 2011, http://law.onecle.com/new-jersey/2c-the-new-jersey-code-of-criminal-justice/5-2.html.

People v. Han, 78 Cal. App. 4th 797, 802 (2000), accessed January 28, 2011, http://caselaw.lp.findlaw.com/data2/californiastatecases/g023433.pdf.

Smith, G., "Courts: Lawsuit Accuses Diocese of Hiding Sex Abuse," *Norwich Bulletin* website, accessed January 4, 2011, http://www.norwichbulletin.com/lifestyles/spirituality/x497774422/Courts-Lawsuit-accuses-diocese-of-hiding-sex-abuse.

Sportsbusinessdaily.com website, "Arbitration Ruling Effectively Ends Loria RICO Suit," accessed June 28, 2011, http://www.sportsbusinessdaily.com/Daily/Issues/2004/11/Issue-46/Franchises/Arbitration-Ruling-Effectively-Ends-Loria-Rico-Suit.aspx.

State v. Bond, 49 Conn. App. 183 (1998), accessed January 1, 2011, http://caselaw.findlaw.com/ct-court-of-appeals/1255702.html.

State v. Lewis, 220 Conn. 602 (1991), accessed January 2, 2011, http://scholar.google.com/scholar_case?case=6997065715061309373&hl=en&as_sdt=2&as_vis=1&oi=scholarr.

State v. Verive, 627 P.2d 721 (1981), accessed January 1, 2011, http://wings.buffalo.edu/law/bclc/web/azverive.htm.

Tenn. Code Ann. §39-12-107(c), accessed January 4, 2011, http://law.justia.com/tennessee/codes/2010/title-39/chapter-12/part-1/39-12-107.

Tex. Penal Code § 15.02, accessed January 3, 2011, http://law.onecle.com/texas/penal/15.02.00.html.

U.S. v. Castaneda, 9 F.3d 761 (1993), accessed January 3, 2011, http://scholar.google.com/scholar_case?case=13576116398000833345&hl=en&as_sdt=2&as_vis=1&oi=scholarr.

USLegal, "Definition of Wharton's Rule," USLegal.com website, accessed January 3, 2011, http://definitions.uslegal.com/w/whartons-rule.

Zimmerman, K., Kent Zimmerman, "Hell's Angel: The Life and Times of Sonny Barger and the Hell's Angels Motorcycle Club," accessed January 4, 2011, http://www.organized-crime.de/revbar01sonnybarger.htm.

18 Pa. Cons. Stat. § 905, accessed January 4, 2011, http://law.onecle.com/pennsylvania/crimes-and-offenses/00.009.005.000.html.

18 U.S.C. § 371, accessed January 1, 2011, http://codes.lp.findlaw.com/uscode/18/I/19/371.

CC licensed content, Shared previously

- Criminal Law. **Provided by**: University of Minnesota Libraries Publishing . **Located at**: http://open.lib.umn.edu/criminallaw/. **License**: *CC BY-NC-SA: Attribution-NonCommercial-ShareAlike*

8.3 Solicitation

Learning Objectives

Explain why solicitation is an inchoate crime.
Define the criminal act element required for solicitation.
Define the criminal intent element required for solicitation.
Determine whether the defense of renunciation is available for solicitation.
Discuss various approaches to solicitation grading.

Solicitation can be a precursor to conspiracy because it criminalizes the *instigation* of an agreement to commit a criminal offense. Solicitation is an inchoate crime because it is possible that the conspiracy will *never be formed*, and the crime that is its object will *not be committed*. Many of the rules that apply to attempt and conspiracy also apply to solicitation, as is discussed in Section 8.3 "Solicitation".

Solicitation Act

The **criminal act** element required for solicitation is generally **words** that *induce* another to commit a capital felony, first-degree felony (Tex. Penal Code, 2011), or any crime (N.Y. Penal Law, 2011). Typical words of inducement are request, command, encourage, hire, procure, entice, and advise. The Model Penal Code defines solicitation as follows: "[a] person is guilty of solicitation to commit a crime if with the purpose of promoting or facilitating its commission he commands, encourages or requests another person to engage in specific conduct which would constitute such crime" (Model Penal Code § 5.02(1)). However, the Model Penal Code does not require direct *communication*, if "conduct was designed to effect such communication." (Model Penal Code § 5.02(2)).

Example of Solicitation Act

Jimmy calls his friend Choo, who is reputed to be a "fence," and asks Choo to help him sell some stolen designer shoes. If Jimmy is in a jurisdiction that criminalizes the "request" to commit *any crime*, Jimmy probably has committed the criminal act element required for solicitation. If Jimmy is in a jurisdiction that only criminalizes solicitation to commit a *capital felony* or *first-degree felony*, then Jimmy probably has not committed the criminal act element required for solicitation because selling stolen property is not generally graded that severely. If Jimmy is in a jurisdiction that follows the Model Penal Code, and Jimmy and Choo had a long-standing arrangement whereby Jimmy puts stolen items in a storage facility so that Choo can sell them, Jimmy will not have to communicate his request to Choo. He simply will have to place the shoes in the storage facility to commit the criminal act element required for solicitation.

Solicitation Intent

The criminal intent element required for solicitation is **specific intent** or **purposely** to promote the crime's commission in most jurisdictions and under the Model Penal Code, as set forth in Section 8.3.1 "Solicitation Act" (Or. Rev. Stat., 2011).

Example of Solicitation Intent

Review the solicitation act example in Section 8 "Example of Solicitation Act". In this example, Jimmy *desires* Choo to commit the crime of selling stolen property so that he can reap a benefit from his stolen designer shoes. Thus Jimmy probably has the criminal intent required for solicitation. If Jimmy is in a jurisdiction that criminalizes solicitation to commit any crime, Jimmy could be charged with and convicted of this offense.

Renunciation as a Defense to Solicitation

Similar to conspiracy, many jurisdictions allow **renunciation** as an **affirmative defense** to solicitation (Ariz. Rev. Stat., 2011). The renunciation must be *voluntary* and *complete* and must *thwart* the crime that is solicited. As the Model Penal Code states, "it is an affirmative defense that the actor, after soliciting another person to commit a crime, persuaded him not to do so or otherwise prevented the commission of the crime, under circumstances manifesting a complete and voluntary renunciation of his criminal purpose" (Model Penal Code § 5.02(3)).

Solicitation Grading

Jurisdictions vary as to how they **grade** solicitation. Some jurisdictions grade solicitation according to the crime solicited, with more serious crimes accorded a more severe solicitation punishment (Ala. Code, 2011). Others grade solicitation the same as the crime solicited, with exceptions (N.H. Rev. Stat. Ann., 2011). Some states grade solicitation as a misdemeanor, *regardless* of the crime solicited (Commonwealth v. Barsell, 2011).

Figure 8.8 Diagram of Solicitation

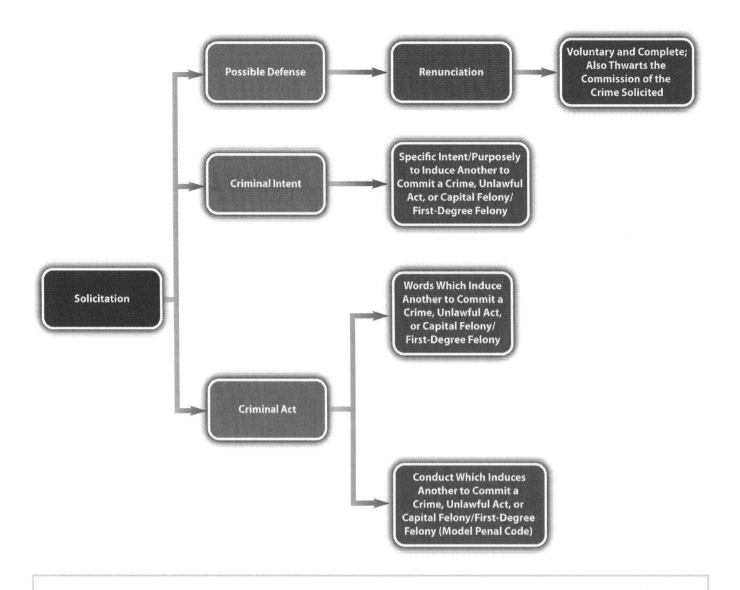

Key Takeaways

- Solicitation is an inchoate crime because the crime that is solicited may not be completed.
- The criminal act element required for solicitation is words or conduct that induces another to commit any crime, a capital felony, or first-degree felony.
- The criminal intent element required for solicitation is specific intent or purposely to induce another to commit any crime, a capital felony, or first-degree felony.
- Renunciation is an affirmative defense to solicitation if the defendant voluntarily and completely renounces his or her criminal purpose and thwarts the commission of the solicited crime.
- Jurisdictions vary in their approach to grading solicitation. Some jurisdictions grade solicitation on a sliding scale according to the crime solicited, some grade solicitation the same as the crime solicited, and some grade solicitation as a misdemeanor, regardless of the crime solicited.

Exercises

Answer the following questions. Check your answers using the answer key at the end of the chapter.

Nancy asks Jennifer to help her counterfeit twenty-dollar bills. Jennifer refuses. Has a crime been committed in this situation?
Read *Planter v. State*, 9 S.W. 3d 156 (1999). In *Planter*, the defendant told a former police officer

wearing a wire that he would kill his estranged son-in-law for ten thousand dollars. The defendant was convicted of solicitation to commit murder. The defendant appealed on the basis that he did not solicit the former police officer to commit murder; he solicited the former police officer to *pay him* to commit murder. Did the Court of Criminal Appeals of Texas uphold the defendant's conviction? The case is available at this link: http://caselaw.findlaw.com/tx-court-of-criminal-appeals/1007515.html.

Read *People v. Dennis*, 340 N.W.2d 81 (1983). In *Dennis*, the defendant was convicted of incitement to murder, which is the Michigan equivalent of solicitation to murder. The defendant appealed based on the fact that she solicited a police officer posing as a hit man, so the police officer did not have the intent to murder, and thus the murder was not possible. Did the Michigan Court of Appeals uphold the defendant's conviction? The case is available at this link: http://scholar.google.com/scholar_case?case=4173359376569096786&hl=en&as_sdt=2002&as_vis =1.

References

Ala. Code § 13A-4-1(f), accessed January 7, 2011, http://law.onecle.com/alabama/criminal-code/13A-4-1.html.

Ariz. Rev. Stat. § 13-1005, accessed January 7, 2011, http://www.azleg.gov/FormatDocument.asp?inDoc=/ars/13/01005.htm&Title=13&DocType=ARS.

Commonwealth v. Barsell, 424 Mass. 737 (1997), accessed January 7, 2011, http://scholar.google.com/scholar_case?case=8677391463974362410&hl=en&as_sdt=2&as_vis=1&oi=scholarr (accessed January 7, 2011).

N.H. Rev. Stat. Ann. § 629:2(IV), accessed January 7, 2011, http://law.justia.com/codes/new-hampshire/2009/TITLELXII/CHAPTER629/629-2.html.

N.Y. Penal Law § 100.00, accessed January 6, 2011, http://law.onecle.com/new-york/penal/PEN0100.00_100.00.html.

Or. Rev. Stat. § 161.435, accessed January 6, 2011, http://law.onecle.com/oregon/161-general-provisions/161.435.html.

Tex. Penal Code § 15.03, accessed January 6, 2011, http://law.onecle.com/texas/penal/15.03.00.html (accessed January 6, 2011).
CC licensed content, Shared previously

- Criminal Law. **Provided by**: University of Minnesota Libraries Publishing . **Located at**: http://open.lib.umn.edu/criminallaw/. **License**: *CC BY-NC-SA: Attribution-NonCommercial-ShareAlike*

8.4 End-of-Chapter Material

Summary

An inchoate crime might never be completed. The rationale of punishing a defendant for an inchoate crime is prevention and deterrence. The three inchoate crimes are attempt, conspiracy, and solicitation.

The criminal act element required for attempt must be more than thoughts or mere preparation. Modern jurisdictions use four tests to ascertain attempt. The proximity test analyzes how close the defendant is to completing the offense by examining how much is left to be done. The defendant may have to come dangerously close to completion but generally does not have to reach the last act before completion. The res ipsa loquitur test looks at the moment in time when the defendant stopped progressing toward completion to see if the defendant's acts indicate that the defendant has no other purpose than commission of the offense. The probable desistance test focuses on how far the defendant has progressed to see if it is probable that the defendant won't desist until the crime is complete. The Model Penal Code substantial steps test has two parts. First, the defendant must take substantial steps toward completion of the crime. Second, the defendant's actions must strongly corroborate the defendant's criminal purpose.

Some jurisdictions also criminalize preparatory crimes such as the manufacture or possession of burglar's tools. Preparatory crimes can be combined with attempt under the appropriate circumstances.

The criminal intent element required for attempt is the specific intent or purposely to commit the crime attempted. Legal impossibility can be a defense to attempt if the defendant mistakenly believes that a legal act attempted is illegal. Factual impossibility is not a defense to attempt if the crime cannot be completed because the facts are not as the defendant believes them to be. Voluntary abandonment is also a defense to attempt in some jurisdictions if the defendant voluntarily and completely renounces the attempted crime.

If a jurisdiction recognizes transferred intent, a defendant can be criminally responsible for attempt against the intended victim and the completed offense against the actual victim. In many jurisdictions, attempt merges into the crime if the crime is completed. Jurisdictions vary as to how they grade attempt; either attempt is graded the same or lower than the completed offense.

The criminal act element required for conspiracy is an agreement to commit any crime, commit a felony, falsely indict another for a crime, or falsely maintain any lawsuit, depending on the jurisdiction. Some jurisdictions also require an overt act in furtherance of the conspiracy that could be a legal or preparatory act.

The criminal intent element required for conspiracy in many jurisdictions is the specific intent or purposely to agree and to commit the crime at issue. In some states, a coconspirator can be prosecuted even if another coconspirator is not prosecuted or acquitted. Coconspirators do not need to know every other coconspirator, as long as they are aware that other coconspirators exist. A wheel conspiracy connects all members to one central member. A chain conspiracy connects members to each other in a linear fashion.

The Pinkerton rule holds coconspirators criminally responsible for every foreseeable crime committed in furtherance of the conspiracy. Wharton's rule creates a judicial presumption that a crime requiring two parties merges into a conspiracy made up of two parties.

Renunciation can be a defense to conspiracy if a coconspirator voluntarily and completely abandons the conspiracy and thwarts the crime that is its object. Conspiracy generally does not merge into the conspired offense. Jurisdictions vary as to how they grade conspiracy. Usually it is graded the same or lower than the crime that is the conspiracy's object, but it is not unconstitutional to punish conspiracy more severely than the conspired offense. The federal RICO statute is targeted at organized crime, including conspiracy.

Solicitation is the instigation of an agreement to commit any crime or, in some jurisdictions, a capital or first-degree felony. The criminal act element required for solicitation is words or conduct of inducement. The criminal intent element required for solicitation is specific intent or purposely to promote the crime solicited.

Renunciation is a defense to solicitation if it is voluntary and complete and thwarts the solicited offense. Jurisdictions vary as to how they grade solicitation. Some grade solicitation the same as the crime solicited, others vary the grading depending on the crime solicited, and still others grade solicitation as a misdemeanor.

You Be the Prosecutor

You are a prosecutor seeking a promotion. You want to win your next case so that you can make a good impression on your superior. Read the prompt, review the case, and then decide whether you would **accept** or **reject** it from a pool of cases available to junior prosecutors. Check your answers using the answer key at the end of the chapter.

The defendant is charged with witness tampering by **attempting** to kill the witness. A witness identified the defendant, a police officer, as someone who sexually assaulted her at gunpoint. The defendant met with two individuals, one of them an FBI informant, and told them that he wanted to kill the witness before trial. He was thereafter apprehended with a gun he had recently test-fired in the vicinity of the witness's house, which he had located with the FBI informant on a previous occasion. The jurisdiction in which you prosecute cases follows the "substantial steps" test for the attempt act element. Will you **accept** or **reject** the case? Read *U.S. v. Contreras*, 950 F.2d 232 (1991). The case is available at this link:
http://law.justia.com/cases/federal/appellate-courts/F2/950/232/110462/.

The defendant, a substitute teacher, is charged with two counts of **attempted** child sexual abuse for blocking the door of his residence and refusing to allow his thirteen-year-old student to leave. The defendant also asked the student for a kiss, was told "no," and moved his face in the proximity of the student's face. Will you **accept** or **reject** the case? Read *People v. Miller*, 856 N.Y.S. 2d 443 (2008). The case is available at this link:
http://scholar.google.com/scholar_case?case=13341924462190148625&q=%22Stan+Miller%22+%22People+v+Miller%22&hl=en&as_sdt=2,5&as_ylo=2007&as_vis=1.

The defendant is charged with **conspiracy** to commit manslaughter and various other crimes (including manslaughter). The defendant and an acquaintance agreed to shoot at some individuals near a housing project and walked over carrying guns. The defendant fired shots at a dumpster with people standing nearby, and one of the people was hit and killed. In your state, the criminal intent required for conspiracy is the specific intent or purposely to agree, and the specific intent or purposely to commit the crime that is the conspiracy's object. Will you **accept** or **reject** the case? Read *State v. Montgomery*, 22 Conn. App. 340 (1990). The case is available at this link:
http://scholar.google.com/scholar_case?case=355479416909506104&hl=en&as_sdt=2&as_vis=1&oi=scholarr

The defendant is charged with **solicitation** to traffic narcotics. The defendant was in a vehicle with other individuals, and a drug dealer approached them. The defendant gave the drug dealer twenty dollars to examine the drugs, gave the drugs back, and got his twenty dollars back. Thereafter, a police officer who had witnessed the transaction arrested everyone in the car. Will you **accept** or **reject** the case? Read *State v. Pinson*, 895 P.2d 274 (1995). The case is available at this link:
http://scholar.google.com/scholar_case?case=1966550891971070482&hl=en&as_sdt=2&as_vis=1&oi=scholarr.

Cases of Interest

- *People v. Hart*, 176 Cal. App. 4th 662 (2009), discusses attempt and the natural and probable consequences doctrine: http://scholar.google.com/scholar_case?case=9438325952737556456&hl= en&as_sdt=2&as_vis=1&oi=scholarr.
- *U.S. v. Guest*, 383 U.S. 745 (1966), discusses conspiracy and the US Constitution: http://www.oyez.org/cases/1960-1969/1965/1965_65.
- *Reynolds v. State*, 2007 Tex. App. LEXIS 6139 (2007), discusses solicitation to commit capital murder: https://casetext.com/case/reynolds-v-state-54.

Articles of Interest

- Criminal attempt: https://www.highbeam.com/doc/1G1-389935141.html
- José Padilla's conspiracy conviction: http://www.nytimes.com/2008/01/23/us/23padilla.html
- Criminal solicitation and entrapment: http://digitalcommons.uconn.edu/cgi/viewcontent.cgi?article =1071&context=econ_wpapers

Websites of Interest

- Discussion on various crimes, including inchoate crimes: http://criminal.laws.com/conspiracy
- Information about the RICO Act: http://www.ricoact.com

CC licensed content, Shared previously

- Criminal Law. **Provided by**: University of Minnesota Libraries Publishing . **Located at**: http://open.lib.umn.edu/criminallaw/. **License**: *CC BY-NC-SA: Attribution-NonCommercial-ShareAlike*

Chapter 9: Criminal Homicide

9.1 Homicide

Bill Salek – Evidence – CC BY-ND 2.0.

[W]hether it is made for the purpose of destroying animal life, or whether it was not made by man at all, or whether it was made by him for some other purpose, if it is a weapon, or if it is a thing with which death can be easily and readily produced, the law recognizes it as a deadly weapon...

—*Acers v. U.S.*, cited in Section 9 "Inference of Intent"

Learning Objectives

Define homicide.
Recognize that all homicides are not criminal.
Identify the corpus delicti components in a criminal homicide.
Compare the definition of fetus in criminal homicide and feticide statutes.
Compare common-law feticide and suicide with modern views.
Ascertain whether it is constitutional to criminalize assisted suicide.

In this section, you learn the definition of homicide and the meaning of *human being*, which vary from state to state. You also learn that suicide is not criminal, but *assisted suicide* might be, depending on the jurisdiction.

Synopsis of the History of Homicide

Homicide is the killing of one human being by another. Homicide is not always criminal. For example, a lawful execution pursuant to the death penalty is *homicide*, but it is not *criminal* homicide.

Homicide law in the United States has its origins in the English common law. Oxford professor Sir William Blackstone defined homicide as justifiable, excusable, or felonious. Justifiable homicides were not criminal because they did not include the concept of guilt. Excusable homicides were not criminal because they included minimal guilt. Felonious homicides were criminal and were considered the most heinous offenses known to man.

Initially at common law, every felonious or criminal homicide was punished by death. Gradually, as the law evolved, unlawful killings were divided into murder and manslaughter based on the defendant's criminal *intent*. Murder had the criminal intent element of malice aforethought and remained a capital offense. Manslaughter was an unlawful killing without malice and was punished by incarceration.

In modern times, most states define criminal homicide and its elements in *statutes*, which often are interpreted by case law. Many jurisdictions continue to follow Blackstone's philosophy and the common-law division between murder and manslaughter, as is discussed in this chapter.

Corpus Delicti in Criminal Homicide

An essential component of *every* criminal case, including criminal homicide, is corpus delicti. Corpus delicti is the substance of the crime at issue. The prosecution must prove corpus delicti beyond a reasonable doubt, with evidence *other than a defendant's confession* (People v. Ochoa, 2011). Although a detailed discussion of corpus delicti is beyond the scope of this text, corpus delicti in a criminal homicide case consists of the death of a victim, caused by the defendant, in an unlawful manner.

Often the victim's body is never discovered, which could make it more difficult for the prosecution to prove corpus delicti but not impossible. If there is sufficient circumstantial or direct evidence, such as bloodstains, surveillance footage, or witness testimony, the prosecution can prove corpus delicti without the victim's body and can convict the defendant of criminal homicide.

Feticide

Feticide is the intentional destruction of a fetus. At common law, a *human being* could not be the victim of criminal homicide unless it was born alive (Keeler v. Superior Court, 2010). The Model Penal Code takes this approach and defines human being as "a person who has been born and is alive" (Model Penal Code § 210.0 (1)). The modern trend in many jurisdictions is to include the fetus as a victim in a criminal homicide or feticide statute, excepting *abortion*. The definition of fetus is either set forth in the criminal homicide or feticide statute or created by case law. Many states and the federal government consider an embryo a fetus from the time of conception (Ala. Code, 2010). Other states determine that a fetus is formed when the child has "quickened," or is able to move within the womb—about four to five months after conception (Fla. Stat., 2010). A few states do not consider the fetus a victim of criminal homicide or feticide until it is viable and can survive outside the womb (Ind. Code, 2010).

Figure 9.1 Crack the Code

Crack the Code

Compare the following state laws:

Ga. Code § 16-5-80:

(a) A person commits the offense of feticide if he willfully kills an unborn child so far developed as to be ordinarily called 'quick' by any injury to the mother of such child, which would be murder if it resulted in the death of such mother.

(b) A person convicted of the offense of feticide shall be punished by imprisonment for life.

Ala. Code § 13A-6-1:

(a) As used in Article 1 and Article 2, the following terms shall have the meanings ascribed to them by this section:

(1) CRIMINAL HOMICIDE. Murder, manslaughter, or criminally negligent homicide.

(2) HOMICIDE. A person commits criminal homicide if he intentionally, knowingly, recklessly or with criminal negligence causes the death of another person.

(3) PERSON. The term, when referring to the victim of a criminal homicide or assault, means a human being, including an unborn child in utero at any stage of development, regardless of viability.

In Georgia, *feticide* is criminal, and a fetus is defined as an unborn child who has "quickened"; in Alabama, a person commits *criminal homicide* when killing an unborn child in utero at any stage of development.

Suicide

At common law, suicide was a crime. The punishment was forfeiture of the lands owned by the deceased. In modern times, most states do not criminalize suicide. However, almost all jurisdictions make it a crime to *assist* a suicide, and the US Supreme Court has held these statutes constitutional (Washington v. Glucksberg, 2010). Several states have special statutes that specifically punish assisted suicide less severely than their first- or second-degree murder statutes (Tex. Penal Code, 2010). A minority of states allow terminally ill patients to end their lives with the assistance of a physician (Or. Rev. Stat., 2010). The Model Penal Code provides that "[a] person who purposely aids or solicits another to commit suicide is guilty of a felony of the second degree if his conduct causes such suicide or an attempted suicide" (Model Penal Code § 210.5(2)).

Key Takeaways

- Homicide is the killing of one human being by another.
- Homicide is not always criminal. For example, a lawful execution pursuant to the death penalty is homicide, but it is not criminal homicide.
- The corpus delicti components in a criminal homicide are the death of the victim, caused by the defendant, in an unlawful manner.
- States that criminalize feticide consider an embryo a fetus at the moment of conception, when it quickens in the womb, or when it is viable and can survive outside the womb.

- In modern times, in many jurisdictions feticide is a crime (excepting abortion), and suicide is not. At common law, the following applied:
  - Feticide was not a crime; only a person "born alive" could be the victim of criminal homicide.
  - Suicide was a crime; the punishment was forfeiture of the deceased's lands.
- The US Supreme Court has held that it is constitutional to criminalize assisted suicide, and most states do. A minority of states allow a physician to legally end the life of a terminally ill patient.

Exercises

Answer the following questions. Check your answers using the answer key at the end of the chapter.

What is the fundamental difference between homicide and suicide?
Read *Washington v. Glucksberg*, 521 U.S. 702 (1997). Which part of the Constitution did the US Supreme Court analyze when it held that it is constitutional to criminalize assisted suicide? The case is available at this link: http://scholar.google.com/scholar_case?case=17920279791882194984&q=Washington+v.+Glucksberg&hl=en&as_sdt=2,5.

References

Ala. Code § 13A-6-1, accessed February 13, 2010, http://www.legislature.state.al.us/codeofalabama/1975/13A-6-1.htm.

Fla. Stat. § 782.09, accessed July 10, 2010, http://www.lawserver.com/law/state/florida/statutes/florida_statutes_782-09.

Ind. Code §35-42-1-1(4), accessed July 10, 2010, http://www.in.gov/legislative/ic/code/title35/ar42/ch1.html.

Keeler v. Superior Court, 2 Cal.3d 619 (1970), accessed July 10, 2010, http://scholar.google.com/scholar_case?case=2140632244672927312&hl=en&as_sdt=2&as_vis=1&oi=scholarr.

Or. Rev. Stat. § 127.800 et seq., accessed July 10, 2010, http://law.onecle.com/oregon/127-powers-of-attorney-advance-directives/index.html.

People v. Ochoa, 966 P.2d 442 (1998), accessed February 13, 2011, http://scholar.google.com/scholar_case?case=13299597995178567741&q=corpus+delicti+criminal+homicide&hl=en&as_sdt=2,5.

Tex. Penal Code § 22.08, accessed July 10, 2010, http://law.onecle.com/texas/penal/22.08.00.html.

Washington v. Glucksberg, 521 U.S. 702 (1997), accessed July 10, 2010, http://scholar.google.com/scholar_case?case=17920279791882194984&q=Washington+v.+Glucksberg&hl=en&as_sdt=2,5.

CC licensed content, Shared previously

- Criminal Law. **Provided by**: University of Minnesota Libraries Publishing . **Located at**: http://open.lib.umn.edu/criminallaw/. **License**: *CC BY-NC-SA: Attribution-NonCommercial-ShareAlike*

9.2 Murder

> ## Learning Objectives
>
> Define the criminal act element required for murder.
> Explain why criminal intent is an important element of murder.
> Identify, describe, and compare the three types of malice aforethought and the three Model Penal Code murder mental states.
> Explain the deadly weapon doctrine.
> Define death.
> Give examples of justifiable and excusable homicides.
> Ascertain which type of criminal homicide the defendant commits when deliberately and inadvertently transmitting AIDS.

Murder is a crime that has the elements of criminal act, criminal intent, causation, and harm. In this section, you learn the *elements* of murder. In upcoming sections, you learn the *factors* that classify murder as first degree, felony, and second degree.

Murder Act

Most jurisdictions define the **criminal act** element of murder as conduct that causes the victim's death (N.Y. Penal Law, 2011). The criminal act could be carried out with a weapon, a vehicle, poison, or the defendant's bare hands. Like all criminal acts, the conduct must be undertaken *voluntarily* and cannot be the result of a *failure to act* unless a duty to act is created by common law or statute.

Murder Intent

It is the criminal intent element that basically separates murder from manslaughter. At common law, the criminal intent element of murder was malice aforethought. In modern times, many states and the federal government retain the malice aforethought criminal intent (Cal. Penal Code, 2011). The Model Penal Code defines murder intent as **purposely**, **knowingly**, or **recklessly** under circumstances manifesting extreme indifference to the value of human life (Model Penal Code § 210.2).

An exception to the criminal intent element of murder is **felony murder**. Most jurisdictions criminalize felony murder, which does not require malice aforethought or the Model Penal Code murder mental states. Felony murder is discussed shortly.

The Meaning of Malice

Malice, as used in the term malice aforethought, is not the intent to vex or annoy. Nor is it hatred of the victim. Malice exists when the defendant desires the victim's death or is indifferent to whether the victim lives or dies. Malice is apparent in three criminal homicide situations: the defendant intends to kill the victim, the defendant intends to cause serious bodily injury to the victim, or the defendant has a depraved heart and does not care if the victim lives or dies.

The specific intent to kill the victim corresponds with the Model Penal Code's **purposely** murder mental state and is often referred to as express malice (N.R.S., 2011). The intent to cause serious bodily injury corresponds with the Model Penal Code's **knowingly** or **recklessly** murder mental states and is often referred to as implied malice. *Serious bodily injury* is a technical term and is generally defined in a state statute or by case law. The Model Penal Code defines serious bodily injury as "bodily injury which creates a substantial risk of death or which causes serious, permanent disfigurement, or protracted loss or impairment of the function of any bodily member or organ" (Model Penal Code § 210.0(3)). The depraved heart intent is also **implied malice** (N.R.S., 2011) and corresponds with the Model Penal Code's **knowingly** or **recklessly** murder mental states, depending on the attendant circumstances.

Example of Intent to Kill

Jay decides he wants to kill someone to see what it feels like. Jay drives slowly up to a crosswalk, accelerates, and then runs down an elderly lady who is crossing the street. Jay is acting with the *intent to kill*, which would be express malice or purposely.

Example of Intent to Cause Serious Bodily Injury

Jay wants to injure Robbie, a track teammate, so that he will be the best runner in the high school track meet. Jay waits for Robbie outside the locker room and when Robbie exits, Jay attacks him and stabs him several times in the knee. Unfortunately, one of Jay's stabbing wounds is in the carotid artery, and Robbie bleeds to death. Jay is acting with the *intent to cause serious bodily injury*, which would be implied malice, or knowingly or recklessly under circumstances manifesting extreme indifference to the value of human life.

Example of Depraved Heart Intent

Jay is angry at Brittany for turning him down when he asks her to the senior prom. Jay decides to teach Brittany a lesson. He knocks her unconscious as she walks home from school and then drives her out to a deserted field and dumps her on the ground. He thereafter leaves, feeling vindicated at the thought of her walking over ten miles to the nearest telephone. Brittany does not regain consciousness and spends the entire night in the field, where temperatures drop to 5°F. Brittany dies of exposure and acute hypothermia. Jay acts with the intent of depraved heart, also called *abandoned and malignant heart*. This criminal intent is another form of implied malice, or knowingly or recklessly under circumstances manifesting extreme indifference to the value of human life.

The Meaning of Aforethought

The term *aforethought* at common law meant that the defendant planned or premeditated the killing. However, this term has lost its significance in modern times and does not modify the malice element in any way. Premeditation is a factor that can elevate murder to first-degree murder, as is discussed shortly.

Inference of Intent

The deadly weapon doctrine creates an inference of murder intent when the defendant uses a deadly weapon (People v. Carines, 2011). A judge may instruct the jury that they can infer the defendant intended the natural and probable consequences of the criminal act, which are *death* when a deadly weapon is utilized. This basically alleviates the burden of having to prove criminal intent for murder.

A deadly weapon is any instrumentality that can kill when used in a manner calculated to cause death or serious bodily injury (Acers v. United States, 2010). The Model Penal Code defines deadly weapon as "any firearm, or other weapon, device, instrument, material or substance, whether animate or inanimate, which in the manner it is used or is intended to be used is known to be capable of producing death or serious bodily injury" (Model Penal Code § 210.0 (4)). Some examples of deadly weapons are knives, guns, broken bottles, or even bare hands if there is a discrepancy in the size of the attacker and the victim. Aside from creating an inference of intent for murder, use of a deadly weapon may also *enhance a sentence* for certain crimes.

Causation Issues in Murder

There is always a causation analysis for murder. The defendant must be the **factual** and **legal cause** of a very specific harm—the victim's death. Causation issues in murder are numerous. If a state has a one or three years and a day rule, this could complicate the causation scenario when a victim's life is artificially extended. One and three years and a day rules are discussed in detail in Chapter 4 "The Elements of a Crime". In addition, *co-felon liability* could extend criminal responsibility to defendants that did not actually kill the victim, as is discussed shortly.

Harm Element of Murder

As stated previously, the **harm** element of murder is a victim's death. With the advent of life-sustaining machines, jurisdictions have had to develop a definition for the term *dead*. A victim is legally dead when there is irreversible cessation of the entire brain, including the brain stem (Uniform Determination of Death Act, 2010).

Figure 9.2 Diagram of Murder

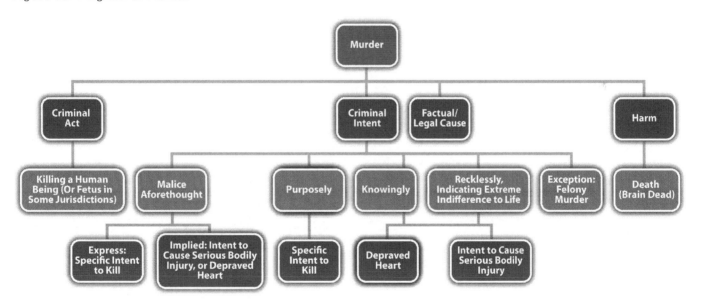

Justification and Excuse

As Blackstone stated, murder cannot be *justified* or *excused*. Justifiable and excusable homicides are *noncriminal*, and thus justification or excuse can operate as an **affirmative defense** in many jurisdictions. A thorough discussion of defenses based on justification and excuse is in Chapter 5 "Criminal Defenses, Part 1" and Chapter 6 "Criminal Defenses, Part 2".

A *justifiable homicide* is a homicide that is warranted under the circumstances. One example of a justifiable homicide is when a law enforcement officer shoots and kills a fleeing felon to prevent imminent great bodily injury or death. This killing is intentional and **purposeful** with **malice aforethought**, but it is noncriminal. The justification negates the criminality and the law enforcement officer will not be convicted of murder. A complete discussion of use of deadly force by law enforcement to arrest or apprehend a criminal defendant is in Chapter 5 "Criminal Defenses, Part 1". Other murder defenses based on justification are self-defense, defense of others, and defense of habitation.

An *excusable homicide* is a homicide that society forgives or pardons. One example of an excusable homicide is a homicide committed by a defendant who is found legally insane. This killing could also be intentional and **purposeful** with **malice aforethought**, but it is noncriminal. The excuse negates the criminality and the defendant will not be convicted of murder. A complete discussion of the insanity defense is in Chapter 6 "Criminal Defenses, Part 2".

AIDS and Homicide

The criminal transmission of AIDS is a new and evolving topic with state and federal courts and criminal codes. Many jurisdictions have statutes specifying that death by the *deliberate* transmission of AIDS is **murder** because murder intent is present (Minn. Stat. Ann., 2010). Death by the *inadvertent* transmission of AIDS is more likely **manslaughter**, although modern courts could begin to imply malice or murder intent in this situation. For states that follow the one or three years and a day rule, the time limit could affect any murder or manslaughter charge because medical breakthroughs have extended the life span of AIDS victims significantly.

Good News: The US Murder Rate Is Declining

Table 9.1 Murder Rate in the United States: Percent Change January–December

Years	Percent Change/Murder Rate
2006/2005	+1.8
2007/2006	−0.6
2008/2007	−3.9
2009/2008	−7.2

Source: Department of Justice, "Crime in the United States; Preliminary Annual Uniform Crime Report," accessed July 28, 2010, http://www.fbi.gov/ucr/prelimsem2009/table_3.html.

Key Takeaways

- The criminal act element required for murder is conduct that causes the victim's death.
- The criminal intent element of murder is important because it distinguishes murder from manslaughter.
- The three types of malice aforethought are intent to kill, intent to cause serious bodily injury, and depraved heart. The three Model Penal Code murder mental states are purposely, knowingly, or recklessly under circumstances manifesting extreme indifference to the value of human life.
- Express malice is the intent to kill the victim, or purposely, under the Model Penal Code. Implied malice is indifference to whether the victim lives or dies, or knowingly or recklessly under circumstances manifesting extreme indifference to the value of human life under the Model Penal Code. Implied malice, knowingly, and recklessly includes the intent to commit serious bodily injury and depraved heart intent.
- The deadly weapon doctrine creates an inference of murder intent when the defendant uses a deadly weapon. If the trier of fact accepts the inference, the prosecution does not have the burden of proving criminal intent.
- A human being is dead when there is irreversible cessation of the entire brain, including the brain stem.

Criminal Law

- An example of a justifiable homicide is a killing by law enforcement to prevent great bodily injury or death. An example of an excusable homicide is a killing perpetrated by a legally insane defendant.
- When a victim dies because of the deliberate transmission of AIDS, the crime is most likely murder because murder intent is present. When a victim dies because of the inadvertent transmission of AIDS, the crime is most likely manslaughter, although modern courts could begin to imply malice or murder intent in this situation.

Exercises

Answer the following questions. Check your answers using the answer key at the end of the chapter.

Jay is angry about the grade he received on his criminal law midterm. Jay pulls a loaded revolver out of his backpack, aims at a tree and fires in an attempt to release his frustrations. Unfortunately, Jay is an inexperienced marksman and the bullet strikes an innocent bystander in the forehead, killing him. What was Jay's criminal intent when shooting the revolver?
A prosecutor reviews the file for Jay's criminal case. After reading the facts, he chuckles and tells his paralegal, "It won't be hard to prove criminal intent in this case." Is this true? Why or why not?
Read *U.S. v. Moore*, 846 F.2d 1163 (1988). Did the US Court of Appeals for the Eighth Circuit hold that teeth are a deadly weapon when the defendant is infected with the HIV virus? The case is available at this link: http://openjurist.org/846/f2d/1163.

References

Acers v. United States, 164 U.S. 388 (1896), accessed February 13, 2010, http://scholar.google.com/scholar_case?case=16538901276155737856&hl=en&as_sdt=2&as_vis=1&oi=scholarr.

Cal. Penal Code § 187, accessed February 4, 2011, http://law.justia.com/california/codes/2009/pen/187-199.html.

Minn. Stat. Ann. § 609.2241, accessed February 24, 2010, https://www.revisor.mn.gov/statutes/?id=609.2241.

N.R.S. § 200.020(1), accessed February 13, 2011, http://law.onecle.com/nevada/crimes/200.020.html.

N.Y. Penal Law § 125.27, accessed February 4, 2011, http://law.onecle.com/new-york/penal/PEN0125.27_125.27.html.

People v. Carines, 597 N.W. 2d 130 (1999), accessed February 13, 2011, http://scholar.google.com/scholar_case?case=6441565823584670121&q=deadly+weapon+doctrine&hl=en&as_sdt=2,5.

Uniform Determination of Death Act, accessed February 14, 2010, http://www.gencourt.state.nh.us/rsa/html/X/141-D/141-D-mrg.htm.
CC licensed content, Shared previously

- Criminal Law. **Provided by**: University of Minnesota Libraries Publishing . **Located at**: http://open.lib.umn.edu/criminallaw/. **License**: *CC BY-NC-SA: Attribution-NonCommercial-ShareAlike*

9.3 First-Degree Murder

Learning Objectives

Ascertain the three types of murder that are typically first degree.
Define premeditated murder.
Explain the significance of the criminal act element of murder in premeditated murder.
Define murder by a specified means.
Give examples of specified means for first-degree murder.
Analyze first-degree murder grading.
Ascertain the circumstances that merit capital punishment.

In this section, you analyze the *factors* that classify a murder as first-degree murder. Keep in mind that the criminal act, criminal intent, causation, and harm elements of murder have already been discussed.

Factors Classifying Murder as First Degree

States and the federal government usually include premeditated murder, murder by a specified means, and very serious **felony murders** in their first-degree murder statutes. Felony murder is discussed shortly.

Premeditated Murder

Premeditated murder was originally and historically the predominant form of murder in any first-degree murder statute. A common statutory definition of first-degree premeditated murder is a willful, deliberate, premeditated killing (Mich. Comp. Laws, 2010).

Definition of Willful, Deliberate, and Premeditated

Most jurisdictions define willful as a **specific intent to kill**, **purposely**, or *express malice*. Jurisdictions differ when interpreting deliberate and premeditated. A minority of jurisdictions equate express malice or purposely with deliberation and premeditation, which means that the prosecution need only prove specific intent to kill for a first-degree premeditated murder conviction (Hawthorne v. State, 2010). However, this interpretation could blur the distinction between first and second-degree murder. The majority of jurisdictions have defined *deliberate* as calm and methodical, without passion or anger (People v. Anderson, 2011). *Premeditated* generally means the defendant reflected on the act or planned ahead (People v. Cole, 2011). In other words, if the defendant specifically intends to kill the victim and rationally, purposefully, takes steps that culminate in the victim's death, the defendant has committed first-degree premeditated murder in many jurisdictions.

Often it is the act itself that proves the killing was willful, deliberate, and premeditated. If the killing is carried out in a manner that indicates a strong and calculated desire to bring about the victim's death, the trier of fact can and often does conclude that the murder was premeditated (State v. Snowden, 2010).

Most jurisdictions agree that an *extended period of time* is not a requirement of premeditation (Commonwealth v. Carroll, 2010). Thus a murder can be premeditated and first degree even if it is conceived only moments before the actual killing (State v. Schrader, 2010). Some jurisdictions do not require *any* appreciable time lapse between the formation of intent and the criminal act (State v. Snowden, 2010).

Example of a Willful, Deliberate, Premeditated Murder

Imagine that Joannie and her husband Tim are in a terrible fight in the kitchen. Tim tells Joannie that he is going to get a divorce and will thereafter seek full custody of their two young children. Joannie states, "Wait here. I need to go to the bathroom. I will be right back." She walks down the hall, but goes into the *bedroom*, rather than the bathroom, and removes a handgun from the nightstand drawer. She then walks to the bathroom and flushes the toilet. Hiding the handgun in the pocket of her bathrobe, she walks back into the kitchen, removes it, and shoots Tim four times in the abdomen, killing him.

In this scenario, Joannie probably could be convicted of premeditated murder in most jurisdictions. Joannie shoots and kills Tim in a calm, methodical manner, evidencing **deliberation**. Her manufactured excuse and flushing of the toilet indicate **planning**. The act of shooting Tim four times shows that Joannie has a **specific intent to kill** and a strong and calculated desire to bring about Tim's death. Note that *timing* is not an issue here. Even a few minutes are enough to carry out a premeditated murder if the proper facts are present.

Example of a Spontaneous Killing

Compare the previous example with this scenario. Frank, Dillon's supervisor, calls Dillon into his office and fires him. Enraged, Dillon grabs a heavy brass paperweight from the top of Frank's desk and strikes him in the forehead, killing him instantly. In this example, Dillon acts in *anger*, not calm, cool, reflection. The act of grabbing a heavy brass paperweight appears *impulsive*, not planned. There is no evidence to indicate that Dillon knew he would be fired or knew that there was a brass paperweight on Frank's desk. In addition, the single blow to the head does not necessarily indicate that Dillon had a strong and calculated desire to *kill* Frank. Dillon's conduct may be supported by **murder intent** (most likely implied malice, knowingly, or recklessly under circumstances manifesting extreme indifference to the value of human life), but there is no evidence of specific intent to kill, deliberation, or premeditation. Thus Frank's killing would probably not be first-degree premeditated murder in most jurisdictions.

Murder by a Specified Means

Murder by a **specified means** is a specific *method* of killing that is extremely heinous. Most states list the specified means in their first-degree murder statutes. Some examples of commonly included specified means are murder by drive-by shooting, destructive device like a bomb, weapon of mass destruction, ammunition designed to puncture a bulletproof vest, poison, torture, or lying in wait, which is an ambush-style killing (Cal. Penal Code, 2010). Note that all the aforementioned *methods* of killing involve premeditation to a certain extent and could also probably qualify as first-degree premeditated murder.

Figure 9.3 Diagram of First-Degree Murder

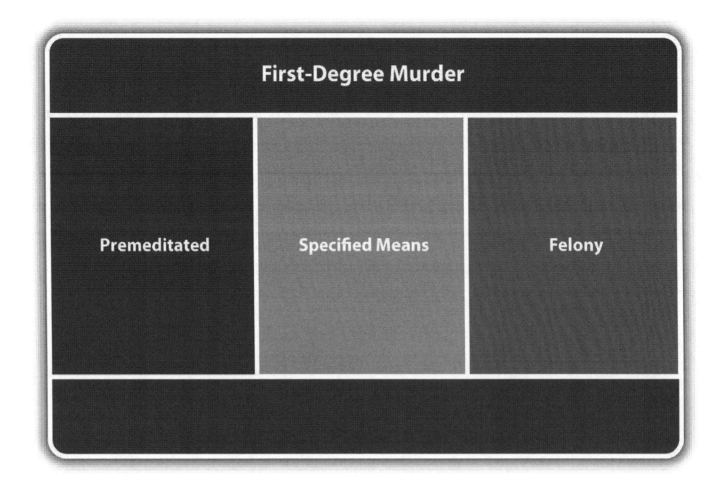

First-Degree Murder Grading

Most states divide murder into **first** and **second degree** (N.R.S., 2011). Some states add a **third degree** of murder that generally includes less serious sentencing options (Pa. Cons. Stat. Ann., 2010). The Model Penal Code classifies *all* murders as felonies of the first degree (Model Penal Code § 210.2(2)).

First-degree murder is the highest classification of murder and results in the most extreme punishment available in a jurisdiction's punishment scheme. If the jurisdiction allows for the death penalty, first-degree murder typically is the only crime against an individual that qualifies the defendant for execution (N.R.S., 2011). If the jurisdiction does not allow for the death penalty, first-degree murder often qualifies the defendant for *life in prison* (Mich. Comp. Laws, 2011).

Capital Punishment

The US Supreme Court has held that criminal homicide is the *only* crime against an individual that can merit the death penalty (Kennedy v. Louisiana, 2010). A discussion of crimes against the government (such as treason) that merit the death penalty is in Chapter 13 "Crimes against the Government".

In states that allow capital punishment, first-degree murder with one or more aggravating factor(s) is generally a capital offense. Examples of aggravating factors are killing more than one person, killing for financial gain, killing with a particularly heinous method, or killing a peace officer (Death Penalty Information Center 1, 2010). In general, the trier of fact must ensure that the aggravating factor(s) are not outweighed by mitigating factor(s). Examples of mitigating factors are the youth of the defendant, the defendant's lack of a criminal history, and the fact that the defendant was acting under extreme emotional or mental disturbance (Death Penalty Information Center 2, 2010).

Figure 9.4 Diagram of Capital Punishment

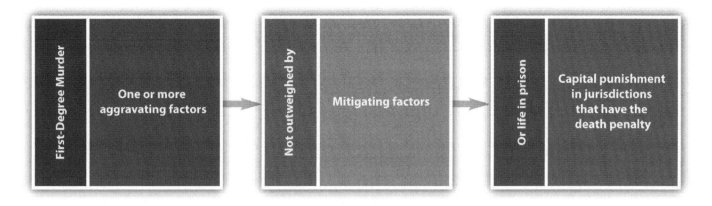

The Peterson Case

A jury convicted Scott Peterson of first-degree premeditated murder for the killing of his pregnant wife Laci Peterson. They also convicted him of second-degree murder for the killing of his unborn son Conner (Montaldo, C. 1, 2010). The governing statute was California Penal Code § 189 (Cal. Penal Code, 2010). After issuing the verdict, the jury sentenced Peterson to death based on the special circumstance of killing more than one person (Montaldo, C. 2, 2010).

The prosecution was successful without *direct evidence* or proof of the *cause of death* (Montaldo, C. 1, 2010).

Congress was inspired by the Peterson case to pass the **Unborn Victims of Violence Act**, 18 U.S.C. § 1841 (18 U.S.C., 2010), creating the new federal crime of killing an unborn child.

Key Takeaways

- Most states and the federal government include premeditated murder, murder by a specified means, and felony murder in their first-degree murder statutes.
- Premeditated murder is typically a purposeful killing committed after calm planning and reflection. An extensive length of time between the formation of criminal intent and the criminal act is not generally a requirement of premeditated murder.
- The criminal act can help prove that a murder was premeditated. If the killing is carried out in a manner that indicates a strong and calculated desire to bring about the victim's death, the trier of fact can conclude that the murder was premeditated.
- When the defendant commits murder with a particularly heinous method, the killing is murder by a specified means.
- First-degree murder statutes often include the following specified means: murder by drive-by shooting, destructive device like a bomb, weapon of mass destruction, ammunition designed to puncture a bulletproof vest, poison, torture, or lying in wait.
- First-degree murder is the highest classification of murder with the most severe sentencing options. If the jurisdiction allows for capital punishment, first-degree murder typically is the only crime against an individual that merits the death penalty. If the jurisdiction does not allow for capital punishment, first-degree murder often qualifies the defendant for life in prison.
- The only crime against an individual that can merit capital punishment is criminal homicide. In most jurisdictions, the defendant must commit first-degree murder combined with one or more aggravating factors that are not outweighed by mitigating factors to receive the death penalty.

Exercises

Answer the following questions. Check your answers using the answer key at the end of the chapter.

Johnnie decides he wants to kill Marcus, the leader of a rival gang. Johnnie knows that Marcus always hangs out in front of the gas station on Friday nights. Johnnie puts his gun in the glove compartment of his car and drives to the gas station on a Friday night. He sees Marcus standing out front. He slowly drives by, takes aim, and shoots Marcus from the car, killing him. Could this be first-degree murder? Explain your answer.

Read *State v. West*, 844 S.W.2d 144 (1992). Did the Supreme Court of Tennessee hold that a defendant's failure to report a shooting to the police for over an hour and concealment of the murder weapon constitutes sufficient evidence to prove premeditated murder? The case is available at this link:
http://scholar.google.com/scholar_case?case=3481778471457660977&hl=en&as_sdt=2002&as_vis=1.

Read *U.S. v. Downs*, 56 F.3d 973 (1995). Identify motive, planning, and preconceived design in this case. The case is available at this link: https://casetext.com/case/us-v-downs-2.

References

Cal. Penal Code § 189, accessed February 18, 2010, http://law.onecle.com/california/penal/189.html.

Commonwealth v. Carroll, 412 Pa. 525 (1963), accessed February 18, 2010, http://scholar.google.com/scholar_case?case=13694151174720667465&hl=en&as_sdt=2&as_vis=1&oi=scholarr.

Death Penalty Information Center 1, "Aggravating Factors for Capital Punishment by State," accessed September 23, 2010, http://www.deathpenaltyinfo.org/aggravating-factors-capital-punishment-state.

Death Penalty Information Center 2, "Terry Lenamon's List of State Death Penalty Mitigation Statutes," accessed September 23, 2010, http://www.jdsupra.com/post/documentViewer.aspx?fid=d61d8c7b-896b-4c1a-bd87-f86425206b45.

Hawthorne v. State, 835 So. 2d 14 (2003), accessed September 19, 2010, http://scholar.google.com/scholar_case?case=6294577581180338458&hl=en&as_sdt=2&as_vis=1&oi=scholarr.

Kennedy v. Louisiana, 128 S. Ct. 2641 (2008), accessed September 21, 2010, http://www.law.cornell.edu/supct/html/07-343.ZO.html.

Mich. Comp. Laws § 750.316, accessed September 19, 2010, http://law.onecle.com/michigan/750-michigan-penal-code/mcl-750-316.html.

Montaldo, C., "The Peterson Verdict: Special Circumstances," About.com website, accessed July 15, 2010, http://crime.about.com/od/news/a/scott_verdict.htm.

Montaldo, C. 1, "Scott Peterson Guilty of first-degree murder," About.com website, accessed July 15, 2010, http://crime.about.com/od/news/a/scott_peterson.htm.

N.R.S. § 200.030, accessed February 13, 2011, http://law.onecle.com/nevada/crimes/200.030.html.

Pa. Cons. Stat. Ann. § 2502, accessed February 14, 2010, http://wings.buffalo.edu/law/bclc/web/pa2501.html.

People v. Anderson, 447 P.2d 942 (1968), accessed February 13, 2011, http://scholar.google.com/scholar_case?case=9215896464929219588&q=definition+of+deliberate+premeditated+murder&hl=en&as_sdt=2,5.

People v. Cole, 95 P.3d 811 (2004), accessed February 13, 2011, http://scholar.google.com/scholar_case?case=18037950298665209340&q=definition+of+deliberate+premeditated+murder&hl=en&as_sdt=2,5.

State v. Schrader, 302 SE 2d 70 (1982), accessed September 19, 2010, http://scholar.google.com/scholar_case?case=287453315188864266&hl=en&as_sdt=2&as_vis=1&oi=scholarr.

State v. Snowden, 313 P.2d 706 (1957), accessed September 19, 2010, http://scholar.google.com/scholar_case?case=16193283019378884065&hl=en&as_sdt=2&as_vis=1&oi=scholarr.

18 U.S.C. § 1841, accessed February 13, 2010, http://crime.about.com/gi/o.htm?zi=1/XJ&zTi=1&sdn=crime&cdn=newsissues&tm=435&gps=634_398_1276_788 &f=10&tt= 2&bt=0&bts=0&zu=http%3A//www.nrlc.org/Unborn_Victims/UVVAEnrolled.html.
CC licensed content, Shared previously

- Criminal Law. **Provided by**: University of Minnesota Libraries Publishing . **Located at**: http://open.lib.umn.edu/criminallaw/. **License**: *CC BY-NC-SA: Attribution-NonCommercial-ShareAlike*

9.4 Felony Murder

Learning Objectives

Define the criminal intent element required for felony murder.

Compare the criminal intent element of felony murder to implied malice, knowingly, or recklessly under circumstances manifesting extreme indifference to human life.

Explain the rule of co-felon liability for felony murder.

Explain an exception to the rule of co-felon liability for felony murder.

Analyze criminal responsibility for felony murder when someone other than a co-felon kills the victim.

Analyze criminal responsibility for felony murder when someone other than a co-felon kills a co-felon.

Describe concurrence of the felony and the homicide for felony murder.

Analyze felony murder grading and ascertain the felonies that typically classify felony murder as first degree.

Felony murder is a criminal homicide that occurs during the commission or attempted commission of a felony. Most states and the federal government include felony murder in their penal codes (18 U.S.C., 2011). However, it has not been universally adopted. The Model Penal Code does not include felony murder per se. It does suggest a rebuttable presumption that killings that occur during the commission of specified dangerous felonies exhibit recklessness under circumstances manifesting extreme indifference to the value of human life (Model Penal Code § 210.2(1)(b)).

Felony Murder Intent

What distinguishes felony murder from murder is the absence of the typical **murder** intent. The criminal intent element required for felony murder is the intent required for a **felony** that causes a victim's death.

Explanation of Felony Murder Intent

When the defendant commits a felony that is inherently dangerous to life, he or she does so knowing that some innocent victim may die. In essence, this awareness is similar to implied malice, knowingly, or recklessly under circumstances manifesting extreme indifference to the value of human life. What is difficult to justify is a conviction for felony murder when the felony is *not* inherently dangerous to life. Thus most jurisdictions limit the felony murder doctrine to felonies that create a foreseeable risk of violence or death. States that include nonviolent felonies in their felony murder statutes generally grade them as **second-** or **third-degree** felony murder (Fla. Stat. Ann., 2010).

Example of Felony Murder Intent

Joaquin, who has just lost his job, decides to burn down his apartment building because he can't afford to pay the rent. Joaquin carefully soaks his apartment with lighter fluid, exits into the hallway, and throws a lit, lighter-fluid-soaked towel into the apartment. He then runs outside to watch the entire building burn down. Several tenants die of smoke inhalation because of the fire. In jurisdictions that recognize felony murder, Joaquin can probably be charged with and convicted of murder for every one of these deaths.

In this example, Joaquin did not *intend to kill* the tenants. However, he did most likely have the criminal intent necessary for **arson**. Therefore, felony murder convictions are appropriate. Note that Joaquin exhibited extreme indifference to whether the tenants in the building lived or died, which could also constitute the criminal intent of **implied malice** or **depraved heart**.

Liability of Co-Felons for Felony Murder

It is common for more than one defendant to cooperate in the commission of a felony. Group participation in criminal conduct could constitute more than one crime—for example, conspiracy—and could also place criminal responsibility squarely on a defendant who did not *commit* the criminal act. The general rule for felony murder in many jurisdictions is that if *one* defendant kills a victim during the commission or attempted commission of a specified felony, *all defendants* involved in the felony are guilty of felony murder (State v. Hoang, 2011).

Example of Co-Felon Liability for Felony Murder

Joe and Jane dream up a plan to rob a local bank. Joe is designated as the primary robber and is supposed to enter the bank and hand a note to the teller demanding all the money in her station. Jane's role in the felony is to drive the getaway vehicle to the bank, wait outside the front door with the motor running, and transport Joe and the money back to their apartment after the bank transaction is completed. Joe takes a handgun hidden beneath his jacket into the bank. He passes the note to the teller, and she frantically summons a security guard. As the security guard starts to approach, Joe pulls out the gun. An elderly lady standing to the left of Joe suffers a heart attack and dies at the sight of the gun. In this case, Joe *and Jane* can probably be convicted of felony murder. Note that Jane did nothing to directly cause the victim's death from a heart attack. However, Jane *did* drive the getaway vehicle with the criminal intent to commit robbery, so Jane is criminally responsible for the consequences in many jurisdictions.

Exception to Co-Felon Liability for Felony Murder

Some jurisdictions provide an **exception to co-felon liability** for felony murder if the defendant did not actually commit the act that killed the victim and had neither knowledge nor awareness that a death might occur (N.Y. Penal Law, 2010).

Example of the Exception to Co-Felon Liability for Felony Murder

Review the example with Joe and Jane in Section 9 "Example of Co-Felon Liability for Felony Murder". Change this example so that Jane is a teller at the local bank. Joe and Jane plan the "robbery" so that Jane is to pretend Joe is a customer, and hand Joe all the money in her station after he enters the bank *unarmed* and passes her a phony check made out to "cash." Without informing Jane, Joe brings a gun into the bank, "just in case." The security guard observes Jane handing Joe large amounts of cash. Suspicious, he begins to approach the station. Joe notices and frantically pulls out the gun and points it at the security guard. The elderly lady standing to the left of Joe suffers a heart attack and dies at the sight of the gun. In this example, Jane may have a valid defense to co-felon liability for the elderly lady's death in some jurisdictions. Although Jane had the intent to commit theft, a trier of fact could determine that Jane had neither the *knowledge* nor *awareness* that a death might occur because she believed she was cooperating in a nonviolent offense. Thus it is possible that in certain jurisdictions only Joe is subject to a conviction of felony murder in this case.

Liability When Someone Other than the Defendant Kills the Victim

Generally, if the felony is inherently dangerous to life, and the defendant or defendants intentionally create a situation that is likely to result in death, if death does result, each and every defendant is guilty of felony murder. In some jurisdictions, this criminal liability exists even *when someone other than a co-felon* kills the victim (People v. Hernandez, 2010). Review the bank robbery committed by Joe and Jane, as discussed in Section 9 "Example of Co-Felon Liability for Felony Murder". If the security guard takes a shot at Joe but misses and kills the bank teller instead, both Joe and Jane are guilty of the bank teller's death pursuant to this interpretation of the felony-murder doctrine.

Some jurisdictions relieve a defendant from criminal liability for felony murder if the death is the *death of a co-felon*, rather than a completely innocent victim (State v. Canola, 2010). In the case of Joe and Jane discussed in Section 9 "Example of Co-Felon Liability for Felony Murder", if the security guard shoots and kills *Joe* in a jurisdiction that recognizes this exception, Jane is not guilty of felony murder.

Concurrence of the Felony and the Death of the Victim

Another important aspect that must be analyzed in any felony murder case is the **concurrence** of the felony and the death of the victim. The felony and the death must be part and parcel of the same continuous transaction. Therefore, there must be a determination of (1) when the felony begins and (2) when the felony ends. If the death occurs *before* or *after* the commission or attempted commission of the felony, the defendant might not be guilty of felony murder.

Example of a Death That Occurs before the Felony Begins

Carlos shoots and kills his drug dealer in a fit of temper because the drugs he bought are placebo. After the killing, it occurs to Carlos that the drug dealer might be carrying significant amounts of cash. Carlos thereafter steals some cash from the drug dealer's pockets and runs off. Although this killing is probably murder, it is *not* **felony murder**. Carlos stole money from his drug dealer, but the theft occurred *after the murder*. Thus the killing did not happen *during* a robbery. If premeditation is proven, this could still be first-degree murder, but it is not first-degree felony murder.

Death That Occurs after the Felony Ends

More commonly, the issue is whether the killing occurs after the felony ends. The general rule is that the felony ends when the defendant has reached *a place of temporary safety* (People v. Young, 2010). This place does *not* have to be the defendant's residence; it could simply be a hiding place. Pursuant to this rule, a death that occurs during a car chase as the defendants flee the scene of the crime is considered felony murder (Del. Code Ann. Tit. 11, 2011).

Figure 9.5 Diagram of Felony Murder

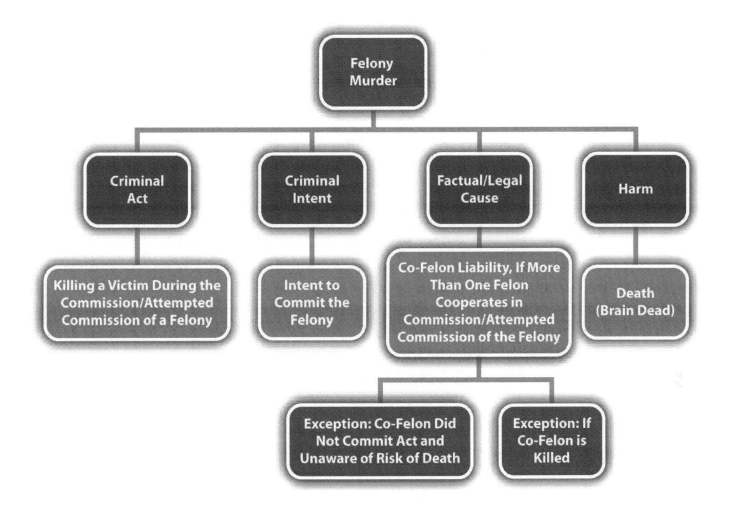

Felony Murder Grading

Felony murder can be **first**, **second**, or **third degree** (Fla. Stat. Ann., 2010). Some common examples of felonies listed in first-degree murder statutes are arson, rape, carjacking, robbery, burglary, kidnapping, and certain forcible sexual felonies (Cal. Penal Code, 2010).

Key Takeaways

- The criminal intent element required for felony murder is the intent required for the underlying felony, not murder intent.
- If a felony is inherently dangerous to life, the defendant may act with implied malice, knowingly, or recklessly manifesting extreme indifference to human life when committing or attempting to commit the felony.
- If more than one defendant commits or attempts to commit a felony, all defendants are guilty of felony murder if a victim is killed during the commission or attempted commission of the felony.
- Some jurisdictions will not find a co-felon criminally responsible for felony murder if the co-felon did not commit the act of killing and was unaware that there was a risk of death.
- In some jurisdictions, all co-felons are criminally responsible for felony murder when someone other than a co-felon kills a victim during the commission or attempted commission of a felony that is inherently dangerous to life.
- In some jurisdictions, all co-felons are not criminally responsible for felony murder when someone other than a co-felon kills a co-felon during the commission or attempted commission of a felony.
- The killing must take place during the commission or attempted commission of a felony for the felony murder rule to apply.
- Felony murder can be first, second, or third degree. Typical felonies that classify felony murder as

first degree are arson, rape, carjacking, robbery, burglary, kidnapping, and certain forcible sexual felonies.

Exercises

Answer the following questions. Check your answers using the answer key at the end of the chapter.

Read *People v. Anderson*, 666 N.W.2d 696 (2003). Did the Minnesota Supreme Court uphold a charge of second-degree felony murder when the underlying felonies were possession of a firearm by a convicted felon and possession of a stolen firearm? The case is available at this link: http://law.justia.com/cases/california/supreme-court/3d/6/628.html.

Kurt robs a convenience store at gunpoint. As the cashier hands him money out of the cash register, Kurt hears a siren and runs outside, stuffing the money in his pockets. He sees a dark alley and dashes into it. While he crouches there waiting for the police to leave, a homeless person living in the alley taps him on the shoulder. Startled, Kurt spins around and shoots and kills the homeless person. Is this felony murder? Explain your answer.

Read *Enmund v. Florida*, 458 U.S. 782 (1982). In *Enmund*, the US Supreme Court held that the death penalty is unconstitutional in a felony murder case for one who neither took life, attempted to take life, nor intended to take life. On which part of the Constitution did the Court rely in reaching this holding? The case is available at this link: http://www.law.cornell.edu/supct/html/historics/USSC_CR_0458_0782_ZO.html.

References

Cal. Penal Code § 189, accessed February 18, 2010, http://law.onecle.com/california/penal/189.html.

Del. Code Ann. Tit. 11 § 636 (a) (2), accessed February 18, 2010, http://law.justia.com/delaware/codes/title11/c005-sc02.html.

Fla. Stat. Ann. § 782.04[4], accessed February 18, 2010, http://law.onecle.com/florida/crimes/782.04.html.

N.Y. Penal Law § 125.25 (3), accessed February 18, 2010, http://law.onecle.com/new-york/penal/PEN0125.25_125.25.html.

People v. Hernandez, 82 N.Y.2d 309 (1993), accessed February 18, 2010, http://scholar.google.com/scholar_case?case=3094702040122584711&q=People+v.+Hernandez+82+N.Y.2d+309&hl=en&as_sdt=2,5.

People v. Young, 105 P.2d 487 (2005), accessed February 18, 2010, http://scholar.google.com/scholar_case?case=5918096649976465300&q=felony+murder+%22temporary+safety%22&hl=en&as_sdt=2,5.

State v. Canola, 73 N.J. 206 (1977), accessed February 18, 2010, http://www.audiocasefiles.com/acf_cases/8722-state-v-canola.

State v. Hoang, 755 P.2d 7 (1988), accessed February 13, 2011, http://scholar.google.com/scholar_case?case=2216953450979337225&q=heart+attack+during+robbery+%22co+felon%22&hl=en&as_sdt=2,5.

18 U.S.C. § 1111, accessed February 4, 2011, http://codes.lp.findlaw.com/uscode/18/I/51/1111.
CC licensed content, Shared previously

- Criminal Law. **Provided by**: University of Minnesota Libraries Publishing . **Located at**: http://open.lib.umn.edu/criminallaw/. **License**: *CC BY-NC-SA: Attribution-NonCommercial-ShareAlike*

9.5 Second-Degree Murder

Learning Objectives

Compare statutory definitions of second-degree murder.
Ascertain two types of murder that are typically second degree.
Analyze second-degree murder grading.

States that classify murder as either first or second degree often define second-degree murder as any murder that is not first-degree murder (Mich. Comp. Laws, 2010). This definition excludes murders that are premeditated or committed with a specified means. It includes *implied malice* murder, such as murder committed with the intent to inflict serious bodily injury and depraved heart murder.

Depraved Heart Murder

Some statutes use the Model Penal Code's language and define second-degree murder as a killing executed recklessly, under circumstances manifesting extreme indifference to the value of human life (K.S.A., 2010). This definition embodies the concept, discussed previously, of murders committed with a depraved or abandoned and malignant heart. The facts that give rise to this type of second-degree murder often indicate the mens rea of *recklessness*, rather than purposeful or knowing intent or express malice. Whether the killing is a second-degree murder or manslaughter is left to the trier of fact and often rests on the **degree** of recklessness exhibited. If the defendant's conduct indicates *extreme* indifference to life, the killing is a depraved heart murder. If the defendant's conduct is simply reckless, the killing is manslaughter. As the Model Penal Code states in its comments, "[w]hether recklessness is so extreme that it demonstrates similar indifference is not a question, it is submitted, that can be further clarified. It must be left directly to the trier of fact under instructions which make it clear that recklessness that can fairly be assimilated to purpose or knowledge should be treated as murder and that less extreme recklessness should be punished as manslaughter" (A.L.I., Model Penal Code & Commentaries Part II § 210.2, Comment. 4, pp. 21–22 (1980)).

Example of a Depraved Heart Murder

After watching his fifth-grade daughter play softball, Doug attends a party with her team and other parents at the local pizza parlor. Doug's daughter leaves the party with her mother, Doug's ex-wife. Doug consumes ten beers and then leaves the party and smokes some crack cocaine in his vehicle. He thereafter begins driving home. As he is driving in a busy section of town, he hears his phone beep, indicating the receipt of a text message. He grabs his phone and starts reading the text. This lapse of attention causes him to run a red light and broadside a vehicle turning left in front of him, killing a child sitting in the passenger seat. Doug puts his vehicle in reverse, drives around the car he hit, and leaves the scene of the accident. These facts could give rise to a conviction for depraved heart second-degree murder. Although Doug did not act with specific intent to kill, his conduct in driving while under the influence of alcohol and crack cocaine, reading a text message while driving impaired in a busy part of town, and leaving the scene of an accident most likely elevate Doug's intent from ordinary recklessness to recklessness indicating extreme indifference to the value of human life. Thus the trier of fact could find Doug guilty of murder rather than manslaughter in this case.

Figure 9.6 Diagram of Second-Degree Murder

Second-Degree Murder Grading

Most jurisdictions **grade** second-degree murder *lower* than first-degree murder and include less serious sentencing options (N.R.S. § 200.030, 2011). Most jurisdictions grade second-degree murder *higher* than manslaughter because it has a more heinous criminal intent (N.R.S. § 200.080, 2011). Manslaughter is discussed shortly.

Key Takeaways

- Second-degree murder is often defined as any murder that is not first-degree murder. Second-degree murder can also be defined as murder committed recklessly, under circumstances evidencing extreme indifference to life.
- Second-degree murder includes implied malice murder, such as murder with the intent to cause serious bodily injury, and depraved heart murders.
- Second-degree murder is graded lower than first-degree murder but higher than manslaughter.

Exercises

Answer the following questions. Check your answers using the answer key at the end of the chapter.

Reread the second question of the exercises in Section 9.4 "Felony Murder". When Kurt shoots the homeless person in the alley, is this killing first or second-degree murder? Explain your answer.
Read *Berry v. Superior Court*, 208 Cal. App. 3d 783 (1989). In *Berry*, the defendant was charged with second-degree murder when his pit bull attacked and killed a young child. The pit bull had never bitten anyone before this incident. Did the California Court of Appeal uphold the defendant's murder charge on a theory of implied malice? The case is available at this link:
http://lawschool.courtroomview.com/acf_cases/9986-berry-v-superior-court.
Read *Dowda v. State*, 776 So.2d 714 (2000). Why did the Mississippi Court of Appeals hold that this killing was a depraved heart murder? The case is available at this link:
http://www.mssc.state.ms.us/images/Opinions/Conv9328.pdf.

References

K.S.A. § 21-3402, accessed September 21, 2010, http://kansasstatutes.lesterama.org/Chapter_21/Article_34/21-3402.html.

Mich. Comp. Laws § 750.317, accessed February 24, 2010, http://www.legislature.mi.gov/(S(gjc5ys55et3ukfj0uq5uehqm))/mileg.aspx?page=GetObject&objectname=mcl-750-317.

N.R.S. § 200.030, accessed February 13, 2011, http://law.onecle.com/nevada/crimes/200.030.html.

N.R.S. § 200.080, accessed February 13, 2011, http://law.onecle.com/nevada/crimes/200.080.html.
CC licensed content, Shared previously

- Criminal Law. **Provided by**: University of Minnesota Libraries Publishing . **Located at**: http://open.lib.umn.edu/criminallaw/. **License**: *CC BY-NC-SA: Attribution-NonCommercial-ShareAlike*

9.6 Manslaughter

Learning Objectives

Compare murder and manslaughter.
Define voluntary manslaughter.
Ascertain the basis of an adequate provocation.
Explain the concurrence of a voluntary manslaughter killing and the heat of passion.
Compare voluntary and involuntary manslaughter.
Describe the three types of involuntary manslaughter.
Analyze manslaughter grading.

What distinguishes murder from manslaughter is the **criminal intent element**. Manslaughter is an unlawful killing *without* malice or murder intent (N.R.S. § 200.040, 2011). The criminal act, causation, and harm elements of manslaughter and murder are fundamentally the same. Thus criminal intent is the only manslaughter offense element that is discussed in this section.

Voluntary Manslaughter

Manslaughter has two basic classifications: **voluntary** and **involuntary**. Voluntary manslaughter has the same criminal intent element as murder. In fact, a voluntary manslaughter killing is typically supported by express malice, specific intent to kill, or purposely. However, in a voluntary manslaughter, an emotional state called a heat of passion negates the murder intent. An adequate provocation from the *victim* inspires the heat of passion (Tenn. Code Ann., 2010). The Model Penal Code does not require adequate provocation from the victim per se, but it does have a similar provision that reduces murder to manslaughter when there is a reasonable explanation or excuse (Model Penal Code § 210.3(1)(b)).

The **adequacy** requirement is essential to any voluntary manslaughter analysis. Many defendants are provoked and thereafter kill with murder intent. Nonetheless, most provocations are not **adequate** to drop the crime from murder to manslaughter. The victim's provocation must be serious enough to goad a *reasonable person* into killing (People v. Steele, 2011). A reasonable person is a fictional and objective standard created by the trier of fact. Of course, *the defendant* must *actually* be provoked, which is a subjective standard (People v. Steele, 2011).

Example of Inadequate Provocation

Revisit the situation discussed in Section 9 "Example of a Spontaneous Killing", in which Dillon kills his supervisor Frank with a brass paperweight after Frank fires him. Clearly, Frank's conduct provokes Dillon into killing Frank. However, getting fired would not provoke a *reasonable person* into a killing frenzy. In fact, reasonable people are fired all the time and learn to live with it peacefully. Therefore, in this example, Dillon's crime is most likely *murder*, not voluntary manslaughter.

Example of Adequate Provocation

A traditional example of provocation that *is* adequate to reduce a crime from murder to manslaughter is an observation by one spouse of another spouse in the act of adultery (Ohio v. Shane, 2011). For example, José comes home from work early and catches his wife in bed with his best friend. He becomes so enraged that he storms over to the dresser, grabs his handgun, and shoots and kills her. Clearly, José acts with intent to kill. However, the victim *provoked* this intent with an act that could cause a *reasonable person to kill*. Thus José has probably committed voluntary manslaughter in this case, not murder.

Other Examples of Adequate Provocation

Other examples of adequate provocation are when the homicide victim batters the defendant and a killing that occurs during a mutual combat (Ohio v. Shane, 2011). Cases have generally held that *words alone* are *not* enough to constitute adequate provocation (Girouard v. State, 2011). Thus in the adequate provocation example in Section 9 "Example of Adequate Provocation", if a friend told José that his wife was committing adultery, and José responded by shooting and killing his wife, this would probably be murder, not voluntary manslaughter.

Concurrence of the Killing and the Heat of Passion

The second requirement of voluntary manslaughter is that the killing occur *during* a heat of passion. Defendants generally exhibit rage, shock, or fright when experiencing a heat of passion. This emotional state negates the calm, deliberate, intent to kill that supports a charge of murder. However, heat of passion mental states are typically brief in duration. Thus there cannot be a *significant time lapse* between the victim's provocation and the killing (State v. Cole, 2010). Analyze the adequate provocation example discussed in Section 9 "Example of Adequate Provocation". If José waits until the next day to shoot and kill his wife, the crime is most likely premeditated first-degree murder, *not* voluntary manslaughter.

Figure 9.7 Diagram of Voluntary Manslaughter

Voluntary Manslaughter		
Adequate *provocation* from the victim		Killing occurs *during* a heat of passion
Enough to cause a reasonable person to kill	The defendant must actually be provoked into killing in a heat of passion	No significant time lapse between heat of passion and the killing

Involuntary Manslaughter

Involuntary manslaughter is an unlawful killing that completely lacks murder intent. Involuntary manslaughter is distinguishable from voluntary manslaughter, which generally includes a murder intent that has been *negated*. Involuntary manslaughter generally can be classified as misdemeanor manslaughter, reckless or negligent involuntary manslaughter, or vehicular manslaughter.

Misdemeanor Manslaughter

Misdemeanor manslaughter, also called **unlawful act manslaughter**, is a criminal homicide that occurs during the commission or attempted commission of a *misdemeanor*. The Model Penal Code completely rejects misdemeanor manslaughter. There is a trend to follow the Model Penal Code's example and abolish misdemeanor manslaughter. Most states that prohibit misdemeanor manslaughter only include misdemeanors that are inherently dangerous to life in the criminal statute, excluding strict liability misdemeanors or malum prohibitum crimes (K.S.A., 2010). A minority of states and the federal government include strict liability or malum prohibitum crimes in their misdemeanor manslaughter statutes (21 O.S., 2010). In either jurisdiction, the defendant need only possess the criminal intent *for the misdemeanor* to be guilty of the killing.

Example of Misdemeanor Manslaughter

Roberta points an unloaded gun at Jennifer to scare her into breaking up with Roberta's ex-boyfriend. This crime is called brandishing a weapon and is often classified as a misdemeanor. At the sight of the gun, Jennifer suffers a heart attack and dies. Roberta has most likely committed misdemeanor manslaughter in this case. Brandishing a weapon is not always inherently dangerous to life. However, if Jennifer has a heart attack and dies because of Roberta's commission of this misdemeanor offense, Roberta still could be criminally responsible for misdemeanor manslaughter in many jurisdictions.

Reckless or Negligent Involuntary Manslaughter

States and the federal government also criminalize **reckless** or **negligent** involuntary manslaughter (Ala. Code, 2011). Reckless or negligent involuntary manslaughter is a more common form of manslaughter than misdemeanor manslaughter. The Model Penal Code defines reckless homicide as *manslaughter* and a felony of the second degree (Model Penal Code § 210.3). The Model Penal Code defines negligent homicide as a felony of the third degree (Model Penal Code § 210.4).

Reckless involuntary manslaughter is a killing supported by the criminal intent element of **recklessness**. Recklessness means that the defendant *is aware* of a risk of death but acts anyway. Negligent involuntary manslaughter is a killing supported by the criminal intent element of **negligence**. Negligence means that the defendant *should be aware* of a risk of death, but is not. This category includes many careless or accidental deaths, such as death caused by firearms or explosives, and a parent's failure to provide medical treatment or necessities for his or her child. Reckless and negligent criminal intent is discussed in detail in Chapter 4 "The Elements of a Crime".

As stated in Section 9.5.1 "Depraved Heart Murder", reckless or negligent involuntary manslaughter is often similar to second-degree depraved heart murder. If the prosecution charges the defendant with both crimes, the trier of fact determines which crime is appropriate based on the attendant circumstances.

Example of Reckless or Negligent Involuntary Manslaughter

Steven, an off-duty sheriff's deputy, brings his shotgun into the local rifle shop to be repaired. Steven thinks that the shotgun is unloaded and hands it to the employee with the *safety off*. Unfortunately, the gun is loaded and discharges, shooting and killing the employee. In this case, Steven *should know* that at certain times the safety on his shotgun must always be on because he is a registered gun owner and a sheriff's deputy who has been trained to handle guns. However, Steven is unaware of the risk and believes that the gun is unloaded. If the employee dies, Steven could be convicted of negligent involuntary manslaughter in jurisdictions that recognize this crime. If Steven is in a jurisdiction that only recognizes **reckless** involuntary manslaughter, the prosecution may have to prove a higher degree of awareness, such as Steven's knowledge that the shotgun was *loaded*.

Vehicular Manslaughter

Vehicular manslaughter is typically either the operation of a motor vehicle with **recklessness** or **negligence** resulting in death or the operation of a motor vehicle *under the influence* of alcohol or drugs resulting in death (N.Y. Penal Law §125.12, 2010). Some states have specific vehicular manslaughter statutes (Cal. Penal Code, 2011). In states that do not, the defendant could be prosecuted under a jurisdiction's misdemeanor or unlawful act manslaughter statute if the defendant violates a vehicle code section. Vehicular manslaughter can also be prosecuted under a jurisdiction's reckless or negligent involuntary manslaughter statute, depending on the circumstances. If the defendant uses a motor vehicle as a weapon to kill the victim, the intent to kill is present and the appropriate crime would be **murder**.

Figure 9.8 Diagram of Involuntary Manslaughter

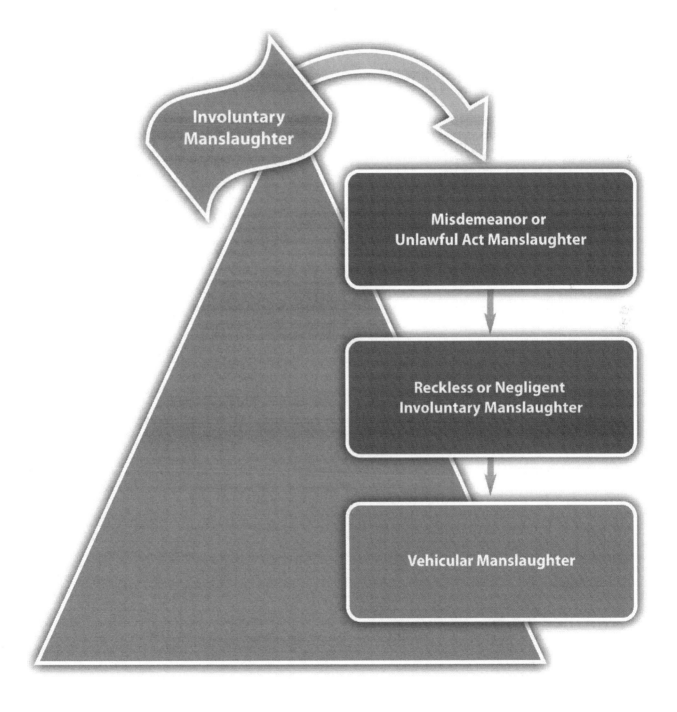

Manslaughter Grading

Voluntary and involuntary manslaughter typically have a more lenient punishment scheme than murder because the criminal intent is less heinous (N.R.S. § 200.080, 2011). Often manslaughter functions as an imperfect *defense* to murder, based on the less serious sentencing options. In general, voluntary manslaughter is **graded** higher than involuntary manslaughter (N.R.S. § 200.090, 2011). Some states divide manslaughter into degrees, rather than classifying it as voluntary and involuntary, with first-degree manslaughter punished more severely than second-degree manslaughter (N.Y. Penal Law §125.20, 2011). The Model Penal Code grades all manslaughter as a felony of the second degree (Model Penal Code § 210.3(2)) and grades negligent homicide as a felony of the third degree (Model Penal Code § 210.4(2)).

Figure 9.9 Diagram of Homicide

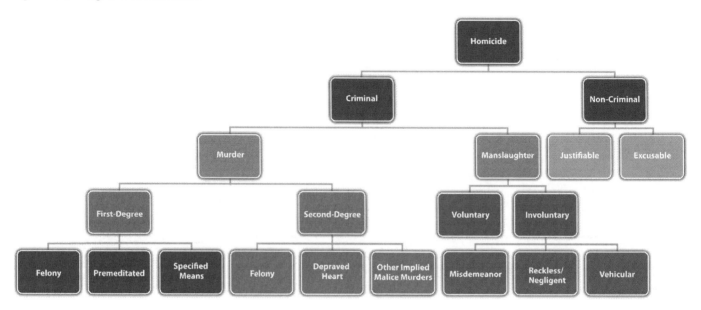

Key Takeaways

- Murder is a killing supported by the criminal intent of malice or purposely, knowingly, or recklessly under circumstances manifesting extreme indifference to life. Manslaughter is a killing supported by malice negated by a heat of passion, reckless, or negligent criminal intent.
- Voluntary manslaughter is a killing that occurs during an adequately provoked heat of passion.
- An adequate provocation is one sufficient to goad a reasonable person into killing and that actually provokes the defendant into killing.
- A killing must occur during a heat of passion to be classified as voluntary manslaughter. If a killing occurs before the heat of passion is provoked or after the heat of passion has cooled, it probably will be classified as murder.
- Voluntary manslaughter is supported by murder intent that has been negated in an adequately provoked heat of passion. Involuntary manslaughter lacks murder intent altogether.
- The three types of involuntary manslaughter are misdemeanor manslaughter, reckless or negligent involuntary manslaughter, and vehicular manslaughter.
- Manslaughter is typically graded lower than murder. Voluntary manslaughter is typically graded higher than involuntary manslaughter. The Model Penal Code grades all manslaughters as felonies of the second degree and grades negligent homicide as a felony of the third degree.

Exercises

Answer the following questions. Check your answers using the answer key at the end of the chapter.

How does the Model Penal Code classify criminal homicides?

Read *Stevens v. State*, 691 N.E.2d 412 (1997). Why did the Indiana Supreme Court affirm the lower court's decision to refuse a jury instruction on voluntary manslaughter in this case? The case is available at this link: http://scholar.google.com/scholar_case?case=1747625552972024733&q=stevens+v.+state+691+ne2d+412&hl=en&as_sdt=2002&as_vis=1.

Read *Tripp v. State*, 374 A.2d 384 (1977). In this case, the defendant killed his ex-girlfriend, her mother, her niece, and her son. Did the Maryland Court of Appeals hold that *the victim* must be the source of adequate provocation in a voluntary manslaughter case? The case is available at this link: http://scholar.google.com/scholar_case?case=17743318345966072534&hl=en&as_sdt=2002&as_vis=1.

Read *Walker v. Superior Court*, 47 Cal.3d 112 (1988). What was the basis for the involuntary manslaughter charge against the defendant in this case? Did the California Supreme Court uphold this charge? The case is available at this link: http://scholar.google.com/scholar_case?case=11713950418773441100&hl=en&as_sdt=2&as_vis=1&oi=scholarr.

Law and Ethics

Should Killing an Abortion Doctor Be Voluntary Manslaughter?

Scott Roeder left his pew during a church service, walked up to a well-known abortion doctor, and deliberately shot him in the head, killing him. During Roeder's trial for first-degree premeditated murder, the defense asked the court to allow a second charge of voluntary manslaughter. The defense claimed that defendant Roeder was acting in *defense of others* in the attempt to save the lives of unborn children (USA Today, 2010).

What are some of the consequences of allowing the charge of voluntary manslaughter in this situation?

Check your answer using the answer key at the end of the chapter.

Scott Roeder Verdict Video

Scott Roeder Convicted of Murder

Scott Roeder's murder verdict is shown in this video:
(click to see video)

References

Ala. Code § 13A-6-3(a) (1), accessed February 13, 2011, http://law.onecle.com/alabama/criminal-code/13A-6-3.html.

Cal. Penal Code § 191.5, accessed February 7, 2011, http://law.onecle.com/california/penal/191.5.html.

Girouard v. State, 583 A.2d 718 (1991), accessed February 24, 2011, http://www.audiocasefiles.com/acf_cases/8711-girouard-v-state.

K.S.A. § 21-3404 (b), accessed July 28, 2010,

http://kansasstatutes.lesterama.org/Chapter_21/Article_34/21-3404.html.

N.R.S. § 200.040, accessed February 13, 2011, http://law.onecle.com/nevada/crimes/200.040.html.

N.R.S. § 200.080, accessed February 13, 2011, http://law.onecle.com/nevada/crimes/200.080.html.

N.R.S. § 200.090, accessed February 13, 2011, http://law.onecle.com/nevada/crimes/200.090.html.

N.Y. Penal Law § 125.12, accessed March 5, 2010, http://wings.buffalo.edu/law/bclc/web/NewYork/ny3%28a%29%281%29-.htm.

N.Y. Penal Law §125.20, accessed February 24, 2011, http://ypdcrime.com/penal.law/article125.htm#125.20.

Ohio v. Shane, 63 Ohio St.3d 630 (1992), accessed February 24, 2011, http://scholar.google.com/scholar_case?case=8752055493993855988&q=voluntary+manslaughter+spouse+act+of+adultery&hl=en&as_sdt=2,5.

People v. Steele, 47 P.2d 225 (2002), accessed February 13, 2011, http://scholar.google.com/scholar_case?case=18208208560981664037&q=voluntary+manslaughter+reasonable+person+adequate+provocation&hl=en&as_sdt=2,5.

State v. Cole, 338 S.C. 97 (2000), accessed March 1, 2010, http://www.judicial.state.sc.us/opinions/htmlfiles/SC/25037.htm.

Tenn. Code Ann. § 39-13-211, accessed February 24, 2010, http://www.lexisnexis.com/hottopics/tncode.

USA Today, "Man Testifies he Killed Kansas Abortion Doctor," accessed July 27, 2010, http://www.usatoday.com/news/nation/2010-01-28-tiller-murder-trial_N.htm.

21 O.S. § 711(1), accessed July 28, 2010, http://www.oscn.net/applications/oscn/DeliverDocument.asp?CiteID=69314.
CC licensed content, Shared previously

- Criminal Law. **Provided by**: University of Minnesota Libraries Publishing . **Located at**: http://open.lib.umn.edu/criminallaw/. **License**: *CC BY-NC-SA: Attribution-NonCommercial-ShareAlike*

9.7 End-of-Chapter Material

Summary

Homicide is the killing of one human being by another. Criminal homicide is either murder or manslaughter. Some states and the federal government also criminalize the killing of a fetus. Suicide is usually not criminal, although assisted suicide could be.

Many jurisdictions follow the common law and define murder as the killing of a victim with malice aforethought. Malice can be either a specific intent to kill, which is express malice, or the intent to do serious bodily injury, or depraved heart, which is implied malice. The Model Penal Code defines murder intent as purposely, knowingly, or recklessly under circumstances indicating extreme indifference to life. A killing by the transmission of AIDS can either be murder, if the transmission is deliberate, or manslaughter, if the transmission is inadvertent.

Most jurisdictions divide murder into degrees of seriousness. First-degree murder is the most serious, can merit the death penalty in certain jurisdictions, and generally includes premeditated murder, murder by a specified means, and serious felony murders. Premeditated murder is typically a killing supported by specific intent to kill combined with cool reflection and planning. Murder by a specified means is killing with a specific heinous method. Felony murder is a homicide that occurs during the commission or attempted commission of a felony. Felony murder lacks murder intent; the defendant need only possess the intent required for the felony. Felony murder can be graded as first, second, or third degree, depending on the felony. The Model Penal Code classifies all murders as first-degree felonies.

Second-degree murder is often defined as any murder that is not first degree. Typically, second-degree murder intent is the intent to inflict serious bodily injury or a depraved heart intent. Second-degree murder is usually graded lower than first-degree murder but higher than manslaughter.

In many jurisdictions, manslaughter is an unlawful killing without murder intent. Most jurisdictions divide manslaughter into voluntary and involuntary. The Model Penal Code classifies all manslaughters as felonies of the second degree. Voluntary manslaughter is a killing that occurs during a heat of passion inspired by adequate provocation from the victim, negating murder intent. Involuntary manslaughter can be a killing that occurs during the commission or attempted commission of a misdemeanor or a reckless or negligent killing, depending on the jurisdiction. Involuntary manslaughter can also be vehicular manslaughter when the killing occurs while driving a vehicle recklessly, negligently, or under the influence of alcohol or drugs. The Model Penal Code classifies negligent killings as negligent homicide and a felony of the third degree.

You Be the Judge

Read the prompt and then decide whether you would **affirm** or **reverse** the lower court. Review the case and see how the judges or justices actually ruled. Check your answers using the answer key at the end of the chapter.

The defendant shot and killed his ex-girlfriend, who was pregnant. The defendant did not know she was pregnant, nor was it obvious from her appearance. The lower court reversed a jury verdict of second-degree murder of the fetus, and the prosecution appealed. Would you **affirm** or **reverse**? *People v. Taylor*, 86 P.3d 881 (2004). The case is available at this link: http://caselaw.lp.findlaw.com/data2/californiastatecases/s112443.pdf.

The defendant held his wife and two small children hostage at gunpoint in a train compartment for three days. The wife died of a bullet wound and one of the children died of dehydration. The defendant was convicted of first-degree murder for the child's death, based on the specified means of "starvation." The defendant appealed because there was *no evidence* of *specific intent to kill* the child. Would you **affirm** or **reverse**? *State v. Evangelista*, 353 S.E.2d 375 (1987). The case is available at this link: http://scholar.google.com/scholar_case?case=587685537389879135&hl=en&as_sdt=2&as_vis=1&oi=scholarr.

The defendant was charged with felony murder for the death of his girlfriend's mother. The underlying felony was cruelty to an elderly person. The defendant and his girlfriend had removed the victim from an assisted living facility so that they could control her Social Security checks. Thereafter, they neglected to care for her and she died from this neglect. The defendant claimed that he had *no duty of care* for his *girlfriend's mother*. The lower court denied his motion for a new trial. Would you **affirm** or **reverse**? *Wood v. State*, 620 S.E.2d 348 (2005). The case is available at this link: http://law.justia.com/cases/georgia/supreme-court/2005/s05a0839-1.html.

The defendant held the victim, his ex-wife, hostage in her home with a gun. When an oil truck pulled into her driveway, she smirked at the defendant because she knew the confrontation was over. The defendant shot and killed her and claimed that the *smirk* was *adequate provocation*. The court held that the defendant was not entitled to a jury instruction on voluntary manslaughter. Would you **affirm** or **reverse**? *State v. Warmke*, 879 A.2d 30 (2005). The case is available at this link: http://scholar.google.com/scholar_case?case=7047276887490940793&q=State+v.+Warmke,+879+A.2d+30+%282005%29.&hl=en&as_sdt=2,6&as_vis=1.

Cases of Interest

- *United States v. Watson*, 501 A.2d 791 (1985), discusses premeditation in a short period of time: http://www.scribd.com/doc/10079243/United-States-v-Watson.
- *Calderon v. Prunty*, 59 F.3d 1005 (1995), discusses lying in wait: http://openjurist.org/59/f3d/1005.
- *Mullaney v. Wilbur*, 421 U.S. 684 (1975), discusses the burden of proof for voluntary manslaughter: http://supreme.justia.com/us/421/684/case.html.

Articles of Interest

- Assisted suicide: http://phoenixcriminallawnews.com/2011/04/lawrence-egbert-of-final-exit-network -acquitted-of-manslaughter.html
- Utah bill that criminalizes miscarriage: http://abcnews.go.com/Health/utah-abortion-bill-punishing-miscarriages-preventing-crime/story?id=9955517
- Prosecution of Michael Jackson's doctor for involuntary manslaughter, http://www.cbsnews.com/stories/2011/01/25/eveningnews/main7282905.shtml
- HIV as a deadly weapon: http://www.johntfloyd.com/is-hiv-a-deadly-weapon/

Websites of Interest

- Fetal homicide statutes: http://www.ncsl.org/research/health/fetal-homicide-state-laws.aspx
- Information about assisted suicide: http://www.assistedsuicide.org
- State statutes on the criminal transmission of HIV: http://www.cdc.gov/hiv/policies/law/states/exposure.html

Statistics of Interest

- Crime, including homicide:
  https://www.fbi.gov/about-us/cjis/ucr/crime-in-the-u.s/2014/crime-in-the-u.s.-2014/offenses-known-to-law-enforcement/expanded-offense

References

People v. Anderson, 666 N.W. 2d 696, 700 (2003), accessed July 30, 2010, http://www.lexisone.com/lx1/caselaw/freecaselaw?action=OCLGetCaseDetail&format=FULL&sourceID=bdjhdg&searchTerm=ejhU.Iaea.aadj.ebKG&searchFlag=y&l1loc=FCLOW.

State v. West, 844 S.W. 2d 144, 147 (1992), accessed July 30, 2010, http://scholar.google.com/scholar_case?case=3481778471457660977&hl=en&as_sdt=2002&as_vis=1.

USA Today, "Man Testifies he Killed Kansas Abortion Doctor," accessed July 27, 2010, http://www.usatoday.com/news/nation/2010-01-28-tiller-murder-trial_N.htm.
CC licensed content, Shared previously

- Criminal Law. **Provided by**: University of Minnesota Libraries Publishing . **Located at**: http://open.lib.umn.edu/criminallaw/. **License**: *CC BY-NC-SA: Attribution-NonCommercial-ShareAlike*

Chapter 10: Sex Offenses and Crimes Involving Force, Fear, and Physical Restraint

10.1 Sex Offenses

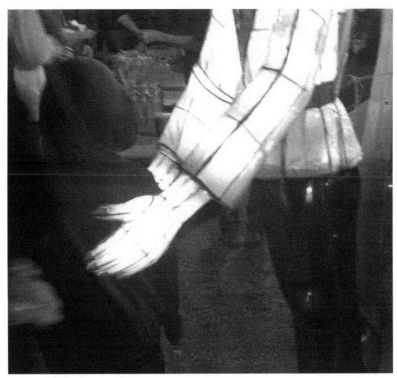

Keoni Cabral – Kidnapped – CC BY 2.0.

Among the evils that both the common law and later statutory prohibitions against kidnapping sought to address were the isolation of a victim from the protections of society and the law and the special fear and danger inherent in such isolation.

—*State v. Salaman*, cited in Section 10.4 "Kidnapping and False Imprisonment"

Learning Objectives

Compare common-law rape and sodomy offenses with modern rape and sodomy offenses.
Define the criminal act element required for rape.
Define the attendant circumstance element required for rape.
Ascertain the amount of resistance a victim must demonstrate to evidence lack of consent.
Ascertain whether the victim's testimony must be corroborated to convict a defendant for rape.
Define the criminal intent element required for rape.
Analyze the relationship between the criminal intent element required for rape and the mistake of fact defense allowed for rape in some jurisdictions.
Define the harm element required for rape.
Identify the primary components of rape shield laws.
Identify the most prevalent issues in acquaintance rape.
Compare spousal rape with rape.

Identify the elements of statutory rape, and compare statutory rape with rape.
Compare sodomy, oral copulation, and incest with rape.
Analyze sex offenses grading.
Identify the primary components of sex offender registration statutes.

In this section, you learn the elements of rape and related sex offenses and examine defenses based on **consent**. In upcoming sections, you analyze the elements of other crimes involving force, fear, and physical restraint, including assault, battery, domestic violence, stalking, and kidnapping.

Synopsis of the History of Rape and Sodomy

The word **rape** has its roots in the Latin word *rapere*, which means to steal or seize. At early common law, rape was a capital offense. The elements of rape were forcible sexual intercourse, by a man, with a woman not the spouse of the perpetrator, conducted without consent, or with consent obtained by force or threat of force (Macnamara, D., 2011). The rape prosecution required evidence of the defendant's use of force, extreme resistance by the victim, and evidence that corroborated the rape victim's testimony. The common law also recognized the crime of **sodomy**. In general, sodomy was the penetration of the male anus by a man. Sodomy was condemned and criminalized even *with consent* because of religious beliefs deeming it a crime against nature (Lawbrain.com, 2011).

In the 1970s, many changes were made to rape statutes, updating the antiquated common-law approach and increasing the chances of conviction. The most prominent changes were eliminating the marital rape exemption and the requirement of evidence to corroborate the rape victim's testimony, creating rape shield laws to protect the victim, and relaxing the necessity for the defendant's use of force or resistance by the victim (Lyon, M. R., 2011). Many jurisdictions also changed the name of rape to sexual battery, sexual assault, or unlawful sexual conduct and combined sexual offenses like rape, sodomy, and oral copulation into one statute. Although some states still have statutes that provide the death penalty for rape, the US Supreme Court has held that rape, even *child rape*, cannot be considered a **capital** offense without violating the Eighth Amendment cruel and unusual punishment clause, rendering these statutes unenforceable (Kennedy v. Louisiana, 2011).

Sodomy law has likewise been updated to make sodomy a gender-neutral offense and preclude the criminalization of consensual sexual conduct between adults. The US Supreme Court has definitively held that consensual sex between adults may be protected by a right of privacy and cannot be criminalized without a sufficient government interest (Lawrence v. Texas, 2011).

Table 10.1 Comparing Common Law Rape and Sodomy with Modern Statutes

Crime	Criminal Act	Lack of Victim Consent?	Victim Resistance?	Other Differences
Common-law rape	Penis-vagina penetration	Yes	Yes, extreme resistance	Corroborative evidence required; no spousal rape; capital crime
Modern rape	Some states include any sexual penetration	Yes	Not if force is used, or threat of force that would deter a reasonable person from resisting (See section 10.1.2.2.2.)	No corroborative evidence required; spousal rape is a crime in some jurisdictions; rape is not a capital crime.
Common-law sodomy	Male penis-male anus penetration	No. Even consensual sodomy was criminal.	No. Even consensual sodomy was criminal.	

Crime	Criminal Act	Lack of Victim Consent?	Victim Resistance?	Other Differences
Modern sodomy	Gender-neutral penis-anus penetration	Yes	Same as modern rape, above	Consensual sodomy in prison or jail is still criminal in some jurisdictions. (See section 10.1.7.)

Rape Elements

In modern times, rape is a crime that has the elements of criminal act, criminal intent, causation, and harm. Rape also has an attendant circumstance element, which is lack of consent by the victim.

Rape Act

The **criminal act** element required for rape in many states is *sexual intercourse*, accomplished by *force or threat* of force (Md. Code Ann. § 3-303, 2011). Sexual intercourse is typically defined as penetration of a woman's vagina by a man's penis and can also be referred to as vaginal intercourse (Md. Code Ann. § 3-301(g), 2011). Some jurisdictions include the penetration of the woman's vagina by other body parts, like a finger, as sexual intercourse (K.S.A., 2011). The Model Penal Code defines the criminal act element required for rape as sexual intercourse that includes "intercourse per os or per anum," meaning oral and anal intercourse (Model Penal Code § 213.0(2)). In most jurisdictions, a man or a woman can commit rape (K.S.A., 2011).

Although it is common to include force or threat of force as an indispensible part of the rape criminal act, some modern statutes expand the crime of rape to include situations where the defendant does *not* use force or threat, but the victim is *extremely vulnerable*, such as an intoxicated victim, an unconscious victim, or a victim who is of tender years (K.S.A., 2011). The Model Penal Code includes force, threat of force, and situations where the defendant has impaired the victim's power to control conduct by administering intoxicants or drugs without the victim's knowledge or sexual intercourse with an unconscious female or a female who is fewer than ten years old (Model Penal Code § 213.1(1)). Other statutes may criminalize **unforced** *nonconsensual* sexual intercourse or other forms of **unforced** *nonconsensual* sexual contact as less serious forms of rape with reduced sentencing options (N.Y. Penal Law, 2011).

Example of Rape Act

Alex and Brad play video games while Brad's sister Brandy watches. Brad tells Alex he is going to go the store and purchase some beer. While Brad is gone, Alex turns to Brandy, pulls a knife out of his pocket, and tells her to take off her pants and lie down. Brandy tells Alex, "No, I don't want to," but thereafter acquiesces, and Alex puts his penis into Brandy's vagina. Alex has probably committed the criminal act element required for rape in most jurisdictions. Although Alex did not use physical force to accomplish sexual intercourse, his *threat* of force by display of the knife is sufficient. If the situation is reversed, and Brandy pulls out the knife and orders Alex to put his penis in her vagina, many jurisdictions would also criminalize Brandy's criminal act as rape. If Alex does not use force or a threat of force, but Brandy is only nine years old, some jurisdictions still criminalize Alex's act as rape, as would the Model Penal Code.

Rape Attendant Circumstance

In many jurisdictions, the **attendant circumstance** element required for rape is *the victim's lack of consent* to the defendant's act (Md. Code Ann § 3-304, 2011). Thus victim's consent could operate as a **failure of proof** or

affirmative defense.

Proving Lack of Consent as an Attendant Circumstance

Proving lack of consent has two components. First, the victim must be legally *capable* of giving consent. If the victim is under the age of consent or is mentally or intellectually impaired because of a permanent condition, intoxication, or drugs, the prosecution does not have to prove lack of consent in many jurisdictions (K.S.A., 2011). Sexual intercourse with a victim under the age of consent is a separate crime, **statutory rape**, which is discussed shortly.

The second component to proving lack of consent is separating true consent from consent rendered *involuntarily*. Involuntary consent is present in two situations. First, if the victim consents to the defendant's act because of fraud or trickery—for example, when the victim is unaware of the *nature* of the act of sexual intercourse—the consent is involuntary. A victim is generally unaware of the nature of the act of sexual intercourse when a doctor shams a *medical procedure* (Iowa v. Vander Esch, 2011). This is called fraud in the factum. Fraud in the inducement, which is a fraudulent representation as to the *circumstances* accompanying the sexual conduct, does not render the consent involuntary in many jurisdictions. An example of fraud in the inducement is a defendant's false statement that the sexual intercourse will *cure* a medical condition (Boro v. Superior Court, 2011).

A more common example of involuntary consent is when the victim consents to the defendant's act because of **force** or **threat** of force. The prosecution generally proves this type of consent is involuntary by introducing evidence of the victim's *resistance*.

Figure 10.1 Diagram of Consent

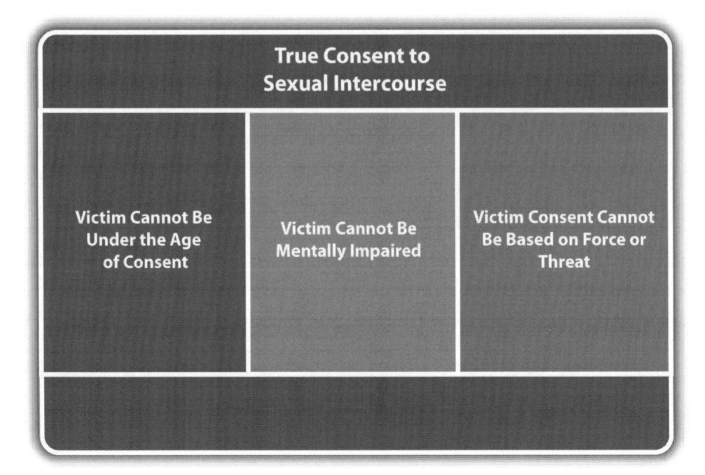

Proving Involuntary Consent by the Victim's Resistance

Under the common law, the victim had to manifest *extreme resistance* to indicate lack of consent. In modern times, the victim does not have to fight back or otherwise endanger his or her life if it would be futile to do so. In most jurisdictions, the victim only needs to resist to the same extent as a reasonable person under similar circumstances, which is an objective standard (Del. Code Ann. tit. II, § 761(j), 2011).

The use of force by the defendant could eliminate *any* requirement of victim resistance to prove lack of consent (N.Y. Penal Law § 130.05, 2011). If the defendant obtains consent using a *threat* of force, rather than force, the victim may not have to resist if the victim experiences subjective fear of serious bodily injury, and a reasonable person under similar circumstances would not resist, which is an objective standard (Minn. Stat. Ann. § 609.343(c), 2011). Threat of force can be accomplished by words, weapons, or gestures. It can also be present when there is a discrepancy in size or age between the defendant and the victim or if the sexual encounter takes place in an isolated location. The Model Penal Code considers it a felony of the third degree and gross sexual imposition when a male has sexual intercourse with a female not his wife by compelling "her to submit by any threat that would prevent resistance by a woman of ordinary resolution" (Model Penal Code § 213.1(2)(a)). Note that the Model Penal Code's position does not require the threat to be a *threat of force*; it can be *any* type of threat that prevents physical resistance.

If the victim does not physically resist the criminal act, the prosecution must prove that the victim affirmatively indicated lack of consent in some other manner. This could be a verbal response, such as saying, "No," but the verbal response must be unequivocal. In the most extreme case, at least one court has held that a verbal "No" *during the act* of sexual intercourse is sufficient, and the defendant who *continues* with sexual intercourse after being told "No" is committing the criminal act of rape (In re John Z., 2011).

Figure 10.2 Proving Lack of Consent

Proving	
Lack of	
Consent	

The Requirement of Corroborative Evidence

At early common law, a victim's testimony was insufficient evidence to meet the burden of proving the elements of rape, including lack of consent. The victim's testimony had to be supported by additional corroborative evidence. Modern jurisdictions have done away with the corroborative evidence requirement and allow the trier of fact to determine the elements of rape or lack of consent based on the victim's testimony alone (State v. Borthwick, 2011). However, statistics indicate that rape prosecutions often result in acquittal. Thus although technically the victim's testimony need not be corroborated, it is paramount that the victim *promptly report* the rape to the appropriate authorities and submit to testing and interrogation to preserve any and all forms of relevant rape evidence.

Example of Rape Attendant Circumstance

Review the example with Brandy and Alex in Section 10 "Example of Rape Act". In this example, after an initial protest, Brandy lies down, takes off her pants, and allows Alex to put his penis in her vagina when he pulls out a knife. It is likely that the trier of fact will find the rape attendant circumstance in this case. Although Brandy acquiesced to Alex's demands *without resisting*, she did so after Alex took a knife out of his pocket, which is a **threat** of force. In addition, Brandy expressed her lack of consent verbally before submitting to Alex's demand. A trier of fact could determine that Brandy experienced a fear of serious bodily injury from Alex's display of the knife, and that a reasonable person under similar circumstances would give in to Alex's demands without physical resistance.

Change this example and assume that after Brad leaves, Alex asks Brandy to have sexual intercourse with him. Brandy responds, "No," but allows Alex to remove her pants and put his penis in her vagina without physically resisting. The trier of fact must make the determination of whether Alex accomplished the sexual act by force or threat of force and without Brandy's consent. If Brandy testifies that she said "No" and did not consent to Alex's act, and Alex testifies that Brandy's verbal response was insufficient to indicate lack of consent, the trier of fact must resolve this issue of fact, and it can do so based on Brandy's testimony, **uncorroborated**, in many jurisdictions. The trier of fact can use the criteria of the difference in age and size between Brandy and Alex, any gestures or words indicating force or threat, and the location and isolation of the incident, among other factors.

Rape Intent

The criminal intent element required for rape in most jurisdictions is the **general intent** or **knowingly** to perform the rape criminal act (State v. Lile, 2011). This may include the intent to use force to accomplish the objective if the state's rape statute includes force or threat of force as a component of the criminal act.

As Chapter 4 "The Elements of a Crime" stated, occasionally, a different criminal intent supports the other elements of an offense. In some states, **negligent** intent supports the rape attendant circumstance of lack of victim consent. This creates a viable **mistake of fact** defense if the defendant has an incorrect perception as to the victim's consent. To be successful with this defense, the facts must indicate that the defendant honestly and reasonably believed that the victim consented to the rape criminal act (People v. Mayberry, 2011). Many jurisdictions expressly disallow the defense, requiring **strict liability** intent for the lack of consent attendant circumstance (State v. Plunkett, 2011).

Example of Rape Intent

Review the example with Alex and Brandy in Section 10 "Example of Rape Act". Change the example so that Alex does not display a knife and simply asks Brandy if she would like to have sex with him. Brandy does not respond. Alex walks over to Brandy and removes her pants. Brandy does not protest or physically resist. Thereafter, Alex asks Brandy if she "likes it rough." Brandy remains silent. Alex physically and forcibly puts his penis in Brandy's vagina. In states that allow a **negligent** intent to support the attendant circumstance of rape, Alex may be able to successfully assert **mistake of fact** as a defense. It appears that Alex has with general intent or knowingly committed forcible sexual intercourse, based on his actions. In most jurisdictions, the jury could be instructed on an *inference* of this intent from Alex's behavior under the circumstances. However, if **negligent** intent is required to support the *attendant circumstance* of the victim's lack of consent, the trier of fact may find that Alex's mistake as to Brandy's consent was honest and reasonable, based on her lack of response or physical resistance. If Alex is in a jurisdiction that requires **strict liability** intent to support the attendant circumstance element, Alex cannot raise the defense because Alex's belief as to Brandy's consent would be irrelevant.

Rape Causation

The defendant's criminal act must be the **factual** and **legal cause** of the harm, which is defined in Section 10 "Rape Harm".

Rape Harm

The **harm** element of rape in most jurisdictions is *penetration*, no matter how slight (Idaho Code Ann. § 18-6101, 2011). This precludes virginity as a defense. In addition, modern statutes do not require male ejaculation, which precludes lack of semen as a defense (Ala. Code § 13A-6-69, 2011).

Example of Rape Harm

Review the example with Alex and Brandy in Section 10 "Example of Rape Act". Assume that Brad walks into the room while Alex and Brandy are engaging in sexual intercourse. Brad tackles Alex and pulls him off Brandy. Alex may be charged with rape, not **attempted** rape, in most jurisdictions. The fact that Alex did not ejaculate does not affect the rape analysis in any way because most jurisdictions do not require ejaculation as a component of the harm element of rape.

Rape Shield Laws

Rape prosecutions can be extremely stressful for the victim, especially when the defendant pursues a **consent** defense. Before the comprehensive rape reforms of the 1970s, rape defendants would proffer any evidence they could find to indicate that the victim was sexually promiscuous and prone to consenting to sexual intercourse. Fearing humiliation, many rape victims kept their rape a secret, not reporting it to law enforcement. This allowed serial rapists to escape punishment and did not serve our criminal justice goal of deterrence.

In modern times, most states protect rape victims with rape shield laws. Rape shield laws prohibit the admission of evidence of the victim's past sexual conduct to prove consent in a rape trial, unless the judge allows it in a pretrial in camera hearing, outside the presence of the jury. Rape shield laws could include the additional protections of the exclusion of evidence relating to the victim's style of dress to prove consent, the exclusion of evidence that the victim requested the defendant to wear a condom to prove consent, and the affirmation that a victim's testimony in a rape trial need not be corroborated by other evidence (Fla. Stat. Ann. § 794.022, 2011). Most courts permit the admission of evidence proving the victim's previous consensual sex *with the defendant* because this evidence is particularly relevant to any consent defense (Colo. Rev. Stat. Ann § 18-3-497(1), 2011).

Example of the Effect of a Rape Shield Law

Review the example with Alex and Brandy in Section 10 "Example of Rape Intent". Assume that the jurisdiction in which the example takes place has a **rape shield law**. If Alex is put on trial for the rape of Brandy and he decides to pursue a consent defense, Alex would *not* be able to introduce evidence of Brandy's sexual history with *other men* unless he receives approval from a judge in an in camera hearing before the trial.

Law and Ethics

Should the Media Be Permitted to Publish Negative Information about a Rape Victim?

In 2003, Kobe Bryant, a professional basketball player, was indicted for sexually assaulting a nineteen-year-old hotel desk clerk. A mistake by a court reporter listed the accuser's name on a court website (MSNBC.com, 2011). The court removed the victim's name after discovery of the mistake, but the damage was done. Thereafter, in spite of a court order prohibiting the publication of the accuser's name, the media, including radio, newspaper, Internet, and television, published the accuser's name, phone number, address, and e-mail address (Kenworty, T. & O'Driscoll, P., 2011). Products like underwear, t-shirts, and coffee mugs with pictures of the accuser and Bryant in sexual positions were widely available for sale, and the accuser received constant harassment, including death threats (Haddad, R., 2011). Although the Colorado Supreme Court ordered pretrial in camera transcripts of hearings pursuant to Colorado's rape shield law to remain confidential, an order that was confirmed by the US Supreme Court (Associated Press et. al. v. District Court for the Fifth Judicial Distric of Colorado, 2011), the accuser was subjected to so much negative publicity that she eventually refused to cooperate and the prosecution dropped the charges in 2004.

Do you think **rape shield laws** should include prohibitions against negative publicity? What are the *constitutional* ramifications of this particular type of statutory protection?

Check your answer using the answer key at the end of the chapter.

Kobe Bryant Video

Kobe Claims Innocence to Sexual Assault Charges

Kobe Bryant and his attorney discuss the charge of rape filed against Kobe in this video:
(click to see video)

Acquaintance Rape

In modern times, rape defendants are frequently known to the victim, which may change the factual situation significantly from stranger rape. Acquaintance rape, also called **date rape**, is a phenomenon that could increase a victim's reluctance to report the crime and could also affect the defendant's need to use force and the victim's propensity to physically resist (The National Center for Victims of Crime, 2011). Although studies indicate that acquaintance rape is on the rise (The National Center for Victims of Crime, 2011), statutes have not entirely addressed the issues presented in an acquaintance rape fact pattern. To adequately punish and deter acquaintance or date rape, rape statutes should punish *nonforcible*, *nonconsensual* sexual conduct *as severely* as forcible rape. Although the majority of states still require forcible sexual intercourse as the rape criminal act element, at least one modern court has rejected the necessity of any force other than what is required to accomplish the sexual intercourse (State of New Jersey in the Interest of M.T.S., 2011). Some rape statutes have also eliminated the requirement that the defendant use force and punish *any* sexual intercourse without consent as rape (Utah Code Ann § 76-5-402(1).

Spousal Rape

As stated previously, at early common law, a man could not rape his spouse. The policy supporting this exemption can be traced to a famous seventeenth-century jurist, Matthew Hale, who wrote, "[T]he husband cannot be guilty of a rape committed by himself upon his lawful wife, for by their mutual matrimonial consent and contract the wife hath given up herself in this kind unto her husband, which she cannot retract" (Hale, History of Pleas of the Crown, p. 629). During the rape reforms of the 1970s, many states eliminated the marital or spousal rape exemption, in spite of the fact that the Model Penal Code does *not* recognize spousal rape. At least one court has held that the spousal rape exemption violates the equal protection clause of the Fourteenth Amendment because it discriminates against *single men* without a sufficient government interest (People v. Liberta, 2011). In several states that criminalize spousal rape, the criminal act, criminal intent, attendant circumstance, causation, and harm elements are exactly the same as the elements of forcible rape (N. H. Rev. Stat. Ann. § 632-A, 2011). Many states also **grade** spousal rape the same as forcible rape—as a serious felony (Utah Code Ann. § 76-5-402(2), 2011). Grading of sex offenses is discussed shortly.

Statutory Rape

Statutory rape, also called **unlawful sexual intercourse**, criminalizes sexual intercourse with a victim who is under the age of legal consent. The age of legal consent varies from state to state and is most commonly sixteen, seventeen, or eighteen (Age of Consent Chart for the U.S.-2010, 2011).

The **criminal act** element required for statutory rape in many jurisdictions is sexual intercourse, although other types of sexual conduct with a victim below the age of consent are also criminal (US Department of Health and Human Services, 2011). The **harm** element of statutory rape also varies, although many jurisdictions mirror the harm element required for rape (US Department of Health and Human Services, 2011). The **attendant circumstance** element required for statutory rape is an underage victim (Cal. Penal Code § 261.5, 2011). There is no requirement for *force* by the defendant. Nor is there an attendant circumstance element of lack of consent because the victim is incapable of legally consenting.

In the majority of states, the criminal intent element of statutory rape is **strict liability** (La. Rev. Stat. Ann. §

14-80, 2011). However, a minority of states require **reckless** or **negligent** criminal intent, allowing for the defense of **mistake of fact** as to the victim's age. If the jurisdiction recognizes mistake of age as a defense, the mistake must be made *reasonably*, and the defendant must take *reasonable* measures to verify the victim's age (Alaska Stat § 11.41.445(b), 2011). The mistake of age defense can be proven by evidence of a falsified identification, witness testimony that the victim lied about his or her age to the defendant, or even the appearance of the victim.

It is much more common to prosecute males for statutory rape than females. The historical reason for this selective prosecution is the policy of preventing teenage pregnancy (Michael M. v. Superior Court, 2011). However, modern statutory rape statutes are gender-neutral (N.Y. Penal Law § 130.30, 2011). This ensures that women, especially women who are older than their sexual partner, are equally subject to prosecution.

Example of Statutory Rape

Gary meets Michelle in a nightclub that only allows entrance to patrons eighteen and over. Gary and Michelle end up spending the evening together, and later they go to Gary's apartment where they have consensual sexual intercourse. In reality, Michelle is actually fifteen and was using false identification to enter the nightclub. If Gary and Michelle are in a state that requires **strict liability** for the criminal intent element of statutory rape, Gary can be subject to prosecution for and conviction of this offense if fifteen is under the age of legal consent. If Gary and Michelle are in a state that allows for **mistake of age** as a defense, Gary could use Michelle's presence in the nightclub as evidence that he acted *reasonably* in believing that Michelle was capable of rendering legal consent. If both Gary and Michelle used false identification to enter the nightclub, and both Gary and Michelle are under the age of legal consent, *both* could be prosecuted for and convicted of statutory rape in most jurisdictions because modern statutory rape statutes are gender-neutral.

Figure 10.3 Comparison of Rape and Statutory Rape

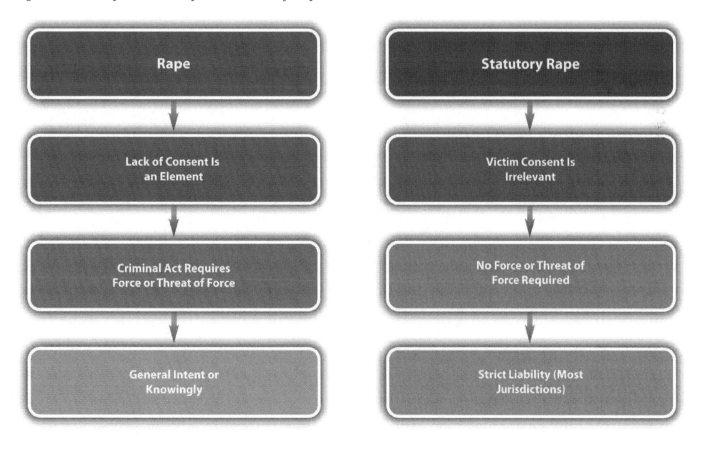

Sodomy and Oral Copulation

As stated previously, some states include rape, sodomy, and oral copulation in a sexual assault or sexual conduct statute that criminalizes a variety of sexual acts involving penetration (Alaska Stat. § 11.41.410, 2011). In states that distinguish between rape and sodomy, the **criminal act** element of sodomy is often defined as forcible *penis to anus* penetration (Cal. Penal Code § 286(a), 2011). Typically, the other sodomy elements, including the lack of consent attendant circumstance, criminal intent, causation, and harm, are the same as the elements of rape. Many jurisdictions also **grade** sodomy the same as rape. Grading is discussed shortly.

Sodomy that is *nonforcible* but committed with an individual below the age of legal consent is also criminal (Cal. Penal Code § 286(b), 2011). As stated previously, the US Supreme Court has held that statutes criminalizing sodomy between consenting adults unreasonably encroach on a right to privacy without a sufficient government interest (Lawrence v. Texas, 2011). In some states, consensual nonforcible sodomy is criminal if it is committed in a *state penitentiary* or *local detention facility* or *jail* (Cal. Penal Code § 286(c), 2011).

In states that distinguish between rape, sodomy, and oral copulation, the **criminal act** element of oral copulation is forcible *mouth to sexual organ* or *anus* penetration (Cal. Penal Code § 288a, 2011). Typically, the other oral copulation elements, including the lack of consent attendant circumstance, criminal intent, causation, and harm, are the same as the elements of rape. Many jurisdictions also **grade** oral copulation the same as rape. Grading is discussed shortly.

A few states still criminalize oral copulation with consent (Ala. Code § 13A-6-65, 2011). Based on the US Supreme Court precedent relating to sodomy, these statutes may be unenforceable and unconstitutional.

Incest

Incest is also criminal in many jurisdictions. The **criminal act** element required for incest is typically sexual intercourse (Fla. Stat. Ann. § 826.04, 2011). The **attendant circumstance** element required for incest is a victim the defendant cannot legally marry because of a family relationship (Del. Code Ann. Tit. 11 § 766, 2011). In the majority of jurisdictions, *force* is not required, and *consent* is not an attendant circumstance element of incest (Del. Code Ann. Tit. 11, 2011). Thus consent by the victim cannot operate as a defense. If the sexual intercourse with a family member is forcible and nonconsensual, the defendant could be charged with and convicted of rape. The criminal intent element required for incest is typically **general intent** or **knowingly** (Fla. Stat. Ann. § 826.04, 2011). The causation and harm elements of incest are generally the same as the causation and harm elements of rape (Fla. Stat. Ann. § 826.04, 2011). However, incest is generally **graded** lower than forcible rape or sexual assault because force and lack of consent are not required (Del. Code Ann. Tit. 11, § 766, 2011).

Example of Incest

Hal and Harriet, brother and sister, have consensual sexual intercourse. Both Hal and Harriet are above the age of legal consent. In spite of the fact that there was no force, threat of force, or fraud, and both parties consented to the sexual act, Hal and Harriet could be charged with and convicted of **incest** in many jurisdictions, based on their *family relationship*.

Sex Offenses Grading

Jurisdictions vary when it comes to **grading** sex offenses. In general, forcible sex crimes involving penetration are graded as serious felonies. Factors that could aggravate grading are gang rape (Fla. Stat. Ann. § 794.023, 2011), the infliction of bodily injury, the use of a weapon, a youthful victim, the commission of other crimes in concert with the sexual offense, or a victim who has mental or intellectual disabilities or who has been compromised by intoxicants (Del. Code Ann. Tit. 11, § 773, 2011). The Model Penal Code grades rape as a felony of the second degree unless the actor inflicts serious bodily injury on the victim or another, or the defendant is a stranger to the victim, in which case the grading is elevated to a felony of the first degree (Model Penal Code § 213.1 (1)).

Sexual offenses that do not include penetration are graded lower (N.Y. Penal Law § 130.52, 2011), along with offenses that could be consensual (Del. Code Ann. Tit. 11, § 766, 2011). Sex offense statutes that criminalize sexual conduct with a victim below the age of legal consent often grade the offense more severely when there is a large age difference between the defendant and the victim, when the defendant is an adult, or the victim is of tender years (Cal. Penal Code § 261.5, 2011).

Figure 10.4 Diagram of Sex Offenses

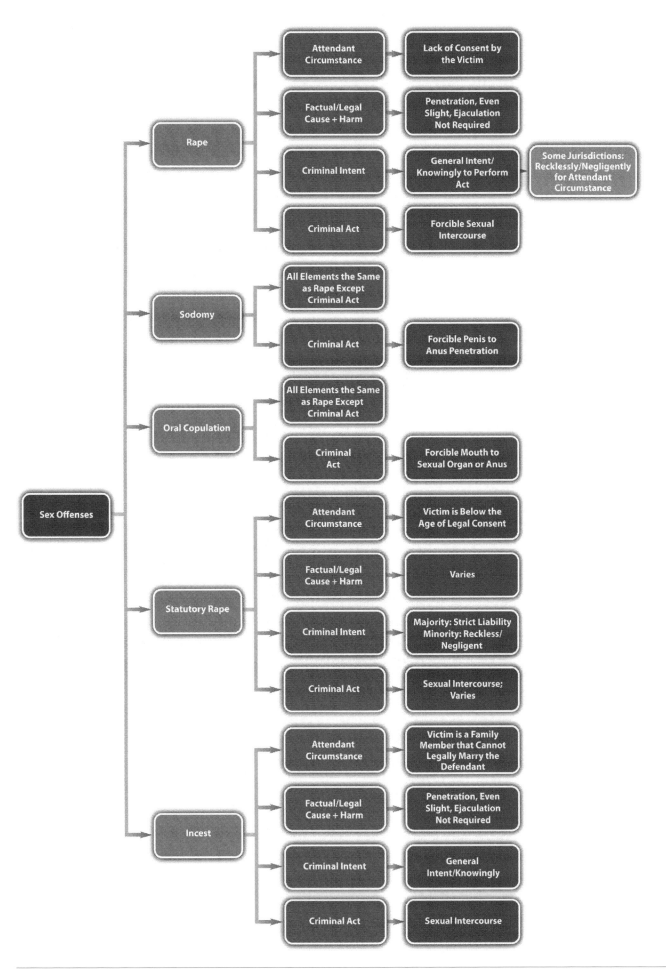

Sex Offender Registration Statutes

Based on a public awareness that sex offenders often reoffend, many states have enacted some form of Megan's law or Jessica's law, which provide for registration, monitoring, control, and elevated sentencing for sex offenders, including those that harm children. Both laws were written and enacted after high-profile cases with child victims became the subject of enormous media attention. Megan's and Jessica's law statutes enhance previously enacted statutes that require the registration of sex offenders with local law enforcement agencies.

Typically, a Megan's law statute provides for registration and notification to the public that a convicted sex offender lives in their area (42 Pa. C. S. § 9799.1, 2011). A Jessica's law statute often includes a stay-away order, mandating that a sex offender cannot live within a certain distance from areas such as a school or park where children tend to congregate. Jessica's law statutes also provide for GPS monitoring and extend the sentencing and parole terms of child sex offenders (Va. Code Ann. § 19.2-295.2:1, 2011).

Figure 10.5 Diagram of Megan's and Jessica's Law Statutes

Megan's Law	
Jessica's Law	

Key Takeaways

- Common-law rape was a capital offense, did not include rape of a spouse, required extreme resistance by the victim, and required evidence to corroborate a victim's testimony. Modern statutes do not make rape a capital offense, often criminalize spousal rape, and do not require extreme resistance by the victim or evidence to corroborate the victim's testimony. At early common law, sodomy was the anal penetration of a man, by a man. Modern statutes make sodomy gender-neutral and only criminalize sodomy without consent.
- The criminal act element required for rape is sexual penetration accomplished with force or threat of force in many jurisdictions.
- The attendant circumstance element required for rape is lack of consent by the victim.
- In many jurisdictions, the victim does not need to resist if the defendant uses force. If the victim is faced with a threat of force rather than force, the victim need not resist if he or she has a subjective fear of serious bodily injury, and this fear is reasonable under the circumstances.
- In modern times, a victim's testimony does not need to be corroborated by other evidence to convict a defendant of rape.
- The criminal intent element required for rape is general intent or knowingly to commit the criminal act.
- In some jurisdictions, the criminal intent element required for the rape attendant circumstance is negligent intent—providing for a defense of mistake of fact as to the victim's consent. In other jurisdictions, the criminal intent element required for the rape attendant circumstance is strict liability, which does not allow for the mistake of fact defense.
- The harm element required for rape is penetration, no matter how slight. Ejaculation is not a requirement for rape in most jurisdictions.
- Rape shield laws generally preclude the admission of evidence of the victim's past sexual conduct in a rape trial, unless it is allowed by a judge at an in camera hearing. Rape shield laws also preclude the admission of evidence of the victim's style of dress and the victim's request that the defendant wear a condom to prove victim consent. Some rape shield laws provide that the victim's testimony need not be corroborated by other evidence to convict the defendant of rape.
- Acquaintance rape often goes unreported and does not necessarily include use of force by the defendant or resistance by the victim.
- States that criminalize spousal rape generally require the same elements for spousal rape as for rape and grade spousal rape the same as rape.
- Statutory rape is generally sexual intercourse with a victim who is under the age of legal consent. Statutory rape does not have the requirement that the intercourse be forcible and does not require the attendant circumstance of the victim's lack of consent because the victim is incapable of rendering legal consent. In the majority of jurisdictions, the criminal intent element required for statutory rape is strict liability. In a minority of jurisdictions, the criminal intent element required

for statutory rape is negligent or reckless intent, providing for a defense of mistake of fact as to the victim's age.

- Sodomy has the same elements as rape except for the criminal act element, which is often defined as forcible penis to anus penetration, rather than penis to vagina penetration. In addition, in some states sodomy is criminal with consent when it occurs in a state prison or a local detention facility or jail. Oral copulation also has the same elements as rape, except for the criminal act element, which is forcible mouth to sexual organ or anus penetration. Incest is sexual intercourse between family members who cannot legally marry.
- Generally, rape, sodomy, and oral copulation are graded as serious felonies. Factors that enhance grading of sex offenses are penetration, gang rape, bodily injury, the use of a weapon, a victim who has intellectual or mental disabilities or is youthful or intoxicated, and the commission of other crimes in concert with the sex offense. Sex offenses committed with the victim's consent and without penetration are typically graded lower. If the victim is below the age of consent, a large age difference exists between the defendant and the victim, the defendant is an adult, or the victim is of tender years, grading typically is enhanced.
- Typically, a Megan's law statute provides for sex offender registration and notification to the public that a convicted sex offender lives in their area. A Jessica's law statute often includes a stay-away order mandating that a sex offender cannot live within a certain distance from areas such as a school or park where children tend to congregate. Jessica's law statutes also provide for GPS monitoring and extend the sentencing and parole terms of child sex offenders.

Exercises

Answer the following questions. Check your answers using the answer key at the end of the chapter.

Jorge and Christina have consensual sexual intercourse. Could this consensual sexual intercourse be criminal? Which crime(s), if any, could exist in this fact pattern?

Read *Toomer v. State*, 529 SE 2d 719 (2000). In *Toomer*, the defendant was convicted of rape after having sexual intercourse with his daughter, who was under the age of fourteen. The jury instruction did not include any requirement for the defendant's use of force or victim resistance. The defendant appealed and claimed that the prosecution should have proven he used force and the victim's resistance because the charge was **rape**, not **statutory rape**. Did the Supreme Court of South Carolina uphold the defendant's conviction? Why or why not? The case is available at this link: http://scholar.google.com/scholar_case?case=3593808516097562509&q=Toomer+v.+State&hl=en&as_sdt=2,5.

Read *Fleming v. State*, 323 SW 3d 540 (2010). In *Fleming*, the defendant appealed his conviction for aggravated sexual assault of a child under fourteen because he was not allowed to present a mistake of age defense. The defendant claimed that the requirement of strict liability intent as to the age of the victim deprived him of **due process of law**. Did the Court of Appeals of Texas agree with the defendant? The case is available at this link: http://scholar.google.com/scholar_case?case=12908572719333538188&q=%22Scott+v.+State+36+SW+3d+240%22&hl=en&as_sdt=2,5.

References

Age of Consent Chart for the U.S.-2010, Ageofconsent.us website, accessed February 14, 2011, http://www.ageofconsent.us.

Ala. Code § 13A-6-60, accessed February 11, 2011, http://law.justia.com/alabama/codes/2009/Title13A/Chapter6/13A-6-60.html.

Ala. Code § 13A-6-65, accessed February 15, 2011, http://www.legislature.state.al.us/CodeofAlabama/1975/13A-6-65.htm.

Alaska Stat. § 11.41.410, accessed February 15, 2011,

http://law.justia.com/alaska/codes/2009/title-11/chapter-11-41/article-04/sec-11-41-410.

Alaska Stat. § 11.41.445(b), accessed February 15, 2011, http://law.justia.com/alaska/codes/2009/title-11/chapter-11-41/article-04/sec-11-41-445.

Associated Press et. al. v. District Court for the Fifth Judicial District of Colorado, 542 U.S. 1301 (2004), accessed February 27, 2011, http://ftp.resource.org/courts.gov/c/US/542/542.US.1301.04.73.html.

Boro v. Superior Court, 163 Cal. App. 3d 1224 (1985), accessed February 17, 2011, http://scholar.google.com/scholar_case?case=8450241145233624189&q=Boro+v.+Superior+Court&hl=en&as_sdt=2,5.

Cal. Penal Code § 261.5, accessed February 15, 2011, http://law.onecle.com/california/penal/261.5.html.

Cal. Penal Code § 286(a), accessed February 15, 2011, http://law.justia.com/california/codes/2009/pen/281-289.6.html.

Cal. Penal Code § 286(b), accessed February 15, 2011, http://law.justia.com/california/codes/2009/pen/281-289.6.html.

Cal. Penal Code § 286(c) (3) (e), accessed February 15, 2011, http://law.justia.com/california/codes/2009/pen/281-289.6.html.

Cal. Penal Code § 288a, accessed February 15, 2011, http://law.onecle.com/california/penal/288a.html.

Colo. Rev. Stat. Ann. § 18-3-407(1) (a), accessed February 14, 2011, http://www.michie.com/colorado/lpext.dll?f=templates&fn=main-h.htm&cp=.

Del. Code Ann. Tit. 11, § 766, accessed February 15, 2011, http://law.justia.com/delaware/codes/2010/title11/c005-sc02.html.

Del. Code Ann. tit. II, § 761(j) (1), accessed February 9, 2011, http://delcode.delaware.gov/title11/c005/sc02/index.shtml#761.

Del. Code Ann. Tit. 11, § 766, accessed February 15, 2011, http://law.justia.com/delaware/codes/2010/title11/c005-sc02.html.

Del. Code Ann. Tit. 11, § 773, accessed February 15, 2011, http://law.justia.com/delaware/codes/2010/title11/c005-sc02.html.

Fla. Stat. Ann. § 794.022, accessed February 11, 2011, http://law.justia.com/florida/codes/2010/TitleXLVI/chapter794/794_022.html.

Fla. Stat. Ann. § 794.023, accessed February 15, 2011, http://law.onecle.com/florida/crimes/794.023.html.

Fla. Stat. Ann. § 826.04, accessed February 15, 2011, http://law.onecle.com/florida/crimes/826.04.html.

Haddad, R., "Shield or Sieve? People v. Bryant and the Rape Shield Law in High-Profile Cases," *Columbia Journal of Law and Social Problems*, accessed February 27, 2011, http://www.columbia.edu/cu/jlsp/pdf/Spring2%202006/Haddad10.pdf.

Idaho Code Ann. § 18-6101, accessed February 10, 2011, http://www.legislature.idaho.gov/idstat/Title18/T18CH61SECT18-6101.htm.

In re John Z., 29 Cal. 4th 756 (2003), accessed February 10, 2011, http://scocal.stanford.edu/opinion/re-john-z-32309.

Iowa v. Vander Esch, 662 N.W. 2d 689 (2002), accessed February 10, 2011, http://scholar.google.com/scholar_case?case=4906781834239023314&q=rape+%22fraud+in+the+inducement%22&hl=en&as_sdt=2,5&as_ylo=2002.

Kennedy v. Louisiana, 128 S. Ct. 2641 (2008), accessed February 8, 2011, http://www.oyez.org/cases/2000-2009/2007/2007_07_343.

K.S.A. § 21-3501(1), accessed February 8, 2011, http://law.justia.com/kansas/codes/2006/chapter21/statute_11553.html.

Kenworty, T., Patrick O'Driscoll, "Judge Dismisses Bryant Rape Case," USAtoday.com website, accessed February 27, 2011, http://www.usatoday.com/sports/basketball/nba/2004-09-01-kobe-bryant-case_x.htm.

La. Rev. Stat. Ann. § 14-80, accessed February 15, 2011, http://law.justia.com/louisiana/codes/2009/rs/title14/rs14-80.html.

Lawbrain.com website, "Sex Offenses," accessed February 8, 2011, http://lawbrain.com/wiki/Sex_Offenses.

Lawrence v. Texas, 539 U.S. 558 (2003), accessed February 8, 2011, http://www.oyez.org/cases/2000-2009/2002/2002_02_102.

Lyon, M. R., "No means No? Withdrawal of Consent During Intercourse and the Continuing Evolution of the Definition of Rape," Findarticles.com website, accessed February 8, 2011, http://findarticles.com/p/articles/mi_hb6700/is_1_95/ai_n29148498/pg_3/?tag=content;col1.

Macnamara, D., "History of Sexual Violence," Interactive theatre.org website, accessed February 8, 2011, http://www.interactivetheatre.org/resc/history.html.

Md. Code Ann. § 3-301(g), accessed February 8, 2011, http://law.justia.com/maryland/codes/2005/gcr/3-301.html.

Md. Code Ann. § 3-303, accessed February 8, 2011, http://law.justia.com/maryland/codes/2005/gcr/3-303.html.

Md. Code Ann. § 3-304, accessed February 8, 2011, http://law.justia.com/maryland/codes/gcr/3-304.html.

Michael M. v. Superior Court, 450 U.S. 464 (1981), accessed February 15, 2011, http://www.oyez.org/cases/1980-1989/1980/1980_79_1344.

Minn. Stat. Ann. § 609.343(c), accessed February 10, 2011, https://www.revisor.mn.gov/statutes/?id=609.343.

MSNBC.com website, "Rape Case against Bryant Dismissed," accessed February 27, 2011, http://nbcsports.msnbc.com/id/5861379.

N. H. Rev. Stat. Ann. § 632-A: 5, accessed February 14, 2011, http://www.gencourt.state.nh.us/rsa/html/LXII/632-A/632-A-5.htm.

The National Center for Victims of Crime, "Acquaintance Rape," Ncvc.org website, accessed February 14, 2011, http://www.ncvc.org/ncvc/main.aspx?dbName=DocumentViewer&DocumentID=32306.

N.Y. Penal Law § 130.05, accessed February 9, 2011, http://law.onecle.com/new-york/penal/PEN0130.05_130.05.html.

N.Y. Penal Law § 130.25(3), accessed February 10, 2011, http://law.onecle.com/new-york/penal/PEN0130.25_130.25.html.

N.Y. Penal Law § 130.30, accessed February 15, 2011, http://law.onecle.com/new-york/penal/PEN0130.30_130.30.html.

N.Y. Penal Law § 130.52, accessed February 15, 2011, http://law.onecle.com/new-york/penal/PEN0130.52_130.52.html.

People v. Liberta, 64 N.Y. 2d 152 (1984), accessed February 14, 2011, http://scholar.google.com/scholar_case?case=1399209540378549726&hl=en&as_sdt=2&as_vis=1&oi=scholarr.

People v. Mayberry, 542 P.2d 1337 (1975), accessed February 11, 2011, http://scholar.google.com/scholar_case?case=6471351898025391619&hl=en&as_sdt=2&as_vis=1&oi=scholarr.

State of New Jersey in the Interest of M.T.S., 609 A.2d 1266 (1992), accessed February 14, 2011, http://www.4lawnotes.com/showthread.php?t=1886.

State v. Borthwick, 880 P.2d 1261 (1994), accessed February 10, 2011, http://www1.law.umkc.edu/suni/CrimLaw/calendar/Class_24_borthwick_case.htm.

State v. Lile, 699 P.2d 456 (1985), accessed February 8, 2011, http://scholar.google.com/scholar_case?case=5958820374035014869&hl=en&as_sdt=2&as_vis=1&oi=scholarr.

State v. Plunkett, 934 P.2d 113 (1997), accessed February 11, 2011, http://scholar.google.com/scholar_case?case=17940293485668190575&hl=en&as_sdt=2&as_vis=1&oi=scholarr.

US Department of Health and Human Services, "Statutory Rape: A Guide to State Laws and Reporting Requirements," ASPE.hhs.gov website, accessed February 16, 2011, http://aspe.hhs.gov/hsp/08/SR/StateLaws/statelaws.shtml.

Utah Code Ann. § 76-5-402(1), accessed February 14, 2011, http://le.utah.gov/~code/TITLE76/htm/76_05_040200.htm.

Utah Code Ann. § 76-5-402(2), accessed February 14, 2011, http://le.utah.gov/~code/TITLE76/htm/76_05_040200.htm.

Va. Code Ann. § 19.2-295.2:1, accessed February 15, 2011, http://leg1.state.va.us/cgi-bin/legp504.exe?000+cod+19.2-295.2C1.

42 Pa. C. S. § 9799.1, accessed February 15, 2011, http://www.pameganslaw.state.pa.us.
CC licensed content, Shared previously

- Criminal Law. **Provided by**: University of Minnesota Libraries Publishing . **Located at**: http://open.lib.umn.edu/criminallaw/. **License**: *CC BY-NC-SA: Attribution-NonCommercial-ShareAlike*

10.2 Assault and Battery

Learning Objectives

Define the criminal act element required for battery.
Define the criminal intent element required for battery.
Define the attendant circumstance element required for battery.
Define the harm element required for battery.
Analyze battery grading.
Distinguish between attempted battery and threatened battery assault.
Define the elements of attempted battery assault.
Define the elements of threatened battery assault.
Analyze assault grading.

Assault and battery are two crimes that are often prosecuted together, yet they are separate offenses with different elements. Although modern jurisdictions frequently combine assault and battery into one statute called **assault**, the offenses are still distinct and are often graded differently. The Model Penal Code calls both crimes assault, simple and aggravated (Model Penal Code § 211.1). However, the Model Penal Code does not distinguish between assault and battery for grading purposes. This section reviews the elements of both crimes, including potential defenses.

Battery Elements

Battery is a crime that has the elements of criminal act, criminal intent, attendant circumstance, causation, and harm as is discussed in the subsections that follow.

Battery Act

The **criminal act** element required for battery in most jurisdictions is an unlawful touching, often described as physical contact (720 ILCS § 12-3, 2011). This criminal act element is what distinguishes assault from battery, although an individual can be convicted of both crimes if he or she commits separate acts supported by the appropriate intent. The defendant can touch the victim with an instrumentality, like shooting the victim with a gun, or can hit the victim with a thrown object, such as rocks or a bottle. The defendant can also touch the victim with a vehicle, knife, or a substance, such as spitting on the victim or spraying the victim with a hose.

Example of Battery Act

Recall from Chapter 1 "Introduction to Criminal Law" an example where Chris, a newly hired employee at McDonald's, spills steaming-hot coffee on his customer Geoff's hand. Although Chris did not touch Geoff with any part of his body, he did pour a substance that unlawfully touched *Geoff's body*, which could be sufficient to constitute the criminal act element for battery in most jurisdictions.

Battery Intent

The criminal intent element required for battery varies, depending on the jurisdiction. At early common law, battery was a purposeful or knowing touching. Many states follow the common-law approach and require **specific intent** or **purposely**, or **general intent** or **knowingly** (Fla. Stat. Ann. § 784.03, 2011). Others include **reckless intent** (K.S.A. § 21-3412, 2011), or **negligent intent** (R.I. Gen. Laws § 11-5-2.2, 2011). Jurisdictions that include reckless or negligent intent generally require actual injury, serious bodily injury, or the use of a deadly weapon. The Model Penal Code requires purposely, knowingly, or recklessly causing bodily injury to another, or negligently causing "bodily injury to another with a deadly weapon" (Model Penal Code § 211.1(1) (b)). If negligent intent is *not* included in the battery statute, certain conduct that causes injury to the victim may not be criminal.

Example of Battery Intent

Review the example with Chris and Geoff in Section 10 "Example of Battery Act". Assume that Chris's act of pouring hot coffee on Geoff's hand occurred when Chris attempted to multitask and hand out change at the same moment he was pouring the coffee. Chris's act of physically touching Geoff with the hot coffee may be supported by negligent intent because Chris is a new employee and is probably not aware of the risk of spilling coffee when multitasking. If the state in which Chris's spill occurs does not include **negligent intent** in its battery statute, Chris probably will *not* be subject to prosecution for this offense. If Chris's state only criminalizes negligent battery when *serious bodily injury* occurs, or when causing bodily injury to another with a *deadly weapon*, Chris will not be subject to prosecution for battery unless the coffee caused a severe burning of Geoff's hand; hot coffee cannot kill and would probably not be considered a deadly weapon.

Battery Attendant Circumstance

The **attendant circumstance** element required for battery in most jurisdictions is that the touching occur without the victim's *consent*. Thus victim's consent can operate as a **failure of proof** or **affirmative defense** in some factual situations.

Example of Battery Consent Defense

Recall from Chapter 5 "Criminal Defenses, Part 1" the example where Allen tackles Brett during a high school football game, causing Brett to suffer a severe injury. Although Allen intentionally touched Brett, and the result is serious bodily injury, Brett **consented** to the touching by voluntarily participating in a sporting event where physical contact is *frequent*. Thus the attendant circumstance element for battery is absent and Allen is probably not subject to prosecution for this offense.

Justification and Excuse Defenses to Battery

In addition to consent, there are also **justification** and **excuse** defenses to battery that Chapter 5 "Criminal Defenses, Part 1" and Chapter 6 "Criminal Defenses, Part 2" discuss in detail. To summarize and review, the justification defenses to battery are self-defense, defense of property and habitation, and the lawful apprehension of criminals. An excuse defense to battery that Chapter 6 "Criminal Defenses, Part 2" explores is the insanity defense. One other excuse defense to battery is the *reasonable discipline* of a child by a parent that is generally regulated by statute and varies from state to state (Kidjacked.com, 2011).

Battery Causation

The defendant's criminal act must be the **factual** and **legal cause** of the harm, which is defined in Section 10 "Battery Harm".

Battery Harm

The **harm** requirement for battery varies, depending on the jurisdiction. Many jurisdictions allow for harmful *or offensive* contact (720 ILCS § 12-3, 2011). Some jurisdictions require an actual injury to the victim (Ala. Code § 13A-6-21, 2011). The severity of the injury can elevate grading, as is discussed in Section 10 "Battery Grading".

Example of Battery Harm

Review the example in Section 10 "Example of Battery Act" where Chris pours hot coffee on Geoff's hand. If Chris and Geoff are in a state that requires *actual injury* to the victim as the harm element of battery, Chris will not be subject to prosecution for this offense unless the hot coffee injures Geoff's hand. If Chris and Geoff are in a state that allows for harmful *or offensive* contact, Chris may be charged with or convicted of battery as long as the battery intent element is present, as discussed in Section 10 "Battery Intent".

Figure 10.6 Diagram of Defenses to Battery

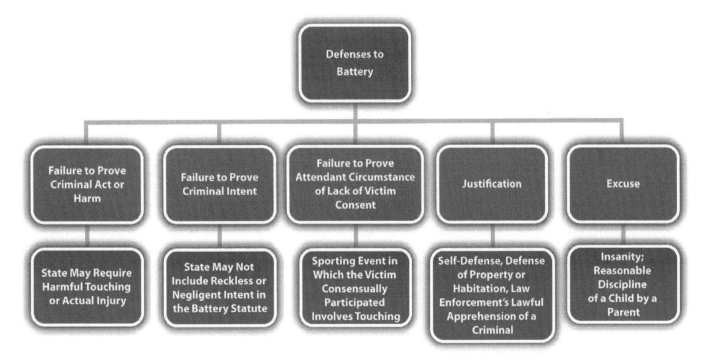

Battery Grading

At early common law, battery was a misdemeanor. The Model Penal Code grades battery (called simple assault) as a misdemeanor unless "committed in a fight or scuffle entered into by mutual consent, in which case it is a petty misdemeanor" (Model Penal Code § 211.1(1)). The Model Penal Code grades *aggravated* battery (called aggravated assault), which is battery that causes serious bodily injury or bodily injury caused by a deadly weapon, as a felony of the second or third degree (Model Penal Code § 211.1(2)). Many states follow the Model Penal Code approach by **grading** battery that causes offense or emotional injury as a misdemeanor (720 ILCS § 12-3, 2011) and battery that causes bodily injury as a gross misdemeanor or a felony (720 ILCS §12-4, 2011). In addition, battery supported by a higher level of intent—such as intent to cause serious bodily injury or intent to maim or disfigure—is often graded higher (Ala. Code § 13A-6-20, 2011). Other factors that can aggravate battery grading are the use of a weapon (R.I. Gen. Laws § 11-5-2, 2011), the commission of battery during the commission or attempted commission of a serious or violent felony (Ala. Code § 13A-6-20, 2011), the helplessness of the victim (Wis. Stat § 940.16(6), 2011), and battery against a teacher (Wis. Stat. § 940.16(5), 2011) or law enforcement officer (Wis. Stat. § 940.20(2), 2011).

Assault Elements

Assault is a crime that has the elements of criminal act and intent. A certain type of assault also has a causation and harm element, as is discussed in Section 10 "Threatened Battery Assault".

Attempted Battery and Threatened Battery Assault

Two types of assault are recognized. In some jurisdictions, assault is an attempted battery. In other jurisdictions, assault is a threatened battery. The Model Penal Code criminalizes both attempted battery and threatened battery assault (Model Penal Code § 211.1). The elements of both types of assault are discussed in Section 10 "Attempted Battery and Threatened Battery Assault".

Attempted Battery Assault

Attempted battery assault is an assault that has every element of battery except for the **physical contact**. The elements of attempted battery assault are criminal act supported by criminal intent. There is no requirement of causation or harm because *attempt* crimes do not have a harm requirement. Although attempted battery assault should allow for the same defense of **consent** as battery, this is not as common with assault as it is with battery, so most statutes do not have the attendant circumstance element of lack of consent by the victim.

Attempted Battery Assault Act

The **criminal act** element required for attempted battery assault is an act that *attempts* to make physical contact with the victim but falls short for some reason. This could be a thrown object that never hits its target, a gunshot that misses, or a punch that doesn't connect. In some states, the defendant must have the **present ability** to cause harmful or offensive physical contact, even though the contact never takes place (Cal. Penal Code § 240, 2011). The present ability requirement is simply an extension of the rule that attempt crimes must progress beyond mere preparation. In the majority of jurisdictions, the criminal act element is measured by the Model Penal Code's substantial steps test described in detail in Chapter 7 "Parties to Crime" (Commonwealth v. Matthews, 2011). To summarize, the substantial steps test requires the defendant to take substantial steps toward completion of the battery, and the defendant's actions must be strongly corroborative of the defendant's criminal purpose (Model Penal Code § 5.01).

Example of Attempted Battery Assault Act

Diana points a loaded pistol at her ex-boyfriend Dan, says, "Prepare to die, Dan," and pulls the trigger. Fortunately for Dan, the gun malfunctions and does not fire. Diana has probably committed **attempted battery assault**. Diana took every step necessary toward completion of battery, and her conduct of aiming a pistol at Dan and pulling the trigger was strongly corroborative of her criminal purpose. In addition, it appears that Diana had the **present ability** to shoot Dan because her gun was loaded. Thus Diana may be charged with and convicted of the offense of attempted battery assault with a deadly weapon. Note that Diana may also be charged with or convicted of attempted murder because it appears that murder intent is present.

Attempted Battery Assault Intent

The criminal intent element required for attempted battery assault is the **specific intent** or **purposely** to cause harmful or offensive contact (People v. Nickens, 2011). Like all attempt crimes, attempted battery assault cannot be supported by reckless or negligent intent.

Example of Attempted Battery Assault Intent

Change the example in Section 10 "Example of Attempted Battery Assault Act" so that Dan hands Diana a pistol and comments that it is unloaded. Diana says, "Really? Well, then, I can do this!" She thereafter points the gun at Dan and playfully pulls the trigger. The gun malfunctions and does not shoot, although it is loaded. Diana probably cannot be charged with or convicted of attempted battery assault in this case. Although Diana took every step necessary toward making harmful physical contact with Dan, she was acting with **negligent**, not **specific** or **purposeful**, intent. Thus the criminal intent element for attempted battery assault is absent, and Diana could only be charged with a lesser offense such as negligent handling of firearms.

Threatened Battery Assault

Threatened battery assault differs from attempted battery assault in that the intent is not to cause physical contact with the victim; the intent is to cause the victim to *fear* physical contact. Thus threatened battery assault is not an attempt crime and has the additional requirement of **causation** and **harm** offense elements.

Threatened Battery Assault Act

The **criminal act** element required for threatened battery assault is conduct that causes the victim apprehension of immediate harmful or offensive physical contact. In general, *words* are *not enough* to constitute the criminal act element required for threatened battery assault (Clark v. Commonwealth, 2011). The words must be accompanied by threatening gestures. In addition, a threat of future harm or a conditional threat is not sufficient (Clark v. Commonwelath, 2011). The physical contact threatened must be unequivocal and immediate. Some jurisdictions still require present ability for threatened battery assault. In others, only **apparent ability** is necessary; this means the victim must *reasonably believe* that the defendant can effectuate the physical contact (Fla. Stat. Ann. § 784.011, 2011).

Example of Threatened Battery Assault Act

Change the example given in Section 10 "Example of Attempted Battery Assault Act" so that Dan's pistol is lying on a table. Diana says to Dan, "If you don't take me back, I am going to shoot you with your own gun!" At this point, Diana has probably not committed the criminal act element required for threatened battery assault. Diana has only used *words* to threaten Dan, and words are generally not enough to constitute the threatened battery assault act. In addition, Diana's threat was **conditional**, not immediate. If Dan agrees to get back together with Diana, no physical contact would occur. Add to the example, and assume that Dan responds, "Go ahead, shoot me. I would rather die than take you back!" Diana thereafter grabs the gun, points it at Dan, and cocks it. At this point, Diana may have committed the criminal act element required for threatened battery assault. Diana's threat is accompanied by a serious *gesture*: cocking a pistol. If the state in which Dan and Diana's example occurs requires **present ability**, then the gun must be loaded. If the state requires **apparent ability**, then Dan must *believe* the gun is loaded—and if he is wrong, Diana could still have committed the criminal act element required for threatened battery assault.

Threatened Battery Assault Intent

The criminal intent element required for threatened battery assault is the **specific intent** or **purposely** to cause *fear* of harmful or offensive contact (Commonwelath v. Porro, 2010). This is different from the criminal intent element required for attempted battery assault, which is the specific intent or purposely to cause *harmful* or *offensive contact*.

Example of Threatened Battery Assault Intent

Review the example in Section 10 "Example of Threatened Battery Assault Act". Change the example so that the gun that Diana grabs is *Diana's* gun, and it is *unloaded*. Diana is aware that the gun is unloaded, but Dan is not. In this example, Diana probably has the intent required for threatened battery assault. Diana's act of pointing the gun at Dan and cocking it, after making a verbal threat, indicates that she has the **specific intent** or **purposely** to cause apprehension in Dan of imminent harmful physical contact. If Diana is in a state that only requires apparent ability to effectuate the contact, Diana has committed the criminal act supported by criminal intent for threatened battery assault. Note that Diana does not have the proper criminal intent for **attempted battery assault** if the gun is *unloaded*. This is because the intent required for attempted battery assault is the intent to *cause harmful or offensive contact*, which Diana clearly cannot intend to do with an unloaded gun.

Threatened Battery Assault Causation

The defendant's criminal act must be the **factual** and **legal** cause of the harm that is defined in Section 10 "Threatened Battery Assault Harm".

Threatened Battery Assault Harm

The **harm** element required for threatened battery assault is the victim's reasonable apprehension of imminent harmful or offensive contact (Commonwelath v. Porro, 2011). Thus the victim's lack of awareness of the defendant's criminal act could operate as a **failure of proof** or **affirmative defense** in many jurisdictions.

Example of Threatened Battery Assault Harm

Review the example in Section 10 "Example of Threatened Battery Assault Act". Change the example so that after Diana verbally threatens Dan, he shrugs, turns around, and begins to walk away. Frustrated, Diana grabs the gun off of the table and waves it menacingly at Dan's back. Dan is unaware of this behavior and continues walking out the door. Diana has probably *not* committed threatened battery assault in this situation. A key component of threatened battery assault is *victim apprehension* or *fear*. If Diana silently waves a gun at Dan's back, it does not appear that she has the specific intent or purposely to inspire fear in Dan of harmful physical contact. In addition, Dan was not cognizant of Diana's action and did not experience the fear, which is the threatened battery assault **harm** element. Thus Diana may not be convicted of assault with a deadly weapon in states that criminalize only threatened battery assault. Note that if the gun is loaded, Diana may have committed **attempted battery assault** in many jurisdictions. Attempted battery assault requires neither intent to inspire fear in the victim nor victim awareness of the defendant's criminal act. A trier of fact could find that Diana took substantial steps toward committing harmful physical contact when she picked up a loaded gun and waved it at Dan's back after making a verbal threat. Attempted battery assault has no harm element, so the crime is complete as soon as Diana commits the criminal act supported by criminal intent.

Figure 10.7 Diagram of Assault Elements

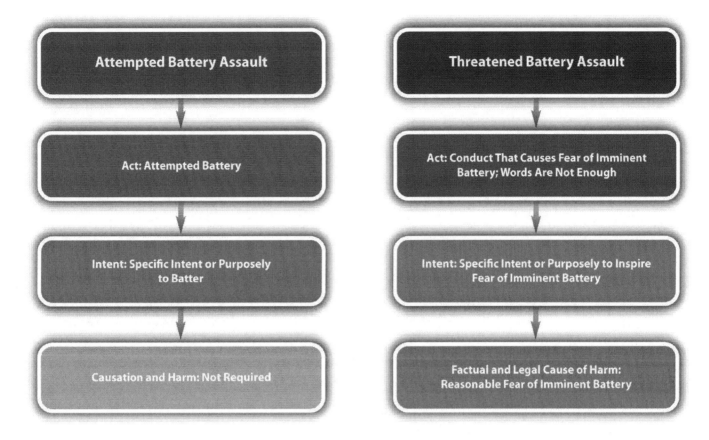

Figure 10.8 Crack the Code

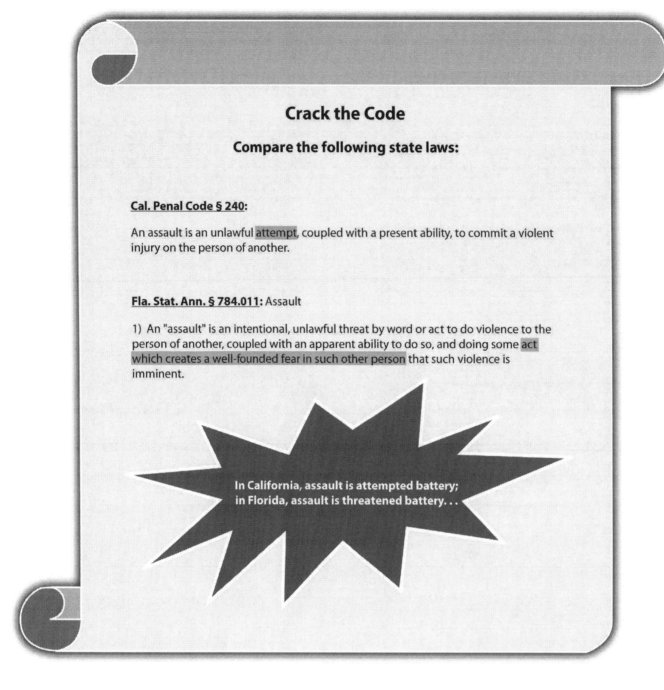

Crack the Code

Compare the following state laws:

Cal. Penal Code § 240:

An assault is an unlawful attempt, coupled with a present ability, to commit a violent injury on the person of another.

Fla. Stat. Ann. § 784.011: Assault

1) An "assault" is an intentional, unlawful threat by word or act to do violence to the person of another, coupled with an apparent ability to do so, and doing some act which creates a well-founded fear in such other person that such violence is imminent.

In California, assault is attempted battery; in Florida, assault is threatened battery...

Assault Grading

Assault **grading** is very similar to battery grading in many jurisdictions. As stated previously, many modern statutes follow the Model Penal Code approach and combine assault and battery into one statute, typically called "assault" (Ariz. Rev. Stat § 13-1203, 2011). Simple assault is generally a misdemeanor (Ariz Rev. Stat. § 13-1203, 2011). Aggravated assault is generally a felony (Ariz. Rev. Stat. § 13-1204, 2011). Factors that could enhance grading of assault are the use of a deadly weapon and assault against a law enforcement officer, teacher, or helpless individual (Ariz. Rev. Stat. § 13-1204, 2011).

Table 10.2 Comparing Battery, Attempted Battery, and Threatened Battery Assault

Crime	Criminal Act	Criminal Intent	Harm	Grading
Battery	Unlawful touching	Specific or purposely, general or knowingly, reckless, or negligent	Harmful or offensive physical contact	Simple: misdemeanor Aggravated: felony
Attempted battery assault	Substantial steps toward a battery plus present ability	Specific or purposely to commit battery	None required	Simple: misdemeanor Aggravated: felony
Threatened battery assault	Conduct that inspires fear of physical contact; words are not enough; may require apparent rather than present ability	Specific or purposely to inspire fear of physical contact	Victim's reasonable fear of imminent physical contact	Simple: misdemeanor Aggravated: felony

Note: **Battery could also include the attendant circumstance element of lack of consent by the victim.**

Key Takeaways

- The criminal act element required for battery is an unlawful touching.
- The criminal intent element required for battery can be specific intent or purposely, general intent or knowingly, recklessly, or negligently, depending on the circumstances and the jurisdiction. Jurisdictions that criminalize reckless or negligent battery generally require actual injury, serious bodily injury, or the use of a deadly weapon.
- The attendant circumstance element required for battery is lack of consent by the victim.
- The harm element of battery is physical contact. Jurisdictions vary as to whether the physical contact must be harmful or if it can be harmful or offensive.
- Battery that causes offense or emotional injury is typically graded as a misdemeanor, and battery that causes physical injury is typically graded as a gross misdemeanor or a felony. Factors that can aggravate grading are a higher level of intent, such as intent to maim or disfigure, use of a weapon, committing battery in concert with other serious or violent felonies, and battery against a helpless victim, teacher, or law enforcement officer.
- Attempted battery assault is an attempt crime that does not require the elements of causation or harm. Threatened battery assault requires causation and harm; the victim must experience reasonable fear of imminent physical contact.
- Attempted battery assault requires the criminal act of substantial steps toward commission of a battery and the criminal intent of specific intent or purposely to commit a battery. Because attempted battery assault is an attempt crime, it also generally requires present ability to commit the battery.
- The criminal act element required for threatened battery assault is conduct that inspires reasonable fear in the victim of imminent harmful or offensive physical contact. Words generally are not enough to constitute the criminal act element, nor are conditional threats. However, because the act need only inspire the fear, rather than culminate in a battery, apparent ability to commit the battery is sufficient in many jurisdictions. The criminal intent element required for threatened battery assault is specific intent or purposely to inspire the victim's reasonable fear. The defendant must also be the factual and legal cause of the harm, which is the victim's reasonable fear of imminent harmful or offensive physical contact.
- Simple assault is generally graded as a misdemeanor; aggravated assault is generally graded as a felony. Factors that can aggravate grading are the use of a weapon or assault against a law enforcement officer, teacher, or helpless victim.

Exercises

Answer the following questions. Check your answers using the answer key at the end of the chapter.

Bob and Rick get into an argument after drinking a few beers. Bob swings at Rick with his fist, but Rick ducks and Bob does not hit Rick. Bob swings again with the other hand, and this time he manages to punch Rick in the stomach. Identify the crimes committed in this situation. If Bob only swings once and misses, which crime(s) have been committed?

Read *State v. Higgs*, 601 N.W.2d 653 (1999). What criminal act did the defendant commit that resulted in a conviction for battery? Did the Court of Appeals of Wisconsin uphold the defendant's conviction? Why or why not? The case is available at this link:
http://scholar.google.com/scholar_case?case=10727852975973050662&q=State+v.+Higgs+601+N.W.2d+653&hl=en&as_sdt=2,5.

Read *Commonwealth v. Henson*, 259 N.E.2d 769 (1970). In *Henson*, the defendant fired blanks at a police officer and was convicted of assault with a deadly weapon. The defendant appealed, claiming that he had no present ability to shoot the police officer because the gun was not loaded with bullets. Did the Supreme Judicial Court of Massachusetts uphold the defendant's conviction? The case is available at this link:
http://scholar.google.com/scholar_case?case=11962310018051202223&hl=en&as_sdt=2002&as_vis=1.

References

Ala. Code § 13A-6-20, accessed February 18, 2011, http://law.onecle.com/alabama/criminal-code/13A-6-20.html.

Ala. Code § 13A-6-20(4), accessed February 18, 2011, http://law.onecle.com/alabama/criminal-code/13A-6-20.html.

Ala. Code § 13A-6-21, accessed February 18, 2011, http://law.onecle.com/alabama/criminal-code/13A-6-21.html.

Ariz. Rev. Stat. § 13-1203, accessed February 20, 2011, http://law.onecle.com/arizona/criminal-code/13-1203.html.

Ariz. Rev. Stat. § 13-1204, accessed February 20, 2011, http://law.onecle.com/arizona/criminal-code/13-1204.html.

Cal. Penal Code § 240, accessed February 19, 2011, http://law.justia.com/california/codes/2009/pen/240-248.html.

Clark v. Commonwealth, 676 S.E.2d 332 (2009), accessed February 19, 2011, http://scholar.google.com/scholar_case?case=12317437845803464805&q=%22assault%22+%2B+%22words+are+not+enough%22&hl=en&as_sdt=2,5.

Commonwealth v. Matthews, 205 PA Super 92 (2005), accessed February 19, 2011, http://scholar.google.com/scholar_case?case=16367791555829234654&q=%22assault%22+%2B+%22conditional+threat%22+%2B+%22not+enough%22&hl=en&as_sdt=2,5.

Commonwealth v. Porro, 458 Mass. 526 (2010), accessed February 20, 2011, http://scholar.google.com/scholar_case?case=13033264667355058927&q=Commonwealth+v.+Porro&hl=en&as_sdt=4,22.

Fla. Stat. Ann. § 784.03, accessed February 18, 2011, http://law.onecle.com/florida/crimes/784.03.html.

K.S.A. § 21-3412, accessed February 18, 2011, http://kansasstatutes.lesterama.org/Chapter_21/Article_34/21-3412.html.

Kidjacked.com website, "United States statutes pertaining to spanking," accessed February 18, 2011, http://kidjacked.com/legal/spanking_law.asp.

People v. Nickens, 685 NW 2d 657 (2004), accessed February 19, 2011, http://scholar.google.com/scholar_case?case=16424953435525763156&hl=en&as_sdt=2&as_vis=1&oi=scholarr.

R.I. Gen. Laws § 11-5-2.2, accessed February 18, 2011, http://law.justia.com/rhodeisland/codes/title11/11-5-2.2.html.

Wis. Stat. §§ 940.19(6) (a), 940.19(6) (b), accessed February 18, 2011, http://nxt.legis.state.wi.us/nxt/gateway.dll?f=templates&fn=default.htm&d=stats&jd=ch.%20940.

Wis. Stat. § 940.20(2), accessed February 18, 2011, http://nxt.legis.state.wi.us/nxt/gateway.dll?f=templates&fn=default.htm&d=stats&jd=ch.%20940.

Wis. Stat. § 940.20(5), accessed February 18, 2011, http://nxt.legis.state.wi.us/nxt/gateway.dll?f=templates&fn=default.htm&d=stats&jd=ch.%20940.

720 ILCS § 12-3, accessed February 18, 2011, http://law.onecle.com/illinois/720ilcs5/12-3.html.

720 ILCS § 12-4, accessed February 18, 2011, http://law.onecle.com/illinois/720ilcs5/12-4.html.
CC licensed content, Shared previously

- Criminal Law. **Provided by**: University of Minnesota Libraries Publishing . **Located at**: http://open.lib.umn.edu/criminallaw/. **License**: *CC BY-NC-SA: Attribution-NonCommercial-ShareAlike*

10.3 Domestic Violence and Stalking

Learning Objectives

Identify the individuals covered by domestic violence statutes.
Identify some of the special features of domestic violence statutes.
Define the criminal act element required for stalking.
Define the criminal intent element required for stalking, and compare various statutory approaches to stalking criminal intent.
Define the harm element required for stalking, and compare various statutory approaches to ascertaining harm.
Analyze stalking grading.

Domestic violence and stalking are modern crimes that respond to societal problems that have escalated in recent years. Domestic violence statutes are drafted to address issues that are prevalent in crimes between family members or individuals living in the same household. Stalking generally punishes conduct that is a *precursor* to assault, battery, or other crimes against the person, as is explored in Section 10.3 "Domestic Violence and Stalking".

Domestic Violence

Domestic violence statutes generally focus on criminal conduct that occurs between **family** members. Although family cruelty or interfamily criminal behavior is not a new phenomenon, enforcement of criminal statutes against family members can be challenging because of dependence, fear, and other issues that are particular to the family unit. In addition, historical evidence indicates that law enforcement can be reluctant to get involved in *family disputes* and often fails to adequately *protect* victims who are trapped in the same residence as the defendant. Specific enforcement measures that are crafted to apply to defendants and victims who are family members are an innovative statutory approach that many jurisdictions are beginning to adopt. In general, domestic violence statutes target crimes against the person, for example, assault, battery, sex offenses, kidnapping, and criminal homicide.

Domestic Violence Statutes' Characteristics

The purpose of many domestic violence statutes is *equal* enforcement and treatment of crimes between family members and *maximum protection* for the domestic violence victim (RCW § 10.99.010, 2011). Domestic violence statutes focus on individuals related by blood or marriage, individuals who share a child, ex-spouses and ex-lovers, and individuals who reside together (Ariz. Rev. Stat. § 13-3601(A), 2011). Domestic violence statutes commonly contain the following provisions:

- Special training for law enforcement in domestic issues (RCW § 10.99.030, 2011)
- Protection of the victim by no-contact orders and nondisclosure of the victim's residence address (RCW § 10.99.040, 2011)

- Duty of law enforcement or prosecutors to inform the victim of the decision of whether to prosecute and the duty to inform the victim of special procedures available to protect domestic violence victims (RCW § 10.99.060, 2011)
- Ability to arrest domestic violence offenders with or without a warrant (Ariz. Rev. Stat. § 13-3601(B), 2011)
- Special factors to consider in the sentencing of domestic violence defendants (RCW § 10.99.100, 2011)
- Peace officer immunity for enforcement of domestic violence provisions (Ariz. Rev. Stat. § 13,3601(G), 2011)

Stalking

California was the first state to enact a stalking law in 1990, in response to the high-profile murder of a young actress named Rebecca Schaeffer whose attacker stalked her for two years. Now *all states* and the federal government have stalking laws (18 U.S.C. § 2261A, 2011). Although statutes criminalizing stalking are gender-neutral, in reality, most stalking victims are women, and most stalking defendants are men.

Before the states enacted stalking laws, a victim who was threatened and harassed but not assaulted had no remedy except to go to court and obtain a restraining order. A restraining order is a court order mandating that the defendant neither contact nor come within a certain distance of the victim. If the defendant violated the restraining order, law enforcement could arrest him or her. Until a restraining order was in place, however, the defendant was free to continue frightening the victim. Restraining orders typically take some time to obtain. The victim must contact and employ an attorney and also set up a court hearing. For this reason, the restraining order method of preventing a defendant from stalking was cumbersome, ineffective, and frequently resulted in force or violence against the stalking victim.

The modern crime of stalking allows law enforcement to arrest and incapacitate defendants *before* they complete an assault, battery, or other violent crime against a victim. Like all crimes, stalking requires the defendant to commit a voluntary act supported by criminal intent. In many jurisdictions, stalking also has the elements of causation and harm, as is discussed in Section 10.3.2 "Stalking".

Stalking Act

Various approaches have been made to criminalize stalking, and a plethora of descriptors now identify the stalking criminal act. In the majority of jurisdictions, the **criminal act** element required for stalking includes *any course of conduct* that **credibly** threatens the victim's safety, including following (Tex. Penal Code § 42.072, 2011), harassing (Cal. Penal Code § 646.9, 2011), approaching (Md. Code Ann. § 3-802, 2011), pursuing, or making an express or implied threat to injure the victim, the victim's family member (Ala. Code § 13A-6-90, 2011), or the victim's property (Tex. Penal Code § 42.072(a), 2011). In general, credible threat means the defendant has the **apparent ability** to effectuate the harm threatened (S. D. Codified Laws § 22-19A-6, 2011). The stalking criminal act is unique among criminal acts in that it must occur on *more than one* occasion or repeatedly (Colo. Rev. Stat. Ann. § 18-3-602, 2011). The popularity of social networking sites and the frequency with which defendants use the Internet to stalk their victims inspired many states to specifically criminalize cyberstalking, which is the use of the Internet or e-mail to commit the criminal act of stalking (Alaska Stat. § 11.41.270, 2011).

Example of a Case Lacking Stalking Act

Elliot tells Lisa on two separate occasions that he loves her. Lisa intensely dislikes Elliot and wants nothing to do with him. Although Elliot's proclamations of love are unwelcome, Elliot probably has not committed the criminal act element required for stalking. Elliot's behavior does not threaten Lisa's *safety* or the safety of her family members or property. Thus Elliot may not be charged with and convicted of stalking in most jurisdictions.

Example of Stalking Act

Change the example in Section 10 "Example of a Case Lacking Stalking Act" so that Elliot tells Lisa he loves her on one occasion. Lisa frowns and walks away. Elliot then follows Lisa and tells her that he will "make her pay" for not loving him. Lisa ignores Elliot's statement, climbs into her car, and drives away. Later that evening, Elliot rings Lisa's doorbell. Lisa does not answer the door but yells at Elliot, telling him to leave. Disgruntled and angry, Elliot carves, "you will die for not loving me" into Lisa's front door with his pocketknife.

Elliot's conduct could constitute the criminal act element required for stalking in most jurisdictions. In this example, Elliot has *followed* Lisa and *approached* her, which is a repeated course of conduct. On two occasions Elliot threatened Lisa: once by telling her he will "make her pay" and again by carving a death threat into her front door. Keep in mind that Elliot's threat to Lisa's safety must be *credible* in many jurisdictions. Thus if Elliot is unable to actually harm Lisa for any reason, the trier of fact could find that he does not have the **apparent ability** to carry out his threat, and he could not be convicted of stalking.

Stalking Intent

The criminal intent element required for stalking also varies, depending on the jurisdiction. In most states, the defendant must commit the criminal act willfully or maliciously (Cal. Penal Code § 646.9, 2011). This indicates a **specific intent** or **purposeful** conduct. However, in states that require the victim to experience **harm**, a different criminal intent could support the harm offense element. States that include bad results or harm in their stalking statutes require either **specific intent** or **purposely**, **general intent** or **knowingly**, **reckless intent**, **negligent intent**, or **strict liability** (no intent) to cause the harm, depending on the state (Ncvc.org, 2011).

Example of Stalking Intent

Review the stalking act example in Section 10 "Example of Stalking Act". In the majority of states, Elliot must make the threatening statement and carve the threatening message into Lisa's front door **willfully** or **maliciously**. However, the requirement that Elliot act with the intent to **cause** Lisa's *reaction* to this conduct varies, depending on the jurisdiction. In some jurisdictions, Elliot must act with the specific intent or purposely to **cause** Lisa to suffer the stalking harm, which is generally *fear* for bodily safety, the safety of family members, or fear of damage to Lisa's property. In others, Elliot can act to cause Lisa's fear with general intent or knowingly, reckless intent, or negligent intent. In some jurisdictions, Elliot's purpose or awareness as to Lisa's feeling of fear is irrelevant because **strict liability** is the intent supporting the harm or bad results requirement.

Stalking Causation

In jurisdictions that require harm for stalking, the defendant's criminal act must be the **factual** and **legal** cause of the harm, which is defined in Section 10 "Stalking Harm".

Stalking Harm

As stated previously, some states require a specific **harm** element in their stalking statutes. This element is defined differently depending on the state but generally amounts to victim **fear**. The fear is typically fear of bodily injury or death of the victim (Ala. Code § 13A-6-90, 2011) or of the victim's family member (Alaska Stat. § 11.41.270, 2011), or damage to the victim's property (Tex Penal Code § 42.072(a), 2011). States also employ different tests to ascertain the harm element. States can require subjective *and* objective fear (Tex. Penal Code § 42.072(a), 2011), *just* subjective fear (Alaska Stat. § 11.41.270, 2011), or *just* objective fear (Md. Code Ann. § 3-802, 2011). Subjective fear means the victim must actually experience fear. Objective fear means a reasonable victim under similar circumstances would experience fear.

Example of Stalking Harm

Review the stalking act example in Section 10 "Example of Stalking Act". In jurisdictions that require subjective **and** objective victim fear as the harm element for stalking, Elliot must cause *Lisa* to experience fear that is *reasonable* under the circumstances. In a jurisdiction that requires only subjective victim fear, Elliot must cause Lisa to feel fear, either reasonably or unreasonably. In a jurisdiction that requires only objective fear, Elliot must act in a manner that would cause a reasonable victim under similar circumstances to experience fear. Keep in mind that if Lisa is aware of a circumstance that makes it unlikely that Elliot can carry out his threat, Elliot *could not* be convicted of stalking in a jurisdiction that requires Lisa to experience *subjective* fear.

Stalking Grading

Jurisdictions vary as to how they **grade** stalking. Many states divide stalking into degrees or grade it as simple and aggravated. First-degree or aggravated stalking is generally graded as a felony, and second-degree or simple stalking is generally graded as a misdemeanor (Alaska Stat. §§ 11.41.260, 2011). Factors that could enhance grading are the violation of a restraining or protective order, the use of a weapon, a youthful victim, or previous convictions for stalking (Alaska Stat. § 11.41.260, 2011).

Figure 10.9 Diagram of Domestic Violence and Stalking

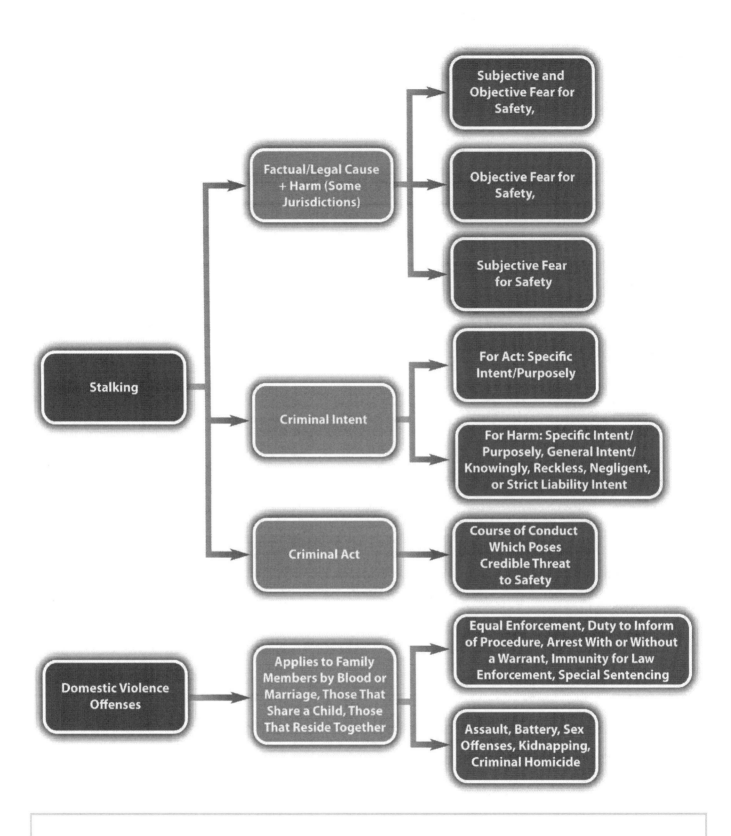

Key Takeaways

- Individuals covered by domestic violence statutes are relatives by blood or marriage, individuals who share a child, ex-spouses and ex-lovers, and individuals who reside together.
- Some special features of domestic violence statutes are special training for law enforcement in domestic issues, protection of the victim by no-contact orders and nondisclosure of the victim's residence address, the duty of law enforcement or prosecutors to inform the victim of the decision of whether to prosecute and the duty to inform the victim of special procedures available to protect

domestic violence victims, the ability to arrest domestic violence offenders with or without a warrant, special factors to consider in the sentencing of domestic violence defendants, and peace officer immunity for enforcement of domestic violence provisions.

- The criminal act element required for stalking varies, but in general it is repeatedly engaging in a course of conduct that poses a credible threat to the victim's safety, including following, harassing, approaching, or pursuing the victim.
- The criminal intent supporting the stalking criminal act is specific intent or purposely in most jurisdictions. Some jurisdictions require a different criminal intent to support the harm requirement: either specific intent or purposely, general intent or knowingly, reckless intent, negligent intent, or strict liability.
- Some jurisdictions require the defendant to cause harm, which is victim fear of serious bodily injury, fear of death of the victim or the victim's family member, or damage to the victim's property. The test for victim fear varies and could be either subjective and objective fear, just subjective fear, or just objective fear.
- It is common to divide stalking into degrees or grade it as simple and aggravated. First-degree or aggravated stalking is generally graded as a felony, and second-degree or simple stalking is generally graded as a misdemeanor. Factors that can aggravate grading are the violation of a restraining or protective order, the use of a weapon, a youthful victim, or previous convictions for stalking.

Exercises

Answer the following questions. Check your answers using the answer key at the end of the chapter.

Chris punches and slaps Rhianna, his roommate and girlfriend. Could this be considered domestic violence?

Read *State v. Holbach*, 2009 ND 37 (2009). In *Holbach*, the defendant appealed a conviction for stalking based on his constitutionally protected right to travel around town and do errands. The defendant was on probation for stalking the victim and subject to conditions of probation, including a stay-away order. However, the victim claimed that she saw the defendant following her around town on many occasions. Did the Supreme Court of North Dakota uphold the defendant's stalking conviction? Why or why not? The case is available at this link: http://scholar.google.com/scholar_case?case=14788412528928431856&q=stalking&hl=en&as_sdt=2,5&as_ylo=2009.

Read *Burke v. State*, 676 S.E.2d 766 (2009). Why did the Court of Appeals of Georgia reverse the defendant's conviction for aggravated stalking in this case? The case is available at this link: http://scholar.google.com/scholar_case?case=14247986447862424093&q=stalking&hl=en&as_sdt=2,5&as_ylo=2009.

References

Ala. Code § 13A-6-90, accessed February 22, 2011, http://www.ncvc.org/src/main.aspx?dbID=DB_Alabama390.

Alaska Stat. §§ 11.41.260, 11.41.270, accessed February 22, 2011, http://www.ncvc.org/src/main.aspx?dbID=DB_Alaska803.

Alaska Stat. § 11.41.270 (a), http://www.ncvc.org/src/main.aspx?dbID=DB_Alaska803.

Alaska Stat. § 11.41.270 (b) (3) (F), accessed February 22, 2011, http://www.ncvc.org/src/main.aspx?dbID=DB_Alaska803.

Ariz. Rev. Stat. § 13-3601(A), accessed February 21, 2011, http://www.azleg.state.az.us/ars/13/03601.htm.

Ariz. Rev. Stat. § 13-3601(B), accessed February 21, 2011, http://www.azleg.state.az.us/ars/13/03601.htm.

Ariz. Rev. Stat. § 13-3601(G), accessed February 21, 2011, http://www.azleg.state.az.us/ars/13/03601.htm.

Cal. Penal Code § 646.9, accessed February 22, 2011, http://www.ncvc.org/src/main.aspx?dbID=DB_California176 (accessed February 22, 1022).

Colo. Rev. Stat. Ann. § 18-3-602, accessed February 22, 2011, http://www.ncvc.org/src/main.aspx?dbID=DB_Colorado285.

Md. Code Ann. § 3-802, accessed February 22, 2011, http://www.ncvc.org/src/main.aspx?dbID=DB_Maryland678.

Ncvc.org website, "Criminal Stalking Laws," accessed February 22, 2011, http://www.ncvc.org/src/main.aspx?dbID=DB_State-byState_Statutes117.

RCW § 10.99.010, accessed February 21, 2011, http://apps.leg.wa.gov/rcw/default.aspx?cite=10.99.010.

RCW § 10.99.030, accessed February 21, 2011, http://apps.leg.wa.gov/rcw/default.aspx?cite=10.99.030.

RCW § 10.99.040, accessed February 21, 2011, http://apps.leg.wa.gov/rcw/default.aspx?cite=10.99.040.

RCW § 10.99.060, accessed February 21, 2011, http://apps.leg.wa.gov/rcw/default.aspx?cite=10.99.060, Ariz. Rev. Stat. § 13-3601(J), accessed February 21, 2011, http://www.azleg.state.az.us/ars/13/03601.htm.

RCW § 10.99.100, accessed February 21, 2011, http://apps.leg.wa.gov/rcw/default.aspx?cite=10.99.100.

S. D. Codified Laws § 22-19A-6, accessed February 22, 2011, http://www.ncvc.org/src/main.aspx?dbID=DB_SouthDakota123.

Tex. Penal Code § 42.072, accessed February 22, 2011, http://www.ncvc.org/src/main.aspx?dbID=DB_Texas176.

Tex. Penal Code § 42.072(a) (1) (c), accessed February 22, 2011, http://www.ncvc.org/src/main.aspx?dbID=DB_Texas176.

18 U.S.C. § 2261A, accessed February 22, 2011, http://www.ncvc.org/src/main.aspx?dbID=DB_Federal_Interstate_Stalking_Institute163#61a.
CC licensed content, Shared previously

- Criminal Law. **Provided by**: University of Minnesota Libraries Publishing . **Located at**: http://open.lib.umn.edu/criminallaw/. **License**: *CC BY-NC-SA: Attribution-NonCommercial-ShareAlike*

10.4 Kidnapping and False Imprisonment

Learning Objectives

Define the criminal act element required for kidnapping.
Define the criminal intent element required for kidnapping.
Define the harm element required for kidnapping.
Define the attendant circumstance element required for kidnapping.
Analyze kidnapping grading.
Compare false imprisonment with kidnapping.
Identify two potential defenses to kidnapping and false imprisonment.
Identify two special features of interference with custody statutes.

Kidnapping and false imprisonment are crimes that involve physical restraint and intrude on the liberty interests of victims. In ancient times, kidnapping was used to remove members of royalty from the kingdom for ransom or to implement the overthrow of the existing monarchy. In the United States, high-profile kidnapping cases, such as the Lindbergh baby kidnapping in the 1930s, and the frequency with which organized crime participated in kidnapping led many states to impose the harshest penalties for this offense: the death penalty or life in prison without the possibility of parole.

In modern times, kidnapping is still a serious **felony**, although the US Supreme Court has held that capital punishment for any crime against an individual other than criminal homicide is unconstitutional. False imprisonment is generally a **lesser included offense** of kidnapping and is graded lower, as is discussed in Section 10.4.2 "False Imprisonment".

Kidnapping Elements

In most jurisdictions, kidnapping has the elements of criminal act, criminal intent, causation, harm, and an attendant circumstance.

Kidnapping Act

The **criminal act** element required for kidnapping is twofold. First, the defendant must **confine** the victim (720 ILC § 5/10-1). Second, in many states, the defendant must move the victim, which is called asportation. One common issue with the kidnapping criminal act is how far the victim must be moved. In the majority of states, the movement can be slight, as long as it is not incidental to the commission of a separate offense (People v. Dominguez, 2011). Other states do not require asportation when the kidnapping is for **ransom** (N.R.S. § 200.310, 2011). Some states have done away with the asportation requirement altogether (N.C. Gen. Stat. § 14-39(a), 2011). The Model Penal Code requires the movement to be from the victim's residence, place of business, or "a substantial distance from the vicinity where he is found" (Model Penal Code § 212.1). However, when the kidnapping is for ransom, for the purpose of committing a felony, to inflict bodily injury or terrorize the victim or another, or to interfere with the performance of a governmental or political function, the Model Penal Code does *not* require asportation, although it does require confinement for a "substantial period in a place of isolation" (Model Penal Code § 212.1).

Example of a Case Lacking Kidnapping Act

Joseph breaks into Abby's home and sees Abby sitting on the couch. A picture window in front of the couch puts Abby in full view of the street and sidewalk. To avoid detection, Joseph grabs Abby off the living room couch and drags her into the bedroom to rape her. Joseph has probably *not* committed the criminal act element required for kidnapping if the kidnapping statute in Joseph's state requires **asportation**. Joseph forcibly confined Abby when he grabbed her. However, his movement of Abby from the couch to the bedroom appears incidental to the crime of rape, which is not sufficient to constitute kidnapping asportation in most jurisdictions.

Kidnapping Intent

The criminal intent element required for kidnapping in many jurisdictions is **specific intent** or **purposely** to commit the criminal act in order to harm or injure the victim or another, confine or hold the victim in secret (N.R.S. § 200.310(2), 2011), receive a ransom, commit a separate offense, subject the victim to involuntary servitude, or interfere with the purpose of the government or some political function (Ariz. Rev. Stat. § 13-1304, 2011).

Example of Kidnapping Intent

Review the example in Section 10 "Example of a Case Lacking Kidnapping Act" with Joseph and Abby. Change this example so that Joseph drags Abby to his car, stuffs her into the trunk, and then drives fifteen miles to a deserted field where he thereafter removes her from the trunk and rapes her. Joseph probably has the criminal intent required for kidnapping in most jurisdictions. Joseph committed the criminal act of forcible confinement and asportation with the purpose of raping Abby, which is **specific intent** or **purposely** to "commit a separate offense." Thus if the other elements of kidnapping are present, Joseph can most likely be charged with and convicted of kidnapping, along with the crime of rape.

Kidnapping Causation

In jurisdictions that require harm for kidnapping, the defendant's criminal act must be the **factual** and **legal** cause of the harm, which is defined in Section 10 "Kidnapping Harm".

Kidnapping Harm

The **harm** element required for kidnapping in most jurisdictions is *confinement* and *asportation*. As stated previously, some jurisdictions have done away with the asportation requirement or do not require asportation when the kidnapping is for ransom.

Kidnapping Attendant Circumstance

In many jurisdictions, the **attendant circumstance** element required for kidnapping is that the confinement or asportation occur against the victim's will or *without* the victim's **consent** (N.C. Gen. Stat. § 14-39, 2011). Thus consent could function as a **failure of proof** or **affirmative defense** to kidnapping.

Example of a Case Lacking Kidnapping Attendant Circumstance

Thomas sees Shawna hitchhiking on the side of a busy freeway at night. Thomas pulls over, rolls down the window, and asks Shawna if she wants a ride. Shawna says, "sure," and climbs into Thomas's vehicle. Thomas drives away with Shawna in the front seat. Thomas has not committed kidnapping in this case. Although Thomas confined and moved Shawna in his vehicle, the facts do not indicate that he has the specific intent to harm her, obtain a ransom, confine her in secret, or commit a separate offense. In addition, Shawna *consented* to the confinement and asportation. Thus the **attendant circumstance** element for kidnapping is also absent and Thomas's conduct may be perfectly legal (unless engaging in hitchhiking is illegal in Thomas's state).

Example of Kidnapping Attendant Circumstance

Change the example given in Section 10 "Example of a Case Lacking Kidnapping Attendant Circumstance" so that after fifty miles of driving, Shawna asks Thomas to pull over and let her out. Thomas refuses, threatens to harm Shawna if she tries to escape, and continues to drive another twenty miles with Shawna in the front seat. If Thomas acted with the proper kidnapping intent, Thomas might have committed kidnapping in this case. Although Shawna's original entrance into Thomas's vehicle and her asportation for the first fifty miles was *consensual*, once Shawna requested that Thomas pull over and let her out, the confinement or asportation was against Shawna's will and *without her consent*. If the trier of fact determines that twenty miles is far enough to constitute sufficient asportation for kidnapping, Thomas could be charged with or convicted of this offense.

Kidnapping Grading

Jurisdictions vary as to how they **grade** kidnapping. The Model Penal Code grades kidnapping as a felony of the first or second degree (Model Penal Code § 212.1). Many states divide kidnapping into degrees or grade it as simple and aggravated (N.R.S. § 200.310, 2011). First-degree or aggravated kidnapping is generally graded as a serious felony, and second-degree or simple kidnapping is generally graded as a lower-level felony (N.R.S. § 200.310, 2011). One factor that could mitigate or reduce grading is the defendant's release of the victim unharmed in a safe place (Ariz. Rev. Stat. § 13-1304(B), 2011). Factors that could enhance grading are the youth of the victim (Ariz. Rev. Stat. § 13-1304, 2011) or the infliction of serious bodily injury (N.C. Gen. Stat. § 14-39, 2011). When kidnapping takes a victim across state lines, the defendant can also be prosecuted for the additional offense of federal kidnapping (18 U.S.C. § 1201, 2011).

False Imprisonment

In many jurisdictions, false imprisonment, also called **felonious restraint**, is a lesser included offense of kidnapping. This means that the crime of false imprisonment is missing one or two of the kidnapping elements and is graded lower than kidnapping. Often, false imprisonment functions as a **partial defense** to kidnapping because of the less serious sentencing options. In general, false imprisonment and felonious restraint under the Model Penal Code require confinement but *not asportation* (Model Penal Code §212.2; 18 Pa. C. S. § 2903, 2011). In some jurisdictions, false imprisonment requires only **general intent** or **knowingly** to commit the criminal act, rather than the **specific intent** or **purposely** to commit other crimes, harm the victim, or receive a ransom (720 ILCS § 5/10-3, 2011). False imprisonment does not require movement and has a lower level of intent, so it is generally **graded** as a gross misdemeanor or a low-level felony (18 Pa. C.S. § 2903, 2011). The Model Penal Code grades felonious restraint as a felony of the third degree (Model Penal Code § 212.2). Factors that can aggravate grading of false imprisonment are the youth of the victim (18 Pa. C. § 2903, 2011) or the use of force or violence to carry out the criminal act (Cal. Penal Code § 237, 2011).

Example of False Imprisonment

Review the case example given in Section 10 "Example of a Case Lacking Kidnapping Attendant Circumstance". Change the facts so that after fifty miles of driving, Shawna asks Thomas to pull over and let her out. Thomas pulls over but thereafter locks all the doors and refuses to let Shawna out for twenty minutes, in spite of her begging and pleading for him to unlock the doors. In this case, Thomas might have committed false imprisonment. Although Shawna's entrance into Thomas's vehicle was *consensual*, when Thomas confined Shawna to his vehicle by locking the doors, he deprived her of her liberty *against her will*. Thomas did not move Shawna without her consent because he pulled over and stopped the vehicle at her request. However, asportation is *not required* for false imprisonment. Although Thomas's actions do not indicate specific intent or purposely to injure Shawna, commit a separate offense, or seek ransom, often **general intent** or **knowingly** to commit the criminal act is sufficient for false imprisonment. Thus these facts indicate the lower-level crime of false imprisonment rather than kidnapping, and Thomas may be charged with and convicted of this offense.

Potential Defenses to Kidnapping and False Imprisonment

As stated previously, consent is a potential **failure of proof** or **affirmative defense** to kidnapping and false imprisonment in some jurisdictions. Another potential defense is **lawful authority** to execute the kidnapping or false imprisonment. Thus when a law enforcement officer or a citizen lawfully arrests a defendant, he or she is not committing kidnapping or false imprisonment. By the same token, if an arrest is executed *unlawfully*, it *might be* kidnapping, false imprisonment, or another related offense (N.C. Gen. Stat. §14-43.1, 2011).

Figure 10.10 Diagram of Defenses to Kidnapping and False Imprisonment

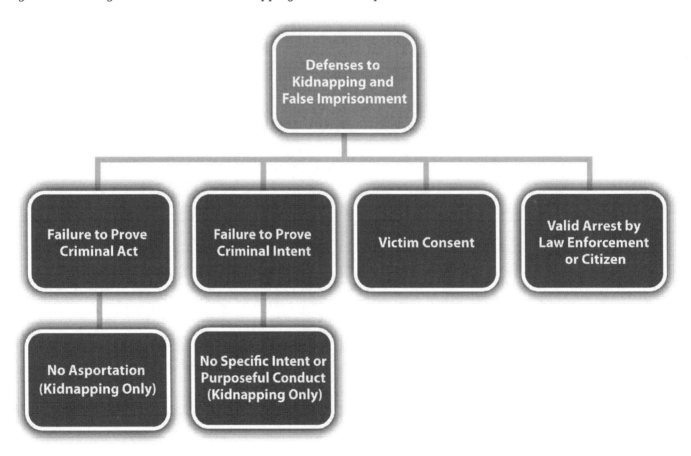

Interference with Custody

Because of a dramatic increase in the abduction of children by their estranged parents and parental interference with child custody and visitation agreements, almost all states have specifically criminalized **interference with the custody of children**(18 Pa. C. S. § 2904, 2011) or **unlawful visitation** (720 ILCS § 5/10-5.5, 2011). The significant features of these modern offenses are their specific applicability to parents as defendants and various defenses based on the good faith belief that the child would be in danger without the allegedly criminal conduct (18 Pa. C. S. § 2904, 2011). **Grading** of these offenses varies, with some states grading nonforcible parental interference with custody as a misdemeanor (720 ILCS § 5/10-5.5, 2011) and others as a low-level felony (18 Pa. C.S. § 2904, 2011).

Table 10.3 Comparing Kidnapping and False Imprisonment

Crime	Criminal Act	Criminal Intent	Harm	Circumstance	Grading
Kidnapping	Confinement plus asportation	Specific or purposely	Confinement plus asportation	Lack of consent	Felony
False imprisonment	Confinement	General or knowingly in some jurisdictions	Confinement	Lack of consent	Gross misdemeanor or low-level felony

Figure 10.11 Diagram of Crimes against the Person

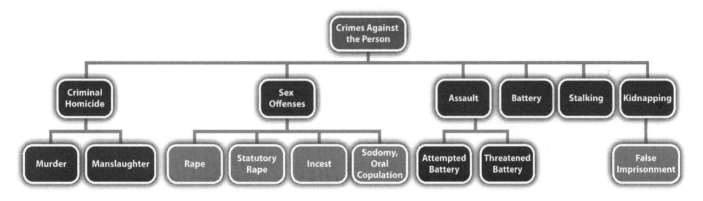

Key Takeaways

- The criminal act element required for kidnapping in many jurisdictions is confinement and asportation of the victim. Some states do not require asportation when the kidnapping is for ransom, and others have done away with the asportation requirement altogether.
- The criminal intent element required for kidnapping in many jurisdictions is the specific intent or purposely to commit the criminal act in order to harm or injure the victim or another, confine or hold the victim in secret, receive a ransom, commit a separate offense, subject the victim to involuntary servitude, or interfere with the purpose of the government or some political function.
- The harm element required for kidnapping in many jurisdictions is confinement and asportation of the victim.
- The attendant circumstance element required for kidnapping is lack of victim consent.
- Kidnapping is generally graded as first degree or aggravated or as second degree or simple. First-degree or aggravated kidnapping is typically a serious felony, while second-degree or simple kidnapping is typically a low-level felony. One factor that could mitigate or reduce grading is the release of the victim unharmed in a safe place. Factors that could aggravate grading are the youth of the victim or the infliction of serious bodily injury.

- False imprisonment is often a lesser included offense of kidnapping, missing the asportation element, and requiring general intent or knowing commission of the criminal act. False imprisonment is also graded lower than kidnapping as either a gross misdemeanor or a low-level felony.
- Two potential defenses to kidnapping and false imprisonment are victim consent and a lawful arrest by a law enforcement officer or citizen.
- Interference with custody statutes specifically include parents as defendants and allow for a good faith defense that a child would suffer injury if not for the allegedly criminal conduct.

Exercises

Answer the following questions. Check your answers using the answer key at the end of the chapter.

Coby is in the process of robbing a bank. When a security guard threatens to shoot Coby, he grabs a customer in the bank and holds a knife to her throat. Coby thereafter demands a getaway vehicle and fifty thousand dollars in cash in exchange for the hostage's release. Has Coby committed **kidnapping** in this case? Why or why not?

Read *State v. Salaman*, 949 A.2d 1092 (2008). In *Salaman*, the defendant grabbed the victim, pinned her to the stairs for five minutes, punched her in the face, and violently stuck his fingers down her throat. He was thereafter convicted of second-degree kidnapping and appealed, claiming his restraint of the victim was merely **incidental** to the crime of assault. In Connecticut, the state where the offense occurred, the kidnapping criminal act is restraint with the specific intent to prevent the victim's liberation. Connecticut also had case precedent holding that restraint that is incidental to the commission of a separate offense is still kidnapping. Did the Supreme Court of Connecticut uphold the defendant's conviction? The case is available at this link: http://scholar.google.com/scholar_case?case=13933358391504195031&q= kidnapping&hl=en&as_sdt=2,5&as_ylo=2008.

Read *Commonwealth v. Rivera*, 828 A.2d 1094 (2003). In *Rivera*, the defendant, who had a court order depriving him of custody, forcibly removed his daughter from her day care and drove around with her in his car, frequently calling and terrorizing the child's mother. The defendant's daughter disappeared, and the defendant was later convicted of felony murder, kidnapping, and other offenses. The underlying felony for the felony murder was **kidnapping**, and the defendant appealed claiming he could not legally kidnap his *own biological child*. Did the Superior Court of Pennsylvania affirm the defendant's felony murder and kidnapping convictions? Why or why not? The case is available at this link: http://scholar.google.com/scholar_case?case=6955582630525573237&q= %22interference+with+the+custody+of+children%22&hl=en&as_sdt=2,5.

References

Ariz. Rev. Stat. § 13-1304, accessed February 24, 2011, http://law.onecle.com/arizona/criminal-code/13-1304.html.

Ariz. Rev. Stat. § 13-1304(B), accessed February 24, 2011, http://law.onecle.com/arizona/criminal-code/13-1304.html.

Cal. Penal Code § 237, accessed February 25, 2011, http://law.onecle.com/california/penal/237.html.

N.C. Gen. Stat. § 14-39, accessed February 24, 2011, http://law.onecle.com/north-carolina/14-criminal-law/14-39.html.

N.C. Gen. Stat. § 14-39(a), accessed February 24, 2011, http://law.onecle.com/north-carolina/14-criminal-law/14-39.html.

N.C. Gen. Stat. § 14-43.1, accessed February 25, 2011, http://law.onecle.com/north-carolina/14-criminal-law/14-43.1.html.

N.R.S. § 200.310, accessed February 24, 2011, http://law.onecle.com/nevada/crimes/200.310.html.

N.R.S. § 200.310(2), accessed February 24, 2011, http://law.onecle.com/nevada/crimes/200.310.html.

People v. Dominguez, 140 P.2d 866 (2006), accessed February 24, 2011, http://scholar.google.com/scholar_case?case=35156125736684840 00&q= People+v.+Dominguez&hl=en&as_sdt=2,5.

18 Pa. C. S. § 2903, accessed February 25, 2011, http://law.onecle.com/pennsylvania/crimes-and-offenses/00.029.003.000.html.

18 U.S.C. § 1201, accessed February 27, 2011, http://www.law.cornell.edu/uscode/18/usc_sec_18_00001201—-000-.html.

720 ILCS § 5/10-1, http://law.onecle.com/illinois/720ilcs5/10-1.html.

720 ILCS § 5/10-3, accessed February 25, 2011, http://law.onecle.com/illinois/720ilcs5/10-3.html.

720 ILCS § 5/10-5.5, accessed February 25, 2011, http://law.onecle.com/illinois/720ilcs5/10-5.5.html.
CC licensed content, Shared previously

- Criminal Law. **Provided by**: University of Minnesota Libraries Publishing . **Located at**: http://open.lib.umn.edu/criminallaw/. **License**: *CC BY-NC-SA: Attribution-NonCommercial-ShareAlike*

10.5 End-of-Chapter Material

Summary

States vary as to how they categorize and grade sex offenses. In general, rape is knowing, forcible sexual intercourse without consent or with consent obtained involuntarily. Although the victim had to resist to indicate lack of consent at early common law, in modern times the victim need not resist if it would be futile to do so. Another modernization from common-law rape is the elimination of an exemption for spousal rape and the elimination of the requirement that victim testimony in a rape case be corroborated. Most states have rape shield laws that govern the admissibility of evidence of the victim's past sexual conduct at a trial for rape. Sodomy and oral copulation are sometimes combined and included with rape in one statute called sexual assault. If sodomy and oral copulation are the subject of separate statutes, sodomy is typically knowing forcible penis to anus penetration, and oral copulation is typically knowing forcible mouth to sexual organ or anus penetration. Statutory rape is generally sexual intercourse with an underage victim either recklessly, negligently, or with strict liability depending on the jurisdiction, and incest is generally knowing sexual intercourse between family members who cannot marry. States vary as to how they grade sex offenses, with force and penetration enhancing the grading to a felony in most jurisdictions.

Assault and battery are often included in the same statute (called assault) but are actually separate offenses with distinct elements. Battery is generally a purposeful, knowing, reckless, or negligent (depending on the jurisdiction) unlawful harmful or offensive touching without victim consent. Assault can be attempted battery, in which case all the elements of battery except the physical contact are present, or threatened battery, which is a purposeful act that causes apprehension of harmful or offensive physical contact in the victim. Simple battery and simple assault are typically misdemeanors, while aggravated versions of these offenses are often felonies. Factors that can aggravate the grading of assault and battery are the use of a weapon or serious injury.

Domestic violence statutes criminalize conduct such as assault, battery, sex offenses, or criminal homicide between family members and have special provisions that pertain to interfamily violence. Stalking criminalizes a purposeful course of conduct that poses a credible threat to the victim's safety. Cyberstalking is the use of the Internet or e-mail to commit stalking. Simple stalking is generally a misdemeanor, while aggravated stalking, which is stalking that causes injury or violates a restraining order, is generally a felony.

Kidnapping is the purposeful confinement and asportation (movement) of a victim for the purpose of injuring or harming the victim or another, hiding the victim in secret, obtaining a ransom, committing a separate offense, subjecting the victim to involuntary servitude, or interfering with the purpose of government or political function. False imprisonment is a lesser included offense of kidnapping that does not include asportation or specific intent. Interference with custody is parental kidnapping or violation of a child custody or visitation agreement. While kidnapping is typically a felony, false imprisonment and interference with custody are generally graded lower, as either a gross misdemeanor or low-level felony.

You Be the Law Enforcement Officer

You are a newly hired law enforcement officer starting out in the file room. You have been given five case files. To properly file them, first read over the facts of each case, determine **which crime** has been committed, and determine whether the crime is a **misdemeanor** or **felony**. Check your answers using the answer key at the end of the chapter.

The defendant was on a date with the victim. After a few drinks, the victim became extremely intoxicated, and the defendant had to have help carrying him to her vehicle. The defendant thereafter drove to a secluded area where she had sexual intercourse with the victim. The victim was unconscious and did not discover the act of sexual intercourse until two months later when the defendant told him she was pregnant. Which **crime** has been committed? Is the crime a **misdemeanor** or a **felony**?

The defendant, a security guard, forced the victim, a shopper in the store, to kiss him by threatening to falsely arrest her for shoplifting if she refused. Which **crime** is this? Is this a **misdemeanor** or a **felony**?

The defendant chased the victim with a knife for two miles. After the defendant was arrested, law enforcement determined that the "knife" was made of rubber and could not cause injury. Which **crime** has been committed? Is the crime a **misdemeanor** or a **felony**?

The defendant grabbed a law enforcement officer's gun and pointed it at him while the law enforcement officer was having coffee in a local restaurant. Which **crime** has been committed? Is the crime a **misdemeanor** or a **felony**?

The defendant, a jilted lover, picked up her ex-boyfriend's child from school and took her to an amusement park where they spent the afternoon going on rides and eating junk food. Which **crime** has been committed? Is the crime a **misdemeanor** or a **felony**?

Cases of Interest

- *U.S. v. Lanier*, 520 U.S. 259 (1997), discusses sexual assault by a judge as the subject of a federal criminal action: http://www.law.cornell.edu/supct/html/95-1717.ZS.html
- *Oregon v. Rangel*, 934 P.2d 1128 (1997), discusses the constitutionality of Oregon's stalking statute under the First Amendment: http://www.publications.ojd.state.or.us/docs/S44151.htm.
- *Chatwin v. U.S.*, 326 U.S. 455 (1946), discusses federal kidnapping in the context of joining a religious cult: http://supreme.justia.com/us/326/455/case.html.

Articles of Interest

- High-profile criminal cases, including rape criminal cases: http://lawdigitalcommons.bc.edu/cgi/viewcontent.cgi?article=2240&context=bclr
- The sexual assault case of former IMF chief, Dominique Strauss-Kahn: http://www.nytimes.com/2011/05/26/nyregion/strauss-kahns-lead-prosecutor-is-said-to-be-replaced.html
- Cyberstalking among college students: http://btci.stanford.clockss.org/cgi/reprint/5/3/279
- Parental kidnapping and domestic violence: http://www.vaw.umn.edu/documents/pkreport/pkreport.html

Websites of Interest

- State statutes on statutory rape: http://aspe.hhs.gov/hsp/08/SR/StateLaws/statelaws.shtml
- Information about various sex offenses: http://criminal.findlaw.com/criminal-charges/sex-crimes.html
- Information about stalking: http://www.stalkingbehavior.com

Statistics of Interest

- Rape and other sex offenses: http://www.rainn.org/statistics
- Nationwide crime by state: http://www.disastercenter.com/crime

CC licensed content, Shared previously

- Criminal Law. **Provided by**: University of Minnesota Libraries Publishing . **Located at**: http://open.lib.umn.edu/criminallaw/. **License**: *CC BY-NC-SA: Attribution-NonCommercial-ShareAlike*

Chapter 11: Crimes against Property

11.1 Nonviolent Theft Crimes

Learning Objectives

Define the criminal act element required for consolidated theft statutes.
Define the criminal intent element required for consolidated theft statutes.
Define the attendant circumstances required for consolidated theft statutes.
Define the harm element required for consolidated theft statutes, and distinguish the harm required for larceny theft from the harm required for false pretenses theft.
Analyze consolidated theft grading.
Define the elements required for federal mail fraud, and analyze federal mail fraud grading.

Although crimes against the person such as murder and rape are considered extremely heinous, crimes against property can cause enormous loss, suffering, and even personal injury or death. In this section, you review different classifications of nonviolent theft crimes that are called white-collar crimes when they involve commercial theft. Upcoming sections analyze theft crimes that involve force or threat, receiving stolen property, and crimes that invade or damage property, such as burglary and arson. Computer crimes including hacking, identity theft, and intellectual property infringement are explored in an exercise at the end of the chapter.

Consolidated Theft Statutes

Historically, nonviolent theft was broken down into three categories: larceny, embezzlement, and false pretenses. The categories differ in the **type of property** that can be stolen and the **method** of stealing. Modern jurisdictions combine all three categories of nonviolent theft into one consolidated theft statute, with a uniform grading system largely dependent on the *value* of the stolen property. The Model Penal Code consolidates *all* nonviolent theft offenses, including receiving stolen property and extortion, under one grading system (Model Penal Code § 223.1). What follows is a discussion of theft as defined in modern consolidated theft statutes, making note of the traditional distinctions among the various theft categories when appropriate. Theft has the elements of criminal act, criminal intent, attendant circumstances, causation, and harm, as is discussed in this chapter.

Consolidated Theft Act

The **criminal act** element required under consolidated theft statutes is stealing real property, personal property, or **services**. **Real property** is land and anything permanently attached to land, like a building. **Personal property** is any movable item. Personal property can be tangible property, like money, jewelry, vehicles, electronics, cellular telephones, and clothing. Personal property can also be intangible property, which means it has value, but it cannot be touched or held, like stocks and bonds. The Model Penal Code criminalizes theft by unlawful taking of movable property, theft by deception, theft of services, and theft by failure to make required disposition of funds received under one consolidated grading provision (Model Penal Code §§ 223.1, 223.2, 223.3, 223.7, 223.8).

The act of stealing can be carried out in more than one way. When the defendant steals by a physical **taking**, the theft is generally a **larceny** theft. The act of taking is twofold. First, the defendant must **gain control** over the item. Then the defendant must **move** the item, which is called **asportation**, as it is with kidnapping (Britt v. Commonwealth, 2011). Although asportation for kidnapping must be a certain distance in many jurisdictions, the asportation for larceny can be any distance—even the slightest motion is sufficient (Britt v. Commonwealth, 2011). Control plus asportation can be accomplished by the defendant's physical act or by deceiving the victim into transferring the property with a false representation of fact. This is called larceny by trick. Because larceny requires a physical taking, it generally only pertains to personal property.

Another way for a defendant to steal property is to **convert** it to the defendant's use or ownership. Conversion generally occurs when the victim transfers *possession* of the property to the defendant, and the defendant thereafter appropriates the property transferred. When the defendant steals by conversion, the theft is generally an **embezzlement** theft (Commonwealth v. Mills, 2011). Embezzlement could occur when the defendant gains possession of property from a friendship or a family relationship or from a paid relationship such as employer-employee or attorney-client. Embezzlement does not require a physical taking, so it can pertain to real or personal property.

When the defendant steals by a false representation of fact, and the subject of the theft is a **service**, the theft is generally a **false pretenses** theft (Cal. Penal Code § 484(a), 2011). False pretenses can *also* be used to steal personal or real property and is very similar to larceny by trick in this regard. What differentiates false pretenses from larceny by trick is the **status** of the property *after* it is stolen, which is discussed under the harm element of consolidated theft statutes.

To summarize, whether the defendant steals by a physical taking, a conversion, or a false representation of fact, and whether the defendant steals real or personal property or a service, the crime is theft under modern consolidated theft statutes and is graded primarily on the value of the property or service stolen.

Example of Consolidated Theft Act

Jeremy stops by the local convenience store on his way to work and buys some cigarettes. Before paying for the cigarettes, Jeremy slips a package of chewing gum into his pocket and does not pay for it. Jeremy continues walking to his job at a local gas station. When one of the customers buys gas, Jeremy only rings him up for half of the amount purchased. Once the gas station closes, Jeremy takes the other half out of the cash register and puts it in his pocket with the chewing gum. After work, Jeremy decides to have a drink at a nearby bar. While enjoying his drink, he meets a patron named Chuck, who is a taxi driver. Chuck mentions that his taxi needs a tune-up. Jeremy offers to take Chuck back to the gas station and do the tune-up in exchange for a taxi ride home. Chuck eagerly agrees. The two drive to the gas station, and Jeremy suggests that Chuck take a walk around the block while he performs the tune-up. While Chuck is gone, Jeremy lifts the hood of the taxi and then proceeds to read a magazine. When Chuck returns twenty-five minutes later, Jeremy tells him the tune-up is complete. Chuck thereafter drives Jeremy home for free.

In this scenario, Jeremy has performed three separate acts of theft. When Jeremy slips the package of chewing gum into his pocket without paying for it, he has physically **taken** personal property, which is a **larceny** theft. When Jeremy fails to ring up the entire sale for a customer and pockets the rest from the cash register, he has **converted** the owner of the gas station's cash for his own use, which is an **embezzlement** theft. When Jeremy **falsely represents** to Chuck that he has performed a tune-up of Chuck's taxi and receives a free taxi ride in payment, he has falsely represented a fact in exchange for a service, which is a **false pretenses** theft. All three of these acts of theft could be prosecuted under *one* consolidated theft statute. The three stolen items have a relatively low value, so these crimes would probably be graded as a misdemeanor. Grading of theft under consolidated theft statutes is discussed shortly.

Figure 11.1 Diagram of Consolidated Theft Act

Larceny	
Embezzlement	
False Pretenses	

In many jurisdictions, all three types of theft are prosecuted under one consolidated theft statute.

Consolidated Theft Intent

The criminal intent element required under consolidated theft statutes is either **specific intent** or **purposely**, or **general intent** or **knowingly** to perform the criminal act, depending on the jurisdiction. The Model Penal Code requires **purposeful** intent for theft by unlawful taking, deception, theft of services, and theft by failure to make required disposition of funds received (Model Penal Code §§ 223.2, 223.3, 223.7, 223.8).

When the criminal intent is specific or purposely, the defendant must intend the criminal act of stealing and must *also* intend to *keep* the stolen property (Itin v. Ungar, 2011). This could create a potential **failure of proof** or **affirmative defense** that the defendant was only "borrowing" property and intended to return it after use. In some jurisdictions, specific or purposeful intent to keep the property does not apply to **embezzlement** theft under the traditional definition (In the Matter of Schwimmer, 2011). Thus in these jurisdictions, a defendant who embezzles property and later replaces it cannot use this replacement as a defense.

Example of a Case Lacking Consolidated Theft Intent

Jorge goes to the nursery and spends hundreds of dollars on plants for his garden. Some of the plants are delicate and must be put into the ground immediately after purchase. When Jorge gets home, he discovers that he has no shovel because he loaned it to his brother-in-law a few weeks ago. He notices that his neighbor's shovel is leaning against his neighbor's garage. If Jorge borrows his neighbor's shovel so that he can get his expensive plants into the ground, this appropriation would probably *not* constitute the crime of theft under a consolidated theft statute in certain jurisdictions. Jorge had the intent to perform the theft act of **taking** personal property. However, Jorge did not have the specific or purposeful intent to deprive his neighbor of the shovel *permanently*, which is often required for larceny theft. Thus in this scenario, Jorge may not be charged with and convicted of a consolidated theft offense.

Example of Consolidated Theft Intent

Review the example with Jeremy given in Section 11 "Example of Consolidated Theft Act". Change this example and assume when Jeremy charged his customer for half of the sale and later pocketed fifty dollars from the cash register, his intent was to *borrow* this fifty dollars to drink at the bar and replace the fifty dollars the next day when he got paid. Jeremy probably has the criminal intent required for theft under a consolidated theft statute in many jurisdictions. Although Jeremy did not have the specific or purposeful intent to permanently deprive the gas station owner of fifty dollars, this is *not* generally required with **embezzlement** theft, which is the type of theft Jeremy committed. Jeremy had the intent to convert the fifty dollars to his own use, so the fact that the conversion was only a *temporary* deprivation may not operate as a defense, and Jeremy may be charged with and convicted of theft under a consolidated theft statute.

Figure 11.2 Crack the Code

Crack the Code

Compare the following state laws:

Colo. Rev. Stat. Ann. § 18-4-401(1) (a): Theft

(1) A person commits theft when he knowingly obtains or exercises control over anything of value of another without authorization, or by threat or deception, and:

(a) Intends to deprive the other person permanently of the use or benefit of the thing of value;

Fla. Stat. Ann. § 812.014: Theft

(1) A person commits theft if he or she knowingly obtains or uses, or endeavors to obtain or to use, the property of another with intent to, either temporarily or permanently:

(a) Deprive the other person of a right to the property or a benefit from the property.

(b) Appropriate the property to his or her own use or to the use of any person not entitled to the use of the property.

In Colorado, theft requires intent to deprive the victim of property permanently; in Florida, intent to *temporarily* deprive the victim of property is sufficient for theft...

Larceny or False Pretenses Intent as to the False Statement of Fact

As stated previously, the **taking** in both larceny by trick and false pretenses occurs when the defendant makes a false representation of fact that induces the victim to transfer the property or services. In many jurisdictions, the defendant must have **general intent** or **knowledge** that the representation of fact is *false* and must make the false representation with the **specific intent** or **purposely** to deceive (People v. Lueth, 2011). The Model Penal Code criminalizes theft by deception when a defendant purposely "creates or reinforces a false impression, including false impressions as to law, value, intention or other state of mind" (Model Penal Code § 223.3(1)).

Example of Larceny or False Pretenses Intent as to the False Representation of Fact

Review the example with Jeremy in Section 11 "Example of Consolidated Theft Act". In this example, Jeremy told Chuck that he performed a tune-up of Chuck's taxi, when actually he just lifted the hood of the taxi and read a magazine. Because Jeremy knew the representation was false, and made the representation with the intent to deceive Chuck into providing him with a free taxi ride home, Jeremy probably has the appropriate intent for theft of a service by false pretenses, and he may be subject to prosecution for and conviction of this offense under a consolidated theft statute.

Consolidated Theft Attendant Circumstance of Victim Ownership

All theft requires the **attendant circumstance** that the property stolen is the property of another (Alaska Stat. § 11.46.100, 2011). The criminal intent element for theft must support this attendant circumstance element. Thus **mistake of fact** or **law** as to the ownership of the property stolen could operate as a **failure of proof** or **affirmative defense** to theft under consolidated theft statutes in many jurisdictions (Haw. Rev. Stat. § 708-834, 2011). The Model Penal Code provides an affirmative defense to prosecution for theft when the defendant "is unaware that the property or service was that of another" (Model Penal Code § 223.1(3) (a)).

Example of Mistake of Fact as a Defense to Consolidated Theft

Review the example of a case lacking consolidated theft intent given in Section 11 "Example of a Case Lacking Consolidated Theft Intent". Change this example so that Jorge arrives home from the nursery and begins frantically searching for his shovel in his toolshed. When he fails to locate it, he emerges from the shed and notices the shovel leaning against his neighbor's garage. Jorge retrieves the shovel, uses it to put his plants into the ground, and then puts it into his toolshed and locks the door. If the shovel Jorge appropriated is actually *his neighbor's* shovel, which is an exact replica of Jorge's, Jorge may be able to use **mistake of fact** as a defense to theft under a consolidated theft statute. Jorge **took** the shovel, but he mistakenly believed that it was *his*, not the property of another. Thus the criminal **intent** for the attendant circumstance of victim ownership is lacking, and Jorge probably will not be charged with and convicted of theft under a consolidated theft statute.

Consolidated Theft Attendant Circumstance of Lack of Consent

Theft under a consolidated theft statute also typically requires the **attendant circumstance** element of lack of victim consent (Tex. Penal Code § 31.03(b), 2011). Thus victim consent to the taking or conversion may operate as a **failure of proof** or **affirmative defense** in many jurisdictions. Keep in mind that all the rules of consent discussed in Chapter 5 "Criminal Defenses, Part 1" and Chapter 10 "Sex Offenses and Crimes Involving Force, Fear, and Physical Restraint" apply. Thus consent obtained *fraudulently*, as in larceny by trick or false pretenses, is not valid and effective and cannot form the basis of a consent defense.

Example of a Consensual Conversion That Is Noncriminal

Review the example given in Section 11 "Example of Consolidated Theft Act" with Jeremy. Change the example so that the owner of the gas station is Jeremy's best friend Cody. Cody tells Jeremy several times that if he is ever short of cash, he can simply take some cash from the register, as long as it is not more than fifty dollars. Assume that on the date in question, Jeremy did *not* ring up half of a sale but simply took fifty dollars from the register because he was short on cash, and he needed money to order drinks at the bar. In this case, Jeremy may have a valid defense of **victim's consent** to any charge of theft under a consolidated theft statute.

Embezzlement Attendant Circumstance of a Relationship of Trust and Confidence

In many jurisdictions, embezzlement theft under a consolidated theft statute requires the **attendant circumstance** element of a relationship of **trust** and **confidence** between the victim and the defendant (Commonwealth v. Mills, 2011). This relationship is generally present in an employer-employee relationship, a friendship, or a relationship where the defendant is paid to care for the victim's property. However, if the attendant circumstance element of trust and confidence is lacking, the defendant will *not* be subject to prosecution for embezzlement under a consolidated theft statute in many jurisdictions.

Example of a Case Lacking Embezzlement Attendant Circumstance

Tran sells an automobile to Lee. Tran's automobile has personalized license plates, so he offers to apply for new license plates and thereafter send them to Lee. Lee agrees and pays Tran for half of the automobile, the second payment to be made in a week. Lee is allowed to take possession of the automobile and drives it to her home that is over one hundred miles away. Tran never receives the second payment from Lee. When the new license plates arrive, Tran phones Lee and tells her he is going to keep them until Lee makes her second payment. In some jurisdictions, Tran has *not* embezzled the license plates. Although Tran and Lee have a relationship, it is *not* a relationship based on **trust** or **confidence**. Tran and Lee have what is called a debtor-creditor relationship (Lee is the debtor and Tran is the creditor). Thus if the jurisdiction in which Tran sold the car requires a special confidential relationship for embezzlement, Tran may not be subject to prosecution for this offense.

Attendant Circumstance of Victim Reliance Required for False Pretenses or Larceny by Trick

A false pretenses or larceny by trick theft under a consolidated theft statute requires the additional **attendant circumstance** element of victim reliance on the false representation of fact made by the defendant (People v. Lueth, 2011). Thus a victim's knowledge that the statement is *false* could operate as a **failure of proof** or **affirmative defense** in many jurisdictions.

Example of a Case Lacking the Attendant Circumstance of Victim Reliance Required for False Pretenses

Review the example with Jeremy and Chuck in Section 11 "Example of Consolidated Theft Act". Change the example so that Chuck does not walk around the block as Jeremy asked him to do. Instead, Chuck walks around the corner and then spies on Jeremy while he reads a magazine with the hood open. Chuck takes out his phone and makes a videotape of Jeremy. After twenty-five minutes, Chuck walks back over to Jeremy and thereafter gives Jeremy the free taxi ride home. When they arrive at Jeremy's house, Chuck shows Jeremy the videotape and threatens to turn it over to the district attorney if Jeremy does not pay him two hundred dollars. In this case, Jeremy probably has a valid **defense** to false pretenses theft. Chuck, the "victim," did not *rely* on Jeremy's false representation of fact. Thus the attendant circumstance element of false pretenses is lacking and Jeremy may not be subject to prosecution for and conviction of this offense. Keep in mind that this is a false pretenses scenario because Chuck gave Jeremy a *service*, and larceny by trick only applies to *personal property*. Also note that Chuck's action in threatening Jeremy so that Jeremy will pay him two hundred dollars may be the criminal act element of **extortion**, which is discussed shortly.

Figure 11.3 Diagram of Defenses to Consolidated Theft

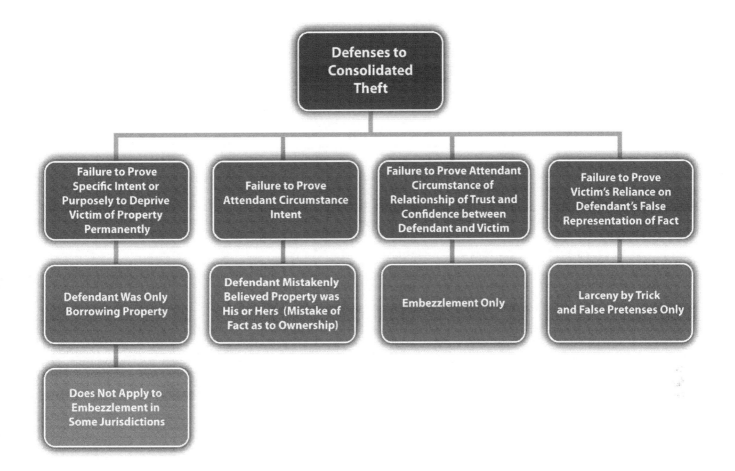

Consolidated Theft Causation

The criminal act must be the **factual** and **legal cause** of the consolidated theft harm, which is defined in Section 11 "Consolidated Theft Harm".

Consolidated Theft Harm

Consolidated theft is a crime that always includes bad results or **harm**, which is the victim's temporary or permanent loss of property or services, no matter how slight the value. In the case of theft by false pretenses and larceny by trick, in some jurisdictions, the status of the property *after* it has been stolen determines which crime was committed. If the defendant becomes the *owner* of the stolen property, the crime is a **false pretenses** theft (People v. Curtin, 2011). If the defendant is merely in *possession* of the stolen property, the crime is **larceny by trick** (People v. Beaver, 2011). When the stolen property is money, the crime is false pretenses theft because the possessor of money is generally the owner (People v. Curtin, 2011).

Example of False Pretenses Theft Harm

Review the example given in Section 11 "Example of a Case Lacking Embezzlement Attendant Circumstance" with Tran and Lee. In this example, Lee paid Tran half of the money she owed him for his vehicle, with a promise to pay the remainder in one week. Assume that Lee never intended to pay the second installment when she made the deal with Tran. Tran signs the ownership documents over to Lee, promises to send Lee the license plates when they arrive, and watches as Lee drives off, never to be seen again. In this example, Lee has most likely committed false pretenses theft, rather than larceny by trick. Lee made a false representation of fact with the intent to deceive and received a vehicle for half price in exchange. The vehicle belongs to Lee, and the ownership documents are in her name. Thus Lee has *ownership* of the stolen vehicle rather than *possession*, and the appropriate offense is **false pretenses** theft.

Example of Larceny by Trick Harm

Jacob, a car thief, runs up to Nanette, who is sitting in her Mercedes with the engine running. Jacob tells Nanette he is a law enforcement officer and needs to take control of her vehicle to pursue a fleeing felon. Nanette skeptically asks Jacob for identification. Jacob pulls out a phony police badge and says, "Madam, I hate to be rude, but if you don't let me drive your vehicle, a serial killer will be roaming the streets looking for victims!" Nanette grudgingly gets out of the car and lets Jacob drive off, never to be seen again. In this example, Jacob has obtained the Mercedes, but the ownership documents are still in Nanette's name. Thus Jacob has *possession* of the stolen vehicle rather than *ownership*, and the appropriate offense is **larceny by trick**.

Consolidated Theft Grading

Grading under consolidated theft statutes depends primarily on the value of the stolen property. Theft can be graded by degrees (Connecticut Jury Instructions § 53a-119, 2011) or as petty theft, which is theft of property with low value, and grand theft, which is theft of property with significant value (Cal. Penal Code § 486, 2011). Petty theft or theft of the second or third degree is generally a misdemeanor, while grand theft or theft of the first degree is generally a felony, felony-misdemeanor, or gross misdemeanor, depending on the amount stolen or whether the item stolen is a firearm (Cal. Penal Code § 489, 2011). The Model Penal Code grades theft as a felony of the third degree if the amount stolen exceeds five hundred dollars or if the property stolen is a firearm, automobile, airplane, motorcycle, or other motor-propelled vehicle (Model Penal Code § 223.1(2)). The Model Penal Code grades all other theft as a misdemeanor or petty misdemeanor (Model Penal Code § 223.1(2)). When determining the value of property for theft, in many jurisdictions, the value is market value, and items can be aggregated if they were stolen as part of a single course of conduct (Connecticut Jury Instructions §§ 53a-119, 2011). The Model Penal Code provides that "[t]he amount involved in a theft shall be deemed to be the highest value, by any reasonable standard...[a]mounts involved in thefts committed pursuant to one scheme or course of conduct, whether from the same person or several persons, may be aggregated in determining the grade or the offense" (Model Penal Code § 223.1(2) (c)).

Table 11.1 Comparing Larceny, Larceny by Trick, False Pretenses, and Embezzlement

Crime	Criminal Act	Type of Property	Criminal Intent	Attendant Circumstance	Harm
Larceny	Taking control plus asportation	Personal	Specific or purposely to deprive victim permanently*	Victim's property (applies to all four theft crimes), lack of victim consent	Property loss
Larceny by trick	Taking by a false representation of fact	Personal	Specific or purposely to deceive*	Victim reliance on false representation	Victim loses possession of property
False pretenses	Taking by a false representation of fact	Personal, real, services	Specific or purposely to deceive*	Victim reliance on false representation	Victim loses ownership of property

Crime	Criminal Act	Type of Property	Criminal Intent	Attendant Circumstance	Harm
Embezzlement	Conversion	Personal, real	Specific or purposely to deprive victim temporarily or permanently*	Relationship of trust and confidence between defendant and victim (some jurisdictions)	Property loss either temporary or permanent

***Some jurisdictions include general intent or knowingly to commit the criminal act.**

Note: **Grading under consolidated theft statutes is based primarily on property value; market value is the standard, and property can be aggregated if stolen in a single course of conduct.**

Federal Mail Fraud

The federal government criminalizes **theft** by use of the federal postal service as federal mail fraud, a felony (18 U.S.C. § 1341, 2011). Like every federal offense, federal mail fraud is criminal in all fifty states. In addition, a defendant can be prosecuted by the federal and state government for *one act of theft* without violating the double jeopardy protection in the Fifth Amendment of the federal Constitution.

The **criminal act** element required for federal mail fraud is perpetrating a "scheme to defraud" using the US mail (18 U.S.C. § 1341, 2011). *Scheme* has been given a broad interpretation and includes "everything designed to defraud by representations as to the past or present, or suggestions and promises as to the future" (Durland v. U.S., 1896). Even one act of mailing is sufficient to subject the defendant to a criminal prosecution for this offense (U.S. v. McClelland, 2011). In addition, the defendant does not need to actually mail anything himself or herself (U.S. v. McClelland, 2011). The criminal intent element required for federal mail fraud is **general intent** or **knowingly** or **awareness** that the mail will be used to further the scheme (U.S. v. McClelland, 2011). The defendant does not have to intend that the US Mail will be used to commit the theft, as long as use of the postal service is reasonably foreseeable in the ordinary course of business (U.S. v. McClelland, 2011). The defendant's criminal act, supported by the appropriate intent, must be the **factual** and **legal cause** of the **harm**, which is the placement of anything in any post office or depository to be sent by the US Postal Service in furtherance of the scheme to defraud 18 U.S.C. § 1341, 2011).

The Mail Fraud Act has been used to punish a wide variety of schemes, including Ponzi schemes, like the recent high-profile Bernie Madoff case (Parten, C., 2011). In a Ponzi scheme, the defendant informs investors that their investment is being used to purchase real estate, stocks, or bonds, when, in actuality, the money is appropriated by the defendant and used to pay earlier investors. Eventually this leads to a collapse that divests all investors of their investment.

Federal statutes also punish bank fraud (18 U.S.C. § 1344, 2011), health care fraud (18 U.S.C. § 1347, 2011), securities fraud (18 U.S.C. § 1348, 2011), and fraud in foreign labor contracting (18 U.S.C. § 1351, 2011). Fraud committed by wire, television, and radio also is federally criminalized (18 U.S.C. § 1343, 2011).

Bernard Madoff Video

Bernard Madoff $50 Billion Ponzi Scheme: How Did He Do It?

The facts behind Bernie Madoff's Ponzi scheme are explained in this video:
(click to see video)

Key Takeaways

- The criminal act element required for consolidated theft statutes is stealing real or personal property or services. The defendant can commit the theft by a physical taking (larceny), conversion of property in the defendant's possession (embezzlement), or a false representation of fact (false pretenses or larceny by trick).
- The criminal intent element required for consolidated theft statutes is either specific intent or purposely, or general intent or knowingly to perform the criminal act, depending on the jurisdiction. When the criminal intent is specific or purposely, the defendant must intend the criminal act of stealing and must also intend to keep the stolen property. For false pretenses or larceny by trick theft, in many jurisdictions the defendant must have general intent or knowledge that the representation of fact is false and must make the false representation with the specific intent or purposely to deceive.

- All theft generally requires the attendant circumstances that the property stolen is the property of another, and victim consent to the taking, conversion, or transfer of ownership is lacking.
  - In many jurisdictions, embezzlement theft under a consolidated theft statute requires the attendant circumstance element of a relationship of trust and confidence between the victim and the defendant.
  - A false pretenses or larceny by trick theft under a consolidated theft statute requires the additional attendant circumstance element of victim reliance on the false representation of fact made by the defendant.
- The harm element required for consolidated theft statutes is the victim's temporary or permanent loss of property or services, no matter how slight the value. When the defendant gains possession of personal property by a false representation of fact, the theft is larceny by trick theft. When the defendant gains ownership of personal property or possession of money, the theft is false pretenses theft.
- Theft can be graded by degrees or as petty theft, which is theft of property with low value, and grand theft, which is theft of property with significant value. Petty theft or theft of the second or third degree is generally a misdemeanor, while grand theft or theft of the first degree is generally a felony, felony-misdemeanor, or gross misdemeanor, depending on the amount stolen or whether the item stolen is a firearm.
- The criminal act element required for federal mail fraud is the use of the federal postal service to further any scheme to defraud. The criminal intent element required for this offense is general intent, knowingly, or awareness that the postal service will be used. The criminal act supported by the criminal intent must be the factual and legal cause of the harm, which is the placement of anything in a depository or postal office that furthers the scheme to defraud. Federal mail fraud is a felony.

Exercises

Answer the following questions. Check your answers using the answer key at the end of the chapter.

Recall a scenario in Chapter 1 "Introduction to Criminal Law" where Linda and Clara browse an expensive department store's lingerie department and Linda surreptitiously places a bra in her purse and leaves the store without paying for it. What type of theft did Linda commit in this scenario?

Ellen goes to the fine jewelry department at Macy's and asks the clerk if she can see a Rolex watch, valued at ten thousand dollars. The clerk takes the watch out of the case and lays it on the counter. Ellen tells the clerk that her manager is signaling. When the clerk turns around, Ellen puts her hand over the watch and begins to slide it across the counter and *into her open purse*. Before the watch slides off the counter, the clerk turns back around and pins Ellen's hand to the counter, shouting for a security guard. Has Ellen committed a crime in this scenario? If your answer is yes, which crime?

Read *State v. Larson*, 605 N.W. 2d 706 (2000). In *Larson*, the defendant, the owner of an automobile leasing company, was convicted of theft by temporary taking under a consolidated theft statute for failing to return security deposits to customers pursuant to their automobile lease contracts. The defendant appealed, claiming that the lease deposits were not the "property of another." Did the Supreme Court of Minnesota uphold the defendant's conviction? Why or why not? The case is available at this link: http://scholar.google.com/scholar_case?case=18374046737925458759&q=

embezzlement+%22temporary+taking%22&hl=en&as_sdt=2,5.

Read *People v. Traster*, 111 Cal. App. 4th 1377 (2003). In *Traster*, the defendant told his employer that it was necessary to purchase computer-licensing agreements, and he was given the employer credit card to purchase them. The defendant thereafter appropriated the money, never purchased the licenses, and quit his job a few days later. The defendant was convicted of theft by false pretenses under a consolidated theft statute. Did the Court of Appeal of California uphold the defendant's conviction? Why or why not? The case is available at this link: http://scholar.google.com/scholar_case?case=14111729725043843748&q= larceny+false+pretenses+possession+ownership&hl=en&as_sdt=2,5&as_ylo=2000.

Read *U.S. v. Ingles*, 445 F.3d 830 (2006). In *Ingles*, the defendant was convicted of federal mail fraud when his son's cabin was burned by arson and his son made a claim for homeowner's insurance. The evidence indicated that the defendant was involved in the arson. The defendant's son was **acquitted** of the arson, and only the insurance company, which sent several letters to the defendant's son, did the acts of mailing. Did the US Court of Appeals for the Fifth Circuit uphold the defendant's conviction? Why or why not? The case is available at this link: http://scholar.google.com/scholar_case?case=6621847677802005327&q= federal+mail+fraud+%22one+letter%22&hl=en&as_sdt=2,5&as_ylo=2000.

References

Alaska Stat. § 11.46.100, accessed March 8, 2011, http://law.justia.com/codes/alaska/2009/title-11/chapter-11-46/article-01/sec-11-46-100.

Britt v. Commonwealth, 667 S.E.2d 763 (2008), accessed March 8, 2011, http://scholar.google.com/scholar_case?case=2834311189194937383&q= larceny+asportation&hl=en&as_sdt=2,5&as_ylo=1999.

Cal. Penal Code § 484(a), accessed March 8, 2011, http://law.onecle.com/california/penal/484.html.

Cal. Penal Code § 486, accessed March 10, 2011, http://law.onecle.com/california/penal/486.html.

Cal. Penal Code § 489, accessed March 10, 2011, http://law.onecle.com/california/penal/489.html.

Commonwealth v. Mills, 436 Mass. 387 (2002), accessed March 7, 2011, http://scholar.google.com/scholar_case?case=14428947695245966729&q= larceny+false+pretenses+embezzlement&hl=en&as_sdt=2,5&as_ylo=1997.

Connecticut Jury Instructions §§ 53a-119, 53a-122 through 53a-125b, accessed March 10, 2011, http://www.jud.ct.gov/JI/criminal/part9/9.1-1.htm.

Durland v. U.S., 161 U.S. 306, 313 (1896), http://supreme.justia.com/us/161/306.

Haw. Rev. Stat. § 708-834, accessed March 8, 2011, http://law.justia.com/codes/hawaii/2009/volume-14/title-37/chapter-708/hrs-0708-0834-htm.

In the Matter of Schwimmer, 108 P.3d 761 (2005), accessed March 8, 2011, http://scholar.google.com/scholar_case?case=6371832289506627584&q= embezzlement+borrowing+%22no+intent+to+permanently+deprive%22&hl= en&as_sdt=2,5&as_ylo=1999.

Itin v. Ungar, 17 P.3d 129 (2000), accessed March 8, 2011, http://scholar.google.com/scholar_case?case=12387802565107699365&q=theft+requires+ specific+intent+to+permanently+deprive&hl=en&as_sdt=2,5&as_ylo=1999.

Parten, C., "After Madoff: Notable Ponzi Schemes," CNBC website, accessed March 11, 2011, http://www.cnbc.com/id/41722418/After_Madoff_Most_Notable_Ponzi_Scams.

People v. Beaver, 186 Cal. App. 4th 107 (2010), accessed March 10, 2011, http://scholar.google.com/scholar_case?case=12194560873043980150&q= false+pretenses+theft+of+a+service&hl=en&as_sdt=2,5&as_ylo=1999.

People v. Curtin, 22 Cal. App. 4th 528 (1994), accessed March 10, 2011, http://scholar.google.com/scholar_case?case=3765672039191216315&q= false+pretenses+theft+of+a+service&hl=en&as_sdt=2,5&as_ylo=1999.

People v. Lueth, 660 N.W.2d 322 (2002), accessed March 9, 2011, http://scholar.google.com/scholar_case?case=16580779180424536816&q= false+pretenses+knowledge+statement+is+false+intent+to+deceive&hl= en&as_sdt=2,5&as_ylo=1999.

Tex. Penal Code § 31.03(b) (1), accessed March 8, 2011, http://law.justia.com/codes/texas/2009/penal-code/title-7-offenses-against-property/chapter-31-theft.

U.S. v. McClelland, 868 F.2d 704 (1989), accessed March 18, 2011, http://scholar.google.com/scholar_case?case=8428034080210339517&q= federal+mail+fraud+%22one+letter%22&hl=en&as_sdt=2,5&as_ylo=2000.

18 U.S.C. § 1341, accessed March 18, 2011, http://www.law.cornell.edu/uscode/18/usc_sec_18_00001341—-000-.html.

18 U.S.C. § 1343, accessed March 11, 2011, http://www.law.cornell.edu/uscode/18/usc_sec_18_00001343—-000-.html.

18 U.S.C. § 1344, accessed March 11, 2011, http://www.law.cornell.edu/uscode/18/usc_sec_18_00001344—-000-.html.

18 U.S.C. § 1347, accessed March 11, 2011, http://www.law.cornell.edu/uscode/18/usc_sec_18_00001347—-000-.html.

18 U.S.C. § 1348, accessed March 11, 2011, http://www.law.cornell.edu/uscode/18/usc_sec_18_00001348—-000-.html.

18 U.S.C. § 1351, accessed March 11, 2011, http://www.law.cornell.edu/uscode/18/usc_sec_18_00001351—-000-.html.
CC licensed content, Shared previously

- Criminal Law. **Provided by**: University of Minnesota Libraries Publishing . **Located at**: http://open.lib.umn.edu/criminallaw/. **License**: *CC BY-NC-SA: Attribution-NonCommercial-ShareAlike*

11.2 Extortion, Robbery, and Receiving Stolen Property

NZ – House in flames – CC BY 2.0.

Arson is one of the easiest crimes to commit on the spur of the moment…it takes only seconds to light a match to a pile of clothes or a curtain…

—*People v. Atkins,* cited in Section 11 "Arson Intent"

Learning Objectives
Define the criminal act element required for extortion.
Define the criminal intent element required for extortion.
Identify a potential defense to extortion.
Define the attendant circumstances required for extortion.
Define the harm element required for extortion.
Analyze extortion grading.
Identify the differences between robbery, larceny, and extortion.
Analyze robbery grading.
Define the criminal act element required for receiving stolen property.
Define the criminal intent element required for receiving stolen property.
Identify a failure of proof or affirmative defense to receiving stolen property in some jurisdictions.
Define the attendant circumstances and harm element required for receiving stolen property.
Analyze receiving stolen property grading.

Extortion

All states and the federal government criminalize extortion, which is also called **blackmail** (K.S.A. § 21-3428, 2011). As stated previously, the Model Penal Code criminalizes theft by extortion and grades it the same as all other nonforcible theft offenses (Model Penal Code § 223.4). Extortion is typically nonviolent, but the elements of extortion are very similar to **robbery**, which is considered a forcible theft offense. Robbery is discussed shortly.

Extortion has the elements of criminal act, criminal intent, attendant circumstances, causation, and harm, as is explored in Section 11.2.1 "Extortion".

Extortion Act

The **criminal act** element required for extortion is typically the theft of property accomplished by a **threat** to cause *future* harm to the victim, including the threat to inflict bodily injury, accuse anyone of committing a crime, or reveal a secret that would expose the victim to hatred, contempt, or ridicule (Ga. Code § 16-8-16, 2011). The Model Penal Code criminalizes theft by extortion when the defendant obtains property of another by threatening to inflict bodily injury on anyone, commit any criminal offense, accuse anyone of a criminal offense, expose any secret tending to subject any person to hatred, contempt, or ridicule or impair his credit and business repute, take or withhold action as an official, bring about a strike or boycott, testify with respect to another's legal claim, or inflict any other harm that would not benefit the actor (Model Penal Code § 223.4). Note that some of these acts could be *legal*, as long as they are not performed with the unlawful intent to steal.

Example of Extortion Act

Rodney tells Lindsey that he will report her illegal drug trafficking to local law enforcement if she does not pay him fifteen thousand dollars. Rodney has probably committed the criminal act element required for extortion in most jurisdictions. Note that Rodney's threat to expose Lindsey's illegal activities is actually *desirable* behavior when performed with the intent to eliminate or reduce crime. However, under these circumstances, Rodney's act is most likely *criminal* because it is supported by the intent to steal fifteen thousand dollars from Lindsey.

Extortion Intent

The criminal intent element required for extortion is typically the **specific intent** or **purposely** to commit the criminal act and to unlawfully deprive the victim of property *permanently* (Connecticut Criminal Jury Instructions

§§53a-119(5), 2011). This intent requirement is similar to the criminal intent element required for larceny and false pretenses theft, as discussed in Section 11 "Consolidated Theft Intent". Some jurisdictions only require **general intent** or **knowingly** to perform the criminal act (Ariz. Rev. Stat. § 13-1804).

Example of a Case Lacking Extortion Intent

Review the example with Rodney and Lindsey in Section 11 "Example of Extortion Act". Change the example and assume that Rodney asks Lindsey to loan him the fifteen thousand dollars so that he can make a balloon payment due on his mortgage. Lindsey refuses. Rodney thereafter threatens to expose Lindsey's drug trafficking if she doesn't loan him the money. In many jurisdictions, Rodney may not have the criminal intent element required for extortion. Although Rodney performed the criminal act of threatening to report Lindsey for a crime, he did so with the intent to *borrow* money from Lindsey. Thus Rodney did not act with the specific intent or purposely to permanently deprive Lindsey of property, which could operate as a **failure of proof** or **affirmative defense** to extortion in many jurisdictions.

Extortion Attendant Circumstance

Extortion is a form of theft, so it has the same **attendant circumstance** required in consolidated theft statutes—the property stolen belongs to *another*. In many jurisdictions, it is an **affirmative defense** to extortion that the property taken by threat to expose a secret or accuse anyone of a criminal offense is taken *honestly*, as compensation for property, or restitution or indemnification for harm done by the secret or crime (Ga. Code § 16-8-16, 2011). The Model Penal Code provides an affirmative defense to extortion by threat of accusation of a criminal offense, exposure of a secret, or threat to take or withhold action as an official if the property obtained was "honestly claimed as restitution or indemnification for harm done in the circumstances to which such accusation, exposure, lawsuit or other official action relates, or as compensation for property or lawful services" (Model Penal Code § 223.4).

Example of Extortion Affirmative Defense

Tara, a real estate broker, hires Trent to be a real estate sales agent in her small realty office. Tara decides she wants to get the property listing of a competitor by using Trent to obtain information. Tara tells Trent to pretend he is a buyer interested in the property. She asks him to make an appointment with the competitor, ask a lot of questions about the owner of the property, and thereafter bring Tara the information. Tara promises to pay Trent one thousand dollars for his time and effort. Trent spends several hours performing this task and thereafter demands his one thousand dollars payment. Tara tells Trent she is experiencing "tough times" and can't afford to pay him. Trent threatens to tell Tara's competitor what she is up to if she doesn't pay him the one thousand dollars. Trent has probably *not* committed extortion in many jurisdictions. Although Trent threatened to expose Tara's secret if she didn't pay him one thousand dollars, Trent *honestly* believed he was owed this money for a job he performed that was *directly related* to the secret. Thus in many jurisdictions, Trent has an **affirmative defense** that the money demanded was compensation for services and not the subject of unlawful theft by extortion.

Attendant Circumstance of Victim Consent

Extortion also requires the **attendant circumstance** of victim consent. With extortion, the victim consensually transfers the property based on **fear** inspired by the defendant's threat (Oklahoma Uniform Jury Instructions No. CR 5-34, 2011).

Example of Attendant Circumstance of Victim Consent for Extortion

Review the example with Rodney and Lindsey in Section 11 "Example of Extortion Act". Assume that Lindsey grudgingly gives Rodney the fifteen thousand dollars so that he will not report her drug trafficking. In this example, Lindsey is *consensually* transferring the money to Rodney to prevent him from making good on his threat. Thus the attendant circumstance of victim **consent** based on **fear** is most likely present, and Rodney could be subject to prosecution for and conviction of extortion in most jurisdictions.

Extortion Causation

The criminal act must be the **factual** and **legal cause** of extortion harm, which is defined in Section 11 "Extortion Harm".

Extortion Harm

The defendant must **obtain** property belonging to another for the completed crime of extortion in most jurisdictions (Oklahoma Uniform Jury Instructions No. CR 5-34, 2011). If the defendant commits the criminal act of threatening the victim with the appropriate criminal intent, but the victim does not actually transfer the property to the defendant, the defendant can only be charged with *attempted* extortion (Oklahoma Uniform Jury Instructions No. CR 5-32, 2011).

Example of a Case Lacking Extortion Harm

Review the example with Rodney and Lindsey in Section 11 "Example of Extortion Act". Assume that after Rodney threatens to report Lindsey's drug trafficking to local law enforcement, Lindsey calls local law enforcement, turns herself in for drug trafficking, and also reports Rodney for making the threat. In this case, because Rodney did not "obtain" property by threat, the crime of extortion is not complete, and *attempted* extortion would be the appropriate charge in most jurisdictions.

Figure 11.4 Diagram of Defenses to Extortion

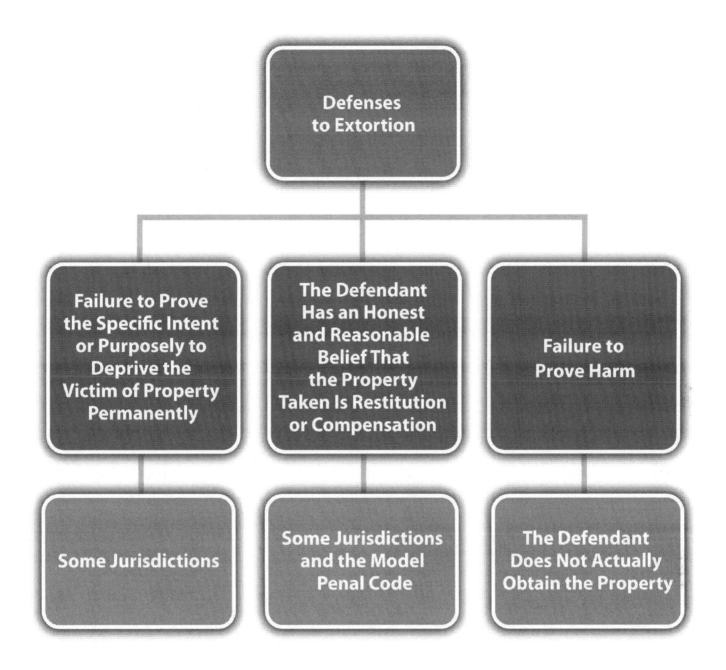

Extortion Grading

Extortion is generally **graded** as a felony in most jurisdictions (Or. Rev. Stat. § 164.075, 2011). As stated previously, the Model Penal Code grades extortion under its consolidated theft offense.

Robbery

Robbery was the first common-law theft crime. The criminalization of robbery was a natural progression from other common-law crimes against the person because robbery always involves force, violence, or threat and could pose a risk of injury or death to the robbery victim, defendant, or other innocent bystanders. Recall from Chapter 9 "Criminal Homicide" that robbery is generally a serious felony that is included in most felony murder statutes as a predicate felony for **first-degree** felony murder. When robbery does not result in death, it is typically graded more severely than theft under a consolidated theft statute. Robbery grading is discussed shortly.

The elements of robbery are very similar to the elements of **larceny** and **extortion**. For the purpose of brevity, only the elements of robbery that are distinguishable from larceny and extortion are analyzed in depth. Robbery has the elements of criminal act, attendant circumstances, criminal intent, causation, and harm, as is explored in Section 11.2 "Extortion, Robbery, and Receiving Stolen Property".

Robbery Act

It is the criminal act element that primarily distinguishes robbery from larceny and extortion. The **criminal act** element required for robbery is a taking of personal property by **force** or **threat** of force (Ind. Code § 35-42-5-1, 2011). Force is generally physical force. The force can be slight, but it must be more than what is required to gain control over and move the property (S.W. v. State, 2011). Many jurisdictions require force *during* the taking, which includes the use of force to prevent the victim from reclaiming the property, or during escape (State v. Handburgh, 2011). The Model Penal Code requires force or threat "in the course of committing a theft" and defines this as occurring in "an attempt to commit theft or in flight after the attempt or commission" (Model Penal Code § 222.1(1)). Threat for robbery is a threat to inflict *imminent* force (Ala. Code § 13A-8-43, 2011).

While larceny and extortion also require a taking, the defendant typically accomplishes the larceny taking by stealth, or a false representation of fact. In extortion, the defendant accomplishes the taking by a threat of *future* harm that may or may not involve *force*.

Example of Robbery Act

Review the example given in Section 11 "Example of Extortion Act" with Rodney and Lindsey. In this example, Rodney threatened to expose Lindsey's drug trafficking if she didn't pay him fifteen thousand dollars. Change the example so that Rodney tells Lindsey he will kill her if she doesn't write him a check for fifteen thousand dollars. Rodney exemplifies his threat by pointing to a bulge in his front jacket pocket that appears to be a weapon. In this scenario, Rodney has most likely committed the criminal act element required for **robbery**, *not* **extortion**. Rodney's threat is a threat of *immediate force*. Compare this threat to Rodney's threat to expose Lindsey's drug trafficking, which is a threat of *future* harm that relates to Lindsey's *arrest* for a crime, rather than force.

Example of a Case Lacking Robbery Act

Peter, a jewelry thief, notices that Cheryl is wearing a diamond ring. Peter walks up to Cheryl and asks her if she wants him to read her palm. Cheryl shrugs her shoulders and says, "Sure! What have I got to lose?" While Peter does an elaborate palm reading, he surreptitiously slips Cheryl's diamond ring off her finger and into his pocket. Peter has probably *not* committed the criminal act element required for robbery in this case. Although Peter used a certain amount of physical force to remove Cheryl's ring, he did not use any force *beyond* what was required to gain control over Cheryl's property and move it into his possession. Thus Peter has probably committed the criminal act element required for **larceny** theft, *not* **robbery**, and is subject to less severe sentencing for this lower-level offense.

Robbery Attendant Circumstances

Another difference between robbery and larceny or extortion is the **attendant circumstances** requirement(s). Robbery requires the same attendant circumstance required for both larceny and extortion—that the property taken belongs to another. It also has the same attendant circumstance as larceny—that the defendant accomplish the taking against the victim's will and without consent. However, robbery has one additional attendant circumstance, which is that the property be taken **from the victim's person** or **presence** (Cal. Penal Code § 211). The property does not need to be in the actual physical possession of the victim, as long as it is under the victim's *control* (Jones v. State, 2011). Thus if the victim could have prevented the taking if not for the force, violence, or threat posed by the defendant, this attendant circumstance is present (Jones v. State, 2011).

Example of Robbery Attendant Circumstances

Review the example given in Section 11 "Example of Robbery Act" with Rodney and Lindsey. In this example, Rodney tells Lindsey he will kill her if she doesn't write him a check for fifteen thousand dollars. Change this example so that Rodney knows Lindsey has recently withdrawn fifteen thousand dollars in cash from the bank. Rodney demands the cash, tells Lindsey he will kill her if she doesn't give it to him, and gestures toward a bulge in his front jacket pocket that appears to be a weapon. Lindsey tells Rodney, "The money is in my purse, but if you take it, you will be ruining my life!" and points to her purse, which is on the kitchen table a few feet away. Rodney walks over to the table, opens Lindsey's purse, and removes a large envelope stuffed with bills. In this scenario, the attendant circumstances for robbery appear to be present. Rodney took the property of another without consent. Although the money was not on Lindsey's person, it was in her **presence** and subject to her **control**. If Rodney had not threatened Lindsey's life, she could have *prevented* the taking. Thus Rodney has most likely committed robbery and is subject to prosecution for and conviction of this offense.

Robbery Intent

The criminal intent element required for robbery is the same as the criminal intent element required for larceny and extortion in many jurisdictions. The defendant must have the **specific intent** or **purposely** to commit the criminal act and to deprive the victim of the property *permanently* (Metheny v. State, 2011). Some jurisdictions do not require the intent to permanently deprive the victim of property and include *temporary* takings in the robbery statute (Fla. Stat. Ann. § 812.13, 2011).

Example of Robbery Intent

Review the example with Rodney and Lindsey in Section 11 "Example of a Case Lacking Extortion Intent". In this example, Rodney demands a loan from Lindsey in the amount of fifteen thousand dollars and threatens to expose her drug trafficking activities if she doesn't comply. Change this example so that Rodney tells Lindsey to loan him fifteen thousand dollars or he will kill her, gesturing at a bulge in his front jacket pocket that appears to be a weapon. In a jurisdiction that requires the criminal intent to **permanently** deprive the victim of property for robbery, Rodney does not have the appropriate criminal intent. In a jurisdiction that allows for the intent to **temporarily** deprive the victim of property for robbery, Rodney has the appropriate criminal intent and may be charged with and convicted of this offense.

Robbery Causation and Harm

The criminal act supported by the criminal intent must be the **factual** and **legal cause** of the robbery **harm**, which is the same as the harm requirement for larceny and extortion: the property must be transferred to the defendant (Oklahoma Uniform Jury Instructions No. CR 4-141, 2011). In some jurisdictions, *no* transfer of property needs to take place, and the crime is complete when the defendant employs the force or threat with the appropriate criminal intent (Williams v. State, 2011).

Example of Robbery Harm

Review the example with Rodney and Lindsey in Section 11 "Example of Robbery Attendant Circumstances". In this example, Rodney threatens to kill Lindsey if she does not give him fifteen thousand dollars out of her purse and gestures to a bulge in his front jacket pocket that appears to be a weapon. Change this example so that Lindsey leaps off of the couch and tackles Rodney after his threat. She reaches into his pocket and determines that Rodney's "gun" is a plastic water pistol. Rodney manages to get out from under Lindsey and escapes. If Rodney and Lindsey are in a jurisdiction that requires a transfer of property for the harm element of robbery, Rodney has probably only committed *attempted* robbery because Rodney did not get the chance to take the money out of Lindsey's purse. If Rodney and Lindsey are in a jurisdiction that does *not* require a transfer of property for the harm element of robbery, Rodney may be subject to prosecution for and conviction of this offense.

Figure 11.5 Diagram of Defenses to Robbery

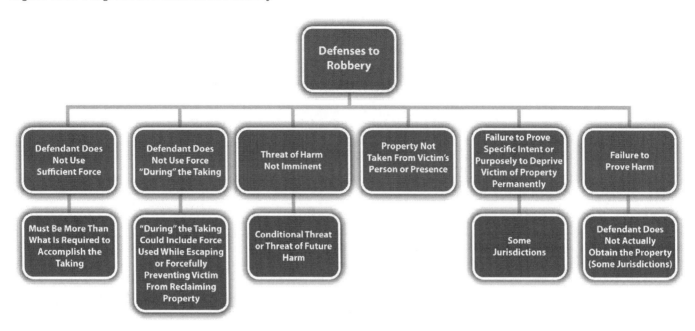

Robbery Grading

As stated previously, robbery is generally **graded** as a serious felony that can serve as the predicate felony for first-degree felony murder (Cal. Penal Code § 189, 2011) and a strike in states that have three strikes statutes (Cal. Penal Code § 1192.7, 2011). Robbery grading is aggravated by the use of a weapon or when the defendant inflicts serious bodily injury (Tex. Penal Code § 29.03, 2011). The Model Penal Code grades robbery as a felony of the second degree, unless the actor attempts to kill anyone or purposely inflicts or attempts to inflict serious bodily injury, in which case it is graded as a felony of the first degree (Model Penal Code § 222.1(2)).

Table 11.2 Comparing Larceny, Extortion, and Robbery

Crime	Criminal Act	Criminal Intent	Attendant Circumstance	Harm
Larceny	Taking by stealth or false representation of fact	Specific or purposely to deprive the victim of property permanently*	Victim's property, lack of victim consent	Property transfer
Extortion	Taking by threat of future harm; not necessarily physical	Specific or purposely to deprive the victim of property permanently*	Victim's property; the victim consents based on fear	Property transfer
Robbery	Taking by force or threat of imminent force	Specific or purposely to deprive the victim of property permanently*	Victim's property, lack of victim consent, property is taken from the victim's person or presence	Property transfer**
*In some jurisdictions, the defendant can intend a temporary taking.				
**In some jurisdictions, the victim does not need to transfer the property to the defendant.				

Receiving Stolen Property

All jurisdictions criminalize receiving stolen property, to deter theft and to break up organized criminal enterprises that benefit from stealing and selling stolen goods. Receiving stolen property criminal statutes often are targeted at pawnbrokers or fences who regularly buy and sell property that is the subject of one of the theft crimes discussed in the preceding sections. As stated, the Model Penal Code includes receiving stolen property in its consolidated theft offense (Model Penal Code §§ 223.1, 223.6). Receiving stolen property has the elements of criminal act, criminal intent, attendant circumstances, causation, and harm, as is explored in Section 11.2.3 "Receiving Stolen Property".

Receiving Stolen Property Act

The **criminal act** element required for receiving stolen property in many jurisdictions is receiving, retaining, disposing of (Ala. Code § 13A-8-16, 2011), selling (Cal. Penal Code § 496, 2011), trafficking in (Fla. Stat. Ann. § 812.019, 2011), buying, or aiding in concealment (Mass. Gen. Laws ch. 266 § 60) of stolen personal property. The Model Penal Code defines the criminal act element as receiving, retaining, or disposing of stolen movable property (Model Penal Code § 223.6(1)). The criminal act does not generally require the defendant to be in actual **physical possession** of the property, as long as the defendant retains *control* over the item(s) (Ga. Code § 16-8-7, 2011). This would be a constructive possession. The Model Penal Code defines receiving as "acquiring possession, control or title, or lending on the security of the property" (Model Penal Code § 223.6(1)). Note that the criminal act element of receiving stolen property includes both **buying** and **selling**. Thus dealers that regularly purchase and then sell stolen items can be prosecuted for both of these acts under the same statute.

Example of Receiving Stolen Property Act

Chanel, a fence who deals in stolen designer perfume, arranges a sale between one of her thieves, Burt, and a regular customer, Sandra. Chanel directs Burt to drop off a shipment of one crate of the stolen perfume at Chanel's storage facility and gives Burt the key. Chanel pays Burt five thousand dollars for the perfume delivery. Chanel thereafter accepts a payment of ten thousand dollars from Sandra and gives Sandra another key with instructions to pick up the perfume the next day after it has been delivered. Chanel could probably be charged with and convicted of receiving stolen property in most jurisdictions. Although Chanel did not ever acquire actual *possession* of the stolen designer perfume, Chanel had *control* over the property or constructive possession through her storage facility. Chanel's acts of **buying** the perfume for five thousand dollars and then **selling** it for ten thousand dollars both would be criminalized under *one* statute in many jurisdictions. Thus Chanel could be prosecuted for *both* acts as separate charges of receiving stolen property.

Receiving Stolen Property Intent

The criminal intent element required for receiving stolen property has two parts. First, the defendant must have the intent to commit the criminal act, which could be **specific intent** or **purposely**, **general intent** or **knowingly**, **recklessly**, or **negligently** to either buy-receive or sell-dispose of stolen personal property, depending on the jurisdiction. This means that the defendant must have **actual knowledge** that the property is stolen (Mass. Gen. Laws ch. 266 § 60, 2011), or the defendant must be aware or should be aware of a **risk** that the property is stolen (Ala. Code § 13A-8-16(a), 2011). The Model Penal Code requires the defendant to purposely commit the act *knowing* that the property is stolen or *believing* that the property has *probably* been stolen (Model Penal Code § 223.6(1)). The Model Penal Code also provides a **presumption** of knowledge or belief when the defendant is a **dealer**, which is defined as a "person in the business of buying or selling goods including a pawnbroker," and has been found in possession or control of property stolen from two or more persons on more than one occasion, or has received stolen property in another transaction within the year preceding the transaction charged, or acquires the property for consideration far below its reasonable value (Model Penal Code § 223.6(2)). Many state statutes have a similar provision (Ala. Code § 13A-8-16, 2011).

The second aspect of criminal intent for receiving stolen property is the defendant's **specific intent** or **purposeful** desire to deprive the victim of the property *permanently*, which is required in some jurisdictions

(Hawaii Criminal Jury Instructions No. 10.00, 10.20, 2011). This creates a **failure of proof** or **affirmative defense** that the defendant received and retained the stolen property with the intent to *return* it to the true owner (Ga. Code § 16-8-7(a), 2011). The Model Penal Code also provides a defense if "the property is received, retained, or disposed of with purpose to restore it to the owner" (Model Penal Code § 223.6(1)).

Example of Receiving Stolen Property Intent

Chip's iPod breaks, so he decides to go to the local electronics store and buy a new one. As he is approaching the store, Heather saunters over from a nearby alley and asks him if he wants to buy a brand new iPod for ten dollars. Suspicious of the price, Chip asks Heather to see the iPod. She hands it to him, and he notices that the box looks like it has been tampered with and a price tag removed. He shrugs, takes ten dollars out of his wallet, and hands it to Heather in exchange for the iPod. In jurisdictions that require **actual knowledge** that the property is stolen, Chip probably does not have the appropriate criminal intent for receiving stolen property because he did not know Heather and had no way of knowing if Heather was selling him stolen property. In jurisdictions that require **awareness of a risk** that the property is stolen, Chip may have the appropriate criminal intent because he knew the price was too low and noticed that the box had been tampered with to remove evidence of an actual price or vendor.

Change the example so that Chip is a pawnshop broker, and Heather brings the iPod into his shop to pawn for the price of ten dollars. In many jurisdictions, if Chip accepts the iPod to pawn, this creates a **presumption** of receiving stolen property criminal intent. Chip is considered a dealer, and in many jurisdictions, dealers who acquire property for consideration that they *know* is *far below* the reasonable value are subject to this type of presumption.

Change the example again so that Chip notices the following message written on the back of the iPod box: "This iPod is the property of Eugene Schumaker." Chip is Eugene Schumaker's friend, so he pays Heather the ten dollars to purchase the iPod so he can return it to Eugene. In many jurisdictions and under the Model Penal Code, Chip can use his intent to return the stolen property to its true owner as a **failure of proof** or **affirmative defense** to receiving stolen property.

Retaining Stolen Property

If **retaining** is the criminal act element described in the receiving stolen property statute, a defendant can still be convicted of receiving stolen property if he or she originally receives the property *without* the appropriate criminal intent, but later keeps the property *after* discovering it is stolen (Connecticut Criminal Jury Instructions §§53a-119(8), 2011).

Example of Retaining Stolen Property

Review the example with Chip and Heather in Section 11 "Example of Receiving Stolen Property Intent". Change this example so that Chip is not a dealer and is offered the iPod for one hundred dollars, which is fairly close to its actual value. Chip purchases the iPod from Heather and thereafter drives home. When he gets home, he begins to open the box and notices the message stating that the iPod is the property of Eugene Schumaker. Chip thinks about it for a minute, continues to open the box, and then retains the iPod for the next six months. If Chip is in a state that defines the criminal act element for receiving stolen property as **retains**, then Chip most likely committed the criminal act with the appropriate criminal intent (knowledge that the property is stolen) and may be subject to prosecution for and conviction of this offense.

Receiving Stolen Property Attendant

Circumstances

The property must be *stolen* for this crime, so the prosecution must prove the **attendant circumstances** that the property belongs to another and lack of victim consent.

Receiving Stolen Property Causation

The criminal act must be the **factual** and **legal cause** of receiving stolen property harm, which is defined in Section 11 "Receiving Stolen Property Harm".

Receiving Stolen Property Harm

The defendant must **buy**, **receive**, **retain**, **sell**, or **dispose of** stolen property for the completed crime of receiving stolen property in most jurisdictions (Ala. Code § 13A-8-16, 2011). If the defendant does not actually gain or transfer control of the property, only *attempted* receiving stolen property can be charged.

Figure 11.6 Diagram of Defenses to Receiving Stolen Property

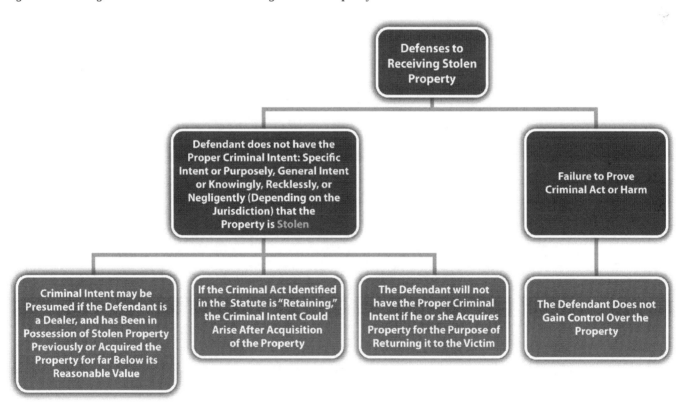

Receiving Stolen Property Grading

Receiving stolen property is **graded** as a felony-misdemeanor (Cal. Penal Code § 496, 2011) or as a misdemeanor if the stolen property is of low value and a felony if the stolen property is of high value (Ga. Code § 16-8-12, 2011).

Figure 11.7 Diagram of Crimes Involving Theft

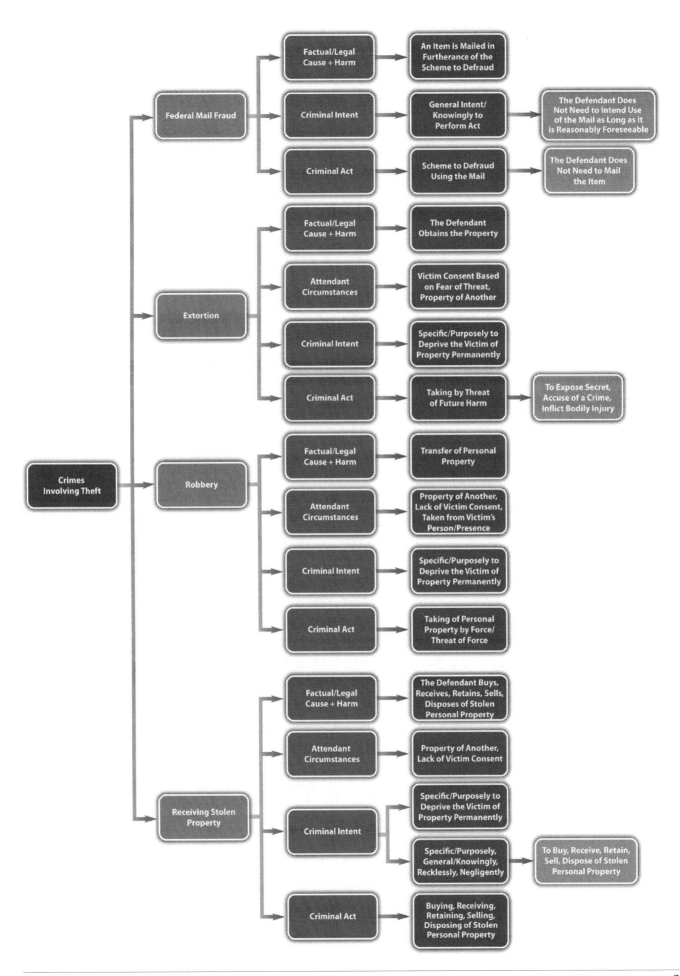

Key Takeaways

- The criminal act element required for extortion is typically a theft of property accomplished by a threat to cause future harm to the victim.
- The criminal intent element required for extortion is typically the specific intent or purposely to unlawfully deprive the victim of property permanently. However, in some jurisdictions, it is the general intent or knowingly to perform the criminal act.
- In many jurisdictions, it is an affirmative defense to extortion that the property taken by threat to expose a secret or accuse anyone of a criminal offense is taken honestly, as compensation for property, or as restitution or indemnification for harm done by the secret or crime.
- The attendant circumstances of extortion are that the property belongs to another and that the victim consents to transferring the property to the defendant based on fear inspired by the defendant's threat.
- The harm element required for extortion is that the defendant obtains the property of another.
- Extortion is graded as a felony in most jurisdictions.
- Robbery requires a taking accomplished by force or threat of imminent force. Extortion requires a taking by threat of future harm that is not necessarily force, and larceny generally requires a taking by stealth or a false representation of fact. Robbery also requires the attendant circumstance that the property be taken from the victim's person or presence and is generally graded more severely than larceny or extortion.
- Robbery is typically graded as a serious felony, which is a strike in jurisdictions that have three strikes statutes, and a predicate felony for first-degree felony murder.
- The criminal act element required for receiving stolen property is typically buying-receiving, retaining, and selling-disposing of stolen personal property.
- The defendant must have the intent to commit the criminal act of receiving stolen property, which could be specific intent or purposely, general intent or knowingly, recklessly, or negligently to either buy-receive or sell-dispose of stolen personal property, depending on the jurisdiction. If "retain" is the criminal act element specified in the receiving stolen property statute, a defendant who obtains property without knowledge that it is stolen commits the offense if he or she thereafter keeps property after discovering that it is stolen. The defendant must also have the specific intent or purposeful desire to deprive the victim of the property permanently in some jurisdictions.
- A failure of proof or affirmative defense to receiving stolen property in some jurisdictions is that the defendant received and retained the stolen property with the intent to return it to the true owner.
- The attendant circumstances for receiving stolen property are that the property belongs to another and lack of victim consent. The harm element of receiving stolen property is that the defendant buy-receive, retain, or sell-dispose of stolen personal property.
- Receiving stolen property is graded as a felony-misdemeanor or a misdemeanor if the stolen property is of low value and a felony if the stolen property is of high value.

Exercises

Answer the following questions. Check your answers using the answer key at the end of the chapter.

Review the example given in Section 11 "Example of a Case Lacking the Attendant Circumstance of Victim Reliance Required for False Pretenses" with Jeremy and Chuck. In this example, Chuck shows Jeremy a video he made of Jeremy reading a magazine instead of tuning up Chuck's taxi. Chuck thereafter threatens to show this video to the district attorney if Jeremy does not pay him two hundred dollars. Has Chuck committed a crime in this scenario? If your answer is yes, which crime? Read *State v. Robertson*, 531 S. E. 2d 490 (2000). In *Robertson*, the Court of Appeals of North Carolina reversed the defendant's conviction for robbery of the victim's purse. What was the basis of the court's reversal of conviction? The case is available at this link: http://scholar.google.com/scholar_case?case=10266690205116389671&q= robbery+%22purse+snatching%22&hl=en&as_sdt=2,5&as_ylo=2000.
Read *People v. Pratt*, 656 N.W.2d 866 (2002). In *Pratt*, the defendant was convicted of receiving stolen property for taking and concealing his girlfriend's vehicle. The defendant appealed, claiming that there was no evidence to indicate that he intended to permanently deprive his girlfriend of the vehicle, and thus it was not "**stolen**." Did the Court of Appeals of Michigan uphold the defendant's

conviction? Why or why not? The case is available at this link: http://scholar.google.com/scholar_case?case=9260508991670862336&q= actual+knowledge+%22receiving+stolen+property%22&hl=en&as_sdt=2,5&as_ylo=2000.

References

Ala. Code § 13A-8-16, accessed March 12, 2011, http://law.onecle.com/alabama/criminal-code/13A-8-16.html.

Ala. Code § 13A-8-43, accessed March 18, 2011, http://law.onecle.com/alabama/criminal-code/13A-8-43.html.

Ariz. Rev. Stat. § 13-1804, http://law.onecle.com/arizona/criminal-code/13-1804.html.

Cal. Penal Code § 189, accessed March 19, 2011, http://law.onecle.com/california/penal/189.html.

Cal. Penal Code § 211, accessed March 19, 2011, http://codes.lp.findlaw.com/cacode/PEN/3/1/8/4/s211.

Cal. Penal Code § 496, accessed March 12, 2011, http://law.onecle.com/california/penal/496.html.

Cal. Penal Code § 1192.7, accessed March 19, 2011, http://law.onecle.com/california/penal/1192.7.html.

Connecticut Criminal Jury Instructions §§53a-119(5) and 53a-122(a) (1), accessed March 12, 2011, http://www.jud.ct.gov/ji/criminal/part9/9.1-11.htm.

Connecticut Criminal Jury Instructions §§53a-119(8) and 53a-122 through 53a-125b, accessed March 13, 2011, http://www.jud.ct.gov/ji/criminal/part9/9.1-15.htm.

Fla. Stat. Ann. § 812.019, accessed March 12, 2011, http://law.onecle.com/florida/crimes/812.019.html.

Fla. Stat. Ann. § 812.13, accessed March 19, 2011, http://law.onecle.com/florida/crimes/812.13.html.

Ga. Code § 16-8-7, accessed March 12, 2011, http://law.onecle.com/georgia/16/16-8-7.html.

Hawaii Criminal Jury Instructions No. 10.00, 10.20, accessed March 13, 2011, http://www.courts.state.hi.us/docs/docs4/crimjuryinstruct.pdf.

Jones v. State, 652 So. 2d 346 (1995), accessed March 19, 2011, http://scholar.google.com/scholar_case?case=11856873917512077763&q= robbery+%22from+the+victim%27s+person%22&hl=en&as_sdt=2,5&as_ylo=2000.

K.S.A. § 21-3428, accessed March 18, 2011, http://kansasstatutes.lesterama.org/Chapter_21/Article_34/21-3428.html.

Ga. Code § 16-8-12, accessed March 13, 2011, http://law.onecle.com/georgia/16/16-8-12.html.

Ga. Code § 16-8-16, accessed March 11, 2011, http://law.onecle.com/georgia/16/16-8-16.html.

Ind. Code § 35-42-5-1, accessed March 18, 2011, http://law.onecle.com/indiana/35/35-42-5-1.html.

Mass. Gen. Laws ch. 266 § 60, http://law.onecle.com/massachusetts/266/60.html.

Metheny v. State, 755 A.2d 1088 (2000), accessed March 19, 2011, http://scholar.google.com/scholar_case?case=10315203348655203542&q= robbery+%22deprive+permanently%22&hl=en&as_sdt=2,5.

Oklahoma Uniform Jury Instructions No. CR 4-141, accessed March 19, 2011, http://www.okcca.net/online/oujis/oujisrvr.jsp?o=248.

Oklahoma Uniform Jury Instructions No. CR 5-34, accessed March 12, 2011, http://www.okcca.net/online/oujis/oujisrvr.jsp?oc=OUJI-CR%205-34.

Or. Rev. Stat. § 164.075, accessed March 12, 2011, http://law.onecle.com/oregon/164-offenses-against-property/164.075.html.

S.W. v. State, 513 So. 2d 1088 (1987), accessed March 18, 2011, http://scholar.google.com/scholar_case?case=8956843531832075141&q= robbery+%22slight+force%22&hl=en&as_sdt=2,5.

State v. Handburgh, 830 P.2d 641 (1992), accessed March 18, 2011, http://scholar.google.com/scholar_case?case=2186457002998894202&q= State+v.+Handburgh&hl=en&as_sdt=2,5.

Tex. Penal Code § 29.03, accessed March 12, 2011, http://law.onecle.com/texas/penal/29.03.00.html.

Williams v. State, 91 S.W. 3d 54 (2002), accessed March 19, 2011, http://scholar.google.com/scholar_case?case=9518129765374420507&q= robbery+%22transfer+of+property%22&hl=en&as_sdt=2,5&as_ylo=2000.

CC licensed content, Shared previously

- Criminal Law. **Provided by**: University of Minnesota Libraries Publishing . **Located at**: http://open.lib.umn.edu/criminallaw/. **License**: *CC BY-NC-SA: Attribution-NonCommercial-ShareAlike*

11.3 Crimes That Invade or Damage Property

Learning Objectives

Define the criminal act element required for burglary.
Define the criminal intent element required for burglary.
Define the attendant circumstances required for burglary.
Analyze burglary grading.
Define the elements of criminal trespass, and analyze criminal trespass grading.
Define the criminal act element required for arson.
Define the criminal intent element required for arson.
Define the attendant circumstances required for arson.
Define the harm element required for arson.
Analyze arson grading.
Define the elements of criminal mischief, and analyze criminal mischief grading.

Burglary

Although burglary is often associated with theft, it is actually an enhanced form of trespassing. At early common law, burglary was the invasion of a man's castle at nighttime, with a sinister purpose. Modern jurisdictions have done away with the common-law attendant circumstances and criminalize the unlawful **entry** into almost *any structure* or *vehicle*, at *any time* of day. Burglary has the elements of criminal act, criminal intent, and attendant circumstances, as is explored in Section 11.3.1 "Burglary".

Burglary Act

The **criminal act** element required for burglary varies, depending on the jurisdiction. Many jurisdictions require breaking and entering into the area described in the burglary statute (Mass. Gen. Laws ch. 266 § 14, 2011). Some jurisdictions and the Model Penal Code only require entering (Model Penal Code § 221.1). Other jurisdictions include **remaining** in the criminal act element (Fla. Stat. Ann. § 810.02(b)).

When criminal breaking is required, generally *any* physical force used to enter the burglarized area is sufficient—even pushing open a closed door (Commonwealth v. Hallums, 2011). **Entry** is generally partial or complete intrusion of either the defendant, the defendant's body part, or a tool or instrument (People v. Nible, 2011). In some jurisdictions, the entry must be *unauthorized* (State v. Hall, 2011), while in others, it could be *lawful* (People v. Nunley, 2011). The Model Penal Code makes an exception for "premises...open to the public" or when the defendant is "licensed or privileged to enter" (Model Penal Code § 221.1(1)). **Remaining** means that the defendant lingers in the burglarized area after an initial lawful or unlawful entry (State v. Allen, 2011).

Example of Burglary Act

Jed uses a burglar tool to remove the window screen of a residence. The window is open, so once Jed removes the screen, he places both hands on the sill, and begins to launch himself upward. The occupant of the residence, who was watching Jed from inside, slams the window down on Jed's hands. Jed has probably committed the criminal act element required for burglary in many jurisdictions. When Jed removed the window screen, he committed a **breaking**. When Jed placed his hands on the windowsill, his fingers intruded into the residence, which satisfies the **entry** requirement. Thus Jed may be subject to a prosecution for burglary rather than *attempted* burglary, even though he never actually damaged or broke the barrier of the residence or managed to gain complete access to the interior.

Burglary Intent

Depending on the jurisdiction, the criminal intent element required for burglary is typically the **general intent** or **knowingly** to commit the criminal act, with the **specific intent** or **purposely** to commit a felony (Mass. Gen. Laws ch. 266 § 14, 2011), any crime (Connecticut Criminal Jury Instructions §53a-102, 2011), or a felony, grand, or petty theft once inside the burglarized area (Cal. Penal Code § 459, 2011). The Model Penal Code describes the criminal intent element as "purpose to commit a crime therein" (Model Penal Code § 221.1(1)).

Example of a Case Lacking Burglary Intent

Hans dares Christian to break into a house in their neighborhood that is reputed to be "haunted." Christian goes up to the front door of the house, shoves it open, steps inside the front hallway, and then hurriedly dashes back outside. Christian probably does not have the criminal intent element required for burglary in this scenario. Although Christian committed the criminal act of breaking and entering, Christian did not have the intent to commit a crime once inside. Christian's conduct is probably criminal, but it is most likely a **criminal trespass**, *not* **burglary**. Criminal trespass is discussed in Section 11.3.2 "Criminal Trespass".

Burglary Attendant Circumstances

Depending on the jurisdiction, burglary often includes the **attendant circumstance** that the area entered is a structure, building, or vehicle belonging to another (Oklahoma Uniform Jury Instructions No. CR 5-13, 2011). However, modern jurisdictions have eliminated the requirement that the property belong to another (Cal. Penal Code § 459, 2011) and prohibit burglarizing property owned by the *defendant*, such as a landlord burglarizing a tenant's apartment. Some jurisdictions require a structure or building to be occupied (Iowa Code § 713.1, 2011), or require it to be a dwelling (Connecticut Criminal Jury Instructions §53a-102, 2011), and require a vehicle to be *locked* (Cal. Penal Code § 459, 2011). A few jurisdictions also retain the common-law attendant circumstance that the burglary take place at nighttime (Mass. Gen. Laws ch. 266 § 15, 2011).

Structure or building generally includes a house, room, apartment, shop, barn, or even a tent (Cal. Penal Code § 459, 2011). The Model Penal Code expressly excludes *abandoned* structures or buildings (Model Penal Code § 221.1(1)). A dwelling is a building used for lodging at night (Connecticut Criminal Jury Instructions § 53a-102, 2011). Occupied means that the structure or building can be used for business or for lodging at night and does not necessarily require the actual presence of a person or victim when the criminal act takes place (Iowa Code § 702.12). Nighttime means the time after sunset and before sunrise when it is too dark to clearly see a defendant's face (State v. Reavis, 2011).

Example of Burglary Attendant Circumstances

Susan breaks down a door and steps inside a building with the intent to commit arson, a felony, once inside. If the building is an empty child's tiny plastic playhouse, the attendant circumstance that the structure be **occupied** or a

dwelling is lacking. If it is twelve noon, the attendant circumstance that the criminal act takes place at **nighttime** is lacking. If it is pitch black outside and 10 p.m. and the building is Susan's ex-boyfriend's residence, then Susan has most likely committed burglary and may be subject to prosecution for and conviction of this offense.

Figure 11.8 Diagram of Defenses to Burglary

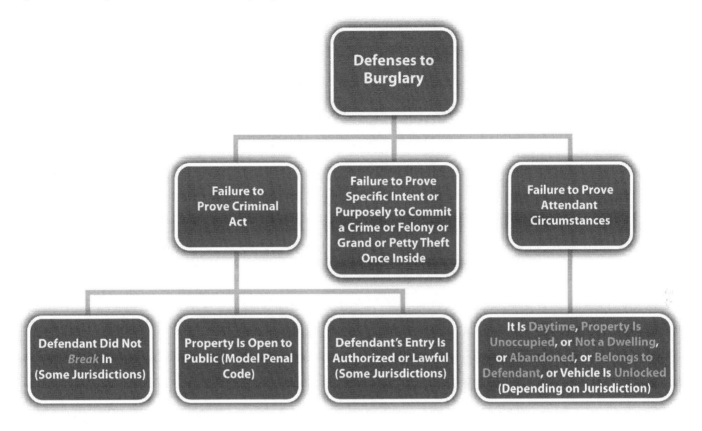

Burglary Grading

Burglary is typically divided into degrees (Iowa Code §§ 713.3, 713.5, 713.6A, 2011). First-degree burglary is generally a serious felony that can serve as the predicate felony for first-degree felony murder (Cal. Penal Code § 189, 2011) and a strike in states that have three strikes statutes (Cal. Penal Code § 1192.7, 2011). Factors that can elevate burglary grading are the use or possession of a weapon, the entry into a residence, dwelling, or building where people are present, the commission of burglary at nighttime, or the infliction of injury or death (Mass. Gen. Laws ch. 266 § 14, 2011). Second- and third-degree burglary generally are still felonies, although less serious than first-degree burglary (Ala. Code § 13A-7-7, 2011). The Model Penal Code grades burglary as a felony of the second degree if perpetrated in the dwelling of another at night, or if the actor purposely, knowingly, or recklessly inflicts or attempts to inflict bodily injury or is armed with explosives or a deadly weapon. Otherwise, the Model Penal Code grades burglary as a felony of the third degree (Model Penal Code § 221.1(2)).

Keep in mind that a defendant can be prosecuted for burglary even if the felony or crime intended after entry *never takes place*. In addition, if the defendant actually commits the felony or crime after entry, the defendant can be prosecuted for *both* burglary and the completed crime without violating the protection against double jeopardy in the Fifth Amendment to the federal Constitution. The Model Penal Code states that a "person may not be convicted both for burglary and for the offense which it was his purpose to commit after the burglarious entry...unless the additional offense constitutes a felony of the first or second degree" (Model Penal Code § 221.1(3)).

Criminal Trespass

As stated previously, criminal trespass is generally charged when one or more of the attendant circumstances of burglary are lacking or when the criminal intent is less heinous. Typically, criminal trespass is an unauthorized (**attendant circumstance**) entry or remaining (**criminal act**) into a building, occupied structure, or place as to which notice against trespassing is given, owned by another (**attendant circumstance**), with **general intent** or **knowingly** that the entry was unauthorized (criminal intent) (18 Pa. C.S. § 3503, 2011). The Model Penal Code states that it is criminal trespass when the defendant "knowing that he is not licensed or privileged to do so…enters or surreptitiously remains in any building or occupied structure…or any place as to which notice against trespass is given" (Model Penal Code § 221.2). Criminal trespass is generally **graded** as a less serious felony than burglary or is graded as a misdemeanor if the trespass is into a place, rather than a building or occupied structure (18 Pa. C.S. § 3503, 2011). The Model Penal Code grades criminal trespass as a misdemeanor if it is committed in a dwelling at night; otherwise, it is graded as a petty misdemeanor or a violation (Model Penal Code § 221.2).

Arson

Arson is one of the most destructive crimes in the United States, costing billions of dollars per year in lost or damaged homes, businesses, and real property. Many jurisdictions punish arson as a high-level felony that could merit a punishment of life in prison and mandatory registration requirements similar to serious sex offenses (730 ILCS 148 § 10, 2011).

At early common law, arson was primarily a crime against **habitation**, rather than a crime against property. The elements of arson at common law were the malicious or intentional burning of a dwelling owned by another. Modern statutes criminalize burning almost *anything*, including the defendant's own property in many instances.

Arson is a crime that has the elements of criminal act, criminal intent, attendant circumstances, causation, and harm, as is explored in Section 11.3.3 "Arson".

Arson Act

The **criminal act** element required for arson is typically setting fire to or burning real or personal property specified in the arson statute (Cal. Penal Code § 451, 2011). This could include buildings, structures, land, and vehicles (Tex. Penal Code § 28.02, 2011). Some states define the criminal act element as "damaging" the specified property by fire or explosives (Ga. Code tit. 16 § 16-7-60, 2011). The Model Penal Code describes the criminal act element as starting a fire or causing an explosion (Model Penal Code § 220.1(1). The **type** or **value** of the property the defendant burns or damages can enhance grading. Grading is discussed shortly.

Example of Arson Act

Clark and Manny are bored and decide to light a fire in the woods near their houses. The grass is damp from a recent rain, so the fire does not spread and burns only a small circle of grass. Clark and Manny give up and walk home. Clark and Manny have probably committed the criminal act element required for arson in most jurisdictions. Although a large destructive fire was not set by Clark and Manny, the two did burn or damage real property and start a fire, which satisfies the criminal act requirement in most jurisdictions and under the Model Penal Code.

Arson Intent

The criminal intent element required for arson in many jurisdictions is the **general intent** or **knowingly** to commit the criminal act (Ga. Code tit. 16 § 16-7-60). Thus the defendant only needs the intent to burn or damage property specified in the arson statute; the defendant does not have to intend to burn a *specific* structure or personal property, even if that is the end result (People v. Atkins, 2011). The Model Penal Code requires starting a fire or causing an explosion "with the purpose of destroying a building or occupied structure of another; or destroying or damaging any property...to collect insurance for such loss" (Model Penal Code § 220.1(1)).

Example of Arson Intent

Review the example with Clark and Manny in Section 11 "Example of Arson Act". Change this example so that Clark and Manny leave the area and a tiny spark from the fire they set begins to ignite. After a few hours, a large and powerful fire starts and burns thousands of acres in the forest. Clark and Manny most likely have the criminal intent element required for arson in many jurisdictions. Although Clark and Manny did not necessarily *want* to burn thousands of acres of forest land, they did **intentionally** or **knowingly** start a fire in the forest, which is all that many modern arson statutes require. Thus even though Clark and Manny did not intend the end result, Clark and Manny are probably subject to prosecution for and conviction of arson for their conduct.

Arson Attendant Circumstances

In most jurisdictions, arson must burn a specific type of property. Although this can be interpreted as an attendant circumstance, it is also a function of **grading**. Thus first-degree arson may focus on arson of a dwelling (Vt. Stat. Ann. tit. 13 § 502, 2011), while second-degree arson focuses on arson of other property (Vt. Stat. Ann. tit 13 § 503, 2011). Many jurisdictions do *not* require the attendant circumstance that property "belongs to another," and therefore the defendant can burn his or her own property and still be guilty of arson. However, the defendant must generally burn his or her property with the **specific intent** or **purposely** to *defraud* for the burning to constitute arson (Ga. Code tit. 16 § 16-7-62, 2011). The Model Penal Code requires "destroying or damaging any property, whether his own or another's, to collect insurance for such loss" (Model Penal Code § 220.1(b)).

Example of a Case Lacking Arson Intent for Burning the Defendant's Property

Tim decides he wants to get rid of all the reminders of his ex-girlfriend. Tim piles all the photographs, gifts, and clothing items that are connected to his relationship with his ex into his fireplace and burns them. In this scenario, Tim probably does *not* have the criminal intent element required for arson in most jurisdictions. Although Tim burned or damaged property, the property belongs to *Tim*, not another. Thus Tim must burn the property with the **specific intent** or **purposely** to defraud—most likely an insurance carrier. Tim burned his own property with only **general intent** or **knowingly**, so Tim may not be charged with and convicted of arson in most jurisdictions.

Arson Causation

The criminal act must be the **factual** and **legal cause** of arson harm, which Section 11 "Example of Arson Causation" defines. As stated previously, the defendant does not have to *intend* to burn a specific structure or personal property, even if that is the end result in many jurisdictions. However, there must be a causation analysis in every arson case because arson is a crime that requires a bad result or harm. Thus the arson **harm** must be *reasonably foreseeable* at the time the defendant commits the criminal act with the accompanying criminal intent.

Example of Arson Causation

Review the example with Clark and Manny in Section 11 "Example of Arson Intent". In this example, Clark and Manny try to light a fire in the forest, but the grass is too damp, so they give up and leave the area. Hours later, a spark from their fire ignites, burning thousands of acres. Clark and Manny could be the **factual** and **legal cause** of this harm in many jurisdictions. Even though the grass was damp and difficult to burn, a trier of fact could find that it is reasonably foreseeable when lighting a fire in the forest that the fire could turn into a massive and destructive blaze. Thus Clark and Manny's act accompanied by the general intent or knowingly to burn **caused** significant harm, and Clark and Manny may be subject to prosecution for arson in this case.

Arson Harm

The **harm** element required for arson is burning, charring, or damage to the property specified in the arson statute. Damage could be damage to even a small part (California Criminal Jury Instructions No. 1515, 2011), and in the most extreme cases, even smoke damage without burning or charring is sufficient (Ursulita v. State, 2011). The Model Penal Code only requires starting a fire or causing an explosion with the appropriate criminal intent, regardless of whether damage to real or personal property ensues (Model Penal Code § 220.1(1)). Some states follow the Model Penal Code approach (Tex. Penal Code § 28.02, 2011).

Example of Arson Harm

Review the example with Clark and Manny in Section 11 "Example of Arson Act". In this example, Clark and Manny started a fire in the woods that burned a small circle of dead grass. This **damage** is probably sufficient to constitute the harm for arson in most jurisdictions. Although the value of the damaged forest land is not *excessive*, excessive damage is not typically a requirement under modern arson statutes—*any* damage is enough. Thus Clark and Manny may be subject to a prosecution for and conviction of this offense in most jurisdictions.

Figure 11.9 Diagram of Defenses to Arson

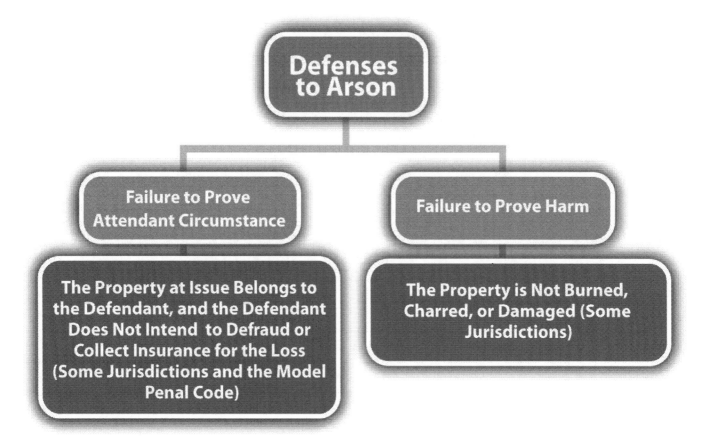

Arson Grading

Arson is typically divided into degrees (Ga. Code tit. 16 § 16-7-60, 2011), or simple and aggravated (Cal. Penal Code § 451.5, 2011). Factors that can elevate **grading** are the burning or damage of another's dwelling (Ga. Code tit. 16 § 16-7-60, 2011), bodily injury or death (Connecticut Criminal Jury Instructions § 53a-111, 2011), extensive property damage, or damage to property of high value (Cal. Penal Code § 451.5, 2011). As stated previously, arson is a serious felony that can result in a sentence of life in prison and mandatory registration requirements similar to serious sex offenses (730 ILCS § 10, 2011). Arson is also generally a strike in states that have three strikes statutes (Cal. Penal Code § 1192.7, 2011) and a predicate felony for first-degree felony murder (Cal. Penal Code § 189, 2010). Many jurisdictions grade even simple arson or second or third-degree arson as a felony (Cal. Penal Code § 451, 2011). The Model Penal Code grades arson as a felony of the second degree (Model Penal Code § 220.1).

Criminal Mischief

Criminal mischief prohibits damaging or destroying property, tampering with property, or deception or threat that leads to a loss of property. Although criminal mischief may be a felony in many jurisdictions, it is generally a less serious felony than arson, either because the defendant inflicts damage to property in a safer manner or because the criminal intent is less heinous. The **criminal act** element required for criminal mischief is damaging (Ala. Code § 13A-7-21, 2011), destroying, interfering with (Or. Rev. Stat. § 164.365, 2011), or tampering with (Alaska Stat. § 11.46.480, 2011) property. The criminal intent element required for criminal mischief varies, depending on the jurisdiction and the degree of the offense. The criminal intent could be **specific intent** or **purposely**, **general intent** or **knowingly**, **reckless**, or **negligent** (18 Pa.C.S. § 3304, 2011). The **attendant circumstances** required for criminal mischief are typically committing the criminal act against the property of another (or property that is government owned) without victim consent or with no right or authorization (Alaska Stat. § 11.46.475, 2011). The **harm** element required for criminal mischief is damage, destruction, or interference to property by fire, explosive, flood, or some other method, or interference with electricity, water, oil or gas (Alaska Stat. § 11.46.475, 2011), or loss of property or money by deception such as causing the victim to purchase a worthless product (18 Pa.C.S. § 3304, 2011). As stated previously, criminal mischief is often a *less serious* felony than arson and could also be graded as a gross misdemeanor or misdemeanor (18 Pa.C.S. § 3304, 2011). Factors that could elevate **grading** of criminal mischief are the extent of the property damage and the severity of the defendant's criminal intent (18 Pa.C.S. § 3304, 2011). The Model Penal Code criminalizes criminal mischief when the defendant purposely, recklessly, or negligently damages tangible property of another by fire, explosives, or other dangerous means, purposely or recklessly tampers with tangible property of another so as to endanger person or property, or purposely or recklessly causes another to suffer pecuniary loss by deception or threat. The Model Penal Code grades criminal mischief as a felony of the third degree, misdemeanor, petty misdemeanor, or violation, depending on the extent of the damage or the criminal intent (Model Penal Code § 220.3).

Figure 11.10 Diagram of Crimes That Invade or Damage Property

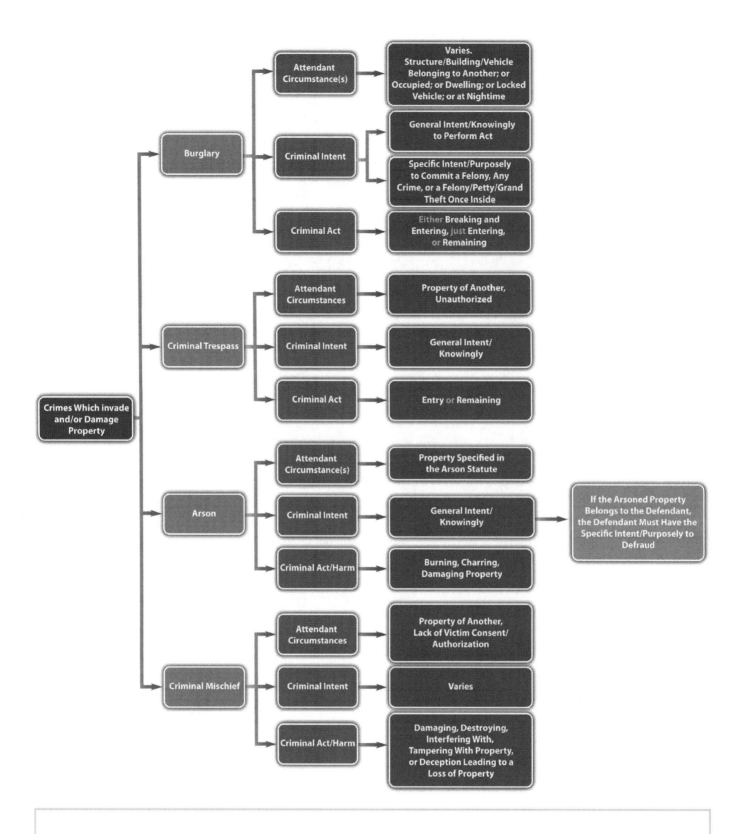

Key Takeaways

- The criminal act element required for burglary is breaking and entering, just entering, or remaining.
- The criminal intent element required for burglary is typically the general intent or knowingly to commit the criminal act and the specific intent or purposely to commit a felony, any crime, or a felony, petty, or grand theft once inside the burglarized area.
- Burglary generally includes the attendant circumstances that the area entered is a structure, building, or vehicle belonging to another, or an occupied building or structure, or a dwelling.

Modern jurisdictions have eliminated the requirement that the property belong to another and prohibit the defendant from burglarizing his or her own property. Some jurisdictions require a vehicle to be locked, and a few jurisdictions require the burglary to take place at nighttime.

- Burglary is typically graded as a felony that is divided into degrees. First-degree burglary is often a strike in jurisdictions that have three strikes statutes and a predicate felony for first-degree felony murder.
- Typically, criminal trespass is an unauthorized (attendant circumstance) entry or remaining (criminal act) into a building, occupied structure, or place as to which notice against trespassing is given, owned by another (attendant circumstance) with general intent or knowingly that the entry was unauthorized (criminal intent). Criminal trespass is generally graded as a felony, albeit a less serious felony than burglary, or a misdemeanor if the area trespassed is a place rather than an occupied building or structure.
- The criminal act element required for arson is starting a fire, burning, or damaging with fire or explosives specified real or personal property.
- The criminal intent element required for arson is the general intent or knowingly to commit the criminal act in many jurisdictions.
- Arson statutes can specify the attendant circumstance that the defendant burns a specific type of property, such as a dwelling or other real or personal property. In most jurisdictions, if the defendant burns his or her own property, the defendant must act with the specific intent or purposely to defraud, typically an insurance carrier.
- The harm element required for arson is burning, charring, damage, or, in the most extreme cases, smoke damage.
- Arson is typically graded as a felony that is divided into degrees. First-degree arson is often a strike in jurisdictions that have three strikes statutes and a predicate felony for first-degree felony murder. Arson could also carry a registration requirement like serious sex offenses.
- The elements of criminal mischief are damaging or destroying property, tampering with property, or deception or threat that leads to a loss of property (criminal act and harm) with specific intent or purposely, general intent or knowingly, recklessly, or negligently. Although criminal mischief may be a felony in many jurisdictions, it is generally a less serious felony than arson and in some jurisdictions it is graded as a gross misdemeanor or misdemeanor.

Exercises

Answer the following questions. Check your answers using the answer key at the end of the chapter.

Why is burglary of a **dwelling** at **nighttime** generally graded higher than other burglaries?
Read *Butler v. Florida*, No. 1D08-0958 (Fla: Dist. Court of Appeals, 2009). In *Butler*, the defendant appealed his convictions for trespass and criminal mischief, based on the trial court's failure to instruct the jury on the defense of **necessity**. The defendant claimed he broke into a residence because he was being chased and feared for his safety. Did the Court of Appeal of Florida reverse the defendant's convictions? Why or why not? The case is available at this link: http://scholar.google.com/scholar_case?case=1710354491441564352&q= burglary+%22necessity+defense%22&hl=en&as_sdt=2,5&as_ylo=2000.
Read *In the Matter of V.V.C.*, No. 04-07-00166 CV (Tex.: Court of Appeals, 2008). In *V.V.C.*, the Court of Appeals of Texas dismissed a minor's adjudication for arson when he started a fire in the boy's restroom of a middle school. What was the basis for the court's dismissal? The case is available at this link: http://scholar.google.com/scholar_case?case=1784800980619654964&q= arson+%22smoke+damage%22&hl=en&as_sdt=2,5&as_ylo=2000.

Law and Ethics

WikiLeaks: Should Exposure of Information Be Criminal?

Julian Assange, famous for his computer hacking skills, is the editor in chief of WikiLeaks, a whistleblower website. WikiLeaks has exposed documents and videos detailing the corruption in Kenya, Guantanamo Bay procedures, and the American involvement in the Afghan and Iraq wars, portions of which were classified

confidential and **secret** (Khatchadourian, R., 2011). The *New York Times* published some of this information (Savage, C., 2011). Although WikiLeaks did not actually "leak" classified material (some of it was allegedly passed to WikiLeaks by a low-level US Army intelligence analyst), the US Department of Justice has launched a criminal investigation regarding the release, and US prosecutors are reportedly considering charges against Assange (Savage, C., 2011).

> Do you think it is ethical to expose or publish "leaked" confidential and secret government information?
> What is the difficulty in prosecuting a defendant for this type of publication?

Check your answers using the answer key at the end of the chapter.

WikiLeaks Video

60 Minutes Interviews Julian Assange

Julian Assange's interview with *60 Minutes* is shown in the following video:
(click to see video)

References

Ala. Code § 13A-7-21, accessed March 24, 2011, http://law.onecle.com/alabama/criminal-code/13A-7-21.html.

Ala. Code § 13A-7-7, accessed March 20, 2011, http://law.onecle.com/alabama/criminal-code/13A-7-7.html.

Alaska Stat. § 11.46.475, accessed March 24, 2011, http://law.justia.com/codes/alaska/2009/title-11/chapter-11-46/article-04/sec-11-46-475.

Alaska Stat. § 11.46.480, accessed March 24, 2011, http://law.justia.com/codes/alaska/2009/title-11/chapter-11-46/article-04/sec-11-46-480.

Cal. Penal Code § 1192.7, accessed March 21, 2011, http://law.onecle.com/california/penal/1192.7.html.

Cal. Penal Code § 189, accessed March 20, 2011, http://law.onecle.com/california/penal/189.html.

Cal. Penal Code § 451, accessed March 22, 2011, http://law.onecle.com/california/penal/451.html.

Cal. Penal Code § 451.5, accessed March 21, 2011, http://law.onecle.com/california/penal/451.5.html.

Cal. Penal Code § 459, accessed March 20, 2011, http://law.onecle.com/california/penal/459.html.

California Criminal Jury Instructions No. 1515, accessed March 22, 2011, http://www.justia.com/criminal/docs/calcrim/1500/1515.html.

Commonwealth v. Hallums, 61 Mass. App. Ct. 50 (2004), accessed March 20, 2011, http://scholar.google.com/scholar_case?case=5153605963860010581&q=burglary+%22breaking+requirement%22&hl=en&as_sdt=2,5&as_ylo=2000.

Connecticut Criminal Jury Instructions § 53a-111, accessed March 22, 2011, http://www.jud.ct.gov/ji/criminal/part9/9.3-1.htm.

Connecticut Criminal Jury Instructions §53a-102, accessed March 20, 2011, http://www.jud.ct.gov/ji/criminal/part9/9.2-3.htm.

Fla. Stat. Ann. § 810.02(b) (2), http://law.justia.com/codes/florida/2010/TitleXLVI/chapter810/810_02.html.

Ga. Code tit. 16 § 16-7-60, accessed March 21, 2011, http://law.onecle.com/georgia/16/16-7-60.html.

Iowa Code § 702.12, http://search.legis.state.ia.us/nxt/gateway.dll/ic?f=templates&fn=default.htm.

Iowa Code § 713.1, accessed March 20, 2011, http://coolice.legis.state.ia.us/cool-ice/default.asp?category=billinfo&service=iowacode&ga=83&input=713.

Iowa Code §§ 713.3, 713.5, 713.6A, accessed March 20, 2011, http://coolice.legis.state.ia.us/cool-ice/default.asp?category=billinfo&service=iowacode&ga=83&input=713.

Khatchadourian, R., "No Secrets," *New Yorker* website, accessed March 29, 2011, http://www.newyorker.com/reporting/2010/06/07/100607fa_fact_khatchadourian?printable=true.

Mass. Gen. Laws ch. 266 § 14, accessed March 20, 2011, http://law.justia.com/codes/massachusetts/2009/PARTIV/TITLEI/CHAPTER266/Section14.html.

Mass. Gen. Laws ch. 266 § 15, accessed March 20, 2011, http://law.onecle.com/massachusetts/266/15.html.

Oklahoma Uniform Jury Instructions No. CR 5-13, accessed March 20, 2011, http://www.okcca.net/online/oujis/oujisrvr.jsp?oc=OUJI-CR%205-13.

Or. Rev. Stat. § 164.365, accessed March 24, 2011, http://law.onecle.com/oregon/164-offenses-against-property/164.365.html.

People v. Atkins, 25 Cal. 4th 76 (2001), accessed March 22, 2011, http://scholar.google.com/scholar_case?case=9598329868727521 80&q=%22mens+rea+for+arson%22&hl=en&as_sdt=2,5.

People v. Nible, 200 Cal. App. 3d 838 (1988), accessed March 20, 2011, http://scholar.google.com/scholar_case?case=2854983864809427191&q=burglary+%22partial+entry%22&hl=en&as_sdt=2,5&as_ylo=2000.

People v. Nunley, 168 Cal. App. 3d 225 (1985), accessed March 20, 2011, http://scholar.google.com/scholar_case?case=13700546275600703774&q=burglary+%22shoplifting%22&hl=en&as_sdt=2,5&as_ylo=2000.

Savage, C., "U.S. Prosecutors Study WikiLeaks Prosecution," *New York Times* website, accessed March 29, 2011, http://www.nytimes.com/2010/12/08/world/08leak.html?_r=2&partner=rss&emc=rss.

State v. Allen, 110 P. 3d 849 (2005), accessed March 20, 2011, http://scholar.google.com/scholar_case?case=8379482139957 51444&q=burglary+%22remaining+means%22&hl=en&as_sdt=2,5&as_ylo=2000.

State v. Hall, 3 P.3d 582 (2000), accessed March 20, 2011, http://scholar.google.com/scholar_case?case=14296917791490578337&q=burglary+%22shoplifting%22&hl=en&as_sdt=2,5&as_ylo=2000.

State v. Reavis, 700 S.E.2d 33 (2010), accessed March 20, 2011, http://scholar.google.com/scholar_case?case=10817450688281022337&q=burglary+%22definition+of+nighttime%22&hl=en&as_sdt=2,5&as_ylo=2000.

Tex. Penal Code § 28.02, accessed March 22, 2011, http://law.onecle.com/texas/penal/28.02.00.html.

Ursulita v. State, 706 S.E.2d 123 (2011), accessed March 22, 2011, http://scholar.google.com/scholar_case?case=8922319356856476558&q=Ursulita+v.+State&hl=en&as_sdt=2,5&as_ylo=2000.

Vt. Stat. Ann. tit. 13 § 502, accessed March 22, 2011, http://law.justia.com/codes/vermont/2009/title-13/chapter-11/502.

Vt. Stat. Ann. tit. 13 § 503, accessed March 22, 2011, http://law.justia.com/codes/vermont/2009/title-13/chapter-11/503.

18 Pa. C.S. § 3503, accessed March 20, 2011, http://law.onecle.com/pennsylvania/crimes-and-offenses/00.035.003.000.html.

18 Pa.C.S. § 3304, accessed March 24, 2011, http://law.onecle.com/pennsylvania/crimes-and-offenses/00.033.004.000.html.

730 ILCS § 10, accessed March 21, 2011, http://law.onecle.com/illinois/730ilcs148/10.html.

730 ILCS 148 § 10, accessed March 21, 2011, http://law.onecle.com/illinois/730ilcs148/10.html.

CC licensed content, Shared previously

- Criminal Law. **Provided by**: University of Minnesota Libraries Publishing . **Located at**: http://open.lib.umn.edu/criminallaw/. **License**: *CC BY-NC-SA: Attribution-NonCommercial-ShareAlike*

11.4 End-of-Chapter Material

Summary

Crimes against property include theft, crimes connected to theft, and crimes that invade or damage property. Modern jurisdictions criminalize several forms of theft under consolidated theft statutes that grade theft primarily on the value of the property stolen. Larceny under a consolidated theft statute in many jurisdictions is the physical taking or gaining possession of a victim's personal property by control and asportation, or a false representation of fact, with the intent to keep the property. Embezzlement under a consolidated theft statute is the conversion of a victim's real or personal property entrusted to the defendant. False pretenses under a consolidated theft statute is the permanent transfer of ownership of real or personal property or services from the victim to the defendant, based on a false representation of fact. The theft of property of low value is typically a misdemeanor (petty theft), while the theft of property of high value (grand theft) is a felony, felony-misdemeanor, or a gross misdemeanor, depending on the circumstances and the jurisdiction. Federal mail fraud, a felony, is the knowing use of the mail to perpetrate a scheme to defraud.

Extortion is the purposeful theft of property by a threat of future harm such as bodily injury or exposure of the victim's crime or secret that subjects the victim to hatred, contempt, or ridicule. Extortion is typically graded as a felony. Robbery is the purposeful theft of property from the victim's person or presence by force or threat of imminent physical harm. Robbery is typically graded as a serious felony. Receiving stolen property is receiving, buying, selling, disposing of, or retaining stolen property with either knowledge or awareness that the property is stolen or knowledge or awareness of a risk that the property is stolen. Receiving stolen property is typically graded as a felony-misdemeanor or a misdemeanor if the property is of low value and a felony if the property is of significant value.

Burglary is either breaking and entering, entering, or remaining on another's property with the intent to commit a felony, any crime, grand theft, or petty theft once inside. In some jurisdictions, the defendant can burglarize his or her own property. Burglary is typically graded as a serious felony. Criminal trespass is a knowing unauthorized entry onto the property of another. Criminal trespass is typically graded as a less serious felony than burglary, or a misdemeanor if the trespass is into a place, rather than an occupied building or structure. Arson is knowingly burning or damaging by fire property described in the arson statute. Arson is typically graded as a serious felony. Criminal mischief is damaging, destroying, or interfering with property with specific intent or purposely, general intent or knowingly, recklessly, or negligently, depending on the jurisdiction and the degree of the offense. Criminal mischief is typically graded as a less serious felony than arson, a gross misdemeanor, or a misdemeanor.

You Be the Legal Textbook Author

Read the statute, and then describe the elements of each of the following crimes. Check your answers using the answer key at the end of the chapter.

Offenses against computer users: Fla. Stat. Ann. § 815.06. The statute is available at this link: http://law.onecle.com/florida/crimes/815.06.html. Identify the criminal **act** (seven possible), criminal **intent**, **attendant circumstance**, and **harm**. How is this crime **graded**?
Identity theft: 18 Pa. C.S. § 4120. The statute is available at this link:

http://law.onecle.com/pennsylvania/crimes-and-offenses/00.041.020.000.html. Identify the criminal **act** (two possible), **criminal intent**, **attendant circumstance**, and **harm**. How is this crime **graded**?

Unlawful duplication of computer-related material in the first degree: N.Y. Penal Law § 156.30. The statute is available at this link: http://law.onecle.com/new-york/penal/PEN0156.30_156.30.html. Identify the criminal **act** (three possible), **criminal intent**, **attendant circumstance**, and **harm**. How is this crime **graded**?

Cases of Interest

- *People v. Beaver*, 186 Cal. App. 4th 107 (2010), illustrates the complexity of prosecuting theft under a consolidated theft statute: http://scholar.google.com/scholar_case?case=12194560873043980150&q=false+pretenses+theft+of+a+service&hl=en&as_sdt=2,5&as_ylo=1999.
- *State v. Castillo*, Docket No. 29, 641 (NM: 2011), discusses the difference between a debit card and credit card for theft: http://scholar.google.com/scholar_case?case=8674118418557512209&q=State+v+Castillo+NM&hl=en&as_sdt=2,5&as_ylo=2010.
- *People v. Nowack*, 614 N.W.2d 78 (2000), discusses the criminal intent element required for arson: http://scholar.google.com/scholar_case?case=3668258956679541189&q=arson+%22specific+intent+crime%22&hl=en&as_sdt=2,5&as_ylo=2000.

Articles of Interest

- Bernie Madoff case: http://papers.ssrn.com/sol3/papers.cfm?abstract_id=1661462
- Largest hedge fund insider trading case in US history: http://www.huffingtonpost.com/2011/03/22/raj-rajaratnam-jury-hears_n_839281.html
- Celebrity burglaries: http://www.nigerianbestforum.com/generaltopics/?p=50094
- Wildland arson: http://www.springerlink.com/content/h4w5015373m2v200

Websites of Interest

- Information on arson: http://www.ncjrs.gov/App/Topics/Topic.aspx?topicid=66
- Cybercrime: http://www.justice.gov/usao/priority-areas/cyber-crime
- US DOJ identity theft information: http://www.justice.gov/criminal/fraud/websites/idtheft.html

Statistics of Interest

- Burglary: http://bjs.ojp.usdoj.gov/index.cfm?ty=tp&tid=321
- Identity theft: http://bjs.ojp.usdoj.gov/index.cfm?ty=tp&tid=42

CC licensed content, Shared previously

- Criminal Law. **Provided by**: University of Minnesota Libraries Publishing . **Located at**: http://open.lib.umn.edu/criminallaw/. **License**: *CC BY-NC-SA: Attribution-NonCommercial-ShareAlike*

Chapter 12: Crimes against the Public

12.1 Quality-of-Life Crimes

Source: Image courtesy of Tara Storm.

The state has not only a right to "maintain a decent society" but an obligation to do so. In the public nuisance context, the community's right to security and protection must be reconciled with the individual's right to expressive and associative freedom. Reconciliation begins with the acknowledgment that the interests of the community are not invariably less important than the freedom of individuals.

—*People v. Acuna*, cited in Section 12 "Civil Responses to Gang Activity"

Learning Objectives

Define the criminal act element required for disorderly conduct.
Define the criminal intent element required for disorderly conduct.
Define the attendant circumstance required for disorderly conduct.
Identify potential constitutional challenges to disorderly conduct statutes.
Analyze disorderly conduct grading.
Identify potential constitutional challenges to vagrancy statutes.
Identify potential constitutional challenges to loitering statutes.
Define the elements of loitering, and analyze loitering grading.
Compare sit-lie laws to loitering statutes.

Crimes against the public include offenses that affect the quality of life, group violence such as gang activity, and vice crimes. Because quality-of-life crimes are often based on *moral* or *value* judgments, these offenses tend to target the poor and downtrodden. If the conduct prohibited involves an individual's **status** in society, **assembling**, or **speech**, the First and Fourteenth Amendments require a narrowly tailored statute supported by a compelling government interest. This creates a conflict between legislators trying to ensure peace and tranquility for citizens and judges upholding the many individual protections included in the Bill of Rights.

The quality-of-life offenses discussed are disorderly conduct, vagrancy, and loitering. Upcoming sections analyze crimes involving group activity, such as unlawful assembly and riot, along with the ever-growing problem of criminal gangs, and novel criminal and civil responses. The final section of this chapter discusses common vice crimes, including possession, sale, and use of controlled substances and prostitution.

Disorderly Conduct

Disorderly conduct, also called **disturbing the peace**, criminalizes conduct that negatively impacts the quality of life for citizens in any given city, county, or state. Although disorderly conduct is typically a low-level offense, the enforcement of disorderly conduct statutes is important to preserve citizens' ability to live, work, and travel in safety and comfort. Disorderly conduct has the elements of criminal act, criminal intent, and an attendant circumstance, as is explored in Section 12.1.1 "Disorderly Conduct".

Disorderly Conduct Act

Three **criminal acts** generally are identified in any disorderly conduct statute. The defendant must either (1) make a loud and unreasonable noise, obscene utterance, or gesture, (2) engage in fighting or threatening, or state fighting words, or (3) create a hazardous condition by an act that does not serve a legitimate purpose (18 Pa. C. S. § 5503, 2011). The Model Penal Code defines disorderly conduct as engaging in fighting or threatening or violent tumultuous behavior, making unreasonable noise or an offensively course utterance, gesture, or display, addressing abusive language to any person present, or creating a hazardous or physically offensive condition by an act that serves no legitimate purpose (Model Penal Code § 250.2). When the criminal act is a loud and unreasonable noise, the quality of the noise is judged in the *setting* where the noise occurred. A noise made in an extremely quiet area can be softer than a noise made in a loud and busy area like a city street during peak hours (Haw. Rev. Stat. § 711-1101(2), 2011). The term "hazardous condition" generally refers to a situation that is dangerous and poses a risk of injury to others in the vicinity of the defendant's conduct (Wolfe v. State, 2011).

Example of Disorderly Conduct Act

David and Daniel leave a party in a quiet neighborhood at three in the morning. Both are inebriated. After walking a couple of blocks and telling stories, they begin singing loudly with their arms wrapped around each other. David stumbles and trips Daniel, who falls heavily to the sidewalk. Daniel gets up and starts screaming and swearing at David, challenging him to fight. David yells back, "Bring it on!" David pushes Daniel, he pushes back, and they begin punching and kicking. In this instance, David and Daniel have probably committed *three* separate disorderly conduct offenses. When David and Daniel began singing at three in the morning on a quiet street, they made a loud and unreasonable noise. When they challenged each other to fight, they uttered threats or stated fighting words. When they engaged in a fistfight, they committed fighting, or created a hazardous condition. Thus David and Daniel are most likely subject to a prosecution for and conviction of three counts of disorderly conduct in many jurisdictions.

Disorderly Conduct Intent

The criminal intent element required for disorderly conduct in many jurisdictions is the **specific intent** or **purposely** to cause public inconvenience, annoyance, or alarm, or the **reckless** intent to cause a *risk* thereof (Ala. Code § 13A-11-7, 2011). The Model Penal Code has the same criminal intent requirement (Model Penal Code § 250.2(1)).

Example of Disorderly Conduct Intent

Review the example given in Section 12 "Example of Disorderly Conduct Act" with David and Daniel. David and Daniel may not have had the **specific intent** to cause public inconvenience, annoyance, or alarm; however, their behavior in a quiet neighborhood late at night displays the **reckless** intent to cause a risk of such inconvenience, annoyance, or alarm. Although David and Daniel are inebriated, recall from Chapter 6 "Criminal Defenses, Part 2" that intoxication is *not* generally a defense to a reckless intent crime. Thus a trier of fact could find that David and Daniel have the appropriate criminal intent for disorderly conduct, and they may both be subject to conviction of this offense.

Disorderly Conduct Attendant Circumstance

In many jurisdictions, disorderly conduct requires the **attendant circumstance** that the conduct occur in a public place (Tex. Penal Code § 42.01, 2011). This goes along with the purposeful or reckless intent to inconvenience, annoy, or alarm the public, or create a risk thereof. The Model Penal Code defines public as "affecting or likely to affect persons in a place to which the public or a substantial group has access...highways, transport facilities, schools, prisons, apartment houses, places of business or amusement, or any neighborhood" (Model Penal Code § 250.2).

Example of Disorderly Conduct Attendant Circumstance

Review the example in Section 12 "Example of Disorderly Conduct Act" with David and Daniel. David and Daniel commit their acts of loud and unreasonable noise, threats, fighting words, fighting, and creating a hazardous condition on a **sidewalk** in a **neighborhood**. Thus in jurisdictions that require the disorderly conduct attendant circumstance of a public place, David and Daniel may be subject to prosecution for and conviction of this offense. If David and Daniel committed exactly the same acts in a private residence located on fifty acres with no neighbors for miles, the attendant circumstance for disorderly conduct would be *lacking*, along with the *criminal intent* to annoy, inconvenience, or alarm the public.

Potential Constitutional Challenges to Disorderly Conduct Statutes

Because disorderly conduct statutes often criminalize **obscene gestures** and **words**, **threats**, and **fighting words**, they are subject to constitutional challenges under the First and Fourteenth Amendments. However, not all speech is protected under the First Amendment. As Chapter 3 "Constitutional Protections" discusses in detail, it is constitutional to regulate *obscenity*, *true threats*, and *fighting words*. Nonetheless, any statute criminalizing speech or expression is subject to strict scrutiny, must be narrowly drafted, and supported by a compelling government interest. Thus two common grounds for challenging disorderly conduct statutes are **void for vagueness** and **overbreadth** (Colten v. Kentucky, 2011).

Example of a Disorderly Conduct Statute That Is Unconstitutional

A state legislature enacts a disorderly conduct statute that prohibits "making rude and annoying comments to another." This statute is most unlikely unconstitutional under the First and Fourteenth Amendments. The words *rude* and *annoying* are ambiguous, which could lead to uneven application by law enforcement and a failure to provide adequate notice to the public of what is criminal. Therefore, the statute can be stricken as **void for vagueness**. In addition, rude and annoying comments are not necessarily fighting words, true threats, or obscenity, so they could be protected under the First Amendment. This means that the statute could also be stricken as **overbroad** because it includes protected and unprotected conduct within its parameters. For a fuller and more detailed description of void for vagueness and overbreadth constitutional challenges, please refer to Chapter 3 "Constitutional Protections".

Figure 12.1 Potential Constitutional Challenges to Disorderly Conduct Statutes

Disorderly Conduct Grading

As stated previously, disorderly conduct is a low-level offense that is typically **graded** as a misdemeanor (N.C. Gen. Stat. § 14-132). The Model Penal Code grades disorderly conduct as a petty misdemeanor if the defendant's purpose is to cause substantial harm or serious inconvenience or if the defendant persists with his or her conduct after a warning. Otherwise, the Model Penal Code grades disorderly conduct as a violation (Model Penal Code § 250.2(2)).

Vagrancy and Loitering

Although the government technically does not have an interest in punishing individuals for who they are, such as an impoverished person or a transient, the public perception of law enforcement is often affected by the presence of so-called vagrants and panhandlers in any given area. Thus virtually every jurisdiction has statutes punishing either vagrancy or loitering. However, these statutes are subject to constitutional attack if they are **void for vagueness**, **overbroad**, or target **status**.

Historically, vagrancy statutes were broadly drafted to allow law enforcement considerable discretion in arresting the unemployed, gamblers, drug addicts, alcoholics, and those who frequented houses of prostitution or other locations of ill repute. In a sense, vagrancy statutes attempted to incapacitate individuals *before* they engaged in criminal activity, to ensure the safety and security of any given area.

In 1972, the US Supreme Court struck down a Florida vagrancy statute in *Papachristou v. City of Jacksonville*, 405 U.S. 156 (1972). The Court held that the statute, which prohibited night walking, living off one's spouse, and frequenting bars or liquor stores was void for vagueness and violated the due process clause in the Fourteenth Amendment. Thereafter, many states repealed or modified vagrancy statutes in lieu of more precisely drafted statutes prohibiting specific criminal conduct such as loitering. The Model Penal Code prohibits public drunkenness and drug incapacitation (Model Penal Code § 250.5) and loitering or prowling (Model Penal Code § 250.6). To summarize US Supreme Court precedent refining loitering statutes: it is unconstitutional to target those who are unemployed (Edwards v. California, 2011) or to enact a statute that is vague, such as a statute that criminalizes loitering in an area "with no apparent purpose," (City of Chicago v. Morales, 2011) or without the ability to provide law enforcement with "credible and reliable identification" (Kolender v. Lawson, 2011).

In a jurisdiction that criminalizes loitering, the **criminal act** element is typically loitering, wandering, or remaining, with the **specific intent** or **purposely** to gamble, beg, or engage in prostitution (Ala. Code § 13A-11-9, 2011). An **attendant circumstance** could specify the location where the conduct takes place, such as a school or transportation facility (Ariz. Rev. Stat. § 13-2905, 2011). Another common attendant circumstance is being masked in a public place while loitering, with an exception for defendants going to a masquerade party or participating in a public parade (Ala. Code § 13A-11-9, 2011). The Model Penal Code prohibits loitering or prowling in a place, at a time, or in a manner not usual for law-abiding individuals under circumstances that warrant alarm for the safety of persons or property in the vicinity (Model Penal Code § 250.6). Loitering is generally **graded** as a misdemeanor (Ariz. Rev. Stat. § 13-2905, 2011) or a violation (Ala. Code § 13A-11-9, 2011). The Model Penal Code grades loitering as a violation (Model Penal Code § 250.6).

Figure 12.2 Crack the Code

Crack the Code

Compare the following state laws:

La. Rev. Stat. Ann. § 14:107: Vagrancy

The following persons are and shall be guilty of vagrancy:

(1) Habitual drunkards; or

(2) Persons who live in houses of ill fame or who habitually associate with prostitutes; or

(3) Able-bodied persons who beg or solicit alms, provided that this article shall not apply to persons soliciting alms for bona fide religious, charitable or eleemosynary organizations with the authorization thereof; or

(4) Habitual gamblers or persons who for the most part maintain themselves by gambling; or

(5) Able-bodied persons without lawful means of support who do not seek employment and take employment when it is available to them; or

(6) Able-bodied persons of the age of majority who obtain their support gratis from persons receiving old age pensions or from persons receiving welfare assistance from the state; or

(7) Persons who loaf the streets habitually or who frequent the streets habitually at late or unusual hours of the night, or who loiter around any public place of assembly, without lawful business or reason to be present;

Ala. Code § 13A-11-9: Loitering

a) A person commits the crime of loitering if he:

(1) Loiters, remains or wanders about in a public place for the purpose of begging; or

(2) Loiters or remains in a public place for the purpose of gambling; or

(3) Loiters or remains in a public place for the purpose of engaging or soliciting another person to engage in prostitution or deviate sexual intercourse; or

(4) Being masked, loiters, remains or congregates in a public place; or

(5) Loiters or remains in or about a school, college or university building or grounds after having been told to leave by any authorized official of such school, college or university, and not having any reason or relationship involving custody of or responsibility for a pupil or any other specific, legitimate reason for being there, and not having written permission from a school, college or university administrator; of value of another without authorization, or by threat or deception, and:

Louisiana has a vagrancy statute subject to constitutional challenge pursuant to *Papchristou*; Alabama has a more precise loitering statute.

Many jurisdictions also criminalize panhandling or **begging**. Panhandling statutes essentially criminalize speech, so they must be narrowly tailored to avoid successful constitutional challenges based on the First Amendment, void for vagueness, or overbreadth. Constitutional panhandling statutes generally proscribe aggressive conduct (Gresham v. Peterson, 2011) or conduct that blocks public access or the normal flow of traffic.

Sit-Lie Laws

One modern statutory approach to preventing homeless individuals and transients from congregating in cities and affecting the quality of life or the prosperity of businesses and tourism are sit-lie laws. Sit-lie laws prohibit sitting or lying on public streets and sidewalks and thereby encourage individuals to move about, rather than block access to businesses, roadways, or transportation facilities. If precisely drafted, sit-lie laws could resemble constitutional **loitering** statutes, substituting sitting or lying down for the criminal act of loitering, wandering, or remaining. However, these statutes are susceptible to the same constitutional challenges as vagrancy and loitering statutes because they target the impoverished, addicts, and the unemployed.

Seattle was the first city in the United States to enact a sit-lie ordinance in 1993 that prohibited sitting or lying on a public sidewalk between the hours of 7 a.m. and 9 p.m. in Seattle's downtown area. The ordinance was attacked and ultimately upheld by the US Court of Appeals for the Ninth Circuit in 1996 (Knight, H., 2011). Los Angeles thereafter enacted a more comprehensive ordinance that banned sitting, lying, or sleeping on public streets and sidewalks at all times and in all places within Los Angeles city limits. This ordinance was stricken by the same court as unconstitutional **cruel and unusual punishment** pursuant to the Eighth Amendment (Jones v. City of Los Angeles, 2011). The court held that the homeless in Los Angeles far outnumbered the amount of space available in homeless shelters, and therefore the ordinance punished defendants for conduct that was *involuntary*. Portland followed Los Angeles with a sidewalk-obstruction ordinance, requiring individuals to keep their personal belongings within two feet of their bodies. This ordinance was stricken as **void for vagueness** in 2009 (Davis, M., 2011).

The most recent enactment of a sit-lie ordinance took place in San Francisco in 2010. The San Francisco ordinance is modeled after the Seattle ordinance and prohibits sitting or lying on a public sidewalk in the city limits between 7 a.m. and 9 p.m., with exceptions for medical emergencies, protests, or those who have disabilities (San Francisco Police Code § 16.8, 2011). The first offense is an infraction, and the second offense is a misdemeanor (San Francisco Police Code § 16.8, 2011). If the San Francisco ordinance successfully reduces the presence of transients and is upheld as constitutional, other cities that desire the same results could soon follow suit.

Figure 12.3 Potential Constitutional Challenges to Loitering, Panhandling, and Sit-Lie Laws

Loitering	
Panhandling	
Sit-Lie	

Table 12.1 Comparing Disorderly Conduct, Loitering, and Sit-Lie Laws

Crime	Criminal Act	Criminal Intent	Attendant Circumstance
Disorderly conduct	Unreasonable noise, obscene utterance or gesture, fighting, threats, fighting words, creating a hazardous condition	Specific or purposely or recklessly to disturb the public or create a risk thereof	Act takes place in public
Loitering	Loitering, wandering, remaining	Specific or purposely to beg, gamble, solicit prostitution	Act takes place near a school, transportation facility: the defendant is masked
Sit-lie law	Sitting or lying down	Strict liability*	Act takes place between certain times of day, in public, on a sidewalk, or on a street
***Exceptions for medical emergencies, people who have disabilities, protests**			

Key Takeaways

- The criminal act element required for disorderly conduct is either when the defendant (1) makes a loud and unreasonable noise, obscene utterance, or gesture, (2) engages in fighting or threatening, or states fighting words, or (3) creates a hazardous condition by an act that does not serve a legitimate purpose.
- The criminal intent element required for disorderly conduct in many jurisdictions is the specific intent or purposely to cause public inconvenience, annoyance, or alarm, or the reckless intent to cause a risk thereof.
- The disorderly conduct attendant circumstance is that the conduct occurs in a public place.
- Disorderly conduct statutes can be constitutionally challenged under the First or Fourteenth Amendments as void for vagueness or overbroad.

- Disorderly conduct is typically graded as a misdemeanor.
- Vagrancy statutes are subject to constitutional challenges if they are void for vagueness, overbroad, or target status.
- Loitering statutes are subject to constitutional challenges if they target the unemployed or are void for vagueness.
- The loitering criminal act element is typically loitering, wandering, or remaining, with the specific intent or purposely to gamble, beg, or engage in prostitution. An attendant circumstance could specify the location the conduct takes place, such as a school or transportation facility. Another common attendant circumstance is being masked in a public place while loitering, with an exception for defendants going to a masquerade party or participating in a public parade. Loitering is typically graded as a misdemeanor or a violation.
- Sit-lie laws typically prohibit sitting or lying on a public sidewalk or street, instead of loitering, wandering, or remaining like loitering statutes.

Exercises

Answer the following questions. Check your answers using the answer key at the end of the chapter.

A city enacts an ordinance that prohibits standing or remaining in a crosswalk for an extended period with a sign. What are three potential constitutional challenges to this ordinance? Can you identify a government interest supporting it?

Read *State v. Russell*, 890 A.2d 453 (2006). Why did the Supreme Court of Rhode Island reinstate a complaint against the defendant for disorderly conduct in this case? The case is available at this link: http://scholar.google.com/scholar_case?case=15220603438033851670&q=State+v+Russell&hl=en&as_sdt=2,5.

Read *People v. Hoffstead*, 905 N.Y.S.2d 736 (2010). Why did the New York Supreme Court overturn the defendant's conviction for loitering in this case? The case is available at this link: http://scholar.google.com/scholar_case?case=16147172189959232373&q=People+v.+Hoffstead&hl=en&as_sdt=2,5.

References

18 Pa. C. S. § 5503, accessed April 2, 2011, http://law.onecle.com/pennsylvania/crimes-and-offenses/00.055.003.000.html.

Ala. Code § 13A-11-7, accessed April 3, 2011, http://law.onecle.com/alabama/criminal-code/13A-11-7.html.

Ala. Code § 13A-11-9, accessed April 5, 2011, http://law.onecle.com/alabama/criminal-code/13A-11-9.html.

Ariz. Rev. Stat. § 13-2905, accessed April 5, 2011, http://law.onecle.com/arizona/criminal-code/13-2905.html.

City of Chicago v. Morales, accessed April 5, 2011, 527 U.S. 41 (1999), http://supreme.justia.com/us/527/41/case.html.

Colten v. Kentucky, 407 U.S. 104 (1972), accessed April 3, 2011, http://scholar.google.com/scholar_case?case=7926620308068158831&q=Colten+v.+Kentucky&hl=en&as_sdt=2,5.

Davis, M., "Sit/Lie Law Unconstitutional," *Portland Mercury* website, accessed April 5, 2011, http://blogtown.portlandmercury.com/BlogtownPDX/archives/2009/02/19/judge_rules_sit_lie_law_uncons.

Edwards v. California, 314 U.S. 160 (1941), accessed April 5, 2011, http://scholar.google.com/scholar_case?case=6778891532287614638&hl=en&as_sdt=2&as_vis=1&oi=scholarr.

Gresham v. Peterson, 225 F.3d 899 (2000), accessed April 5, 2011, http://scholar.google.com/scholar_case?case=12046859312956994237&q=%22Gresham+v.+Peterson%22&hl=en&as_sdt=2,5.

Haw. Rev. Stat. § 711-1101(2), accessed April 2, 2011, http://www.capitol.hawaii.gov/hrscurrent/vol14_Ch0701-0853/HRS0711/HRS_0711-1101.htm.

Jones v. City of Los Angeles, 444 F.3d 1118 (2006), accessed April 5, 2011, http://scholar.google.com/scholar_case?case=4259488333208893136&q=Jones+v.+City+of+Los+Angeles+2005&hl=en&as_sdt=2,5&as_ylo=2004.

Knight, H., "San Francisco Looks to Seattle: Did Sidewalk Sitting Ban Help?" seattlepi.com website, accessed April 5, 2011, http://www.seattlepi.com/default/article/San-Francisco-looks-to-Seattle-Did-sidewalk-888774.php.

Kolender v. Lawson, accessed April 5, 2011, 461 U.S. 352 (1983), http://supreme.justia.com/us/461/352.

N.C. Gen. Stat. § 14-132, http://law.onecle.com/north-carolina/14-criminal-law/14-132.html.

San Francisco Police Code § 16.8, accessed April 5, 2011, http://www.sfgov2.org/ftp/uploadedfiles/elections/candidates/Nov2010_CivilSidewalks.pdf.

Tex. Penal Code § 42.01, accessed April 2, 2011, http://law.onecle.com/texas/penal/42.01.00.html.

Wolfe v. State, 24 P.3d 1252 (2001), accessed April 2, 2011, http://scholar.google.com/scholar_case?case=8611678948602739716&q=disorderly+conduct+%22hazardous+condition%22&hl=en&as_sdt=2,5&as_ylo=2000.
CC licensed content, Shared previously

- Criminal Law. **Provided by**: University of Minnesota Libraries Publishing . **Located at**: http://open.lib.umn.edu/criminallaw/. **License**: *CC BY-NC-SA: Attribution-NonCommercial-ShareAlike*

12.2 Crimes Targeting Group Conduct

Learning Objectives

Define the elements of unlawful assembly and failure to disperse.
Identify potential constitutional challenges to unlawful assembly and failure to disperse statutes.
Analyze unlawful assembly and failure to disperse grading.
Define the elements of riot, and analyze riot grading and the potential for constitutional challenges to riot statutes.
Define criminal gang and criminal gang member.
Compare gang participation and gang-enhancement statutes.
Analyze two civil responses to the criminal gang problem.
Identify potential constitutional challenges to gang activity statutes.

Group conduct, if criminal, can enhance the potential for violence and injury and is punishable as the crimes of unlawful assembly, riot, or criminal gangs. However, the right to *peacefully* **assemble** is guaranteed in the First Amendment, so statutes codifying these offenses can be subject to constitutional attack similar to disorderly conduct, vagrancy, and loitering statutes. In addition, the problem of criminal gangs has proven to be so stubborn that it has produced some novel criminal *and civil* responses. The following sections discuss group activity offenses as well as their potential constitutional defenses.

Unlawful Assembly and Failure to Disperse

Unlawful assembly can be the predicate offense to riot, which is discussed shortly. The elements required for unlawful assembly are the assembling (Ala. Code § 13A-11-5, 2011) or meeting (Fla. Stat. Ann. § 870.02, 2011) (**criminal act**) of a group, with the **specific intent** or **purposely** to commit a breach of the peace, some other unlawful act (Fla. Stat. Ann. § 870.02, 2011), or riot (Ala. Code § 13A-11-5, 2011). Some jurisdictions and the Model Penal Code punish the failure to disperse (**criminal act**) when a peace officer or public servant orders a group participating in disorderly conduct likely to cause substantial harm, serious annoyance, or alarm to do so (Mass. Gen. Laws ch. 269 § 1, 2011) (Model Penal Code § 250.1(2)). The criminal intent element for failure to disperse is **general intent** or **knowingly** (N.J. Stat. § 2C:33-1, 2011) (Model Penal Code § 250.1(2)).

Jurisdictions vary as to the **attendant circumstance** for unlawful assembly and failure to disperse, which is the size of the group. Some common group minimums are **two** (Cal. Penal Code § 407, 2011), **three** (Fla. Stat. Ann. § 870.02, 2011), or **five** (N.J. Stat. § 2C:33-1, 2011). The Model Penal Code requires three or more persons (Model Penal Code § 250.1(2)).

Example of Unlawful Assembly and Failure to

Disperse

Six neighbors are sitting on their porches, peacefully chatting. One of the neighbors, Buck, notices a pro-choice group with signs in the park across the street. Annoyed, Buck tells the group, "Let's go show those losers what it's like to fear for your life!" He marches angrily over to the park, and the other neighbors follow. Buck begins chanting, "How would you like to be aborted?" and the other neighbors join in. The individuals in the pro-choice group stand their ground, and the decibel of the chanting increases. Buck and his neighbors form a ring around the group and move in closer, almost touching the individuals and their signs. A park ranger hears the noise, walks over to Buck and his neighbors, and tells them to "move along." Buck spits at the ranger's feet and starts up the chant again. The other neighbors laugh and join him.

In this scenario, Buck and his neighbors have most likely committed unlawful assembly and failure to disperse in many jurisdictions. Buck and his neighbors number six, which generally meets the minimum unlawful assembly and failure to disperse attendant circumstance requirement. When Buck and his neighbors go to the park in a group, they are assembling. Their chant, "How would you like to be aborted?" is directed at a pro-choice group, so it is evident that Buck and his neighbors have the specific intent or purposely to cause a breach of the peace. In addition, the increasing decibel of the chanting and the neighbors' close proximity to the pro-choice group indicates an intent to intimidate, threaten, and possibly commit an unlawful act such as false imprisonment, assault, battery, or riot. When the park ranger, who is most likely a peace officer, tells Buck and his neighbors to "move along," he is ordering them to disperse. Buck's response in spitting at the ranger's feet and starting up the chant again is probably a failure to disperse committed with general intent or knowingly. Thus Buck and his neighbors may be subject to prosecution for and conviction of *both* of these offenses in many jurisdictions.

Potential Constitutional Challenges to Unlawful Assembly and Failure to Disperse Statutes

The offenses of unlawful assembly and failure to disperse target conduct that, if *peaceful*, is protected by the First Amendment. Therefore, similar to disorderly conduct offenses, statutes proscribing this type of conduct are subject to strict scrutiny, must be narrowly tailored, and must be supported by a compelling government interest, or they are vulnerable to attack under the **First Amendment** (People v. Sanchez, 2011) or as **void for vagueness** and **overbroad**.

Figure 12.4 Potential Constitutional Challenges to Unlawful Assembly and Failure to Disperse Statutes

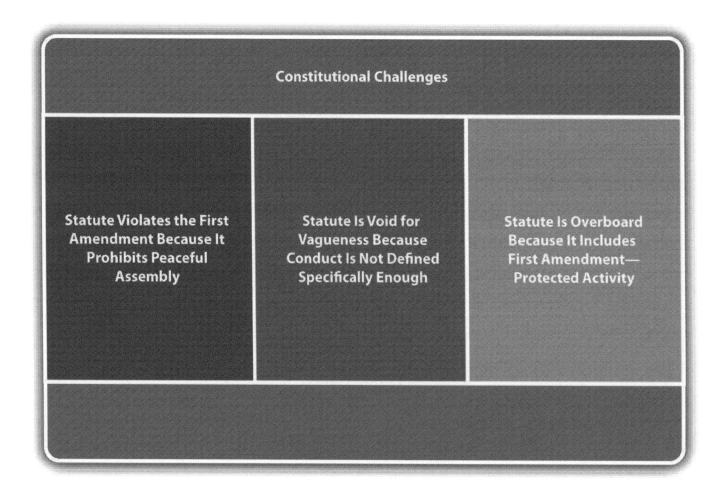

Constitutional Challenges

| Statute Violates the First Amendment Because It Prohibits Peaceful Assembly | Statute Is Void for Vagueness Because Conduct Is Not Defined Specifically Enough | Statute Is Overboard Because It Includes First Amendment—Protected Activity |

Unlawful Assembly and Failure to Disperse Grading

Unlawful assembly and failure to disperse are generally **graded** as misdemeanors (Ala. Code § 13A-11-5, 2011). The Model Penal Code grades failure to disperse as a misdemeanor (Model Penal Code § 250.1(2)).

Riot

Riot can be the result of an unlawful assembly that escalates, an **incitement to riot** (discussed in Chapter 3 "Constitutional Protections"), or can occur spontaneously without any planning or predicate activity. The **criminal act** element required for riot in many jurisdictions is group commission of an unlawful act of violence or a lawful act in a violent and tumultuous manner (Ga. Code tit. 16 § 16-11-30, 2011). The Model Penal Code criminalizes riot when a group participates in a course of disorderly conduct (Model Penal Code § 250.1). The criminal intent element for riot varies, depending on the jurisdiction. Some jurisdictions and the Model Penal Code require **specific intent** or **purposely** to commit or facilitate a felony or misdemeanor, or to prevent or coerce official action, or **general intent** or **knowledge** that anyone plans to use a firearm or deadly weapon (N.J. Stat. § 2C:33-1, 2011) (Model Penal Code § 250.1). Others make riot a **strict liability** offense (Cal. Penal Code § 404, 2011; Ga. Code tit. 16 § 16-11-30). In many jurisdictions, riot also has the requirement that the defendant(s) be the **factual** and **legal cause** of **harm**, which is public terror and alarm or a risk thereof (Ala. Code § 13A-11-3, 2011).

Jurisdictions vary as to the **attendant circumstance** for riot, which is the size of the group. Some common group minimums are **two** (Ga. Code tit. 16 § 16-11-30, 2011), **five** (N.J. Stat. § 2C:33-1, 2011), and **six** (Ala. Code § 13A-11-3, 2011). The Model Penal Code requires **three** or more persons (Model Penal Code § 250.1). Riot is **graded** as a misdemeanor (Ala. Code § 13A-11-3, 2011), or a felony if a firearm is used (Va. Code Ann. § 18.2-405,

2011) or there is property damage or physical injury to an individual other than the defendants (N.Y. Penal § 240.06, 2011). The Model Penal Code grades riot as a felony of the third degree (Model Penal Code § 250.1).

Example of Riot

Review the example with Buck and his neighbors in Section 12 "Example of Unlawful Assembly and Failure to Disperse". Assume that after the park ranger orders Buck and his neighbors to disperse, Buck spits at the ranger's feet, continues chanting, and thereafter becomes so enraged that he grabs a sign out of one of the pro-choice individual's hands and begins beating him over the head with it. The other neighbors follow suit and within minutes they are all wielding signs and hitting the pro-choice individuals with them. In this scenario, Buck and his neighbors have most likely committed riot. Buck and his neighbors number six, which meets the minimum group requirement in many riot statutes. Buck and his neighbors have also *assaulted* and *battered* some of the pro-choice individuals, which are unlawful acts of violence. The statement made by Buck about showing the pro-choice group what it means to fear for your life indicates a specific intent or purposely to commit a felony or misdemeanor, which is the intent requirement in many jurisdictions. If the riot statute in Buck's state requires factual and legal causation and the harm of public terror and alarm, the beating constitutes the causation and harm requirement. Thus Buck and his neighbors' conduct probably falls within the parameters of most riot statutes, and Buck and his neighbors may be subject to prosecution for and conviction of this offense in many jurisdictions.

Potential Constitutional Challenges to Riot Statutes

Because statutes criminalizing riot include the requirement of *force* or *violence*, they do not target protected conduct under the First Amendment and are not as prone to a constitutional challenge. Of course, any criminal statute must be precisely drafted so that it is not void for vagueness. However, riot statutes are not generally subject to strict scrutiny because the First Amendment does not include forceful or violent expression within the definition of speech.

Rodney King Riots Video

KTLA News, April 30, 1992, 6:50 p.m., King Riots

News clips of the riots that occurred subsequent to the Rodney King trial are shown in this video: (click to see video)

Criminal Gangs

Many jurisdictions have statutes, both criminal and civil, that address the ongoing dilemma of criminal gangs. However, gang activity remains a problem in major cities and even smaller, rural areas. Criminal gangs can create a stigma that attaches to a location, affecting property values and residents' attitudes about the effectiveness of law enforcement and the justice system in general. Commentators and legislators differ as to the most effective remedies for the gang problem, leading to a plethora of diverse statutory responses.

What follows is a discussion of modern statutes targeting gang activity and the potential constitutional challenges.

Criminal Gang Definitions

It is important for a jurisdiction's gang statute to define criminal gang and criminal gang member precisely, to avoid constitutional challenges under the First Amendment or void for vagueness and overbreadth. This is because gang membership involves assembly, which, if *peaceful,* is protected under the First Amendment.

Federal law defines a criminal street gang as an ongoing group, club, organization, or association of **five** or more that has as one of its primary purposes the commission of specific criminal offenses or activities that affect interstate or foreign commerce (18 U.S.C. 521(a), 2011). Federal law defines a gang member as someone who participates in a criminal street gang with the **general intent** or **knowledge** that its members engage in a continuing series of specified crimes, or an individual who **intends to promote** or **further** the felonious activities of the criminal street gang (18 U.S.C. 521(d), 2011). One representative state statutory definition of criminal gang is a group of **three** or more persons who have in common a name, identifying sign, symbol, tattoo, style of dress, or use of hand signs and who have committed or attempted to commit specified crimes for the benefit of the group (Alaska Stat. § 11.81.900, 2011). Criminal gang member could be statutorily defined as any person who engages in a pattern of criminal gang activity and who meets two or more of the following criteria: (1) admits to gang membership; (2) is identified as a gang member; (3) resides in or frequents a particular gang's area and adopts its style of dress, use of hand signs, or tattoos; (3) associates with known gang members; or (4) has been arrested more than once in the company of identified gang members for offenses consistent with gang activity (Idaho Code Ann. § 18-8502(2), 2011).

Example of Criminal Gang Definitions

The North Side Boys are a group of **fifty-five** members who have a special **tattoo**, wear the **colors** black and white daily, and pride themselves on their **illegal** controlled substances distribution. Mike decides he wants to be a North Side Boy. Mike participates in a special initiation process that includes selling a specified quantity of an illegal controlled substance in a certain location over a period of two weeks. After Mike completes the initiation, he gets the North Side Boys' tattoo, wears the North Side Boys' colors daily, and spends all his time with the North Side Boys, hanging out and also contributing to their illegal activities. The North Side Boys probably meets the criteria for a **criminal gang**, and Mike is most likely a **criminal gang member** under many modern statutes. The North Side Boys has an identifiable tattoo and style of dress and furthers a criminal activity, which is the distribution of illegal controlled substances. Mike can be identified as a gang member by other North Side Boys members, frequents the North Side Boys' gang area, and adopts the gang's style of dress and tattoos along with furthering its criminal enterprise. Thus the North Side Boys and Mike fit the definition of criminal gang and gang member in many jurisdictions, and Mike may be subject to prosecution for and conviction of criminal gang activity if he commits crimes at the direction of or in furtherance of the gang, as is analyzed in Section 12 "Criminal Gang Activity".

Criminal Gang Activity

States generally criminalize gang participation (Ohio Rev. Code Ann. § 2923.42, 2011), *enhance* the *penalty* for a crime when it is committed in furtherance of a gang (Fla. Stat. Ann. § 874.04, 2011), or **both** (Cal. Penal Code § 186.22). If a state enacts a gang participation statute, the **criminal act** element is generally described as actively participating in a criminal gang and promoting, furthering, or assisting in any felony, with the **general intent** or **knowingly** that members of the gang engage in a pattern of criminal gang activity (Del. Code Ann. tit. 11 § 616, 2011). Gang participation is generally **graded** as a felony (Del. Code Ann. tit. 11 § 616, 2011). Gang enhancement statutes enhance the defendant's sentence for actually committing a misdemeanor or felony with the **specific intent** or **purposely** to benefit, promote, or further the interests of the criminal gang (Fla. Stat. Ann. § 874.04, 2011). Some jurisdictions only provide gang enhancement for the commission of a felony (Del. Code. Ann. tit. 11 § 616, 2011).

Example of Criminal Gang Activity

Review the example with Mike and the North Side Boys given in Section 12 "Example of Criminal Gang Definitions". Assume that Mike resumes selling illegal controlled substances *at the behest* of the North Side Boys after his initiation and is arrested. If the state where Mike sells illegal controlled substances has a gang participation statute and grades the crime of sale of illegal controlled substances as a felony, Mike could be prosecuted for and convicted of this crime. He furthered and assisted in the North Side Boys' sale of illegal controlled substances with the general intent or knowingly that members of the North Side Boys engaged in this pattern of criminal gang activity. If the state also has a gang enhancement statute, Mike could have his sentence for sale of illegal controlled substances *enhanced* because he committed the sale of illegal controlled substances in furtherance of the criminal gang. In either situation, Mike will be punished *more severely* for the sale of illegal controlled substances than an individual defendant who sells illegal controlled substances on his or her own, rather than at the direction or in furtherance of a criminal gang.

Figure 12.5 Diagram of Typical Modern Gang Statutes

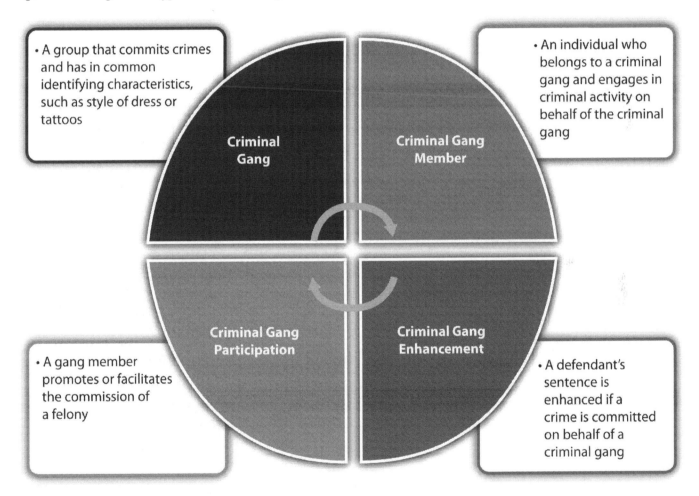

Civil Responses to Gang Activity

As stated previously, the problem of criminal gangs is challenging and has proven resistant to criminal remedies. Thus many jurisdictions have also enacted civil gang control statutes, along with resorting to the remedy of civil gang injunctions to try to curb the multitude of harms that gangs inflict.

Civil gang control statutes generally provide for damages, often enhanced, for coercion, intimidation, threats, or other harm caused by a gang or gang member (Fla. Stat. Ann. § 874.06, 2011). A common provision of civil gang control statutes is the ability of a resident *or state agency* to sue as a plaintiff (Fla. Stat. Ann. § 874.06, 2011).

Figure 12.6 Example of a Civil Gang Control Statute

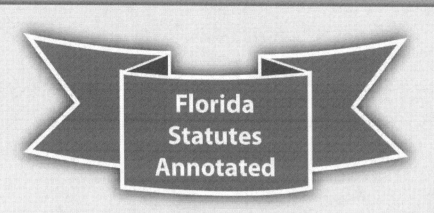

(1) A person or organization establishing, by clear and convincing evidence, coercion, intimidation, threats, or other harm to that person or organization in violation of this chapter has a civil cause of action for treble damages, an injunction, or any other appropriate relief in law or equity. Upon prevailing, the plaintiff may recover attorney's fees in the trial and appellate courts and the costs of investigation and litigation that are reasonably incurred.

(2)(a) For purposes of this subsection, the term "state" includes any of the state's agencies, instrumentalities, subdivisions, or municipalities, and includes, but is not limited to, state attorneys and the Office of Statewide Prosecution of the Department of Legal Affairs.

(b) In addition to any remedies provided for by ss. 60.05 and 823.05, the state has a civil cause of action against any person or organization if it proves by clear and convincing evidence that it has been injured by reason of a violation of this chapter by the person or organization. The state has a civil cause of action for treble damages, injunctive relief, or any other relief in law or equity which the court deems appropriate. If the state prevails, it may also recover attorney's fees in the trial and appellate courts and the costs of investigation and litigation that are reasonably incurred.

Civil gang injunctions (CGIs) are precisely drafted orders prohibiting gang members from associating with other gang members or entering certain areas known for gang activity (Tex. Penal Code § 125.065, 2011). A state agency or an individual resident can typically make a motion requesting a CGI (Tex. Penal Code § 125.064, 2011). The basis for a CGI motion is the tort of public nuisance, which requires proof that the gang is disturbing the enjoyment of life and property for those living in the community (People v. Acuna, 2011). Common provisions of CGIs are a prohibition on associating with known gang members, wearing gang colors, flashing gang hand signs, or loitering in areas known for gang activity (Shiner, M., 2011). Violation of a CGI could constitute the crime of **contempt**, resulting in fines or incarceration (Tex. Penal Code § 125.066, 2011).

Example of Civil Responses to Gang Activity

Review the example with Mike and the North Side Boys in Section 12 "Example of Criminal Gang Definitions". Mike and the North Side Boys are subject to a criminal prosecution for gang **participation** for their sale of illegal controlled substances. They also are subject to gang *enhancements* for any felony committed at the direction or in furtherance of the North Side Boys. In addition, if the state where Mike and the North Side Boys are located has statutes providing **civil** remedies and **CGI**s, both Mike and the North Side Boys members are subject to a civil suit for damages if they coerce, intimidate, or injure another. They also are subject to an injunction constraining their ability to meet, associate, wear black and white, flash gang hand signs, or loiter in certain areas. If a CGI is in place, and Mike or the North Side Boys violate it, a potential exists for criminal charges of **contempt**, leading to fines or incarceration.

Colton Gang Injunction

News Story of the Colton Civil Gang Injunction

The civil gang injunction in Colton, California, is discussed in this video:
(click to see video)

Potential Constitutional Challenges to Gang Statutes

Gang activity and gang association require assembly, which, if *peaceful*, is protected by the First Amendment. Thus statutes proscribing gang conduct are subject to attack under the **First Amendment** or **void for vagueness** and **overbreadth**. CGIs have the same constitutional concerns as criminal gang activity statutes because their violation can lead to a criminal prosecution for contempt (People v. Acuna, 2011).

In *City of Chicago v. Morales*, 527 U.S. 41 (1999), the US Supreme Court struck down Chicago's Gang Congregation Ordinance as void for vagueness. The ordinance prohibited criminal street gang members from "loitering in public." The term *loitering* was defined as remaining in any one place with *no apparent purpose*. When a Chicago law enforcement officer observed a gang member loitering, he was obligated to order the gang member to disperse, and if the gang member refused, the gang member was subject to arrest for violating the ordinance. The Court held that the ordinance did not give the public notice of what was criminal, as required by the due process clause of the Fourteenth Amendment, and allowed too much discretion to law enforcement to unevenly enforce its provisions.

Under *Morales*, modern statutes targeting gang activity and association must precisely define criminal conduct, avoid vague terms such as "no apparent purpose," and ensure that First Amendment protected activity is not included within the statute's reach. CGIs should support a significant government interest, be narrowly tailored to avoid constitutionally protected activity, and be buttressed by evidence that the CGI is the least restrictive means to carry out the interest stated (Shiner, M., 2011).

Figure 12.7 Potential Constitutional Challenges to Statutes Targeting Gangs

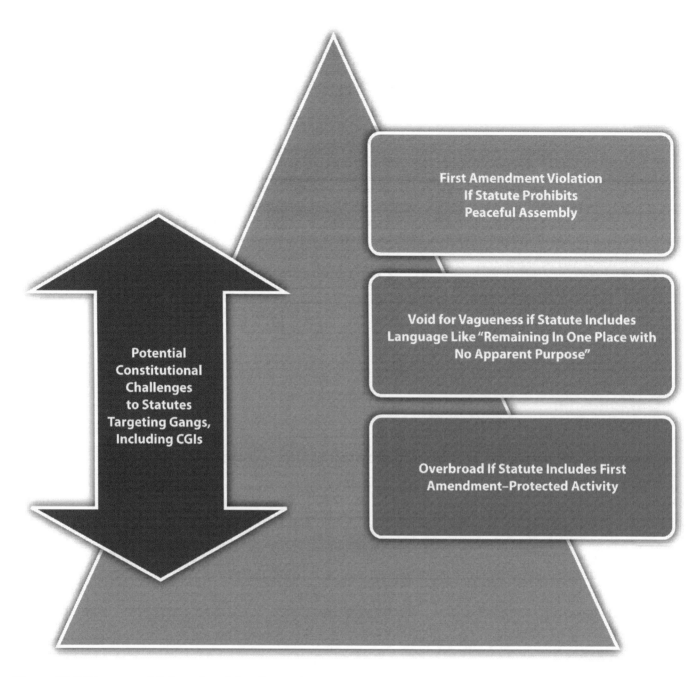

Figure 12.8 Diagram of Crimes Involving Group Activity

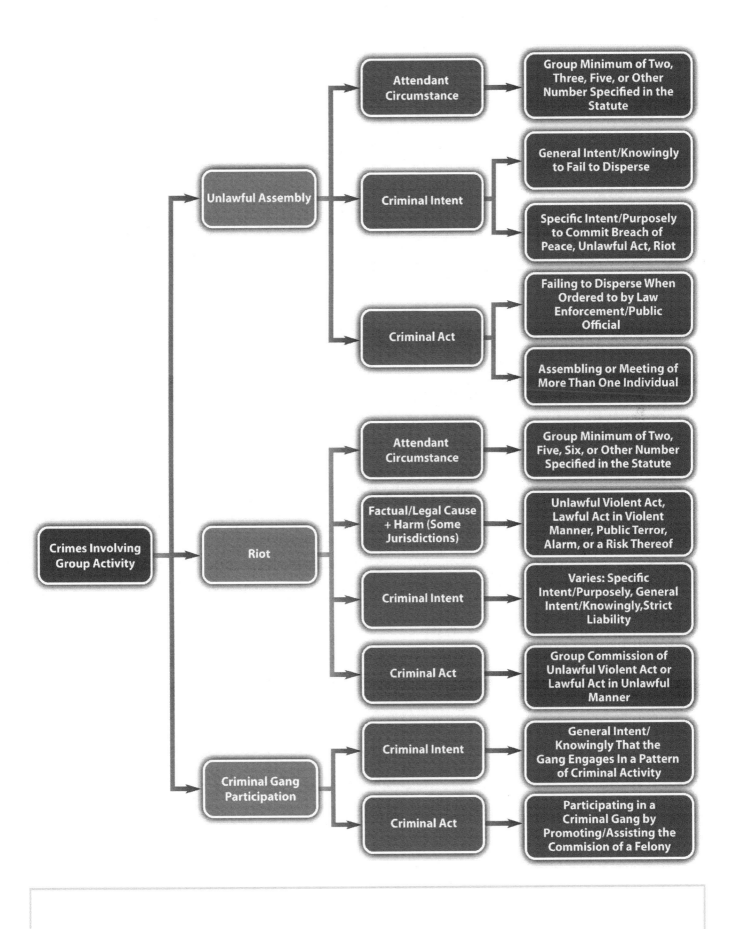

Key Takeaways

- The elements of unlawful assembly are the assembling or meeting of a group (criminal act) with the specific intent or purposely to commit breach of the peace, some other unlawful act, or riot. Some jurisdictions punish the failure to disperse (criminal act) with general intent or knowingly when a peace officer or public servant orders a group likely to cause substantial harm, serious annoyance, or alarm to do so. Jurisdictions vary as to the attendant circumstance, which is the group minimum, identifying two, three, five, or some similar number, depending on the statute.
- Unlawful assembly and failure to disperse statutes can be constitutionally challenged under the First Amendment, as void for vagueness, or overbroad.
- Unlawful assembly and failure to disperse are typically graded as misdemeanors.
- Riot is group commission of an unlawful violent act or a lawful act in a violent manner (criminal act) with either the specific intent or purposely to commit a felony or misdemeanor or prevent official action, or the general intent or knowingly that someone in the group possesses a firearm, or with strict liability intent. Some jurisdictions require the criminal act and intent to be the factual and legal cause of harm, which is public terror, alarm, or a risk thereof. The attendant circumstance, which is the group minimum, could be two, five, six, or some similar number, depending on the statute. Riot is often graded as a misdemeanor, or a felony if a firearm is used or there is property damage or physical injury to someone other than a defendant. Because riot statutes criminalize conduct involving force or violence, riot statutes are not as prone to constitutional challenges as disorderly conduct, vagrancy, loitering, and unlawful assembly statutes.
- Criminal gang could be defined as a group of a statutorily specified number that engages in a pattern of criminal activity and has in common hand signs, tattoos, and style of dress. Criminal gang member could be defined as someone who is identified as a gang member, admits to gang membership, associates with gang members, adopts the hand signs, tattoos, and style of dress of gang members, and commits crimes at the behest of the gang.
- Gang participation statutes criminalize actively participating in a criminal gang and promoting, furthering, or assisting (criminal act) the commission of a felony on behalf of a criminal gang with the general intent or knowingly that the gang participates in a pattern of criminal activity. Gang participation is typically graded as a felony. Gang enhancement statutes enhance a sentence for a misdemeanor or felony committed with the specific intent or purposely to promote or further a criminal gang. Some states only provide gang enhancement statutes for the commission of a felony.
- Civil responses to the gang problem include civil gang control statutes that allow plaintiffs, including state agencies, to sue for enhanced damages for threats, intimidation, or physical injury caused by a gang or gang member and civil gang injunctions (CGIs) that prohibit gang members from associating or congregating in certain areas frequented by criminal gangs.
- Statutes targeting gangs can be constitutionally challenged under the First Amendment or as void for vagueness or overbroad.

Exercises

Answer the following questions. Check your answers using the answer key at the end of the chapter.

A law enforcement officer arrests a group of individuals for standing outside a Jewish temple with signs that indicate a disbelief in the holocaust. The officer tells the individuals that he is arresting them for unlawful assembly. What are some potential constitutional problems with this arrest?

Read *Ortiz v. NYS Parole in Bronx*, 586 F.3d 149 (2009). In *Ortiz*, the defendant was found guilty of several counts of riot under New York's first-degree riot statute for conduct that occurred *after* he left the scene of the riot. Did the US Court of Appeals for the Second Circuit uphold the defendant's conviction? Why or why not? The case is available at this link:
http://scholar.google.com/scholar_case?case=2710893752280724993&q=%22riot+statute%22&hl=en&as_sdt=2,5&as_ylo=2002.

Read *People v. Englebrecht*, 88 Cal. App. 4th 1236 (2001). Did the California Court of Appeal hold that the defendant, an alleged gang member, had the right to a jury trial on the issue of his gang membership for the purpose of a civil gang injunction? The case is available at this link:
http://scholar.google.com/scholar_case?case=449430704300565285&q=unconstitutional+%22civil+gang+injunction%22&hl=en&as_sdt=2,5&as_ylo=1997.

References

Ala. Code § 13A-11-3, accessed April 9, 2011, http://law.onecle.com/alabama/criminal-code/13A-11-3.html.

Ala. Code § 13A-11-5, accessed April 9, 2011, http://law.onecle.com/alabama/criminal-code/13A-11-5.html.

Alaska Stat. § 11.81.900 (13), accessed April 12, 2011, http://law.justia.com/codes/alaska/2009/title-11/chapter-11-81/article-07/sec-11-81-900.

Cal. Penal Code § 186.22, http://law.justia.com/codes/california/2010/pen/186.20-186.33.html.

Cal. Penal Code § 404, accessed April 9, 2011, http://law.onecle.com/california/penal/404.html.

Cal. Penal Code § 407, accessed April 9, 2011, http://law.onecle.com/california/penal/407.html.

Del. Code Ann. tit. 11 § 616 (2)(b), accessed April 13, 2011, http://law.justia.com/codes/delaware/2010/title11/c005-sc02.html.

Fla. Stat. Ann. § 870.02, accessed April 9, 2011, http://law.onecle.com/florida/crimes/870.02.html.

Fla. Stat. Ann. § 874.04, accessed April 14, 2011, http://law.onecle.com/florida/crimes/874.04.html.

Fla. Stat. Ann. § 874.06, accessed April 14, 2011, http://law.onecle.com/florida/crimes/874.06.html.

Ga. Code tit. 16 § 16-11-30, accessed April 9, 2011, http://law.onecle.com/georgia/16/16-11-30.html.

Idaho Code Ann. § 18-8502(2), accessed April 12, 2011, http://law.justia.com/codes/idaho/2010/title18/t18ch85sect18-8502.html.

Mass. Gen. Laws ch. 269 § 1, accessed April 9, 2011, http://law.onecle.com/massachusetts/269/1.html.

N.J. Stat. § 2C:33-1, accessed April 9, 2011, http://law.onecle.com/new-jersey/2c-the-new-jersey-code-of-criminal-justice/33-1.html.

N.Y. Penal § 240.06, accessed April 9, 2011, http://law.onecle.com/new-york/penal/PEN0240.06_240.06.html.

Ohio Rev. Code Ann. § 2923.42, accessed April 14, 2011, http://law.justia.com/codes/ohio/2010/title29/chapter2923/2923_42.html.

People v. Acuna, 14 Cal. 4th 1090 (1997), accessed April 14, 2011, http://scholar.google.com/scholar_case?case=10825872110148502169&hl=en&as_sdt=2&as_vis=1&oi=scholarr (accessed April 15, 2011).

People v. Sanchez, 888 N.Y.S. 2d 352 (2009), accessed April 9, 2011, http://scholar.google.com/scholar_case?case=15178974598569042123&q=unconstitutional+%22unlawful+assembly+statute%22&hl=en&as_sdt=2,5&as_ylo=1992.

Shiner, M., "Civil Gang Injunctions a Guide for Prosecutors," Ndaa.org website, accessed April 14, 2011, http://www.ndaa.org/pdf/Civil_Gang_Injunctions_09.pdf.

Tex. Penal Code § 125.065, accessed April 14, 2011, http://law.onecle.com/texas/civil/125.065.00.html.

Tex. Penal Code § 125.066, accessed April 14, 2011, http://law.onecle.com/texas/civil/125.066.00.html.

Va. Code Ann. § 18.2-405, accessed April 9, 2011, http://law.onecle.com/virginia/crimes-and-offenses-generally/18.2-405.html.

18 U.S.C. 521(a), accessed April 12, 2011, http://www.law.cornell.edu/uscode/18/usc_sec_18_00000521—-000-.html.

18 U.S.C. 521(d), accessed April 12, 2011, http://www.law.cornell.edu/uscode/18/usc_sec_18_00000521—-000-.html.
CC licensed content, Shared previously

- Criminal Law. **Provided by**: University of Minnesota Libraries Publishing . **Located at**: http://open.lib.umn.edu/criminallaw/. **License**: *CC BY-NC-SA: Attribution-NonCommercial-ShareAlike*

12.3 Vice Crimes

Learning Objectives

Identify the sources of federal and state drug laws.
Describe a drug schedule.
Analyze various drug crimes and their grading.
Identify two modern trends in state drug crimes statutes.
Identify a potential constitutional challenge to a state's medical marijuana statute.
Analyze prostitution, pimping, and pandering and their grading.

Vice crimes offend the sensibilities, yet are often *victimless* and *harmless*, other than harm done to the defendant or society in general. Section 12.3.1 "Drug Crimes" explores drug crimes, including manufacture or cultivation, possession, sale, and under the influence offenses. Upcoming sections analyze prostitution, pimping, and pandering. In the final section, various vice statutes are available for review, including statutes criminalizing gambling and conduct involving alcohol.

Drug Crimes

All states and the federal government criminalize the **manufacture** or **cultivation**, **possession**, **sale**, and **use** of specified drugs. Many modern statutes focus on **rehabilitation** for *nonviolent* drug offenders, rather than incarceration, because this has proven effective in reducing recidivism and freeing up jails and prisons for defendants who pose a greater security risk to society. In addition, marijuana, a drug that has demonstrated valid therapeutic qualities, has been legalized by many states for **medicinal** purposes, which poses interesting constitutional questions, as is discussed in Section 12 "Modernization of Drug Crimes Statutes".

Federal and State Drug Schedules

Federal criminal statutes targeting illegal drugs are part of the Comprehensive Drug Abuse Prevention and Control Act of 1970, commonly known as the Controlled Substances Act (21 U.S.C. § 801, 2011). The states follow one of the three versions of the Uniform Controlled Substances Act (Uniform Controlled Substances Act, 2011), which was drafted by a commission striving for uniformity in state and federal laws. For the purpose of drug crimes, the states and the federal government categorize illegal drugs in drug schedules (21 U.S.C. § 812, 2011). The schedules generally focus on the harmful or addictive qualities of the drug, with Schedule I drugs being the most harmful or addictive; the remaining schedules reflect less harmful or addictive drugs, including drugs that are legal with a prescription (Minn. Stat. Ann. § 152.02, 2011).

Example of a Drug Schedule

The North Carolina drug schedule is located in N.C. Gen. Stat. § 90-89-90-94 (N.C. Gen. Stat. § 90-89-90-94, 2011). Review the schedule and note that heroin, a highly addictive drug that can cause death if a user ingests too much, is listed in Schedule I, while marijuana, a less addictive drug that is generally not as harmful as heroin, is listed in Schedule VI.

Federal and State Drug Crimes

The federal government and all fifty states criminalize the manufacture and cultivation, possession, sale, and use of drugs categorized in a jurisdiction's drug schedule, with exceptions for validly prescribed drugs and drugs involved in scientific or medical research. As discussed in Chapter 4 "The Elements of a Crime", the government cannot criminalize the *status* of being a drug addict (Robinson v. California, 2011). However, there is no constitutional impediment to punishing **criminal acts** involving controlled substances, even though it may be more difficult for an addict to control drug-related criminal behavior.

In most jurisdictions, the manufacture of scheduled drugs is a felony (Ala. Code § 13A-12-217, 2011), with a more severe penalty for the accompanying use of a firearm or the furtherance of a clandestine laboratory operation (Ala. Code § 13A-12-218, 2011). Cultivation of marijuana, which must be done with **general intent** or **knowingly**, can be a misdemeanor or a felony, depending on the quantity cultivated (Ohio Rev. Code Ann. § 2925.04, 2011).

Possession of scheduled drugs is typically **graded** based on the quantity possessed, the drug's classification in the schedule, and whether or not the possession is for the purpose of distribution, with the penalties ranging from a misdemeanor for simple possession to a serious felony for possession with intent to sell (Ohio Rev. Code Ann. § 2925.11, 2011). As is discussed more fully in Chapter 4 "The Elements of a Crime", possession can be *actual*, meaning the drug is located on or very near the defendant's person, or *constructive*, meaning the drug is within the defendant's control (Connecticut Jury Instructions No. 2.11-1, 2010). Constructive possession can be *joint*, meaning between two or more (Connecticut Jury Instructions No. 2.11-1, 2010). Simple possession typically must be with **general intent** or **knowingly**, while possession for the purpose of distribution or sale must be with **specific intent** or **purposely** (People v. Parra, 2011). In many states, possession of marijuana is graded lower than possession of other scheduled drugs—even as low as an *infraction* if the quantity is less than one ounce (Cal. Health and Safety Code § 11357(b), 2011).

The sale, **distribution**, or **trafficking** of scheduled drugs is generally a felony, with more severe penalties for drugs in a higher schedule (N.C. Gen. Stat. § 90-95, 2011), the sale of larger quantities (Ala. Code § 13A-12-231, 2011), a sale by an adult to a minor (Ala. Code § 13A-12-215, 2011), or a sale near school grounds (Ala. Code § 13A-12-250, 2011).

Scheduled drug use, also designated as being **under the influence of a controlled substance**, is typically a misdemeanor with more severe penalties for habitual offenders (Cal. Health and Safety Code § 11550, 2011).

Example of Drug Crimes

Charlene decides she wants to make some extra money by growing and selling marijuana. Charlene acquires some marijuana seeds and plants a marijuana garden in her backyard. Once her plants are ready for harvest, Charlene harvests some buds, weighs and packages them, and then puts some of the packages into her backpack and walks to a street corner known for drug sales. After she arrives at the street corner, Rick drives up, rolls down his window, and asks Charlene if she knows where he can "score." Charlene replies, "I have some pot if that is what you are looking for." Rick responds affirmatively, so Charlene gets into Rick's car and they drive to a local park. Rick insists on trying the marijuana before he buys it. Charlene takes out a joint, and Rick and Charlene smoke it. Thereafter, Rick buys one of Charlene's packages that weighs half an ounce and drops Charlene off back at the street corner.

In this example, Charlene has probably committed *every* drug crime discussed in Section 12 "Federal and State Drug Crimes". When Charlene planted the marijuana garden, she committed cultivation of a scheduled drug. Harvesting and packaging the marijuana is possession for sale. Smoking the marijuana with Rick is use, or under the influence of a controlled substance. Selling Rick a half-ounce of marijuana is drug sale, distribution, or trafficking. Rick has also probably committed two drug offenses. Smoking the marijuana with Charlene is use, or under the influence of a controlled substance. When Rick took the package of marijuana from Charlene, he committed possession (which may be an infraction in some states because he bought less than an ounce). Thus, in this example, Charlene and Rick may be subject to prosecution for and conviction of the stated drug offenses in most jurisdictions.

Modernization of Drug Crimes Statutes

Two new trends in state drug crimes statutes are the emphasis on *rehabilitation* for nonviolent drug offenders and the legalization of **marijuana** for **medical** use.

Modern statutes allow nonviolent drug offenders to go through a specialized drug court that typically sentences the offenders to probation and rehabilitation, rather than incarceration (Ariz. Rev. Stat. § 13-3422, 2011). Common offenses for drug courts are simple possession and use of drugs listed in a jurisdiction's drug schedule (Ariz. Rev. Stat. § 13-3422, 2011). Typically, the drug court offender must participate in a rehabilitation program that includes counseling and detoxification within a specified time period (Tex. Penal Code § 469.001, 2011). During the rehabilitation, the offender is frequently drug tested to ensure compliance. If the drug offender tests positive, reoffends, or does not complete the program within the specified time limits, the offender will be found guilty of the original nonviolent drug offense and sentenced accordingly (Ariz. Rev. Stat. § 13-3422, 2011).

Legalization of marijuana for medical use is another modern statutory trend among the states. Currently, sixteen states and the District of Columbia legalize medical marijuana (Procon.org, 2011). The criteria under these statutes vary, but in general a qualified individual can gain a prescription for marijuana from a caregiver, usually a physician, and thereafter obtain, possess, and use a specified quantity of marijuana (Alaska Stat. §§ 17.37.010-17.37.070, 2011). In some states, limited cultivation is also permissible (Cal. Health and Safety Code §§ 11362.7-11362.83, 2011).

The legalization of marijuana for medical use presents an interesting constitutional dilemma because federal law lists marijuana as a Schedule 1 drug and does not permit its possession, use, or sale for medicinal purposes (21 U.S.C. § 812, 2011). Technically, the legalization of marijuana for medical use violates the **Supremacy Clause** in the federal Constitution, which Chapter 2 "The Legal System in the United States" and Chapter 3 "Constitutional Protections" discuss in detail. However, the US Supreme Court has not invalidated any state's medical marijuana statutory scheme on this basis, although the Court has upheld federal Congress's authority to prohibit the possession and use of small quantities of marijuana under the Federal Controlled Substances Act (Gonzales v. Raich, 2011) and has rejected a medical necessity exception for the possession and use of marijuana (U.S. v. Oakland Cannavis Buyer's Cooperative, 2011).

Example of the Modernization of Drug Crimes Statutes

Remy lives in a state that legalizes marijuana for medical use and also has a drug court program. Remy obtains a prescription from an authorized caregiver and then buys the maximum amount of marijuana permitted under her state's medical marijuana statute at a medical marijuana distribution center. As Remy leaves the distribution center, Donny, a drug dealer standing nearby, asks Remy if she would like to buy some cocaine. Remy agrees and buys a gram of cocaine from Donny. Unfortunately for Remy, Donny is a federal Drug Enforcement Agent who thereafter arrests Remy for possession of marijuana and cocaine.

In this example, the federal government can most likely prosecute Remy for possession of both *marijuana and cocaine*, even though her state legalizes marijuana for medical use and Remy has complied with the requirements of the state medical marijuana statute. The US Supreme Court has held that the federal government may criminalize the possession of small amounts of marijuana, and there is no federal medical necessity exemption. Thus Remy may be subject to prosecution for and conviction of both of these offenses under **federal law**. Remy's state also can prosecute Remy for possession of cocaine. Remy's state has a drug court program, so Remy may be qualified to go through drug court for the possession of cocaine charge and may face only probation and rehabilitation for this offense rather than incarceration.

Figure 12.9 Diagram of Modern Drug Crimes Statutes

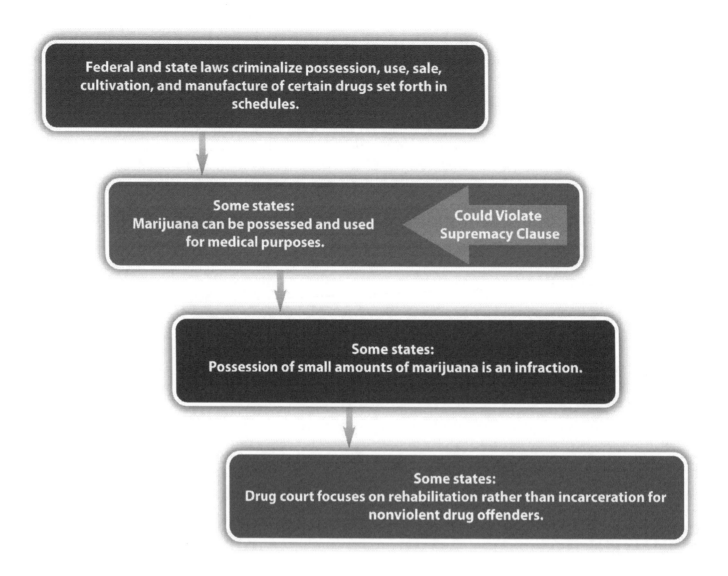

Crimes Involving Prostitution

Every state except Nevada criminalizes prostitution. In Nevada, legal prostitution must follow specific guidelines and can occur only in a licensed house of prostitution (N.R.S. 201.354, 2011).

The **criminal act** element required for prostitution varies, depending on the jurisdiction. In many states, prostitution is offering, agreeing, or engaging (N.Y. Penal Law § 230.00, 2011) in sexual conduct for money (N.Y. Penal Law § 230.00, 2011), property, or anything of value (720 ILCS § 5/11-14, 2011). Agreeing and engaging are both considered prostitution, so the prostitute and the prostitute's *client* could be prosecuted for and convicted of prostitution in most jurisdictions. The Model Penal Code criminalizes loitering in or within view of any public place for the purpose of being hired to engage in sexual activity and an inmate of a house of prostitution engaging in sexual activity as a business (Model Penal Code § 251.1(1)). The sexual conduct or sexual activity specified in statutes criminalizing prostitution generally includes sexual penetration, touching, or fondling sexual organs for sexual gratification (720 ILCS § 5/11-14, 2011). The Model Penal Code includes homosexual and deviate activity (Model Penal Code § 251.1).

The criminal intent element required for prostitution is either **strict liability** (N.Y. Penal Law § 230.00, 2011) or **general intent** or **knowingly** in most jurisdictions (N.M. Stat. § 30-9-2, 2011). The Model Penal Code requires **purposeful intent** if the defendant is loitering to engage in prostitution or **strict liability** if an inmate in a house of prostitution engages in prostitution as a business (Model Penal Code § 251.1). Prostitution is typically **graded** as a misdemeanor, with sentencing enhancements for habitual offenders, prostitution that occurs near a school (720 ILCS § 5/11-14, 2011), or clients who patronize juvenile prostitutes (N.Y. Penal Law § 230.06, 2011). The Model Penal Code grades prostitution as a petty misdemeanor (Model Penal Code § 251.1(1)).

Two crimes associated with prostitution are pimping and pandering. Although the elements of these offenses vary depending on the jurisdiction, in general, the **criminal act** element required for pimping is receiving anything of value from a prostitute with the **general intent** or **knowingly** that it was earned by prostitution (720 ILCS § 5/11-19, 2011). Pimping is generally **graded** as a misdemeanor (720 ILCS § 5/11-19, 2011) or felony (N.M. Stat. § 30-9-4.1, 2011), with sentencing enhancements if intimidation or force is used to compel an act of prostitution (N.Y. Penal Law § 230.33, 2011) or if the prostitute is a juvenile (N.Y. Penal Law § 230.32, 2011).

Pandering is generally procuring another (**criminal act**) with the **specific intent** or **purposely** to commit an act of prostitution (Cal. Penal Code § 266 i, 2011). Pandering is typically **graded** as a felony, with sentencing enhancement if the pandering occurs near a school (720 ILCS § 5/11-16, 2011). The Model Penal Code criminalizes a broad spectrum of conduct as promoting prostitution, including encouraging and inducing another purposely to become or remain a prostitute (Model Penal Code § 251.1(2) (c)). The Model Penal Code grades these acts of promoting prostitution as felonies of the third degree (Model Penal Code § 251.1(3) (a)).

Example of Crimes Involving Prostitution

Daniel approaches Penelope, a sixteen-year-old, as she wanders down the sidewalk. Daniel asks Penelope if she would like to earn a little extra cash. Penelope responds affirmatively, and Daniel asks her if she will have sexual intercourse with John (who is an adult) for one hundred and fifty dollars. Penelope eagerly agrees. Daniel walks Penelope over to the entrance of a motel where John is waiting. John and Penelope enter the motel, and John rents a room where they engage in sexual intercourse. Afterward, John pays Penelope the one hundred and fifty dollars. As Penelope leaves the motel, Daniel swiftly walks over, grabs Penelope by the wrist, and demands the one hundred and fifty dollars. Penelope protests, but Daniel twists her arm behind her back, and she grudgingly hands him the money. Daniel removes twenty dollars, hands it to Penelope, and informs her that it is her "share," and if she wants more, she needs to engage in another act of sexual intercourse.

In this example, Penelope and John have probably committed prostitution, and Daniel has most likely committed pimping and pandering in many jurisdictions. When Penelope has sexual intercourse with John for one hundred and fifty dollars, she is engaging in sexual conduct for money with general intent or knowingly, which constitutes prostitution in most jurisdictions. When John has sexual intercourse with Penelope and thereafter pays her one hundred and fifty dollars, he is engaging in sexual conduct for money with general intent or knowingly, which is also generally criminal prostitution. Penelope is a juvenile, so John's sentence may be **enhanced** and more severe than Penelope's. When Daniel procures John and Penelope for the purpose of committing prostitution, he is most likely committing pandering. When Daniel takes money from Penelope with the general intent or knowingly that it was earned by prostitution, he is probably committing pimping. The use of *force* to obtain the money and Penelope's *age* could **enhance** Daniel's sentence for both crimes in many jurisdictions. Thus Penelope, John, and Daniel may be subject to prosecution for and conviction of the stated crimes of prostitution, pimping, and pandering in most jurisdictions.

Prostitution Video

"The Yard Blues": A Reality of Drugs and Prostitution

A prostitute's life is described in this video:
(click to see video)

Eliot Spitzer Video

New York Governor Eliot Spitzer Resigns after Sex Scandal

This video shows former New York Governor Spitzer resigning after being exposed for his connection with a prostitution ring (Hakim, D., Rashbaum, W. K., 2011):
(click to see video)

Figure 12.10 Diagram of Vice Crimes

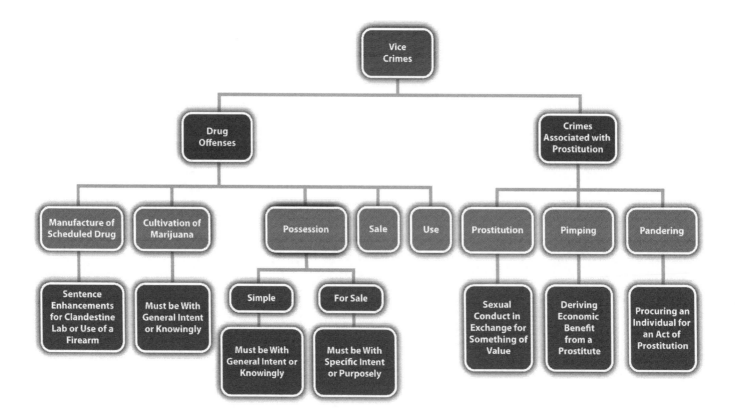

Various Vice Statutes

Most states criminalize **gambling** (18 Pa. C.S. § 5513, 2011), **drunkenness in public** (Cal. Penal Code § 647(f), 2011), and **driving while under the influence** (Or. Rev. Stat. § 813.010, 2011). Review the representative state statutes in the Notes for the elements of these vice crimes.

Key Takeaways

- Federal criminal statutes targeting illegal drugs are part of the Comprehensive Drug Abuse Prevention and Control Act of 1970, commonly known as the Controlled Substances Act. The states follow one of the three versions of the Uniform Controlled Substances Act, which was drafted by a commission striving for uniformity in state and federal laws.
- For the purpose of drug crimes, the states and the federal government categorize illegal drugs in schedules. The schedules generally focus on the harmful or addictive qualities of the drug, with Schedule I drugs being the most harmful or addictive, and the remaining schedules reflecting less harmful or addictive drugs, including drugs that are legal with a prescription.
- In most jurisdictions, the manufacture of scheduled drugs is a felony, and cultivation of marijuana, which must be done with general intent or knowingly, can be a misdemeanor or a felony, depending on the quantity cultivated. Possession of scheduled drugs is typically graded based on the quantity, schedule classification, and whether or not the possession is for sale, with penalties ranging from a misdemeanor for simple possession to a serious felony for possession with intent to sell. Possession of less than an ounce of marijuana is graded lower than possession of other scheduled drugs in many jurisdictions. Sale, distribution, or trafficking of scheduled drugs is generally graded as a felony, with sentencing enhancements for drugs in a higher schedule, the sale of larger quantities, a sale by an adult to a minor, or a sale near school grounds. Scheduled drug use is typically a misdemeanor with more severe penalties for habitual offenders.
- Two modern trends in state drug crimes statutes are the emphasis on rehabilitation for nonviolent drug offenders, which drug courts provide through sentencing, and the legalization of marijuana for medical use in sixteen states and the District of Columbia.
- Technically, a state's legalization of marijuana for medical use violates the Supremacy Clause because federal law classifies marijuana as a Schedule I drug and does not allow its possession,

sale, or use for any purpose.

- Prostitution is generally offering, agreeing, or engaging in sexual conduct for money or anything of value (criminal act), with general intent or knowingly, or strict liability. Prostitution is typically graded as a misdemeanor, with sentencing enhancements for habitual offenders, prostitution that occurs near a school, or clients who patronize juvenile prostitutes. Pimping is generally receiving anything of value from a prostitute (criminal act), with general intent or knowingly that it was earned by prostitution in many jurisdictions, and is typically graded as a misdemeanor or felony, with sentencing enhancements if intimidation or force is used to compel an act of prostitution or if the prostitute is a juvenile. Pandering is generally procuring another (criminal act) with specific intent or purposely to commit an act of prostitution and is typically graded as a felony with sentencing enhancement if the pandering takes place near a school.

Exercises

Answer the following questions. Check your answers using the answer key at the end of the chapter.

Anita lives in a state that permits the possession and use of marijuana for medical reasons. Anita obtains some marijuana and uses it to treat her medical condition, carefully following her state's statutory requirements. Has Anita committed a crime(s)?

Read *Poindexter v. State*, 153 S.W. 3d 402 (2005). In *Poindexter*, the defendant purchased cocaine from a confidential informant inside his house. After the defendant left, a subsequent law enforcement search uncovered the cocaine inside a tin breath mints can hidden in the ceiling of the master bedroom closet. The defendant was convicted at trial, but the appellate court reversed, based on the fact that another individual was seen on the premises, so there was *insufficient* proof of the defendant's possession. Did the Court of Criminal Appeals of Texas affirm the court's reversal? Why or why not? The case is available at this link:
http://scholar.google.com/scholar_case?case=10968287895213637721&q=possession+of+drugs+roommate+control+%22joint+possession%22&hl=en&as_sdt=2,5&as_ylo=2002.

Read *People v. Watson*, No. 90962 (Ohio 2120 2009). In *Watson*, the defendant was convicted of compelling prostitution. The defendant appealed on the grounds that the proper interpretation of compelling prostitution under the Ohio statute requires force, duress, or coercion and the defendant merely arranged it so that the prostitute had no money for shelter, clothes, and food if she did not continually commit prostitution. Did the Court of Appeals of Ohio uphold the defendant's conviction? Why or why not? The case is available at this link:
http://scholar.google.com/scholar_case?case=5203798681398361958&q=prostitution+client+acquitted+%22convicted+of+prostitution+%22&hl=en&as_sdt=2,5&as_ylo=2002.

Law and Ethics

Should Convicted Prostitutes Be Subjected to Involuntary AIDS Testing?

Read *Love v. Superior Court*, 226 Cal. App. 3d 736 (1990). The case is available at this link: http://scholar.google.com/scholar_case?case=16603325888575880385&q=Love+v.+Superior+Court&hl=en&as_sdt=2,5. In *Love*, the defendants, convicted prostitutes, challenged the constitutionality of a California statute that required AIDS testing and counseling for those convicted of prostitution and other sex offenses (Cal. Penal Code § 1202.1, 2011). The defendants claimed the statute was an unreasonable search pursuant to the Fourth Amendment and also violated the due process and the equal protection clauses. The California Court of Appeals upheld the statute, holding that the "special need" of preventing the spread of AIDS was a valid exercise of state police power, and the statute was a reasonable means to effectuate that interest. In California, soliciting or agreeing to exchange sexual conduct for money constitutes prostitution (Cal. Penal Code § 647(b), 2011), so a conviction for prostitution does not necessarily indicate an exchange of bodily fluids that could spread AIDS.

Do you think it is ethical to require all convicted prostitutes to submit to AIDS testing, whether or not they engaged in sexual intercourse? Why or why not?

Check your answer using the answer key at the end of the chapter.

References

Gonzales v. Raich, 545 U.S. 1 (2005), accessed April 17, 2011, http://www.oyez.org/cases/2000-2009/2004/2004_03_1454.

People v. Parra, 70 Cal. App. 4th 222 (1999), accessed April 17, 2011, http://scholar.google.com/scholar_case?case=5809016451778310933&q=People+v.+Parra+70+Cal.+App.+4th+222&hl=en&as_sdt=2,5.

Robinson v. California, 370 U.S. 660 (1962), accessed April 18, 2011, http://scholar.google.com/scholar_case?case=3358010003227436496&hl=en&as_sdt=2&as_vis=1&oi=scholarr.

U.S. v. Oakland Cannabis Buyers' Cooperative, 532 U.S. 483 (2001), accessed April 17, 2011, http://www.oyez.org/cases/2000-2009/2000/2000_00_151.

18 Pa. C.S. § 5513, accessed April 21, 2011, http://law.onecle.com/pennsylvania/crimes-and-offenses/00.055.013.000.html.

21 U.S.C. § 801 et seq., accessed April 17, 2011, http://www.deadiversion.usdoj.gov/21cfr/21usc/index.html.

21 U.S.C. § 812, accessed April 17, 2011, http://www.law.cornell.edu/uscode/21/usc_sec_21_00000812—-000-.html.

720 ILCS § 5/11-14, accessed April 21, 2011, http://law.onecle.com/illinois/720ilcs5/11-14.html.

720 ILCS § 5/11-16, accessed April 21, 2011, http://law.onecle.com/illinois/720ilcs5/11-16.html.

Ala. Code § 13A-12-217, accessed April 17, 2011, http://law.onecle.com/alabama/criminal-code/13A-12-217.html.

Ala. Code § 13A-12-218, accessed April 17, 2011, http://law.onecle.com/alabama/criminal-code/13A-12-218.html.

Ala. Code § 13A-12-231, accessed April 17, 2011, http://law.onecle.com/alabama/criminal-code/13A-12-231.html.

Ala. Code § 13A-12-250, accessed April 17, 2011, http://law.onecle.com/alabama/criminal-code/13A-12-250.html.

Alaska Stat. §§ 17.37.010-17.37.070, accessed April 17, 2011, http://medicalmarijuana.procon.org/sourcefiles/alaska-ballot-measure-8.pdf.

Ariz. Rev. Stat. § 13-3422, accessed April 17, 2011, http://law.onecle.com/arizona/criminal-code/13-3422.html.

Cal. Health and Safety Code § 11357(b), accessed April 18, 2011, http://www.canorml.org/laws/hsc11357.html#b.

Cal. Health and Safety Code § 11550, accessed April 17, 2011, http://law.onecle.com/california/health/11550.html.

Cal. Health and Safety Code §§ 11362.7-11362.83, accessed April 17, 2011, http://medicalmarijuana.procon.org/view.resource.php?resourceID=000881#California.

Cal. Penal Code § 1202.1, accessed April 22, 2011, http://law.onecle.com/california/penal/1202.1.html.

Cal. Penal Code § 266 i, accessed April 21, 2011, http://law.onecle.com/california/penal/266i.html.

Cal. Penal Code § 647(b), accessed April 2, 2011, http://law.onecle.com/california/penal/647.html.

Cal. Penal Code § 647(f), accessed April 21, 2011, http://law.onecle.com/california/penal/647.html.

Connecticut Jury Instructions No. 2.11-1, http://www.jud.ct.gov/ji/criminal/part2/2.11-1.htm (accessed February

13, 2010).

Hakim, D., William K. Rashbaum, "Spitzer Is Linked to Prostitution Ring," *New York Times* website, accessed September 4, 2011, http://www.nytimes.com/2008/03/10/nyregion/10cnd-spitzer.html.

Minn. Stat. Ann. § 152.02, accessed April 17, 2011, https://www.revisor.mn.gov/statutes/?id=152.02 (accessed April 17, 2011).

N.C. Gen. Stat. § 90-89-90-94, accessed April 17, 2011, http://www.ncga.state.nc.us/EnactedLegislation/Statutes/HTML/ByArticle/Chapter_90/Article_5.html.

N.C. Gen. Stat. § 90-95, accessed April 17, 2011, http://www.ncga.state.nc.us/EnactedLegislation/Statutes/HTML/ByArticle/Chapter_90/Article_5.html.

N.M. Stat. § 30-9-2, accessed April 21, 2011, http://law.justia.com/codes/new-mexico/2009/chapter-30/article-9/section-30-9-2.

N.M. Stat. § 30-9-4.1, accessed April 21, 2011, http://law.justia.com/codes/new-mexico/2009/chapter-30/article-9/section-30-9-4-1.

N.R.S. 201.354, accessed April 18, 2011, http://law.onecle.com/nevada/crimes/201.354.html.

N.Y. Penal Law § 230.00, accessed April 21, 2011, http://law.onecle.com/new-york/penal/PEN0230.00_230.00.html.

N.Y. Penal Law § 230.06, accessed April 21, 2011, http://law.onecle.com/new-york/penal/PEN0230.06_230.06.html.

N.Y. Penal Law § 230.32, accessed April 21, 2011, http://law.onecle.com/new-york/penal/PEN0230.32_230.32.html.

N.Y. Penal Law § 230.33, accessed April 21, 2011, http://law.onecle.com/new-york/penal/PEN0230.33_230.33.html.

Ohio Rev. Code Ann. § 2925.04, accessed April 17, 2011, http://codes.ohio.gov/orc/2925.04.

Ohio Rev. Code Ann. § 2925.11, accessed April 17, 2011, http://codes.ohio.gov/orc/2925.

Or. Rev. Stat. § 813.010, et seq., accessed April 21, 2011, http://law.onecle.com/oregon/813-driving-under-the-influence-of/index.html.

Procon.org website, "Medical Marijuana Summary Chart," accessed April 17, 2011, http://medicalmarijuana.procon.org/view.resource.php?resourceID=000881.

Tex. Penal Code § 469.001, accessed April 17, 2011, http://codes.lp.findlaw.com/txstatutes/HS/6/B/469/469.001.

Uniform Controlled Substances Act (1994), accessed April 17, 2011, http://www.law.upenn.edu/bll/archives/ulc/fnact99/1990s/ucsa94.pdf.
CC licensed content, Shared previously

- Criminal Law. **Provided by**: University of Minnesota Libraries Publishing . **Located at**: http://open.lib.umn.edu/criminallaw/. **License**: *CC BY-NC-SA: Attribution-NonCommercial-ShareAlike*

12.4 End-of-Chapter Material

Summary

States have an interest in protecting the quality of life of citizens, and therefore prohibit crimes against the public. Most jurisdictions criminalize disorderly conduct, which is making a loud and unreasonable noise, obscene utterance or gesture, fighting, threatening or stating fighting words, or creating a hazardous condition in public, with the specific intent or purposely or reckless intent to cause public inconvenience and alarm or a risk thereof. Disorderly conduct statutes target speech, so they are subject to constitutional challenges under the First and Fourteenth Amendments. Disorderly conduct is typically graded as a misdemeanor. Unconstitutionally vague statutes criminalizing vagrancy have been supplanted by precisely drafted statutes criminalizing loitering, which is loitering, wandering, or remaining with specific intent or purposely to gamble, beg, or commit prostitution in a specified area. Loitering is typically graded as a misdemeanor or a violation. Panhandling or begging is also criminal in many jurisdictions, and panhandling statutes should be narrowly tailored to target aggressive conduct or conduct that blocks public access or the normal flow of traffic. Sit-lie laws prohibit sitting or lying down with strict liability intent in public or on a sidewalk during specified times in certain areas. Sit-lie laws are subject to constitutional challenges as cruel and unusual punishment or void for vagueness and are typically graded as an infraction.

Group conduct tends to enhance the potential for force and violence. Most jurisdictions criminalize unlawful assembly, which is purposefully assembling or meeting to cause a breach of the peace, and failure to disperse, which is the knowing refusal or failure to disperse when ordered to by law enforcement. Both unlawful assembly and failure to disperse statutes are subject to constitutional challenges under the First Amendment or as void for vagueness and overbroad, require the attendant circumstance of a group minimum of two, three, or five, and are graded as a misdemeanor. Most jurisdictions also criminalize riot, which is group commission of an unlawful act of violence or a lawful act in an unlawful manner, with the specific intent or purposely to commit or facilitate a misdemeanor or felony or prevent official action, or the general intent or knowingly that one of the group plans to use a firearm or deadly weapon. In some jurisdictions, riot is a strict liability offense. A few jurisdictions require the defendants to be the factual and legal cause of riot harm, which is public terror and alarm. Riot typically requires the attendant circumstance of a group minimum of two, five, or six and is graded as a misdemeanor or a felony if a firearm is used or if there is property damage or physical injury to someone other than the defendants.

Gang conduct is prohibited federally and in state statutes. States either criminalize gang conduct as gang participation, enhance a penalty for a crime committed by a criminal gang or gang member, or both. Gang participation is generally furthering the commission of a felony for the benefit of a criminal gang with the general intent or knowingly that other members participate in gang activity and is a felony. Gang enhancement statutes enhance the penalty for the commission of a felony or misdemeanor at the direction of or to further a criminal gang. Civil responses to gang conduct are civil gang activity statutes providing for damages and civil gang injunctions, which prohibit gang association, hand signs, wearing of gang colors, and loitering in areas known for gang activity. Statutes regulating gangs are subject to constitutional challenges under the First Amendment and as void for vagueness or overbroad.

All states and the federal government criminalize specific controlled substances offenses. Jurisdictions classify drugs in schedules, based on their harmful or addictive qualities, and punish drug offenses accordingly. Common offenses are the manufacture, cultivation, possession for personal use or sale, sale, and use of scheduled drugs, with the grading ranging from a felony to an infraction, depending on the offense and the drug. Some jurisdictions provide rehabilitation combined with probation as a penalty for nonviolent offenders through a drug court procedure. Some jurisdictions also legalize marijuana for medical use, which could violate federal supremacy because the federal government does not legalize marijuana for this purpose.

All states except Nevada criminalize prostitution. In Nevada, only prostitution that occurs in a licensed house of prostitution is noncriminal. Prostitution is offering, agreeing, or engaging in specified sexual conduct for money or anything of value, with strict liability or general intent or knowingly in most jurisdictions, and is typically graded as a misdemeanor with sentencing enhancements for habitual offenders, prostitution that occurs near a school, or patronizing a juvenile prostitute. Pimping is generally receiving something of value from a prostitute, with general intent or knowingly that it was earned by prostitution, and is graded as a misdemeanor or a felony with sentencing enhancements if the defendant uses force or the prostitute is a juvenile. Pandering is generally procuring another for an act of prostitution with specific intent or purposely and is typically graded as a felony with sentencing enhancement if the pandering takes place near a school.

You Be the Legislator

You are a legislator with a perfect record for voting on statutes that are constitutional. You have been presented with four proposed statutes. Read each one, and then read the case analyzing a replica statute for constitutionality. Decide whether you should vote **for** or **against** the proposed statute if you want to keep your perfect record. Check your answers using the answer key at the end of the chapter.

The proposed statute is *Disorderly Conduct* and reads as follows: It is a misdemeanor to engage in indecent or disorderly conduct in the presence of another in a public place. This statute was analyzed for constitutionality by *Satterfield v. State*, 395 S.E. 2d 816 (1990). The case is available at this link: http://scholar.google.com/scholar_case?case=8539981756406627329&q= Satterfield+v.+State+395&hl=en&as_sdt=2,5. Should you vote **for** or **against** the statute?

The proposed statute is *Loitering for prostitution* and reads as follows: It is unlawful for any person to loiter in or near any public place in a manner and under circumstances manifesting the purpose of inducing, enticing, soliciting for or procuring another to commit an act of prostitution. Among the circumstances that may be considered in determining whether such purpose is manifested are that such person repeatedly beckons to, stops, or attempts to stop or engages persons passing by in conversation, or repeatedly stops or attempts to stop motor vehicle operators by hailing, waving of arms or any other bodily gesture. This statute was analyzed for constitutionality by *Silvar v. Dist. Ct.*, 129 P.3d 682 (2006). The case is available at this link: http://scholar.google.com/scholar_case?case=15323479136078401167&q= Silvar+v.+Dist.+Ct.&hl=en&as_sdt=2,5. Should you vote **for** or **against** the statute?

The proposed statute is *Gang Violence and Juvenile Crime Prevention Act* and reads as follows: State Prosecutors are hereby authorized to bring specified crime charges against minors fourteen and older in the criminal division of adult court rather than in the juvenile division without a judicial determination that the minor is unfit for a juvenile court disposition. This statute was analyzed for constitutionality by *Manduley v. Superior Court*, 41 P.3d 3 (2002). The case is available at this link: http://scholar.google.com/scholar_case?case=14196981766707899172&q= Manduley+v.+Superior+Court&hl=e.n&as_sdt=2,5. Should you vote **for** or **against** the statute?

The proposed statute is *Mere Possession* and reads as follows: It is a crime to possess an unprescribed controlled substance. This statute was analyzed for constitutionality by *State v. Bradshaw*, 98 P.3d 1190 (2004). The case is available at this link: http://scholar.google.com/scholar_case?case=33245956757868529&q= State+v.+Bradshaw+98&hl=en&as_sdt=2,5. Should you vote **for** or **against** the statute?

Cases of Interest

- *Roulette v. City of Seattle*, 97 F.3d 300 (1996), discusses sit-lie laws: http://scholar.google.com/scholar_case?case=11766310634401293489&q= %22sit+lie+%22&hl=en&as_sdt=2,5.

- *Noy v. State*, 83 P.3d 538 (2003), discusses Alaska's possession of marijuana law: http://scholar.google.com/scholar_case?case=17763301345063946977&q=%22Noy+v.+State%22&hl=en&as_sdt=2,5.
- *Phillips v. State*, 25 So. 3d 404 (2010), discusses the right to participate in drug court: http://scholar.google.com/scholar_case?case=706671360238134410&q=%22drug+court%22&hl=en&as_sdt=2,5&as_ylo=2009.
- *In re BW*, 313 S.W. 3d 818 (2010), discusses juvenile prostitution: http://scholar.google.com/scholar_case?case=13593192130854531269&q=%22prostitution+statute%22&hl=en&as_sdt=2,5&as_ylo=2009.

Articles of Interest

- True threats and the First Amendment: http://works.bepress.com/cgi/viewcontent.cgi?article=1018&context=mark_strasser
- Gang injunctions: http://digitalcommons.law.ggu.edu/cgi/viewcontent.cgi?article=1736&context=ggulrev
- Substance abuse in America: http://works.bepress.com/cgi/viewcontent.cgi?article=1000&context=edward_perez

Websites of Interest

- Information about the homeless: http://www.nationalhomeless.org
- Information about gangs: http://www.nationalgangcenter.gov
- Information about the legalization of prostitution: http://prostitution.procon.org

Statistics of Interest

- Homelessness: http://www.nationalhomeless.org/factsheets
- Gang violence: http://www.ncjrs.gov/app/QA/Detail.aspx?Id=11&context=9
- Drug crime: http://www.dea.gov/druginfo/factsheets.shtml

CC licensed content, Shared previously

- Criminal Law. **Provided by**: University of Minnesota Libraries Publishing . **Located at**: http://open.lib.umn.edu/criminallaw/. **License**: *CC BY-NC-SA: Attribution-NonCommercial-ShareAlike*

Chapter 13: Crimes against the Government

13.1 Crimes Involving National Security

Source: Image courtesy of Tara Storm.

Bribery, of course, connotes a voluntary offer to obtain gain, where extortion connotes some form of coercion.

—*U.S. v. Adcock*, cited in Section 13.3.2 "Bribery Elements"

Learning Objectives

Define the elements of treason, and analyze treason's evidentiary requirements and grading.
Define the elements of sedition, and analyze sedition grading.
Define the elements of various forms of sabotage, and analyze sabotage grading.
Define the elements of espionage, and analyze espionage grading.

The government is tasked with keeping the nation safe from domestic and international attacks on the government and citizens. National security is an issue that affects the entire country, so most of the regulation in this area is *federal*, rather than *state* (Pennsylvania v. Nelson, 2011). Criminal statutes protecting the government can encroach on the individual freedom to protest government action and can also affect privacy interests, which subjects them to enhanced constitutional scrutiny similar to the crimes against the public reviewed in Chapter 12 "Crimes against the Public". This section explores crimes against the nation, such as treason, sedition, sabotage, and espionage. Section 13.2 "Crimes Involving Terrorism" examines terrorism and the USA PATRIOT Act. The last section of this chapter discusses other crimes against the government that are primarily *state* regulated, such as perjury, bribery, and obstruction of justice.

Treason

Article III § 3 of the US Constitution defines treason and specifies the evidentiary requirements for any treason trial. The founding fathers wanted to ensure that the government would not charge an individual with treason without significant and reliable proof. Treason was punishable by death in England, so it was a constant threat to anyone who disagreed with the ruling party. Although the treason clause in the Constitution is modeled after the early English law defining treason, it omits a section that criminalized "imagining the death of the King" and also limits Congress's authority to extend or expand the crime of treason or to lighten the evidentiary requirements.

The pertinent section of the Constitution states, "Treason against the United States shall consist only in levying War against them, or, in adhering to their Enemies, giving them Aid and Comfort. No Person shall be convicted of Treason unless on the Testimony of two Witnesses to the same overt Act, or on Confession in open Court."

Treason Elements and Grading

The **criminal act** element required for treason is levying war against the United States **or** adhering to the enemy by giving aid and comfort (18 U.S.C. § 2381, 2011). Prosecutions for treason are practically nonexistent, so case law in this area is dated, yet still constitutes viable precedent. In *U.S. v. Burr*, 25 F Cas 55 (1807), a case involving then-vice president Aaron Burr's prosecution for treason, the US Supreme Court held that levying war means an actual assembling of men, not a **conspiracy** to levy war, nor a mere *enlistment* of men. In *Haupt v. U.S.*, 330 U.S. 631 (1947), the US Supreme Court held that the defendant's acts of harboring and sheltering his son in his home, helping him to purchase an automobile, and obtain employment constituted providing aid and comfort to the enemy because the defendant's son was a spy and saboteur. The criminal intent element required for treason is most likely the **general intent** or **knowingly** to commit an act of levying war or the **specific intent** or **purposely** to betray the United States by giving aid and comfort to enemies (Cramer v. U.S., 1945). The *Constitution* specifies the evidentiary requirements that two witnesses testify to an overt act of treason or that the defendant confess in open court, although this is not set forth in the federal treason statute (18 U.S.C., 2011). As stated in *Cramer v. U.S.*, 325 U.S. 1, 34, 35 (1945), "Every act, movement, deed, and word of the defendant charged to constitute treason must be supported by the testimony of two witnesses," and it is not enough that the elements of treason can be *inferred* from the witness statements. Treason is **graded** as a felony that can merit the death penalty or prohibit the defendant from ever holding federal office (18 U.S.C. § 2381, 2011).

Example of a Case Lacking Treason Elements and Evidentiary Requirements

Benedict is identified as a person of interest in a treason case. A government agent posing as an enemy spy invites Benedict to dinner, and they discuss the decline of the United States and whether or not they should "do something about it." At the conclusion of the dinner, Benedict picks up the tab. Thereafter, Benedict is arrested for treason and refuses to incriminate himself by responding to law enforcement interrogation. It is unlikely that Benedict will be convicted of treason in this case. Benedict paid for the government agent's dinner, which could constitute providing **aid** to the enemy. However, Benedict indicated a hesitancy to take further action, which does not satisfy the requirement that he act with the **specific intent** or **purposely** to *betray* the United States. In addition, only the government agent can testify as to Benedict's act of paying for a meal because Benedict is asserting his right to remain silent. Therefore, the constitutional requirement that two witnesses testify about the overt act charged as treason is not satisfied. The intent element and evidentiary requirement for treason are lacking, so Benedict probably will not be subject to prosecution for and conviction of this offense.

Figure 13.1 Crack the Code

Crack the Code

Compare the following state laws:

<u>18 U.S.C. § 2381</u>: **Treason**

Whoever, owing allegiance to the United States, levies war against them or adheres to their enemies, giving them aid and comfort within the United States or elsewhere, is guilty of treason and shall suffer death, or shall be imprisoned not less than five years and fined under this title but not less than $10,000; and shall be incapable of holding any office under the United States.

<u>720 ILCS 5/30-1</u>: **Treason**

Sec. 30-1. Treason.

(a) A person owing allegiance to this State commits treason when he or she knowingly:

   (1) Levies war against this State; or

   (2) Adheres to the enemies of this State, giving them aid or comfort.

(b) No person may be convicted of treason except on the testimony of 2 witnesses to the same overt act, or on his confession in open court.

(c) Sentence. Treason is a Class X felony for which an offender may be sentenced to death under Section 5-5-3 of the Unified Code of Corrections.

The federal treason statute does not include the Constitution's requirement that two witnesses testify and corroborate an overt act of treason unless the defendant confesses in open court; the Illinois treason statute does. . .

Sedition

Sedition criminalizes the incitement of insurrection or revolution by seditious speech or writings and, as such, is subject to the restrictions set forth in the First Amendment. The first federal law prohibiting sedition was the Sedition Act enacted in 1798 and repealed by Thomas Jefferson after his election as president. The current federal statute criminalizing sedition was originally enacted in 1940 and is codified at 18 U.S.C. § 2385. Conspiracy to commit sedition is codified at 18 U.S.C. § 2384. Many states have similar provisions (51 Pa. Cons. Stat. Ann. § 6018, 2011). Like treason, sedition is rarely prosecuted.

The **criminal act** element required for sedition is either advocating, aiding, teaching, organizing or printing, publishing, or circulating written matter that advocates, aids, or teaches the overthrow of the US government or any state, district, or territory thereof by *force* or *violence* (18 U.S.C. § 2385, 2011). The criminal intent element required for sedition is the **general intent** or **knowingly** to advocate, aid, teach, or organize, or the **specific intent** or **purposely** to print, publish, or circulate written matter that advocates, aids, or teaches the violent government overthrow. In *Yates v. U.S.*, 354 U.S. 298 (1957), the US Supreme Court held that only advocacy directed at *promoting unlawful action* could be constitutionally prohibited. Advocacy of an "abstract doctrine" was protected by the First Amendment as free speech (Yates v. U.S., 2011). Sedition is **graded** as a felony that can prohibit the defendant from obtaining employment with the US government for a minimum of five years postconviction (18 U.S.C. § 2385, 2011).

Example of Sedition

Mo, a disgruntled immigrant who has been denied citizenship, decides he wants to overthrow the US government and supplant it with a new government that will grant the citizenship privileges he desires. Mo prints up leaflets advocating the overthrow of the government by placing a series of bombs in strategic and specifically named places and passes them out every Saturday in front of varied places known for ethnic diversity throughout the city. Mo has most likely committed sedition in this example. Mo **printed written matter** advocating the overthrow of the US government by *unlawful* action, using *force* and *violence*. Mo's intent was to get rid of the current government so that he could gain citizenship, which is **specific intent** or **purposely**. Thus Mo's conduct probably constitutes sedition, and he may be subject to prosecution for and conviction of several counts of this offense.

Figure 13.2 Diagram of Sedition

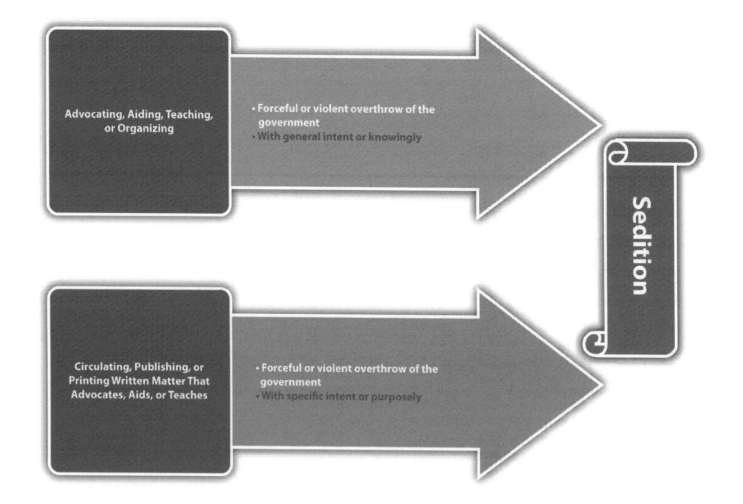

Sabotage

Sabotage is criminalized at 18 U.S.C. § 2151 et seq., which includes several different forms of this offense. Many states have similar provisions (RCW § 9.05.060, 2011). In general, sabotage is destroying, damaging, or defectively producing (**criminal act** and **harm**) property with the **specific intent** or **purposely**, **general intent** or **knowingly**, or **negligently** to impede the nation's ability to prepare for or participate in war and national defense and is detailed in the following United States Codes:

- 18 U.S.C. § 2152 focuses on destroying or damaging harbor-defense property.
- 18 U.S.C. § 2153 focuses on destroying or damaging war material, premises, or utilities.
- 18 U.S.C. § 2154 focuses on producing defective war materials, premises, or utilities.
- 18 U.S.C. § 2155 focuses on destroying or damaging national defense material, premises, or utilities.
- 18 U.S.C. § 2156 focuses on producing defective national defense material, premises, or utilities.

Both 18 U.S.C. §§ 2153 and 2154 have the **attendant circumstance** that the conduct occur during *war* or a *national emergency*. All the sabotage statutes **grade** sabotage as a felony, with sentences ranging from five to thirty years' incarceration in federal prison.

Sabotage is prosecuted more often than treason and sedition, and there have been some extremely interesting criminal sabotage cases, including sabotage indictments against a corporation manufacturing defective raincoats for the armed forces during wartime, a sabotage trial for the burning of an ROTC building on the Washington University campus after the Kent State University riots, a sabotage trial for defendants who stole copper wire from a railroad track that was used to ship war materials, and the sabotage indictment of Osama bin Laden for extraterritorial (outside the United States) activity.

Example of Sabotage

Review the example in Section 13 "Example of Sedition" with Mo. Add to this example and imagine that Mo gets no response to his fliers and becomes enraged. He decides to get back at the United States for not allowing him to become a US citizen by harming its national security and exposing it to attack by enemy forces. He thereafter hacks into the computer system used by the US Department of Defense and damages it so that it is out of commission for two weeks. Mo has most likely committed the federal crime of **sabotage**. Mo **damaged** national defense material with the **specific intent** or **purposely** to interfere with the nation's security and defense, which is prohibited under 18 U.S.C. § 2155, whether or not it is wartime or during a national emergency. Thus Mo may be subject to prosecution for and conviction of this offense and could face many years of incarceration for his conduct.

Figure 13.3 Diagram of Sabotage

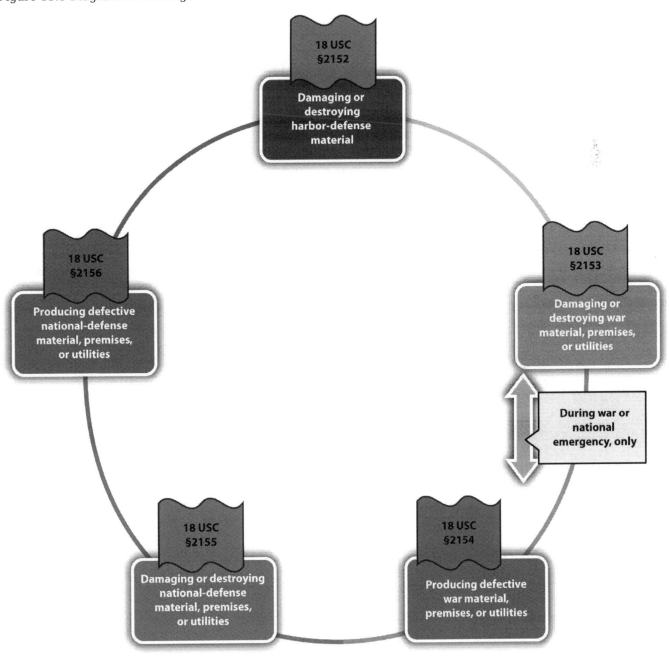

Espionage

Espionage, also known as "spying," is criminalized at 18 U.S.C. § 792 et seq. Originally part of one of the early versions of the Sedition Act of 1918, the crime of espionage has a colorful history and many interesting criminal prosecutions similar to criminal sabotage. Federal espionage statutes criminalize various acts, depending on whether the conduct occurs during *peace* or during *war*. During times of peace, it is criminal espionage to gather, transmit, or attempt to gather or transmit defense information (**criminal act**) with **general intent** or **knowingly**, or with the **specific intent** or **purposely** that it will be used to damage the United States or assist any foreign nation (18 U.S.C. § 793, 2011). During times of war, it is criminal espionage to collect, record, publish, or communicate information about military activities or to attempt any of the foregoing (**criminal act**) with the **specific intent** or **purposely** that the information will be transmitted to the enemy (18 U.S.C. § 794(b), 2011). Espionage is graded as a **felony**, with potential sentencing of life in prison or the death penalty (18 U.S.C. § 792 et seq., 2011).

Some interesting criminal espionage cases are the Rosenberg case, where a married couple conspired to pass nuclear secrets to the Soviets and were later executed pursuant to the death penalty, the Hanssen case, where an FBI agent sold state secrets to Moscow for $1.4 million in cash and diamonds, and the Aragoncillo case, where a White House employee stole intelligence documents from White House computers and e-mailed them to the Philippines.

Example of Espionage

Review the example given in Section 13 "Example of Sabotage" with Mo and his computer hacking. Change the example so that before Mo damages the US Department of Defense computer system, he copies some information from different top-secret sites and sends them to operatives in an enemy nation with this message: "I have stolen this information directly from the US Department of Defense. I have also disabled their computer system, which will probably take some time to repair. Now is an excellent time to attack the United States." He thereafter severely damages the computer system. In this example, Mo has most likely committed both sabotage and espionage. As stated in Section 13 "Example of Sabotage", Mo probably committed sabotage when he **damaged** national defense material with the **specific intent** or **purposely** to interfere with the nation's security and defense. When Mo copied top-secret information and sent it to an enemy nation, along with informing the nation that the US Department of Defense computer system was disabled, he **gathered** and **transmitted** information with the **specific intent** or **purposely** that it be used to injure the United States. Thus Mo has probably committed both sabotage and espionage and may be subject to prosecution for and conviction of these offenses.

Video of the President Informing the Nation bin Laden Is Dead

President Obama on the Death of Osama bin Laden

President Obama's speech explaining Osama bin Laden's death is shown in this video:

(click to see video)

Table 13.1 Comparing Treason, Sedition, Sabotage, and Espionage

Crime	Criminal Act or Harm	Criminal Intent	Attendant Circumstance(s)
Treason*	Levy war, or give aid and comfort to enemies	Most likely, general intent or knowingly to levy war, specific intent or purposely to betray the United States with aid and comfort	

Crime	Criminal Act or Harm	Criminal Intent	Attendant Circumstance(s)
Sedition	Advocating or printing matter that advocates the forceful or violent overthrow of the US government	General intent or knowingly to advocate, specific intent or purposely when printing matter that advocates the forceful or violent overthrow of the US government	
Sabotage	Varies: either destroying, damaging, or producing defective property that impedes US defense capabilities	Varies: specific intent or purposely, general intent or knowingly or negligently	Certain conduct must take place during war or a national emergency
Espionage	Spying	Varies: either general intent or knowingly, or specific intent or purposely that information will be transmitted to the enemy	Certain conduct must take place during war

*Includes the evidentiary requirement of the testimony of two witnesses or the defendant's confession in open court

Key Takeaways

- The criminal act element required for treason is levying war against the United States or adhering to the enemy by giving the enemy aid and comfort. The criminal intent element required for treason is most likely the general intent or knowingly to commit an act of levying war, or the specific intent or purposely to betray the United States by giving aid and comfort to enemies. Treason also has the constitutional evidentiary requirement that two witnesses corroborate the acts of treason or that the defendant confess in open court. Treason is graded as a felony.
- The criminal act element required for sedition is advocating, aiding, teaching, organizing, or printing, publishing, or circulating written matter that advocates, aids, or teaches the overthrow of the US government by force or violence. The criminal intent element required for sedition is the general intent or knowingly to advocate, aid, teach, or organize or the specific intent or purposely to print, publish, or circulate written matter that advocates, aids, or teaches the forceful or violent government overthrow. Sedition is graded as a felony.
- The criminal act and harm elements required for sabotage vary but are generally damaging, destroying, or producing defective property that impedes the US national defense or ability to participate in or prepare for war. The criminal intent element required for sabotage also varies but is either specific intent or purposely, general intent or knowingly, or negligent intent, depending on the criminal act. Some forms of sabotage require the attendant circumstance that the conduct occurs during wartime or a national emergency. Sabotage is graded as a felony.
- Espionage is spying (criminal act) with general intent or knowingly, or the specific intent or purposely to transmit information to another nation. Some forms of espionage require the attendant circumstance that the conduct occurs during wartime. Espionage is graded as a felony.

Exercises

Answer the following questions. Check your answers using the answer key at the end of the chapter.

Stephanie stands in front of a mosque and advocates for the overthrow of the US government. Is Stephanie committing **sedition**? Why or why not?
Read *U.S. v. Kabat*, 797 Fed.2d 580 (1986). Did the US Court of Appeals for the Eighth Circuit

uphold the defendants' convictions for sabotage when, as nuclear protestors, they intentionally damaged US missiles? Why or why not? The case is available at this link: http://scholar.google.com/scholar_case?case=5276967647790252481&q= sabotage+%222155%22&hl=en&as_sdt=2,5&as_ylo=1992.

Read *In re Squillacote*, 790 A.2d 514 (2002). Did the District of Columbia Court of Appeals hold that conspiracy to commit espionage and attempted espionage are crimes of **moral turpitude** that could support the defendant's disbarment? The case is available at this link: http://scholar.google.com/scholar_case?case=8408409521873710428&q= espionage+%22793%22&hl=en&as_sdt=2,5&as_ylo=2000.

References

Cramer v. U.S., 325 U.S. 1 (1945), http://supreme.justia.com/us/325/1.

Pennsylvania v. Nelson, accessed May 1, 2011, 350 U.S. 497 (1956), http://supreme.justia.com/us/350/497/case.html.

RCW § 9.05.060, accessed May 1, 2011, http://apps.leg.wa.gov/rcw/default.aspx?cite=9.05.060.

Yates v. U.S., 354 U.S. 298, 318 (1957), accessed April 30, 2011, http://scholar.google.com/scholar_case?case=14369441513839511604&q= Yates+v.+U.S.&hl=en&as_sdt=2,5.

18 U.S.C. § 792 et seq., accessed May 1, 2011, http://www.law.cornell.edu/uscode/718/usc_sup_01_18_10_I_20_37.html.

18 U.S.C. § 793, accessed May 1, 2011, http://www.law.cornell.edu/uscode/718/usc_sec_18_00000793—-000-.html.

18 U.S.C. § 794(b), accessed May 1, 2011, http://www.law.cornell.edu/uscode/718/usc_sec_18_00000794—-000-.html.

18 U.S.C. § 2381, accessed April 29, 2011, http://www.law.cornell.edu/uscode/718/usc_sec_18_00002381—-000-.html.

18 U.S.C. § 2385, accessed April 30, 2011, http://www.law.cornell.edu/uscode/718/usc_sec_18_00002385—-000-.html.

51 Pa. Cons. Stat. Ann. § 6018, accessed April 30, 2011, http://law.onecle.com/pennsylvania/military-affairs/00.060.018.000.html.
CC licensed content, Shared previously

- Criminal Law. **Provided by**: University of Minnesota Libraries Publishing . **Located at**: http://open.lib.umn.edu/criminallaw/. **License**: *CC BY-NC-SA: Attribution-NonCommercial-ShareAlike*

13.2 Crimes Involving Terrorism

Learning Objectives

Identify three federal statutory schemes targeting terroristic conduct.
Ascertain the function of the Department of Homeland Security.
Define international and domestic terrorism.
Identify crimes involving terrorism.
Identify potential constitutional challenges to the USA PATRIOT Act.

In recent years, crimes involving terrorism have escalated both in the United States and abroad. The federal government's response has been to enact comprehensive criminal statutes with severe penalties targeting terroristic conduct. In this section, federal statutes criminalizing acts of terrorism are reviewed, along with potential constitutional challenges.

Statutory Schemes Targeting Terrorism

Before the September 11, 2001, terrorist attacks on the United States, the primary federal statutes criminalizing terrorism were the Omnibus Diplomatic Security and Antiterrorism Act of 1986 and the Antiterrorism and Effective Death Penalty Act of 1996 (AEDPA), which was enacted after the Oklahoma City bombings. After September 11, 2001, Congress enacted the USA PATRIOT Act, which stands for Uniting and Strengthening America by Providing Appropriate Tools Required to Intercept and Obstruct Terrorism Act of 2001.

The USA PATRIOT Act changed and strengthened existing laws targeting terrorism and enhanced US capabilities to prosecute terrorism committed abroad. Specifically, the USA PATRIOT Act increases federal jurisdiction over crimes committed outside the United States (USA PATRIOT Act, Tit. VIII § 804, 2011), creates new crimes involving financial support of terrorism or terrorists abroad (USA PATRIOT Act, Tit. VIII § 805, 2011), and provides for the civil forfeiture of assets connected to terrorism (USA PATRIOT Act, Tit. VIII § 806, 2011). Other fundamental changes incorporated in the USA PATRIOT Act are the expansion of government surveillance capabilities, including telephone interception and scrutiny of e-mails (USA PATRIOT Act, Tit. II, § 203 et seq.).

In 2002, Congress created the Department of Homeland Security (DHS) under the authority of the Homeland Security Act. DHS enforces provisions of federal laws against terrorism and includes the following agencies: the Secret Service, Customs, the Federal Emergency Management Agency, United States Coast Guard, Border Patrol, Transportation Security Administration, and Citizenship and Immigration Services (Department of Homeland Security website, 2011).

Criminal Terroristic Conduct

International terrorism is defined as violent acts committed *outside* the United States that would be criminal if committed in the United States, and that appear to be intended to influence a civilian population or government by intimidation, **or** to affect the conduct of government by mass destruction, assassination, or kidnapping (18

U.S.C. § 2331(1), 2011). Specific crimes such as murder, attempted murder, and conspiracy to commit murder committed against an American national (defined as an American citizen or individual who owes permanent allegiance to the United States)(18 U.S.C. § 1101(a), 2011) while *outside* the United States are graded as high-level **felonies** with all ranges of sentencing options available, including the death penalty (18 U.S.C. § 2332, 2011).Domestic terrorism is defined exactly the same as international terrorism, except that the violent acts are committed *within* the territorial jurisdiction of the United States (18 U.S.C. § 2331(5), 2011). Prohibited as terrorism are the use of a weapon of mass destruction, which is defined as any destructive device or weapon designed to cause death or serious bodily injury through the release of chemicals, toxins, or radioactivity (18 U.S.C. § 2332A(c), 2011), bombings of places of public use—including public transportation systems (18 U.S.C. § 2332F, 2011)—financing of terrorism (18 U.S.C. § 2339C, 2011), harboring or concealing terrorists (18 U.S.C. § 2339, 2011), or attempt or conspiracy to do any of the foregoing. All these crimes are **graded** as serious felonies.

Example of Terrorism

Zacarias Moussaoui, a French citizen, was the *only* defendant prosecuted for the September 11, 2001, terrorist attacks. Although Moussaoui was not onboard any of the planes that crashed into the World Trade Center, Pentagon, and a Pennsylvania field because he was in federal custody, he was **indicted** (Zacarias Moussaoui indictment, 2011) for several counts of conspiracy to commit terrorism and aircraft piracy and **pleaded guilty** to all charges. Specifically, Moussaoui pleaded guilty to conspiracy to commit acts of terrorism transcending national boundaries, conspiracy to commit aircraft piracy, conspiracy to destroy aircraft, conspiracy to use weapons of mass destruction, conspiracy to murder US employees, and conspiracy to destroy property of the United States. After the extended trial, during which Moussaoui attempted to represent himself, and the resulting guilty pleas, the jury carefully considered and recommended against the death penalty for Moussaoui, who was thereafter sentenced to life in prison (Markon, J. & Dwyer, T., 2011). Moussaoui later moved to withdraw his guilty pleas, but his motion was rejected by the US District Court for the Eastern District of Virginia (U.S. v. Moussaoui, 2011), whose decision was later affirmed by the US Court of Appeals for the Fourth Circuit (U.S. v. Moussaoui, 2011).

Figure 13.4 Moussaoui Indictment

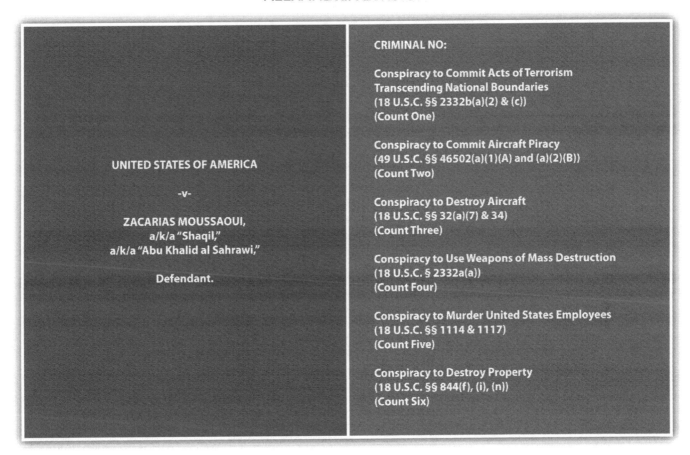

IN THE UNITED STATES DISTRICT COURT
FOR THE EASTERN DISTRICT OF VIRGINIA
ALEXANDRIA DIVISION

UNITED STATES OF AMERICA

-v-

ZACARIAS MOUSSAOUI,
a/k/a "Shaqil,"
a/k/a "Abu Khalid al Sahrawi,"

Defendant.

CRIMINAL NO:

Conspiracy to Commit Acts of Terrorism
Transcending National Boundaries
(18 U.S.C. §§ 2332b(a)(2) & (c))
(Count One)

Conspiracy to Commit Aircraft Piracy
(49 U.S.C. §§ 46502(a)(1)(A) and (a)(2)(B))
(Count Two)

Conspiracy to Destroy Aircraft
(18 U.S.C. §§ 32(a)(7) & 34)
(Count Three)

Conspiracy to Use Weapons of Mass Destruction
(18 U.S.C. § 2332a(a))
(Count Four)

Conspiracy to Murder United States Employees
(18 U.S.C. §§ 1114 & 1117)
(Count Five)

Conspiracy to Destroy Property
(18 U.S.C. §§ 844(f), (i), (n))
(Count Six)

DECEMBER 2001 TERM - AT ALEXANDRIA
INDICTMENT

Constitutional Challenges to the USA PATRIOT Act

Portions of the USA PATRIOT Act provide for enhanced government surveillance capabilities, which are considered a search, so constitutional implications are present pursuant to the **Fourth Amendment**, which prohibits unreasonable search and seizure. In addition, provisions of the Act that prohibit financing terrorists and terrorism have been attacked as violative of the **First Amendment's** protection of free speech, free association, and freedom of religion. Litigation involving these challenges is ongoing and was filed on behalf of citizens by the American Civil Liberties Union (ACLU) (Kranich, N., 2011).

Figure 13.5 Diagram of Crimes Involving National Security and Terrorism

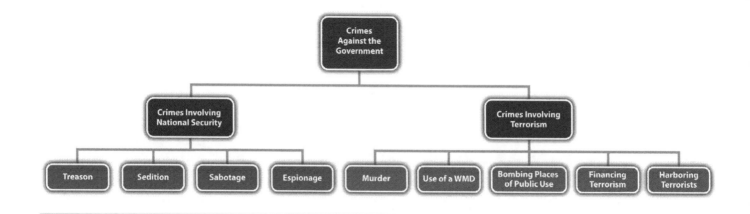

Key Takeaways

- Three statutory schemes targeting terroristic conduct are the Omnibus Diplomatic Security and Antiterrorism Act of 1986, the Antiterrorism and Effective Death Penalty Act of 1996, and the USA PATRIOT Act.
- The Department of Homeland Security enforces terrorism laws.
- The definition of international terrorism is violent acts committed outside the United States that would be criminal if committed in the United States and that appear to be intended to influence a civilian population or government by intimidation, or to affect the conduct of government by mass destruction, assassination, or kidnapping. The definition of domestic terrorism is exactly the same, except the criminal acts take place within the territorial jurisdiction of the United States.
- Examples of crimes involving terroristic conduct are murder, use of a weapon of mass destruction, bombing places of public use, financing terrorism, harboring a terrorist, and conspiracy or attempt to commit any of the foregoing.
- The USA PATRIOT Act expands government surveillance capabilities, so it is subject to a Fourth Amendment challenge as an unreasonable search, and also prohibits financing terrorism, so it is subject to a First Amendment challenge as a prohibition on free speech, freedom of religion, and freedom to associate.

Exercises

Answer the following questions. Check your answers using the answer key at the end of the chapter.

Joshua shoots and kills Khalid in front of the Pakistani Embassy in Washington, DC. Is this an act of domestic terrorism? Why or why not?

Read *Humanitarian Law Project v. Reno*, 205 F.3d 1130 (2000). Did the US Court of Appeals for the Ninth Circuit uphold 18 U.S.C. § 2339, which prohibits providing material support to terrorists? What were the constitutional challenges to this federal statute? The case is available at this link: http://scholar.google.com/scholar_case?case=6926778734800618484&q= convicted+%222339%22&hl=en&as_sdt=2,5&as_ylo=2000.

Read *Humanitarian Law Project v. U.S. Department of Justice*, 352 F.3d 382 (2003). In this case, the same federal statute was analyzed (18 U.S.C. § 2339) as in *Humanitarian Law Project v. Reno*, in Exercise 2. Did the US Court of Appeals for the Ninth Circuit uphold the statute in the face of a Fifth Amendment challenge that the statute deprived the defendants of due process of law? Why or why not? The case is available at this link: http://scholar.google.com/scholar_case?case=2048259608876560530&q= convicted+%222339%22&hl=en&as_sdt=2,5&as_ylo=2000.

References

Department of Homeland Security website, accessed May 4, 2011, http://www.dhs.gov/index.shtm.

Kranich, N., "The Impact of the USA PATRIOT Act: An Update," Fepproject.org website, accessed May 4, 2011, http://www.fepproject.org/commentaries/patriotactupdate.html.

Markon, J., Timothy Dwyer, "Jurors Reject Death Penalty for Moussaoui," *Washington Post* website, accessed May 11, 2011, http://www.washingtonpost.com/wp-dyn/content/article/2006/05/03/AR2006050300324.html.

U.S. v. Moussaoui, Criminal No. 01-455-A (2003), accessed May 4, 2011, http://law2.umkc.edu/faculty/projects/ftrials/moussaoui/withdrawguilty.pdf.

USA PATRIOT Act, Tit. II, § 203 et seq., http://frwebgate.access.gpo.gov/cgi-bin/getdoc.cgi?dbname=107_cong_public_laws&docid=f:publ056.107.pdf.

USA PATRIOT Act, Tit. VIII § 804, accessed May 4, 2011, http://frwebgate.access.gpo.gov/cgibin/getdoc.cgi?dbname=107_cong_public_laws&docid=f:publ056.107.pdf.

USA PATRIOT Act, Tit. VIII § 805, accessed May 4, 2011, http://frwebgate.access.gpo.gov/cgi-bin/getdoc.cgi?dbname=107_cong_public_laws&docid=f:publ056.107.pdf.

USA PATRIOT Act, Tit. VIII § 806, accessed May 4, 2011, http://frwebgate.access.gpo.gov/cgi-bin/getdoc.cgi?dbname=107_cong_public_laws&docid=f:publ056.107.pdf.

Zacarias Moussaoui indictment, Justice.gov website, accessed May 4, 2011, http://www.justice.gov/ag/moussaouiindictment.htm.

18 U.S.C. § 1101(a) (22), accessed May 3, 2011, http://www.law.cornell.edu/uscode/html/uscode08/usc_sec_08_00001101—-000-.html.

18 U.S.C. § 2331(1), accessed May 3, 2011, http://www.law.cornell.edu/uscode/718/usc_sec_18_00002331—-000-.html.

18 U.S.C. § 2331(5), accessed May 3, 2011, http://www.law.cornell.edu/uscode/718/usc_sec_18_00002331—-000-.html.

18 U.S.C. § 2332, accessed May 3, 2011, http://www.law.cornell.edu/uscode/718/usc_sec_18_00002332—-000-.html.

18 U.S.C. § 2332A(c) (2), accessed May 4, 2011, http://www.law.cornell.edu/uscode/718/usc_sec_18_00002332—a000-.html.

18 U.S.C. § 2332F, accessed May 4, 2011, http://www.law.cornell.edu/uscode/718/usc_sec_18_00002332—f000-.html.

18 U.S.C. § 2339, accessed May 3, 2011, http://www.law.cornell.edu/uscode/718/usc_sec_18_00002339—-000-.html.

18 U.S.C. § 2339C, accessed May 3, 2011, http://www.law.cornell.edu/uscode/718/usc_sec_18_00002339—C000-.html.

CC licensed content, Shared previously

- Criminal Law. **Provided by**: University of Minnesota Libraries Publishing . **Located at**: http://open.lib.umn.edu/criminallaw/. **License**: *CC BY-NC-SA: Attribution-NonCommercial-ShareAlike*

13.3 Perjury, Bribery, and Obstruction of Justice

Learning Objectives

Define the elements of perjury.
Identify the issues commonly encountered in a perjury prosecution.
Identify a potential defense to perjury.
Define perjury by inconsistent statements and subornation of perjury.
Analyze perjury and subornation of perjury grading.
Define the elements of bribery, identify the primary difficulty in a prosecution for this offense, and analyze bribery grading.
Define the elements of various forms of obstruction of justice, and analyze obstruction of justice grading.

Crimes against the administration of justice impede the government's ability to carry out the important functions of prosecuting and convicting criminals, which, in turn, destroys citizens' confidence that the US legal system is effective in ensuring individual safety and security. This section analyzes perjury, bribery, and obstruction of justice, along with the issues commonly encountered when prosecuting these offenses. Additional statutes criminalizing contempt of court, resisting arrest, and escape are also available for review.

Perjury History and Elements

Witness testimony is important in a variety of settings. Juries depend on witness testimony to reach a fair and impartial verdict in civil and criminal trials, and grand juries depend on witness testimony to indict defendants for criminal conduct. Thus modern laws of perjury are calculated to ensure that witnesses testify truthfully so that justice can be done in each individual case.

In the Middle Ages, the witnesses were the jurors, so the criminalization of false witness testimony did not occur until the sixteenth century when the idea of a trial by an impartial jury emerged. The first common-law prohibition against witness perjury criminalized **false** testimony, given under **oath**, in a **judicial proceeding**, about a **material** issue. This definition was also incorporated into early American common law (Jrank.org, 2011).

In modern times, every state prohibits perjury, as well as the federal government (18 U.S.C. § 1621, 2011). Most state statutes or state common law, in states that allow common-law crimes, define perjury as a false material statement (**criminal act**), made with the **specific intent** or **purposely** to deceive, or the **general intent** or **knowingly** that the statement was false, in a judicial or official proceeding (**attendant circumstance**), under oath (**attendant circumstance**) (Ga. Code tit. 16 § 16-10-70, 2011). The Model Penal Code defines perjury as a false material statement, that the defendant does not believe to be true, made under oath in any official proceeding (Model Penal Code § 241.1(1)). The biggest issues commonly encountered in any perjury prosecution are proving the validity of the oath, the defendant's criminal intent, the materiality of the false statement, and any requirement of corroborative evidence.

Necessity of a Valid Oath

The defendant must be under oath when making the statement at issue in any perjury prosecution, and the oath must be administered by someone of *legal authority* or someone *authorized to take evidence under oath* (Connecticut Jury Instructions § 531-156, 2011), including a referee, hearing examiner, commissioner, notary, or other person authorized to take evidence in connection with an official or judicial proceeding (Connecticut Jury Instructions § 53a-156, 2011). Federally and in many jurisdictions, the false statement can be **written**, as long as it is *certified*, such as a signature on an income tax return (18 U.S.C. § 6065, 2011) or a report (Cal. Penal Code § 129, 2011). The Model Penal Code also considers a false **written** statement perjury, as long as the document containing the statement is made upon oath or affirmation (Model Penal Code § 241.1(3)). In spite of the **attendant circumstance** requirement that the statement be made under oath, many jurisdictions disallow a defense to a prosecution for perjury based on the assertion that the oath or affirmation was administered or taken in an *irregular* manner (Ala. Code § 13A-10-108, 2011). The Model Penal Code has a similar provision (Model Penal Code § 241.1(3)). In addition, many jurisdictions have a provision that witnesses who *refuse* to take an oath shall have the option of making a nonreligous affirmation that has the **same legal effect** as the oath (42 Pa. Cons. Stat. Ann. § 5901, 2011). The Model Penal Code allows for an "oath or equivalent affirmation" (Model Penal Code § 241.1(1)).

Perjury Criminal Intent

As stated previously, in many jurisdictions, the defendant must **know** that a statement is false or must make the statement with the **specific intent** or **purposely** to *deceive*. When the intent requirement is general intent or knowledge that the statement is false, proof that the statement is false could give rise to an inference of intent (State v. Kimber, 2011).

Materiality Requirement

Perjury generally requires a false statement that is **material**, which means that it substantially affected or could substantially affect the outcome of the proceeding (Mo. Ann. Stat. § 575.040, 2011). In many jurisdictions and federally, materiality is a question of fact for the trier of fact, which could be a **jury** (U.S. v. Guadin, 2011). The Model Penal Code defines materiality as a statement that could have affected the course or outcome of the proceeding and declares that materiality should be a question of law, which means it should be determined by a **judge**, *not a jury* (Model Penal Code § 241.1(2)). Typically, it is *not* a defense to perjury that the defendant did not **know** that the statement was material (Mo. Ann. Stat. § 575.040(3), 2011). The Model Penal Code has a similar provision (Model Penal Code § 241.1(2)).

Corroborative Evidence Requirement

Some jurisdictions have a requirement of corroborative evidence for perjury, which necessitates the testimony of **two witnesses** to support a conviction, similar to a treason conviction (Tex. Code of Criminal Procedure, § 38.18, 2011). The Model Penal Code also has this corroborative evidence requirement (Model Penal Code § 241.1(6)).

Defense of Retraction

Many jurisdictions provide a defense to perjury if the defendant **retracts** his or her false statement in the course of the same proceeding in which it was made before it becomes manifest that the falsification will be exposed (Ala. Code § 13A-10-107, 2011). The Model Penal Code has a similar provision (Model Penal Code § 241.1(4)).

Example of a Case Lacking an Element of Perjury

Marcus is a witness in a civil suit for damages against Lindsay. Macy's department store is suing Lindsay for the alleged theft of a diamond necklace. Marcus takes an oath sworn by the court commissioner. He thereafter testifies that he saw Lindsay try on the necklace and then walk out of the store without paying for it. When the Macy's attorney asks Marcus what he was doing at Macy's, Marcus responds that he was buying some jewelry as a gift for his wife. In actuality, Marcus was shopping for jewelry as a gift for his *girlfriend*. Marcus has probably not committed perjury in this case. Marcus is testifying as a witness in a *civil* rather than *criminal* trial, but this satisfies the perjury requirement that the testimony be offered during a **judicial** or **official** proceeding. Before testifying, Marcus took an oath that was administered by a court commissioner, also satisfying the perjury requirement that the defendant take an oath administered by someone with the *legal authority* or *authorization* to take evidence under oath. Marcus's statement is *false*, and he made the statement with **knowledge** of its falsity, which satisfies the perjury criminal intent requirement. However, Marcus's statement does not appear to be **material** to this judicial proceeding because the reason for Marcus's presence at Macy's will not affect the outcome of Lindsay's civil theft trial (usually called the tort of conversion). Thus Marcus is probably not subject to prosecution for and conviction of perjury, based on his testimony in this case.

Example of Perjury

Review the example in Section 13 "Example of a Case Lacking an Element of Perjury" with Marcus. Change this example so that Marcus testifies that he did *not* see Lindsay walk out of the Macy's department store without paying for the necklace because he does not want to admit that he was shopping for jewelry to buy his girlfriend. Anthony, the Macy's civil trial attorney, cross-examines Marcus, and forces him to admit that he saw Lindsay steal the necklace, and that he was *lying* previously. Marcus has most likely committed perjury in this example. Marcus made a **false** statement, under a validly administered **oath**, in a **judicial** proceeding, with **knowledge** of its falsity. Marcus's statement was **material** because, if believed, it would have helped exonerate Lindsay in her civil case. In many jurisdictions, the trier of fact, which could be a judge *or jury*, determines whether or not the statement is material. Marcus's admission that he was lying is not a **retraction** that could serve as a defense because it was not made until the lie was about to be exposed. Thus all the elements of perjury appear to be present, and Marcus may be subject to prosecution for and conviction of this offense.

Figure 13.6 Diagram of Defenses to Perjury

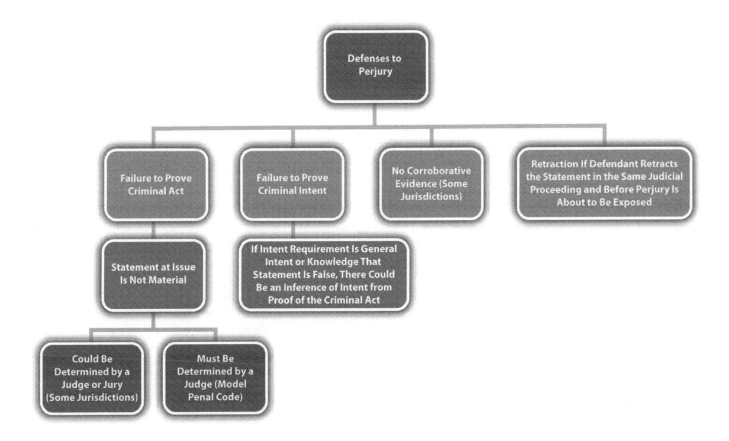

Perjury by Inconsistent Statements

Some jurisdictions criminalize perjury by inconsistent or contradictory statements, which is slightly different from criminal perjury (Ala. Code § 13-10-104, 2011).3 Perjury by inconsistent statements is easier to prove than traditional perjury because the prosecution can simply offer evidence that the defendant made statements that are inconsistent, in a judicial proceeding, after taking a validly administered oath. Corroborative evidence is not required, and the prosecution does not have the burden of proving that one of the statements is false, just that one or the other was false and not believed by the defendant to be true (Ala. Code § 13A-10-104, 2011). The Model Penal Code has a similar provision (Model Penal Code § 241.1(5)).

Example of Perjury by Inconsistent Statements

Review the example with Marcus in Section 13 "Example of Perjury". If Marcus's jurisdiction criminalizes perjury by inconsistent statements, Marcus could most likely be prosecuted for this offense. Marcus made two inconsistent statements while under a validly administered oath in Lindsay's conversion trial, which is a judicial proceeding. In Marcus's criminal perjury by inconsistent statements prosecution, the prosecutor need only offer evidence of the inconsistent statements to the trier of fact. The prosecutor does *not* have to provide corroborative evidence and does *not* have the burden of proving that the first statement was **false**, which will simplify and expedite the trial and may subject Marcus to conviction of this offense.

Subornation of Perjury

Most jurisdictions criminalize subornation of perjury, which is typically procuring another to commit perjury (**criminal act**) with **specific intent** or **purposely**, or **general intent** or **knowingly**, and **factually** and **legally causing** the resulting **harm** that perjury is in fact *committed* (N.C. Gen. Stat. § 14-210, 2011).

Example of a Case Lacking an Element of Subornation of Perjury

Review the example given with Marcus in Section 13 "Example of Perjury". Add to this example and assume that Marcus begs Janelle, another witness in Lindsay's conversion trial, to say that she did not see him at Macy's the day Lindsay stole the necklace. Janelle flatly refuses. Marcus has not committed subornation of perjury in this case. Although Marcus *tried* to procure Janelle to commit **perjury**, with **specific intent** or **purposely**, Janelle did not cooperate and did not commit the perjury. Thus the **harm** element of subornation of perjury is *lacking*, and Marcus can be prosecuted only for *attempted* subornation of perjury or *solicitation* to commit perjury, rather than the completed offense.

Figure 13.7 Comparison of Perjury by Inconsistent Statements and Subornation of Perjury

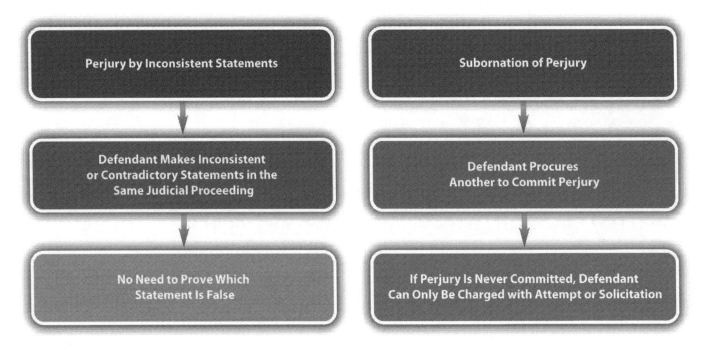

Perjury Grading

Perjury is generally **graded** as a felony (N.C. Gen. Stat. § 14-209, 2011), with a potential sentencing enhancement for committing perjury that causes another to be sentenced to prison or the death penalty (Ga. Code tit. 16, § 16-10-70, 2011). The Model Penal Code grades perjury as a felony of the third degree (Model Penal Code § 241.1(1)). Subornation of perjury is also **graded** as a felony (N.C. Gen. Stat. § 14-210, 2011). However, because of the procedural difficulties in successfully convicting a defendant of perjury and subornation of perjury, these crimes are not often prosecuted. Nonetheless, the threat of a felony conviction still serves as a deterrent and helps to ensure that witnesses testify truthfully in judicial and official proceedings and give accurate statements in certified writings.

Bribery Elements

Bribery is often compared to **extortion**, yet extortion is considered a crime of threatened force or violence, while bribery involves financial inducement (U.S. v. Adcock, 2011). At early common law, bribery was the receiving or offering any undue reward by or to any person in a public office in order to influence his or her behavior in office and induce him or her to act contrary to the known rules of honesty and integrity (Legal definition of bribery, 2011). In modern times, many criminal statutes define bribery as conferring, offering, agreeing to confer, or soliciting, accepting, or agreeing to accept any *benefit* upon a public official (**criminal act**) with the **specific** intent or **purposely** or the **general intent** or **knowingly** to form an agreement or understanding that the public official's vote, opinion, judgment, action, decision, or exercise of discretion will be *influenced* by the benefit (N.Y. Penal Law § 200.00, 2011; N.Y. Penal Law § 200.10). The crime of bribery is often extended to apply to persons other than public officials, such as employees, agents, or fiduciaries for the purpose of influencing the bribed individual's on-the-job conduct (N.Y. Penal Law § 180.00, 2011). This type of bribery is typically called commercial bribery (N.Y. Penal Law § 180.00, 2011). Bribery can also cover members of a state legislature (Cal. Penal Code § 85, 2011; Cal. Penal Code § 86; Cal. Penal Code § 93), any judicial officer, juror, referee, umpire (Cal. Penal Code § 92, 2011), or witness (Or. Rev. Stat. § 162.265, 2011; Or. Rev. Stat. §162.275, 2011) when a bribe is conferred or offered, asked for, received, or agreed to be received to influence their vote or decision. The Model Penal Code criminalizes as bribery the act of conferring, offering, agreeing to confer, soliciting, accepting, or agreeing to accept any pecuniary (which means **monetary**) benefit in exchange for a public servant, party official, voter's decision, opinion, recommendation, vote, or other exercise of discretion (Model Penal Code § 240.1(1)). The Model Penal Code also criminalizes as bribery the act of conferring, offering, agreeing to confer, soliciting, accepting, or agreeing to accept *any* benefit in exchange for a judicial or administrative officer's decision, vote, recommendation, or other exercise of official discretion (Model Penal Code § 240.1(2)).

Prosecutorial Burden in Bribery Prosecutions

Similar to perjury, bribery is notoriously *difficult* to *prove*, which is a factor prosecutors must consider when deciding whether or not to charge an individual(s) with this offense. The most difficult bribery element to prove beyond a reasonable doubt is the criminal intent element of **specific intent** or **purposely** or **general intent** or **knowingly** to enter into an agreement that *influences* the bribed individual's decision.

Example of Bribery

Isabel, a defendant on trial for perjury, notices the judge presiding in her case shopping at Macy's department store. Isabel thereafter buys an expensive watch, has it wrapped, walks up to the judge, and offers it to him as a gift. Isabel has most likely committed bribery in this case. Although the judge did not accept Isabel's "gift," most states criminalize as bribery the **offer** of any benefit, so the act of bribery is complete when Isabel proffers the watch. In addition, based on these facts, Isabel's connection to the judge is only through her perjury prosecution, so her act appears calculated to influence his decision in that case, especially because the watch is expensive and not merely a token. Note that a prosecutor is required to prove *beyond a reasonable doubt* Isabel's **specific intent** or **purposely** or **general intent** or **knowingly** to enter into an agreement with the judge influencing his decision, which is challenging even under the obvious circumstances apparent in this case.

Another Example of Bribery

Review the example with Isabel in Section 13 "Example of Bribery". Add to this example and assume that the judge graciously accepts Isabel's gift and thereafter rules in her favor, *acquitting* her of perjury. In this example, *both* the judge and Isabel have likely committed bribery because most states criminalize the conferring, offering, *and* **accepting** and **receiving** a bribe as the criminal act elements. Thus both Isabel and the judge may be subject to prosecution for and conviction of this offense, and the judge's acquittal of Isabel will ease the prosecutor's burden in proving the **specific intent** or **purposely** or **general intent** or **knowingly** to enter into an agreement corruptly influencing the decision making in this case.

Example of a Case Lacking an Element of Bribery

Isabel notices a gentleman struggling to pay his bill at a local coffee shop. Isabel steps up and charitably offers to pay the gentleman's bill. Later in the day, while watching her son's professional baseball game, Isabel notices that the umpire looks familiar. After pondering it for a few minutes, she realizes that he is the same gentleman who could not pay his bill at the coffee shop. Isabel and the umpire probably have *not* committed bribery in this case.

Although Isabel gave the umpire money, and he was the decision maker in her son's baseball game, Isabel did not give the money, nor did the umpire accept it, with the **specific intent** or **purposely** or **general intent** or **knowingly** to enter into an agreement *influencing* the umpire's decisions. Thus the criminal intent element for bribery appears to be lacking, and neither Isabel nor the umpire are subject to prosecution for and conviction of this offense.

Bribery When No Authority to Act Is Present

In many states and under the Model Penal Code, it is *no defense* to bribery that the individual bribed does *not* have the **authority** to act or make the decision that is the subject of the bribe (Model Penal Code § 240.1) (Ala. Code § 13A-10-61, 2011).

Example of Bribery When No Authority to Act Is Present

Review the example with Isabel and the judge in Section 13 "Another Example of Bribery". Change this example and assume that the "judge" in question is an imposter who is merely masquerading as a judge to live out a lifelong fantasy. Isabel and the "judge" may still be prosecuted for and convicted of bribery in many jurisdictions and under the Model Penal Code because **lack of authority** is typically *not a defense* to bribery under modern statutes criminalizing this offense.

Figure 13.8 Diagram of Defenses to Bribery

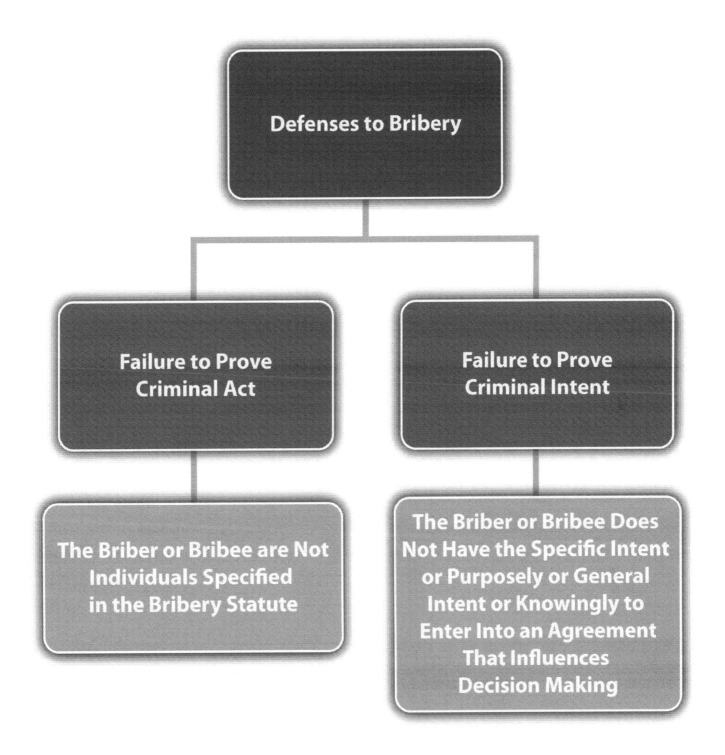

Bribery Grading

Bribery is typically **graded** as a felony (N.Y. Penal Law § 200.00, 2011) with enhancements for bribery that is carried out with a larger sum of money (N.Y. Penal Law § 200.03, 2011) or bribery that results in someone's prosecution or incarceration for a felony (N.Y. Penal Law § 200.04, 2011). When a state legislator (Cal. Penal Code § 88, 2011) or a public official (Cal. Penal Code § 74, 2011) commits bribery, it is typical to **disqualify** that individual from his or her office for life, in addition to any other sentence.

Obstruction of Justice

Obstruction of justice takes many forms and is a classic example of an offense against the administration of justice. States and the federal government exercise broad latitude in enacting statutes that criminalize interference with any aspect of law enforcement procedure or the prosecution and conviction of criminal offenders. Some typical examples of obstruction of justice are as follows: giving false identification to a law enforcement officer (720 ILCS § 5/31-4.5, 2011), impersonating a law enforcement officer (Fla. Stat. Ann. § 843.08, 2011), refusing to aid a law enforcement officer when requested (N.Y. Penal Law § 295.10, 2011), giving false evidence (720 ILCS § 5/31-4, 2011), hiding or concealing oneself and refusing to give evidence (720 ILCS § 5/31-4, 2011), tampering with evidence (Or. Rev. Stat. § 162.295, 2011), and tampering with a witness (18 U.S.C. § 1512, 2011) or juror (Ariz. Rev. Stat. § 13-2807, 2011). All these acts are generally supported by **specific intent** or **purposely** or **general intent** or **knowingly**. The Model Penal Code prohibits threatening unlawful harm to any person or public servant with purpose to influence his decision, opinion, recommendation, vote, or other exercise of discretion (Model Penal Code § 240.2). Obstruction of justice offenses are most often **graded** as a misdemeanor or felony, depending on the offense.

Example of Obstruction of Justice

Barry Bonds, a baseball player and record-breaking home run hitter for the San Francisco Giants, was found guilty by a federal jury for **obstruction of justice**, based on his refusal to answer a question during a grand jury investigation of his steroid use (Macur, J., 2011). Bonds was also charged with three counts of **perjury**, but the jury could not agree to convict, resulting in a mistrial on all three counts (Ortiz, J. L., 2011). The perjury charges stemmed from Bonds's claim while testifying under oath that he never knowingly used steroids, never knowingly used human growth hormones, and was never injected with a substance by anyone other than his trainer. The obstruction of justice conviction resulted from Bonds's evasive answer to the question of whether his personal trainer had ever injected him with steroids (Macur, J., 2011). Instead of answering yes or no to this question, Bonds began reminiscing about his friendship with the trainer, who went to prison four times in five years for also refusing to testify in the investigation (Macur, J., 2011). The perjury charges support the obstruction of justice charge, so the defense asked for a court dismissal of the obstruction of justice conviction in order to clear the way for an appeal (Ortiz, J. L., 2011). Note that Bonds's **obstruction of justice** charge of evading the question and refusing to give evidence appears *easier* to prove than the **perjury** charges, which have a daunting criminal intent requirement, as discussed in Section 13 "Perjury Criminal Intent".

The Barry Bonds Verdict Video

Associated Press: Bonds Guilty of Obstruction, Jury Hung on Others

The verdict in the federal Barry Bonds case is explained in this video:
(click to see video)

Additional Crimes against the Government

Additional crimes against the government that impair the orderly administration of justice are **contempt** (N.C. Gen. Stat. § 5A-11, et seq., 2011), **resisting arrest** (18 Pa. Cons. Stat. Ann. § 5104, 2011), and **escape** (Tex. Penal Code § 38.06, 2011). Review the statutes in the endnotes for common elements and grading of these offenses.

Figure 13.9 Diagram of Perjury, Bribery, and Obstruction of Justice

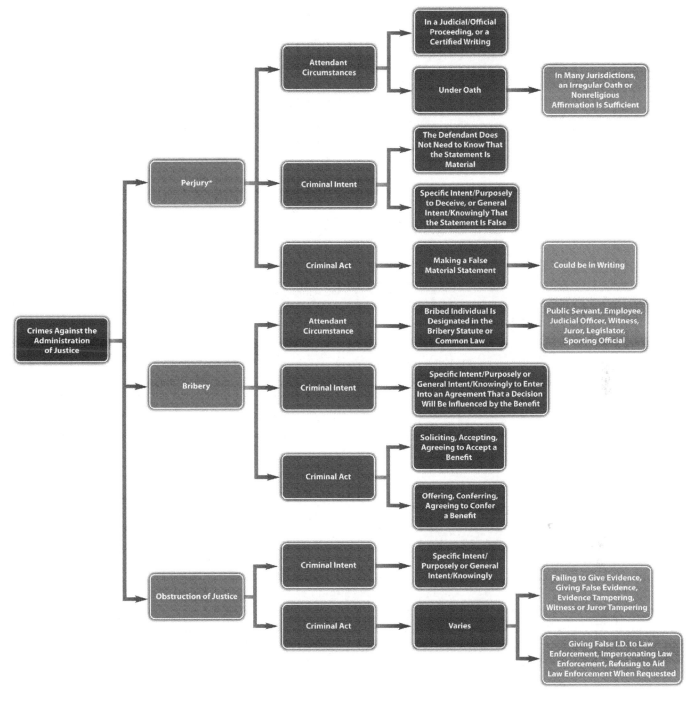

* Requires testimony of two witnesses as corroborative evidence in some jurisdictions

Key Takeaways

- Most jurisdictions define perjury as a false material statement (criminal act), made with specific intent or purposely to deceive, or the general intent or knowingly that the statement was false, in a judicial or official proceeding, or in a certified writing (attendant circumstance), under oath (attendant circumstance).
- The issues commonly encountered in any perjury prosecution are proving the validity of the oath, the defendant's criminal intent, or the materiality of the false statement, and any requirement of corroborative evidence.
- Many jurisdictions provide a defense to perjury if the defendant retracts his or her false statement in the course of the same proceeding in which it was made before it becomes manifest that the

falsification will be exposed.

- Perjury by inconsistent statements is when the defendant makes statements that are inconsistent (criminal act), in a judicial proceeding (attendant circumstance), after taking a validly administered oath (attendant circumstance). The prosecution does not need to prove which statement is false for this offense. Subornation of perjury is procuring another to commit perjury (criminal act), with specific intent or purposely, or general intent or knowingly, and factually and legally causing the resulting harm that perjury is actually committed.
- Perjury is generally graded as a felony, with a potential sentencing enhancement for committing perjury that causes another to be sentenced to prison or the death penalty. Subornation of perjury is also graded as a felony.
- Many criminal statutes define bribery as conferring, offering, agreeing to confer, or soliciting, accepting, or agreeing to accept, any benefit upon a public official (criminal act) with the specific intent or purposely, or the general intent or knowingly to form an agreement or understanding that the public official's decision making will be influenced by the benefit. The crime of bribery is often extended to apply to persons other than public officials, such as employees, agents, or fiduciaries for the purpose of influencing the bribed individual's on-the-job conduct, which is called commercial bribery. Bribery can also cover members of a state legislature, any judicial officer, juror, referee, umpire, or witness. The primary issue in a bribery prosecution is proving the defendant's criminal intent to enter into an agreement that influences the bribed individual's decision making. Bribery is typically graded as a felony, with enhancements for a bribe that is a large sum of money or bribery that results in incarceration for a felony, along with a disqualification from office.
- Some typical examples of obstruction of justice are as follows: giving false identification to a law enforcement officer, impersonating a law enforcement officer, refusing to aid a law enforcement officer when requested, giving false evidence, hiding or concealing oneself and refusing to give evidence, tampering with evidence, and tampering with a witness or juror. All these acts are generally supported by specific intent or purposely, or general intent or knowingly. Obstruction of justice is graded anywhere from a misdemeanor to a felony, depending on the offense.

Exercises

Answer the following questions. Check your answers using the answer key at the end of the chapter.

Susannah, a Hollywood movie star, is a witness in a civil personal injury case. Susannah saw a car accident and is subpoenaed to testify that the defendant was at fault. After the court commissioner administers an oath to tell the truth, Susannah takes the witness stand. She knows the case will generate significant publicity, so Susannah shaves ten years off of her age when asked routine background questions by the prosecutor. If Susannah is thereafter caught in this lie and prosecuted for **perjury**, what will be the primary issue in her perjury prosecution? How will this issue be resolved?

Read *State v. Carr*, 172 Conn. 458 (1977). In this case, the defendant was convicted of bribery when he paid an undercover detective to refrain from investigating narcotics crimes in the area. The defendant appealed, claiming the jury should have been instructed on the lesser included offense of offering gifts to state police officers. Did the Supreme Court of Connecticut uphold the defendant's bribery conviction? Why or why not? The case is available at this link: http://scholar.google.com/scholar_case?case=14705028387089517508&q= %22State+v.+Carr%22&hl=en&as_sdt=2,5.

Read *People v. Silverberg*, 771 N.Y.S. 2d 274 (2003). In this case, the defendant was convicted of witness tampering for a single telephone call he made to an attorney that implied he would send letters to a grievance committee if the attorney did not drop charges against him. Did the Supreme Court of New York uphold the defendant's conviction? Why or why not? The case is available at this link: http://scholar.google.com/scholar_case?case=3089258849772766127&q= %22witness+tampering%22&hl=en&as_sdt=4,33&as_ylo=2003.

Law and Ethics

Should Former President Clinton Have Been Criminally Prosecuted for Perjury and Obstruction of Justice?

On May 6, 1994, Paula Jones filed a civil lawsuit for sexual harassment against then-president Bill Clinton. The US Supreme Court ruled that the president was not immune to this lawsuit, allowing it to continue (Clinton v. Jones, 2011). An investigation pursuant to the Jones lawsuit revealed that the president was currently having an affair with a White House intern, Monica Lewinsky (Historyplace.com website, 2011). During a Jones lawsuit deposition, the president stated under oath that he did not have sexual relations with Ms. Lewinsky pursuant to the definition of sexual relations given by the questioning attorneys (Deposition excerpts, 2011). He also stated that he could not recall ever being alone with Lewinsky at the White House (Deposition excerpts, 2011). After the deposition, he was involved in an effort to get Ms. Lewinsky a federal job outside Washington, DC (Historyplace.com, 2011). Although the Jones lawsuit was dismissed, the president was evasive when asked questions regarding the Lewinsky affair during a grand jury investigation instigated by Prosecutor and former Solicitor General Kenneth Starr. The evening of the grand jury investigation, the president appeared on national TV and admitted, "Indeed, I did have a relationship with Ms. Lewinsky that was not appropriate. In fact, it was wrong. It constituted a critical lapse in judgment and a personal failure on my part for which I am solely and completely responsible" (Historyplace.com, 2011). The House of Representatives later **impeached** Clinton for perjury and obstruction of justice, based on the statements he made at the grand jury investigation and his conduct during the Jones deposition. After a trial in the Senate, he was **acquitted** of both counts and thereafter served out his term as president (Historyplace.com, 2011). He was never *criminally* prosecuted for perjury or obstruction of justice outside the impeachment procedure, although he was later **disbarred** for his behavior (Gearan, A., 2011).

> Is it **ethical** to allow the president to avoid a criminal prosecution for perjury and obstruction of justice **while he is in office**? Why or why not?

Check your answer using the answer key at the end of the chapter.

Clinton Declaration and Admission Videos

Clinton: "I did not have sexual relations with that woman…"

In this video, President Clinton denies that he had sexual relations with Monica Lewinsky: (click to see video)

President Clinton Apologizes to the Nation

In this video, President Clinton admits that he had an inappropriate relationship with Monica Lewinsky: (click to see video)

References

Ala. Code § 13A-10-104, accessed May 6, 2011, http://law.onecle.com/alabama/criminal-code/13A-10-104.html.

Ala. Code § 13A-10-107, accessed May 6, 2011, http://law.onecle.com/alabama/criminal-code/13A-10-107.html.

Ala. Code § 13A-10-108, accessed May 5, 2011, http://law.onecle.com/alabama/criminal-code/13A-10-108.html.

Ala. Code § 13A-10-61, accessed May 7, 2011, http://law.onecle.com/alabama/criminal-code/13A-10-61.html.

Ariz. Rev. Stat. § 13-2807, accessed May 7, 2011, http://law.onecle.com/arizona/criminal-code/13-2807.html.

Cal. Penal Code § 129, accessed May 5, 2011, http://law.onecle.com/california/penal/129.html.

Cal. Penal Code § 74, accessed May 7, 2011, http://law.onecle.com/california/penal/74.html.

Cal. Penal Code § 85, accessed May 6, 2011, http://law.onecle.com/california/penal/85.html.

Cal. Penal Code § 86, http://law.onecle.com/california/penal/86.html.

Cal. Penal Code § 88, accessed May 7, 2011, http://law.onecle.com/california/penal/88.html.

Cal. Penal Code § 92, accessed May 6, 2011, http://law.onecle.com/california/penal/92.html.

Cal. Penal Code § 93, http://law.onecle.com/california/penal/93.html.

Clinton v. Jones, 520 U.S. 681 (1997), accessed May 9, 2011, http://www.law.cornell.edu/supct/html/95-1853.ZS.html.

Connecticut Jury Instructions § 53a-156, accessed May 5, 2011, http://www.jud.ct.gov/ji/criminal/part4/4.5-9.htm.

Deposition excerpts, Jones v. Clinton deposition, Historyplace.com website, accessed May 9, 2011, http://www.historyplace.com/unitedstates/impeachments/jones-deposition.htm.

Fla. Stat. Ann. § 843.08, accessed May 7, 2011, http://law.onecle.com/florida/crimes/843.08.html.

Ga. Code tit. 16 § 16-10-70, accessed May 5, 2011, http://law.onecle.com/georgia/16/16-10-70.html.

Gearan, A., "Clinton Disbarred by Supreme Court," Famguardian.org website, accessed May 9, 2011, http://famguardian.org/Subjects/LawAndGovt/News/ClintonDisbar-011001.htm.

Historyplace.com website, "Presidential Impeachment Proceedings," accessed May 9, 2011, http://www.historyplace.com/unitedstates/impeachments/clinton.htm.
Jrank.org website, "Perjury—Perjury at Common Law," accessed May 5, 2011, http://law.jrank.org/pages/1632/Perjury-Perjury-at-common-law.html.

Legal definition of bribery, Duhaime.org website, accessed May 6, 2011, http://www.duhaime.org/LegalDictionary/B/Bribery.aspx.

Macur, J., "Bonds Guilty of Obstruction, but Not of Perjury," *New York Times* website, accessed May 8, 2011, http://www.nytimes.com/2011/04/14/sports/baseball/14bonds.html?pagewanted=1&_r=1.

Mo. Ann. Stat. § 575.040, accessed May 5, 2011, http://www1.law.umkc.edu/suni/CrimLaw/calendar/Class_4_Mo_perjury.htm.

Mo. Ann. Stat. § 575.040(3) (1), accessed May 5, 2011, http://www1.law.umkc.edu/suni/CrimLaw/calendar/Class_4_Mo_perjury.htm.

N.C. Gen. Stat. § 14-209, accessed May 6, 2011, http://law.onecle.com/north-carolina/14-criminal-law/14-209.html.

N.C. Gen. Stat. § 14-210, accessed May 6, 2011, http://law.onecle.com/north-carolina/14-criminal-law/14-210.html.

N.C. Gen. Stat. § 5A-11, et seq., accessed May 8, 2011, http://law.onecle.com/north-carolina/5a-contempt/index.html.

N.Y. Penal Law § 180.00, accessed May 6, 2011, http://law.onecle.com/new-york/penal/PEN0180.00_180.00.html.

N.Y. Penal Law § 195.10, accessed May 7, 2011, http://law.onecle.com/new-york/penal/PEN0195.10_195.10.html.

N.Y. Penal Law § 200.00, accessed May 6, 2011, http://law.onecle.com/new-york/penal/PEN0200.00_200.00.html.

N.Y. Penal Law § 200.03, accessed May 6, 2011, http://law.onecle.com/new-york/penal/PEN0200.03_200.03.html.

N.Y. Penal Law § 200.04, accessed May 6, 2011, http://law.onecle.com/new-york/penal/PEN0200.04_200.04.html.

N.Y. Penal Law § 200.10, http://law.onecle.com/new-york/penal/PEN0200.10_200.10.html.

Or. Rev. Stat. § 162.265, accessed May 6, 2011, http://law.onecle.com/oregon/162-offenses-against-the-state-and/162.265.html.

Or. Rev. Stat. § 162.295, accessed May 7, 2011,

http://law.onecle.com/oregon/162-offenses-against-the-state-and/162.295.html.

Or. Rev. Stat. §162.275, accessed May 7, 2011, http://law.onecle.com/oregon/162-offenses-against-the-state-and/162.275.html.

Ortiz, J. L., "Verdict in: Bonds Found Guilty, but Case Not Closed Yet," USA TODAY website, accessed May 8, 2011, http://www.usatoday.com/sports/baseball/2011-04-13-verdict-barry-bonds-guilty_N.htm.

State v. Kimber, 48 Conn. App. 234 (1998), accessed May 5, 2011, http://scholar.google.com/scholar_case?case=17399056576949304157&q=State+v.+Kimber+48&hl=en&as_sdt=2,5.

Tex. Code of Criminal Procedure, § 38.18, accessed May 5, 2011, http://law.onecle.com/texas/criminal-procedure/38.18.00.html.

Tex. Penal Code § 38.06, accessed May 8, 2011, http://law.onecle.com/texas/penal/38.06.00.html.

U.S. v. Adcock, 558 F.2d 397 (1977), accessed May 6, 2011, http://scholar.google.com/scholar_case?case=189694239263939940&hl=en&as_sdt=2&as_vis=1&oi=scholarr.

U.S. v. Gaudin, 515 U.S. 506 (1995), accessed May 5, 2011, http://scholar.google.com/scholar_case?case=12281686524757008977&hl=en&as_sdt=2&as_vis=1&oi=scholarr.

18 Pa. Cons. Stat. Ann. § 5104, accessed May 8, 2011, http://law.onecle.com/pennsylvania/crimes-and-offenses/00.051.004.000.html.

18 U.S.C. § 1512, accessed May 7, 2011, http://www.law.cornell.edu/uscode/718/usc_sec_18_00001512—-000-.html.

18 U.S.C. § 1621, accessed May 5, 2011, http://www.law.cornell.edu/uscode/718/usc_sec_18_00001621—-000-.html.

18 U.S.C. § 6065, accessed May 5, 2011, http://www.law.cornell.edu/uscode/26/usc_sec_26_00006065—-000-.html.

42 Pa. Cons. Stat. Ann. § 5901, accessed May 5, 2011, http://law.onecle.com/pennsylvania/judiciary-and-judicial-procedure/00.059.001.000.html.

720 ILCS § 5/31-4, accessed May 7, 2011, http://law.onecle.com/illinois/720ilcs5/31-4.html.

720 ILCS § 5/31-4.5, accessed May 7, 2011, http://law.onecle.com/illinois/720ilcs5/31-4.5.html.
CC licensed content, Shared previously

- Criminal Law. **Provided by**: University of Minnesota Libraries Publishing . **Located at**: http://open.lib.umn.edu/criminallaw/. **License**: *CC BY-NC-SA: Attribution-NonCommercial-ShareAlike*

13.4 End-of-Chapter Material

Summary

The federal government protects national security by primarily regulating crimes against the United States. One of the only crimes defined in the Constitution, treason, prohibits levying war against the United States, most likely with general intent or knowingly, or providing aid and comfort to the enemy with the specific intent or purposely to betray the United States, and is graded as a serious felony with all sentencing options available, including capital punishment. The Constitution specifies the evidentiary requirement that treason be proven by the testimony of two witnesses or the defendant's confession in open court. Sedition criminalizes the advocating, aiding, organizing, or teaching with general intent or knowingly, or publishing, printing, or circulating writings that advocate, aid, or teach with specific intent or purposely the forceful or violent overthrow of the US government and is graded as a serious felony that can prohibit the defendant from holding federal office for five years postconviction. Sabotage is destroying, damaging, or defectively producing specified property with specific intent or purposely, general intent or knowingly, or negligently to impede national defense and is graded as a serious felony. Espionage is gathering or transmitting defense information with general intent or knowingly or the specific intent or purposely to damage the United States or assist any foreign nation, during peace or war, and is graded as a serious felony with all range of sentencing options available, including capital punishment.

The federal government also primarily regulates terrorism and terroristic acts using the Omnibus Diplomatic Security and Antiterrorism Act of 1986, the Antiterrorism and Effective Death Penalty Act of 1996, and the USA PATRIOT Act. The Department of Homeland Security enforces criminal laws targeting terrorism. Terrorism is violent acts committed inside (domestic) or outside (international) the United States that appear to be intended to influence a civilian population or government by intimidation or to affect the conduct of government by mass destruction, assassination, or kidnapping. Currently prohibited as terrorism or terroristic conduct are murder, use of a weapon of mass destruction, bombing places of public use, financing terrorism, harboring a terrorist, and conspiracy or attempt to commit any of the foregoing. The USA PATRIOT Act expands government surveillance capabilities, so it is subject to a Fourth Amendment challenge as an unreasonable search, and also prohibits financing terrorism, so it is subject to a First Amendment challenge as a prohibition on free speech, freedom of religion, and freedom to associate.

The state and federal government both criminalize conduct that impedes the administration of justice, including perjury, bribery, and obstruction of justice. Perjury is typically defined as a false material oral or written statement made under oath or affirmation with the specific intent or purposely to deceive, or the general intent or knowingly that the statement is false, in a judicial or official proceeding or in a certified writing. The biggest issues encountered in a perjury prosecution are proving the validity of the oath, the defendant's criminal intent, the materiality of the false statement, and any requirement of corroborative evidence. One defense to perjury is retraction of the false material statement during the same judicial or official proceeding before it becomes manifest that the falsity will be exposed. Many jurisdictions also criminalize perjury committed by inconsistent statements made under oath or affirmation in an official or judicial proceeding and subornation of perjury, which is procuring another to commit perjury with specific intent or purposely. Perjury and subornation of perjury are typically graded as felonies. Bribery is conferring, offering, agreeing to confer, or soliciting, accepting, or agreeing to accept a benefit upon a public official, employee, legislator, participant in a judicial proceeding, or sports official with the specific intent or purposely, or the general intent or knowingly to influence the bribed individual's decision making. The most difficult bribery element to prove is the criminal intent element. Bribery is typically graded as a felony. Obstruction of justice crimes interfere with the orderly administration of justice. Examples of obstruction of justice offenses are giving false identification to a law enforcement officer, impersonating a law enforcement officer, refusing to aid a law enforcement officer when requested, giving false evidence, hiding or concealing oneself and refusing to give evidence, tampering with evidence, and tampering with a witness or juror, with specific intent or purposely, or general intent or knowingly. Obstruction of justice is graded as a misdemeanor or felony, depending on the offense.

You Be the USA

You are an assistant US attorney starting your first day on the job. You have been presented with four case files and told to review them and recommend criminal prosecutions based on the facts. Read each one and then decide which **crime should be prosecuted**. Check your answers using the answer key at the end of the chapter.

The defendant, an army intelligence analyst stationed near Baghdad, Iraq, downloaded thousands of classified Iraq and Afghanistan documents and confidential cables and released them to an ex-computer hacker who thereafter exposed them to the public. **Which crime** should be prosecuted: **treason** or **obstruction of justice**? Read about this case at this link: http://coto2.wordpress.com/2011/03/02/bradley-manning-charged-with-22-crimes-including-capital-offense-aiding-the-enemy.

The defendant typed up notes while her husband was analyzing sketches of a top-secret bomb's design for the purpose of passing the design on to another nation. **Which crime** should be prosecuted: **conspiracy to commit espionage** or **sabotage**? Read about this case at this link: http://law2.umkc.edu/faculty/projects/ftrials/rosenb/ROS_ACCT.HTM.

The defendant, a cosmetic company, paid Chinese officials to obtain direct licensing of its product in China. Which crime should be prosecuted: **harboring terrorists abroad** or **bribery**? Read about this case at this link: http://fortune.com/2014/12/17/avon-bribery-probe-settlement/.

The defendant, a corrections officer, lied to federal law enforcement during an investigation of her role in the assault of an inmate. Which crime should be prosecuted: **perjury** or **obstruction of justice**? Read about this case at this link: http://www.stltoday.com/news/local/crime-and-courts/article_3d7cd11a-8f67-11df-bc07-00127992bc8b.html.

Cases of Interest

- *Kawakita v. U.S.*, 343 U.S. 717 (1952), discusses a treason conviction based on the treatment of American POWs: http://scholar.google.com/scholar_case?case=14270191881160802490&q=%22treason%22&hl=en&as_sdt=2,5.
- *U.S. v. Rosen*, 445 F.Supp.2d 602 (2006), discusses prosecution under the Espionage Act: http://scholar.google.com/scholar_case?case=18013989744527722325&q=%2218+U.S.C.+793%22&hl=en&as_sdt=2,5.
- *Schultz v. Sykes*, 638 N.W. 2d 604 (2001), discusses the dismissal of a civil case based on subornation of perjury: http://scholar.google.com/scholar_case?case=3885876526561644390&q=%22subornation+of+perjury%22&hl=en&as_sdt=2,5&as_ylo=2000.

Articles of Interest

- Treason prosecutions in modern times: http://www.nysun.com/editorials/time-of-treason/41533
- The trial of Faisal Shahzad: http://www.csmonitor.com/USA/Justice/2010/1005/Life-sentence-for -Faisal-Shahzad-could-join-shoe-bomber-in-Colorado
- The extension of certain portions of the USA PATRIOT Act: http://www.washingtonpost.com/politics/patriot-act-extension-signed-into-law-despite-bipartisan-resistance-in-congress/2011/05/27/AGbVlsCH_story.html

- The famous perjury trial of Alger Hiss: http://www.history.com/this-day-in-history/alger-hiss -convicted-of-perjury
- High-profile bribery cases: http://www.reuters.com/article/2010/04/01/bribery-usa-cases-idUSN0121072820100401
- The criminal prosecution of a sitting president: http://www.justice.gov/sites/default/files/olc/opinions/2000/10/31/op-olc-v024-p0222.pdf

Websites of Interest

- The *U.S. v. Lindh* case: http://notablecases.vaed.uscourts.gov/1:02-cr-00037/Index.html
- Information about terrorism: http://www.fema.gov/pdf/areyouready/terrorism.pdf
- Information about the USA PATRIOT Act: http://civilrights.uslegal.com/usa-patriot-act
- The Department of Homeland Security: http://www.dhs.gov/index.shtm

Statistics of Interest

- Terrorism: http://www.fbi.gov/stats-services/publications
- Bribery: http://www.oecd.org/corruption/

CC licensed content, Shared previously

- Criminal Law. **Provided by**: University of Minnesota Libraries Publishing . **Located at**: http://open.lib.umn.edu/criminallaw/. **License**: *CC BY-NC-SA: Attribution-NonCommercial-ShareAlike*

Chapter 14: Appendix A: Case Listings

14.1 Appendix A: Case Listings

Chapter 1 "Introduction to Criminal Law"

- *BMW of North America, Inc. v. Gore*, 517 U.S. 559 (1996)
- *Gonzales v. Oregon*, 546 U.S. 243 (2006)
- *Payton v. New York*, 445 U.S. 573 (1980)
- *Johnson v. Pearce*, 148 N.C.App. 199 (2001)
- *State v. Gillison*, 766 N.W. 2d 649 (2009)
- *Campbell v. State*, 5 S.W.3d 693 (1999)
- *Keeler v. Superior Court*, 470 P.2d 617 (1970)
- *Texas v. Johnson*, 491 U.S. 397 (1989)
- *Marbury v. Madison*, 5 U.S. (1 Cranch) 137 (1803)
- *Shaw v. Murphy*, 532 U.S. 223 (2001)
- *Lawrence v. Texas*, 539 U.S. 558 (2003)
- *Cetacean Community v. Bush*, 386 F.3d 1169 (9th Cir. 2004)
- *People v. Wrotten*, 2010 NY Slip Op 04501 (2010)
- *Wilson v. Layne*, 526 U.S. 603 (1999)
- *Padilla v. Gonzales,* 397 F.3d 1016 (2005)
- *Rogers v. Tennessee*, 532 U.S. 451 (2001)
- *Roe v. Wade*, 410 U.S. 113 (1973)
- *Bowers v. Hardwick*, 478 U.S. 186 (1986)
- *United States v. Hudson & Goodwin*, 11 U.S. 32 (1812)
- *Alabama v. Shelton*, 535 U.S. 654 (2002)

Chapter 2 "The Legal System in the United States"

- *Gonzales v. Raich*, 545 U.S. 1 (2005)
- *U.S. v. Morrison*, 529 U.S. 518 (2000)
- *Pennsylvania v. Nelson*, 350 U.S. 497 (1956)
- *Youngstown Sheet & Tube Co. v. Sawyer*, 343 U.S. 579 (1952)
- *Hamdi v. Rumsfeld*, 542 U.S. 507 (2004)
- *United States v. P.H.E., Inc.*, 965 F.2d 848 (1992)
- *Hertz Corp. v. Friend*, 130 S.Ct. 1181 (2010)
- *Patterson v. New York*, 432 U.S. 197 (1977)
- *Sullivan v. Louisiana*, 508 U.S. 275 (1993)
- *Robles v. State*, 758 N.E. 2d 581 (2001)
- *Donahue v. Burl Cain*, 231 F.3d 1000 (2000)
- *State v. Hall*, 966 P.2d 208 (1998)
- *Richards v. Florida*, No. 4008-4216 (2010)
- *Clinton v. Jones*, 520 U.S. 681 (1997)
- *Sabri v. United States*, 541 U.S. 600 (2004)
- *U.S. v. Comstock*, 627 F.3d 513 (2010)
- *McCulloch v. Maryland*, 17 U.S. (4 Wheat.) 316 (1819)

- *Commonwealth v. Webster*, 59 Mass. 295 (1850)
- *In re Winship*, 397 U.S. 358 (1970)
- *U.S. v. Arizona*, No. CV 10-1413-PHX-SRB (2010)

Chapter 3 "Constitutional Protections"

- *Duncan v. Louisiana*, 391 U.S. 145 (1968)
- *Smith v. Doe*, 538 U.S. 84 (2003)
- *Stogner v. California*, 539 U.S. 607 (2003)
- *Smith v. Goguen*, 415 U.S. 566 (1974)
- *Grayned v. City of Rockford*, 408 U.S. 104 (1972)
- *Lawrence v. Texas*, 539 U.S. 558 (2003)
- *R.A.V. v. St. Paul*, 505 U.S. 377 (1992)
- *Miller v. California*, 413 U.S. 15 (1973)
- *Jenkins v. Georgia*, 418 U.S. 153 (1974)
- *United States v. Stevens*, 552 U.S. 442 (2010)
- *Wisconsin v. Mitchell*, 508 U.S. 47 (1993)
- *Reno v. American Civ. Liberties Union*, 521 U.S. 844 (1997)
- *Holder v. Humanitarian Law Project*, 130 S. Ct. 2705 (2010)
- *Griswold v. Connecticut*, 381 U.S. 479 (1965)
- *Roe v. Wade*, 410 U.S. 113 (1973)
- *Planned Parenthood v. Casey*, 505 U.S. 833 (1992)
- *District of Columbia v. Heller*, 128 S.Ct. 2783 (2008)
- *McDonald v. Chicago*, No. 08-1521 (2010)
- *Lewis v. U.S.*, 445 U.S. 55 (1980)
- *U.S. v. Lopez*, 514 U.S. 549 (1995)
- *Furman v. Georgia*, 408 U.S. 238 (1972)
- *Gregg v. Georgia*, 428 U.S. 153 (1976)
- *Baze v. Rees*, 128 S. Ct. 1520 (2008)
- *Coker v. Georgia*, 433 U.S. 584 (1977)
- *Kennedy v. Louisiana*, 128 S. Ct. 2641 (2008)
- *Apprendi v. New Jersey*, 530 U.S. 466 (2000)
- *U.S. v. Booker*, 543 U.S. 220 (2005)
- *Blakely v. Washington*, 542 U.S. 296 (2004)
- *Lockyer v. Andrade*, 538 U.S. 63 (2003)
- *Fierro v. Gomez*, 77 F.3d 301 (1996)
- *Gall v. U.S.*, 128 S. Ct. 586 (2007)
- *South Dakota v. Asmussen*, 668 N.W.2d 725 (2003)
- *Christian Legal Society v. Martinez*, 130 S. Ct. 2971 (2010)
- *U.S. v. Alvarez*, 617 F.3d 1198 (2010)
- *Snyder v. Phelps*, No. 09-751 (2011)
- *Robinson v. California*, 370 U.S. 660 (1962)
- *U.S. v. Brown*, 381 U.S. 437 (1965)
- *U.S. v. White*, 882 F.2d 250 (1989)
- *Connally v. General Construction Co.*, 269 U.S. 385 (1926)
- *Bolling v. Sharpe*, 347 U.S. 497 (1954)
- *Loving v. Virginia*, 388 U.S. 1 (1967)
- *Gitlow v. New York*, 268 U.S. 652 (1925)
- *Tinker v. Des Moines Independent Community School District*, 393 U.S. 503 (1969)
- *R.A.V. v. St. Paul*, 505 U.S. 377 (1992)
- *Sable Communis. of California, Inc. v. FCC*, 492 U.S. 115 (1989)
- *Schenck v. U.S.*, 249 U.S. 47 (1919)
- *Chaplinsky v. New Hampshire*, 315 U.S. 568, 572 (1942)
- *Lewis v. City of New Orleans*, 415 U.S. 130 (1974)
- *Gooding v. Wilson*, 405 U.S. 518 (1972)
- *Brandenburg v. Ohio*, 395 U.S. 444 (1969)
- *Virginia v. Black*, 535 U.S. 343 (2003)
- *Roth v. United States*, 354 U.S. 476 (1957)
- *City of Erie et al v. Pap's A.M.*, 529 U.S. 277 (2000)
- *Gonzales v. Carhart*, 127 S.Ct. 1610 (2007)

- *Roper v. Simmons*, 543 U.S. 551 (2005)
- *Ford v. Wainwright*, 477 U.S. 399 (1986)
- *Atkins v. Virginia*, 536 U.S. 304 (2002)
- *Ewing v. California*, 538 U.S. 11 (2003)

Chapter 4 "The Elements of a Crime"

- *State ex rel. Kuntz v. Thirteenth Jud. Dist.*, 995 P.2d 951 (2000)
- *Robinson v. California*, 370 U.S. 660 (1962)
- *Powell v. Texas*, 392 U.S. 514 (1968)
- *Oler v. State*, 998 S.W.2d 363 (1999)
- *Staples v. U.S.*, 511 U.S. 600 (1994)
- *Morissette v. U.S.*, 342 U.S. 246 (1952)
- *State v. Crosby*, 154 P.3d 97 (2007)
- *State v. Horner*, 126 Ohio St. 3d 466 (2010)
- *Dean v. U.S.*, 129 S.Ct. 1849 (2009)
- *Bullock v. State*, 775 A.2d. 1043 (2001)
- *Commonwealth v. Casanova*, 429 Mass. 293 (1999)
- *State v. Andrews*, 572 S.E.2d 798 (2002)
- *State v. Sowry*, 155 Ohio App. 3d 742 (2004)
- *Regalado v. U.S.*, 572 A.2d 416 (1990)
- *State v. Slayton*, 154 P.3d 1057 (2007)
- *State v. Kanavy*, 4 A.3d 991 (2010)
- *U.S. v. Grajeda*, 581 F.3d 1186 (2009)
- *People v. Roberts*, 826 P.2d 274 (1992)
- *Govt. of Virgin Islands v. Smith*, 278 F.2d 169 (1960)
- *State ex rel. Kuntz v. Thirteenth Jud. Dist.*, 995 P.2d 951 (2000)
- *Jones v. U.S.*, 308 F.2d 307 (1962)
- *State v. Davis*, 84 Conn. App. 505 (2004)
- *U.S. v. Pompanio*, 429 U.S. 10 (1976)
- *People v. McDaniel*, 24 Cal. 3d 661 (1979)
- *Commonwealth v. Ely*, 444 N.E. 2d 1276 (1983)
- *State v. Huff*, 469 A.2d 1251 (1984)
- *Key v. State*, 890 So. 2d 1043 (2002)

Chapter 5 "Criminal Defenses, Part 1"

- *State v. Burkhart*, 565 S.E.2d 298 (2002)
- *Hoagland v. State*, 240 P.3d 1043 (2010)
- *Rodriguez v. State*, 212 S.W.3d 819 (2006)
- *Shuler v. Babbitt*, 49 F.Supp.2d 1165 (1998)
- *Menendez v. Terhune*, 422 F.3d 1012 (2005)
- *Tennessee v. Garner*, 471 U.S. 1 (1985)
- *Commonwealth v. Alexander*, 531 S.E.2d 567 (2000)
- *Dutton v. Hayes-Pupko*, No. 03-06-00438 (2008)
- *People v. Lovercamp*, 43 Cal. App. 3d 823 (1974)
- *State v. Daoud*, 141 N.H. 142 (1996)
- *Donaldson v. Lungren*, 2 Cal. App. 4th 1614 (1992)
- *Ramey v. State*, 417 S.E.2d 699 (1992)
- *State v. Perez*, 840 P.2d 1118 (1992)
- *Allison v. Birmingham*, 580 So.2d 1377 (1991)
- *Roy v. Inhabitants of Lewiston*, 42 F.3d 691 (1994)
- *U.S. v. Oakland Cannabis Buyers' Cooperative*, 532 U.S. 483 (2001)
- *Acers v. United States*, 164 U.S. 388 (1896)
- *Graham v. Connor*, 490 U.S. 386 (1989)
- *State v. Rogers*, 912 S.W.2d 670 (1995)
- *State v. Williams* 644 P.2d 889 (1982)

- *State v. Belgard*, 410 So.2d 720 (1982)
- *State v. Taylor*, 858 P.2d 1358 (1993)
- *Bechtel v. State*, 840 P.2d 1 (1992)
- *State v. Sandoval*, 130 P.3d 808 (2006)
- *State v. Faulkner*, 483 A.2d 759 (1984)
- *People v. Kurr*, 654 N.W.2d 651 (2002)
- *Commonwealth v. Miranda*, No. 08-P-2094 (2010)
- *State v. Curley*, Docket # 0000011.WA, (Wash. App. 2010)
- *People v. Ceballos*, 12 Cal.3d 470 (1974)
- *State v. Holmes*, 129 Ohio Misc. 2d 38 (2004)

Chapter 6 "Criminal Defenses, Part 2"

- *Durham v. U.S.*, 214 F.2d 862 (1954)
- *U.S. v. Brawner,* 471 F.2d 969 (1972)
- *State v. Guido*, 191 A.2d 45 (1993)
- *State v. Hornsby*, 484 S.E.2d 869 (1997)
- *People v. Register*, 60 N.Y.2d 270 (1983)
- *Garnett v. State*, 632 A.2d 797 (1993)
- *Sosa v. Jones*, 389 F.3d 644 (2004)
- *Farley v. State*, 848 So.2d 393 (2003)
- *Clark v. Arizona*, 548 U.S. 735 (2006)
- *State v. Ramer*, 86 P.3d 132 (2004)
- *People v. Garcia*, 87 P.3d 159 (2003)
- *Sebesta v. State*, 783 S.W.2d 811 (1990)
- *U.S. v. Hinckley*, 493 F.Supp. 2d 65 (2007)
- *Legue v. State*, 688 N.E.2d 408 (1997)
- *U.S. v. Albertini*, 830 F.2d 985 (1987)
- *Queen v. M'Naghten*, 10 Clark & F.200, 2 Eng. Rep. 718 (H.L. 1843)
- *State v. Crenshaw*, 659 P.2d 488 (1983)
- *State v. Skaggs*, 586 P.2d 1279 (1978)
- *State v. Worlock*, 569 A.2d 1314 (1990)
- *State v. White*, 270 P.2d 727 (1954)
- *Kent v. United States*, 383 U.S. 541 (1966)
- *Hopkins v. State*, 69 A.2d 456 (1949)
- *People v. Olsen*, 685 P.2d 52 (1984)
- *People v. Barraza*, 23 Cal.3d 675 (1979)
- *Graham v. Florida*, 130 S.Ct. 2011 (2010)

Chapter 7 "Parties to Crime"

- *New York Central R. Co. v. U.S.*, 212 U.S. 481 (1909)
- *State v. Ulvinen*, 313 N.W.2d 425 (1981)
- *People v. Premier House, Inc.*, 662 N.Y.S 2d 1006 (1997)
- *Commonwealth v. Life Care Centers of America, Inc.*, 456 Mass. 826 (2010)
- *U.S. v. Hill*, 268 F.3d 1140 (2001)
- *State v. Truesdell*, 620 P.2d 427 (1980)
- *Collins v. State,* 438 So. 2d 1036 (1983)
- *State v. Jackson*, 137 Wn. 2d 712 (1999)
- *U.S. v. L.E. Meyers Co.,* 562 F.3d 845 (2009)
- *State v. Melvin*, No. 382PA09 (North Carolina 2010)
- *State v. Merida-Medina*, 191 P.3d 708 (2008)
- *State v. Guminga*, 395 N.W.2d 344 (1986)
- *Staten v. State*, 519 So. 2d 622 (1988)
- *Commonwealth v. Hargrave*, 745 A.2d 20 (2000)
- *People v. Rolon*, 160 Cal. App. 4th 1206 (2008)
- *People v. Lauria*, 251 Cal. App. 2d 471 (1967)

- *Bogdanov v. People*, 941 P.2d 247, 251 n. 8 (1997)
- *Standefer v. U.S.*, 447 U.S. 10 (1980)
- *State v. Akers*, 400 A.2d 38 (1979)
- *Joubert v. State*, 235 S.W.3d 729 (2007)

Chapter 8 "Inchoate Offenses"

- *People v. Hart*, 176 Cal. App. 3d 662 (2009)
- *U.S. v. Guest*, 383 U.S. 745 (1966)
- *Reynolds v. State*, 207 Tex. App. LEXIS 6139 (2007)
- *Rex v. Scofield*, Cald. 397 (1784)
- *Rex v. Higgins*, 102 Eng. Rep. 269 (K.B. 1801)
- *State v. Withrow*, 8 S.W.3d 75 (1999)
- *People v. Strand*, 539 N.W.2d 739 (1995)
- *Pinkerton v. U.S.*, 328 U.S. 640 (1946)
- *State v. Blackmer*, 816 A.2d 1014 (2003)
- *Commonwealth v. Roux*, 350 A.2d 867 (1976)
- *People v. Han*, 78 Cal. App. 4th 797 (2000)
- *Planter v. State*, 9 S.W. 3d 156 (1999)
- *People v. Dennis*, 340 N.W.2d 81 (1983)
- *U.S. v. Contreras*, 950 F.2d 232 (1991)
- *People v. Miller*, 856 N.Y.S. 2d 443 (2008)
- *State v. Montgomery*, 22 Conn. App. 340 (1990)
- *State v. Pinson*, 895 P.2d 274 (1995)
- *Grill v. State*, 337 Md. 91 (1995)
- *People v. Luna*, 170 Cal. App. 4th 535 (2009)
- *Commonwealth v. Hamel*, 52 Mass. App. Ct. 250 (2001)
- *People v. Dillon*, 668 P.2d 697 (1983)
- *Hamiel v. Wisconsin*, 285 N.W.2d 639 (1979)
- *U.S. v. Mandujano*, 499 F.2d 370, 373 fn. 5, (1974)
- *Dennis v. U.S.*, 341 U.S. 494 (1951),
- *State v. Bond*, 49 Conn. App. 183 (1998)
- *State v. Verive*, 627 P.2d 721 (1981)
- *State v. Lewis*, 220 Conn. 602 (1991)
- *U.S. v. Castaneda*, 9 F.3d 761 (1993)
- *Ianelli v. U.S*, 420 U.S. 770, 785 (1975)
- *Callanan v. U.S.*, 364 U.S. 587 (1961)
- *Clune v. U.S.*, 159 U.S. 590 (1895)
- *Commonwealth v. Barsell*, 424 Mass. 737 (1997)

Chapter 9 "Criminal Homicide"

- *People v. Cole*, 95 P.3d 811 (2004)
- *Washington v. Glucksberg*, 521 U.S. 844 (1997)
- *U.S. v. Moore*, 846 F.2d 1163 (1988)
- *State v. West*, 844 S.W.2d 144 (1992)
- *U.S. v. Downs*, 56 F.3d 973 (1995)
- *People v. Anderson*, 666 N.W.2d 696 (2003)
- *Enmund v. Florida*, 458 U.S. 782 (1982)
- *Berry v. Superior Court*, 208 Cal. App. 3d 783 (1989)
- *Dowda v. State*, 776 So.2d 714 (2000)
- *Stevens v. State*, 691 N.E.2d 412 (1997)
- *Tripp v. State*, 374 A.2d 384 (1977)
- *Walker v. Superior Court*, 47 Cal.3d 112 (1988)
- *People v. Taylor*, 86 P.3d 881 (2004)
- *State v. Evangelista*, 353 S.E.2d 375 (1987)
- *Wood v. State*, 620 S.E.2d 348 (2005)

- *State v. Warmke*, 879 A.2d 30 (2005)
- *United States v. Watson*, 501 A.2d 791 (1985)
- *Calderon v. Prunty*, 59 F.3d 1005 (1995)
- *Mullaney v. Wilbur*, 421 U.S. 684 (1975)
- *People v. Ochoa*, 966 P.2d 442 (1999)
- *Keeler v. Superior Court*, 2 Cal.3d 619 (1970)
- *Washington v. Glucksberg*, 521 U.S. 844 (1997)
- *People v. Carines*, 597 N.W. 2d 130 (1999)
- *Acers v. United States*, 164 U.S. 388 (1896)
- *Hawthorne v. State*, 835 So. 2d 14 (2003)
- *People v. Anderson*, 447 P.2d 942 (1968)
- *State v. Snowden*, 313 P.2d 706 (1957)
- *Commonwealth v. Carroll*, 412 Pa. 525 (1963)
- *State v. Schrader*, 302 SE 2d 70 (1982)
- *Kennedy v. Louisiana*, 128 S. Ct. 2641 (2008)
- *State v. Hoang*, 755 P.2d 7 (1988)
- *People v. Hernandez*, 82 N.Y.2d 309 (1993)
- *State v. Canola*, 73 N.J. 206 (1977)
- *People v. Young*, 105 P.2d 487 (2005)
- *People v. Steele*, 47 P.2d 225 (2002)
- *Ohio v. Shane*, 63 Ohio St.3d 630 (1992)
- *Girouard v. State*, 583 A.2d 718 (1991)
- *State v. Cole*, 338 S.C. 97 (2000)
- *State v. Doub III*, 32 Kan.App.2d 1087 (2004)

Chapter 10 "Sex Offenses and Crimes Involving Force, Fear, and Physical Restraint"

- *State v. Salaman*, 949 A.2d 1092 (2008)
- *Toomer v. State*, 529 SE 2d 719 (2000)
- *Fleming v. State*, 323 SW 3d 540 (2010)
- *State v. Higgs*, 601 N.W.2d 653 (1999)
- *Commonwealth v. Henson*, 259 N.E.2d 769 (1970)
- *State v. Holbach*, 2009 ND 37 (2009)
- *Burke v. State*, 676 S.E.2d 766 (2009)
- *Commonwealth v. Rivera*, 828 A.2d 1094 (2003)
- *U.S. v. Lanier*, 520 U.S. 259 (1997)
- *Oregon v. Rangel*, 934 P.2d 1128 (1997)
- *Chatwin v. U.S*, 326 U.S. 455 (1946)
- *Kennedy v. Louisiana*, 128 S.Ct. 2641 (2008)
- *Lawrence v. Texas*, 539 U.S. 558 (2003)
- *Iowa v. Vander Esch*, 662 N.W. 2d 689 (2002)
- *Boro v. Superior Court*, 163 Cal. App. 3d 1224 (1985)
- *In re John Z.*, 29 Cal. 4th 756 (2003)
- *State v. Borthwick*, 880 P.2d 1261 (1994)
- *State v. Lile*, 699 P.2d 456 (1985)
- *People v. Mayberry*, 542 P.2d 1337 (1975)
- *State v. Plunkett*, 934 P.2d 113 (1997)
- *Associated Press et. al. v. District Court for the Fifth Judicial District of Colorado*, 542 U.S. 1301 (2004)
- *State of New Jersey in the Interest of M.T.S.*, 609 A.2d 1266 (1972)
- *People v. Liberta*, 64 N.Y. 2d 152 (1984)
- *Michael M. v. Superior Court*, 450 U.S. 464 (1981)
- *Lawrence v. Texas*, 539 U.S. 558 (2003)
- *Commonwealth v. Matthews*, 205 PA Super 92 (2005)
- *People v. Nickens*, 685 NW 2d 657 (2004)
- *Clark v. Commonwealth*, 676 S.E.2d 332 (2009)
- *Commonwealth v. Porro*, 458 Mass. 526 (2010)
- *People v. Dominguez*, 140 P.2d 866 (2006)

Chapter 11 "Crimes against Property"

- *State v. Larson*, 605 N.W. 2d 706 (2000)
- *People v. Traster*, 111 Cal. App. 4th 1377 (2003)
- *U.S. v. Ingles*, 445 F.3d 830 (2006)
- *State v. Robertson*, 531 S. E. 2d 490 (2000)
- *People v. Pratt*, 656 N.W.2d 866 (2002)
- *Butler v. Florida*, (Fla: Dist. Court of Appeals, 2009)
- *In the Matter of V.V.C.*, No. 04-07-00166 CV (Tex.: Court of Appeals, 2008)
- *People v. Beaver*, 186 Cal. App. 4th 107 (2010)
- *State v. Castillo*, Docket No. 29, 641 (NM: 2011)
- *People v. Nowack*, 614 N.W.2d 78 (2000)
- *Britt v. Commonwealth*, 667 S.E.2d 763 (2008)
- *Commonwealth v. Mills*, 436 Mass. 387 (2002)
- *Itin v. Ungar*, 17 P.3d 129 (2000)
- *In the Matter of Schwimmer*, 108 P.3d 761 (2005)
- *People v. Lueth*, 660 N.W.2d 322 (2002)
- *People v. Curtin*, 22 Cal. App. 4th 528 (1994)
- *People v. Beaver*, 186 Cal. App. 4th 107 (2010)
- *Durland v. U.S.*, 161 U.S. 306, 313 (1896),
- *U.S. v. McClelland*, 868 F.2d 704 (1989)
- *S.W. v. State*, 513 So. 2d 1088 (1987)
- *State v. Handburgh*, 830 P.2d 641 (1992)
- *Jones v. State*, 652 So. 2d 346 (1995)
- *Metheny v. State*, 755 A.2d 1088 (2000)
- *Williams v. State*, 91 S.W. 3d 54 (2002)
- *Commonwealth v. Hallums*, 61 Mass. App. Ct. 50 (2004)
- *People v. Nible*, 200 Cal. App. 3d 838 (1988)
- *State v. Hall*, 3 P.3d 582 (2000)
- *People v. Nunley*, 168 Cal. App. 3d 225 (1985)
- *State v. Allen*, 110 P. 3d 849 (2005)
- *State v. Reavis*, 700 S.E.2d 33 (2010)
- *People v. Atkins*, 25 Cal. 4th 76 (2001)
- *Ursulita v. State*, Docket No. A10A1733 (Georgia 2011)

Chapter 12 "Crimes against the Public"

- *People v. Acuna*, 14 Cal. 4th 1090 (1997)
- *Papachristou v. City of Jacksonville*, 405 U.S. 156 (1972)
- *State v. Russell*, 890 A.2d 453 (2006)
- *People v. Hoffstead*, 905 N.Y.S.2d 736 (2010)
- *City of Chicago v. Morales*, 527 U.S. 41 (1999)
- *Ortiz v. NYS Parole in Bronx*, 586 F.3d 149 (2009)
- *People v. Englebrecht*, 88 Cal. App. 4th 1236 (2001)
- *Poindexter v. State*, 153 S.W. 3d 402 (2005)
- *People v. Watson*, No. 90962, (Ohio 2120 2009)
- *Love v. Superior Court*, 226 Cal. App. 3d 736 (1990)
- *Satterfield v. State*, 395 S.E. 2d 816 (1990)
- *Silvar v. Dist. Ct.*, 129 P.3d 682 (2006)
- *Manduley v. Superior Court*, 41 P.3d 3 (2002)
- *State v. Bradshaw*, 98 P.3d 1190 (2004)
- *Roulette v. City of Seattle*, 97 F.3d 300 (1996)
- *Noy v. State*, 83 P.3d 538 (2003)
- *Phillips v. State*, 25 So. 3d 404 (2010)
- *In re BW*, 313 S.W. 3d 818 (2010)
- *Wolfe v. State*, 24 P.3d 1252 (2001)
- *Colten v. Kentucky*, 407 U.S. 104 (1972)
- *Edwards v. California*, 314 U.S. 160 (1941)
- *City of Chicago v. Morales*, 527 U.S. 41 (1999)

- *Kolender v. Lawson*, 461 U.S. 352 (1983)
- *Gresham v. Peterson*, 225 F.3d 899 (2000)
- *Jones v. City of Los Angeles*, 444 F.3d 1118 (2006)
- *People v. Sanchez*, 888 N.Y.S. 2d 352 (2009)
- *Robinson v. California*, 370 U.S. 660 (1962)
- *People v. Parra*, 70 Cal. App. 4th 222 (1999)
- *Gonzales v. Raich*, 545 U.S. 1 (2005)
- *U.S. v. Oakland Cannabis Buyers' Cooperative*, 532 U.S. 483 (2001)

Chapter 13 "Crimes against the Government"

- *U.S. v. Adcock*, 558 F.2d 397 (1977)
- *U.S v. Burr*, 25 F Cas 55 (1807)
- *Haupt v. U.S.*, 330 U.S. 631 (1947)
- *Cramer v. U.S.*, 325 U.S. 1, 34, 35 (1945)
- *Yates v. U.S.*, 354 U.S. 298 (1957)
- *U.S. v. Kabat*, 797 Fed.2d 580 (1986)
- *In re Squillacote*, 790 A.2d 514 (2002)
- *Humanitarian Law Project v. Reno*, 205 F.3d 1130 (2000)
- *Humanitarian Law Project v. U.S. Department of Justice*, 352 F.3d 382 (2003)
- *State v. Carr*, 172 Conn. 458 (1977)
- *People v. Silverberg*, 771 N.Y.S. 2d 274 (2003)
- *Kawakita v. U.S.*, 343 U.S. 717 (1952)
- *U.S. v. Rosen*, 445 F.Supp.2d 602 (2006)
- *Schultz v. Sykes*, 638 N.W. 2d 604 (2001)
- *Pennsylvania v. Nelson*, 350 U.S. 497 (1956)
- *U.S. v. Moussaoui*, 591 F.3d 236 (2010)
- *State v. Kimber*, 48 Conn. App. 234 (1998)
- *U.S. v. Gaudin*, 515 U.S. 506 (1995)
- *Clinton v. Jones*, 520 U.S. 681 (1997)

CC licensed content, Shared previously

- Criminal Law. **Provided by**: University of Minnesota Libraries Publishing . **Located at**: http://open.lib.umn.edu/criminallaw/. **License**: *CC BY-NC-SA: Attribution-NonCommercial-ShareAlike*

26869029R00257

Made in the USA
Columbia, SC
20 September 2018